Teach Yourself VISUALLY™ COMPLETE

Mac Pro®

D1296375

Paul McFedries

BOOK SOLD
NO LONGER R.H.P.L.
PROPERTY

Visual®
A Wiley Brand

RICHMOND HILL
PUBLIC LIBRARY

MAY 0 1 2014

RICHMOND GREEN
905-780-0711

RG

Teach Yourself VISUALLY™ Complete Mac Pro®

Published by
John Wiley & Sons, Inc.
10475 Crosspoint Boulevard
Indianapolis, IN 46256

www.wiley.com

Published simultaneously in Canada

Copyright © 2014 by John Wiley & Sons, Inc., Indianapolis, Indiana

No part of this publication may be reproduced, stored in a retrieval system or transmitted in any form or by any means, electronic, mechanical, photocopying, recording, scanning or otherwise, except as permitted under Sections 107 or 108 of the 1976 United States Copyright Act, without either the prior written permission of the Publisher, or authorization through payment of the appropriate per-copy fee to the Copyright Clearance Center, 222 Rosewood Drive, Danvers, MA 01923, 978-750-8400, fax 978-646-8600. Requests to the Publisher for permission should be addressed to the Permissions Department, John Wiley & Sons, Inc., 111 River Street, Hoboken, NJ 07030, 201-748-6011, fax 201-748-6008, or online at www.wiley.com/go/permissions.

Wiley publishes in a variety of print and electronic formats and by print-on-demand. Some material included with standard print versions of this book may not be included in e-books or in print-on-demand. If this book refers to media such as a CD or DVD that is not included in the version you purchased, you may download this material at http://booksupport.wiley.com. For more information about Wiley products, visit www.wiley.com.

Library of Congress Control Number: 2013954184

ISBN: 978-1-118-82645-4

Manufactured in the United States of America

10 9 8 7 6 5 4 3 2 1

Trademark Acknowledgments

Wiley, Visual, the Visual logo, Teach Yourself VISUALLY, Read Less - Learn More and related trade dress are trademarks or registered trademarks of John Wiley & Sons, Inc. and/or its affiliates. Mac Pro is a registered trademark of Apple, Inc. All other trademarks are the property of their respective owners. John Wiley & Sons, Inc. is not associated with any product or vendor mentioned in this book. *Teach Yourself VISUALLY Complete Mac Pro* is an independent publication and has not been authorized, sponsored, or otherwise approved by Apple, Inc.

LIMIT OF LIABILITY/DISCLAIMER OF WARRANTY: THE PUBLISHER AND THE AUTHOR MAKE NO REPRESENTATIONS OR WARRANTIES WITH RESPECT TO THE ACCURACY OR COMPLETENESS OF THE CONTENTS OF THIS WORK AND SPECIFICALLY DISCLAIM ALL WARRANTIES, INCLUDING WITHOUT LIMITATION WARRANTIES OF FITNESS FOR A PARTICULAR PURPOSE. NO WARRANTY MAY BE CREATED OR EXTENDED BY SALES OR PROMOTIONAL MATERIALS. THE ADVICE AND STRATEGIES CONTAINED HEREIN MAY NOT BE SUITABLE FOR EVERY SITUATION. THIS WORK IS SOLD WITH THE UNDERSTANDING THAT THE PUBLISHER IS NOT ENGAGED IN RENDERING LEGAL, ACCOUNTING, OR OTHER PROFESSIONAL SERVICES. IF PROFESSIONAL ASSISTANCE IS REQUIRED, THE SERVICES OF A COMPETENT PROFESSIONAL PERSON SHOULD BE SOUGHT. NEITHER THE PUBLISHER NOR THE AUTHOR SHALL BE LIABLE FOR DAMAGES ARISING HEREFROM. THE FACT THAT AN ORGANIZATION OR WEBSITE IS REFERRED TO IN THIS WORK AS A CITATION AND/OR A POTENTIAL SOURCE OF FURTHER INFORMATION DOES NOT MEAN THAT THE AUTHOR OR THE PUBLISHER ENDORSES THE INFORMATION THE ORGANIZATION OR WEBSITE MAY PROVIDE OR RECOMMENDATIONS IT MAY MAKE. FURTHER, READERS SHOULD BE AWARE THAT INTERNET WEBSITES LISTED IN THIS WORK MAY HAVE CHANGED OR DISAPPEARED BETWEEN WHEN THIS WORK WAS WRITTEN AND WHEN IT IS READ.

FOR PURPOSES OF ILLUSTRATING THE CONCEPTS AND TECHNIQUES DESCRIBED IN THIS BOOK, THE AUTHOR HAS CREATED VARIOUS NAMES, COMPANY NAMES, MAILING, E-MAIL AND INTERNET ADDRESSES, PHONE AND FAX NUMBERS AND SIMILAR INFORMATION, ALL OF WHICH ARE FICTITIOUS. ANY RESEMBLANCE OF THESE FICTITIOUS NAMES, ADDRESSES, PHONE AND FAX NUMBERS AND SIMILAR INFORMATION TO ANY ACTUAL PERSON, COMPANY AND/OR ORGANIZATION IS UNINTENTIONAL AND PURELY COINCIDENTAL.

Contact Us

For general information on our other products and services please contact our Customer Care Department within the U.S. at 877-762-2974, outside the U.S. at 317-572-3993 or fax 317-572-4002.

For technical support please visit www.wiley.com/techsupport.

RICHMOND HILL
PUBLIC LIBRARY

MAY 0 1 2014

RICHMOND GREEN
905-780-0711

Sales | Contact Wiley at (877) 762-2974 or fax (317) 572-4002.

Credits

Acquisitions Editor
Aaron Black

Sr. Project Editor
Sarah Hellert

Technical Editor
Dennis Cohen

Copy Editor
Scott Tullis

Director, Content Development & Assembly
Robyn Siesky

Vice President and Executive Group Publisher
Richard Swadley

About the Author

Paul McFedries is a full-time technical writer. He has been authoring computer books since 1991 and has more than 85 books to his credit, including *Teach Yourself VISUALLY Windows 8.1, Windows 8.1 Simplified, Windows 8 Visual Quick Tips, Excel Data Analysis: Your visual blueprint for analyzing data, charts, and PivotTables*, 4th Edition, *Teach Yourself VISUALLY Excel 2013, Teach Yourself VISUALLY OS X Mavericks, The Facebook Guide for People Over 50, iPhone 5s and 5c Portable Genius*, and *iPad Portable Genius*, 2nd Edition, all available from Wiley. Paul's books have sold more than 4 million copies worldwide. Paul is also the proprietor of Word Spy (www.wordspy.com), a website that tracks new words and phrases as they enter the English language. Paul invites you to drop by his personal website at www.mcfedries.com, or you can follow him on Twitter @paulmcf and @wordspy.

Author's Acknowledgments

It goes without saying that writers focus on text and I certainly enjoyed focusing on the text that you will read in this book. However, this book is more than just the usual collection of words and phrases designed to educate and stimulate the mind. A quick thumb through the pages will show you that this book is also chock full of treats for the eye, including copious screen shots, meticulous layouts, and sharp fonts. Those sure make for a beautiful book and that beauty comes from a lot of hard work by Wiley's immensely talented group of designers and layout artists.

They are all listed in the Credits section on the previous page, and I thank them for creating another gem. Of course, what you read in this book must also be accurate, logically presented, and free of errors. Ensuring all of this was an excellent group of editors that I got to work with directly, including project editor Sarah Hellert, copy editor Scott Tullis, and technical editor Dennis Cohen. Thanks to all of you for your exceptional competence and hard work. Thanks, as well, to Wiley Acquisitions Editor Aaron Black for asking me to write this book.

How to Use This Book

Who This Book Is For

This book is for the reader who has never used this particular technology or software application. It is also for readers who want to expand their knowledge.

The Conventions in This Book

1 Steps

This book uses a step-by-step format to guide you easily through each task. Numbered steps are actions you must do; bulleted steps clarify a point, step, or optional feature; and indented steps give you the result.

2 Notes

Notes give additional information — special conditions that may occur during an operation, a situation that you want to avoid, or a cross reference to a related area of the book.

3 Icons and Buttons

Icons and buttons show you exactly what you need to click to perform a step.

4 Tips

Tips offer additional information, including warnings and shortcuts.

5 Bold

Bold type shows command names, options, and text or numbers you must type.

6 Italics

Italic type introduces and defines a new term.

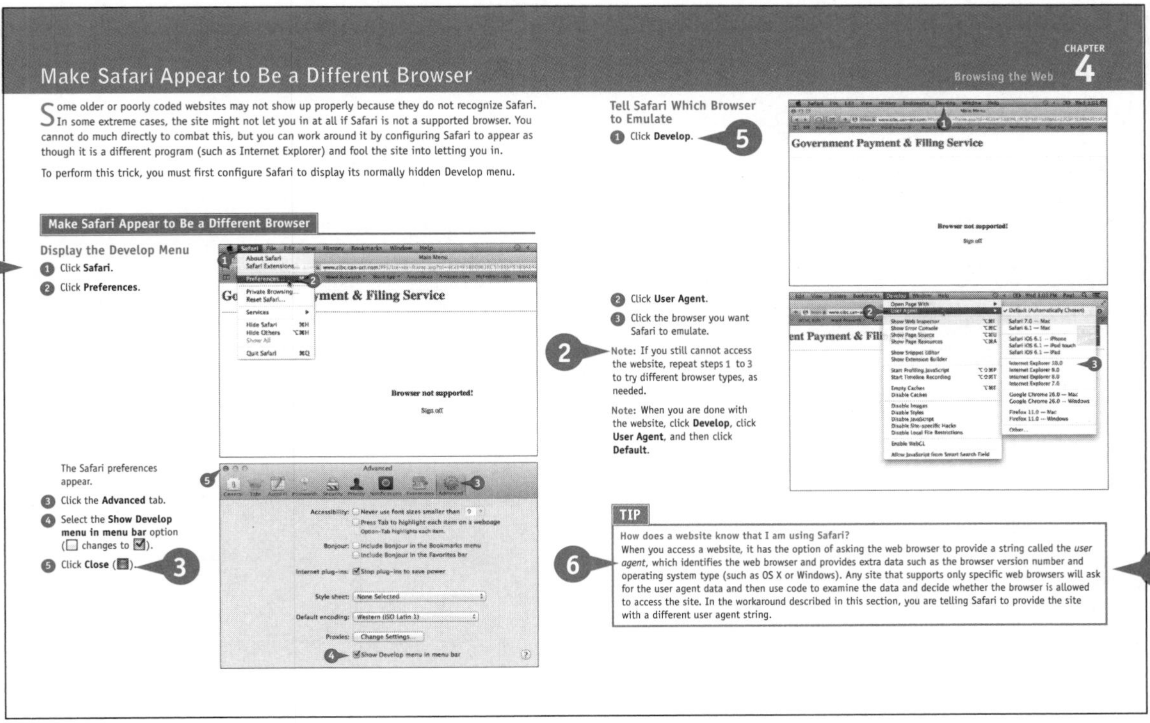

Make Safari Appear to Be a Different Browser

CHAPTER 4 Browsing the Web

Some older or poorly coded websites may not show up properly because they do not recognize Safari. In some extreme cases, the site might not let you in at all if Safari is not a supported browser. You cannot do much directly to combat this, but you can work around it by configuring Safari to appear as though it is a different program (such as Internet Explorer) and fool the site into letting you in.

To perform this trick, you must first configure Safari to display its normally hidden Develop menu.

Make Safari Appear to Be a Different Browser

Display the Develop Menu

1 Click **Safari**.

2 Click **Preferences**.

The Safari preferences appear.

3 Click the **Advanced** tab.

4 Select the **Show Develop menu in menu bar** option (☐ changes to ☑).

5 Click **Close** (■).

Tell Safari Which Browser to Emulate

1 Click **Develop**.

2 Click **User Agent**.

3 Click the browser you want Safari to emulate.

Note: If you still cannot access the website, repeat steps 1 to 3 to try different browser types, as needed.

Note: When you are done with the website, click **Develop**, click **User Agent**, and then click **Default**.

TIP

How does a website know that I am using Safari?

When you access a website, it has the option of asking the web browser to provide a string called the *user agent*, which identifies the web browser and provides extra data such as the browser version number and operating system type (such as OS X or Windows). Any site that supports only specific web browsers will ask for the user agent data and then use code to examine the data and decide whether the browser is allowed to access the site. In the workaround described in this section, you are telling Safari to provide the site with a different user agent string.

Table of Contents

Chapter 1 Learning Basic Program Tasks

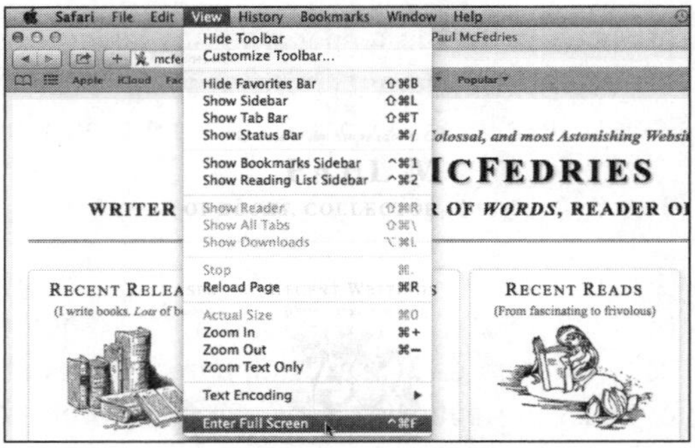

Chapter 2 Learning Basic Document Tasks

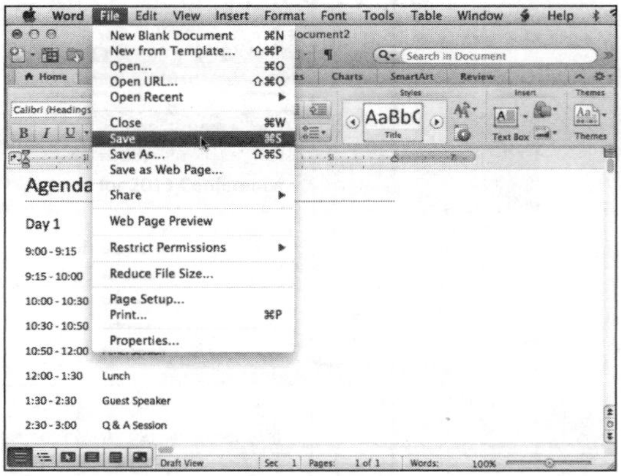

Chapter 3 Connecting Devices

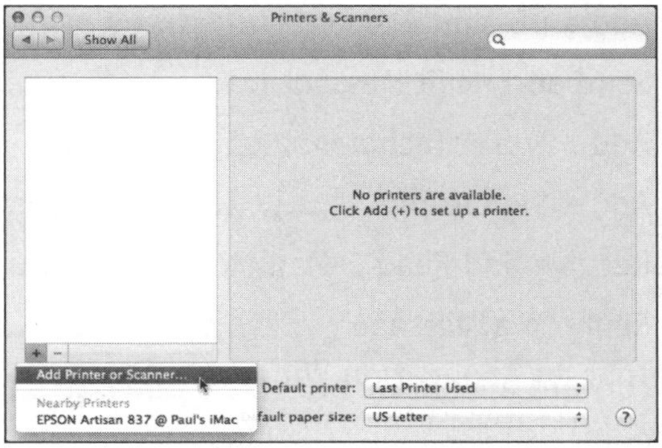

Chapter 4 Browsing the Web

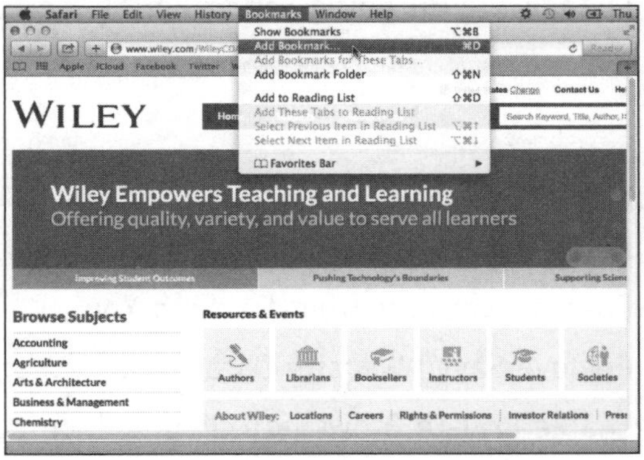

Table of Contents

Chapter 5 Communicating via E-Mail

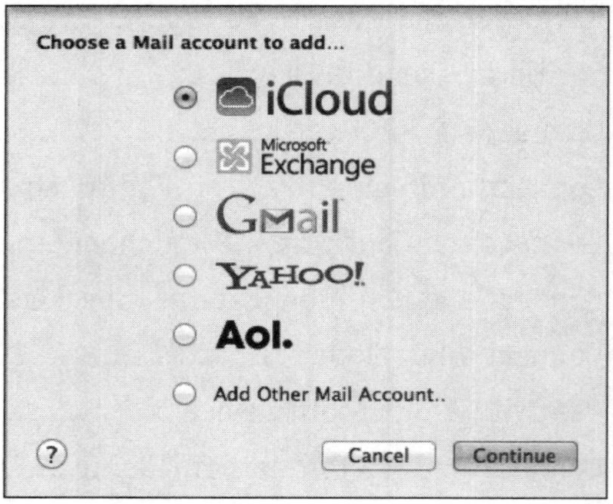

Chapter 6 Enhancing Online Security

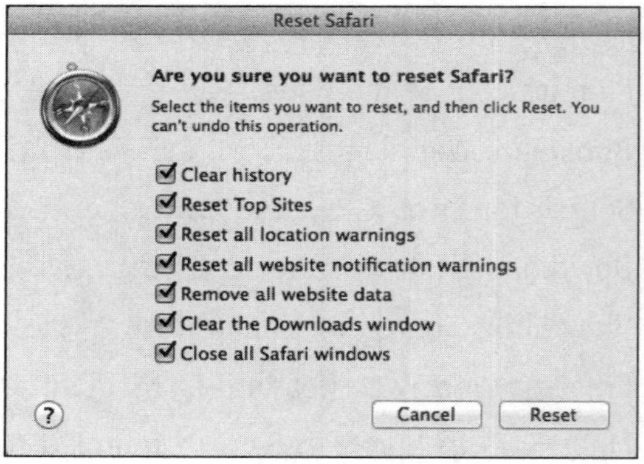

Chapter 7 Talking via Messages and FaceTime

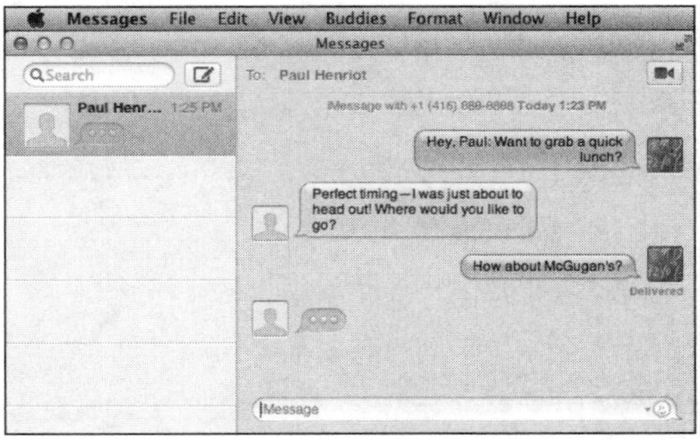

Chapter 8 Tracking Contacts and Events

Chapter 9 Connecting to Social Networks

Chapter 10 Learning Useful Mac Pro Tasks

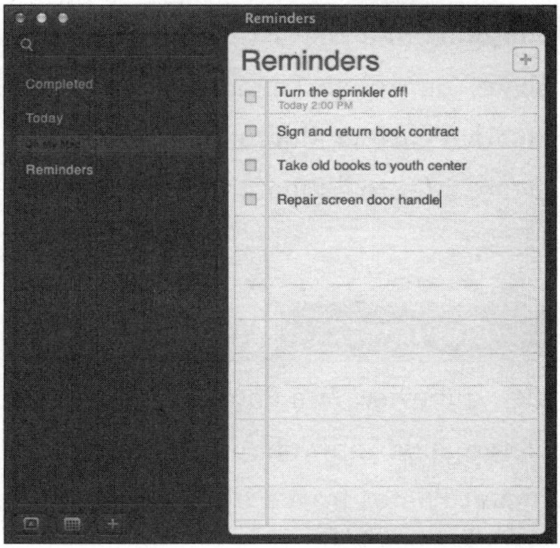

Chapter 11 Playing Mac Pro Audio

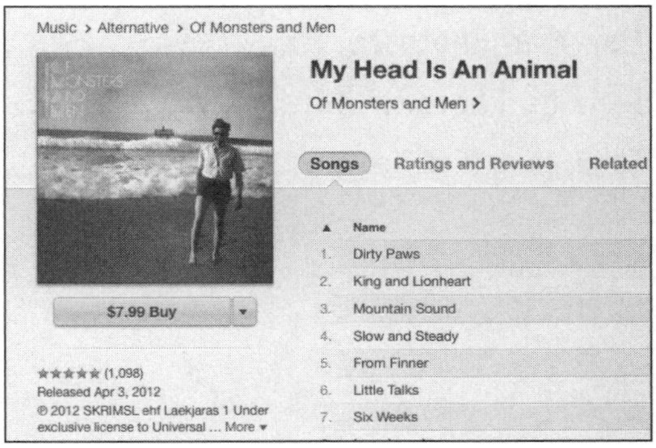

Table of Contents

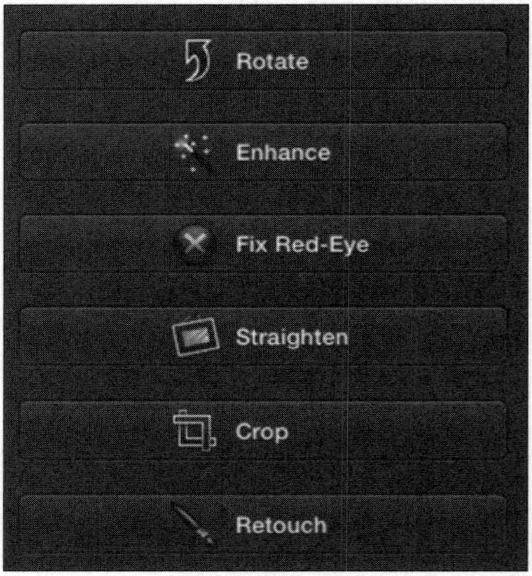

Chapter 13 Playing and Creating Videos

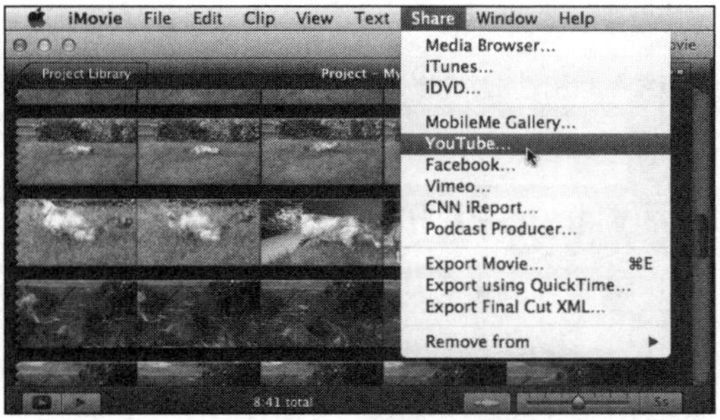

Chapter 14 Customizing Mac Pro

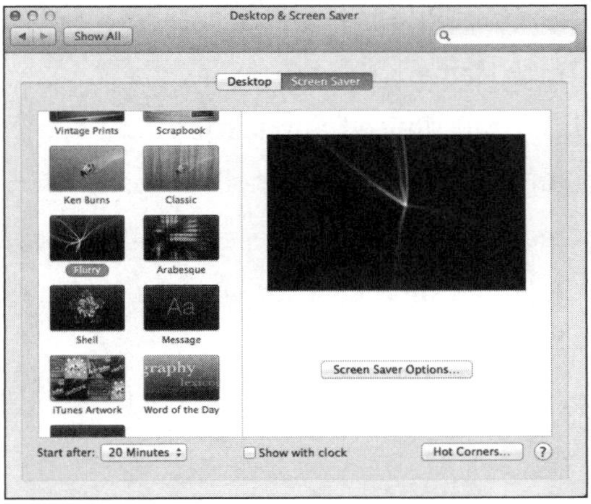

Table of Contents

Chapter 15 Working with Disks

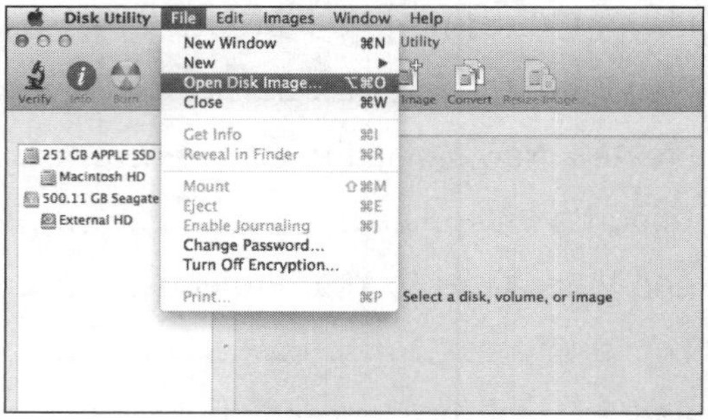

Chapter 16 Maintaining Mac Pro

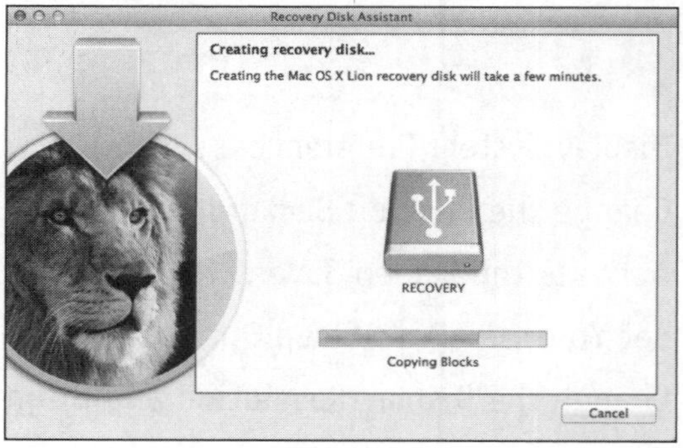

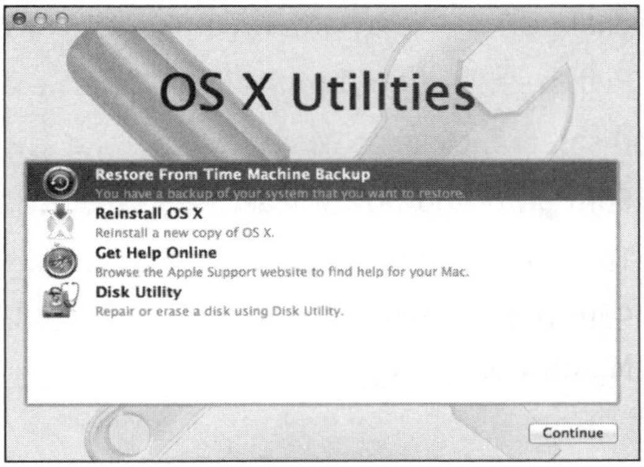

OS X Utilities
Restore From Time Machine Backup
Reinstall OS X
Reinstall a new copy of OS X.
Get Help Online
Browse the Apple Support website to find help for your Mac.
Disk Utility
Repair or erase a disk using Disk Utility.
Continue

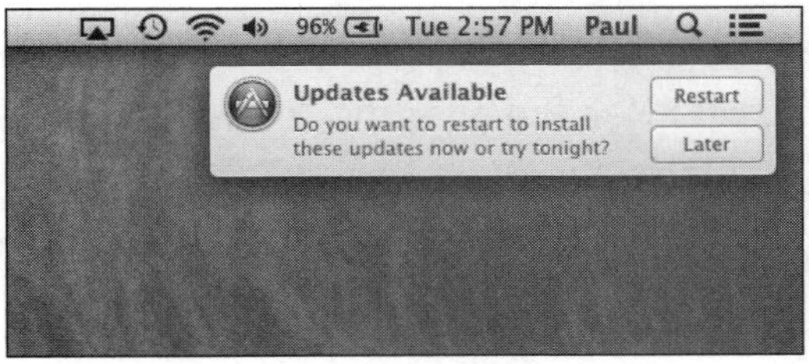

96%
Tue 2:57 PM
Paul
Updates Available
Do you want to restart to install these updates now or try tonight?
Restart
Later

Table of Contents

Chapter 19 Securing Mac Pro

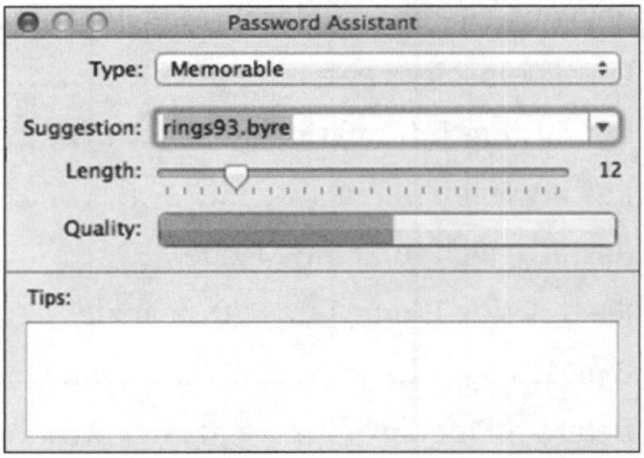

Chapter 20 Working with iCloud

Chapter 21 Networking with Mac Pro

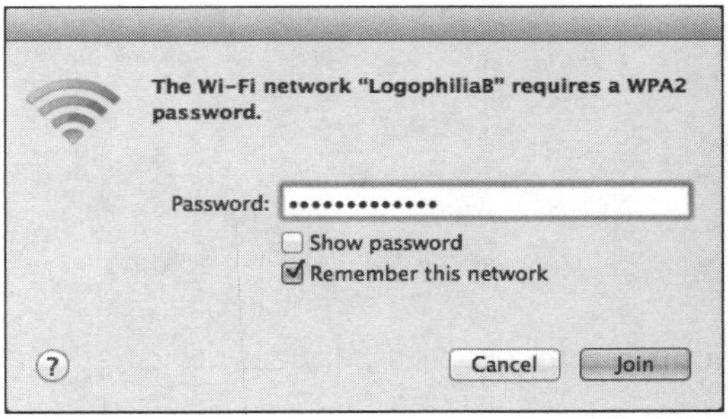

Chapter 22 Running Windows on Mac Pro

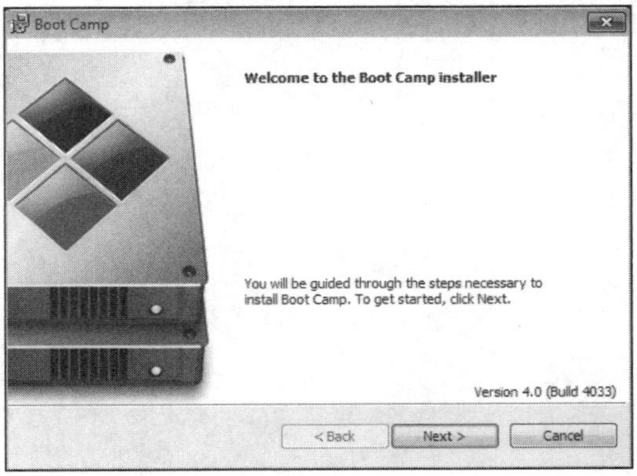

CHAPTER 1

Learning Basic Program Tasks

One of the most crucial Mac Pro concepts is the *application* (also called a *program*), because you perform all Mac Pro tasks using applications. Therefore, it is important to have a basic understanding of how to start and manage applications with your Mac Pro.

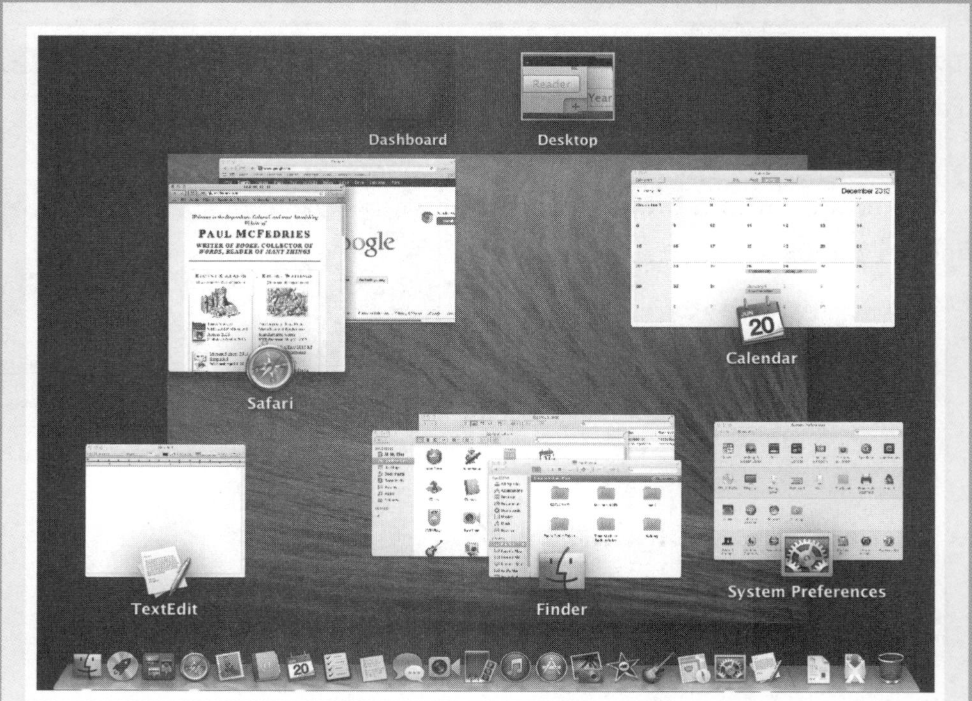

Explore the OS X Screen

Before you can begin to understand how the OS X operating system works, you should become familiar with the basic screen elements. These elements include the OS X menu bar, the desktop, desktop icons, and the Dock. Understanding where these elements appear on the screen and what they are used for will help you work through the rest of the sections in this book and will help you navigate OS X and its applications on your own.

A Menu Bar

The menu bar contains the pull-down menus for OS X and most Mac Pro software.

B Desktop

This is the OS X work area, where you work with your applications and documents.

C Mouse Pointer

The pointer follows the movement of your mouse or your finger on a trackpad or Magic Mouse.

D Desktop Icon

An icon on the desktop represents an application, a folder, a document, or a device attached to your Mac Pro, such as a hard drive, a CD or DVD, or an iPod.

E Dock

The Dock contains several icons, each of which gives you quick access to a commonly used application.

Tour the Dock

The Dock is the strip that runs along the bottom of the Mac Pro screen. The Dock is populated with several small images called *icons*. Each icon represents a particular component of your Mac Pro — an application, a folder, a document, and so on — and clicking the icon opens the component. This makes the Dock one of the most important and useful Mac Pro features because it gives you one-click access to applications, folders, and documents. The icons shown here are typical, but your Mac Pro may display a different arrangement.

A Finder

Work with the files on your computer.

B Launchpad

View, organize, and start your applications.

C Mission Control

Locate and navigate running applications.

D Safari

Browse the World Wide Web on the Internet.

E Mail

Send and receive e-mail messages.

F Contacts

Store and access people's names, addresses, and other contact information.

G Calendar

Record upcoming appointments, birthdays, meetings, and other events.

H Reminders

Set reminders for upcoming tasks.

I Notes

Record to-do lists and other short notes.

J Messages

Send instant messages to other people.

K FaceTime

Place video calls to other FaceTime users.

L Photo Booth

Take a picture using the camera on your Mac Pro.

M iTunes

Play music and other media, and add media to your iPod, iPhone, or iPad.

N App Store

Install new applications and upgrade existing ones.

O iPhoto

Import and edit digital photos and other images.

P iMovie

Import video footage and edit your own digital movies.

Q GarageBand

Create songs, podcasts, and other audio files.

R Maps

Find and get directions to locations.

S System Preferences

Customize and configure your Mac Pro.

T Documents

Display the contents of your Documents folder.

U Downloads

Display the contents of your Downloads folder.

V Trash

Delete files, folders, and applications.

Start an Application

To perform tasks of any kind in OS X, you use one of the applications installed on your Mac Pro. The application you use depends on the task you want to perform. For example, if you want to surf the World Wide Web, you use a web browser application, such as the Safari program that comes with Mac Pro. Before you can use an application, however, you must first tell Mac Pro which application you want to run. Mac Pro launches the application and displays it on the desktop. You can then use the application's tools to perform your tasks.

Start an Application

1 Click the **Finder** icon.

Note: If the application that you want to start has an icon in the Dock, you can click the icon to start the application and skip the steps in this section.

The Finder window appears.

2 Click **Applications**.

Note: You can also navigate to Applications in any Finder window by pressing Shift+⌘+A or by choosing **Go** and then clicking **Applications**.

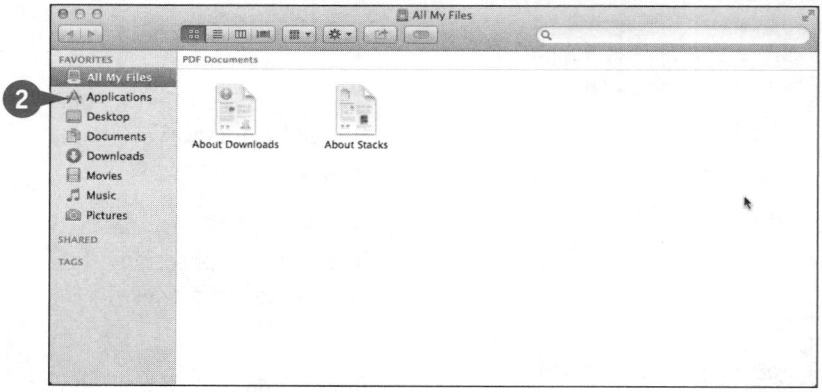

The Applications window appears.

3. Double-click the icon of the application that you want to start.

Note: If you see a folder icon ( ), it means that the application resides in its own folder, which is a storage area on the computer. Double-click to open the folder and then double-click the application icon.

- A The application appears on the desktop.
- B Mac Pro adds a button for the application to the Dock.
- C The menu bar displays the menus associated with the application.

Note: Another common way to launch an application is to use Finder to locate a document with which you want to work and then double-click that document.

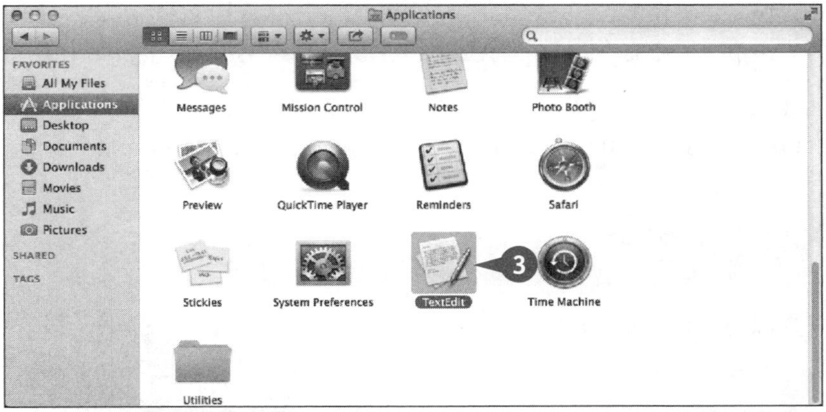

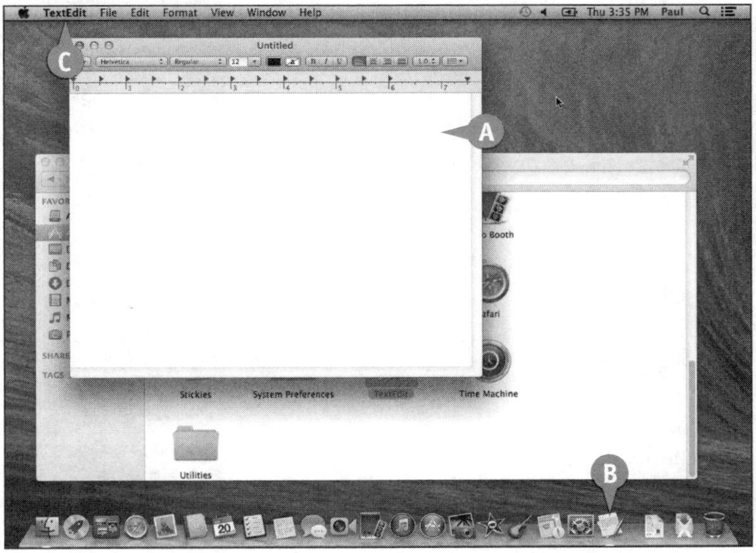

TIPS

How do I add an icon to the Dock for an application I use frequently?
To add an icon to the Dock, repeat steps 1 to 3 in this section. Right-click the application's Dock icon, click **Options**, and then click **Keep in Dock**.

How do I shut down a running application?
To shut down a running application, right-click the application's Dock icon and then click **Quit**. Alternatively, you can switch to the application and press ⌘+Q.

Start an Application Using Launchpad

You can start an application using the Launchpad feature. This is often faster than using the Applications folder, particularly for applications that do not have a Dock icon.

Launchpad is designed to mimic the Home screens of the iPhone, iPad, and iPod touch. So if you own one or more of these devices, then you are already familiar with how Launchpad works.

Start an Application Using Launchpad

1. Click the **Launchpad** icon ( ).

The Launchpad screen appears.

2. If the application you want to start resides in a different Launchpad screen, click the dot that corresponds to the screen.

Note: If you are not sure where to find the application, start typing its name, and then click its icon when it appears.

Launchpad switches to the screen and displays the applications.

3. If the application you want to start resides within a folder, click the folder.

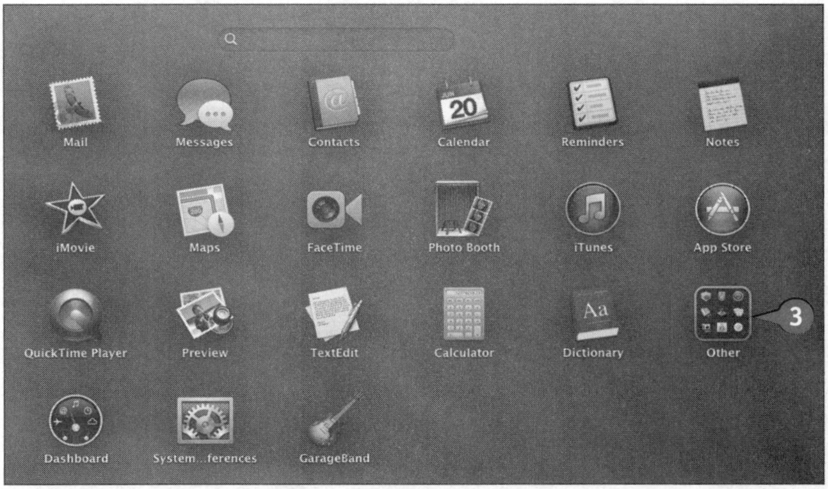

Launchpad opens the folder.

4. Click the icon of the application you want to start.

Mac Pro starts the application.

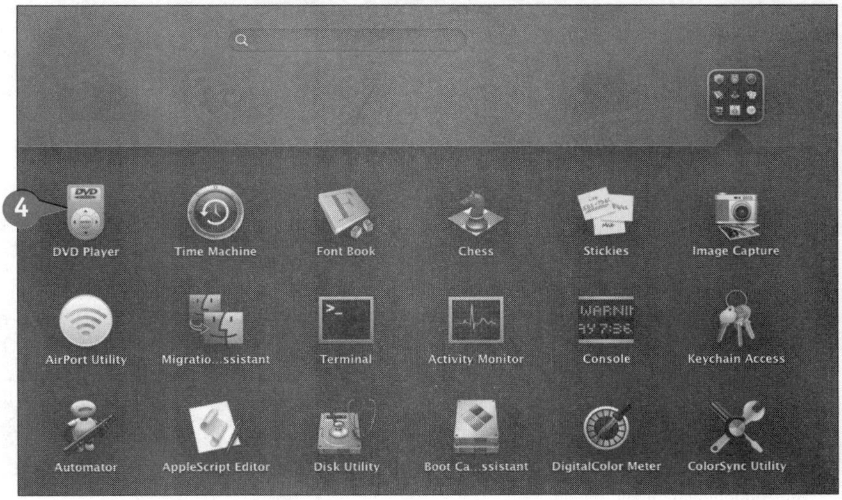

TIP

Is there an easier way to navigate the Launchpad screens?

Yes. Apple has designed Launchpad to work like the iPhone, iPad, and iPod touch, which you navigate by using a finger to swipe the screen right or left. With your Mac Pro, you can also navigate the Launchpad screens by swiping. In this case, however, you must use two fingers, and you swipe right or left on either a trackpad or the surface of a Magic Mouse.

You can also use a trackpad gesture to open Launchpad: Place four fingers lightly on the trackpad and pinch them together.

Switch Between Applications

If you plan on running multiple applications at the same time, you need to know how to easily switch from one application to another. In Mac Pro, after you start one application, you do not need to close that application before you open another one. Mac Pro supports a feature called *multitasking*, which means running two or more applications simultaneously. This is handy if you need to use several applications throughout the day.

Switch Between Applications

1 Click the Dock icon of the application to which you want to switch.

Ⓐ Mac Pro brings the application window(s) to the foreground.

Ⓑ The menu bar displays the menus associated with the application.

Note: To switch between applications from the keyboard, press and hold ⌘ and repeatedly press Tab until the application that you want is highlighted in the list of running applications. Release ⌘ to switch to the application.

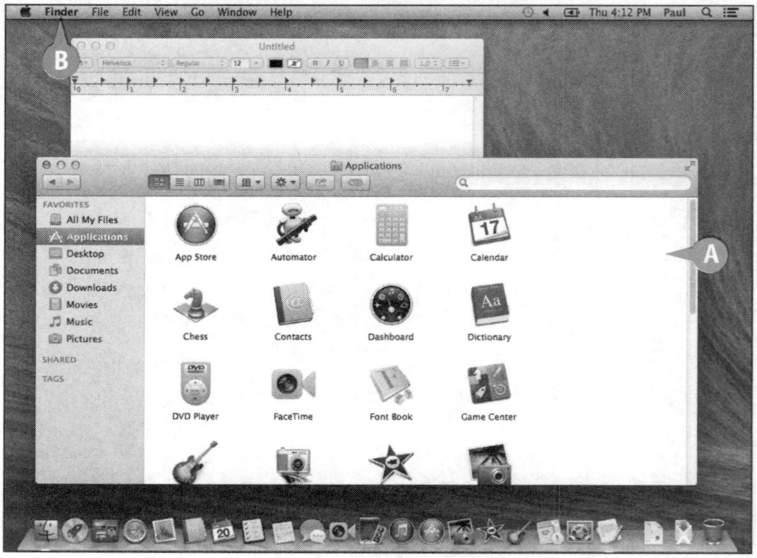

View Running Applications with Mission Control

CHAPTER 1

The Mission Control feature makes it easier for you to navigate and locate your running applications. Mac Pro allows you to open multiple applications at the same time, and the only real limit to the number of open applications you can have is the amount of memory contained in your Mac Pro. In practical terms, this means you can easily open several applications, some of which may have multiple open windows. To help locate and navigate to the window you need, use the Mission Control feature.

View Running Applications with Mission Control

1. Click **Mission Control** ( ).

Note: You can also invoke Mission Control by pressing F3, by placing four fingers on a trackpad and swiping up, or by double-tapping with two fingers on a trackpad or Magic Mouse.

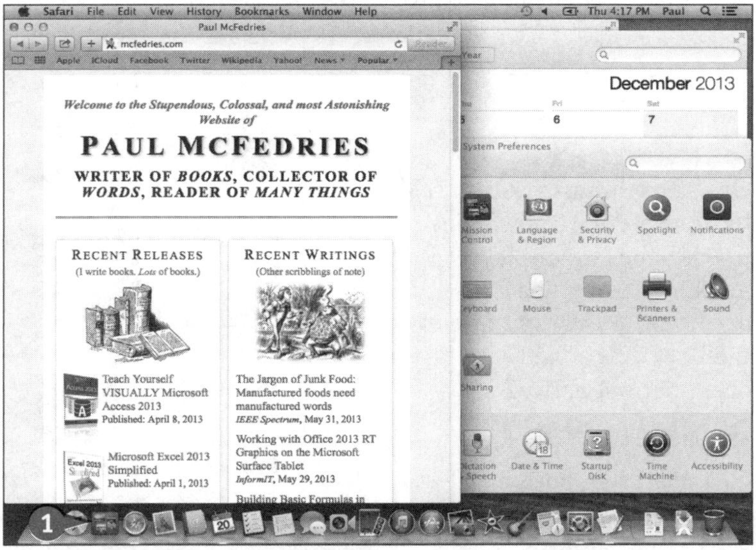

Ⓐ Mission Control displays each open window.

Ⓑ Mission Control groups windows from the same application.

To switch to a particular window, click it.

Ⓒ To close Mission Control without selecting a window, click **Desktop** or press Esc.

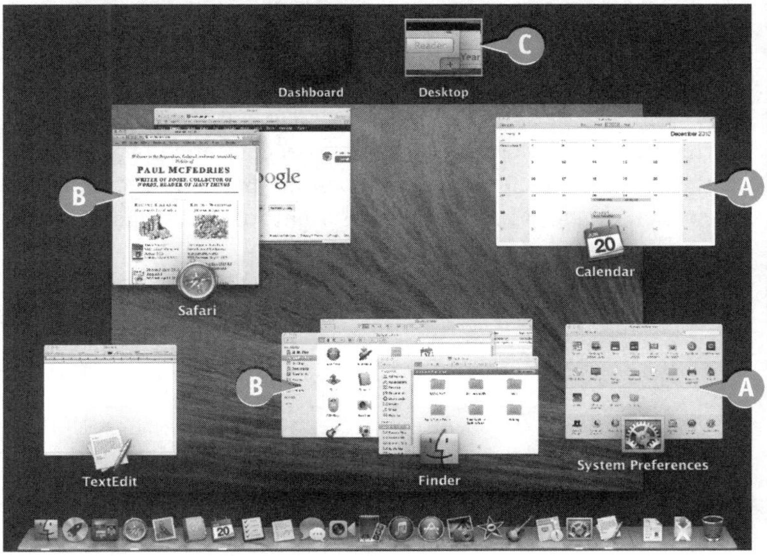

Tour an Application Window

When you start an application, it appears on the OS X desktop in its own window. Each application has a unique window layout, but almost all application windows have a few features in common. To get the most out of your applications and to start working quickly and efficiently in an application, you need to know what these common features are and where to find them within the application window.

A Close Button

Click the **Close** button to remove the application window from the desktop, usually without exiting the application.

B Minimize Button

Click the **Minimize** button to remove the window from the desktop and display an icon for the currently open document in the right side of the Dock. The window is still open, but not active.

C Zoom Button

Click the **Zoom** button to enlarge the window so that it can display all of its content, or as much of its content as can fit the screen.

D Toolbar

The toolbar contains buttons that offer easy access to common application commands and features, although not all applications have toolbars. To move the window, click and drag the toolbar.

E Vertical Scroll Bar

Click and drag the vertical scroll bar to navigate up and down in a document. In some cases, you can also click and drag the horizontal scroll bar to navigate left and right in a document.

F Resize Control

Click and drag any edge or corner of the window to make the window larger or smaller.

G Status Bar

The status bar displays information about the current state of the application or document.

Run an Application Full Screen

You can maximize the viewing and working areas of an application by running that application in full-screen mode. When you switch to full-screen mode, Mac Pro hides the menu bar, the application's status bar, the Dock, and the top section of the application window (the section that includes the Close, Minimize, and Zoom buttons). Mac Pro then expands the rest of the application window so that it takes up the entire screen. You must be running OS X Lion or later to use full-screen mode. Note, too, that not all programs are capable of switching to full-screen mode.

Run an Application Full Screen

1. Click **View**.
2. Click **Enter Full Screen**.

   You can also press Control + ⌘ + F.

(A) You can also click **Full Screen** (⤢).

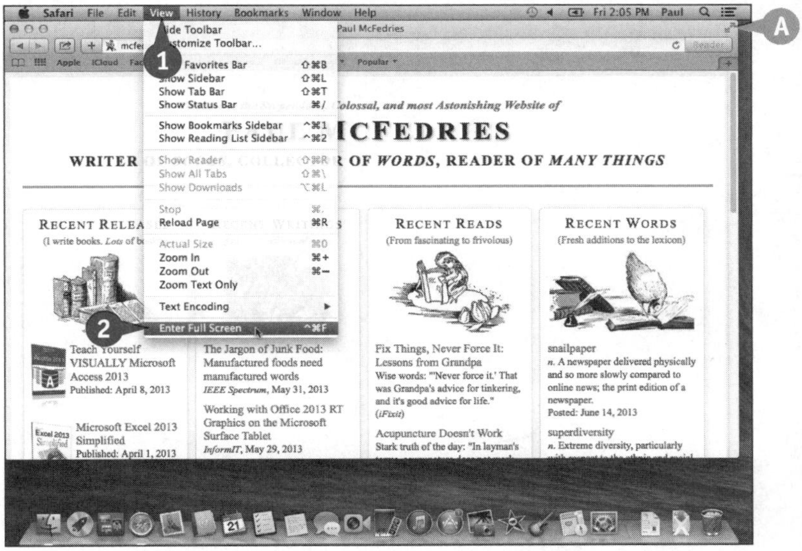

Mac Pro expands the application window to take up the entire screen.

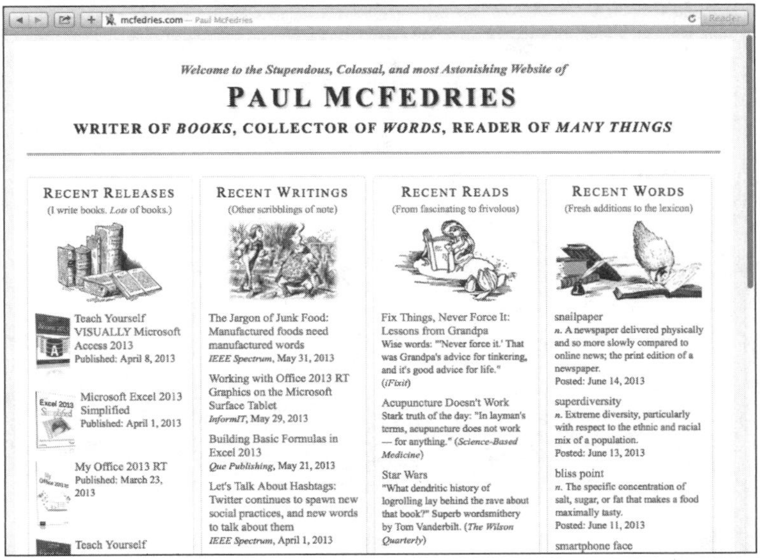

Note: To exit full-screen mode, move the mouse (pointer) up to the top of the screen to reveal the menu bar, click **View**, and then click **Exit Full Screen**. You can also press Esc.

CHAPTER 2

Learning Basic Document Tasks

Much of the work you do with Mac Pro involves documents, which are files that contain text, images, and other data. These tasks include saving, opening, printing, and editing documents, as well as copying and renaming files.

Save a Document

After you create a document and make changes to it, you can save the document to preserve your work. When you work on a document, OS X stores the changes in your Mac Pro's memory. However, OS X erases the contents of the Mac Pro's memory each time you shut down or restart the computer. This means that the changes you make to your document are lost when you turn off or restart your Mac Pro. Saving the document preserves your changes on your Mac Pro's hard drive.

Save a Document

1 Click **File**.

2 Click **Save**.

In most applications, you can also press ⌘+S.

If you have saved the document previously, your changes are now preserved, and you do not need to follow the rest of the steps in this section.

If this is a new document that you have never saved before, the Save As dialog appears.

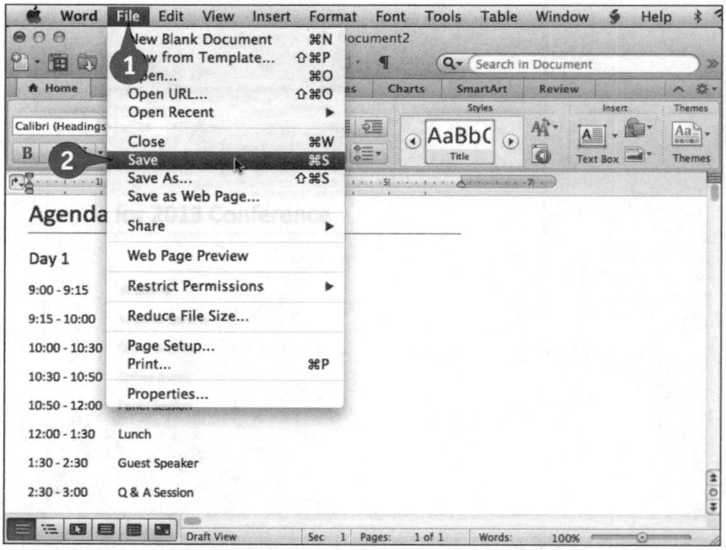

3 Type the filename you want to use in the Save As text box.

A To store the file in a different folder, you can click the **Where** ⇕ and then select the location that you prefer from the pop-up menu.

4 Click **Save**.

The application saves the file.

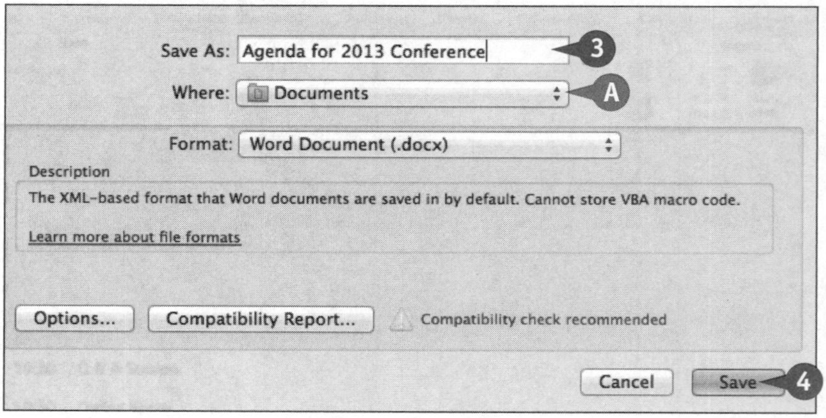

Open a Document

To work with a document that you have saved in the past, you can open it in the application that you used to create it. When you save a document, you save its contents to your Mac Pro's hard drive, and those contents are stored in a separate file. When you open the document using the same application that you used to save it, OS X loads the file's contents into memory and displays the document in the application. You can then view or edit the document as needed.

Open a Document

1. Start the application with which you want to work.
2. Click **File**.
3. Click **Open**.

   In most applications, you can also press ⌘+O.

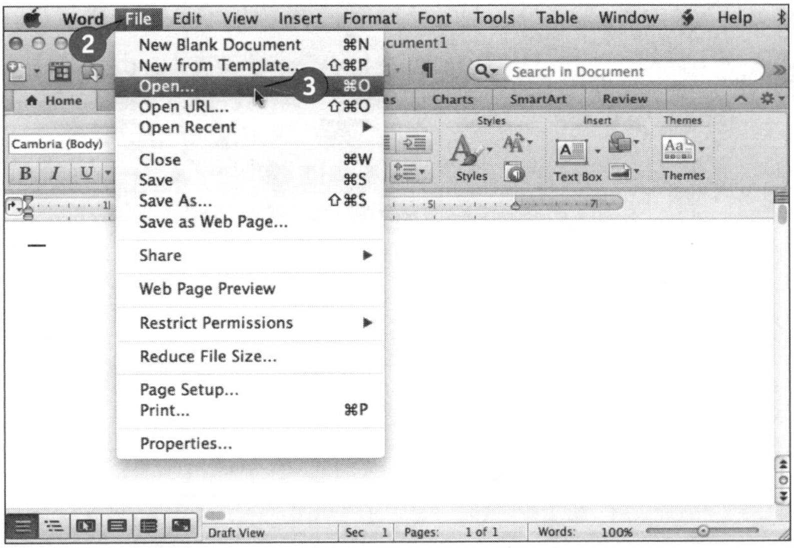

The Open dialog appears.

A. To select a different folder from which to open a file, you can click ⬍ and then click the location that you prefer.

4. Click the document.
5. Click **Open**.

   The document appears in a window on the desktop.

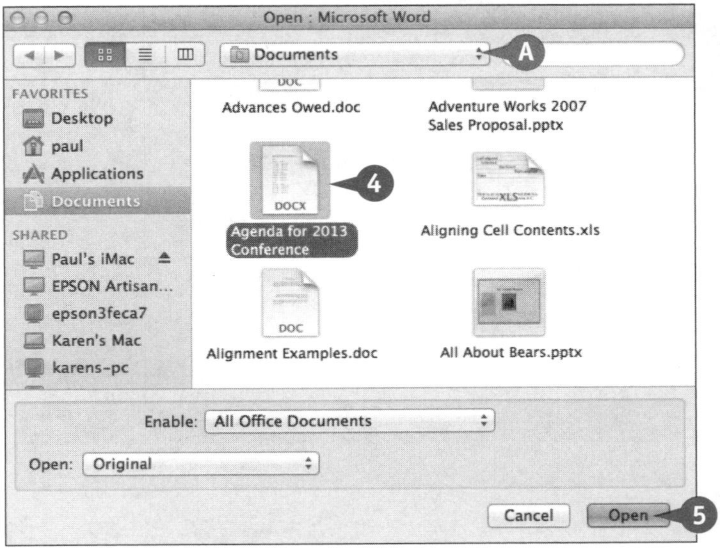

Print a Document

When you need a hard copy of your document, either for your files or to distribute to someone else, you can send the document to your printer. Most applications that deal with documents also come with a Print command. When you run this command, the Print dialog appears. You use the Print dialog to choose the printer you want to use, as well as to specify how many copies you want to print. Most Print dialogs also enable you to see a preview of your document before printing it.

Print a Document

1. Turn on your printer.
2. Open the document that you want to print.

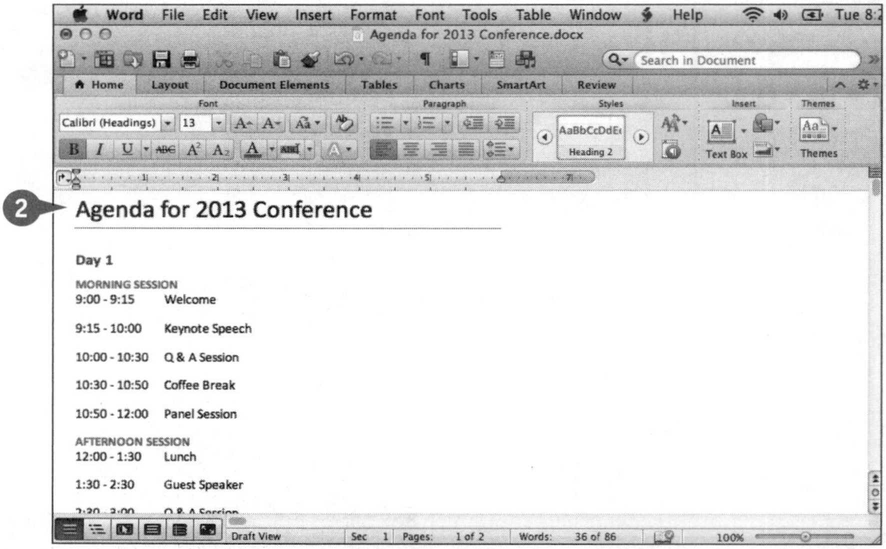

3. Click **File**.
4. Click **Print**.

   In most applications, you can select the Print command by pressing ⌘+P.

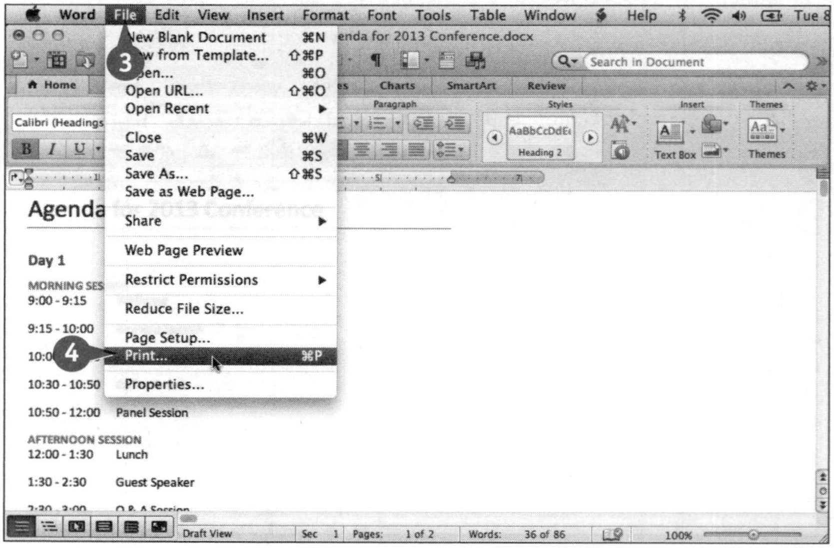

The Print dialog appears.

The layout of the Print dialog varies from application to application. The version shown here is a typical example.

5 If you have more than one printer, click the **Printer** to select the printer that you want to use.

6 To print more than one copy, type the number of copies to print in the Copies text box.

7 Click **Print**.

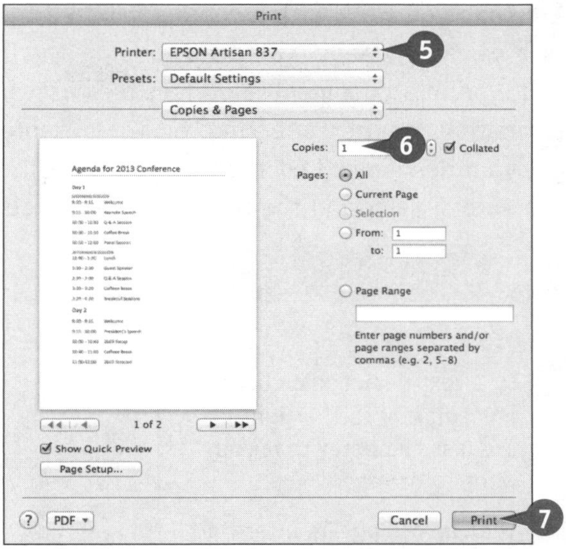

A Mac Pro prints the document. The printer's icon appears in the Dock while the document prints.

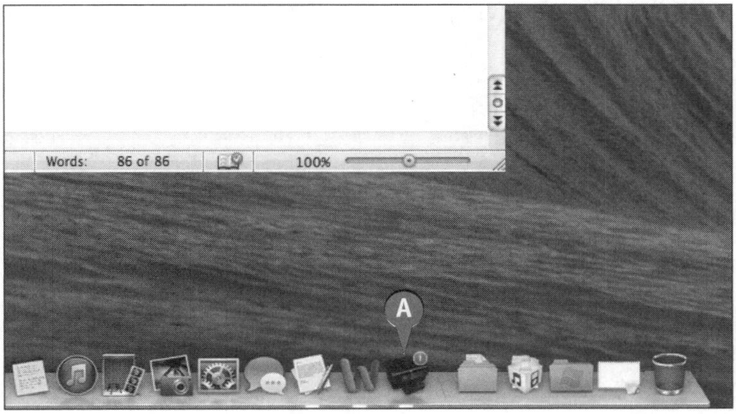

TIP

Can I print only part of my document?

Yes, you can print a range of pages by selecting the **From** option (○ changes to ◉) and then using the two text boxes to type the numbers of the first and last pages you want to print.

If you just want to print one page, click anywhere within the page before running the Print command; then select the **Current Page** option (○ changes to ◉) or the **From** option (○ changes to ◉) and type the page number in both text boxes.

If you just want to print a section of the document, select the text before running the Print command and then select the **Selection** option (○ changes to ◉).

Edit Document Text

When you work with a character-based file, such as a text or word processing document or an e-mail message, you need to know the basic techniques for editing text. It is rare that any text you type in a document is perfect the first time through. It is more likely that the text contains errors that require correcting, or words, sentences, or paragraphs that appear in the wrong place. To get your document text the way you want it, you need to know how to edit text, including deleting characters, selecting the text with which you want to work, and copying and moving text.

Edit Document Text

Delete Characters

1 In a text document, click immediately to the right of the last character that you want to delete.

A The cursor appears after the character.

Agenda for 2013 Conference

Day 1

MORNING SESSION

9:00 - 9:15	Welcome
9:15 - 10:00	Keynote Speech
10:00 - 10:30	Q & A Session
10:30 - 10:50	Coffee Break
10:50 - 12:00	Panel Session
12:00 - 1:30	Lunch

AFTERNOON SESSION

1:30 - 2:30	Guest Speaker
2:30 - 3:00	Q & A Session
3:00 - 3:20	Coffeee Break
3:20 - 4:00	A Look at the Future of the Industry
4:00 - 5:00	Breakout Sessions

2 Press Delete until you have deleted all the characters you want.

If you make a mistake, immediately click **Edit** and then click **Undo**. You can also press ⌘+Z.

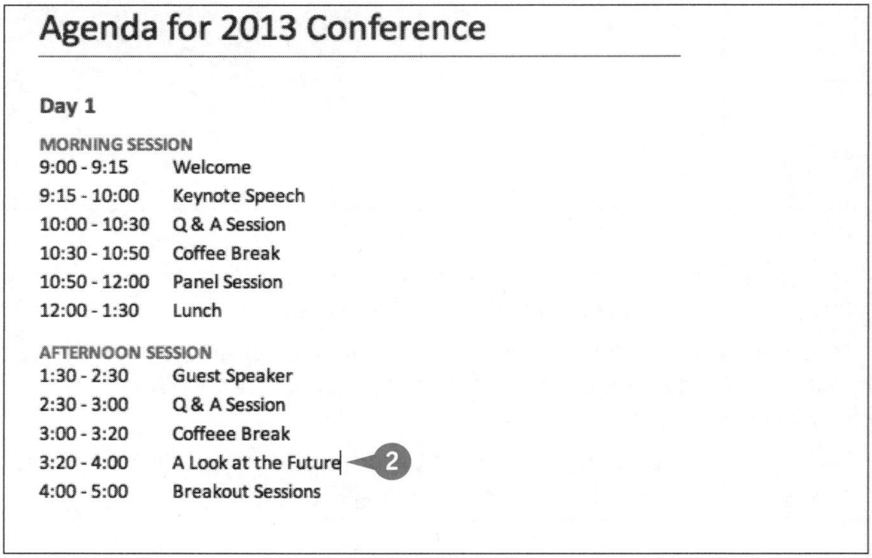
Agenda for 2013 Conference

Day 1

MORNING SESSION

9:00 - 9:15	Welcome
9:15 - 10:00	Keynote Speech
10:00 - 10:30	Q & A Session
10:30 - 10:50	Coffee Break
10:50 - 12:00	Panel Session
12:00 - 1:30	Lunch

AFTERNOON SESSION

1:30 - 2:30	Guest Speaker
2:30 - 3:00	Q & A Session
3:00 - 3:20	Coffeee Break
3:20 - 4:00	A Look at the Future
4:00 - 5:00	Breakout Sessions

Select Text for Editing

1. Click and drag across the text that you want to select.

2. Release the mouse button.

B The application highlights the selected text.

TIP

Are there any shortcut methods for selecting text?

Yes, most applications have shortcuts you can use. Here are the most useful ones:

- Double-click a word to select it.
- Press and hold Shift and press → or ← to select entire words.
- Press and hold Shift and ⌘ and press → to select to the end of the line, or ← to select to the beginning of the line.
- Triple-click inside a paragraph to select it.
- Click **Edit** and then click **Select All**, or press ⌘+A to select the entire document.

continued ►

Once you select text, you can then copy or move the text to another location in your document. Copying text is often a useful way to save work. For example, if you want to use the same passage of text elsewhere in the document, you can copy it instead of typing it from scratch. If you need a similar passage in another part of the document, copy the original and then edit the copy as needed. If you type a passage of text in the wrong position within the document, you can fix that by moving the text to the correct location.

Edit Document Text (continued)

Copy Text

1. Select the text that you want to copy.
2. Click **Edit**.
3. Click **Copy**.

   In most applications, you can also press ⌘+C.

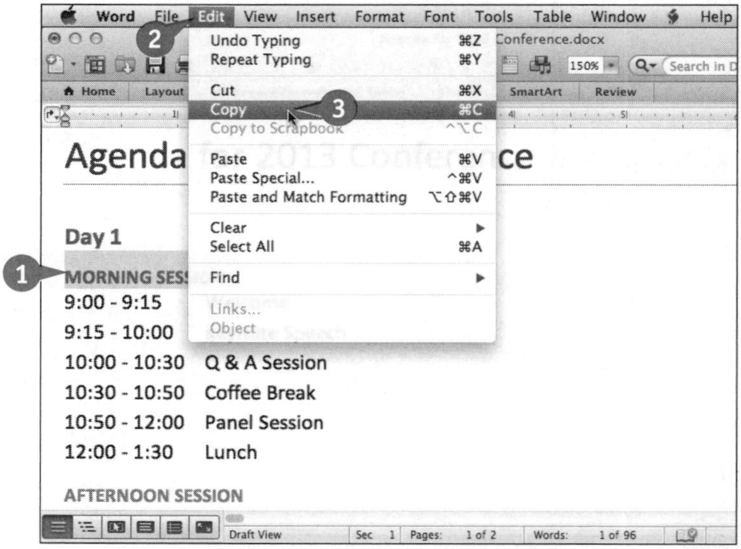

4. Click inside the document where you want the copied text to appear.

   The cursor appears in the position where you clicked.
5. Click **Edit**.
6. Click **Paste**.

   In most applications, you can also press ⌘+V.

Ⓐ The application inserts a copy of the selected text at the cursor position.

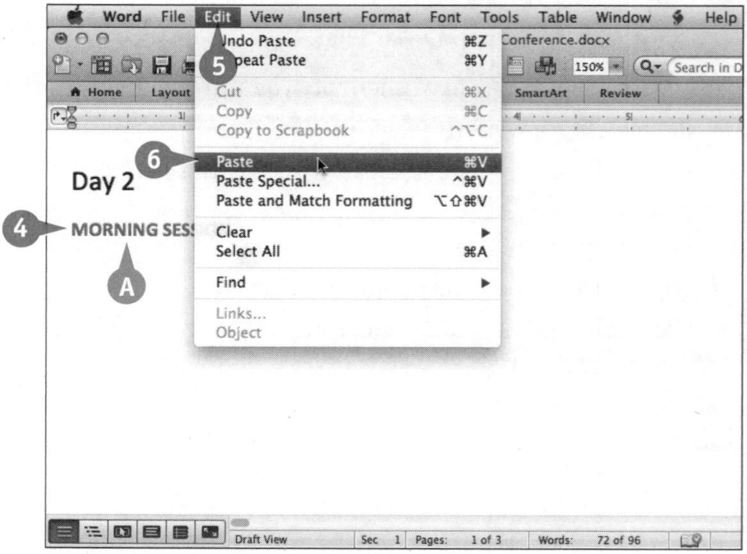

Move Text

1. Select the text that you want to move.
2. Click **Edit**.
3. Click **Cut**.

   In most applications, you can also press ⌘+X.

   The application removes the text from the document.

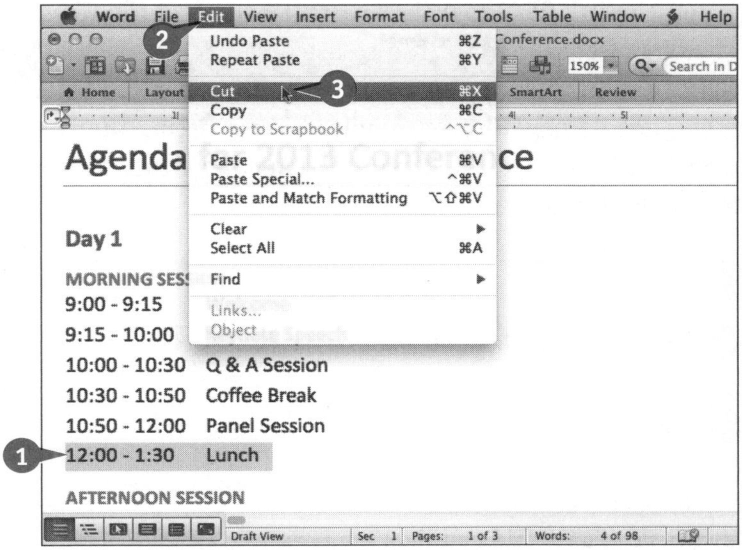

4. Click inside the document where you want to move the text.

   The cursor appears at the position where you clicked.

5. Click **Edit**.
6. Click **Paste**.

   In most applications, you can also press ⌘+V.

B The application inserts the text at the cursor position.

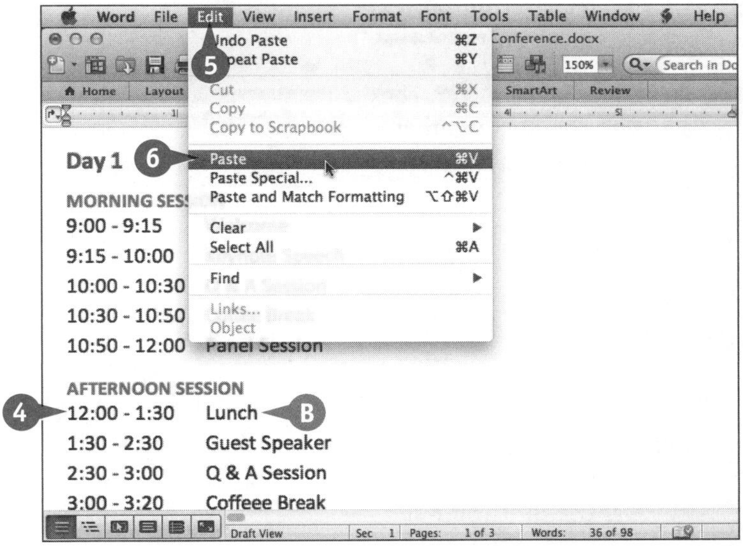

TIP

How do I move and copy text with my mouse?

To move and copy text with your mouse, select the text that you want to move or copy. To move the selected text, position the mouse over the selection and then click and drag the text to the new position within the document.

To copy the selected text, position the mouse pointer over the selection, press and hold Option, and then click and drag the text (the mouse changes to) to the new position within the document.

Copy a File

You can use OS X to make an exact copy of a file. This is useful when you want to make an extra copy of an important file to use as a backup. Similarly, you might require a copy of a file if you want to send the copy on a disk to another person. Finally, copying a file is also a real timesaver if you need a new file very similar to an existing file: You copy the original file and then make the required changes to the copy. You can copy either a single file or multiple files. You can also use this technique to copy a folder.

Copy a File

1. Locate the file that you want to copy.
2. Open the folder to which you want to copy the file.

   To open a second folder window, click **File** and then click **New Finder Window** or press ⌘+N.
3. Press and hold Option, click and drag the file, and then drop it inside the destination folder.

- A The original file remains in its folder.
- B A copy of the original file appears in the destination folder.

You can also make a copy of a file in the same folder, which is useful if you want to make major changes to the file and you would like to preserve a copy of the original. Click the file, click **File**, and then click **Duplicate**, or press ⌘+D. Mac Pro creates a copy with the word "copy" added to the filename.

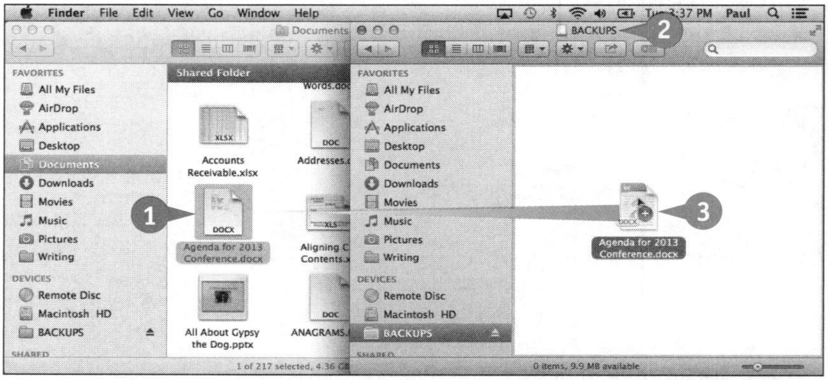

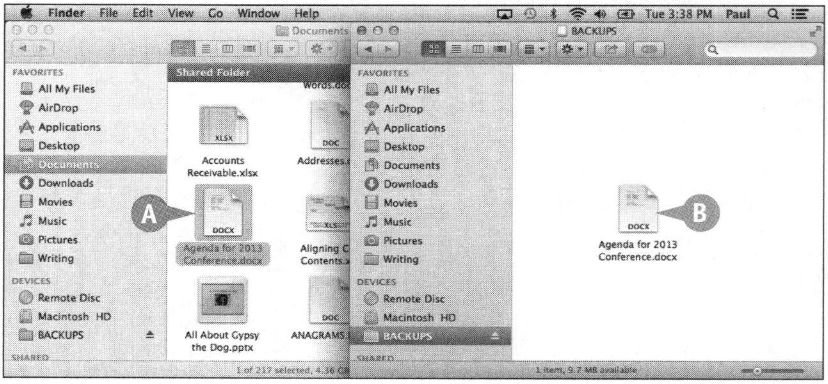

Move a File

When you need to store a file in a new location, the easiest way is to move the file from its current folder to another folder on your Mac Pro. When you save a file for the first time, you specify a folder on your Mac Pro's hard drive. This original location is not permanent, however. Using the technique in this section, you can move the file to another location on your Mac Pro's hard drive. You can use this technique to move a single file, multiple files, and even a folder.

Move a File

1. Locate the file that you want to move.
2. Open the folder to which you want to move the file.

   To create a new destination folder in the current folder, click **File** and then click **New Folder** or press Shift + ⌘ + N.
3. Click and drag the file and drop it inside the destination folder.

Note: If you are moving the file to another drive, you must hold down ⌘ while you click and drag the file.

- A The file disappears from its original folder.
- B The file moves to the destination folder.

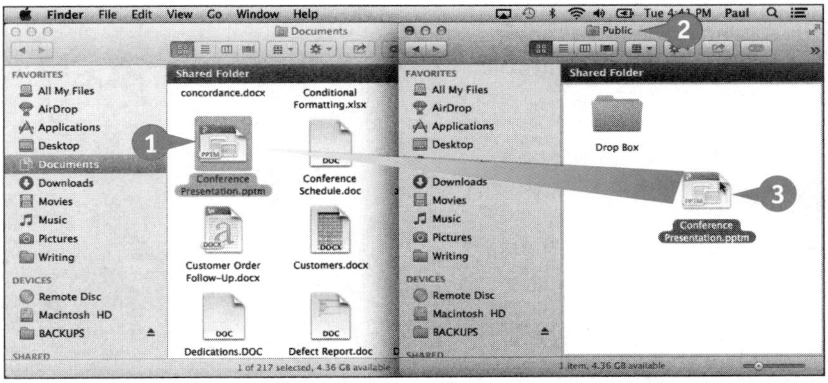

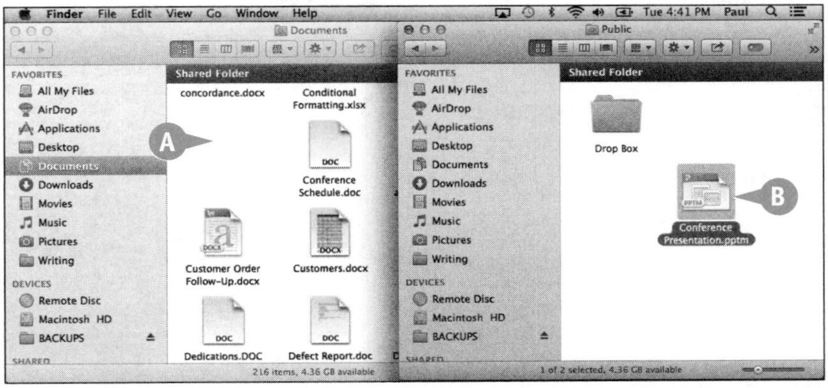

Rename a File

You can change the name of a file, which is useful if the current filename does not accurately describe the contents of the file. Giving your document a descriptive name makes it easier to find the file later. You should rename only those documents that you have created or that someone else has given to you. Do not try to rename any of the Mac Pro system files or any files associated with your applications, or your computer may behave erratically or even crash.

Rename a File

1. Open the folder containing the file that you want to rename.
2. Click the file.
3. Press Return.

Ⓐ A text box appears around the filename.

You can also rename any folders that you have created.

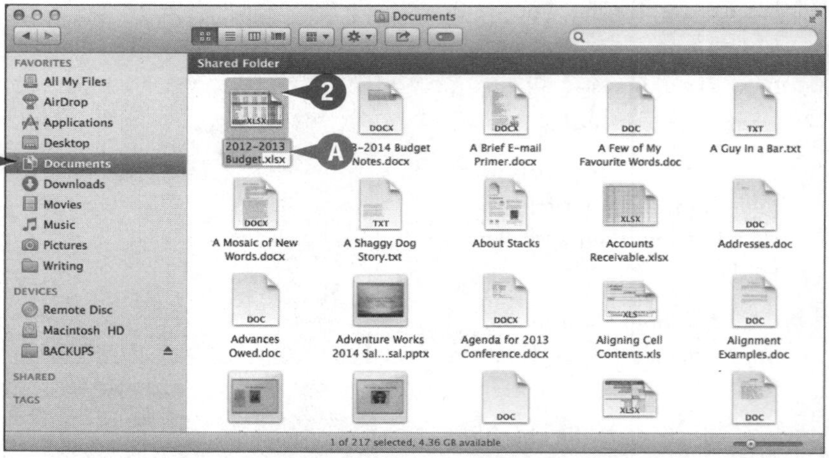

4. Edit the existing name or type a new name that you want to use for the file.

If you decide that you do not want to rename the file after all, you can press Esc to cancel the operation.

5. Press Return or click an empty section of the folder.

Ⓑ The new name appears under the file icon.

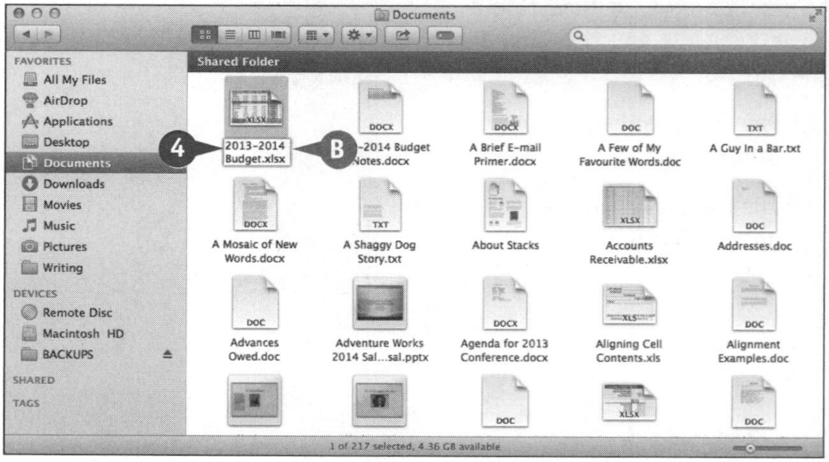

Delete a File

When you no longer need a file, you can delete it. This helps to prevent your hard drive from becoming cluttered with unnecessary files. You should ensure that you delete only those documents that you have created or that someone else has given to you. Do not delete any of the Mac Pro system files or any files associated with your applications, or your computer may behave erratically or even crash.

Delete a File

1. Locate the file that you want to delete.
2. Click and drag the file and drop it on the Trash icon in the Dock.

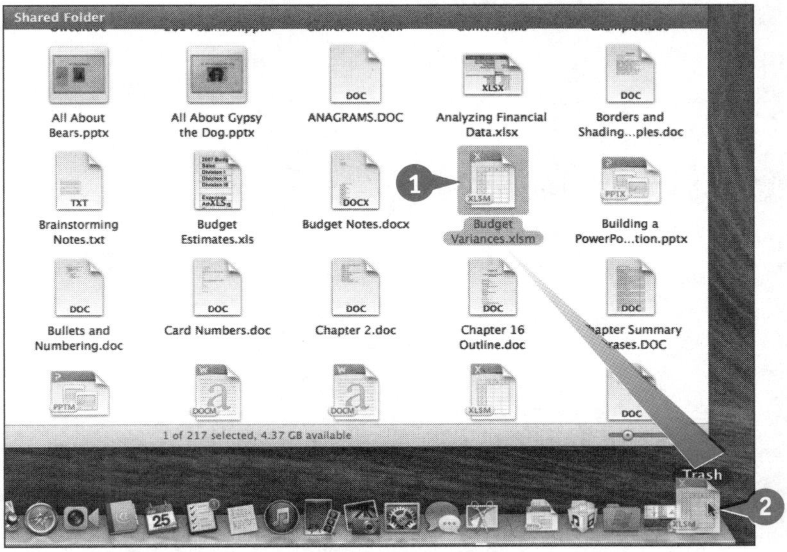

Ⓐ The file disappears from the folder.

You can also delete a file by clicking it and then pressing ⌘+Delete.

If you delete a file accidentally, you can restore it. Simply click the Dock's Trash icon to open the Trash window. Click and drag the file from the Trash window and drop it back in its original folder.

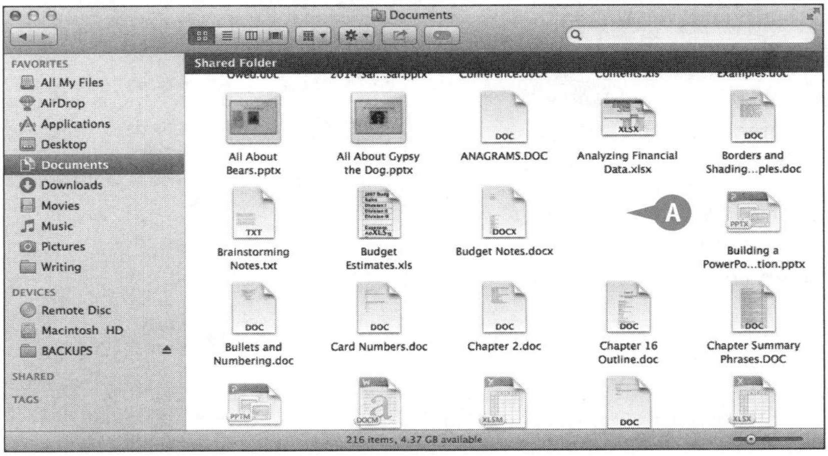

Open a Folder in a Tab

You can make it easier to work with multiple folders simultaneously by opening each folder in its own tab within a single Finder window. As you work with your documents, you may come upon one or more folders that you want to keep available while you work with other folders. Instead of cluttering the desktop with multiple Finder windows, Mac Pro enables you to use a single Finder window that displays each open folder in a special section of the window called a *tab*. To view the contents of any open folder, you need only click its tab.

Open a Folder in a Tab

Open a Folder in a New Tab

1. Right-click the folder you want to open.
2. Click **Open in New Tab**.

Ⓐ A new tab appears for the folder.

Ⓑ The folder's contents appear here.

Ⓒ Click any tab to display its contents in the Finder window.

Ⓓ To close a tab, position the mouse over the tab and then click **Close Tab** ().

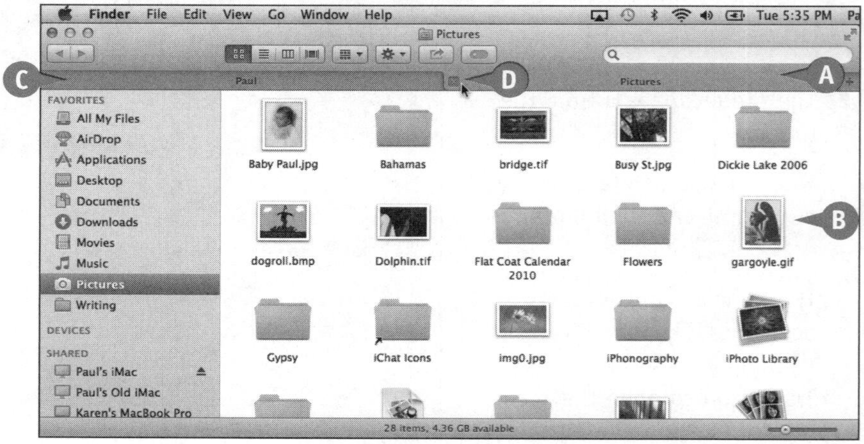

Create a New Tab

1. Click **File**.
2. Click **New Tab**.

E. If you already have two or more tabs open, you can also click the **Create a new tab** icon (+).

Finder creates a new tab.

Merge Open Folder Windows into Tabs

1. Click **Window**.
2. Click **Merge All Windows**.

Finder moves all the open folder windows into tabs in a single Finder window.

Note: To copy or move a file to a folder open in another tab, click and drag the file from its current folder and drop it on the other folder's tab.

TIP

Are there any shortcuts I can use to work with folders in tabs?

Yes, here are a few useful keyboard techniques you can try:

- In a folder, press and hold ⌘ and double-click a subfolder to open it in a tab. Press and hold ⌘+Shift instead to open the subfolder in a tab without switching to the tab.
- In the sidebar, press and hold ⌘ (or ⌘+Shift) and click a folder to open it in a tab.
- Press Shift+⌘+] or Shift+⌘+[to cycle through the tabs.
- Press ⌘+W to close the current tab.
- Press Option and click ☒ to close every tab but the one you clicked.

CHAPTER 3

Connecting Devices

When you plug a device into your Mac Pro, most of the time the device works right away. However, some devices require a bit of extra effort on your part to get them connected and configured. This chapter takes you through a few such devices, including an external display, printer, iPod touch, iPhone, iPad, Bluetooth device, and even another Mac.

Reviewing the Mac Pro Ports

You can connect your Mac Pro to a wide variety of external devices such as displays, hard drives, printers, digital cameras, iPhones, speakers, and microphones. Although your Mac Pro does support wireless device connections using Bluetooth (see the section "Pair with a Bluetooth Device"), most device connections occur by running a cable from the device to a port on your Mac Pro. To help you purchase your devices and to help you make the device connections, you need to understand the different types of ports that come with Mac Pro.

USB Ports

Your Mac Pro comes with four Universal Serial Bus (USB) ports for connecting devices such as hard drives, printers, digital cameras, iPhones, and iPads. Your Mac Pro supports USB 3, which is the latest and fastest version of USB. However, the Mac Pro USB ports are also compatible with the earlier USB 1 and USB 2, so you can still use cables and devices that only support these older versions.

Thunderbolt Ports

Your Mac Pro comes with six Thunderbolt ports for connecting peripherals such as displays, hard drives, and video-editing devices. You can connect Thunderbolt devices directly to Mac Pro, or you can *daisy-chain* devices. This means that if, say, device A comes with multiple Thunderbolt ports, you can connect device B to device A and then connect device A to Mac Pro. Your Mac Pro supports Thunderbolt 2, but is also backward-compatible with Thunderbolt 1 cables and devices.

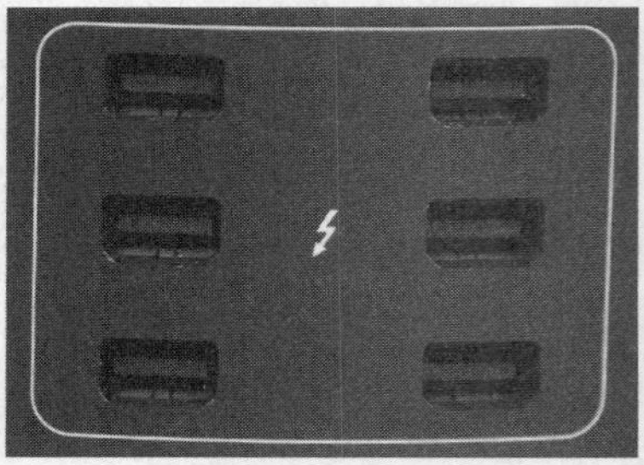

Network Ports

The Mac Pro supports Gigabit Ethernet for a physical connection to a network (wireless connections are also possible; see Chapter 21). *Gigabit* means that Mac Pro supports network connections up to one billion bits per second, although its ports are also compatible with slower networks. Mac Pro comes with two Gigabit Ethernet network ports, which allows Mac Pro to connect to two different networks.

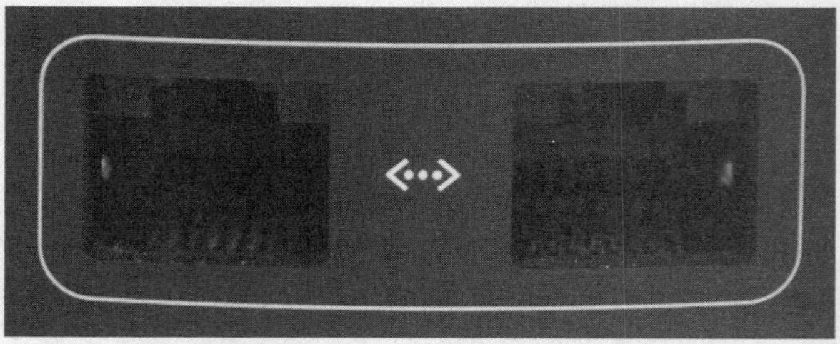

Microphone Port

Your Mac Pro comes with a microphone port that serves as an audio input connection. This enables you to provide audio for apps that support it, such as FaceTime, which you use to make Internet or network-based video phone calls (see Chapter 7), and Messages, which you use to conduct audio chats (also covered in Chapter 7).

Speaker Port

Your Mac Pro comes with a speaker port that serves as an audio output connection. This enables you to send the audio created by applications such as FaceTime, Messages, iTunes (see Chapter 11), and iMovie (see Chapter 13) to speakers, a sound system, or headphones.

HDMI Port

The Mac Pro comes with a High-Definition Multimedia Interface (HDMI) port for connection to a monitor, high-definition TV, or projector that has an HDMI port. You can use the connected HDMI device as an extra Mac Pro display (see the section "Set Up a Second Display") or you can send the Mac Pro screen output to a TV (see the section "Connect Mac Pro to a TV").

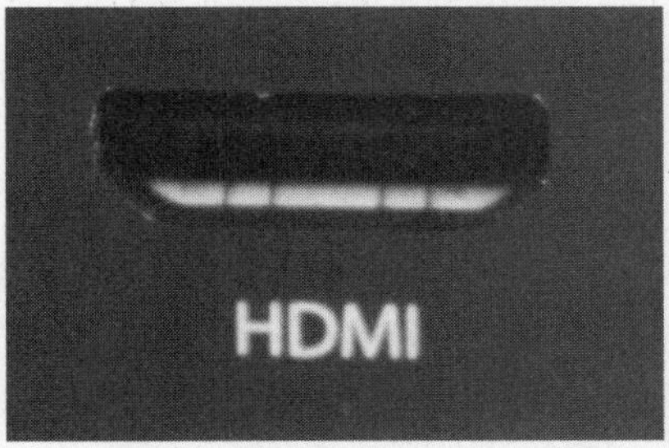

Set Up a Second Display

You can improve your productivity and efficiency by connecting a second monitor to your Mac Pro. For this to work, your extra display must have a video input port that matches an unused video output port on your Mac Pro, such as a Thunderbolt port or the HDMI port for connection to an HDTV. If you do not have such a port, check with Apple or the display manufacturer to see if an adapter is available that enables your Mac Pro to connect with the second display. After you connect your Mac Pro to the display, you can extend the OS X desktop across both monitors.

Set Up a Second Display

1. Connect the second monitor to your Mac Pro.
2. Click **System Preferences** ( ).

   The System Preferences appear.
3. Click **Displays**.

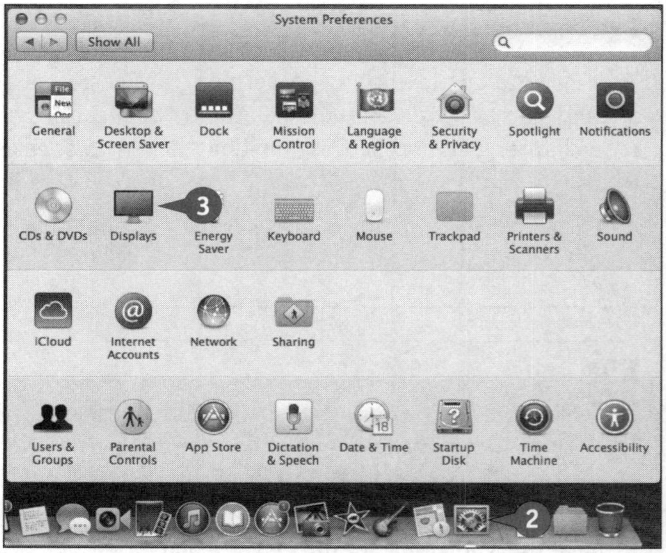

The Displays preferences appear.

4. Click the **Arrangement** tab.

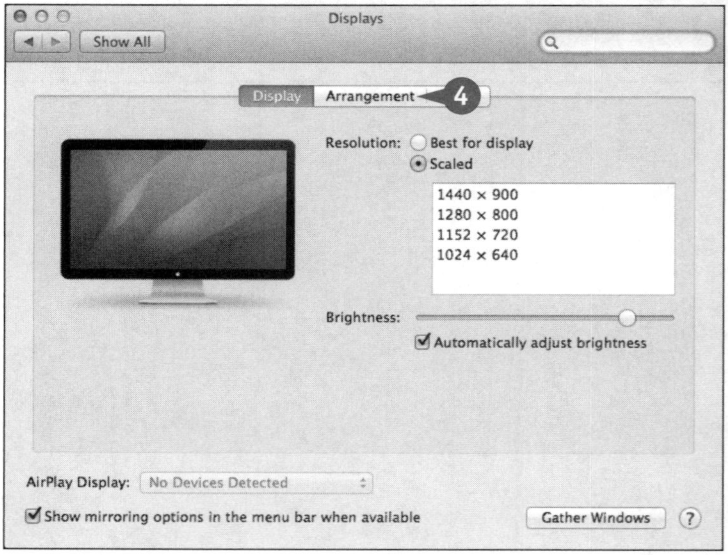

Ⓐ This window represents your Mac Pro's main display.

Ⓑ This window represents the second display.

Ⓒ This white strip represents the OS X menu bar.

5 Click and drag the windows to set the relative arrangement of the two displays.

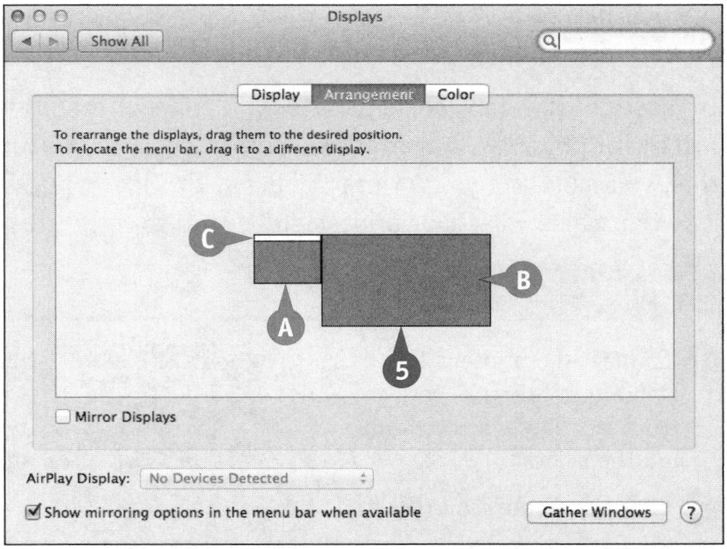

6 To move the menu bar and Dock to the second display, click and drag the menu bar and drop it on the second display.

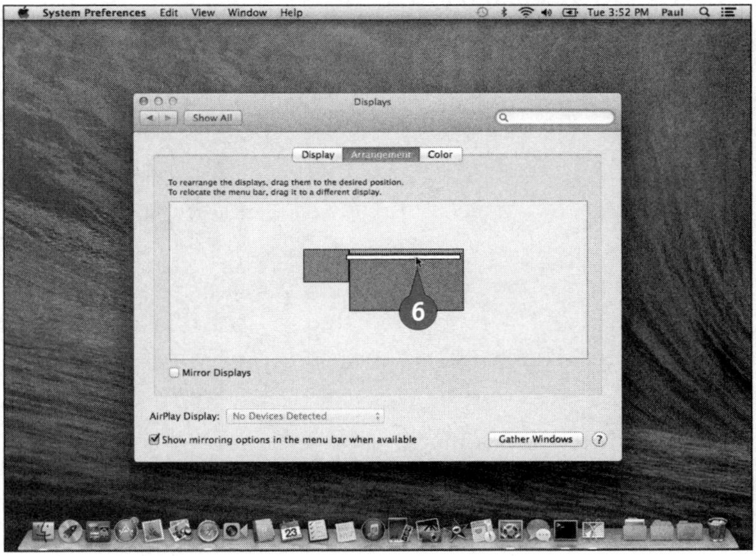

TIPS

Can I use a different desktop background in each display?

Yes. To set the desktop background on the second display, open System Preferences and click **Desktop & Screen Saver**. On the second display, you see the Secondary Desktop dialog. Use that dialog to set the desktop picture or color, as described in Chapter 14.

Can I just use the second display to show my main OS X desktop?

Yes. This is called *mirroring* the main display because the second display shows exactly what appears on your Mac Pro's main monitor, including the mouse pointer. Follow steps 1 to 4 to display the Arrangement tab and then select the **Mirror Displays** option (☐ changes to ☑).

Connect a Printer

If you have a printer that you want to use to make hard copies of some of your documents, you must first connect the printer to your Mac Pro.

In most cases, a few moments after you connect the printer, Mac Pro will recognize the printer and install it right away. However, you should check that your printer installed correctly. If it did not, then you must add your printer by hand. In some rare cases, you may need to insert the installation disc that came with your printer, so be sure to have the disc at hand just in case you need it.

Connect a Printer

1. Connect the printer's USB cable to a free USB port on your Mac Pro and then turn on the printer.
2. Click the **Apple** icon ( ).
3. Click **System Preferences.**

Note: You can also click the **System Preferences** icon ( ) in the Dock.

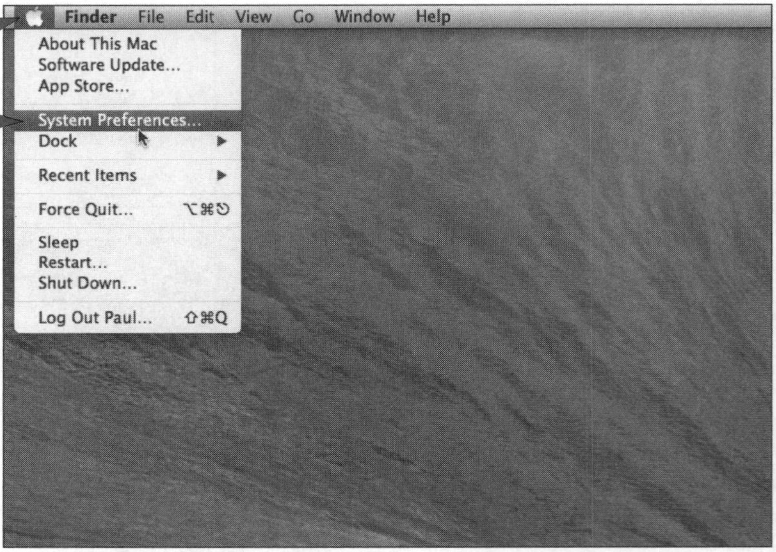

The System Preferences appear.

4. Click **Printers & Scanners.**

The Printers & Scanners preferences appear.

Ⓐ If you see your printer in the Printers list, skip the rest of the steps in this section.

5 Click **Add** (+).

6 Click **Add Printer or Scanner**.

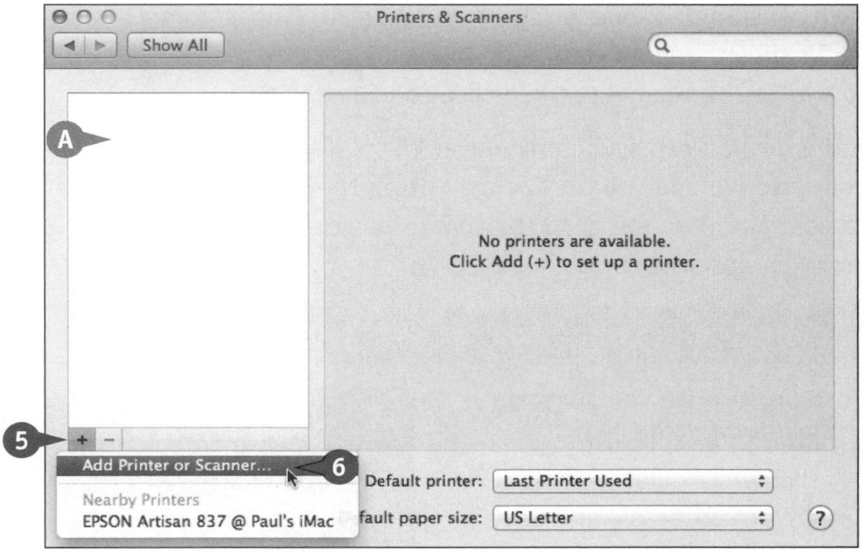

The Add dialog appears.

7 Click the **Default** tab.

8 Click your printer.

9 Click **Add**.

Mac Pro installs the printer, returns you to the Printers & Scanners preferences, and displays your printer.

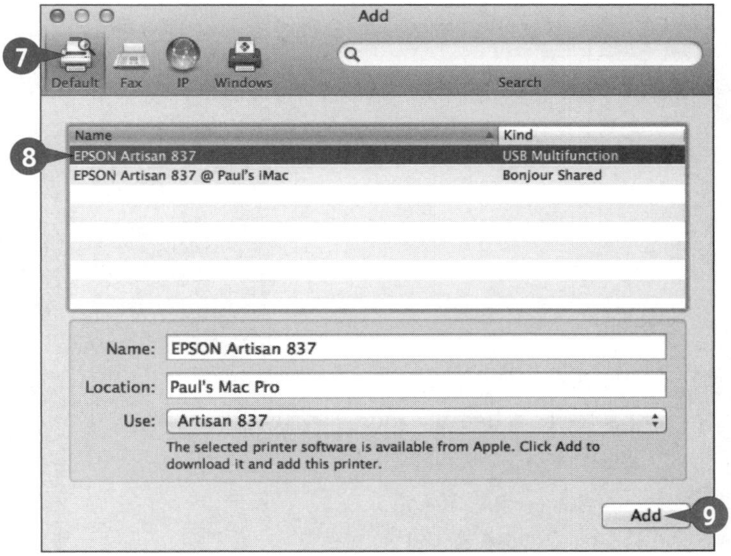

TIPS

Can I configure my printer?

Yes. In the Printers & Scanners preferences, click your printer. Click **Options & Supplies** to see the settings, which vary depending on the printer. For example, you can use the Options tab to set printer options, the Supply Levels tab to monitor ink levels, and the Utility tab to perform tasks such as printing a test page and cleaning the print heads.

What should I do if Mac Pro does not recognize my printer?

If you have an optical drive connected to Mac Pro, insert the disc that came with your printer and then run the installation program. If that does not work, follow steps 1 to 8, click the **Use** ⬍, and then click **Other**. Click the printer disc, locate and choose the printer driver, and then click **Open**.

Connect an iPhone, iPad, or iPod touch

To synchronize some or all of your Mac Pro iTunes library — including music, podcasts, audiobooks, TV shows, and movies — as well as your photos and e-books, with your iPhone, iPad, or iPod touch, you can connect the device to your Mac Pro.

Although you can synchronize over Wi-Fi, if your device is not running a recent version of iOS, or if your Mac Pro and your device are not on the same network, you must physically connect your device to your Mac Pro. You need the USB cable that came with the device package. You can also connect using an optional dock.

Connect an iPhone, iPad, or iPod touch

Connect the Device Directly

1. Attach the USB cable's Lightning connector to the device's port.

2. Attach the cable's USB connector to a free USB port on your Mac Pro.
3. If your device asks if you trust this computer, tap **Trust** on the device and click **Continue** on your Mac Pro.

   Your Mac Pro launches iTunes and automatically begins synchronizing the device.

Connect the Device Using the Dock

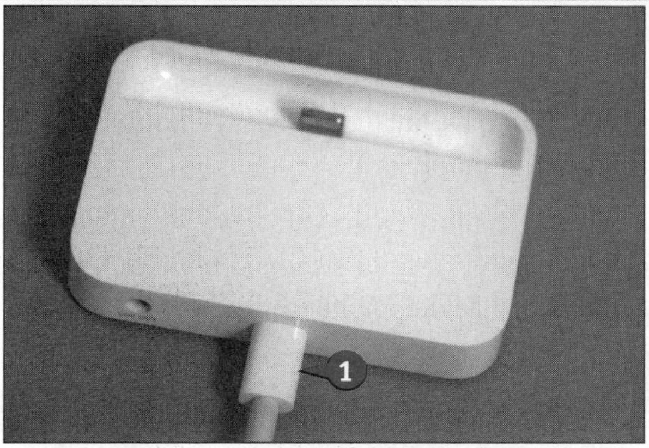

1. Attach the USB cable's Lightning connector to the dock's port.

2. Insert the device into the dock.

3. Attach the cable's USB connector to a free USB port on your Mac Pro.
4. If your device asks if you trust this computer, tap **Trust** on the device and click **Continue** on your Mac Pro.

   Your Mac Pro launches iTunes and automatically begins synchronizing the device.

TIP

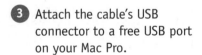

Do I have to eject my device before disconnecting it?

No, you can disconnect the device at any time as long as no sync is in progress. If a sync is in progress and you need to disconnect, first click **Cancel Sync** (⊠) in the iTunes status window and then disconnect your device.

Connect and Configure a Microphone

If you want to supply audio input to your Mac Pro, you must connect an external microphone, which could either be a standalone mic or a headset. This enables you to provide voice input for a number of apps, including FaceTime (for video phone calls), Messages (for audio chats), and iMovie (for adding narration).

Although in most cases your Mac Pro automatically configures the connected microphone as your default audio input device, you should check that this is the case and set up the microphone as your audio input device by hand if needed.

Connect and Configure a Microphone

Connect the Microphone

1. Connect the microphone's stereo mini plug to the Microphone port on the Mac Pro.

A. If your microphone is a USB device, connect it to a USB port, instead.

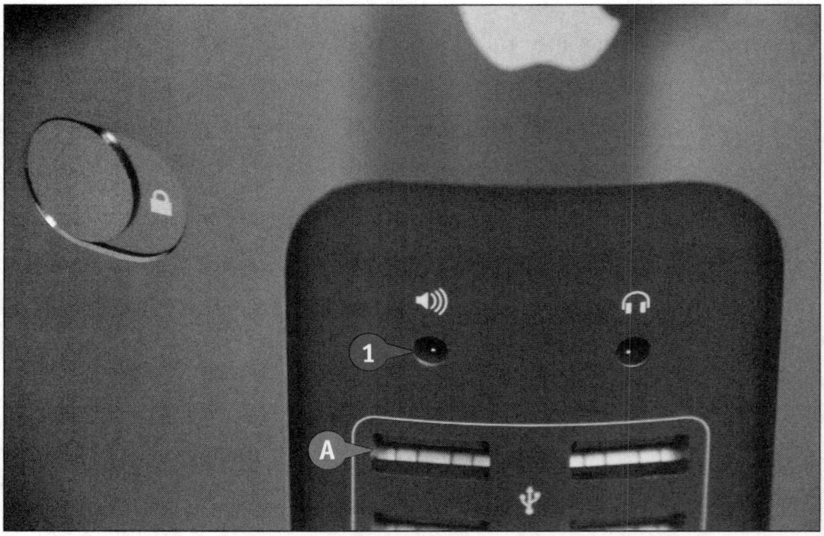

Configure the Microphone

1. Click the **Apple** icon (■).
2. Click **System Preferences**.

Note: You can also click the **System Preferences** icon (■) in the Dock.

The System Preferences appear.

3 Click **Sound**.

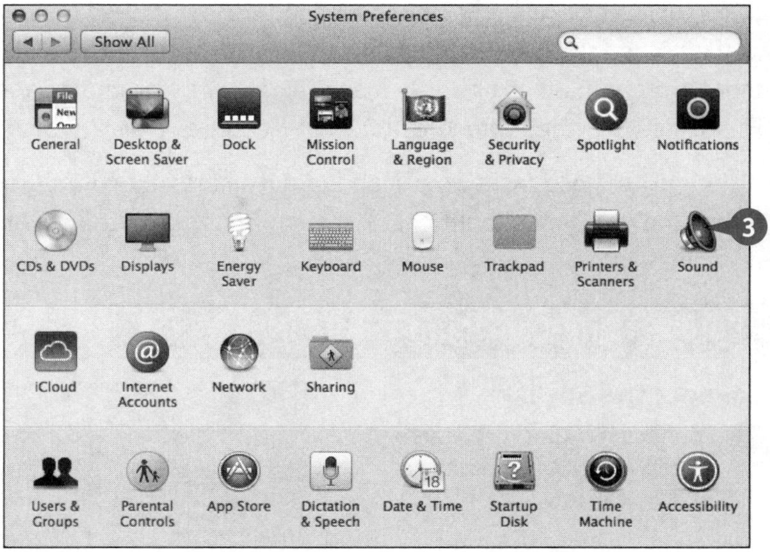

The Sound preferences appear.

4 Click the **Input** tab.

5 Click your microphone or headset.

Mac Pro now uses the microphone or headset as the default audio input device.

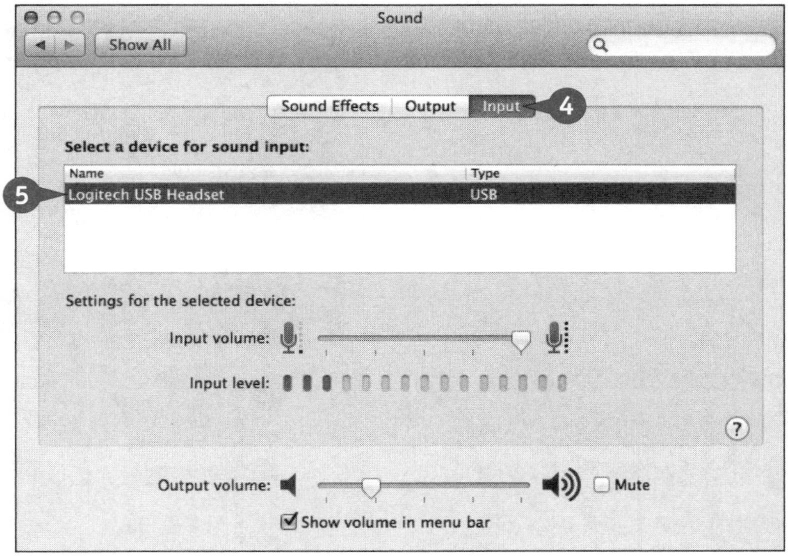

TIPS

Can I connect a musical instrument or professional mic?

Yes, but not usually directly. In most cases, you need an adapter, either a 1/8-inch stereo mini plug to 1/4-inch phono adapter, or a 1/8-inch stereo mini plug to XLR connector adapter.

My voice input is too loud. Can I turn it down?

Yes. Click **System Preferences** ( ), click **Sound**, and then click the **Input** tab. Click and drag the **Input volume** slider ( ) to the left to reduce the volume to an acceptable level. To test the volume, speak into the mic and watch the **Input level** meter. When you are speaking in a normal voice, this meter should not exceed the halfway point.

Connect and Configure External Speakers

If you want to hear the sounds made both by your Mac Pro and by your apps, you must connect your Mac Pro to a set of speakers, a headset, or an audio system. This enables you to hear audio input from a number of apps, including iTunes (for music, audiobooks, TV shows, and movies), FaceTime (for video phone calls), and Messages (for audio chats).

Although in most cases your Mac Pro automatically configures the speakers as your default audio output device, you should check this and configure the speakers as your audio output device manually if needed.

Connect and Configure External Speakers

Connect the Speakers

1. Connect the speakers' stereo mini plug to the Speaker port on the Mac Pro.

A. If your speakers use a USB connection, connect them to a USB port, instead.

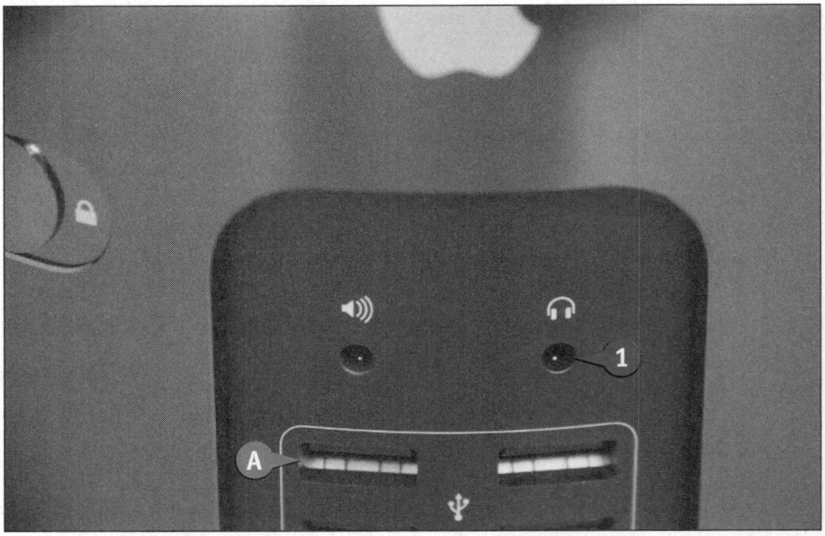

Configure the Speakers

1. Click the **Apple** icon (■).
2. Click **System Preferences**.

Note: You can also click the **System Preferences** icon (▣) in the Dock.

The System Preferences appear.

3 Click **Sound**.

The Sound preferences appear.

4 Click the **Output** tab.

5 Click your speakers.

Mac Pro now uses the speakers as the default audio output device.

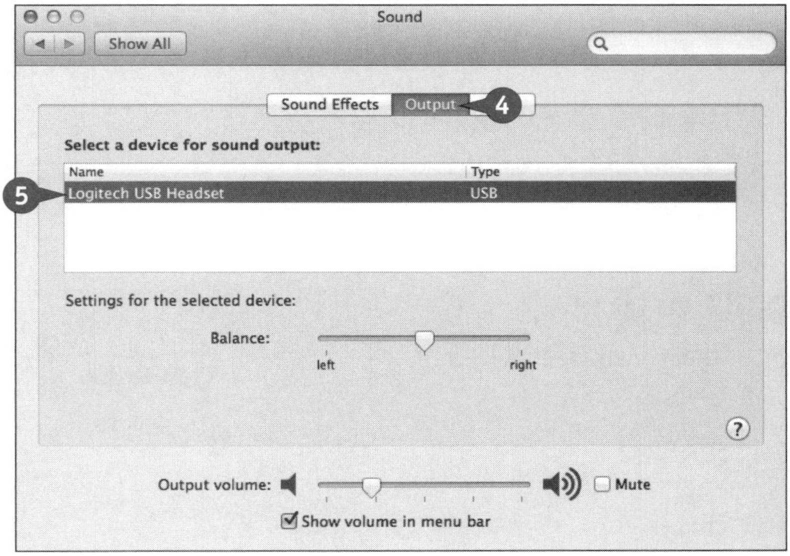

TIP

How do I adjust the sound output volume?

Click **System Preferences** (), click **Sound**, and then click the **Output** tab. Make sure your speakers are selected in the **Select a device for sound output** list. Click and drag the **Output volume** slider () either to the left to reduce the volume, or to the right to increase the volume.

You can also leave the **Show volume in menu bar** option selected () and then click the **Volume** icon () in the menu bar to adjust the output volume.

Connect a Fax Modem

If you want to send or receive faxes using your Mac Pro, you must connect an external fax modem. Faxing has long been superseded by e-mail as the preferred way of sending documents and images. However, faxing still has a place in the world for those times when you need to send a document that shows your signature or contains handwritten annotations. Note that Apple's USB Modem is not compatible with OS X Lion or later.

Connect a Fax Modem

1. Connect the fax modem to a free USB port on your Mac.
2. Follow steps 2 to 5 in the section "Connect a Printer" to display the Add Printer dialog.

3. Click the **Fax** tab.
4. In the Name list, click your modem.

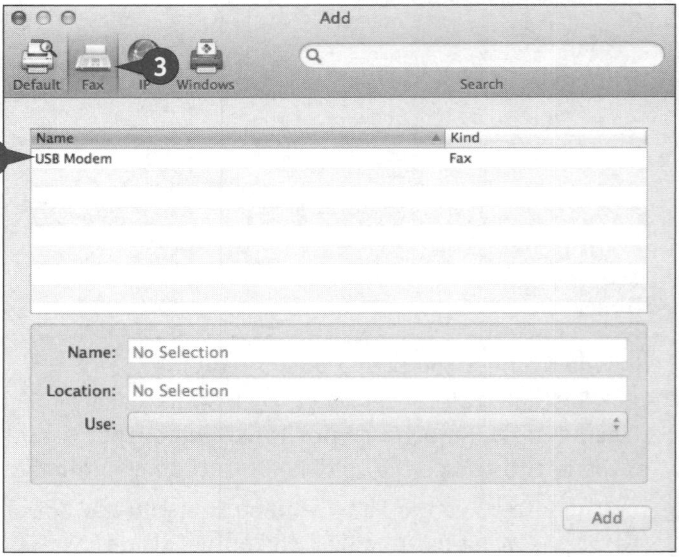

5. Use the Name text box to edit the modem name.
6. Click **Add**.

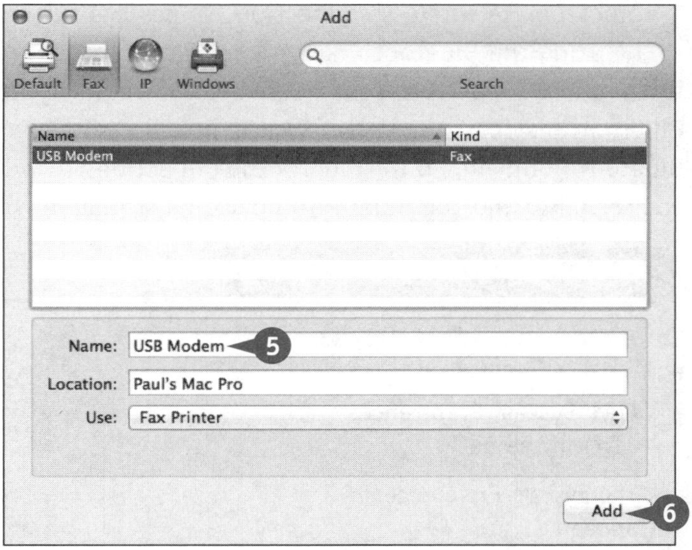

A. Mac Pro adds the modem to the Faxes list.

7. Click **Close** (■).

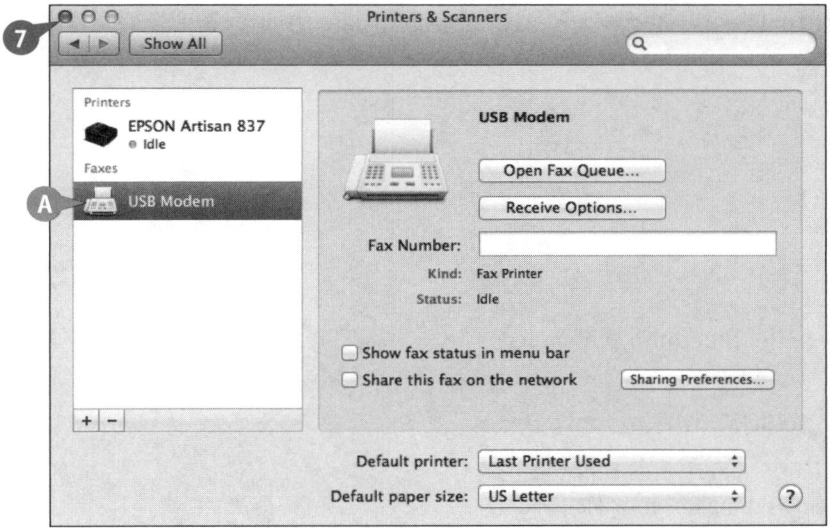

TIP

What do I do if my modem has a serial port instead of a USB port?

Although almost all new modems come with USB ports, many older modems use a serial port instead. Your Mac Pro does not have a corresponding serial port, so you need to purchase a serial-to-USB adapter or cable, which has a serial connector on one end and a USB connector on the other. You will also likely need to locate a device driver that enables your Mac Pro to communicate with the modem. Check the manufacturer's website to see if a 64-bit Mac driver is available.

Pair with a Bluetooth Device

You can make wireless connections to devices such as mice, keyboards, headsets, and cell phones by using the Bluetooth networking technology. The networking tasks that you learn about in Chapter 21 require special equipment to connect your computers and devices. However, with Bluetooth devices, the networking is built in, so no extra equipment is needed. Your Mac Pro has Bluetooth built in, so for Bluetooth connections to work, your device must be Bluetooth-enabled and your Mac Pro and the Bluetooth device must remain within about 30 feet of each other.

Pair with a Bluetooth Device

Connect a Bluetooth Device without a Passkey

1. Click **System Preferences** ( ) in the Dock.

   The System Preferences appear.

2. Click **Bluetooth**.

The Bluetooth preferences appear.

3. Click **Turn Bluetooth On**.

   OS X activates Bluetooth and makes your Mac Pro discoverable.

4 Perform whatever steps are necessary to make your Bluetooth device discoverable.

Note: For example, if you are connecting a Bluetooth mouse, the device often has a separate switch or button that makes the mouse discoverable, so you need to turn on that switch or press that button.

A A list of the available Bluetooth devices appears here.

5 Click **Pair** beside the Bluetooth device you want to connect.

6 Perform the steps required to pair your Mac Pro and your device.

B Your Mac Pro connects with the device.

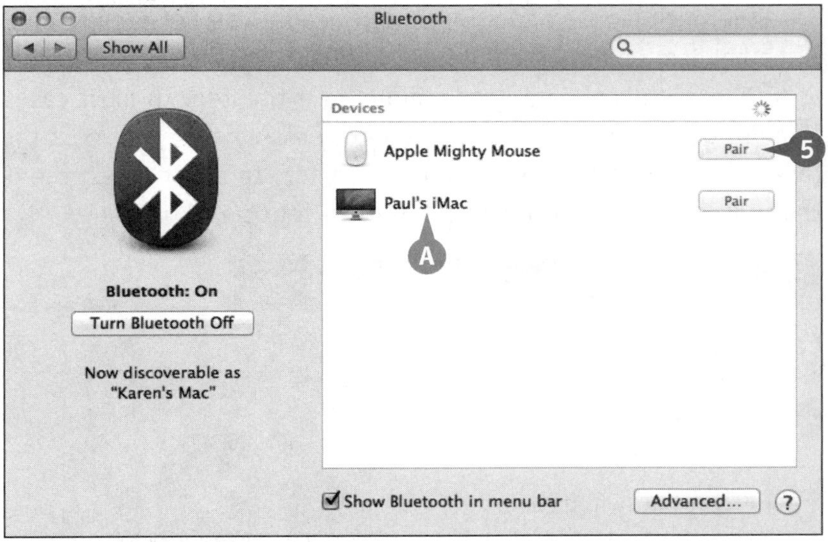

TIPS

What does it mean to make a device discoverable?

This means that you configure the device to broadcast its availability for a Bluetooth connection. Controlling the broadcast is important because you usually want to use a Bluetooth device such as a mouse or keyboard with only a single computer.

What does pairing mean?

As a security precaution, many Bluetooth devices do not connect automatically to other devices. This makes sense, because otherwise it means a stranger with a Bluetooth device could connect to your cell phone or even your Mac Pro. To prevent this, most Bluetooth devices require you to type a password before the connection is made. This is known as *pairing* the two devices.

continued ►

A Bluetooth mouse and a Bluetooth headset do not require any extra pairing steps, although with a headset you must configure Mac Pro to use it for sound output. However, pairing devices such as a Bluetooth keyboard does require an extra step. In most cases, pairing is accomplished by your Mac Pro generating a six- or eight-digit *passkey* that you must then type into the Bluetooth device (assuming that it has some kind of keypad). In other cases, the device comes with a default passkey that you must type into your Mac Pro to set up the pairing.

Pair with a Bluetooth Device (continued)

Connect a Bluetooth Device with a Passkey

1. Turn on the device, if required.
2. Turn on the switch that makes the device discoverable, if required.
3. Follow steps **1** and **2** in the subsection "Connect a Bluetooth Device without a Passkey" to display a list of available Bluetooth devices.
4. Click **Pair** beside your Bluetooth device.

   The Bluetooth Setup Assistant displays a passkey.
5. Use the Bluetooth device to type the displayed passkey.
6. Press Return.

   OS X connects to the device. If you see the Keyboard Setup Assistant, follow the on-screen instructions to set up the keyboard for use with your Mac Pro.

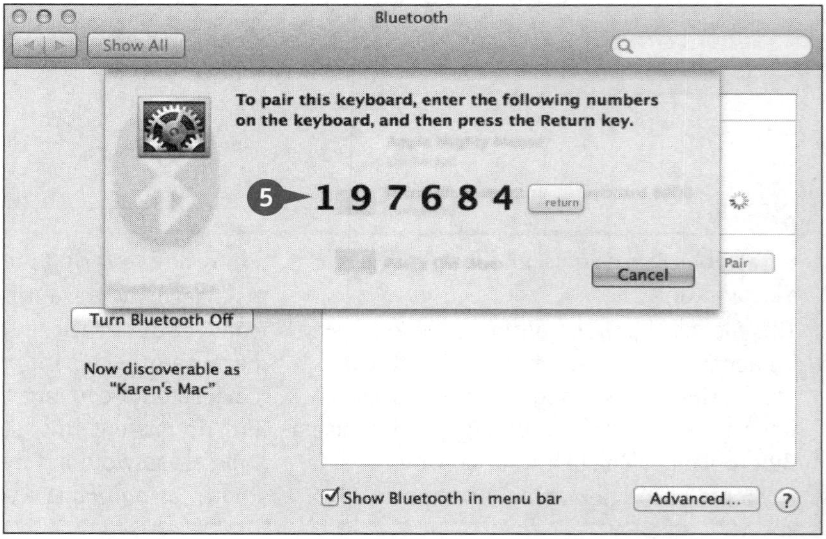

Listen to Audio through Bluetooth Headphones

1. Click **System Preferences** ( ) in the Dock.

   The System Preferences appear.

2. Click **Sound**.

   The Sound preferences appear.

3. Click **Output**.

4. Click the Bluetooth headphones.

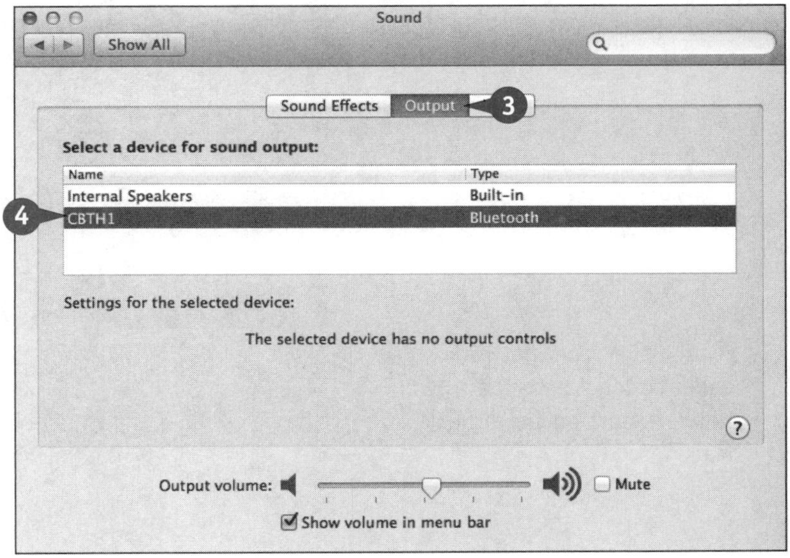

TIP

How do I remove a Bluetooth device?

To remove a Bluetooth device, first follow steps 1 and 2 in the subsection "Connect a Bluetooth Device without a Passkey." Position the mouse ( ) over the device you want to disconnect and then click **Disconnect** ( ). When Mac Pro asks you to confirm, click **Remove.** Mac Pro removes the device. Alternatively, click the **Bluetooth status** icon ( ) in the menu bar, click the device you want to remove, and then click **Disconnect**.

Connect Mac Pro to Another Mac

You can share data such as documents, bookmarks, and downloads between two Macs by connecting those Macs directly using a network cable. Once the connection is made, Mac Pro can see the other Mac's shared folders and can work with them based on the permissions assigned to those folders.

This section assumes that you do not have a local area network set up, so you need to connect the two Macs directly. In either case, you must enable file sharing to share data between the Macs.

Connect Mac Pro to Another Mac

Connect Using a Network Cable

1. Attach one of the network cable's connectors to a network port on your Mac Pro.

2. Attach the other network cable connector to the network port on the other Mac.

Enable File Sharing

1. Click the **Apple** icon (🍎).
2. Click **System Preferences**.

The System Preferences appear.

3. Click **Sharing**.

TIPS

Can I connect my Mac Pro to a MacBook Air, which does not have a network port?
Yes. However, you will need to use a USB network adapter to make the connection. Good examples are the Apple Thunderbolt to Gigabit Ethernet Adapter ($29) and the Apple USB Ethernet Adapter ($29).

Can I connect Mac Pro to another Mac using a Thunderbolt cable?
Yes, but OS X does not set up a network interface between the two machines. Instead, you must start up the other Mac in *target disk mode*, which configures the other Mac to appear as an external hard disk on your Mac Pro. To get the other Mac into target disk mode, start it and hold down T.

continued ▶

The purpose of connecting one Mac to another is to share documents, photos, and other data between the two Macs. By default, a Mac is not configured to share its data with other computers, so you must enable file sharing on both Macs.

Once file sharing is turned on, after you make the Thunderbolt or network cable connection you can see the files shared on the other Mac by accessing Finder's Network folder. You can also control which folders each Mac shares.

Connect Mac Pro to Another Mac (continued)

The Sharing preferences appear.

4 Select the **File Sharing** option (☐ changes to ☑).

Note: See the tip in this section to learn how to share other folders on your Mac Pro.

5 Click **Close** (■).

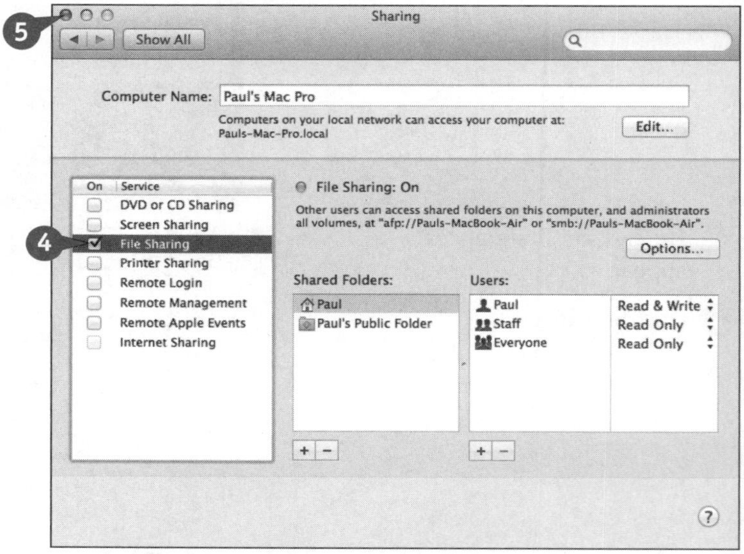

View the Other Mac's Files

1 Click **Finder** (not shown).

2 Click the icon for the other Mac.

Note: If you do not see an icon for the other Mac, click **Go** and then click **Network**, or press Shift+⌘+K.

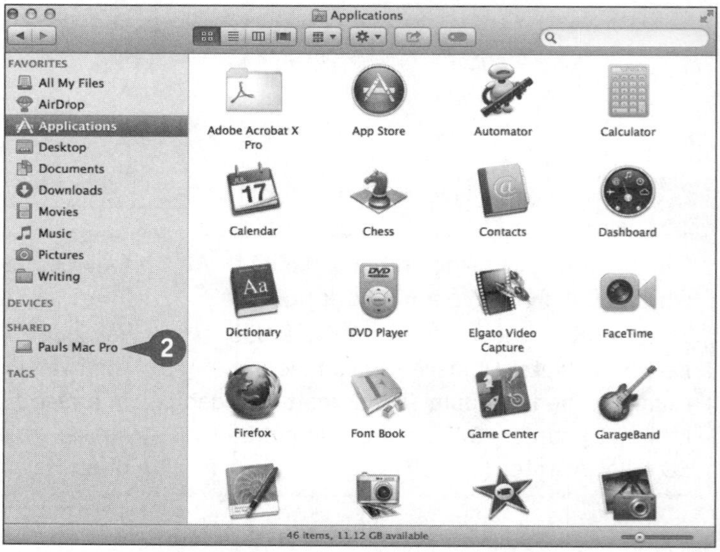

Ⓐ Your Mac connects to the other Mac using the Guest account.

❸ Click **Connect As**.

Your Mac Pro prompts you to log in to the other Mac.

❹ Select the **Registered User** option (◯ changes to ◉).

❺ Type the user name of an account on the other Mac.

❻ Type the account password.

❼ Select the **Remember this password in my keychain** option (☐ changes to ☑).

❽ Click **Connect**.

Your Mac Pro logs in to the other Mac.

Ⓑ You see the folder associated with the user account that you used to log in to the other Mac.

❾ Click a folder to see and work with its contents.

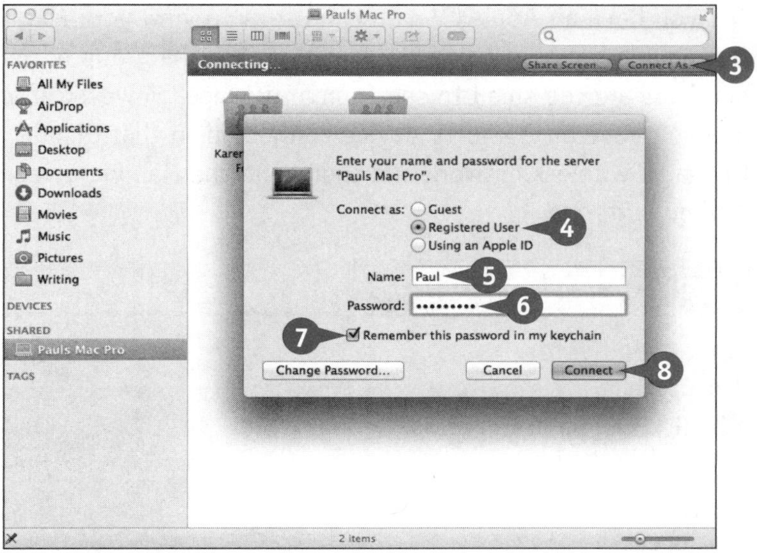

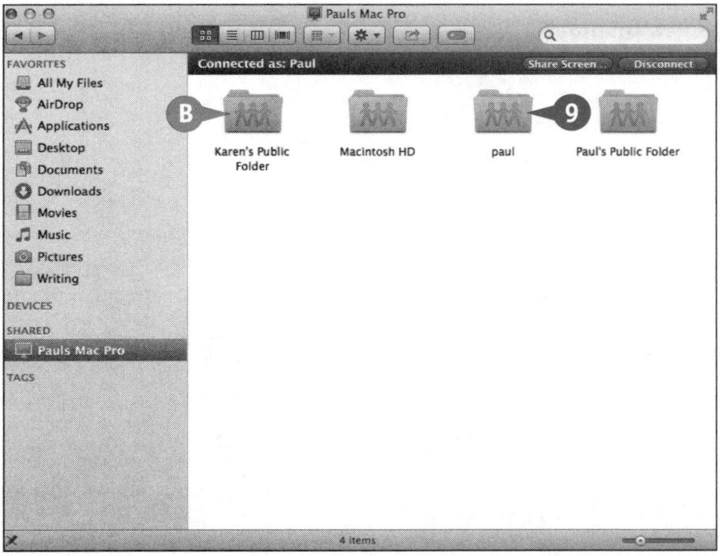

TIP

How do I share other folders?

Click the **Apple** icon (■) and then click **System Preferences** to open the System Preferences. Click **Sharing** and then click **File Sharing**. Under the Shared Folders list, click **Share** (■), click the folder you want to share, and then click **Add**.

Connect Mac Pro to a TV

If you have an Apple TV, you can use it to view your Mac Pro screen on your TV. If you want to demonstrate something on your Mac Pro to a group of people, it is often difficult because most monitors are too small to see from a distance. However, if you have a TV or a projector nearby and you have an Apple TV device connected to that display, you can connect your Mac Pro to the same wireless network and then send the Mac Pro screen to the TV or projector. This is called *AirPlay mirroring*.

Connect Mac Pro to a TV

Mirror via System Preferences

1. Click **System Preferences** ( ) in the Dock.

   The System Preferences appear.

2. Click **Displays.**

The Displays preferences appear.

3. Click the **AirPlay Display** and then click your Apple TV.

   OS X displays your Mac Pro's screen on your TV.

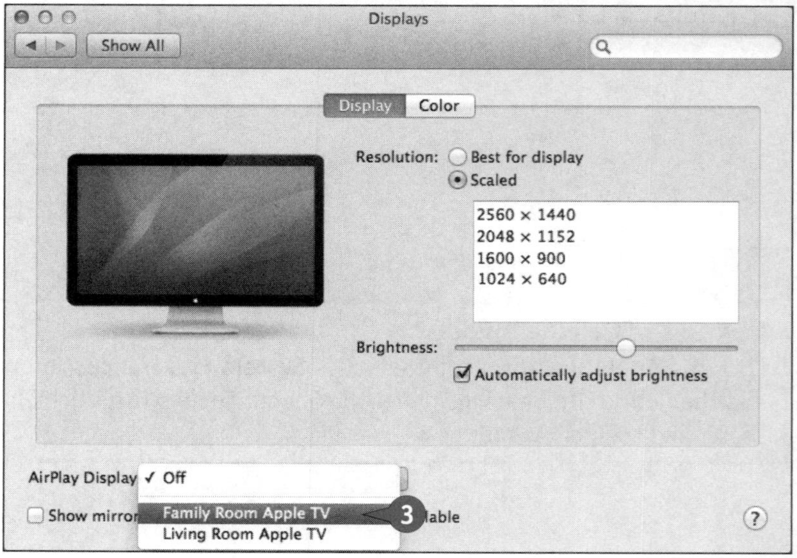

Mirror via the Menu Bar

1. Follow steps 1 and 2 in the subsection "Mirror via System Preferences" to open the Displays preferences.
2. Select the **Show mirroring options in the menu bar when available** option (☐ changes to ☑).

A. OS X adds the AirPlay Mirroring icon (▭) to the menu bar.

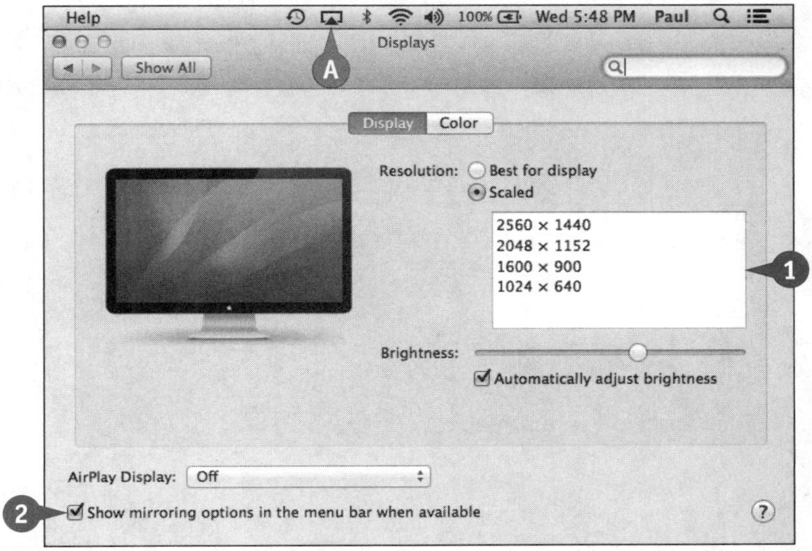

3. Click ▭.
4. Click your Apple TV.

OS X displays your Mac Pro's screen on your TV (▭ changes to ▭).

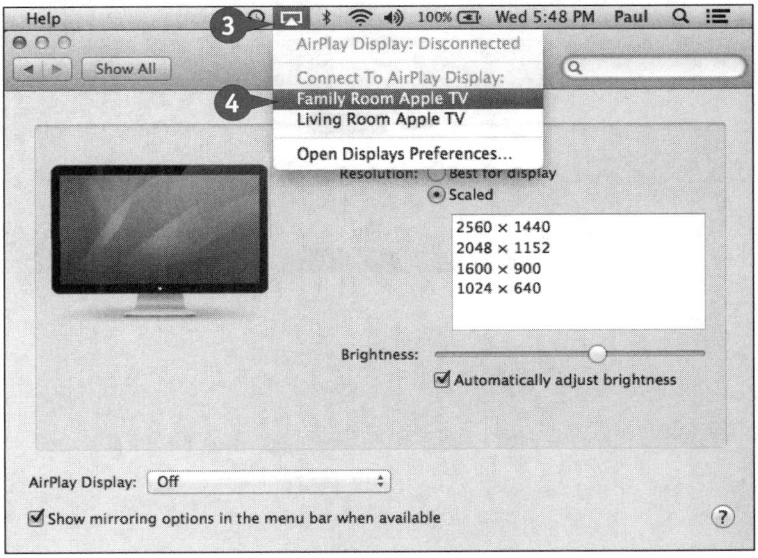

TIPS

Is there an easy way to make my Mac Pro's screen fit my TV screen?

Yes. If you have a high-resolution TV, the Mac Pro screen might look a bit small on the TV. To fix that, click ▭ and then, in the Match Desktop Size To section of the AirPlay Mirroring menu, click your Apple TV.

Can I use my TV as a second monitor for the Mac Pro desktop?

Yes. This is useful if you need extra screen real estate to display the Mac Pro desktop and applications. To configure the TV as a second monitor, click ▭ and then in the Use AirPlay Display To section of the AirPlay Mirroring menu, click **Extend Desktop**.

CHAPTER 4

Browsing the Web

If your Mac Pro is connected to the Internet, you can use the Safari browser to navigate, or *surf*, websites. Safari offers features that make it easy to browse the web. For example, you can open multiple pages in a single Safari window, and you can save your favorite sites for easier access.

Select a Link

Almost all web pages include links to other pages that contain related information. When you select a link, your web browser loads the other page. Web page links come in two forms: text and images. Text links consist of a word or phrase that usually appears underlined and in a different color from the rest of the page text. However, web page designers can control the look of their links, so text links may not always stand out in this way. Therefore, knowing which words, phrases, or images are links is not always obvious. The only way to tell for sure is to position the mouse over the text or image; if the mouse changes to a pointing finger, you know the item is a link.

Select a Link

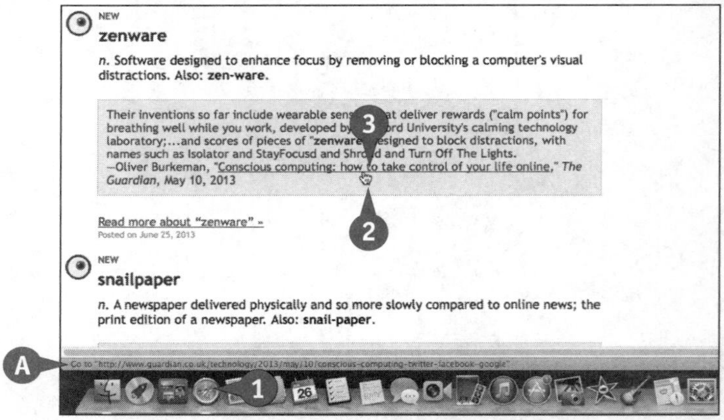

1. In the Dock, click the **Safari** icon ( ).
2. Position the mouse over the link (changes to).
3. Click the text or image.

   A The status bar shows the address of the linked page.

Note: The address shown in the status bar when you point at a link may be different from the one shown when the page is downloading. This occurs when the website *redirects* the link.

Note: If you do not see the status bar, click **View** and then click **Show Status Bar**.

The linked web page appears.

B The web page title and address change after the linked page is loaded.

Enter a Web Page Address

Every web page is uniquely identified by an address called the Uniform Resource Locator, or URL. You can type the address into the web browser to display the page.

The URL is composed of four parts: the *transfer method* (usually HTTP, which stands for Hypertext Transfer Protocol), the *domain name*, the *directory* where the web page is located on the server, and the *filename*. The domain name suffix most often used is .com (commercial), but other common suffixes include .gov (government), .org (nonprofit organization), .edu (education), and country domains such as .ca (Canada).

Enter a Web Page Address

1. Click inside the address bar.
2. Press **Delete** to delete the existing address.
3. Type the address of the web page you want to visit.
4. Press **Return**.

Ⓐ You can also click the site if it appears in the list of suggested sites.

The web page appears.

Ⓑ The web page title changes after the page is loaded.

Open a Web Page in a Tab

You can make it easier to work with multiple web pages and sites simultaneously by opening each page in its own tab. As you surf the web, you may come upon a page that you want to keep available while you visit other sites. Instead of leaving the page and trying to find it again when you need it, Safari lets you leave the page open in a special section of the browser window called a *tab*. You can then use a second tab to visit your other sites, and to resume viewing the first site, you need only click its tab.

Open a Web Page in a Tab

Open a Link in a New Tab

1. Right-click the link you want to open.
2. Click **Open Link in New Tab**.

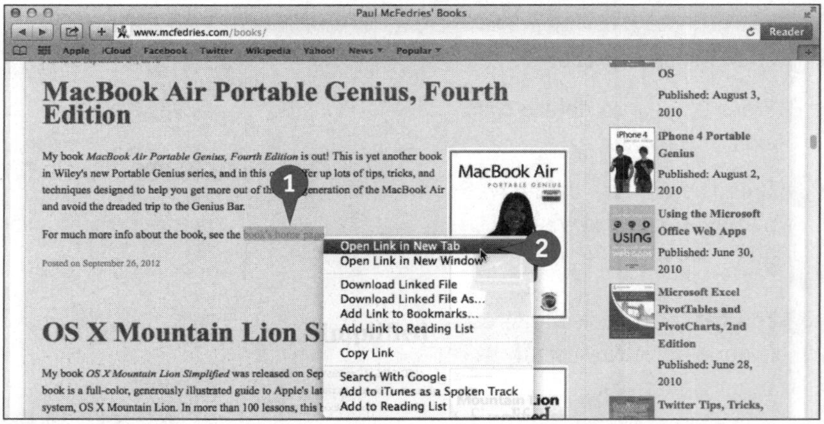

- **A** A new tab appears with the page title.

3. Click the tab to display the page.

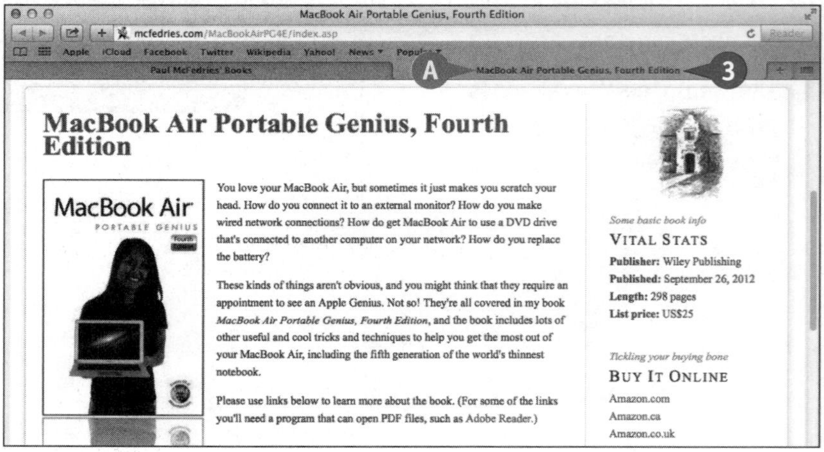

Create a New Tab

1. Click **File**.
2. Click **New Tab**.

B If you already have two or more tabs open, you can also click the **Create a new tab** icon (+).

C Safari creates a new tab and displays the Top Sites page.

After you have used Safari for a while, the Top Sites page lists the websites that you have visited most often.

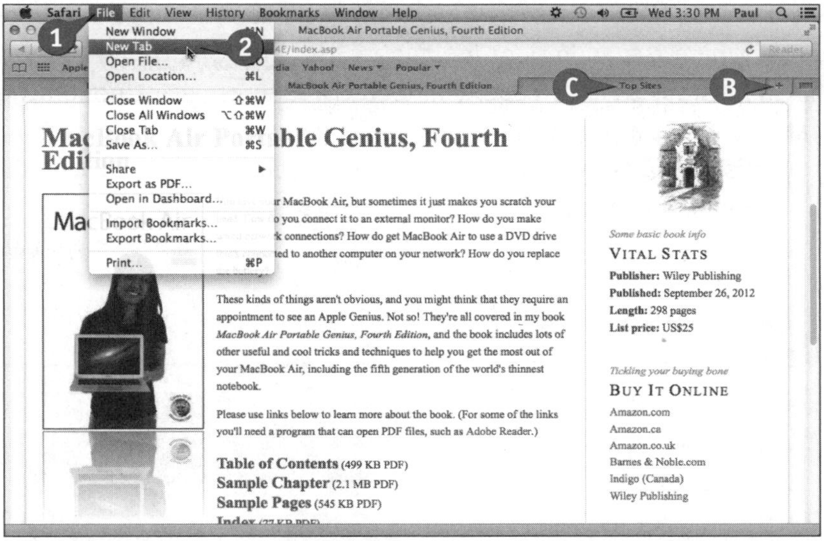

3. Type the address of the page you want to load into the new tab.
4. Press Return.

D Safari displays the page in the tab.

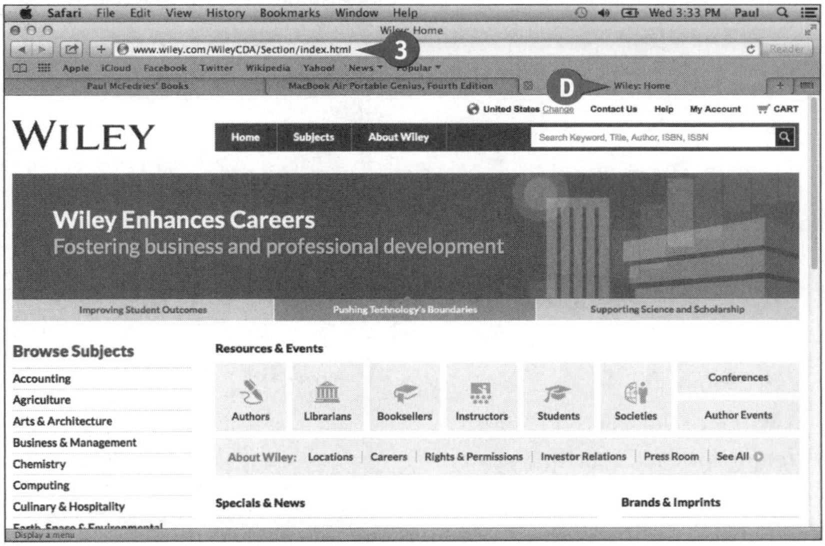

TIP

Are there any shortcuts I can use to open web pages in tabs?

Yes, here are a few useful keyboard techniques you can use:

- Press and hold ⌘ and click a link to open the page in a tab.
- Type an address and then press ⌘+Return to open the page in a new tab.
- Press Shift+⌘+] or Shift+⌘+[to cycle through the tabs.
- Press ⌘+W to close the current tab.

Navigate Web Pages

After you have visited several pages, you can return to a page you visited earlier. Instead of retyping the address or looking for the link, Safari gives you some easier methods. When you navigate from page to page, you create a kind of path through the web. Safari keeps track of this path by maintaining a list of the pages you visit. You can use that list to go back to a page you have visited. After you go back to a page you have visited, you can use the same list to go forward through the pages again.

Navigate Web Pages

Go Back One Page

1. Click the **Previous Page** icon (◀).

   The previous page you visited appears.

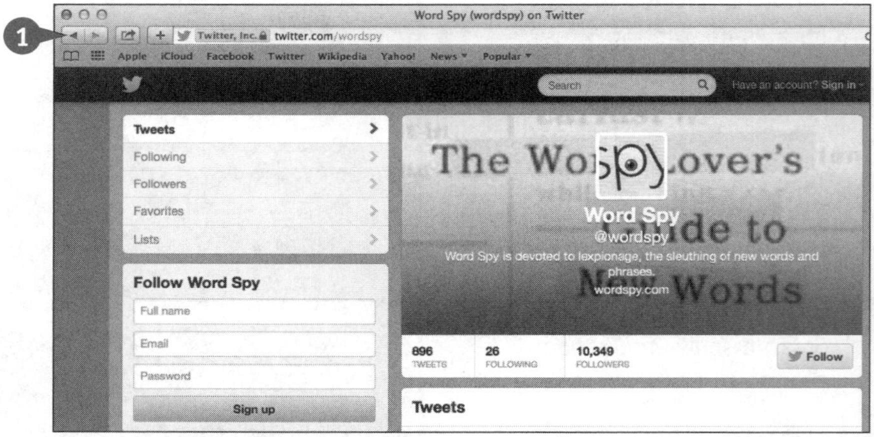

Go Back Several Pages

1. Click and hold down the mouse on ◀.

Note: The list of visited pages is different for each tab that you have open. If you do not see the page you want, you may need to click a different tab.

   A list of the pages you have visited appears.

2. Click the page you want to revisit.

   The page appears.

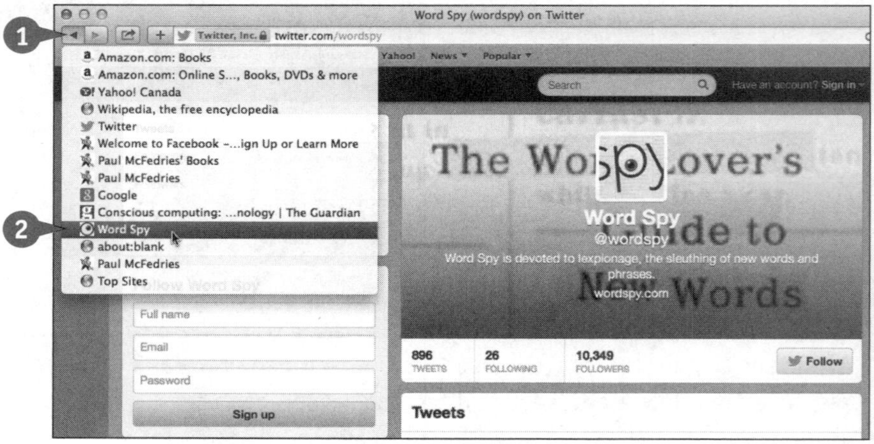

Go Forward One Page

1. Click the **Next Page** icon (▶).

   The next page appears.

Note: If you are at the last page viewed up to that point, ▶ is not active.

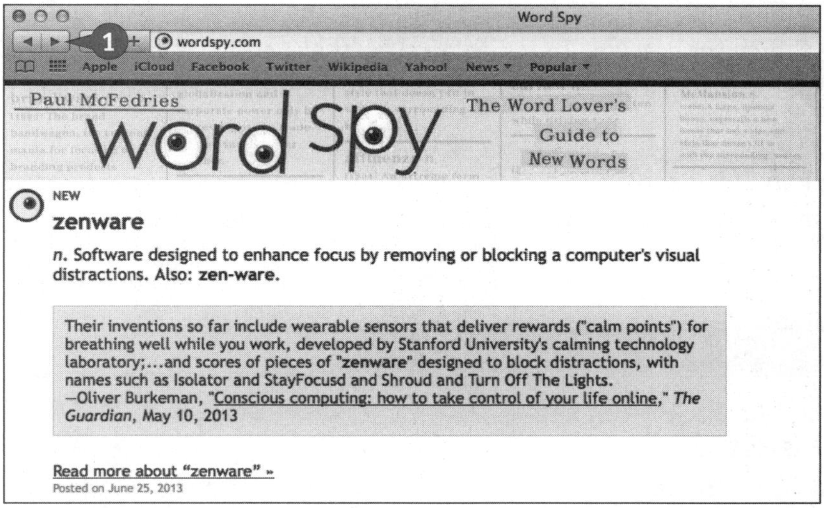

Go Forward Several Pages

1. Click and hold down the mouse on ▶.

   A list of the pages you have visited appears.

Note: The list of visited pages is different for each tab that you have open. If you do not see the page you want, you may need to click a different tab.

2. Click the page you want to revisit.

   The page appears.

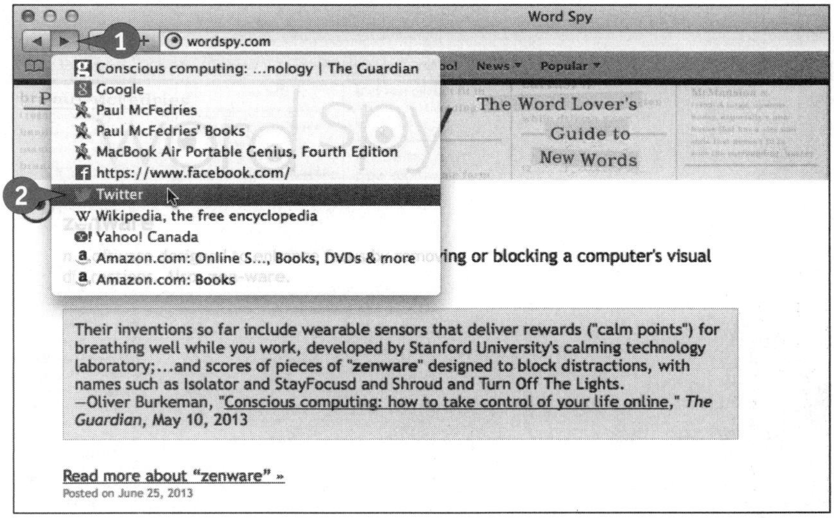

TIP

Are there any shortcuts I can use to navigate web pages?

Yes. Here are a few useful keyboard shortcuts you can use:

- Press ⌘+[to go back one page.
- Press ⌘+] to go forward one page.
- Press Shift+⌘+H to return to the Safari home page (the first page you see when you open Safari).

Navigate with the History List

The Previous Page and Next Page buttons (◀ and ▶) enable you to navigate pages in the current browser session. To redisplay sites that you have visited in the past few days or weeks, you need to use the History list, which is a collection of the websites and pages you have visited over the past month.

If you visit sensitive places such as an Internet banking site or your corporate site, you can increase security by clearing the History list so that other people cannot see where you have been.

Navigate with the History List

Load a Page from the History List

1 Click **History**.

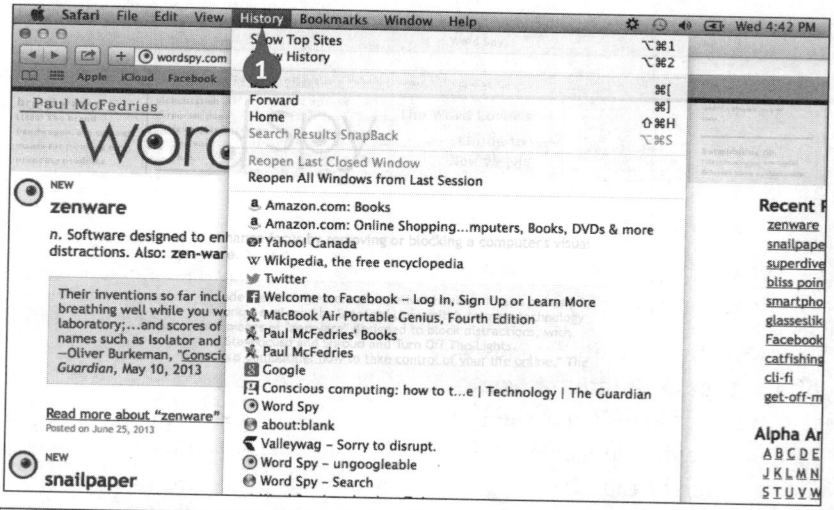

2 Click the date when you visited the page.

A submenu of pages that you visited during that day appears.

3 Click the page you want to revisit.

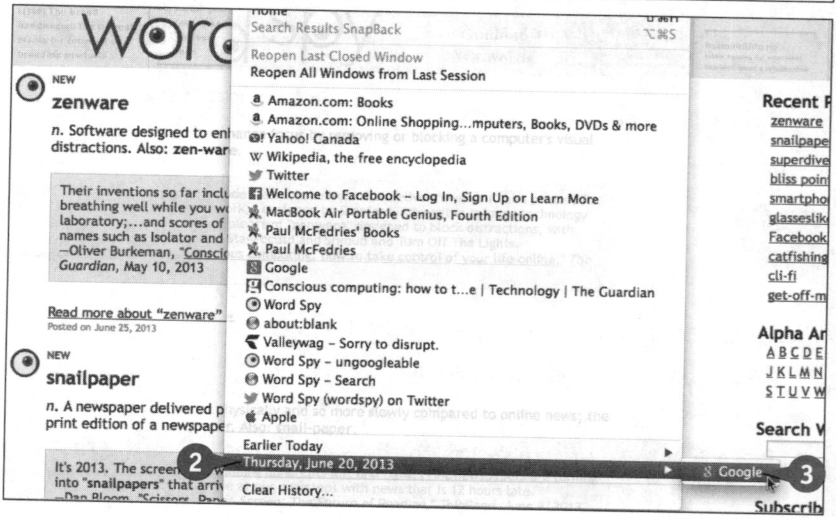

Ⓐ The page appears.

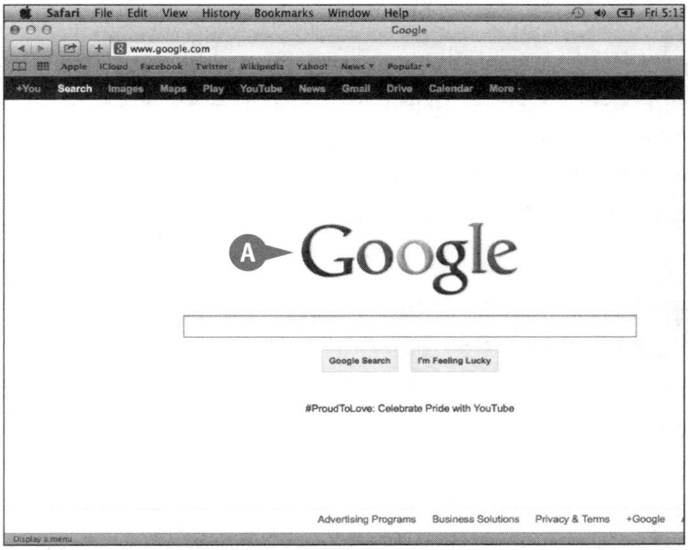

Clear the History List

1. Click **History**.
2. Click **Clear History**.

   Safari deletes all the pages from the history list.

TIP

How can I control the length of time that Safari keeps track of the pages I visit?
In the menu bar, click **Safari** and then **Preferences**. The Safari preferences appear. Click the **General** tab. Click the **Remove history items** and then select the amount of time you want Safari to track your history (Ⓐ). Click **Close** to close the Safari preferences.

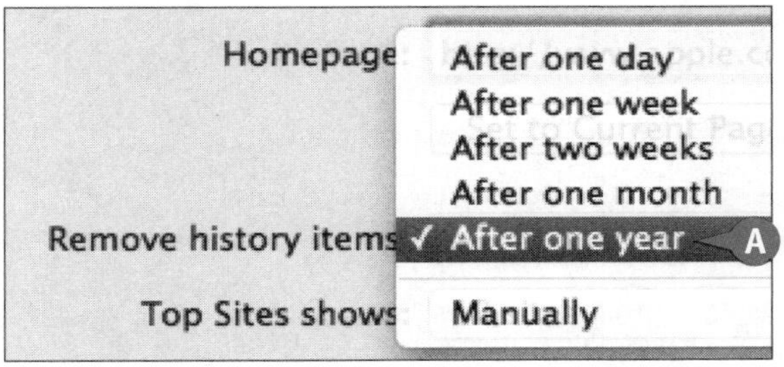

Change Your Home Page

Your home page is the web page that appears when you first start Safari. The default home page is usually the Apple.com Start page, but you can change that to any other page you want, or even to an empty page. This is useful if you do not use the Apple.com Start page, or if you always visit another page at the start of your browsing session. For example, if you have your own website, it might make sense to always begin there. Safari also comes with a command that enables you to view the home page at any time during your browsing session.

Change Your Home Page

Change the Home Page

1. Display the web page that you want to use as your home page.

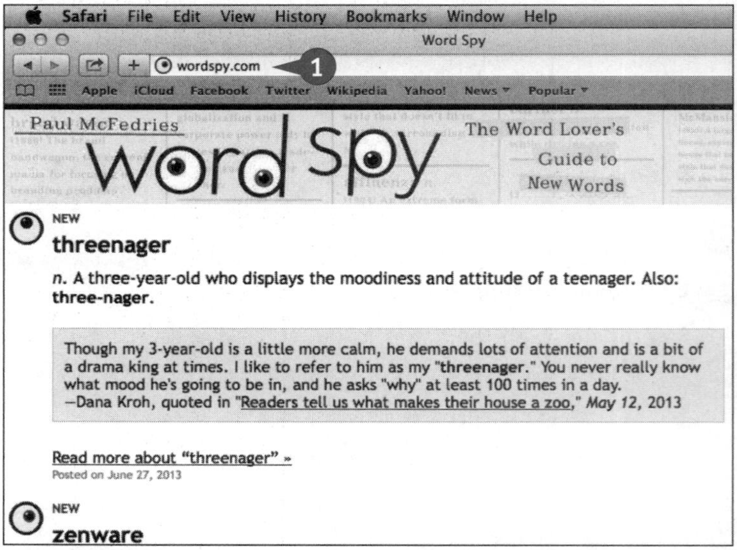

2. Click **Safari**.
3. Click **Preferences**.

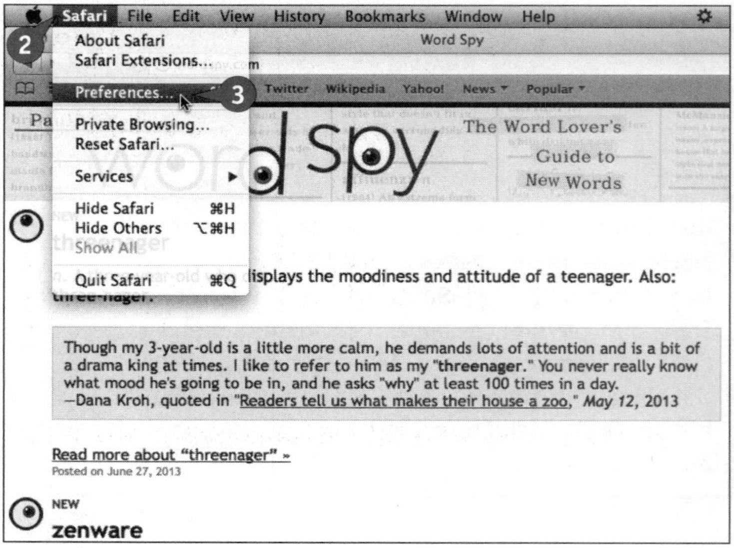

The Safari preferences appear.

4 Click the **General** tab.

5 Click **Set to Current Page.**

A Safari inserts the address of the current page in the Homepage text box.

Note: If your Mac Pro is not currently connected to the Internet, you can also type the new home page address manually using the Homepage text box.

6 Click **Close** ( ).

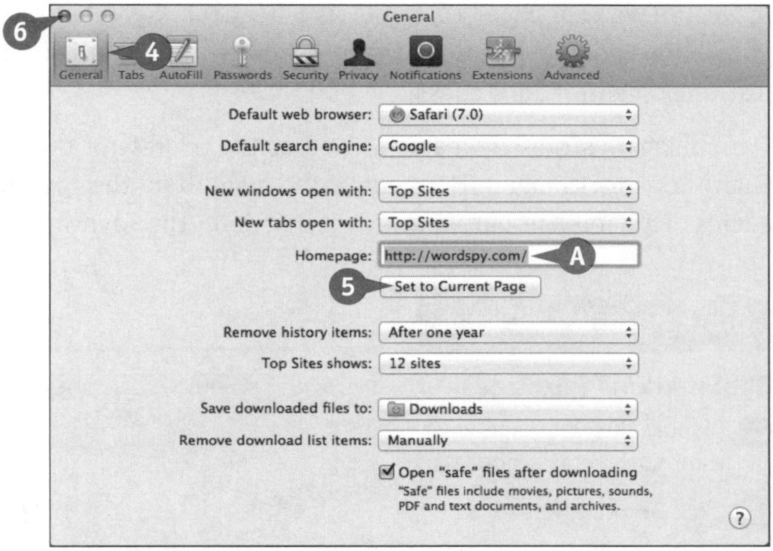

View the Home Page

1 Click **History**.

2 Click **Home**.

Note: You can also display the home page by pressing Shift+⌘+H.

Safari displays the home page.

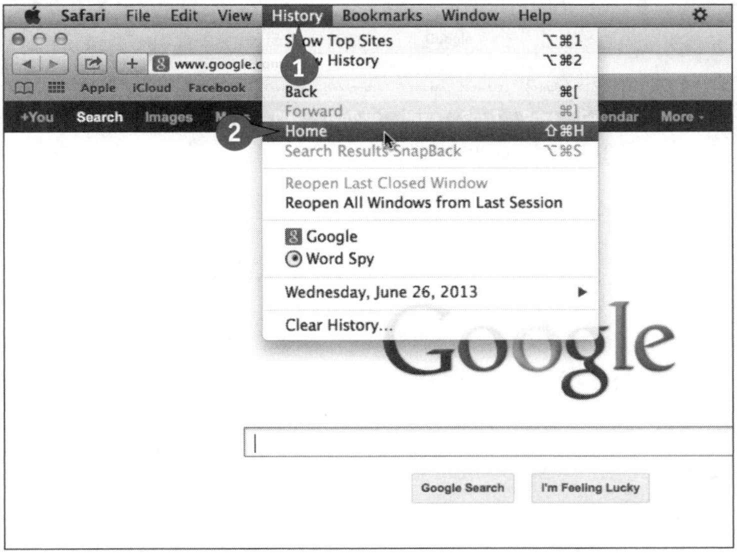

TIP

How can I get Safari to open a new window without displaying the home page?

In the menu bar, click **Safari** and then **Preferences**. The Safari preferences appear. Click the **General** tab. Click the **New windows open with** and then select **Empty Page** (A) from the pop-up menu. Click **Close** ( ) to close the Safari preferences.

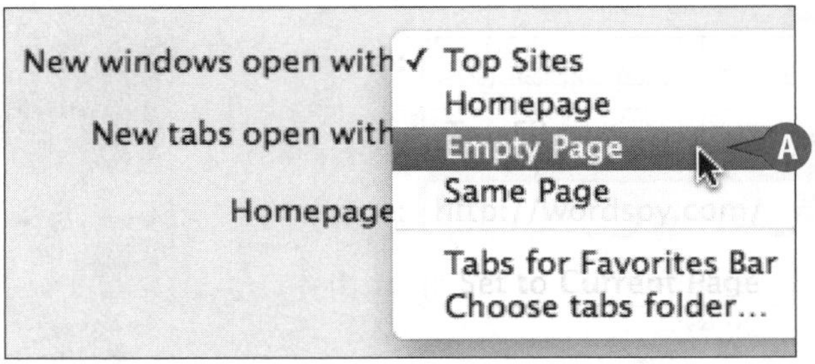

Bookmark Web Pages

If you have web pages that you visit frequently, you can save yourself time by storing those pages as bookmarks — also called favorites — within Safari. This enables you to display the pages with just a couple of mouse clicks.

The bookmark stores the name as well as the address of the page. Most bookmarks are stored on the Safari Bookmarks menu. However, Safari also offers the Favorites bar, which appears just below the address bar. You can put your favorite sites on the Favorites bar for easiest access.

Bookmark Web Pages

Bookmark a Web Page

1. Display the web page you want to save as a bookmark.
2. Click **Bookmarks**.
3. Click **Add Bookmark**.

Ⓐ You can also run the Add Bookmark command by clicking **Share** (↗) and then clicking **Add Bookmark**.

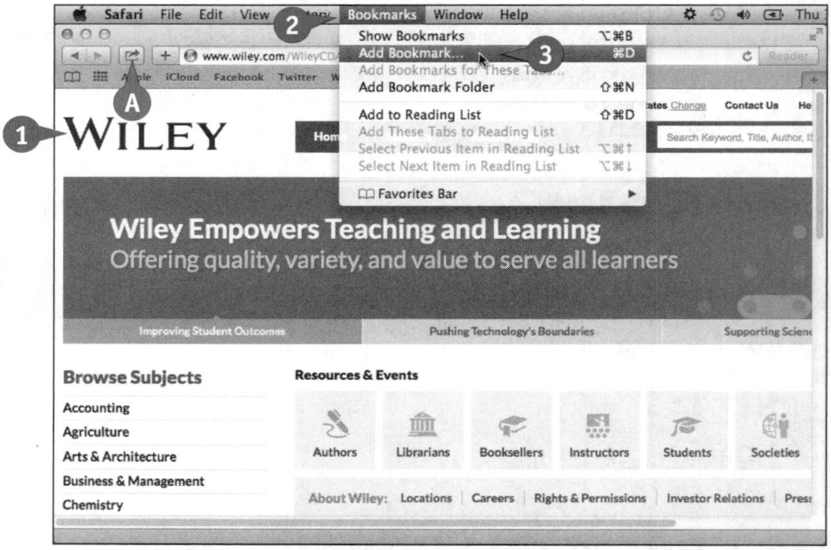

The Add Bookmark dialog appears.

Note: You can also display the Add Bookmark dialog by pressing ⌘+D.

4. Click ⬍ and then click the location where you want to store the bookmark.
5. Edit the page name, if necessary.
6. Click **Add**.

Safari adds a bookmark for the page.

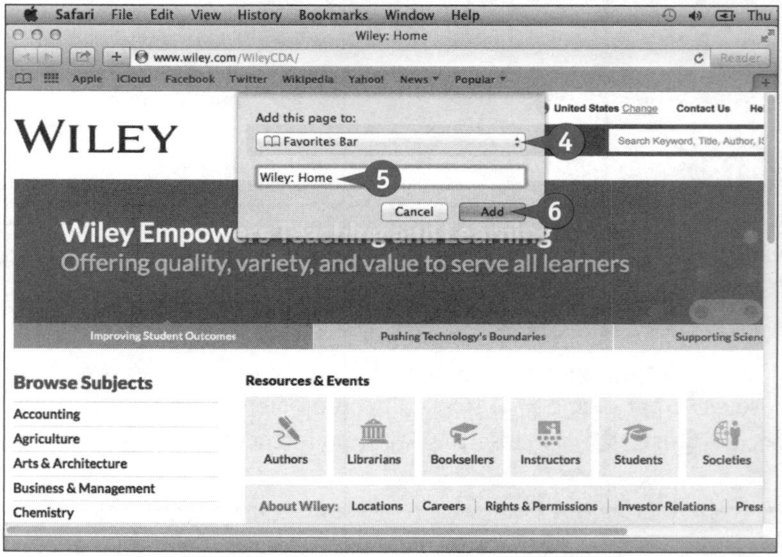

Display a Bookmarked Web Page

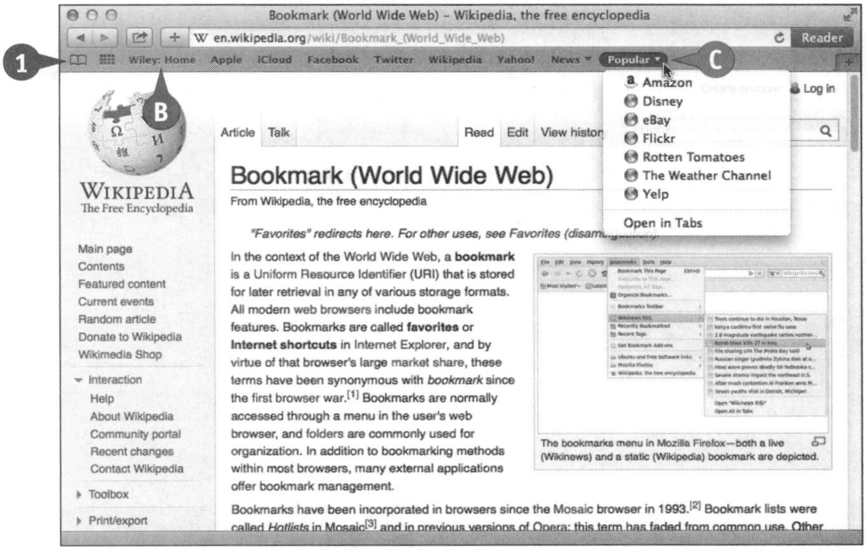

1. Click the **Show all bookmarks** button (📖).

Ⓑ If you added the bookmark to the Favorites bar, click the page name.

Ⓒ If you added the bookmark to a folder, click the folder and then click the page name.

The Bookmarks sidebar appears.

2. Click the location of the bookmark, such as the **Favorites Bar**.
3. Click the folder that contains the bookmark you want to display.
4. Double-click the bookmark.

The web page appears.

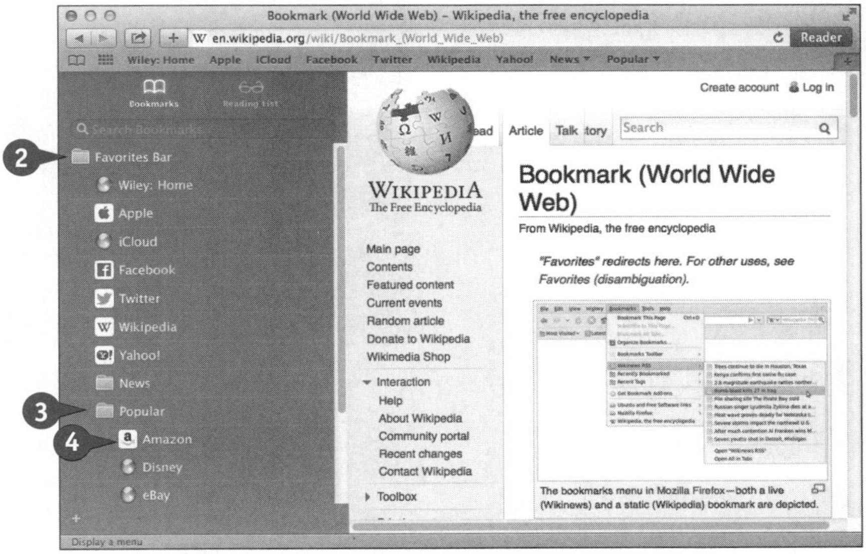

TIPS

I use my Favorites bar a lot. Is there an easier way to display these pages?

Yes. Safari automatically assigns keyboard shortcuts to the first nine bookmarks, counting from left to right and not including folders. For example, you display the leftmost bookmark by pressing ⌘+1. Moving to the right, the shortcuts are ⌘+2, ⌘+3, and so on.

How do I delete a bookmark?

If the site is on the Favorites bar, right-click the bookmark and then click **Delete**, or hold down ⌘ and drag it off the bar. For all other bookmarks, click **Show all bookmarks** button (📖) to display the Bookmarks sidebar. Locate the bookmark you want to remove, right-click the bookmark, and then click **Delete**. You can also click the bookmark and then press Delete.

Search for Sites

If you need information on a specific topic, Safari has a built-in feature that enables you to quickly search the web for sites that have the information you require. The web has a number of sites called *search engines* that enable you to find what you are looking for. By default, Safari uses the Google search site (www.google.com). Simple, one-word searches often return tens of thousands of *hits*, or matching sites. To improve your searching, type multiple search terms that define what you are looking for. To search for a phrase, enclose the words in quotation marks.

Search for Sites

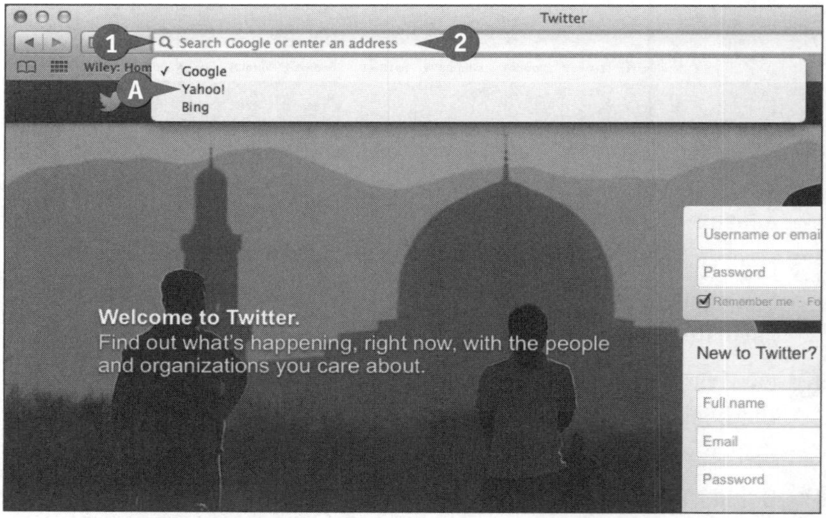

1 Click in the address bar.

2 Press **Delete** to delete the address.

A You can click an item in this list to select the search engine you prefer to use.

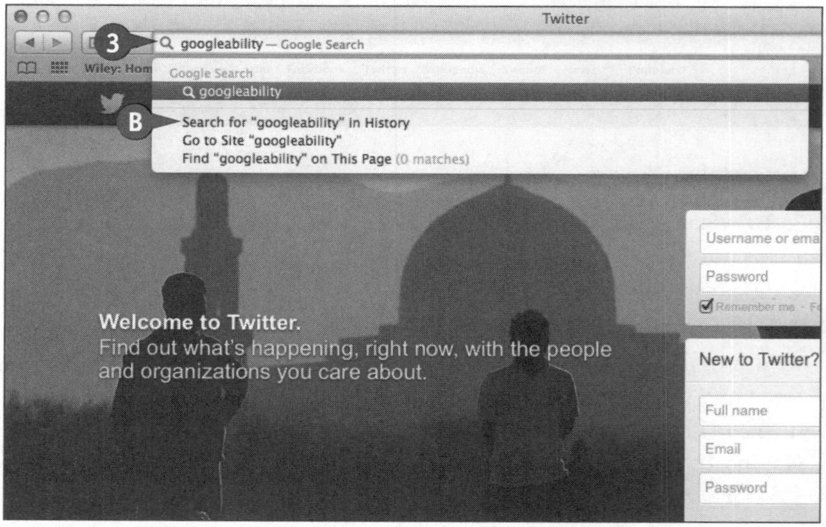

3 Type a word, phrase, or question that represents the information you want to find.

B If you see the search text you want to use in the list of suggested searches, click the text and skip step 4.

4 Press **Return**.

Ⓒ A list of pages that matches your search text appears.

5 Click a web page.

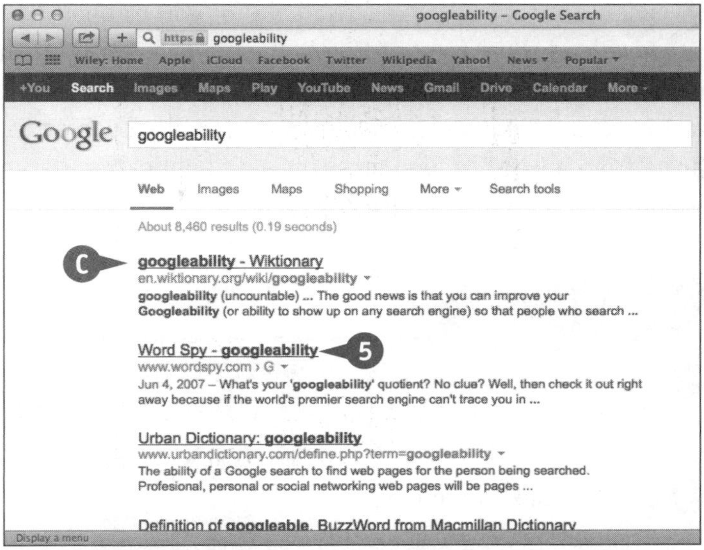

The page appears.

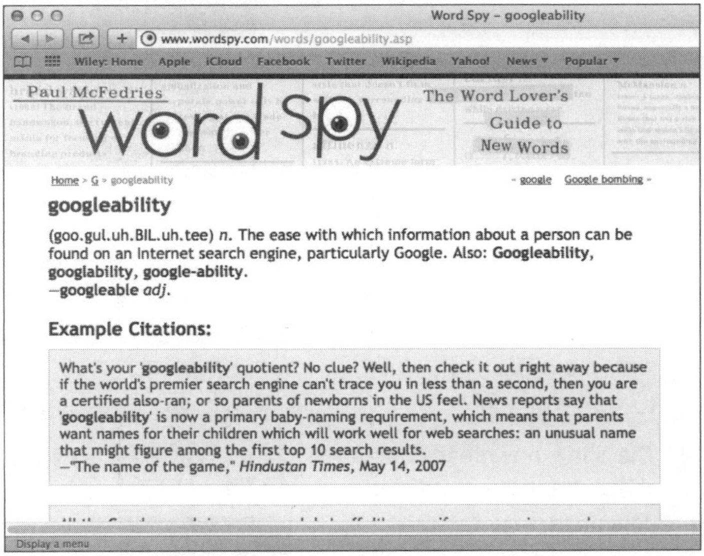

TIP

Is there an easy way that I can rerun a recent search?

Yes. Follow these steps to quickly rerun your search:

1 Click **History**.

2 Click **Search Results SnapBack**.

You can also press Option + ⌘ + S.

Safari sends the search text to Google again.

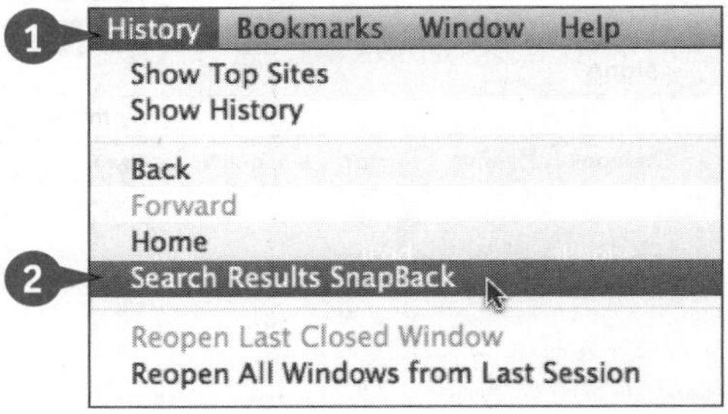

Download a File

Some websites make files available for you to open on your Mac Pro. To use these files, you can download them to your Mac Pro using Safari. Saving data from the Internet to your computer is called *downloading*. For certain types of files, Safari may display the content right away instead of letting you download it. This happens for files such as text documents and PDF files. In any case, to use a file from a website, you must have an application designed to work with that particular file type. For example, if the file is an Excel workbook, you need either Excel for the Mac or a compatible program.

Download a File

1. Navigate to the page that contains the link to the file.
2. Click the link to the file.

Safari downloads the file to your Mac Pro.

Ⓐ The Show Downloads button shows the progress of the download.

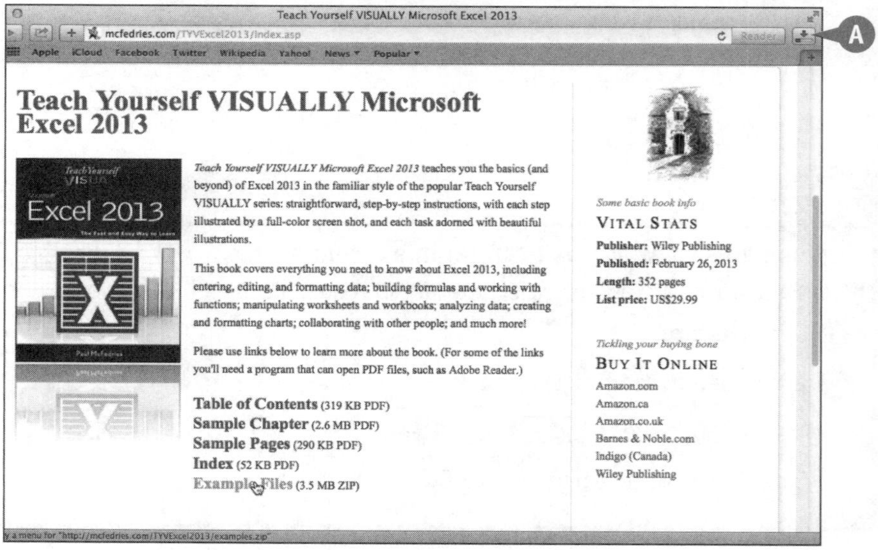

3 When the download is complete, click the **Show Downloads** button ( ).

4 Right-click the file.

B You can also double-click the icon to the left of the file.

C You can click **Show in Finder** ( ) to view the file in the Downloads folder.

5 Click **Open**.

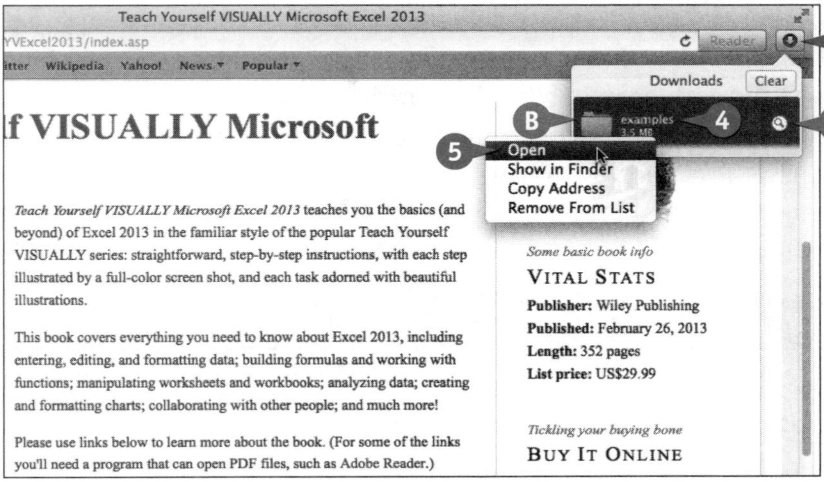

The file opens in Finder (in the case of a compressed Zip file, as shown here) or in the corresponding application.

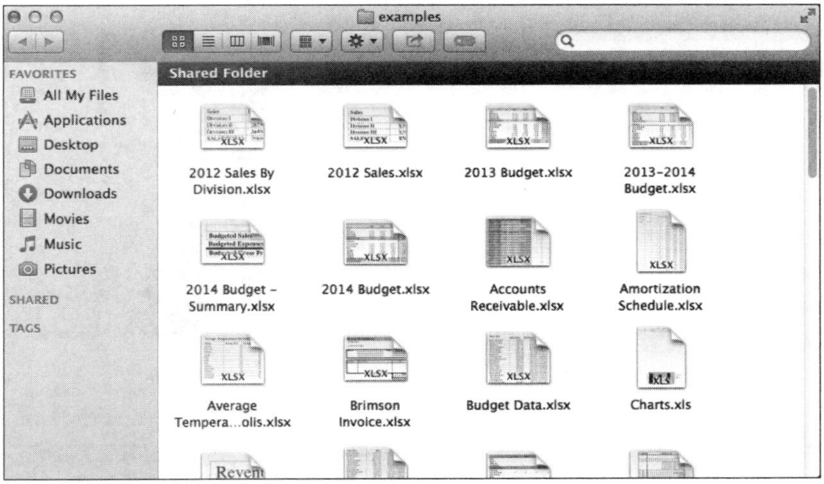

TIPS

If Safari displays the file instead of downloading it, how do I save the file to my Mac Pro?

Click **File** and then click **Save As**. Type a name for the new file, choose a folder, and then click **Save**.

Is it safe to download files from the web?

Yes, as long as you download files only from sites you trust. If you ever notice that Safari is attempting to download a file without your permission, cancel the download immediately because the file likely contains a virus or other malware. If you do not completely trust a file that you have downloaded, use an antivirus program, such as ClamXav at www.clamxav.com, to scan the file before you open it.

View Links Shared on Social Networks

You can make your web surfing more interesting and your social networking more efficient by using Safari to directly access links shared by the people you follow. Social networks are about connecting with people, but a big part of that experience is sharing information, particularly links to interesting, useful, or entertaining web pages. You normally have to log in to the social network to see these links, but if you have used OS X to sign in to your accounts, you can use Safari to directly access links shared by your Twitter and LinkedIn connections. For more information on signing in to your social networking accounts, see Chapter 9.

View Links Shared on Social Networks

1. Click the **Show all bookmarks** button (📖).

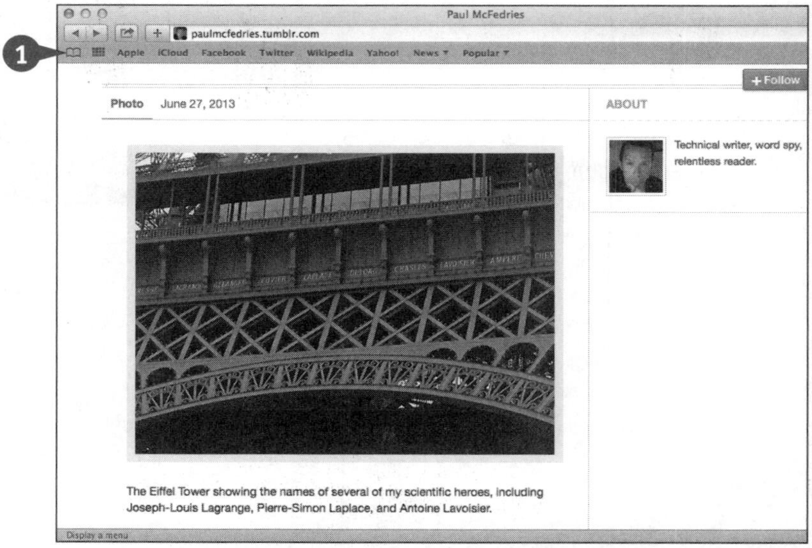

The Bookmarks sidebar appears.

2. Click **Shared Links**.

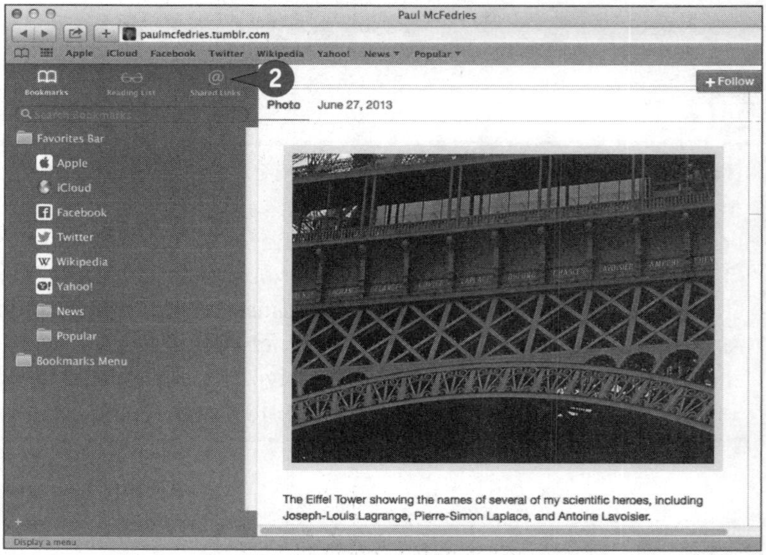

Safari displays the Shared Links sidebar, which lists the most recent links shared by the people you follow on Twitter and LinkedIn.

3. Click the shared link you want to view.

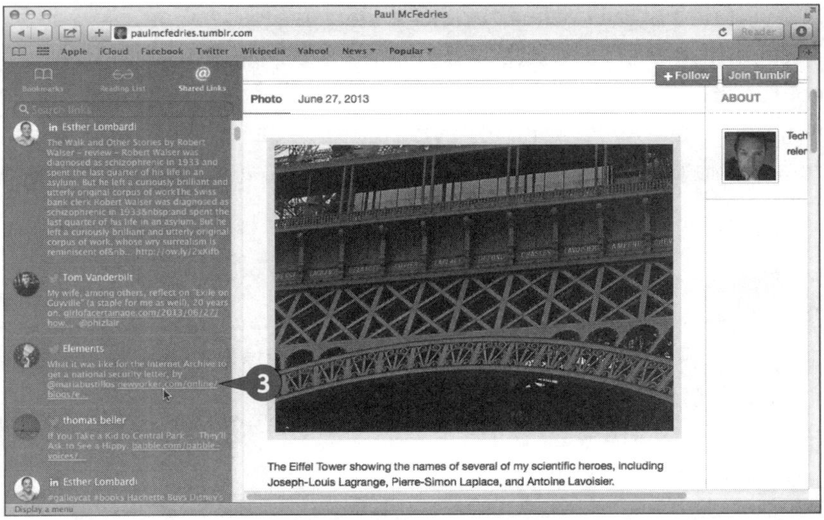

A. Safari displays the linked web page.

B. For a Twitter link, if you want to retweet the link to your followers, click **Retweet**.

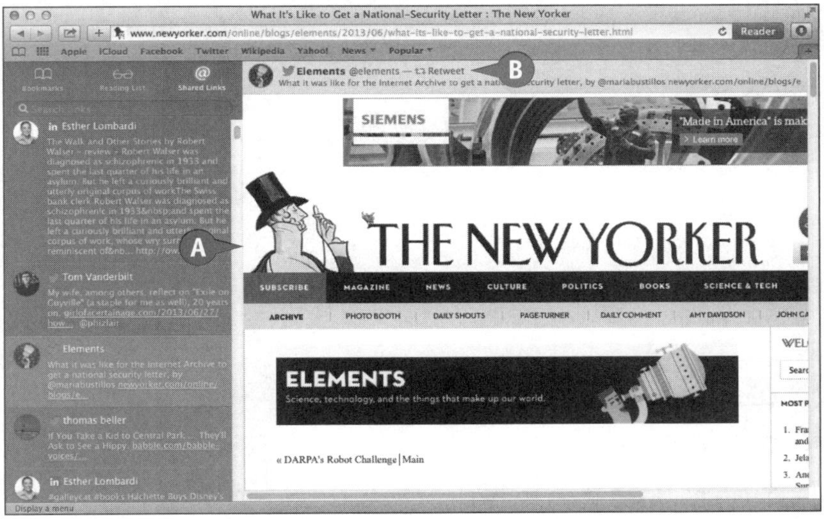

TIPS

How can I be sure that I am seeing the most recent shared links?

Safari usually updates the Shared Links list each time you open it. However, to be sure that you are seeing the most recent links shared by people you follow on Twitter or are connected to on LinkedIn, click the **View** menu and then click **Update Shared Links**.

How do I hide the Shared Links sidebar when I do not need it?

To give yourself more horizontal screen area for viewing pages, hide the sidebar by clicking the **Show all bookmarks** button (📖) again. You can also toggle the Shared Links sidebar on and off by pressing Control + ⌘ + 3.

Create a Web Page Reading List

If you do not have time to read a web page now, you can add the page to your Reading List and then read the page later when you have time. You will often come upon a page with fascinating content that you want to read, but lack the time. You could bookmark the article, but bookmarks are really for pages you want to revisit often, not for those you might read only once. A better solution is to add the page to the Reading List, which is a simple list of pages you save to read later.

Create a Web Page Reading List

Add a Page to the Reading List

1. Navigate to the page you want to read later.

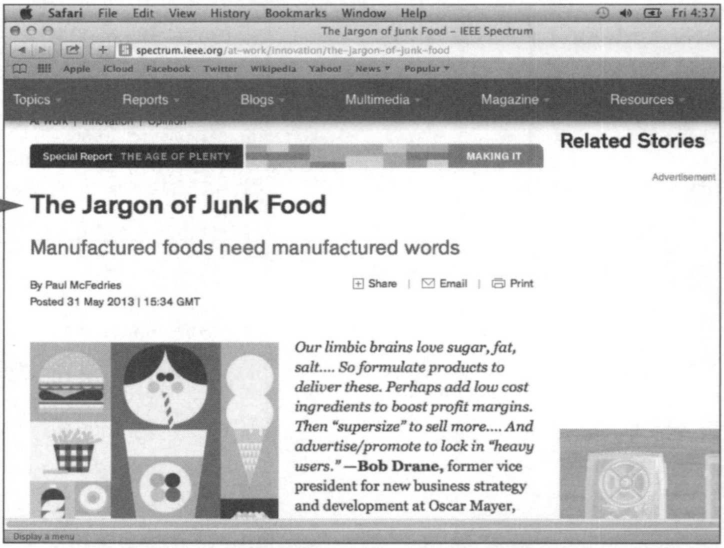

2. Click **Bookmarks**.
3. Click **Add to Reading List**.

   Safari adds the page to the Reading List.

Select a Page from the Reading List

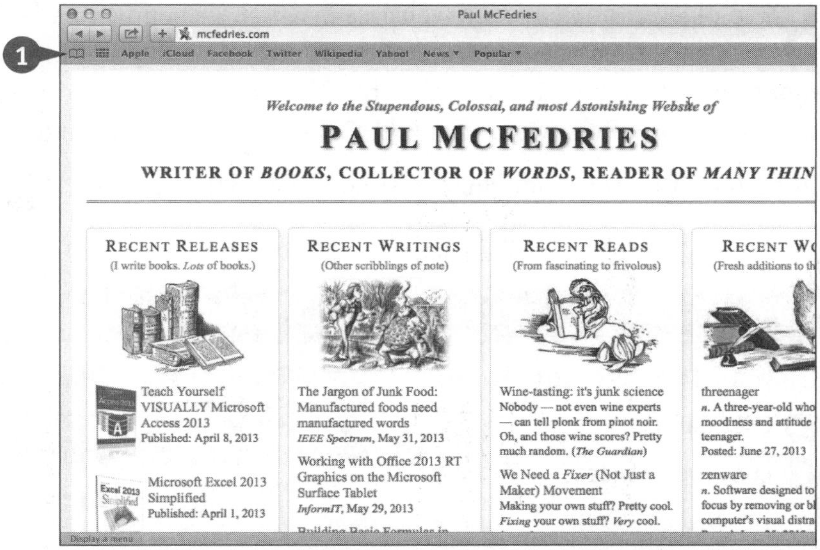

1. Click the **Show all bookmarks** button (📖).

   The Bookmarks sidebar appears.

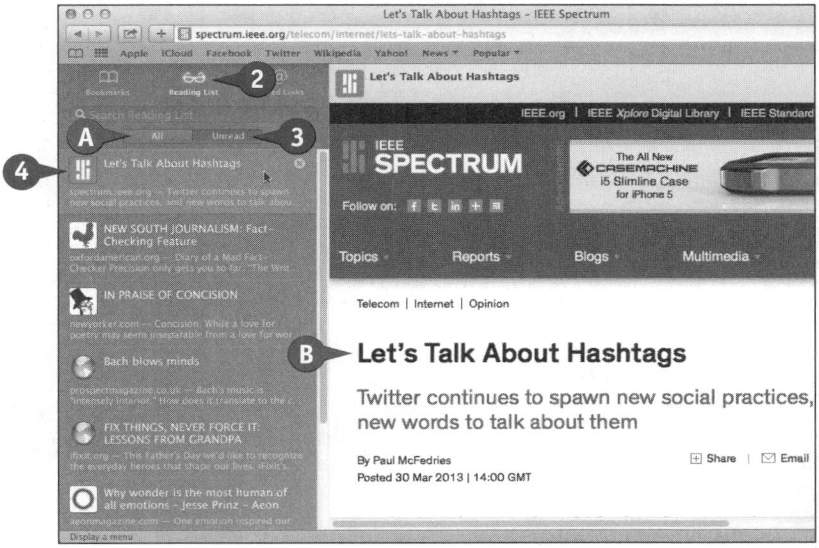

2. Click **Reading List**.
3. Click **Unread**.

   A. If you want to reread a page you have read previously, click **All** instead.

4. Click the page.

   B. Safari displays the page.

TIP

Are there easier ways to add a web page to my Reading List?

Yes, Safari offers several shortcut methods you can use. The easiest is to navigate to the page and then click **Add to Reading List** (+) to the left of the address bar. You can also add the current page to the Reading List by pressing Shift+⌘+D. To add all open tabs to the Reading List, click **Bookmarks** and then click **Add These Tabs to Reading List**. To add a link to the Reading List, hold down Shift and click the link.

Make Safari Appear to Be a Different Browser

Some older or poorly coded websites may not show up properly because they do not recognize Safari. In some extreme cases, the site might not let you in at all if Safari is not a supported browser. You cannot do much directly to combat this, but you can work around it by configuring Safari to appear as though it is a different program (such as Internet Explorer) and fool the site into letting you in.

To perform this trick, you must first configure Safari to display its normally hidden Develop menu.

Make Safari Appear to Be a Different Browser

Display the Develop Menu

1. Click **Safari**.
2. Click **Preferences**.

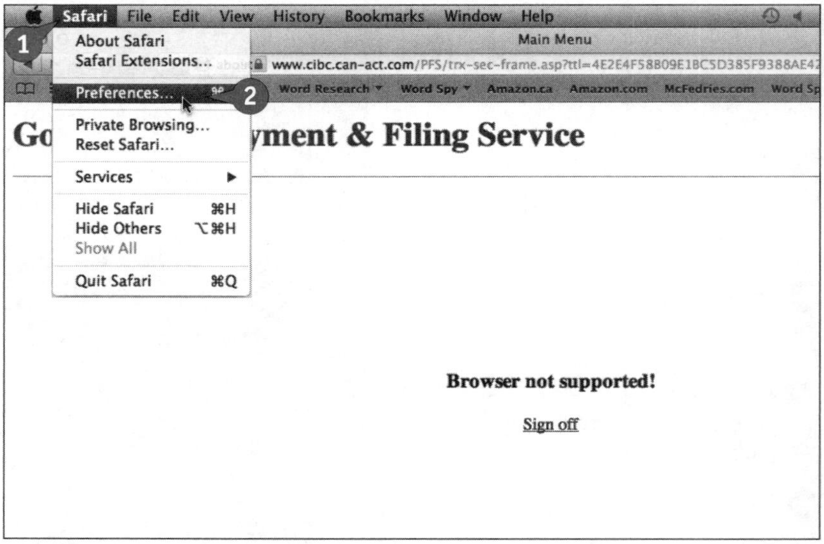

The Safari preferences appear.

3. Click the **Advanced** tab.
4. Select the **Show Develop menu in menu bar** option (☐ changes to ☑).
5. Click **Close** (■).

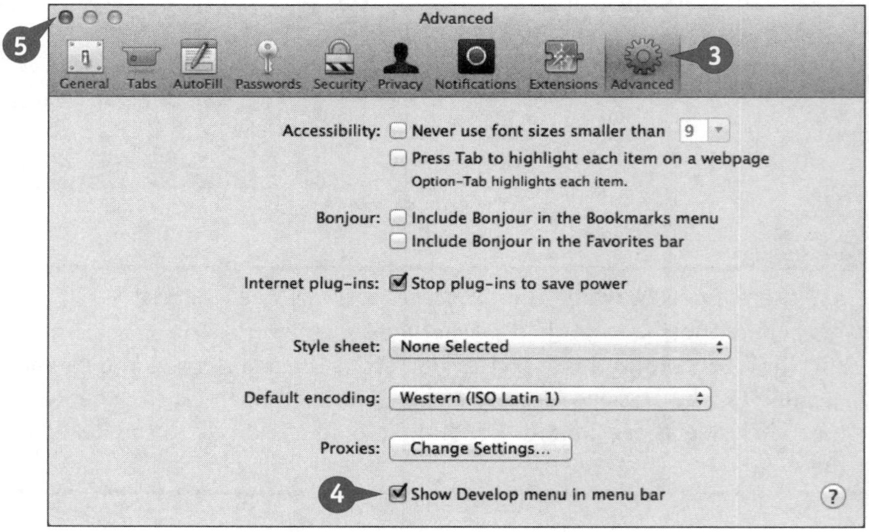

Tell Safari Which Browser to Emulate

1. Click **Develop**.

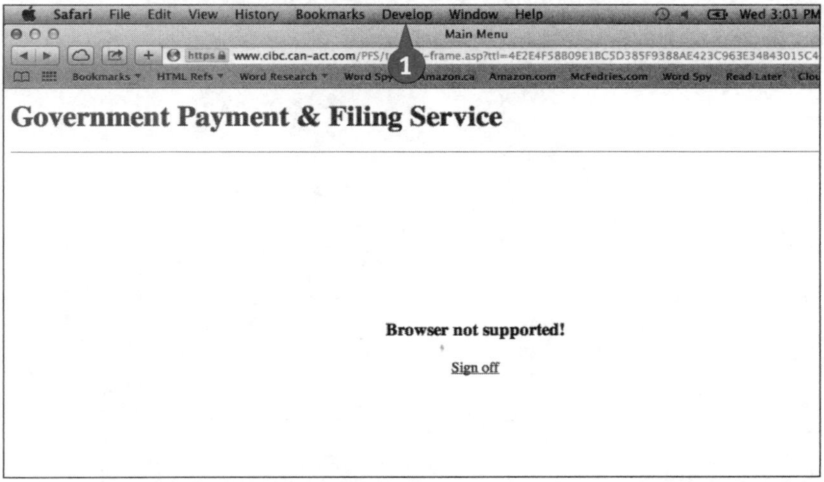

2. Click **User Agent**.
3. Click the browser you want Safari to emulate.

Note: If you still cannot access the website, repeat steps **1** to **3** to try different browser types, as needed.

Note: When you are done with the website, click **Develop**, click **User Agent**, and then click **Default**.

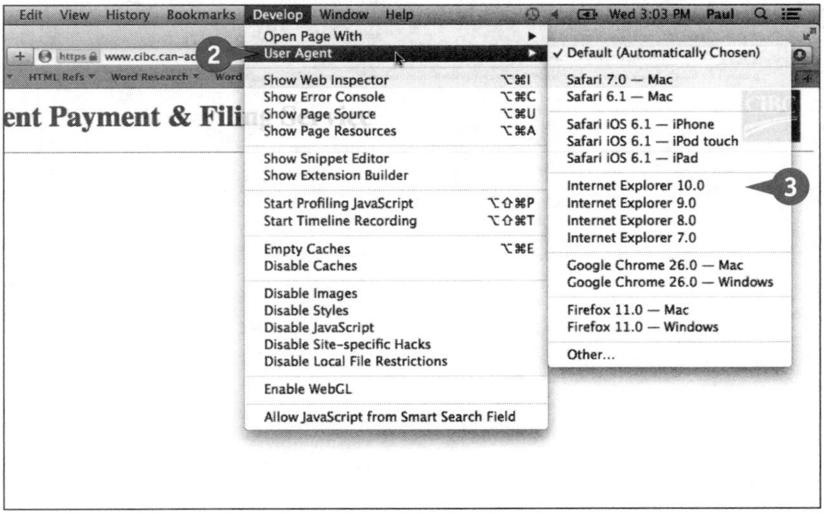

TIP

How does a website know that I am using Safari?

When you access a website, it has the option of asking the web browser to provide a string called the *user agent*, which identifies the web browser and provides extra data such as the browser version number and operating system type (such as OS X or Windows). Any site that supports only specific web browsers will ask for the user agent data and then use code to examine the data and decide whether the browser is allowed to access the site. In the workaround described in this section, you are telling Safari to provide the site with a different user agent string.

CHAPTER 5

Communicating via E-Mail

Mac Pro comes with the Mail application that you can use to exchange e-mail messages. After you type your account details into Mail, you can send e-mail to friends, family, colleagues, and even total strangers almost anywhere in the world.

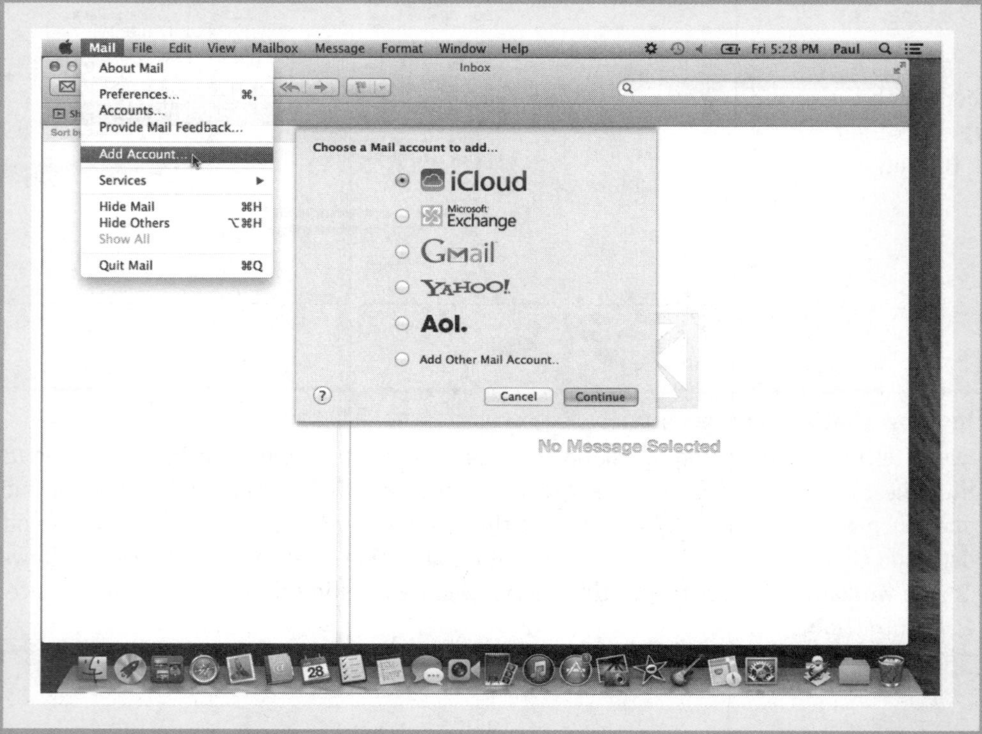

Add an E-Mail Account

To send and receive e-mail messages, you must add your e-mail account to the Mail application. Your account is usually a POP (Post Office Protocol) account supplied by your Internet service provider, which should have sent you the account details. You can also use services such as Gmail to set up a web-based e-mail account, which enables you to send and receive messages from any computer. If you have an Apple ID — that is, an account for use on the Apple iCloud service (www.icloud.com) — you can also set up Mail with your Apple account details.

Add an E-Mail Account

Get Started Adding an Account

1. In the Dock, click the **Mail** icon ().
2. Click **Mail**.
3. Click **Add Account**.

Note: If you are just starting Mail and the Welcome to Mail dialog is on-screen, you can skip steps 2 and 3.

4. Select the type of account you are adding (changes to).
5. Click **Continue**.

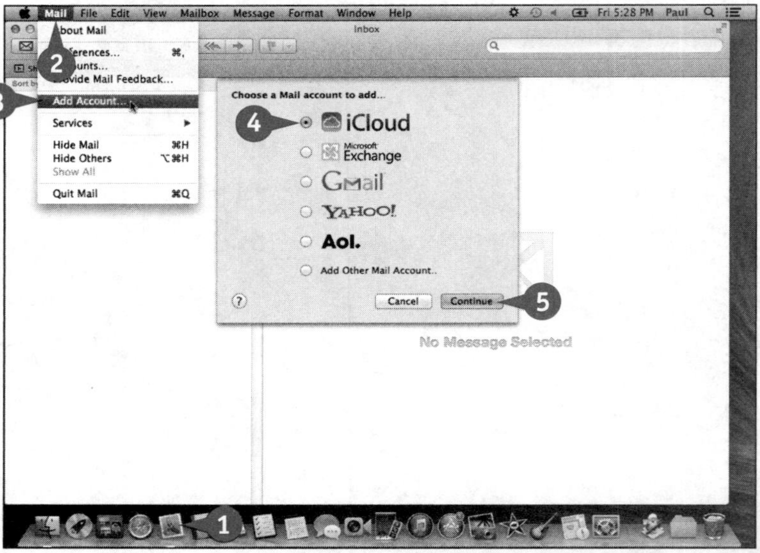

Add an iCloud Account

Note: Complete the following steps if you chose the iCloud option in step 4 of the subsection "Get Started Adding an Account."

1. Type your iCloud account address.
2. Type your iCloud account password.
3. Click **Sign In**.

   Mail signs in to your iCloud account.

Note: Mail prompts you to choose which services you want to use with iCloud. See Chapter 20 to learn more.

4. Click **Add Account** (not shown).

   Mail adds your iCloud account.

Add a POP Account

Note: Complete the following steps if you chose the Add Other Mail Account option in step 4 of the subsection "Get Started Adding an Account."

1. Type your name.
2. Type your POP account address.
3. Type your POP account password
4. Click **Create**.
5. Click the **POP** tab.
6. Type the address of the account's incoming mail server.
7. Edit the User Name text as required.
8. Click **Next**.
9. Type the address of the outgoing mail server, which is sometimes called the SMTP server.
10. Type the outgoing mail server username and password, if your ISP requires them.
11. Click **Create**.

Note: If you see a Verify Certificate dialog, click **Connect**.

12. Click **Create** (not shown).

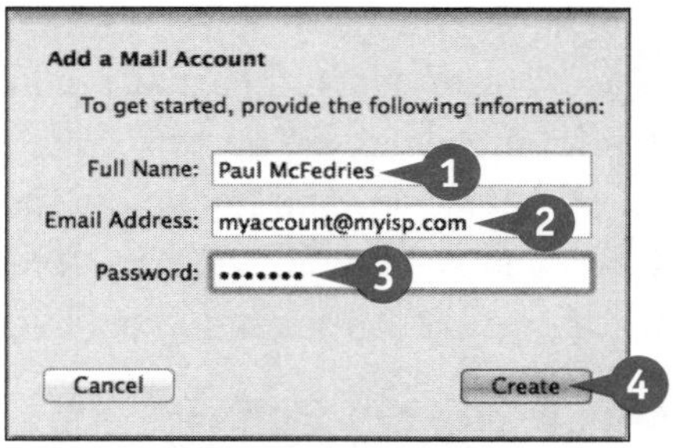

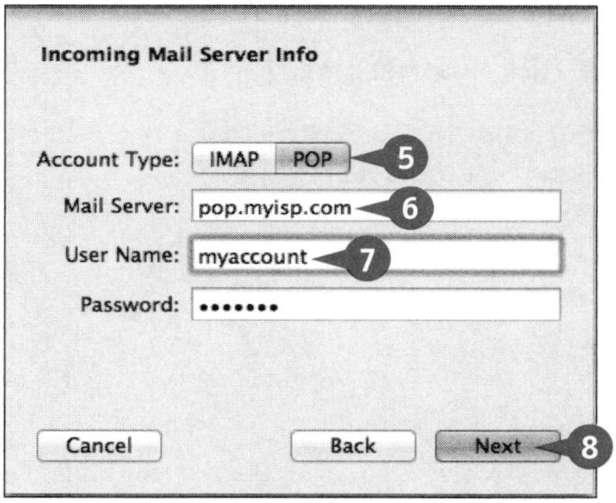

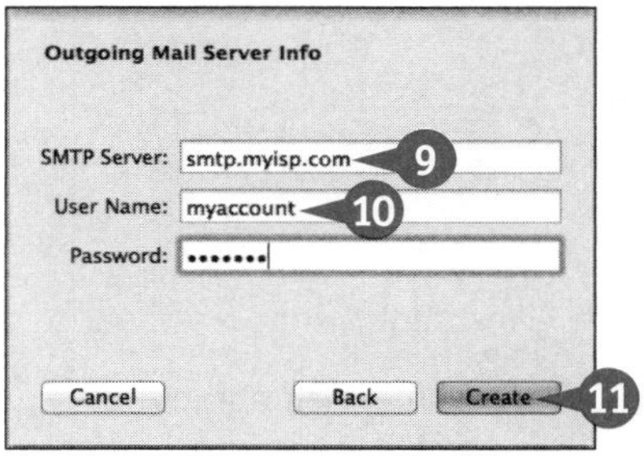

TIPS

What information do I need to add a Microsoft Exchange account?

You need to know your Exchange e-mail address and your account password. You also need to know the address of the Exchange mail server, and in some cases you also need to know your Exchange domain name and user name.

How do I make changes to an account?

After you set up an account, Mail adds it to the preferences. To see your accounts, click **Mail**, click **Preferences**, and then click the **Accounts** tab. Click the account you want to edit and then use the Account Information, Mailbox Behaviors, and Advanced tabs to make your changes. When you click **Close** ( ), Mail prompts you to save your changes, so be sure to click **Save**.

Send an E-Mail Message

If you know the recipient's e-mail address, you can send a message to that address. An e-mail address is a set of characters that uniquely identifies the location of an Internet mailbox. Each address takes the form *username@domain*, where *username* is the name of the person's account with the ISP or with an organization, and *domain* is the Internet name of the company that provides the person's account. When you send a message, it travels through your ISP's outgoing mail server, which routes the messages to the recipient's incoming mail server, which then stores the message in the recipient's mailbox.

Send an E-Mail Message

1. Click **New Message** (✎).

Note: You can also start a new message by pressing ⌘+N.

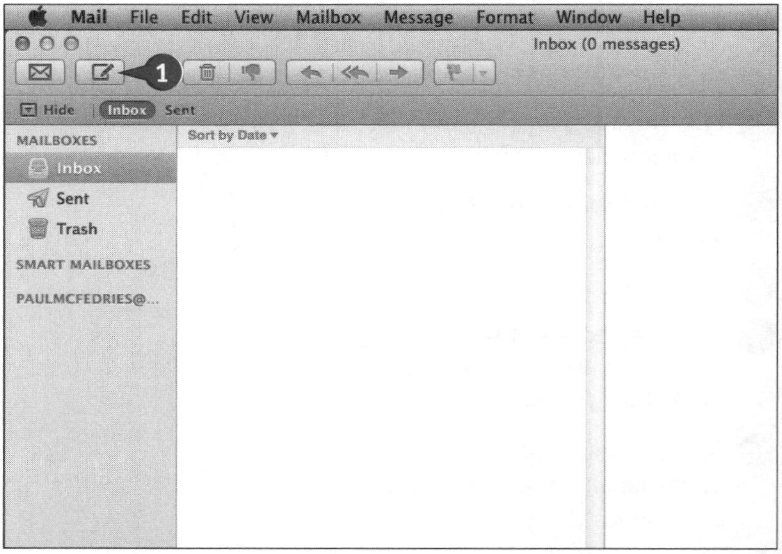

A message window appears.

2. Type the e-mail address of the person to whom you are sending the message in the To field.
3. Type the e-mail address of the person to whom you are sending a copy of the message in the Cc field.

Note: You can add multiple e-mail addresses in both the To field and the Cc field by separating each address with a comma (,).

4. Type a brief description of the message in the Subject field.

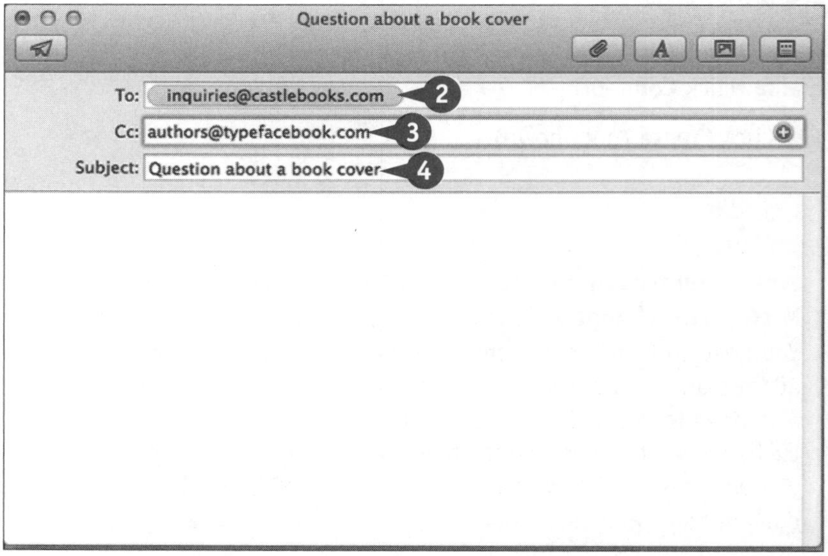

5 Type the message.

A To change the message font, click **Fonts** (A) to display the Font panel.

B To change the overall look of the message, click **Show Stationery** (▤) and then click a theme.

Note: Many people use e-mail programs that cannot process text formatting. Unless you are sure your recipient's program supports formatting, it is best to send plain-text messages. To do this, click **Format** and then click **Make Plain Text**.

6 Click **Send** (✈).

Mail sends your message.

Note: Mail stores a copy of your message in the Sent folder.

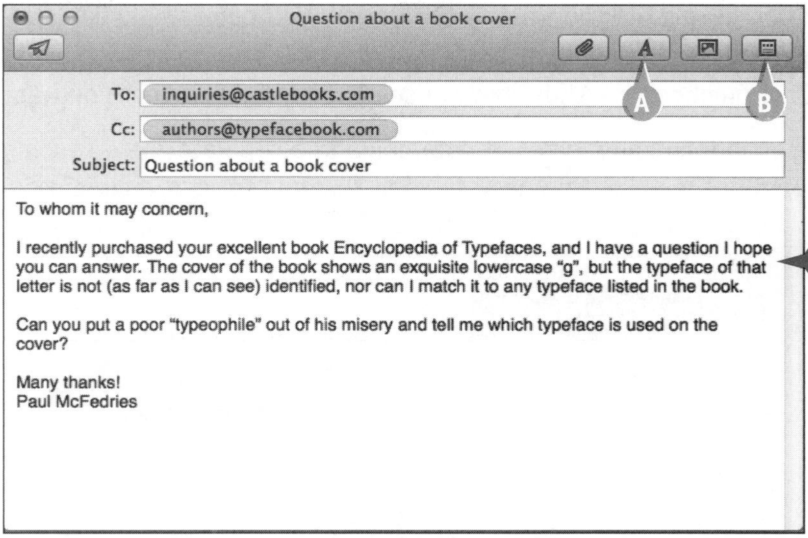

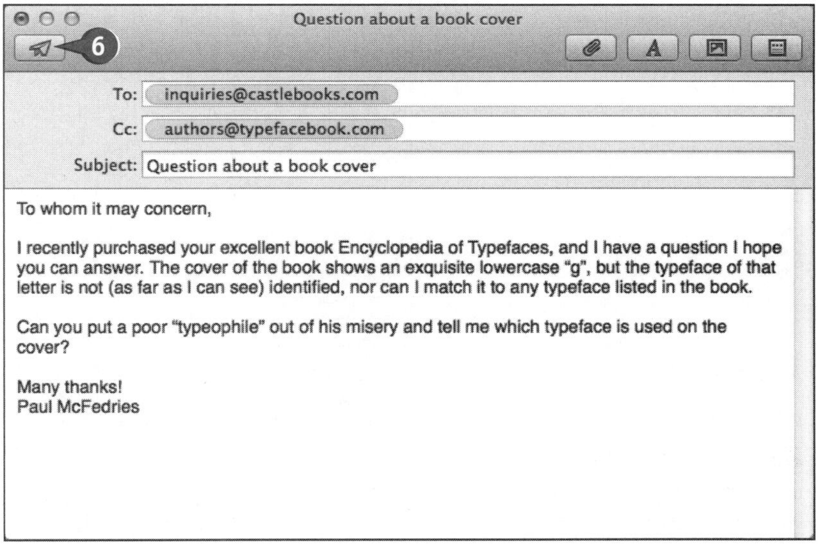

TIP

How can I compose a large number of messages offline?

While disconnected from the Internet, click **Mail** (icon) in the Dock to start Mail. To ensure you are working offline, click **Mailbox**. If the Take All Accounts Offline command is enabled, click that command. Compose and send the message. Each time you click **Send** (✈), your message is stored temporarily in the Outbox folder. When you are done, connect to the Internet. After a few moments, Mail automatically sends all the messages in the Outbox folder.

Add a File Attachment

If you have a file you want to send to another person, you can attach it to an e-mail message. A typical message is fine for short notes, but you may have something more complex to communicate, such as budget numbers or a slide show, or some form of media that you want to share, such as an image.

These more complex types of data come in a separate file — such as a spreadsheet, presentation file, or picture file — so you need to send that file to your recipient. You do this by attaching the file to an e-mail message.

Add a File Attachment

1. Click **New Message** ( ).

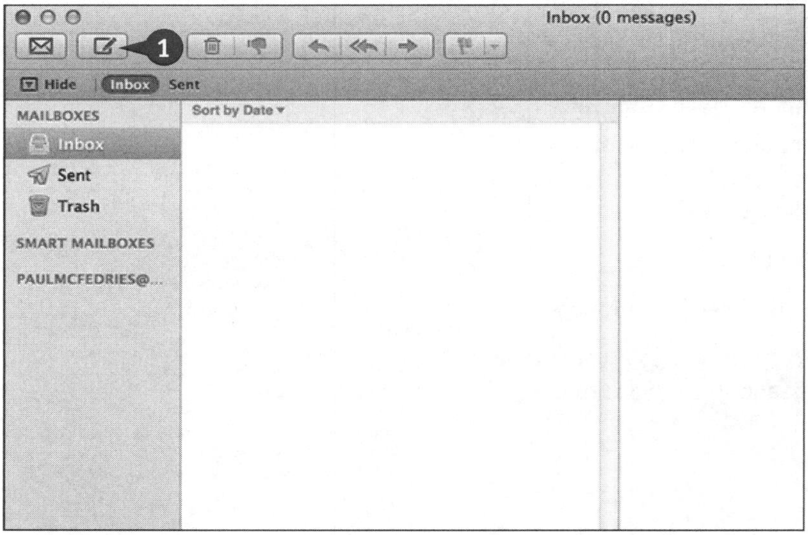

A message window appears.

2. Fill in the recipients, subject, and message text as described in the previous section, "Send an E-Mail Message."
3. Press Return two or three times to move the cursor a few lines below your message.
4. Click **Attach** ( ).

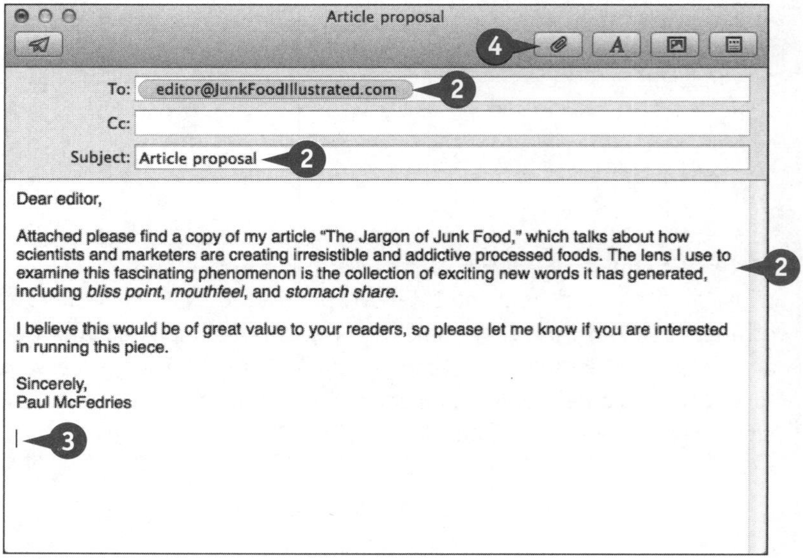

A file selection dialog appears.

5. Click the file you want to attach.
6. Click **Choose File**.

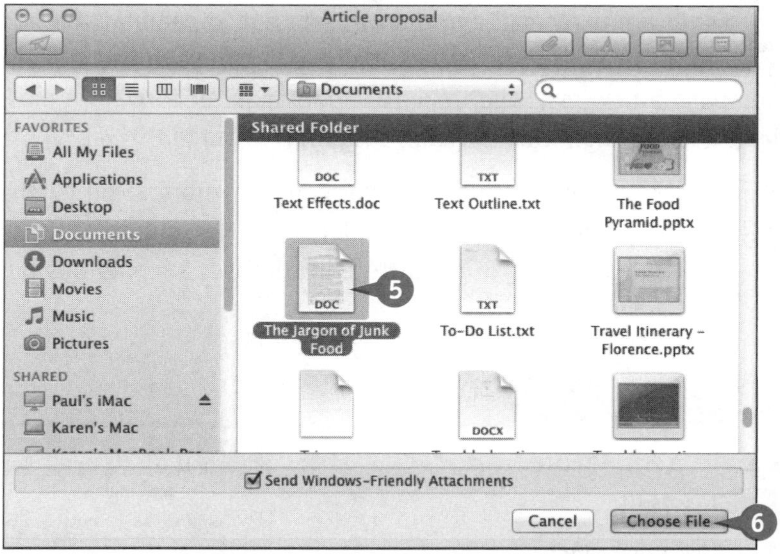

A. Mail attaches the file to the message.

Note: Another way to attach a file to a message is to click and drag the file from Finder and drop it inside the message.

7. Repeat steps 4 to 6 to attach additional files to the message.
8. Click **Send** (✈).

   Mail sends your message.

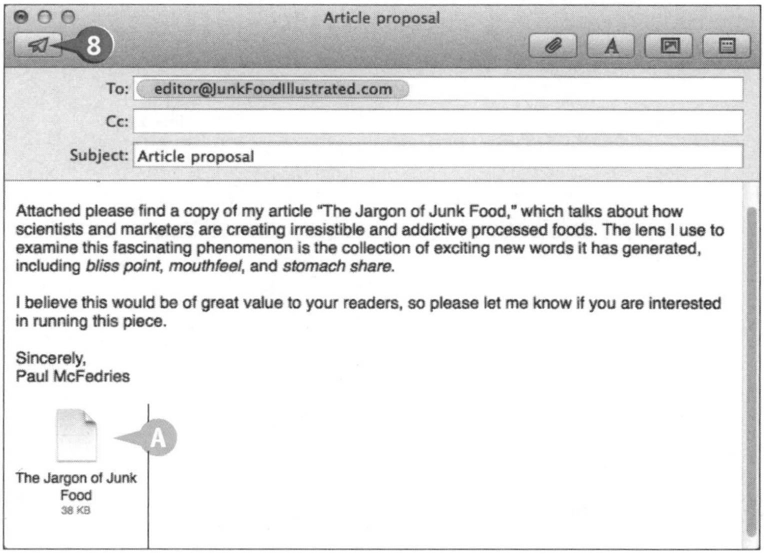

TIP

Is there a limit to the number of files I can attach to a message?

The number of files you can attach to the message has no practical limit. However, you should be careful with the total *size* of the files you send to someone. If either of you has a slow Internet connection, then sending or receiving the message can take an extremely long time. Also, many ISPs place a limit on the size of a message's attachments, which is usually between 2MB and 5MB. In general, use e-mail to send only a few small files at a time.

Add a Signature

A *signature* is a small amount of text that appears at the bottom of an e-mail message. Instead of typing this information manually, you can save the signature in your Mail preferences. When you compose a new message, reply to a message, or forward a message, you can click a button to have Mail add the signature to your outgoing message.

Signatures usually contain personal contact information, such as your phone numbers, business address, and e-mail and website addresses. Mail supports multiple signatures, which is useful if you use multiple accounts or for different purposes such as business and personal.

Add a Signature

Create a Signature

1. Click **Mail.**
2. Click **Preferences.**

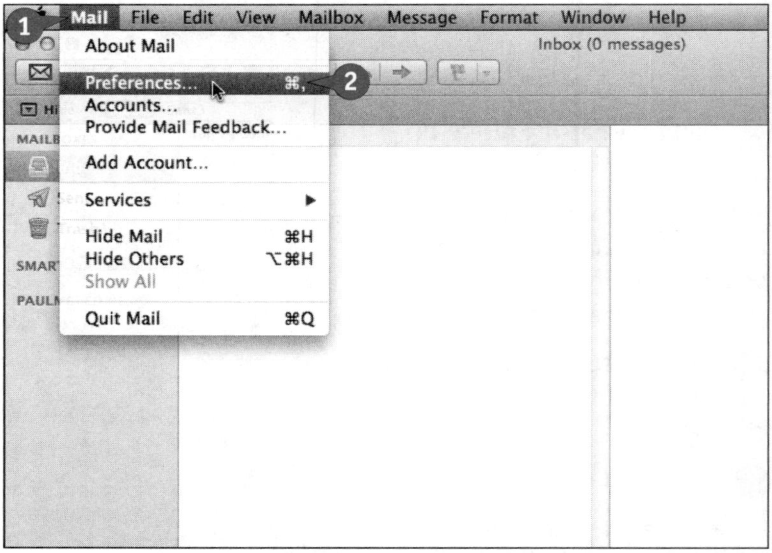

The Mail preferences appear.

3. Click the **Signatures** tab.
4. Click the account for which you want to use the signature.
5. Click **Create a signature** (+).

Mail adds a new signature.

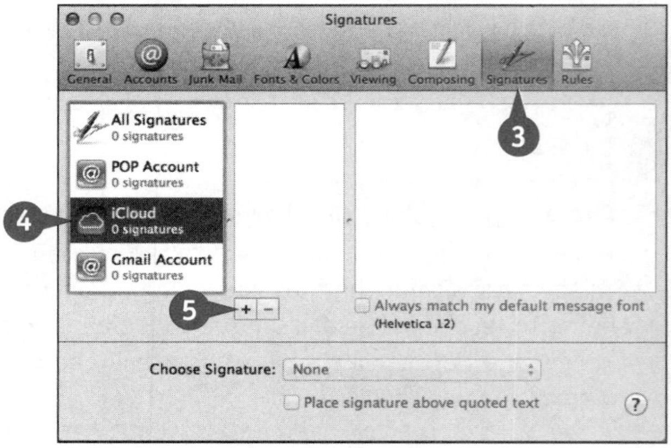

6 Type a name for the signature.

7 Type the signature text.

8 Repeat steps 4 to 7 to add other signatures, if required.

Note: You can add as many signatures as you want. For example, you may want to have one signature for business use and another for personal use.

9 Click **Close** (■).

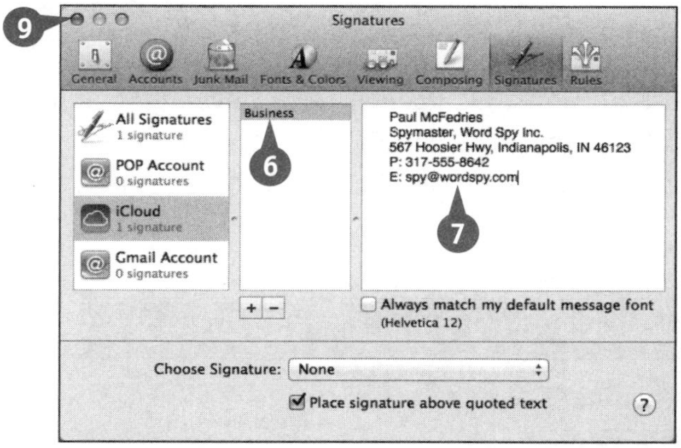

Insert the Signature

1 Click **New Message** (✎) to start a new message.

Note: To start a new message, see the section "Send an E-Mail Message."

2 In the message text area, move the insertion point to the location where you want the signature to appear.

3 Click the **Signature** ⬍ and then click the signature you want to insert.

A The signature appears in the message.

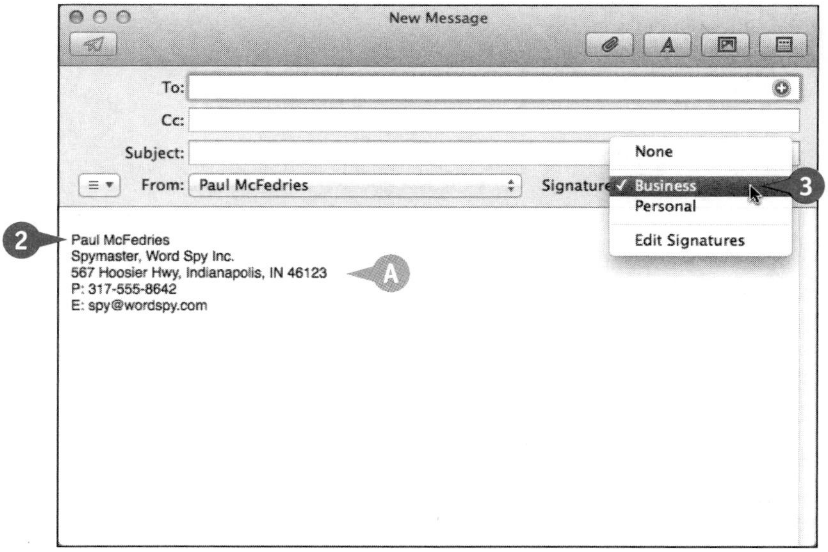

TIP

When I have multiple signatures, how can I choose which signature Mail adds automatically?
Follow steps 1 to 4 to display the signature preferences and choose an account. Click ⬍ and then click the signature you want to insert automatically into each message. If you prefer to add a signature manually, click **None** instead of a signature. Click **Close** (■) to close the Mail preferences.

Receive and Read E-Mail Messages

When another person sends you an e-mail, that message ends up in your account mailbox on the incoming mail server maintained by your ISP or e-mail provider. Therefore, you must connect to the incoming mail server to retrieve and read messages sent to you. You can do this using Mail, which takes care of the details behind the scenes. By default, Mail automatically checks for new messages while you are online, but you can also check for new messages at any time.

Receive and Read E-Mail Messages

Receive E-Mail Messages

1. Click **Get Mail** (✉).

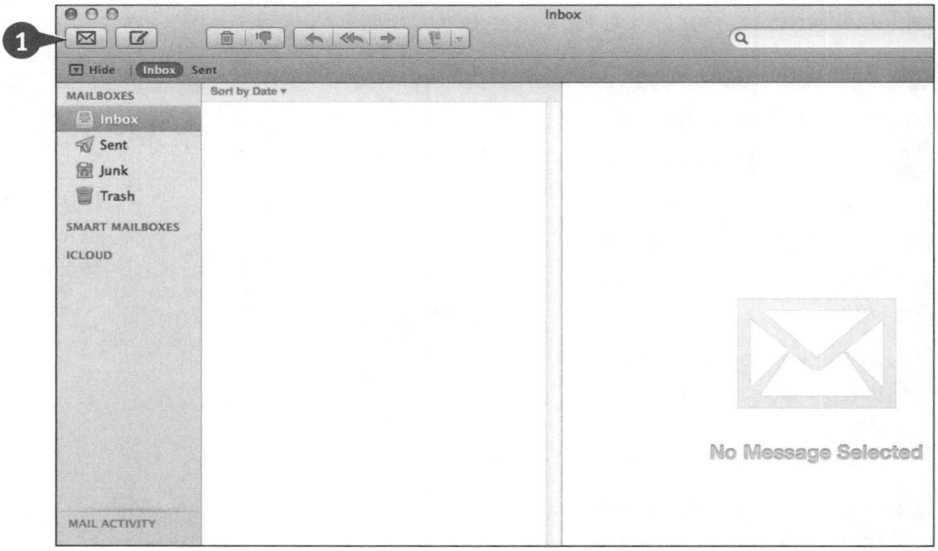

A The Mail Activity area lets you know if you have any incoming messages.

B If you have new messages, they appear in your Inbox folder with a blue dot in this column.

C The Mail icon (Mail icon) in the Dock shows the number of unread messages in the Inbox folder.

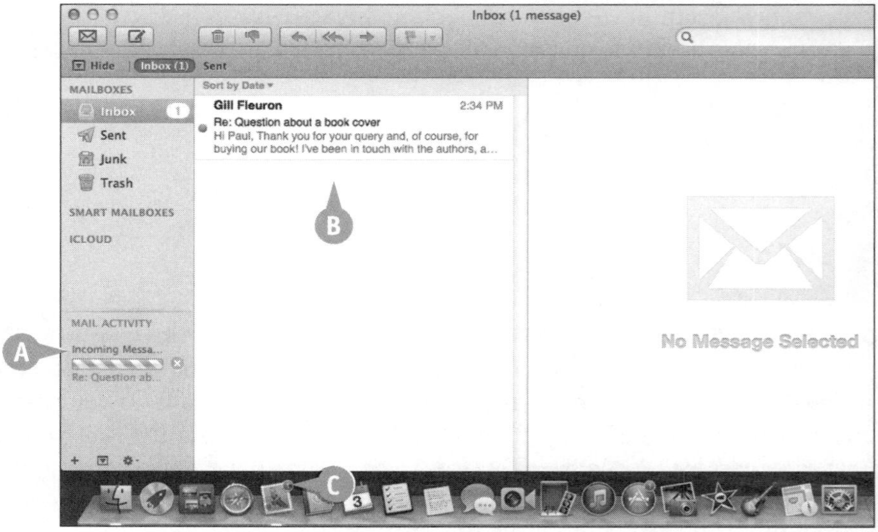

Read a Message

1. Click the message.

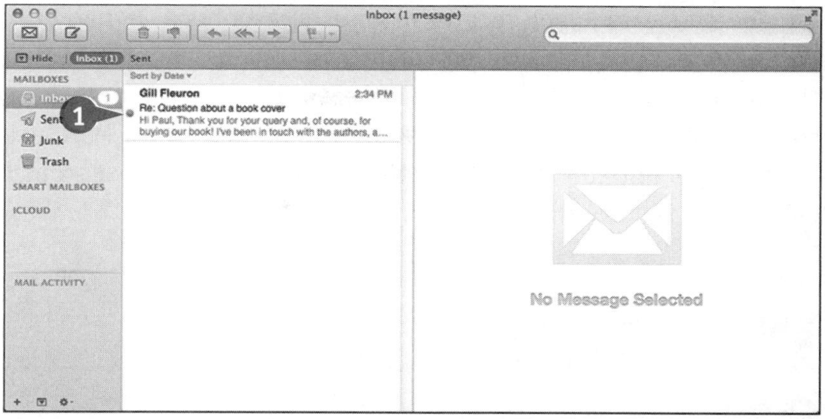

Mail displays the message text in the preview pane.

2. Read the message text in the preview pane.

Note: If you want to open the message in its own window, double-click the message.

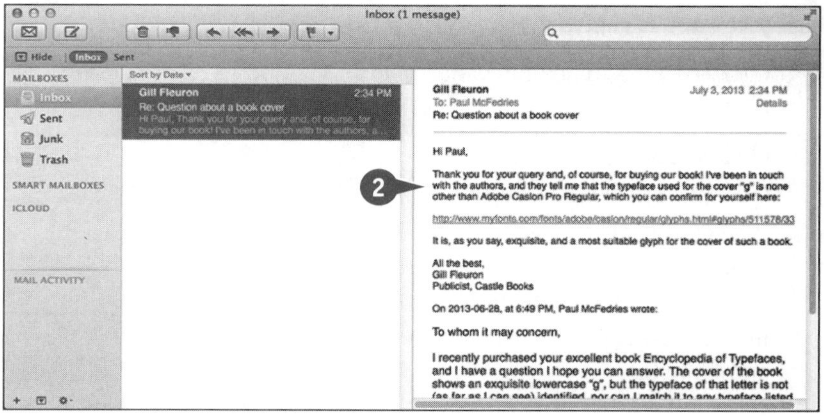

TIP

Can I change how often Mail automatically checks for messages?

Yes. Click **Mail** and then click **Preferences**. The Mail preferences appear. Click the **General** tab. Click the **Check for new messages** ⇕ and then click the time interval that you want Mail to use when checking for new messages automatically. If you do not want Mail to check for messages automatically, click **Manually** instead. Click **Close** (■) to close the Mail preferences.

Reply to a Message

When a message you receive requires a response — whether it is answering a question, supplying information, or providing comments — you can reply to that message. Most replies go only to the person who sent the original message. However, you can also send the reply to all the people who were included in the original message's To and Cc fields. Mail includes the text of the original message in the reply, but you should edit the original message text to include only enough of the original message to put your reply into context.

Reply to a Message

1. Click the message to which you want to reply.
2. Click the reply type you want to use.

   Click **Reply** () to respond only to the person who sent the message.

   Click **Reply All** () to respond to all the addresses in the message's From, To, and Cc fields.

   A message window appears.

- A Mail automatically inserts the recipient addresses.
- B Mail also inserts the subject field, preceded by Re:.
- C Mail includes the original message text at the bottom of the reply.

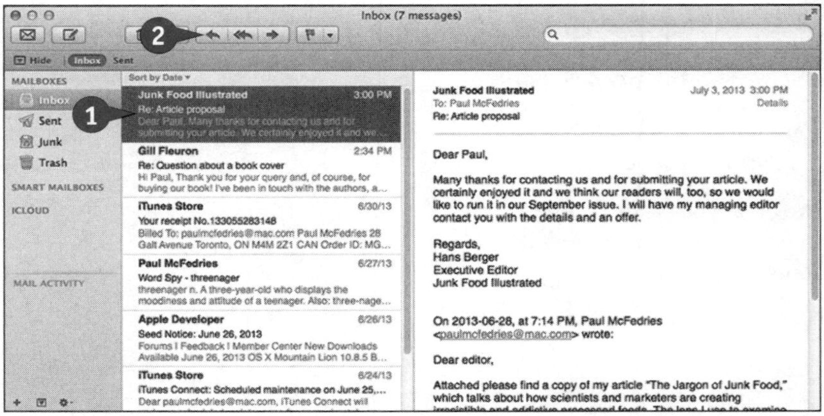

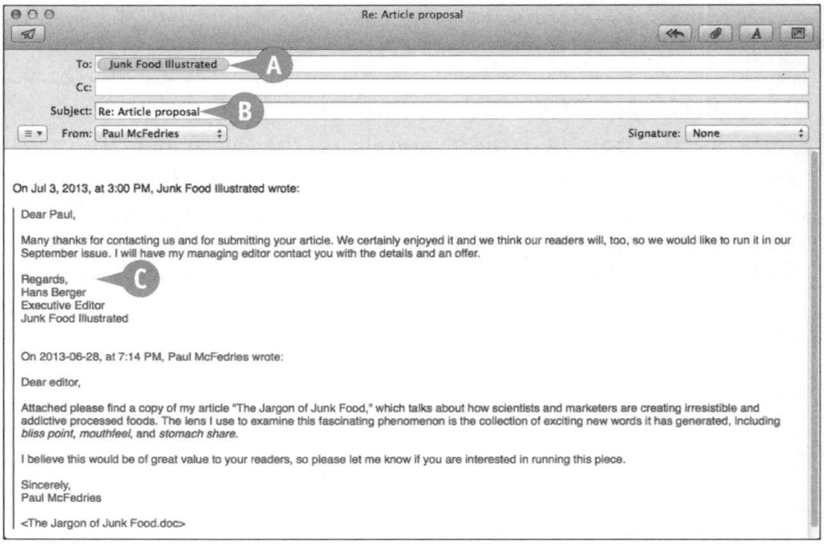

3 Edit the original message to include only the text relevant to your reply.

Note: You can automatically include just the relevant text in the reply by selecting that text before clicking Reply.

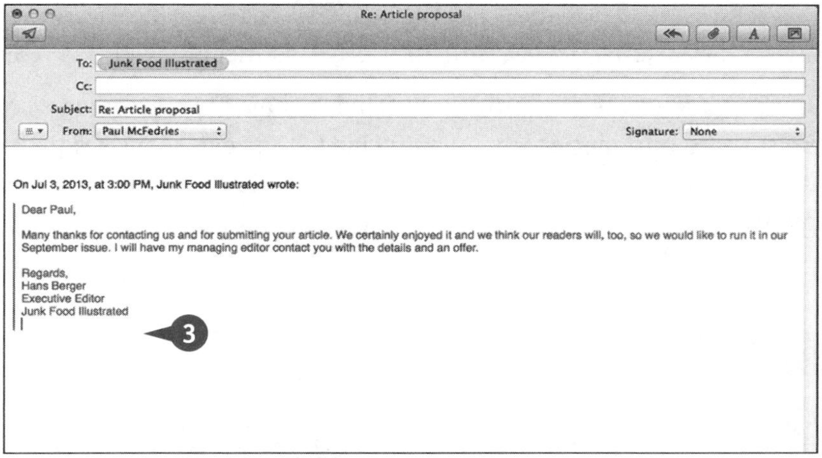

4 Click the area above the original message text and type your reply.

5 Click **Send** ( ).

Mail sends your reply.

Note: Mail stores a copy of your reply in the Sent folder.

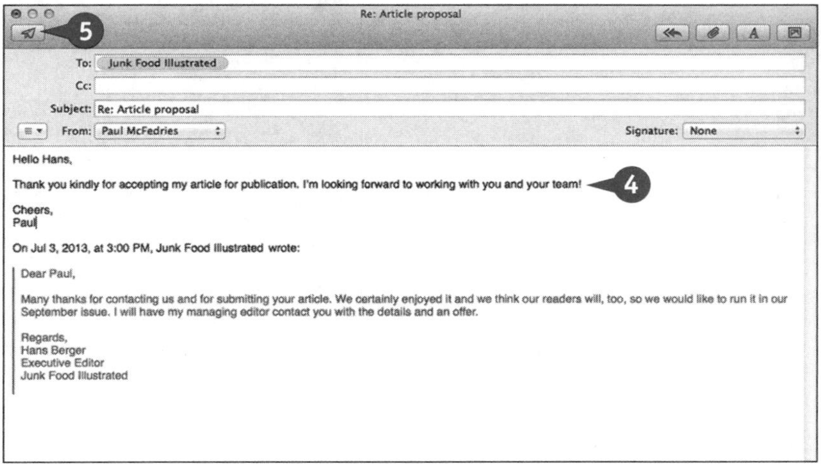

TIP

I received a message inadvertently. Is there a way that I can pass it along to the correct recipient?

Yes. Mail comes with a feature that enables you to pass along inadvertent messages to the correct recipient. Click the message that you received inadvertently, click **Message**, and then click **Redirect** (or press Shift+⌘+E). Type the recipient's address and then click **Send**. Replies to this message will be sent to the original sender, not to you.

Forward a Message

If a message has information relevant to or that concerns another person, you can forward a copy of the message to that person. You can also include your own comments in the forward.

In the body of the forward, Mail includes the original message's addresses, date, and subject field. Below this information Mail also includes the text of the original message. In most cases, you will leave the entire message intact so your recipient can see it. However, if only part of the message is relevant to the recipient, you should edit the original message accordingly.

Forward a Message

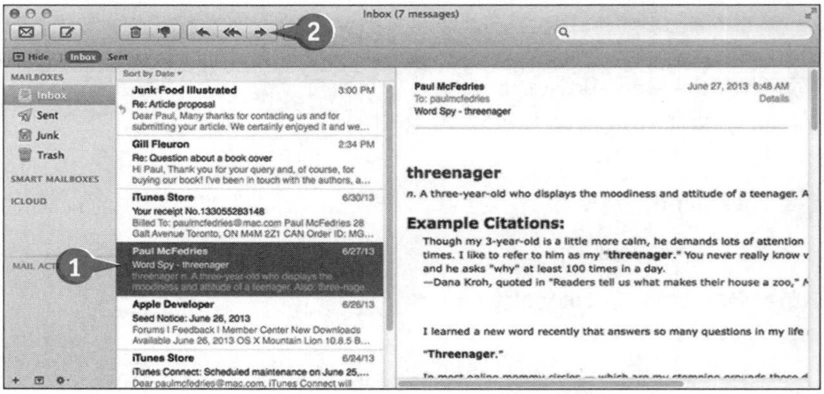

1. Click the message that you want to forward.
2. Click **Forward** (➡).

Note: You can also press Shift+⌘+F.

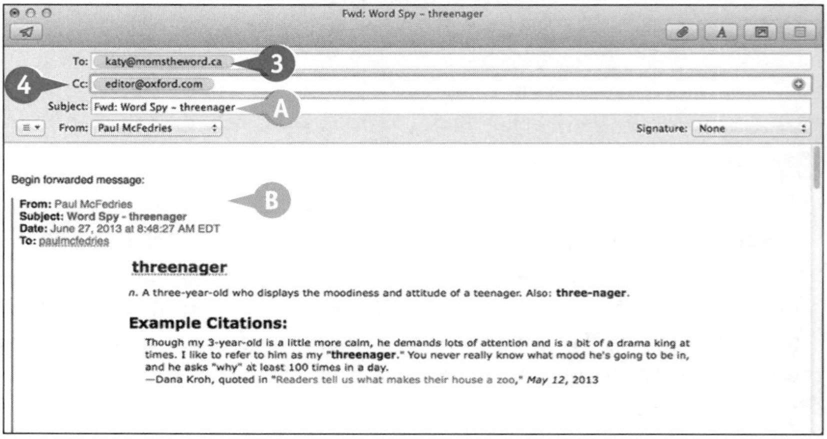

A message window appears.

- **A** Mail inserts the subject field, preceded by Fwd:.
- **B** The original message's addressees (To and From), date, subject, and text are included at the top of the forward.

3. Type the e-mail address of the person to whom you are forwarding the message.
4. To send a copy of the forward to another person, type that person's e-mail address in the Cc field.

5. Edit the original message to include only the text relevant to your forward.

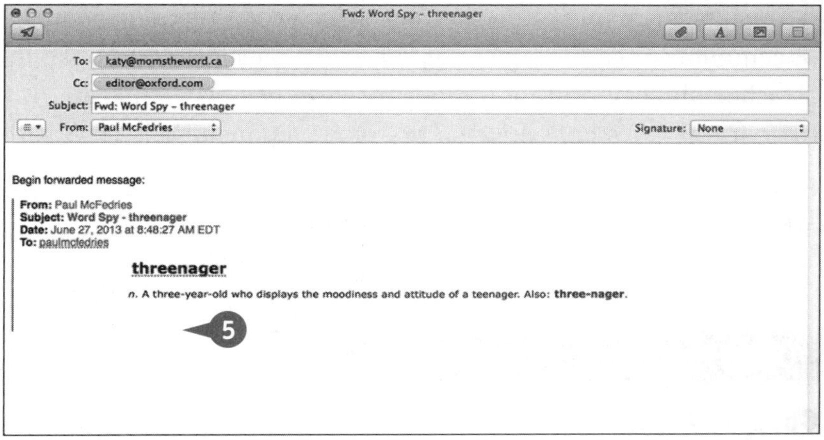

6. Click the area above the original message text and type your comments.

7. Click **Send** ( ).

   Mail sends your forward.

Note: Mail stores a copy of your forward in the Sent folder.

Note: You can forward someone a copy of the actual message instead of just a copy of the message text. Click the message, click **Message**, and then click **Forward As Attachment**. Mail creates a new message and includes the original message as an attachment.

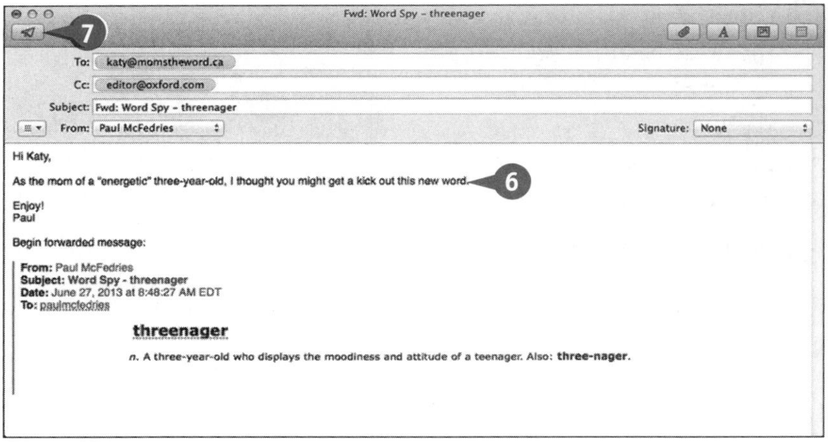

TIP

Mail always formats my replies as rich text, even when the original message is plain text. How can I fix this problem?

You can configure Mail to always reply using the same format as the original message. To do this, click **Mail** and then click **Preferences** to open the Mail preferences. Click the **Composing** tab. Select the **Use the same message format as the original message** option (changes to) and then click **Close** ( ) to close the Mail preferences.

Open and Save an Attachment

If you receive a message that has a file attached, you can open the attachment to view the contents of the file. However, although some attachments only require a quick viewing, other attachments may contain information that you want to keep. In this case, you should save these files to your Mac Pro's hard drive so that you can open them later without having to launch Mail.

Be careful when dealing with attached files. Computer viruses are often transmitted by e-mail attachments.

Open and Save an Attachment

Open an Attachment

1. Click the message that has the attachment, as indicated by the Attachment symbol (📎).

   A. An icon appears for each message attachment.

2. Double-click the attachment you want to open.

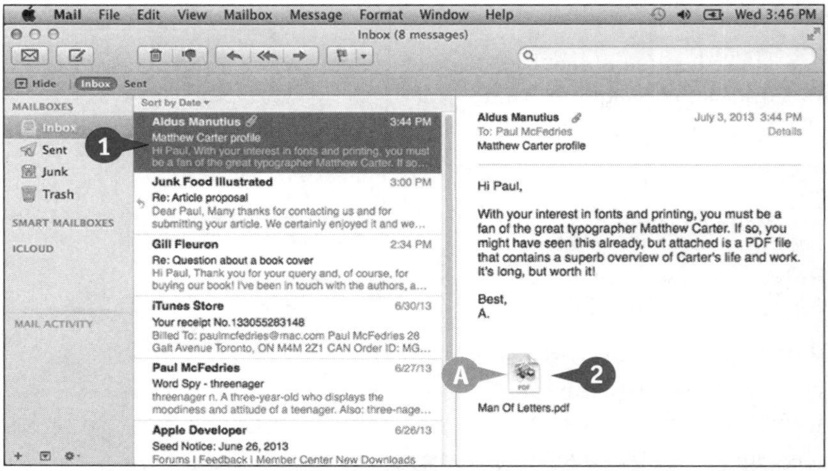

The file opens in the associated application.

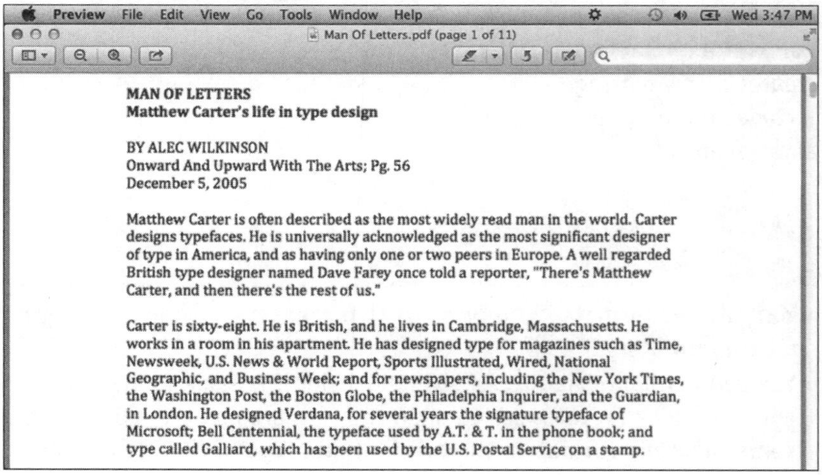

Save an Attachment

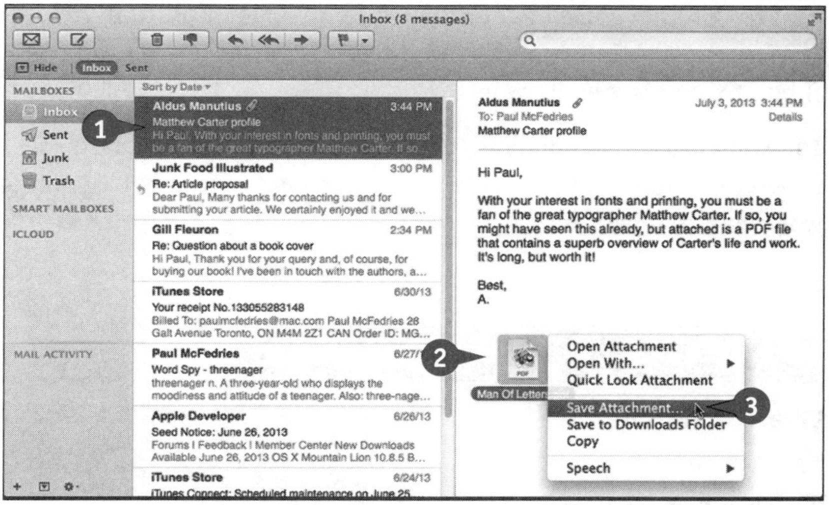

1. Click the message that has the attachment, as indicated by the Attachment symbol ( ).
2. Right-click the attachment you want to save.
3. Click **Save Attachment**.

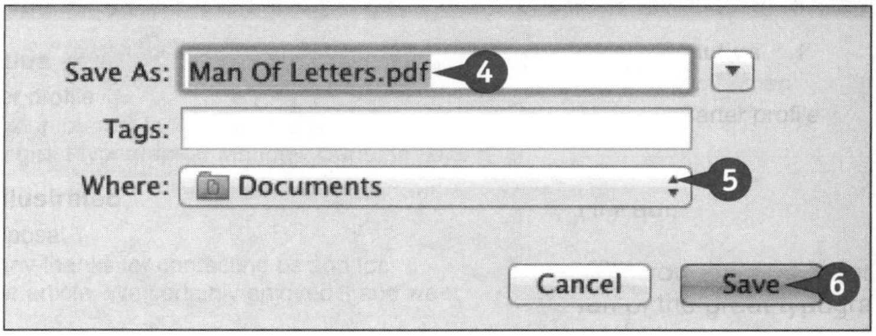

Mail prompts you to save the file.

4. Click in the Save As text box and edit the filename, if desired.
5. Click the **Where** and select the folder into which you want the file saved.
6. Click **Save**.

Note: Another way to save an attachment is to drag it from the message and drop it within a Finder window.

TIPS

Can I open an attachment using a different application?
In most cases, yes. Mac Pro usually has a default application that it uses when you double-click a file attachment. However, it also usually defines one or more other applications capable of opening the file. To check this out, right-click the icon of the attachment you want to open and then click **Open With**. In the menu that appears, click the application that you prefer to use to open the file.

Are viruses a big problem on the Mac?
No, not yet. Most viruses target Windows PCs, and only a few malicious programs target the Mac. However, as the Mac becomes more popular, expect to see more Mac-targeted virus programs. Therefore, you should still exercise caution when opening e-mail attachments.

Create a Mailbox for Saving Messages

After you have used Mail for a while, you may find that you have many messages in your Inbox. To keep the Inbox uncluttered, you can create new mailboxes and then move messages from the Inbox to the new mailboxes.

You should use each mailbox you create to save related messages. For example, you could create separate mailboxes for people you correspond with regularly, projects you are working on, different work departments, and so on.

Create a Mailbox for Saving Messages

Create a Mailbox

1. Click **Mailbox**.
2. Click **New Mailbox**.

The New Mailbox dialog appears.

3. Click the **Location** ⬍ and then click where you want the mailbox located.
4. Type the name of the new mailbox.
5. Click **OK**.

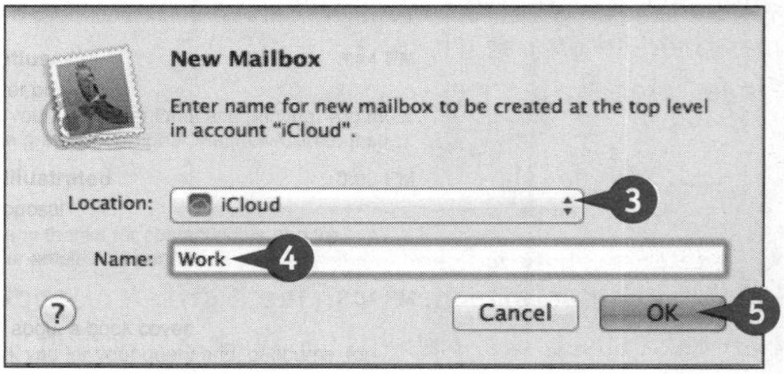

Ⓐ The new mailbox appears in the Mailbox list.

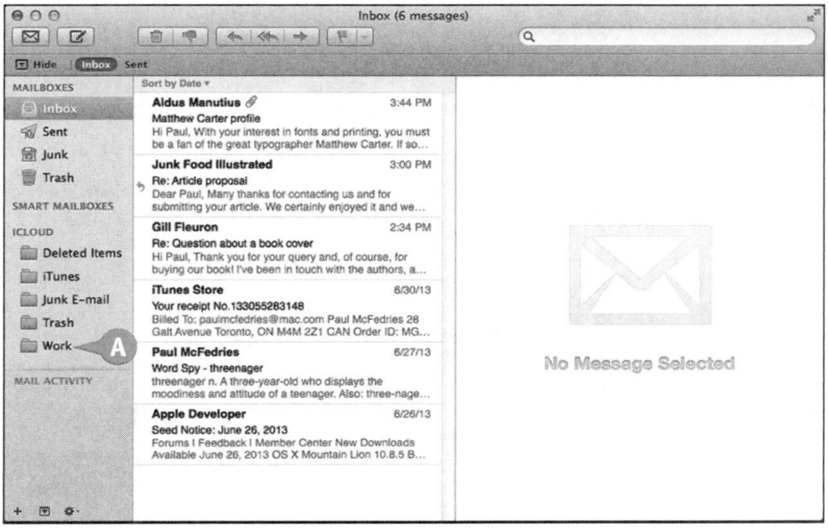

Move a Message to Another Mailbox

1. Position the mouse over the message you want to move.

2. Click and drag the message and drop it on the mailbox to which you want to move it.

   Mail moves the message.

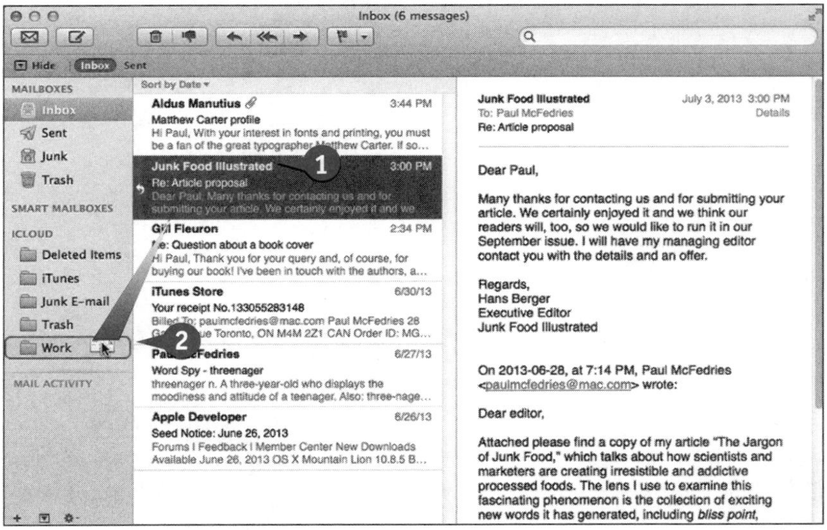

TIPS

How do I rename a mailbox?

Right-click the mailbox and then click **Rename Mailbox.** Type the new name and then press Return. Note that Mail does not allow you to rename any of the built-in mailboxes, including Inbox, Drafts, and Trash.

How do I delete a mailbox?

Right-click the mailbox and then click **Delete**. When Mail asks you to confirm the deletion, click **Delete**. Note that Mail does not allow you to delete any of the built-in mailboxes, including Inbox, Drafts, and Trash. Remember, too, that when you delete a mailbox, you also delete any messages stored in that mailbox.

Create Rules to Filter Incoming Messages

You can make your e-mail chores faster and more efficient if you create *rules* that automatically handle incoming messages.

A rule combines a condition and an action. The condition is one or more message criteria, such as the address of the sender or words in the subject field. Mail applies the rule only to messages that meet these criteria. The action is what happens to a message that satisfies the condition. Example actions include moving the message to another folder or sending a reply.

Create Rules to Filter Incoming Messages

1. Click **Mail.**
2. Click **Preferences.**

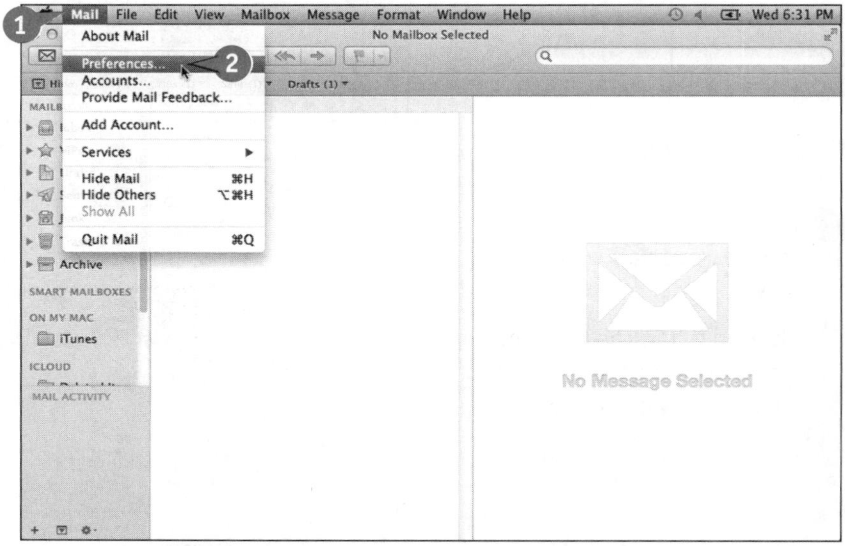

The Mail preferences appear.

3. Click the **Rules** tab.
4. Click **Add Rule**.

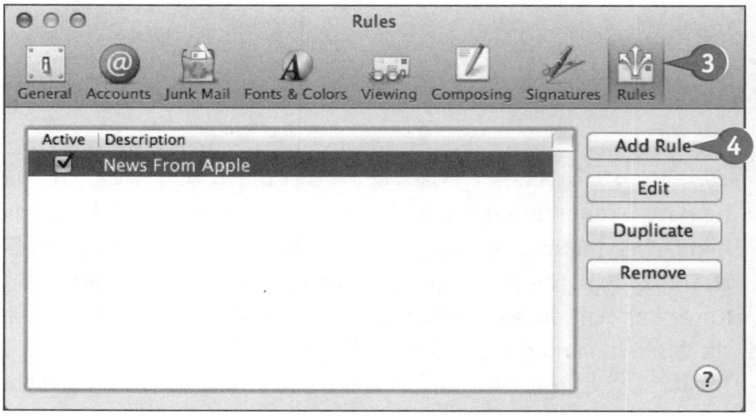

Mail begins a new rule.

5. Type a name for the rule.
6. Click ⬍ and then click the object of the condition.
7. Click ⬍ and then click an operator.
8. Type the value you want to match in the text box.

Note: Not all conditions require an operator or a value.

9. To add another condition, click **Add** (+) and repeat steps 6 to 8.
10. Click ⬍ and then click the type of action.
11. Click ⬍ and then click the action.

Note: Not all conditions require a specific action.

12. To add another action, click **Add** (+) and repeat steps 10 and 11.
13. Click **OK**.

If your Inbox contains messages that match the rule condition, Mail asks if you want to apply the rule now.

14. Click **Apply**.

Mail applies the new rule and adds the rule to the Rules tab.

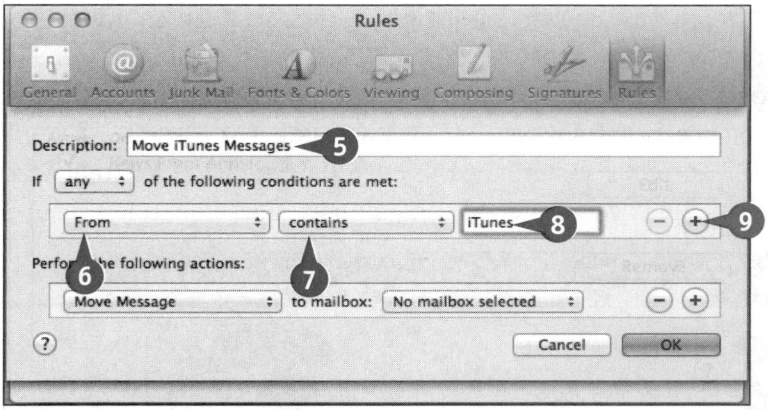

TIP

Can I create a rule that looks for messages that meet *all* the conditions I specify?

Yes. By default, Mail applies a rule on messages that meet any one of the conditions you add. However, you can create more specific rules by telling Mail to match only those messages that satisfy all the criteria you add. In the new rule dialog, click the **If** ⬍ and then click **all**.

Send All Messages from the Same Account

If you have multiple e-mail accounts, you can configure Mail to always send your new messages from one of those accounts. When you compose an e-mail, the message window includes a From field that displays the account from which you will be sending the message. However, the account you see is not always the same account. For example, if you have both an iCloud account and a POP account, sometimes the From field shows the iCloud account. At other times, it shows the POP account. If you prefer to send all messages from one account, you must configure Mail to do this.

Send All Messages from the Same Account

1. Click **Mail**.
2. Click **Preferences**.

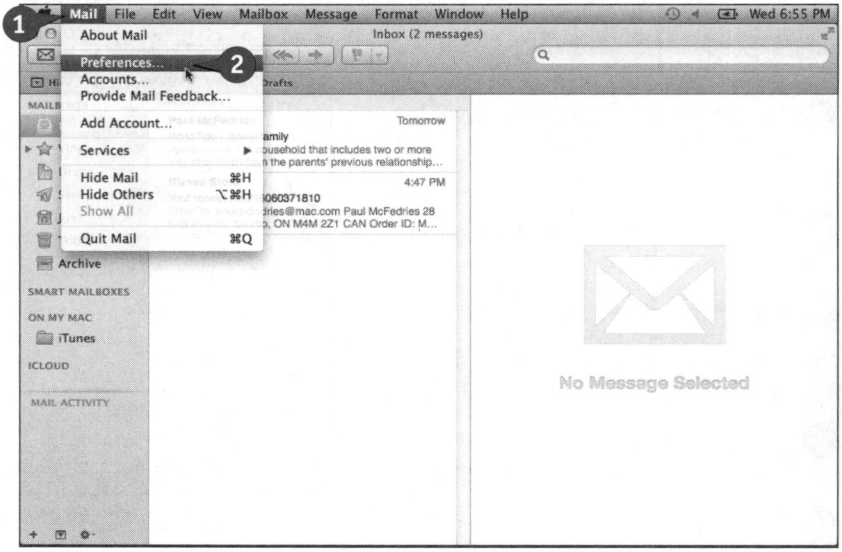

The Mail preferences appear.

3. Click the **Composing** tab.

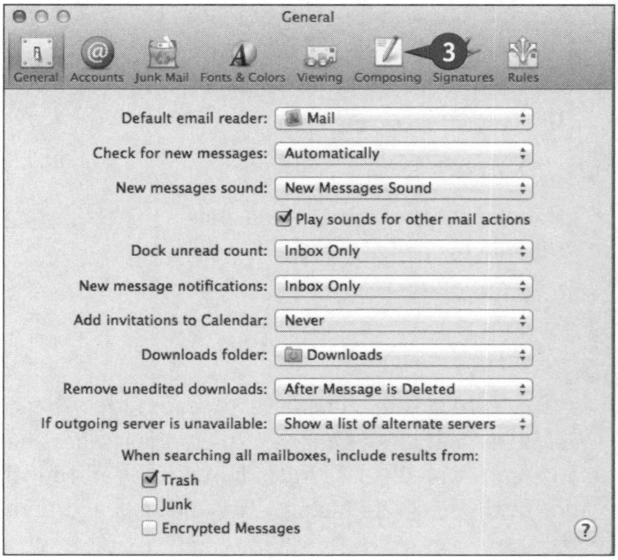

4. Click the **Send new messages from** .

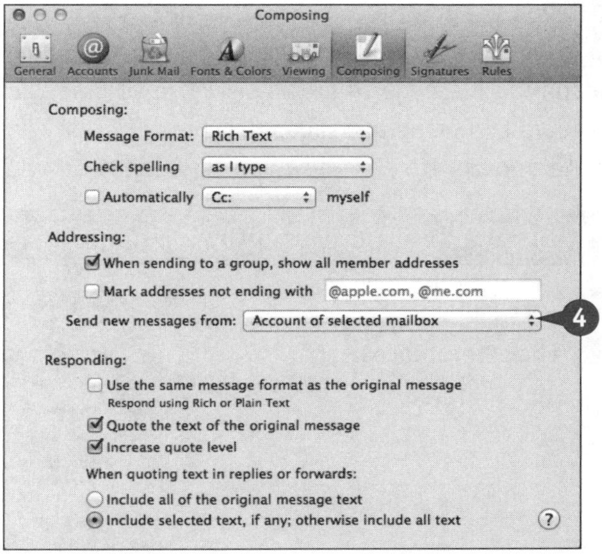

Mail displays a list of your e-mail accounts.

5. Click the account you want to use for sending messages.
6. Click **Close** ( ).

Mail puts the new setting into effect.

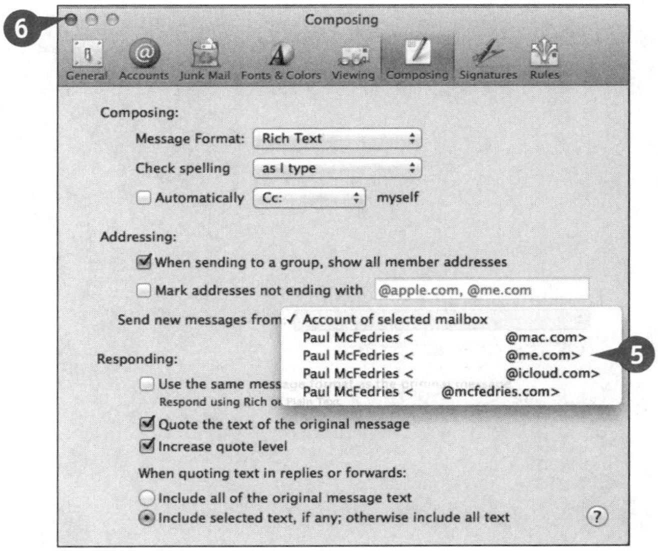

TIP

Why does Mail change the account I use for sending e-mail?

The reason is that Mail keeps track of the last mailbox you viewed, and it uses the account associated with that mailbox in the From list when you next go to compose a message. That actually makes a bit of sense when you think about it. For example, if you are currently working in a mailbox associated with your iCloud account and you start a new message, chances are good that you want to send that message using your iCloud account. However, most people prefer to send messages using a single account.

Control When Mail Removes Incoming Messages from the Server

If you use multiple devices to check your e-mail, you should configure Mail to not remove messages from your ISP's POP server until you no longer need them. By default, Mail does not remove an incoming message from the server until one week after you retrieve the message. If you find you receive too many messages on your other devices, use a shorter interval. If you find that you do not have enough time to view your messages on your other devices, use a longer interval.

Control When Mail Removes Incoming Messages from the Server

1. Click **Mail**.
2. Click **Preferences**.

The Mail preferences appear.

3. Click the **Accounts** tab.
4. Click the icon for the POP account with which you want to work.
5. Click the **Advanced** tab.

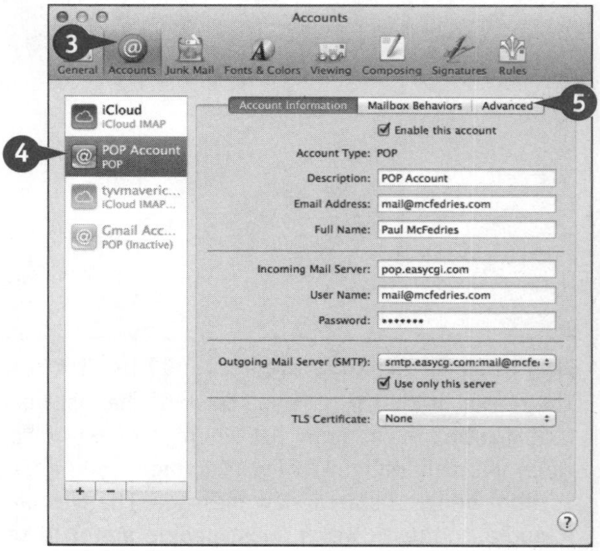

6. Make sure the **Remove copy from server after retrieving a message** option is selected (☑).

7. Click ⇕.

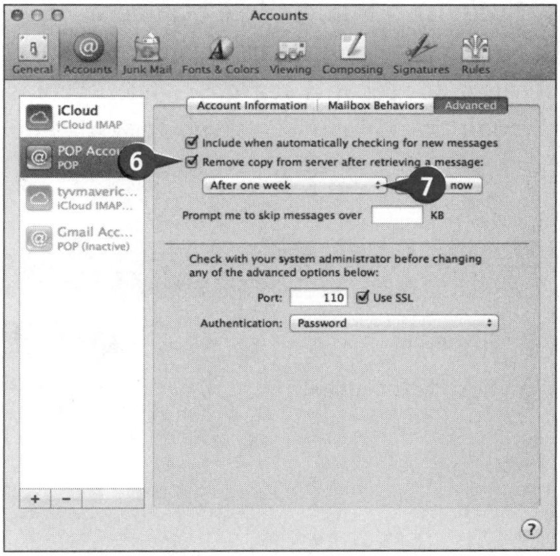

8. Click the interval after which you want each incoming message removed from the server.

9. Click **Close** (●).

   Mail puts the new setting into effect.

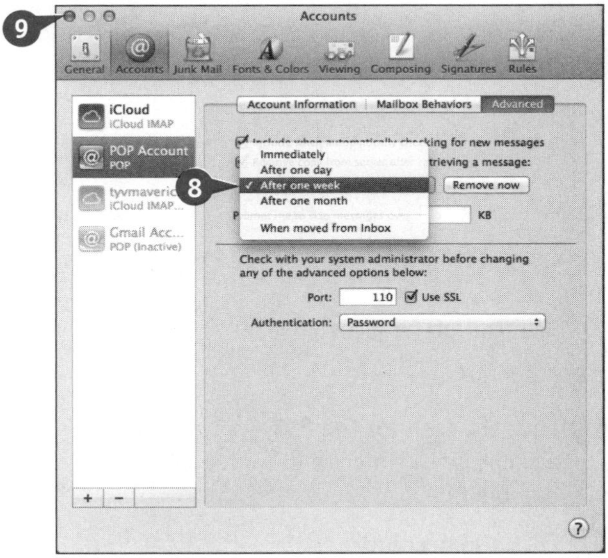

TIPS

What does a POP server do?
A message sent to you does not come directly to your Mac Pro. Instead, it goes to the POP server that your ISP uses to handle incoming messages. When Mail checks for new messages, it asks the POP server if any messages are waiting in your account. If so, Mail downloads those messages but leaves copies of the messages on the server.

How should I configure message removal on my Mac notebook?
Your Mac Pro should be the computer that controls the message deletion. On your Mac notebook, follow steps 1 to 5 and then deselect the **Remove copy from server after retrieving a message** option (☑ changes to ☐) to prevent it from removing messages.

Change the Outgoing Server Port

If you use a third-party e-mail account — such as an account provided by your website hosting provider — you might run into problems when you try to send messages. These problems arise because, for security reasons, some ISPs insist that all their customers' outgoing mail must be routed through the ISP's SMTP server. To work around this problem, many third-party hosts offer access to their SMTP server via a port other than the standard port 25.

Change the Outgoing Server Port

1 Click **Mail**.

2 Click **Preferences**.

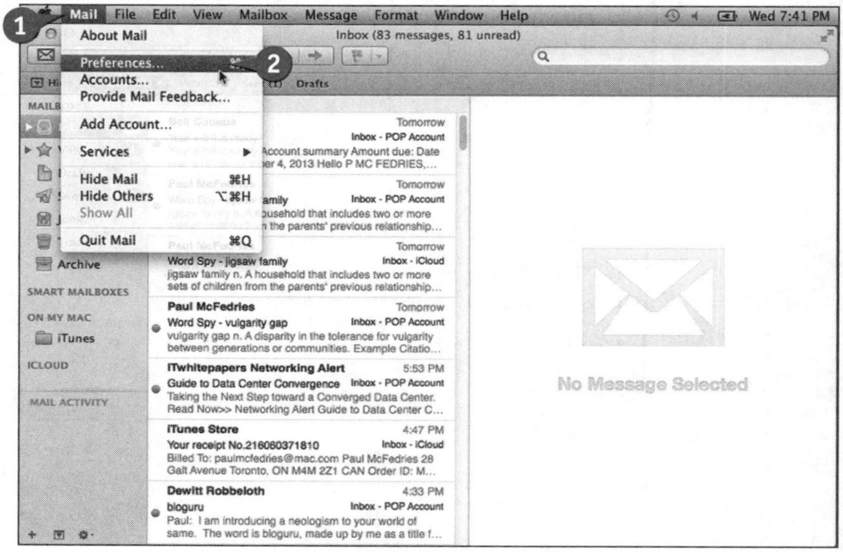

The Mail preferences appear.

3 Click the **Accounts** tab.

4 Click the icon for the POP account with which you want to work.

5 Click the **Account Information** tab.

6 Click the **Outgoing Mail Server (SMTP)** ⇕ and then click **Edit SMTP Server List**.

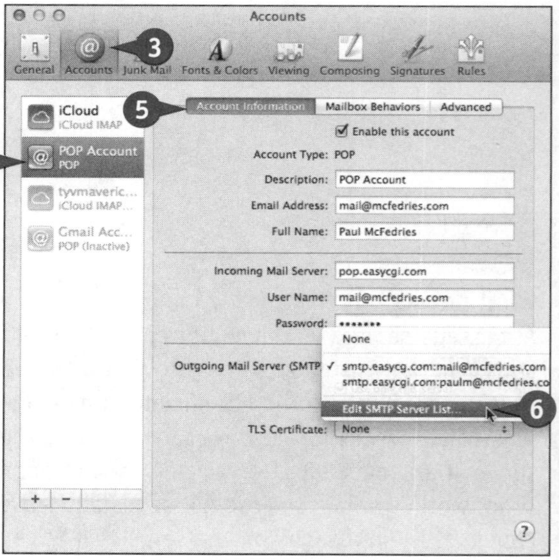

7. Click the server with which you want to work.
8. Click the **Advanced** tab.

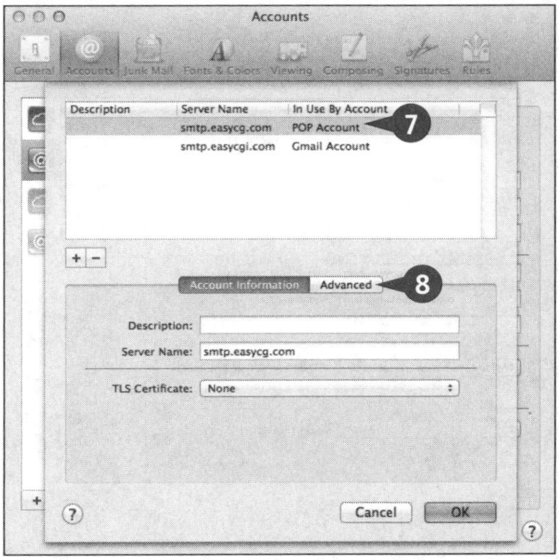

9. Select the **Use custom port** option (changes to).
10. Type the port number you want to use.
11. Click **OK.**
12. Click **Close** ( ).

Mail uses the new server port for all outgoing mail sent from the account.

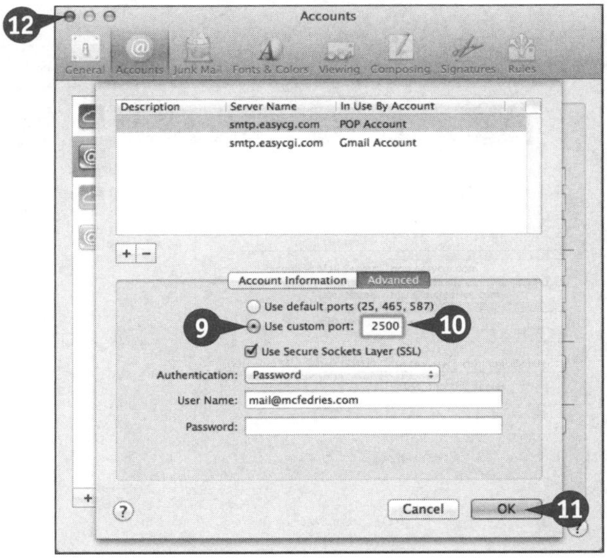

TIP

What kinds of problems can I expect when I use a third-party e-mail account?

- Your ISP might block messages sent using the third-party account because it thinks you are trying to relay the message through the ISP's server (a technique often used by spammers).
- You might incur extra charges if your ISP allows only a certain amount of SMTP bandwidth per month, or a certain number of sent messages, whereas the third-party account offers higher limits or no restrictions at all.
- You might have performance problems, such as the ISP's server taking much longer to route messages than the third-party host.

CHAPTER 6

Enhancing Online Security

This chapter helps you stay secure online by showing you a number of tasks designed to make your Internet sessions as safe and as private as possible. You learn how to delete your browsing history, prevent ad sites from tracking you online, browse the web privately, control junk e-mail, and more.

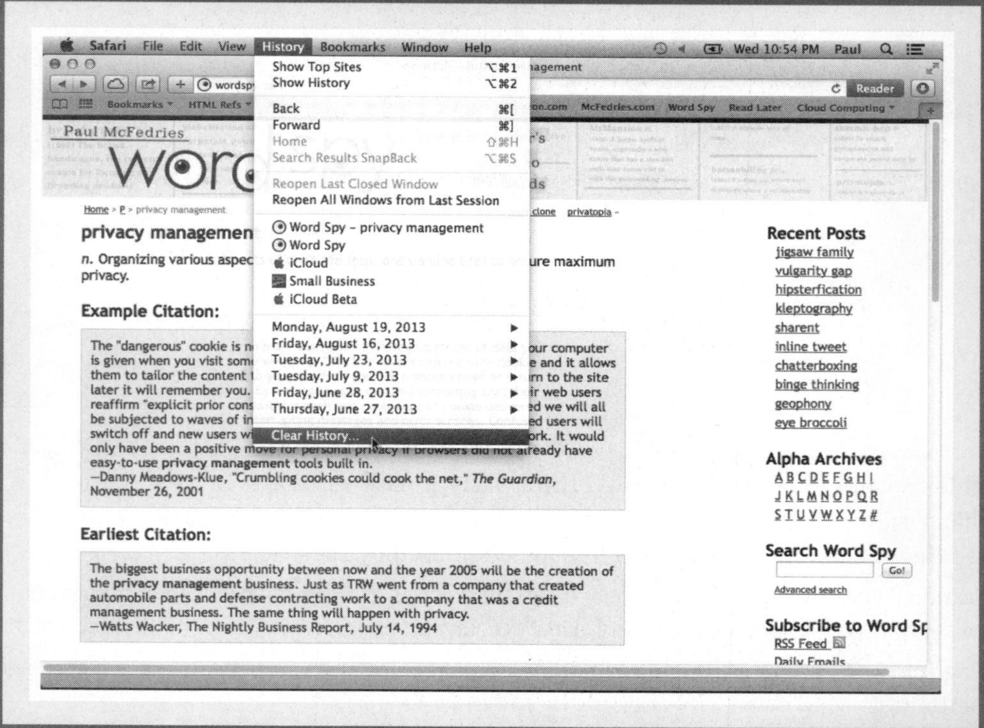

Delete a Site from Your Browsing History

You can enhance your privacy as well as the safety of other people who use your Mac Pro by removing a private or dangerous site from your browsing history. Safari maintains your *browsing history*, which is a list of the sites you have visited. If you share your Mac Pro with others, you might not want them to access certain private sites in your history. Similarly, if you accidentally stumble upon a dangerous or inappropriate site, you likely do not want others to see it. To help prevent both scenarios, you can delete the site from your browsing history.

Delete a Site from Your Browsing History

Delete a Single Site

1. Click **History**.
2. Click **Show History**.

   You can also run the Show History command by pressing Option + ⌘ + 2.

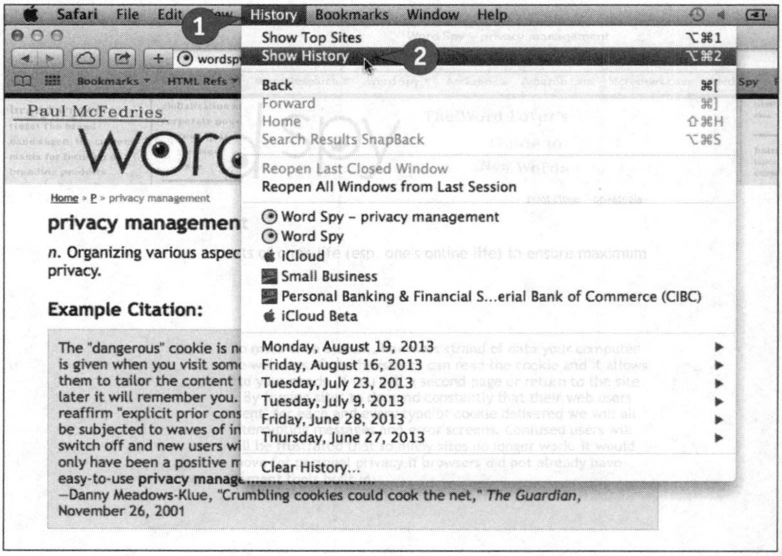

The History tab appears.

3. Right-click the site you want to remove.
4. Click **Delete**.

   Safari deletes the site from your browsing history.

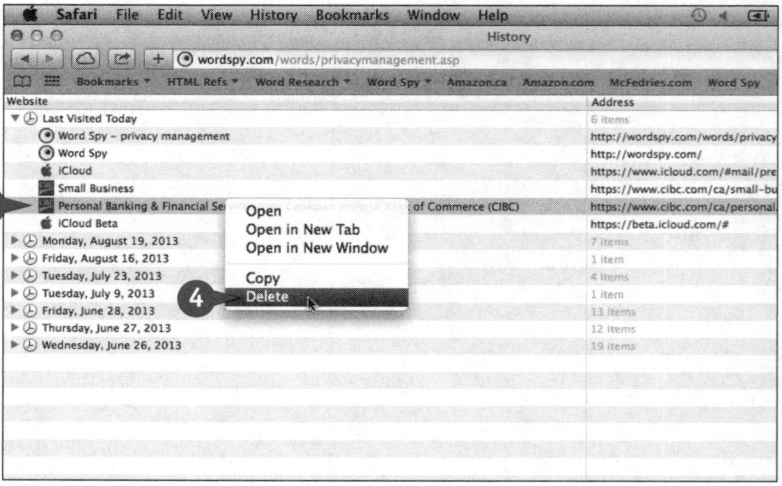

Clear Your Browsing History

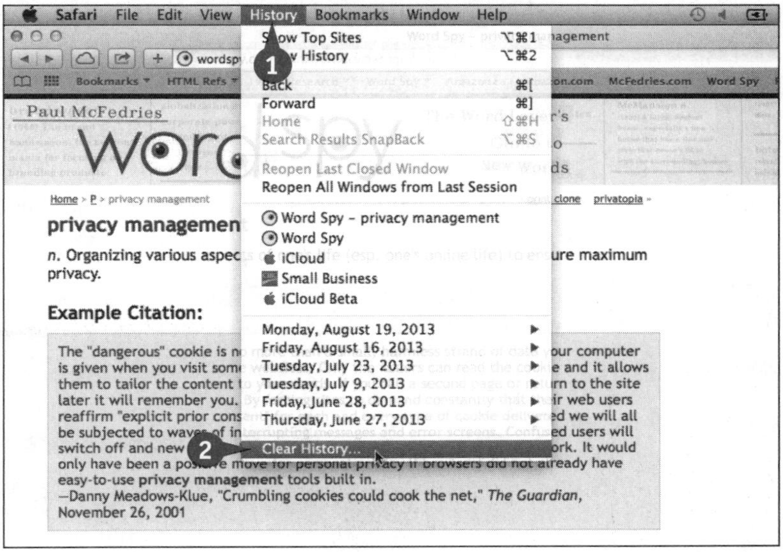

1. Click **History**.
2. Click **Clear History**.

Safari asks you to confirm that you want to delete all the sites in your browsing history.

3. Click **Clear**.

Safari clears every site from your browsing history.

TIP

Is there a way to clear my browsing history automatically?

Yes. If you regularly delete all your browsing history, constantly running the Clear History command can become tiresome. Fortunately, you can configure Safari to make this chore automatic. Click **Safari** and then click **Preferences** to display the Safari preferences. Click the **General** tab. Click the **Remove history items** and then click the length of time after which you want Safari to automatically remove an item from your browsing history. For example, if you click **After one day**, Safari clears out your browsing history daily.

Prevent Websites from Tracking You

You can prevent advertising sites from tracking your online movements by blocking the tracking files that they store on your Mac Pro, as well as other mechanisms that they use for tracking users. Advertisers want to track the sites that you visit in order to deliver ads targeted to your likes and preferences. However, you cannot be sure how these sites are using the information they store about you. Therefore, many people prefer to configure Safari to prevent websites from using their tracking features. Note, however, that there is no guarantee as yet that websites will honor a so-called *Do Not Track* request.

Prevent Websites from Tracking You

1. Click **Safari**.
2. Click **Preferences**.

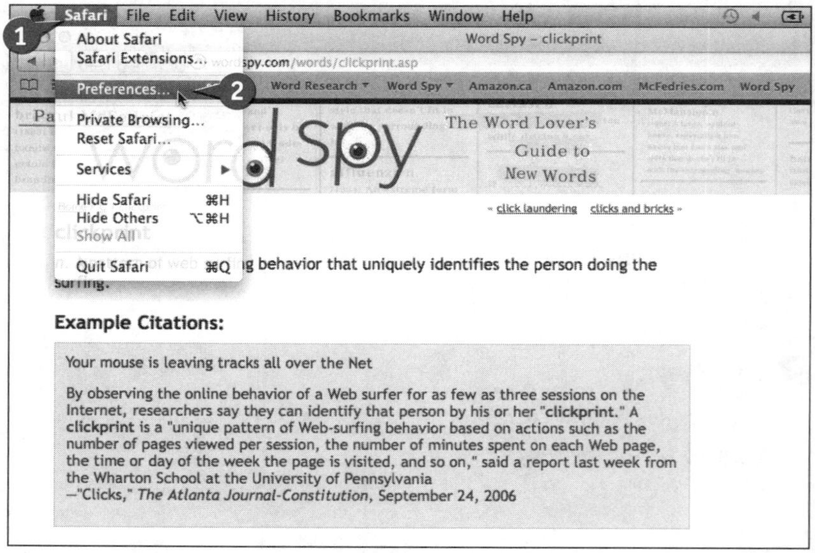

The Safari preferences appear.

3. Click the **Privacy** tab.

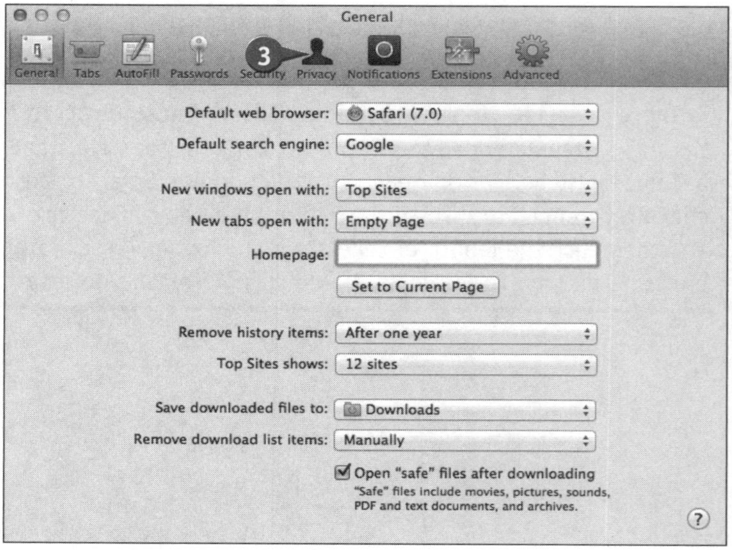

4 Select the **From third parties and advertisers** option (○ changes to ◉).

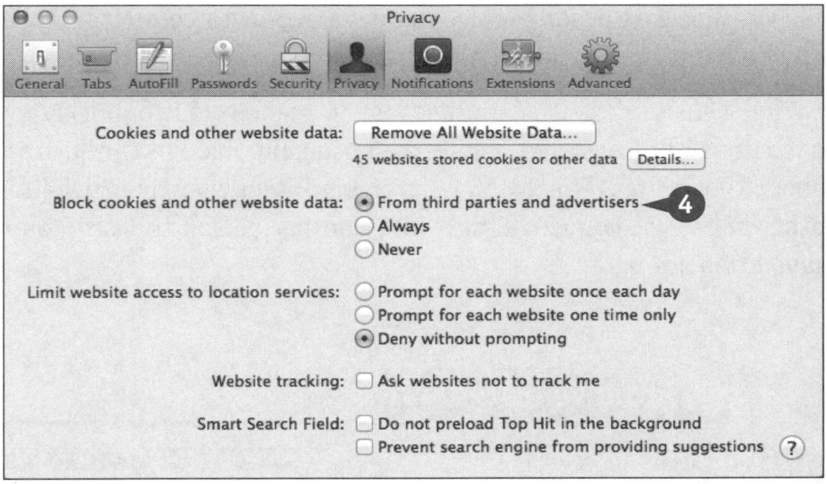

5 Select the **Ask websites not to track me** option (☐ changes to ☑).

6 Click **Close** (■).

Safari no longer accepts cookies from third-party sites and sends all websites a Do Not Track request.

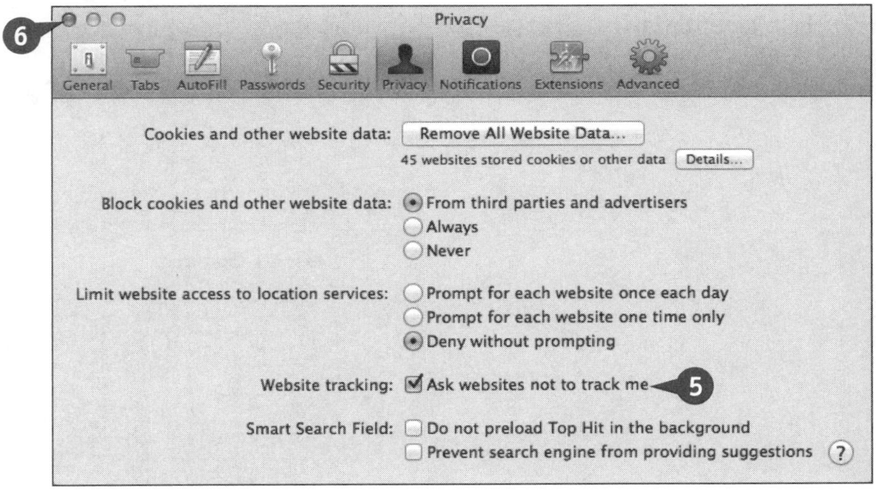

TIP

How can a website track me online?

The most common method is by using a *cookie*, a small text file that it stores on your Mac Pro. Cookies are used routinely by any website that needs to "remember" information about your session at that site: shopping cart data, page customizations, usernames, and so on.

A *third-party cookie* is a cookie set by a site other than the one you are viewing. An advertising site might store information about you in a third-party cookie and then use that cookie to track your online movements and activities. The advertiser can do this because it might have an ad on dozens or hundreds of websites, and that ad is the mechanism that enables the site to set and read its cookies.

Remove Saved Website Data

To ensure that other people who have access to your Mac Pro cannot view information from sites you have visited, you can delete Safari's saved website data.

Saving website data is useful because it enables you to quickly revisit a site. However, it is also dangerous because other people who use your Mac Pro can just as easily visit or view information about those sites. This can be a problem if you visit financial sites, private corporate sites, or some other page that you would not want another person to visit. You reduce this risk by deleting your saved website data.

Remove Saved Website Data

1. Click **Safari**.
2. Click **Reset Safari**.

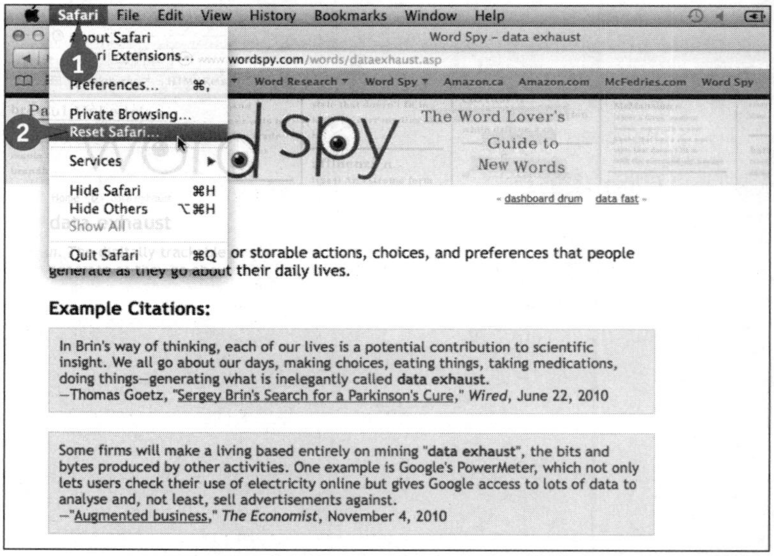

The Reset Safari dialog appears.

3. To delete the list of websites you have visited, select the **Clear history** option (☐ changes to ☑).
4. To clear the list of sites you have visited most often, select the **Reset Top Sites** option (☐ changes to ☑).

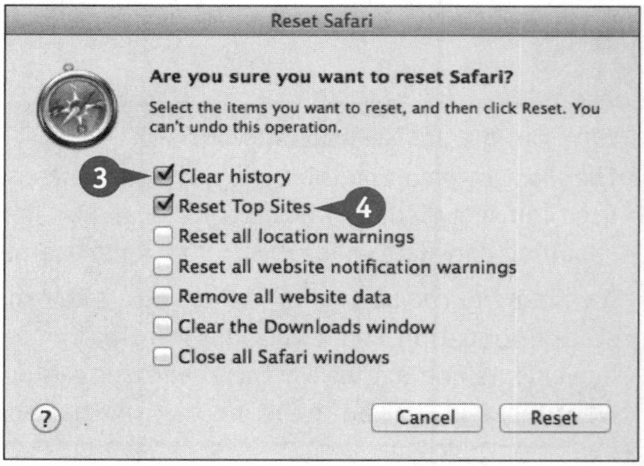

5 To delete information that websites have saved about your location, select the **Reset all location warnings** option (☐ changes to ☑).

6 To clear the list of sites that you have given permission to access the Notification Center, select the **Reset all website notification warnings** option (☐ changes to ☑).

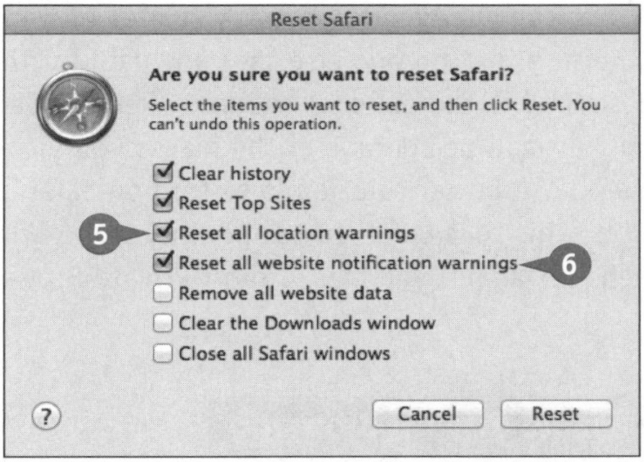

7 To delete saved website data, select the **Remove all website data** option (☐ changes to ☑).

8 To delete the list of files that you have downloaded, select the **Clear the Downloads window** option (☐ changes to ☑).

9 To close your open browser windows, select the **Close all Safari windows** option (☐ changes to ☑).

10 Click **Reset**.

Safari deletes the selected website data.

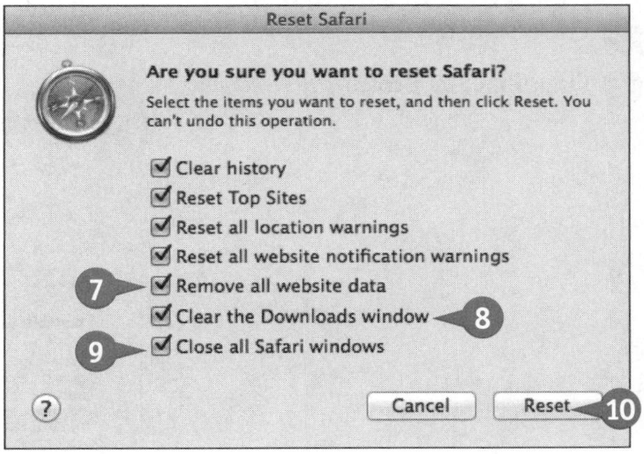

TIP

What types of website data does Safari save?

Besides your browsing history, as discussed in the section "Delete a Site from Your Browsing History," the website data that Safari stores includes copies of page text, images, and other content so that sites load faster the next time you view them. Safari also tracks what sites you visit most often and uses that data to populate the Top Sites page that appears when you open a new tab or window.

Safari also saves the names of files you have downloaded, the names of websites that you have given permission to use your current location, and the names of websites that you have given permission to use the Notification Center.

Enable Private Browsing

If you regularly visit private websites or websites that contain sensitive or secret data, you can ensure that no one else sees any data for these sites by deleting Safari's saved website data, as described in the previous section, "Remove Saved Website Data." However, if these sites represent only a small percentage of the places you visit on the web, deleting your all your website data is overkill. A better solution is to turn on Safari's Private Browsing feature before you visit private sites. This tells Safari to temporarily stop saving any website data. When you are ready to surf regular websites again, you can turn off Private Browsing to resume saving your website data.

Enable Private Browsing

1. Click **Safari**.
2. Click **Private Browsing**.

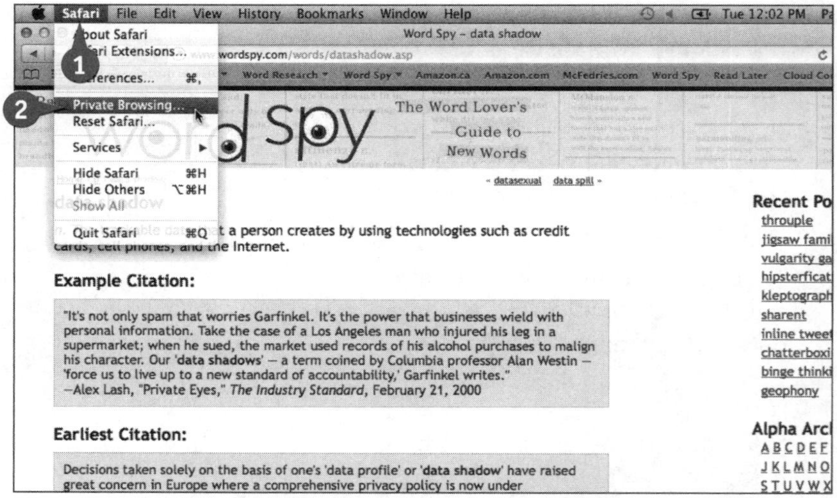

Safari asks you to confirm that you want to turn on Private Browsing.

3. Click **OK**.

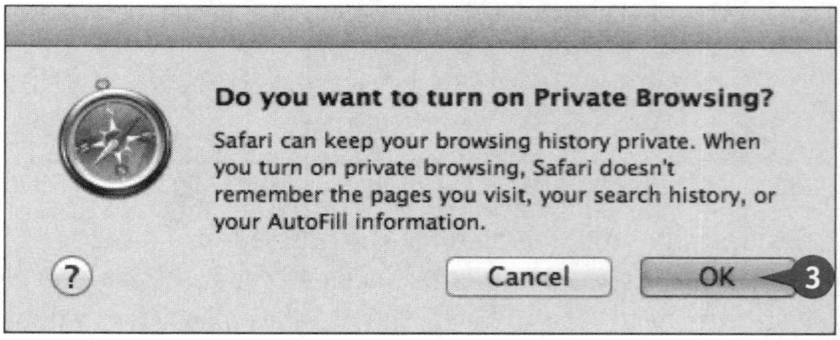

Safari activates the Private Browsing feature.

A The Private indicator tells you that Private Browsing is turned on.

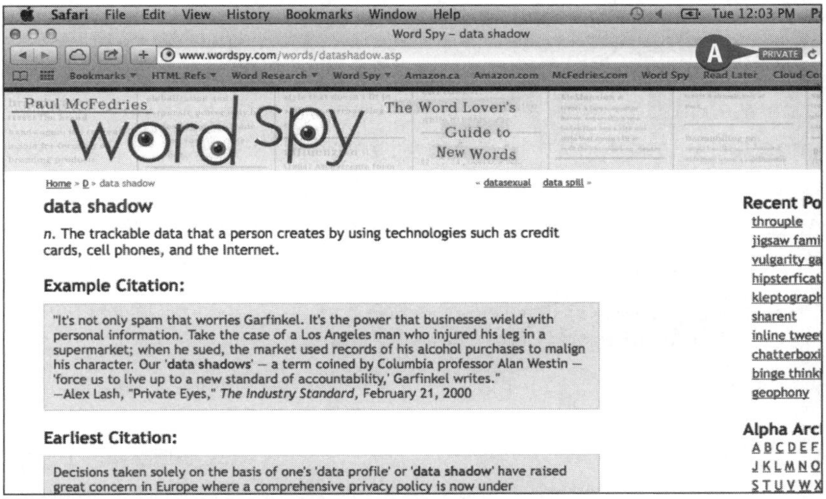

4 Visit the sites you want to see during your private browsing session.

5 When you are done, click **Safari**.

6 Click **Private Browsing**.

B You can also click the **Private** indicator and then click **OK**.

Safari turns off the Private Browsing feature.

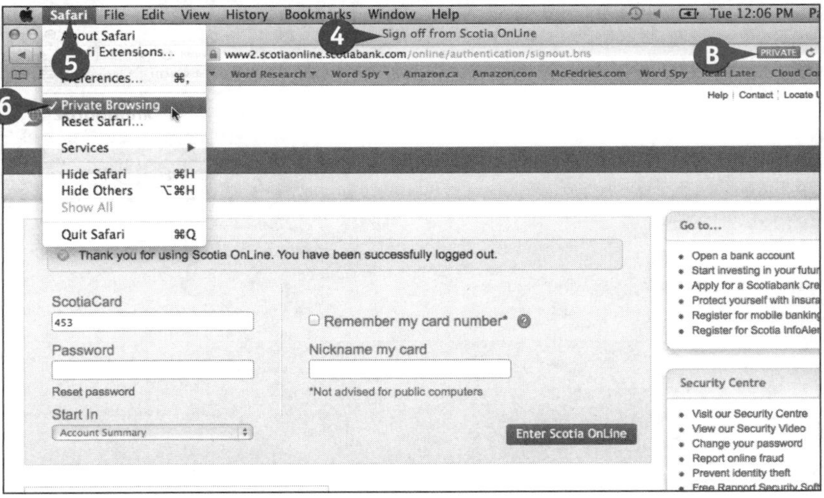

TIPS

Can I prevent websites from requesting my location without having to activate Private Browsing?

Yes, you can configure Safari to reject all website requests for your location. Click **Safari** and then click **Preferences** to open the Safari preferences. Click the **Privacy** tab. In the Limit Website Access to Location Services section, select the **Deny without prompting** option (☐ changes to ◉) and then click **Close** (■).

Safari's Search box displays suggestions based on my previous entries. Can I prevent this?

Yes. Click **Safari** and then click **Preferences** to open the Safari preferences. Click the **Privacy** tab. In the Smart Search Field section, select the **Prevent search engine from providing suggestions** option (☐ changes to ☑) and then click **Close** (■).

Delete a Saved Website Password

You can avoid unauthorized access to a website by removing the site's password that you saved earlier using Safari.

Many websites require a password, along with a username or e-mail address. When you fill in this information and log on to the site, Safari offers to save the password so that you do not have to type it again when you visit the same page in the future. This is convenient, but it has a downside: Anyone who uses your Mac Pro can also access the password-protected content. If you do not want this to happen, you can tell Safari to remove the saved password.

Delete a Saved Website Password

1 Click **Safari**.

2 Click **Preferences**.

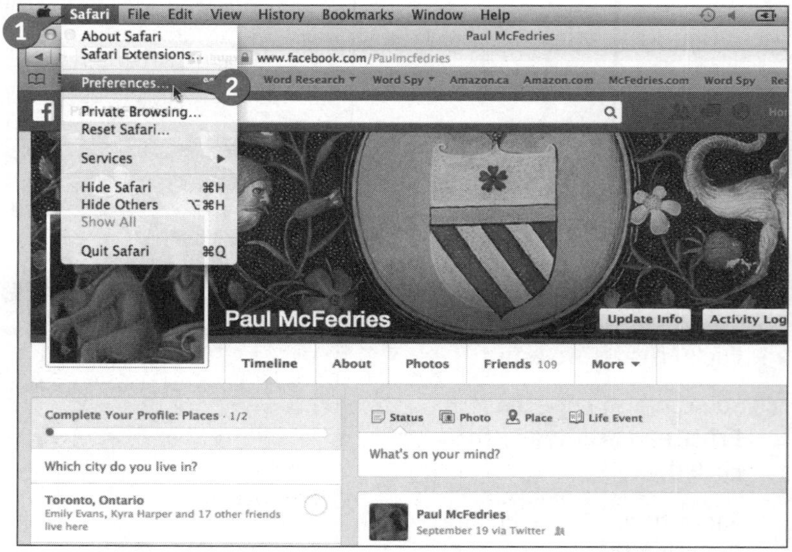

The Safari preferences appear.

3 Click the **Passwords** tab.

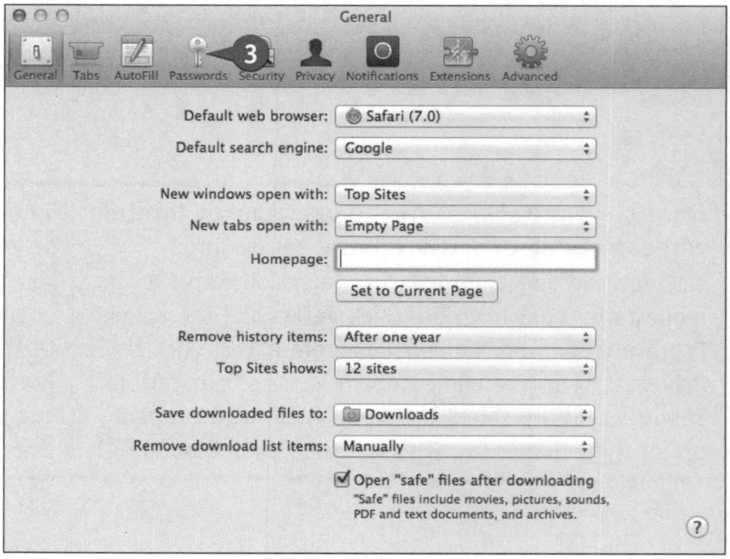

4. Click the web password you want to remove.
5. Click **Remove**.

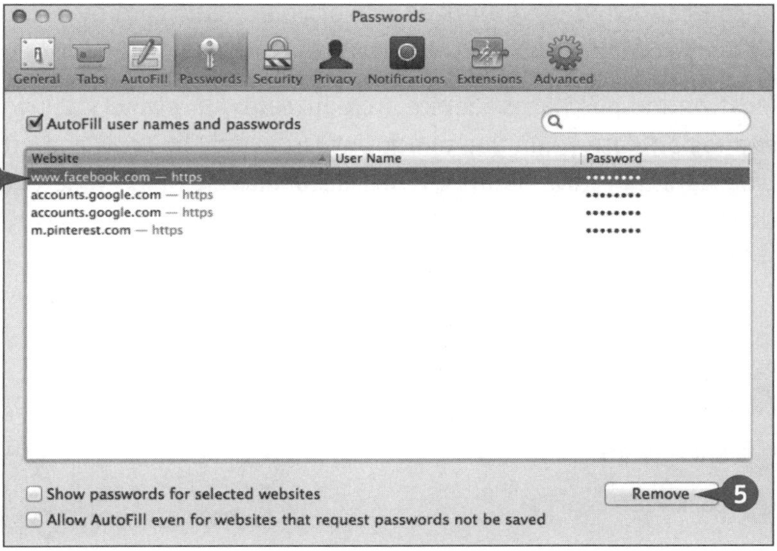

Safari removes the password.

A. If you want to remove all your saved website passwords, click **Remove All**.

B. If you no longer want Safari to save your website passwords, deselect the **AutoFill user names and passwords** option (☑ changes to ☐).

TIP

Are there other website password security risks?

Yes. Many websites offer to "remember" your login information. They do this by placing your username and password in a cookie stored on your Mac Pro. Although convenient, other people who use your Mac Pro to surf to the same sites can also access the password-protected content. Deselect the website option (A) that asks if you want to save your login data (☑ changes to ☐).

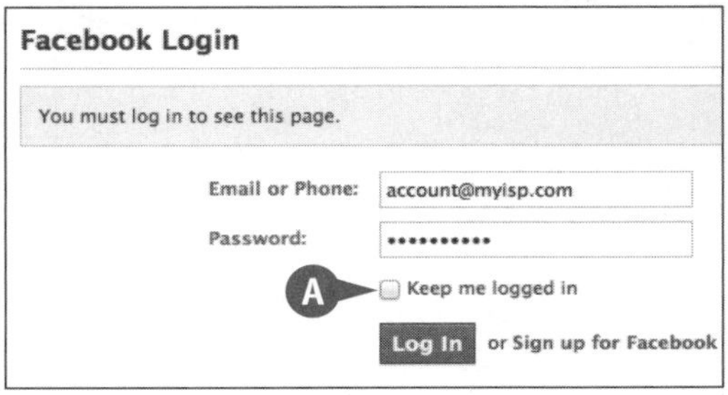

Delete Saved Credit Card Data

You can avoid unauthorized use of your credit card by deleting card data that you saved earlier using Safari.

Most online purchases require a credit card, so retailers ask you to enter your card number and expiration date when you check out. To avoid the time and effort this requires, you can save your card data and have Safari enter it automatically each time you make a purchase. However, the downside to this convenience is that anyone who uses your Mac Pro can also use your credit card information. To prevent this, you can delete the saved credit card data.

Delete Saved Credit Card Data

1. Click **Safari**.
2. Click **Preferences**.

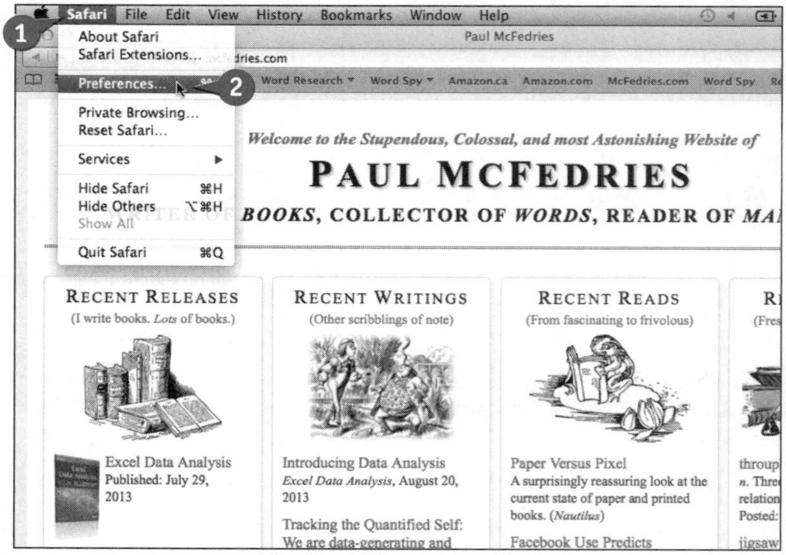

The Safari preferences appear.

3. Click the **AutoFill** tab.
4. Click **Edit**.

Safari displays the list of your saved credit cards.

5. Click the credit card data you want to remove.

6. Click **Remove**.

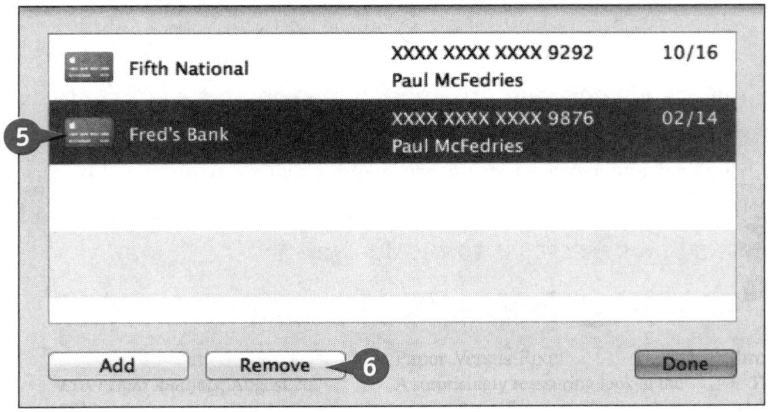

Safari removes the saved credit card data.

7. Click **Done**.

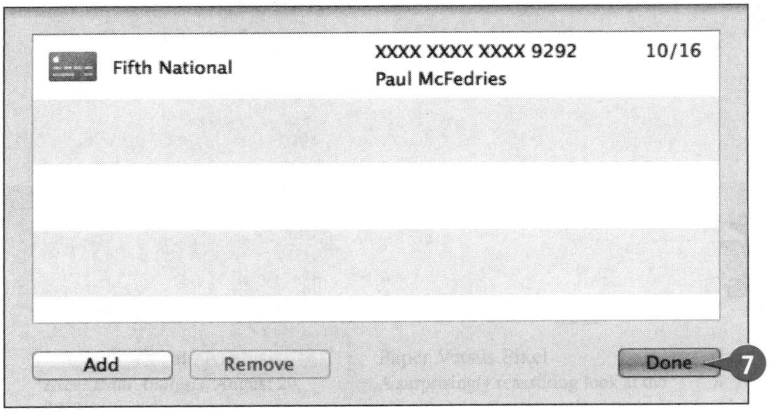

TIP

Does Safari offer to save credit cards that I enter into a web form?

No, you must enter your credit card data by hand. To do this, click **Safari**, click **Preferences**, and then click the **AutoFill** tab. Click **Edit** to the right of the Credit Cards option to display the credit card list. Click **Add** to create a new credit card entry. Type the credit card description and press Tab. Type the credit card number and press Tab. Type the credit card expiry date and press Tab. Type the name that appears on the credit card and then click **Done**.

Move Spam to the Junk Mailbox Automatically

Junk e-mail — or *spam* — refers to unsolicited, commercial e-mail messages that advertise anything from baldness cures to cheap printer cartridges. Many spams advertise deals that are simply fraudulent, and others feature such unsavory practices as linking to adult-oriented sites, and sites that install spyware. Mail enables *junk mail filtering*, which looks for spam as it arrives in your Inbox and then marks each such message as junk. This enables you to quickly recognize junk mail and either delete it or move it to the Junk mailbox. However, you can customize Mail to automatically move all junk messages to the Junk mailbox.

Move Spam to the Junk Mailbox Automatically

1. Click **Mail**.
2. Click **Preferences**.

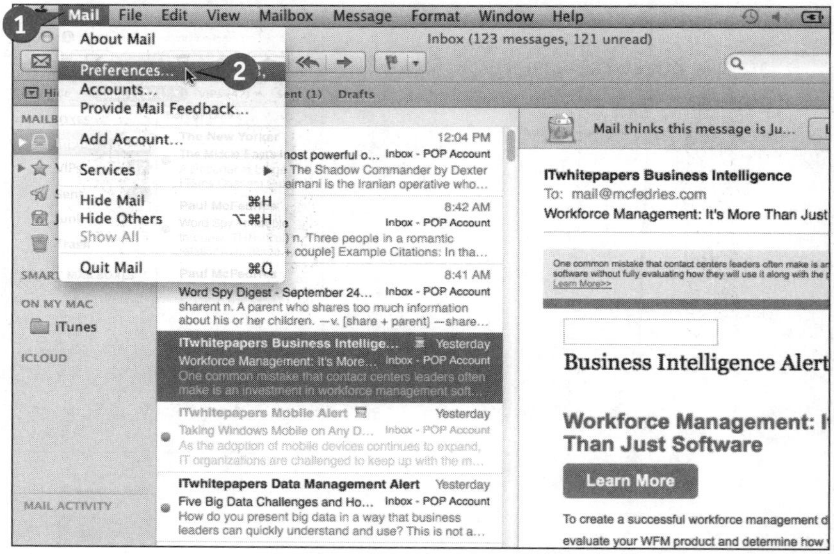

The Mail preferences appear.

3. Click the **Junk Mail** tab.

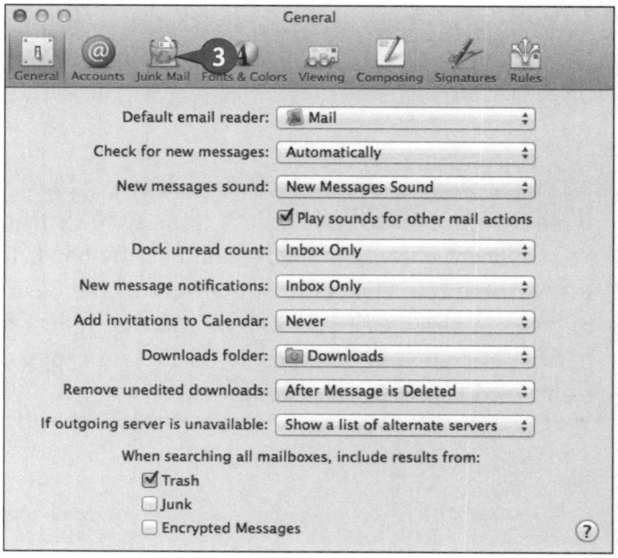

4. Select the **Move it to the Junk mailbox** option (changes to).

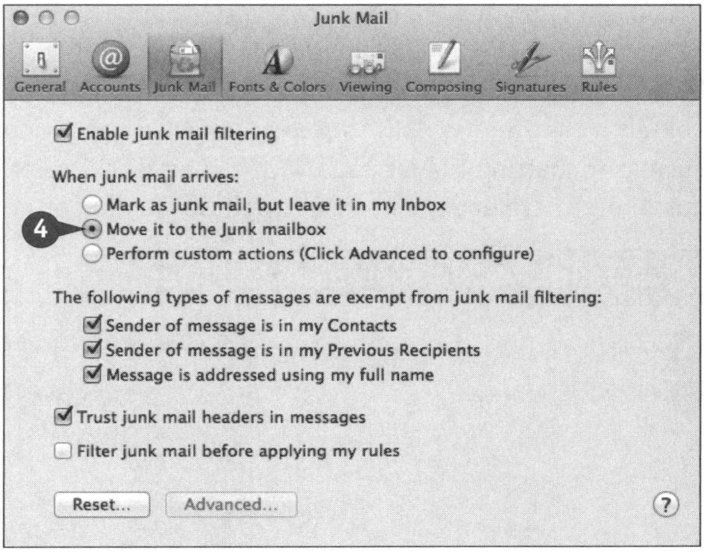

5. Click **Close** ( ).

   Mail closes the preferences and puts the new setting into effect.

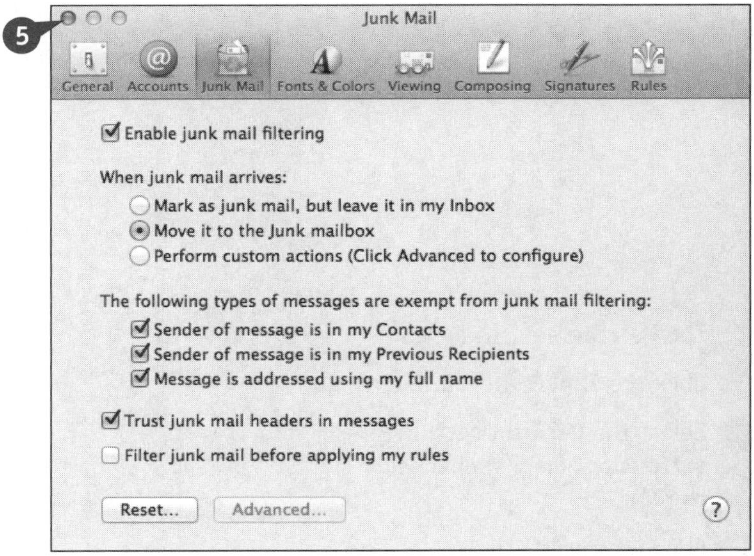

TIPS

Why does Mail not mark some spam messages as junk?
Mail does not recognize all spam varieties, so you may receive some messages that do not get marked as junk. Also, Mail does not mark as junk any message addressed using your full name. To override this, click **Mail**, click **Preferences**, and then click the **Junk Mail** tab. Deselect the **Message is addressed using my full name** option (changes to).

Is there a downside to automatically moving spam to the Junk mailbox?
Yes. Mail occasionally marks legitimate messages as junk. These are called *false positives*, and you should check for them by periodically opening the Junk mailbox. If you see one, click the message, click **Not Junk** in the preview pane, and then move the message to the Inbox.

Configure Advanced Junk Mail Filtering

You can gain greater control over Mail's junk mail filtering by configuring the advanced filtering options. These options are organized as a set of conditions that each message must meet before Mail marks it as junk, such as the sender not being in your contacts and the message containing spam content. The filtering options also specify a set of actions to perform on any message marked as junk, such as formatting the message with a special text color and moving it to the Junk mailbox. You can customize these options by deleting those you do not need and by adding new conditions and actions.

Configure Advanced Junk Mail Filtering

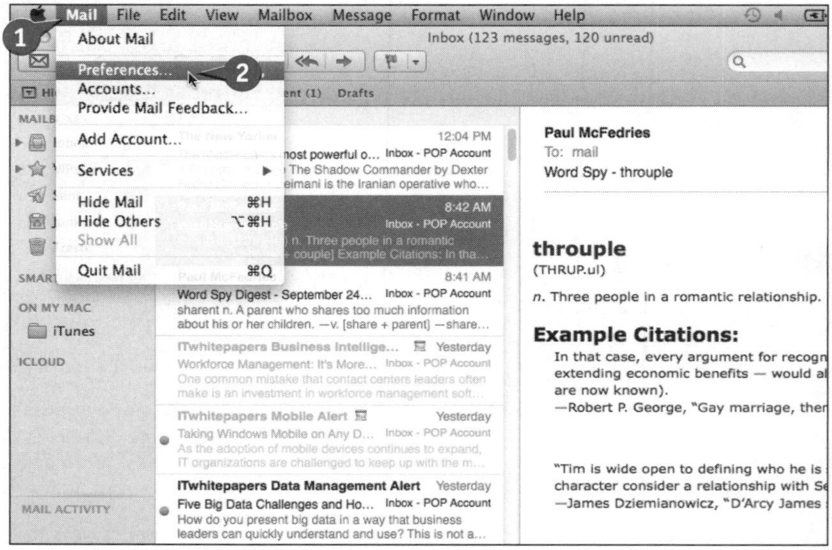

1. Click **Mail**.
2. Click **Preferences**.

The Mail preferences appear.

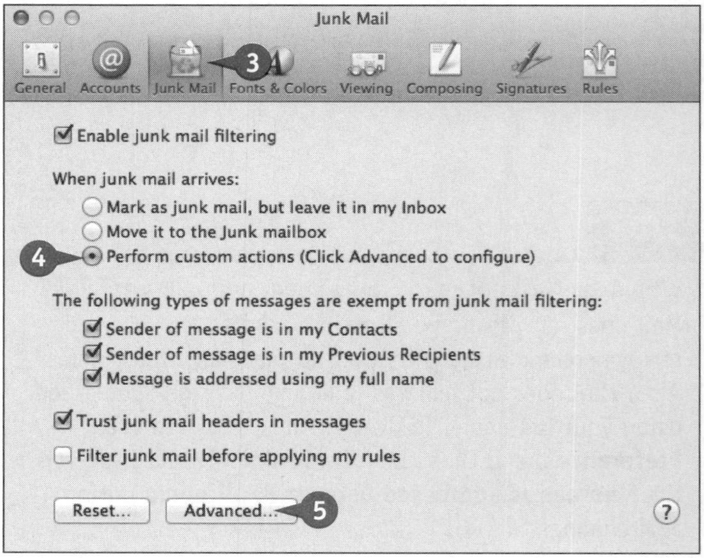

3. Click the **Junk Mail** tab.
4. Select the **Perform custom actions** option (changes to).
5. Click **Advanced**.

Safari displays the advanced junk mail filtering dialog.

A Mail marks a message as junk if it meets all these conditions.

6 Click a condition's **Remove** icon (−) to delete it.

7 Click an **Add** icon (+) to create a new condition.

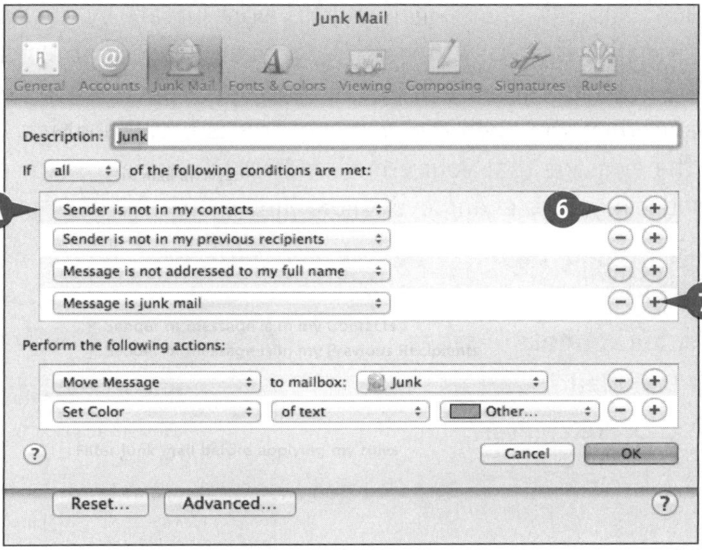

8 If you added a condition, use the pop-up menus and text box to define it.

9 Remove or add actions, as required.

10 Click **OK**.

Mail closes the dialog and puts the new filtering rules into effect.

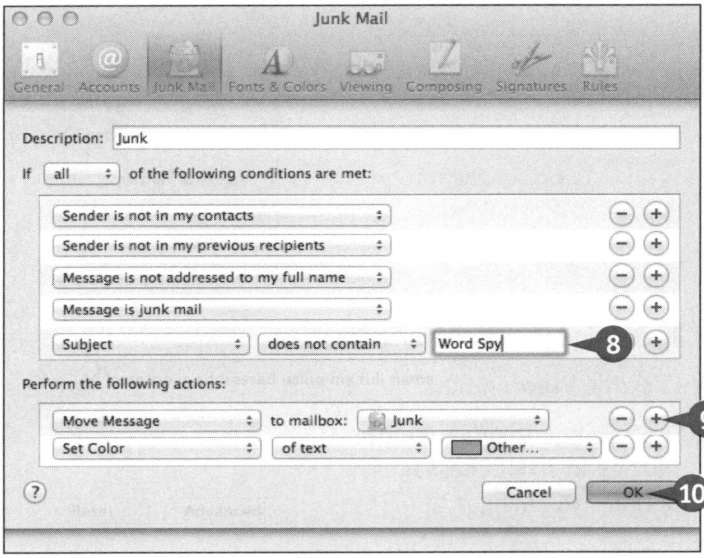

TIP

Almost all the spam I receive contains particular words in the subject or the message text. Can I set up junk mail filtering to handle this?

Yes. Click the **Remove** icon (−) beside each existing condition. In the list of conditions, click the **Add** icon (+). Click the first ⬍ and then click either **Subject** or **Message** content. In the second ⬍, click **contains.** In the text box, type the spam word. Repeat this procedure for each spam word you want include in your filter. Click the **If** ⬍ and then click **any** in the pop-up menu. Click **OK.**

Disable Remote Images

You can make your e-mail address more private by thwarting the remote images inserted into some e-mail messages. A *remote image* is an image that resides on an Internet server computer instead of being embedded in the e-mail message. A special code in the message tells the server to display the image when you open the message. This is usually benign, but the same code can also alert the sender of the message that your e-mail address is working. If the sender is a spammer, then this usually results in you receiving even more junk e-mail. You can prevent this by disabling remote images.

Disable Remote Images

Disable Remote Images

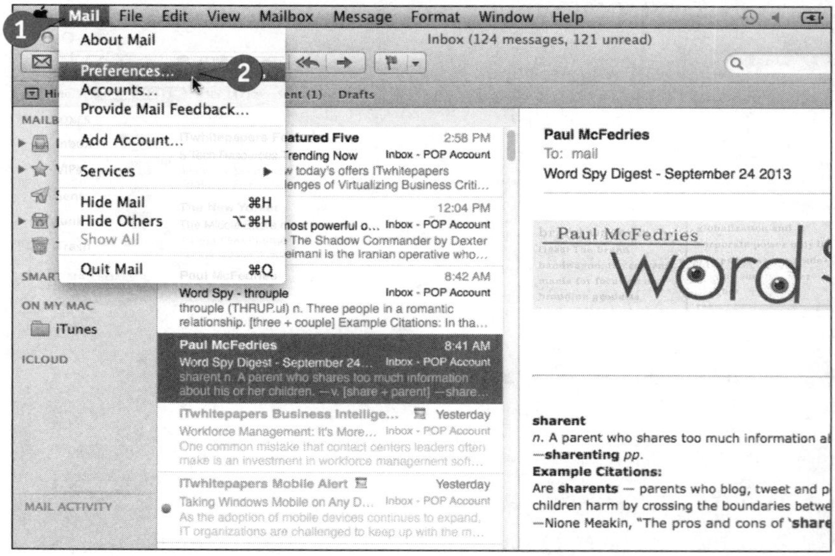

1. Click **Mail**.
2. Click **Preferences**.

The Mail preferences appear.

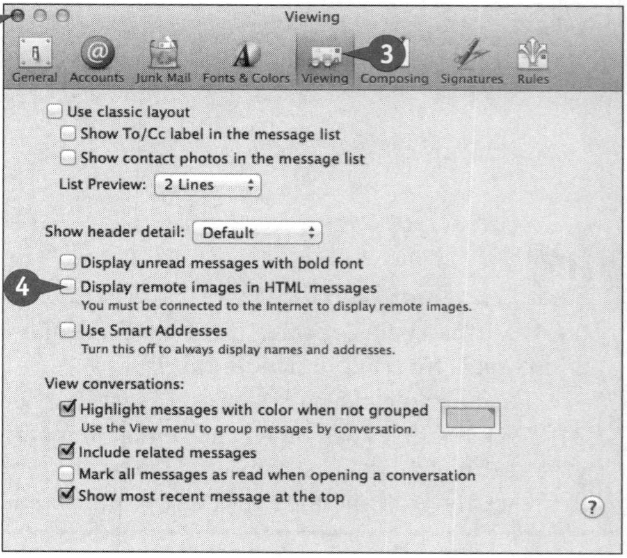

3. Click the **Viewing** tab.
4. Deselect the **Display remote images in HTML messages** option (☑ changes to ☐).
5. Click **Close** (■).

Mail blocks remotes images in your messages.

Display Remote Images in a Message

1. Click the message.

   A. Mail displays a rectangle in place of each remote image.

2. Click **Load Images**.

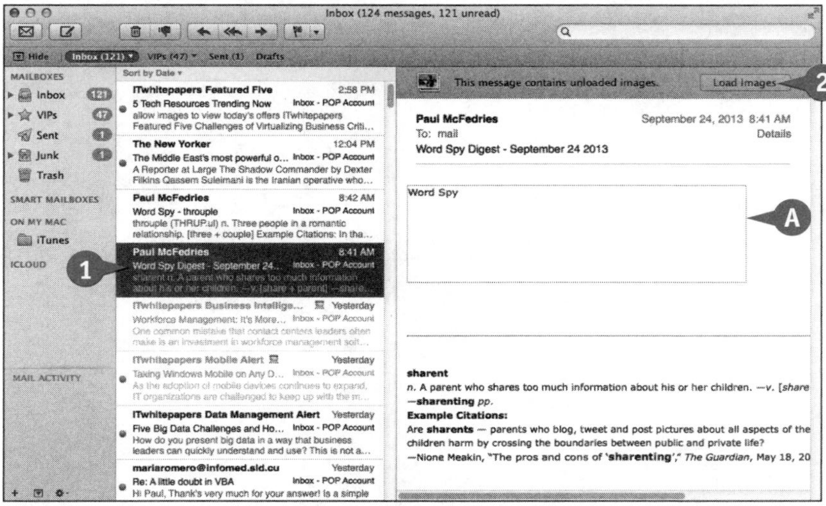

B. Mail displays the message's remote images.

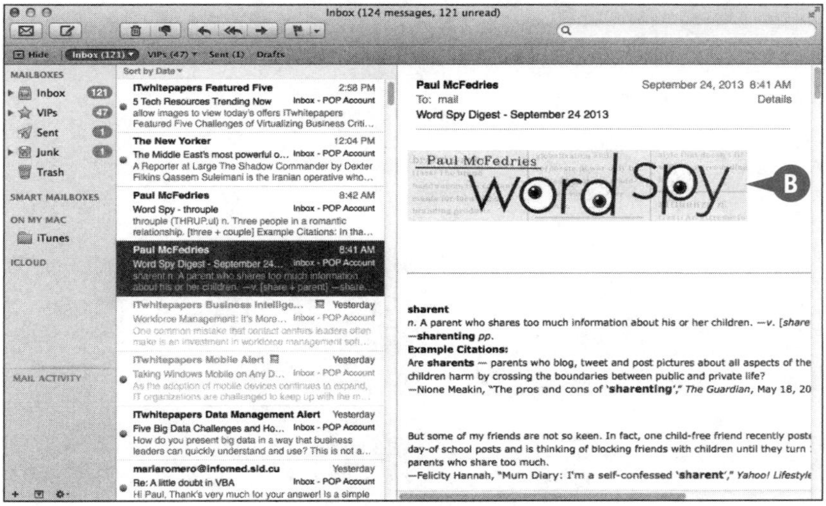

TIP

How do remote images cause me to receive more spam?

Many spammers include in their messages a *web bug*, which is a small and usually invisible image, the code for which is inserted into the e-mail message. That code specifies a remote address from which to download the web bug image when you open or preview the message. However, the code also includes a reference to your e-mail address. The remote server makes note of the fact that you received the message, which means your address is a working one and is therefore a good target for further spam messages. By blocking remote images, you also block web bugs, which means you undermine this confirmation and so receive less spam.

CHAPTER 7

Talking via Messages and FaceTime

You can use the Messages application to exchange instant messages and conduct audio and video chats. You can also use FaceTime to make video calls.

Configure Messages

Mac Pro comes with the Messages application to enable you to use the iMessage technology to exchange instant messages with other people who are online, as well as conduct audio and video chats. The first time you open Messages, you must run through a short configuration process to set up your account. This process involves signing in with your Apple ID and deciding whether you want Messages to send out notifications that tell people when you have read the messages they send to you.

Configure Messages

1. Click **Messages** (💬).

The iMessage dialog appears.

2. Type your Apple ID.
3. Type your Apple ID password.
4. Click **Sign In**.

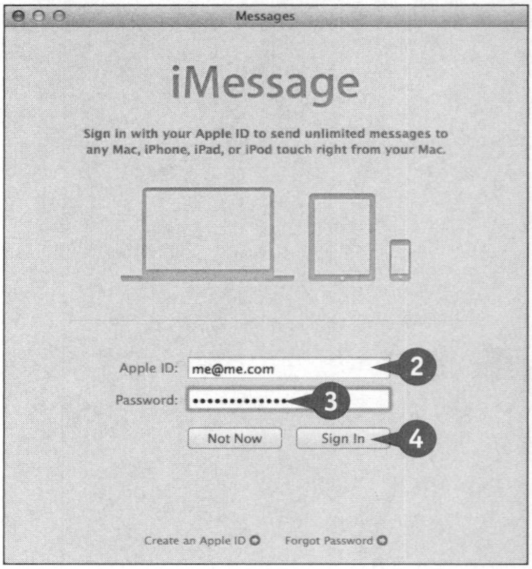

5 Deselect each phone number and e-mail address that you do not want to use with Messages (☑ changes to ☐).

6 If you want other people to know when you have read their messages, select the **Send read receipts** option (☐ changes to ☑).

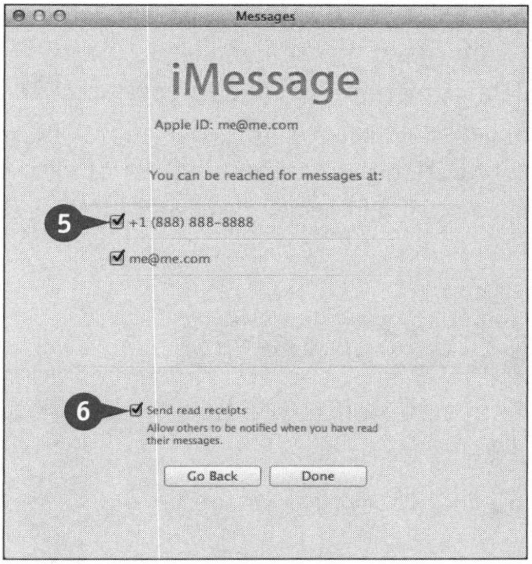

7 Click **Done**.

Messages is now ready to use.

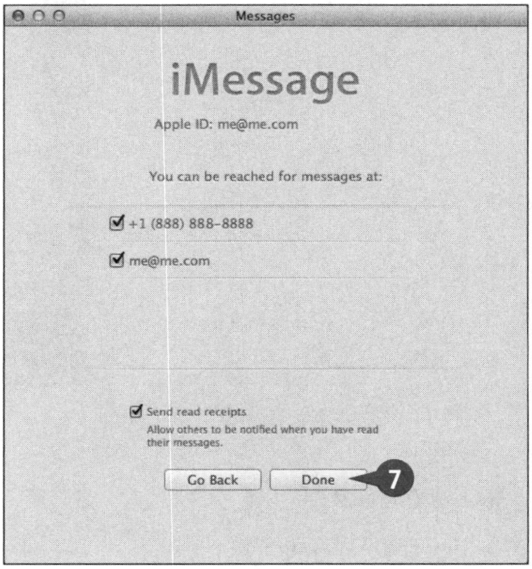

TIP

What if I do not have an Apple ID?

You can create a new Apple ID during the configuration process. Follow steps 1 and 2 to open the iMessage dialog and then click **Create an Apple ID**. In the dialog that appears, type your name, the e-mail address you want to use as your Apple ID, and the password you want to use. You must also choose a secret question and specify your birthday. Click **Create Apple ID** to complete the operation.

Change Your Picture

You can make your instant messaging conversations and your audio chats easier for your buddies by changing the default picture on your account to something memorable or recognizable. The default picture assigned to your account is a generic silhouette of a person's head and shoulders. Because a text or audio chat might show to other people only your e-mail address or phone number, configuring your account with a proper picture helps other users recognize you. Also, a well-chosen image can add a bit of fun and interest to your chats.

Change Your Picture

Choose a Default Picture

1. Click **Messages.**
2. Click **Change My Picture.**

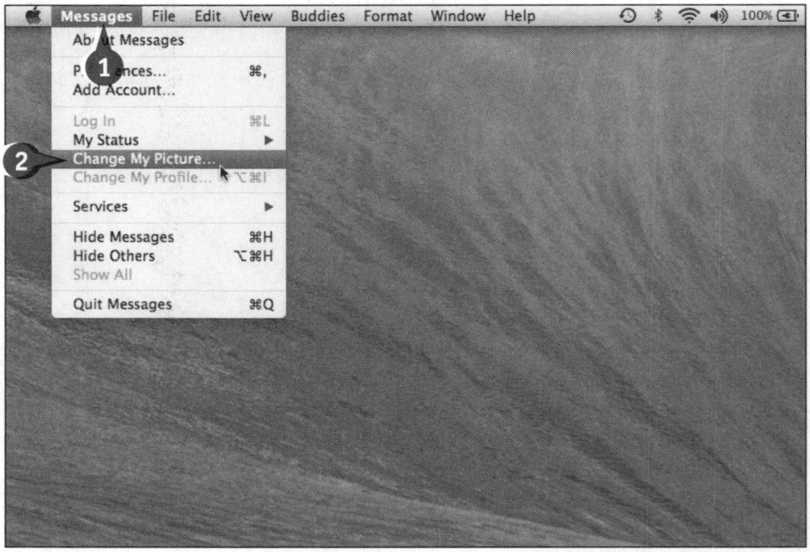

The Edit Picture dialog appears.

3. Click **Defaults.**
4. Click the image you want to use.
5. Click **Done.**

Messages applies the picture to your account.

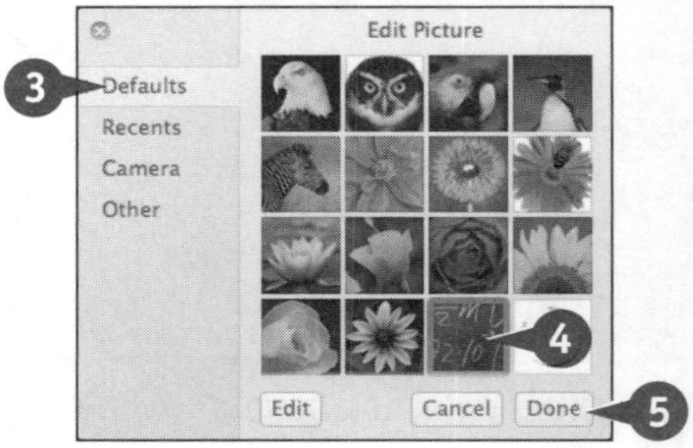

Choose an Image File

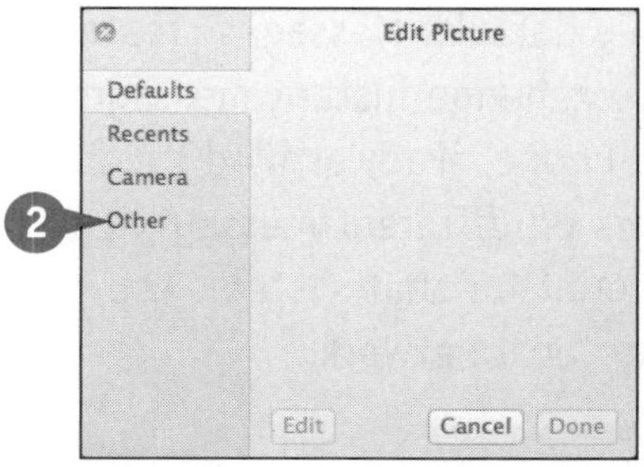

1. Follow steps 1 and 2 in the subsection "Choose a Default Picture" to open the Edit Picture dialog.
2. Click **Other**.

   The Open dialog appears.
3. Click the image you want to use.
4. Click **Open**.
5. Click **Done**.

   Messages applies the picture to your account.

TIP

Can I take a photo of myself instead of using an existing picture?

Yes, assuming your monitor has a built-in camera or you have connected an external camera to your Mac Pro. This is a useful technique to know if none of your existing photos are right for your Messages picture, and if you do not like any of Messages' default pictures.

First, turn on the camera and, if necessary, change the camera mode so that it displays a live feed. Click **Messages** and then click **Change My Picture** to open the Edit Picture screen. Click the **Camera** tab to see the live feed from the camera. When you are ready, click the **Take a picture** icon (📷). Messages counts down from three and snaps the picture. Click **Done**.

Add a Messaging Account

By default, Messages creates an iMessage account using your Apple ID, which enables you to exchange instant messages with other iMessage users, including any of your friends who use an iPhone, iPad, or iPod touch. If you also want to exchange text, audio, or video messages with users on different messaging systems such as AOL, Google, and Yahoo!, you must set up a messaging account for that system. You can also set up a Bonjour account to exchange messages with people on your local network.

Add a Messaging Account

1. Click **Messages.**
2. Click **Add Account.**

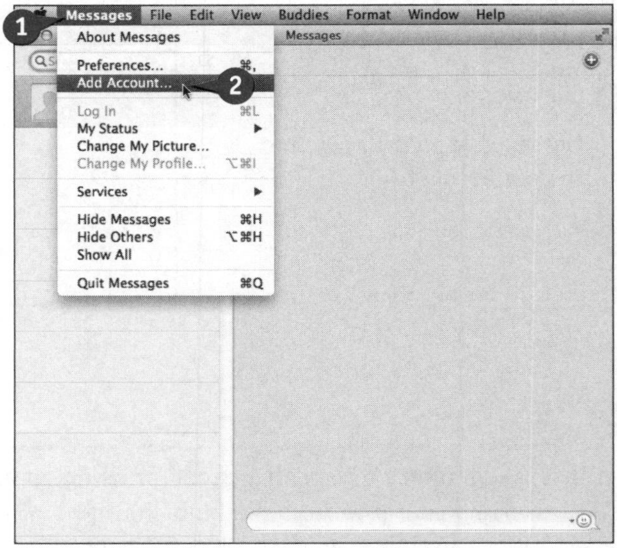

Messages prompts you to select an account type.

3. Select the account type (○ changes to ◉).
4. Click **Continue.**

Messages asks for the account details.

5 Edit your name, if desired.

6 Type your account e-mail address.

7 Type your account password.

8 Click **Set Up**.

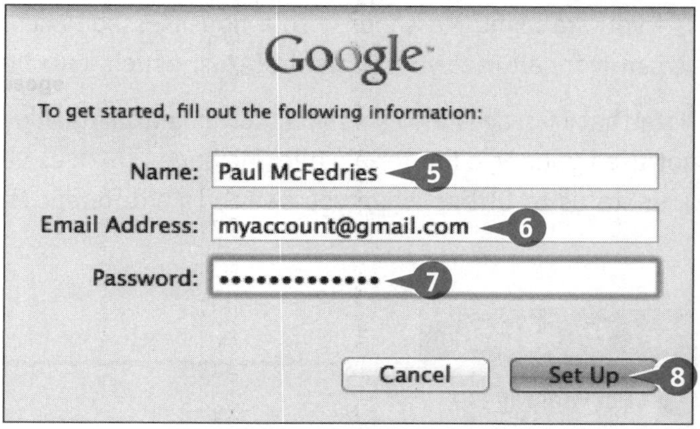

Messages prompts you to choose which apps to use with the account.

9 Select each app you want to use (☐ changes to ☑).

A Make sure you leave the **Messages** option selected (☑).

10 Click **Done**.

Messages adds the account.

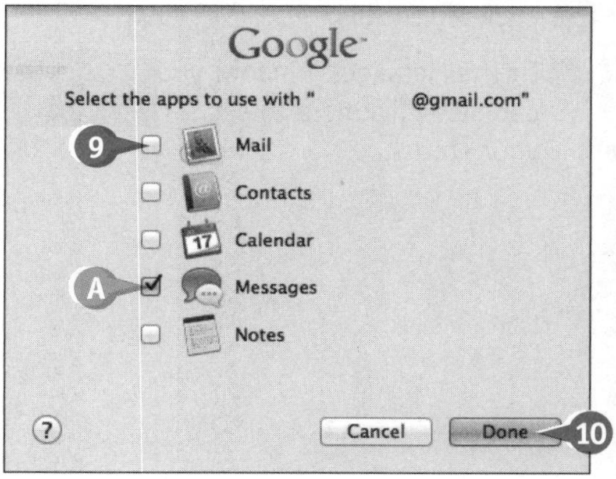

TIPS

How do I set up a Bonjour account?
The Messages app comes with a default Bonjour account, but it is disabled by default. To enable this account, click **Messages** and then click **Preferences** to open the Messages preferences. Click the **Accounts** tab, click the **Bonjour** account, and then select the **Enable Bonjour instant messaging** option (☐ changes to ☑). Click **Close** (■) to return to the Messages app.

How do I disable an account that I am not going to use for a while?
Click **Messages** and then click **Preferences** to open the Messages preferences. Click the **Accounts** tab, click the account, and then deselect the **Enable this account** option (☑ changes to ☐). Click **Close** (■) to return to the Messages app.

Set Your Status

If you are using Messages with a non-iMessage account, such as Google or AOL, or with Bonjour, you can manually set your current status, which your buddies will see when they try to chat with you.

Note that Messages also sets your status automatically in certain situations. For example, when you have not used your Mac Pro for a while, Messages changes your status to Away. Similarly, Messages changes your status to Offline when you switch to a different Mac Pro user account or when you quit Messages.

Set Your Status

1. Click **Messages**.
2. Click **My Status**.

Ⓐ In the Messages window, you can also click here to set your status.

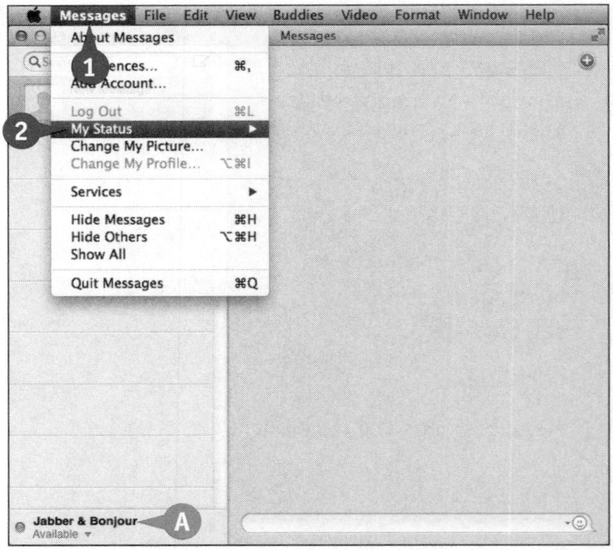

Messages displays a list of statuses.

3. Click the status you want to display.

Ⓑ You can click **Offline** to indicate you are not available to receive messages.

Ⓒ You can click any status with a green dot to indicate that you are available to respond to messages.

Ⓓ You can click any status with a red dot to indicate that you are not available to respond to messages.

Messages changes your status.

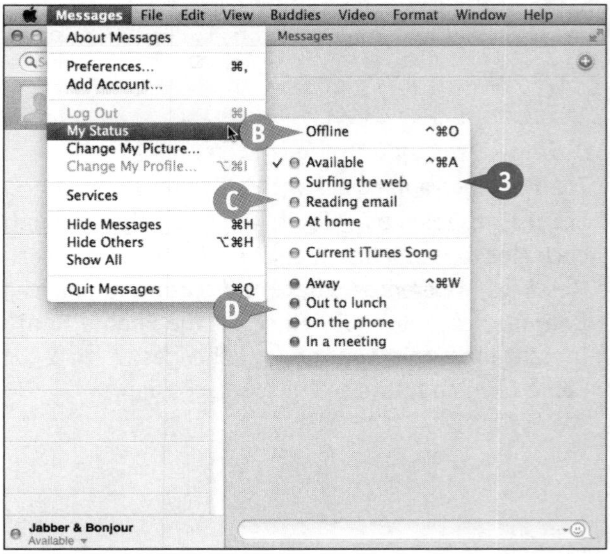

Disable Read Receipts

If you are using the iMessage system for online instant messaging through your iCloud account, when you read a buddy's message, the Messages app sends that person a *read receipt*. This notification tells the other person you have read the message. If you find this to be either an invasion of privacy or a waste of time, you can configure Messages not to send read receipts.

Disable Read Receipts

1. Click **Messages**.
2. Click **Preferences**.

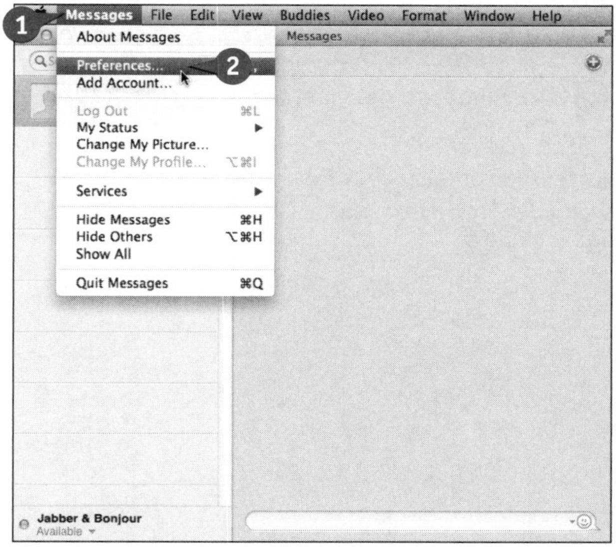

The Messages preferences appear.

3. Click the **Accounts** tab.
4. Click your iMessage account.
5. Deselect the **Send read receipts** option (☑ changes to ☐).
6. Click **Close** (■).

Send a Message

In the Messages app, you use the iMessage system to conduct instant messaging conversations, which are the exchange of text messages between two or more people who are online and available to chat. With iMessage, you can exchange instant messages with other iMessage users who are using a Mac, an iPhone, an iPad, or an iPod touch, as long as they have the Messages app installed.

If you are looking to conduct an instant messaging conversation with someone on a non-iMessage system, such as Google or AOL, see the section "Start a Text Chat."

Send a Message

1 Click **Compose new message** (✎).

Note: You can also click **File** and then click **New Message**, or press ⌘+N.

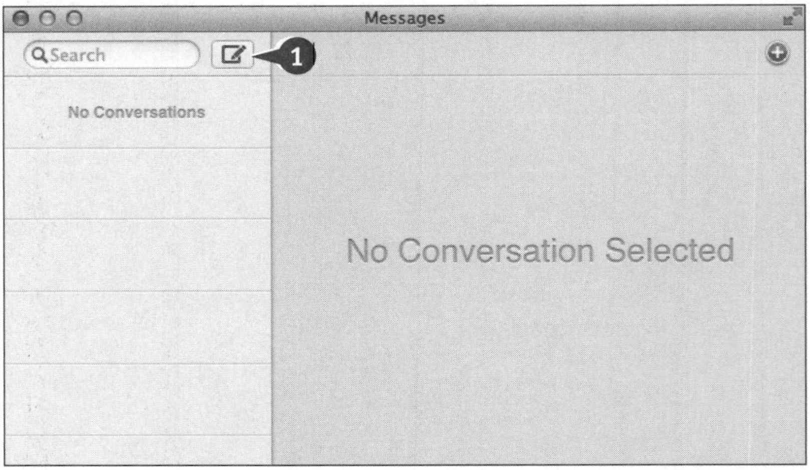

Messages begins a new conversation.

2 In the To field, type the message recipient using one of the following:

The person's e-mail address.

The person's mobile phone number.

The person's name, if that person is in your Contacts list.

A You can also click **Add Contact** (⊕) to select a name from your Contacts list.

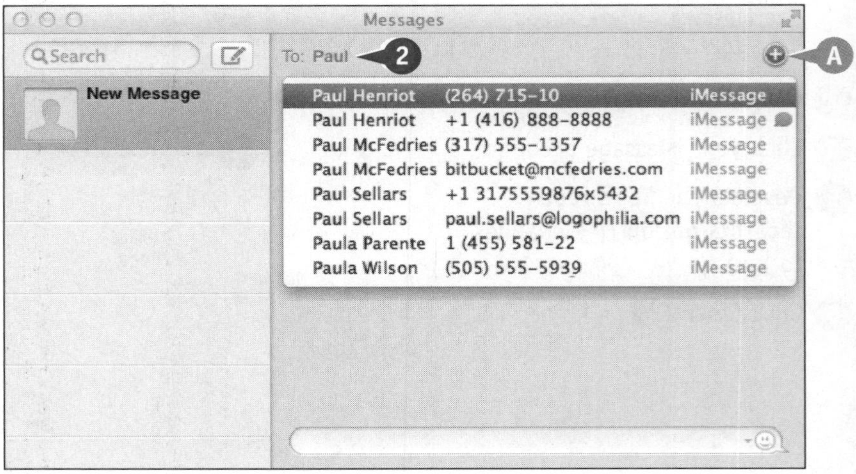

3 Type your message.

B You can also click here if you want to insert a smiley or other emoticon symbol into your message.

4 Press Return.

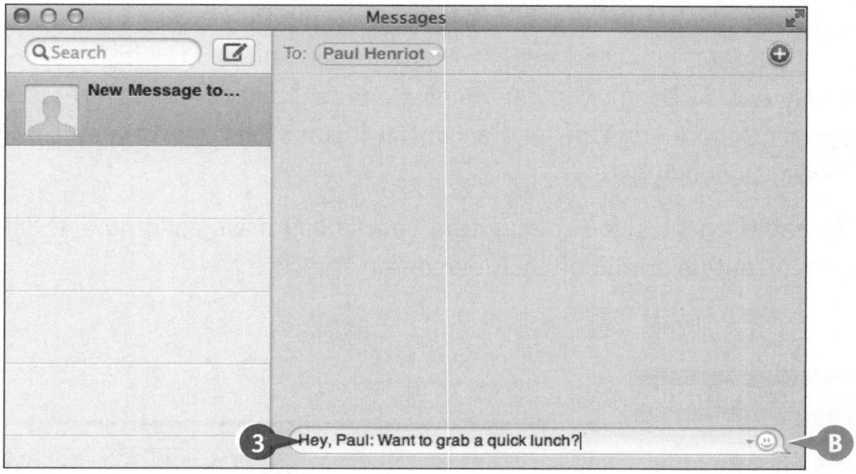

Messages sends the text to the recipient.

C The recipient's response appears in the transcript window.

D You see the ellipsis symbol (…) when the other person is typing.

5 Repeat steps 3 and 4 to continue the conversation.

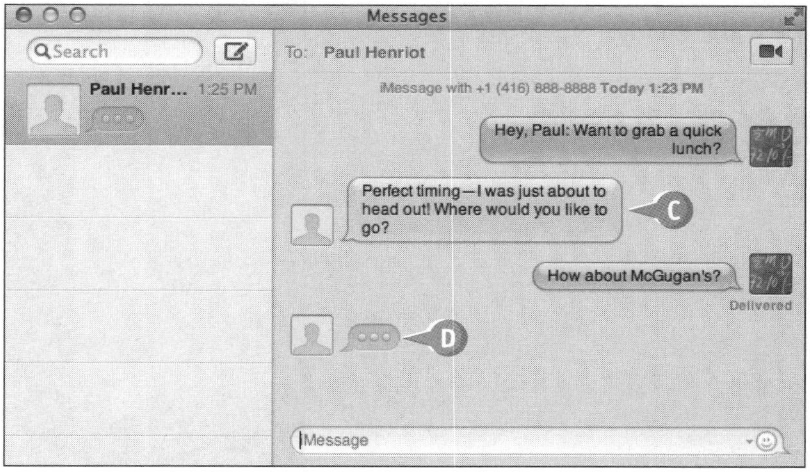

TIP

Can I change the look of my instant messaging conversations?

Yes, you can format the font, font color, and message background color. Click **Messages**, click **Preferences**, and then click the **Viewing** tab.

To format your messages, click the **My background color** ⬍ and then click a color for the message background. Click the **My font color** ⬍ and the **My font** ⬍ to set the color and typeface for your message text.

To format your buddies' messages, click the **Sender's background color** ⬍ and then click a color for the background. Click the **Sender's font color** ⬍ and the **Sender's font** ⬍ to set the color and typeface for your buddies' text.

Add a Buddy

When you are using a non-iMessage account — such as Google or AOL — or when you are using Bonjour, you send instant messages to, and receive instant messages from, the people in your *buddy list*. Although you can receive and respond to instant messages from anyone on the same system, before you can send an initial instant message to a person, you must add the person to your Messages buddy list.

Messages enables you to maintain your buddy list by adding and deleting people, and it tells you the current online status of each person on the list.

Add a Buddy

1 Click **Buddies**.

2 Click **Add Buddy**.

Note: You can also run the Add Buddy command by pressing Shift + ⌘ + A.

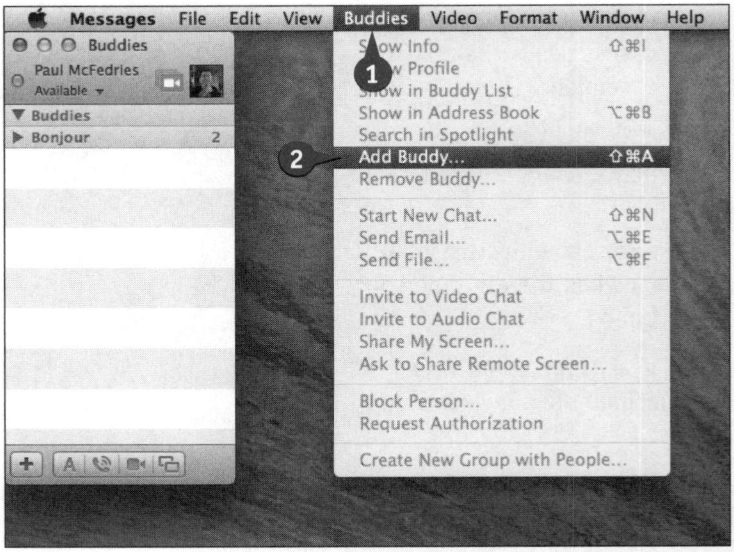

Messages prompts you for the buddy's account information.

3 Use the Account Name text box to specify your buddy's screen name or e-mail address.

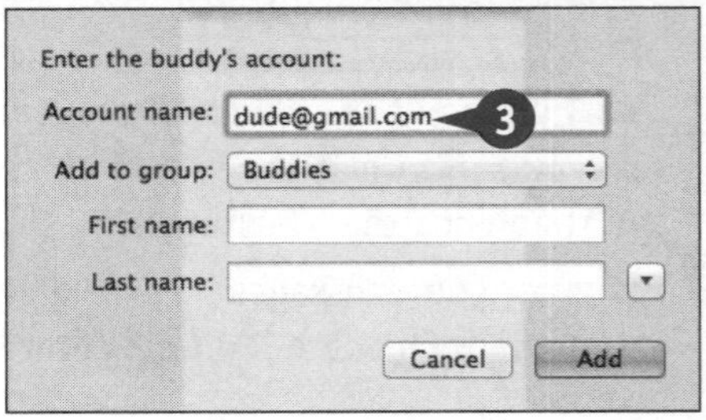

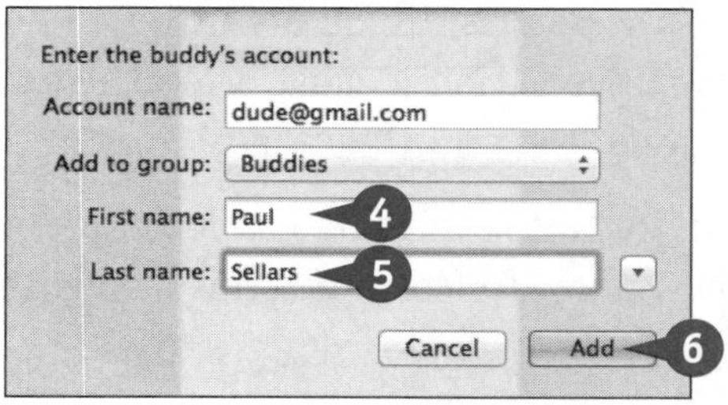

4. Use the First Name text box to type your buddy's first name.
5. Use the Last Name text box to type your buddy's last name.
6. Click **Add**.

A. Messages adds the person to the buddies list.

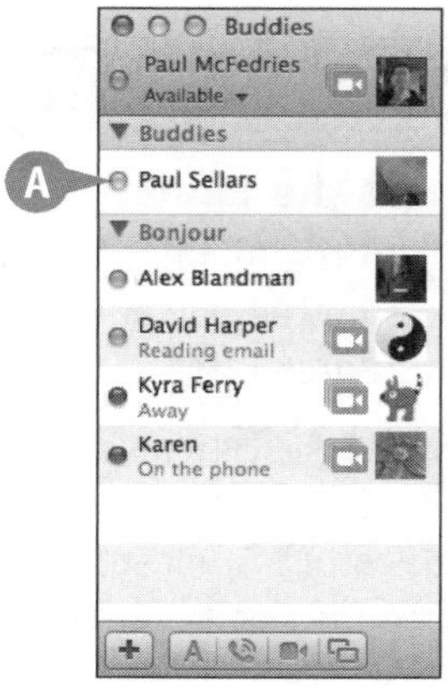

TIP

Is there a way to change the picture that Messages uses for my buddy?

Yes. By default, Messages uses whatever picture your buddy has configured for himself or herself. To display a different picture, follow these steps:

1. Click the buddy.
2. Click **Buddies**.
3. Click **Show Info**.
4. Click **Address Card**.
5. Select the **Always use this picture** option (☐ changes to ☑).
6. Click and drag the picture you want to use and drop it on the Picture box.
7. Click **Close** (■).

Start a Text Chat

In Messages, if you are using a non-iMessage account or Bonjour, then an instant messaging conversation is most often the exchange of text messages between two or more people who are online — or, in the case of Bonjour, on the same network — and available to chat.

An instant messaging conversation begins by one person inviting another person to exchange messages. In Messages, this means sending an initial instant message, and the recipient then responds.

Start a Text Chat

Start the Chat

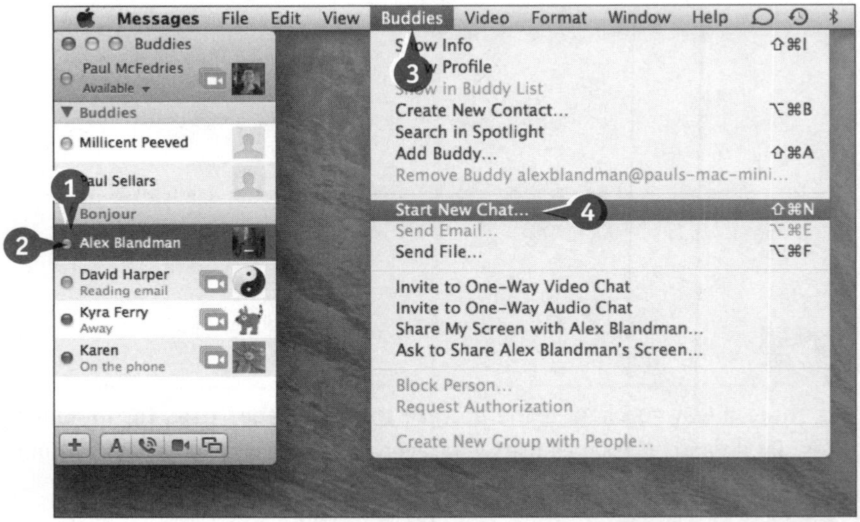

1. In the Buddies list, make sure the person's status icon is green ( ).

Note: The icon means that the person is available to chat; a red icon ( ) means that the person is not available to chat.

2. Click the person you want to chat with.
3. Click **Buddies**.
4. Click **Start New Chat**.

A chat window appears.

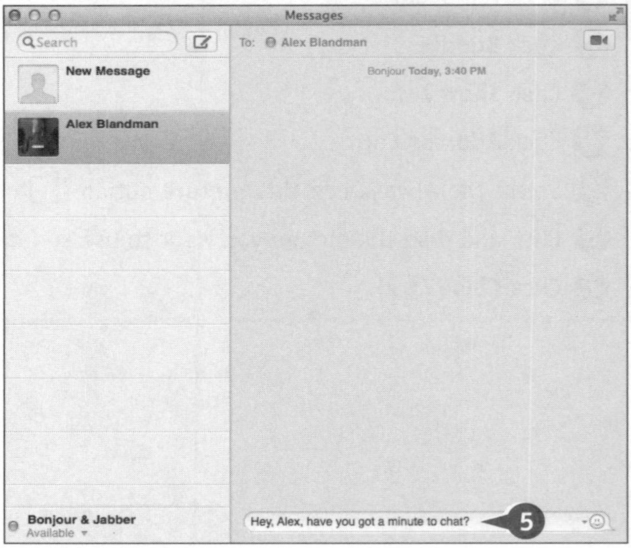

5. Type your message.
6. Press Return.

The message appears on the other person's computer.

Continue the Chat

1 Click the conversation.

2 Type a response.

3 Press Return.

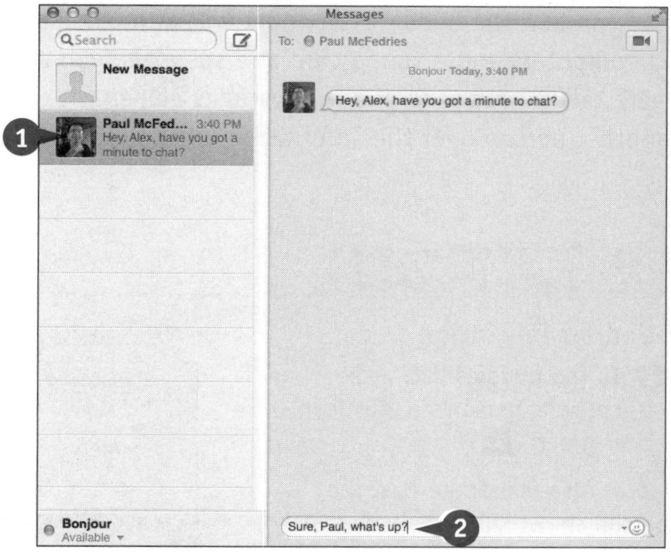

A The response appears in the chat window.

4 Repeat steps 5 and 6 in the subsection "Start the Chat" to continue chatting.

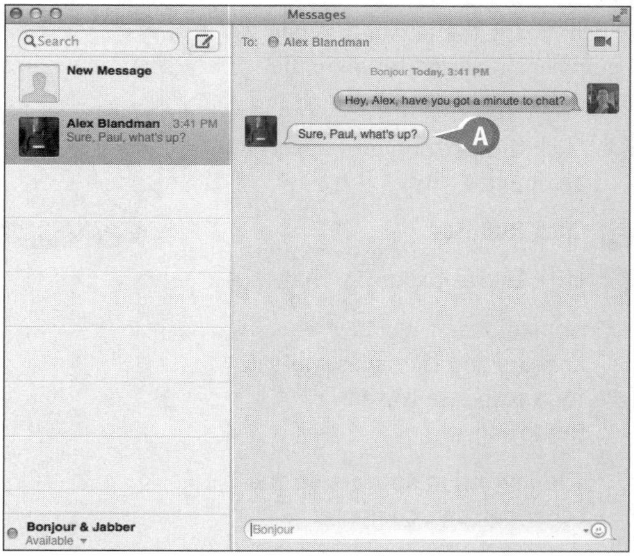

TIPS

Are there faster methods I can use to start a text chat?

Yes. Use the Buddies list to click the person you want to chat with and then click the **Start a text chat** button. You can also start a text chat with the selected buddy by pressing Shift + ⌘ + N.

Can I change or turn off the sound that Messages plays when a new message arrives?

Yes. Click **Messages** and then click **Preferences** to open the Messages preferences. Click the **General** tab. To change the sound, click the **Message received sound** and then click the sound you want. To turn off all Messages sound effects, deselect the **Play sound effects** option (☑ changes to ☐).

Start an Audio Chat

If you and the buddy with whom you want to converse both have a microphone attached to your computers and a sound card and speakers, you can converse with each other just as though you were talking over the phone. Messages comes with an *audio chat* feature that enables you to speak to another person over the Internet or, in the case of a Bonjour buddy, over your local network.

Start an Audio Chat

Send an Invitation

1. In the Buddies list, make sure the person's status icon is green ( ).

Note: Also make sure that the person shows the telephone icon ( ) or the camera icon ( ), which means the person has the equipment required for an audio chat.

2. Click the person you want to audio chat with.
3. Click **Buddies**.
4. Click **Invite to Audio Chat**.

A. An audio chat window appears and Messages waits for a response to the invitation.

The invitation appears on the other person's computer.

Accept an Invitation

1 Click the invitation.

2 Click **Accept**.

B If you prefer to text chat, click **Text Reply** to begin a separate text chat.

C If you cannot chat right now, click **Decline**.

Messages sets up the audio connection.

3 Use your microphone to converse with the other person.

D You can click and drag the slider to control the chat volume.

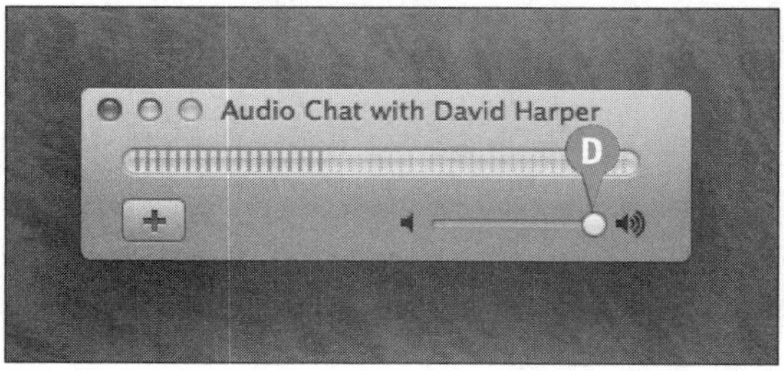

TIPS

Can I start a video chat?

Yes, as long as you both have a webcam, microphone, sound card, and speakers attached to your computers, you can both see and talk to each other using Messages' *video chat* feature. If the other person shows the camera icon (), click that person, click **Buddies**, and then click **Invite to Video Chat**.

Are there faster methods I can use to start an audio or video chat?

Yes. First, use the Buddies list to click the person you want to chat with. For an audio chat, click the **Start an Audio Chat** button (); for a video chat, click the **Start a Video Chat** button ().

Send a File in a Message

If, during an instant messaging conversation, you realize you need to send someone a file, you can save time by sending the file directly from the Messages application.

When you need to send a file to another person, your first thought might be to attach that file to an e-mail message. However, if you happen to be in the middle of an instant messaging conversation with that person, it is easier and faster to use Messages to send the file.

Send a File in a Message

1. Start the conversation with the person to whom you want to send the file.
2. Click **Buddies**.

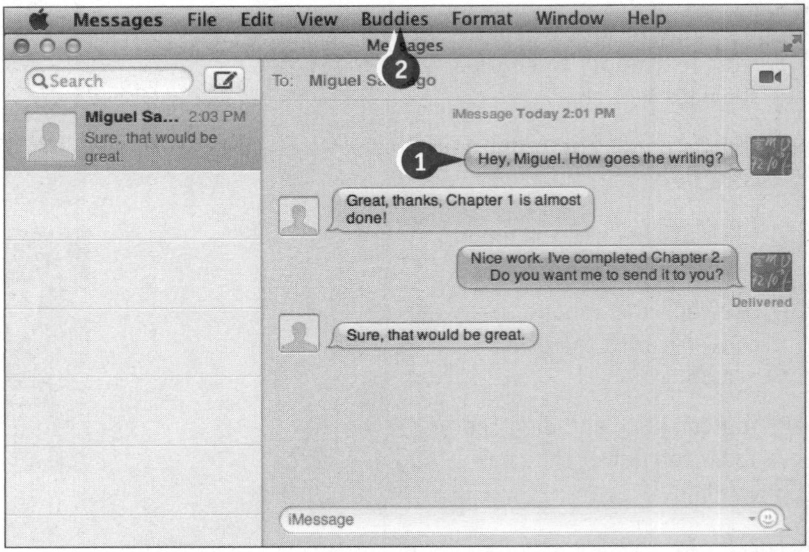

3. Click **Send File**.

Note: You can also press Option + ⌘ + F.

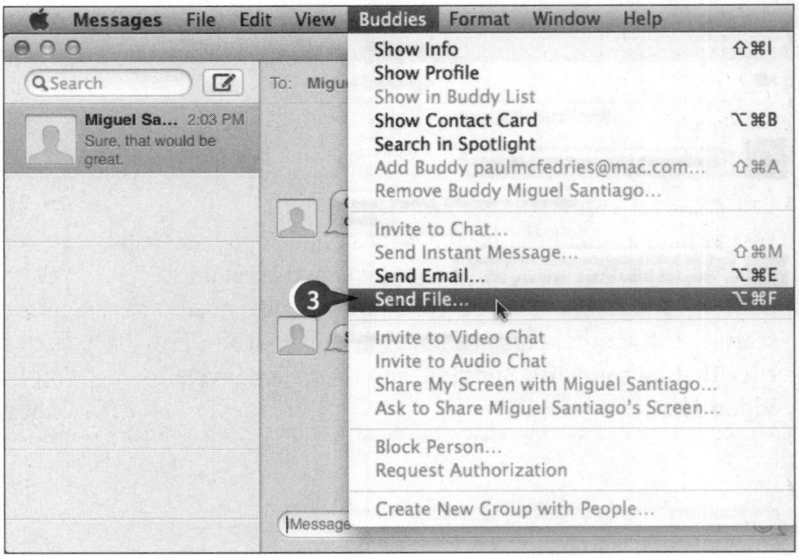

Messages displays a file selection dialog.

4. Click the file you want to send.
5. Click **Send**.

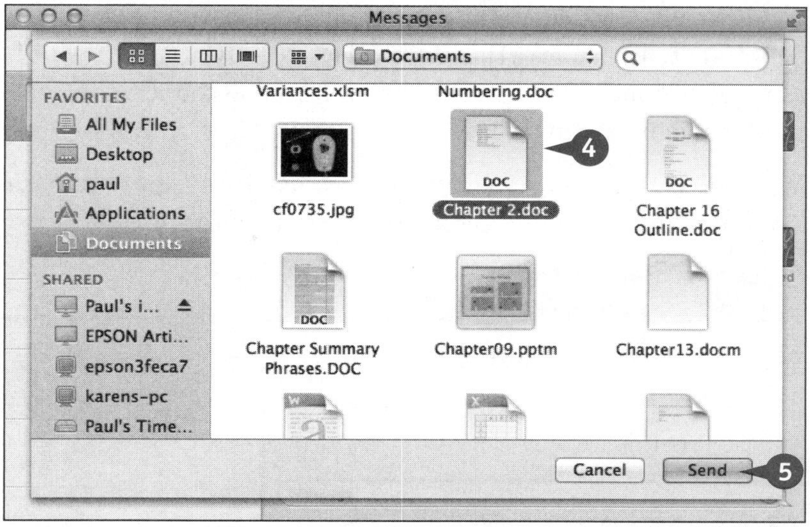

A. Messages adds an icon for the file to the message box.

6. Type your message.
7. Press Return.

Messages asks the other person for permission to receive a file. If the person accepts, Messages sends the message and adds the file as an attachment.

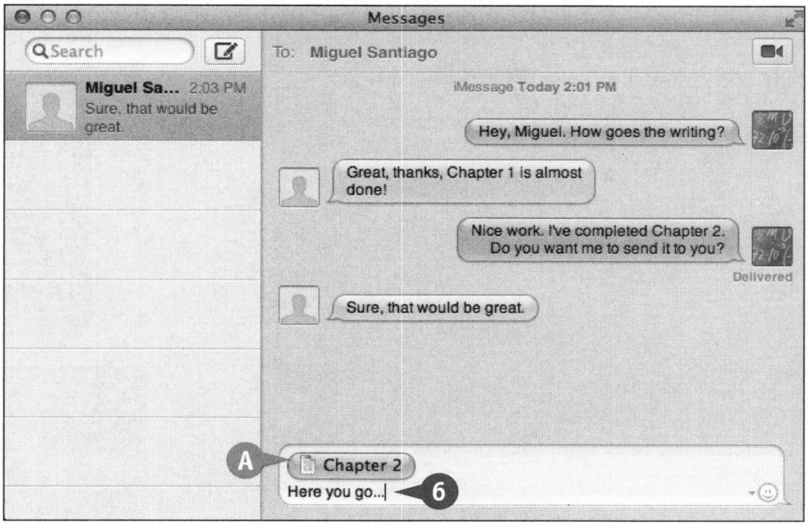

TIP

How do I save a file that I receive during a conversation?

When you receive a message that has a file attachment, the message shows the name of the file, with the file's type icon to the left and a downward-pointing arrow (⬇) to the right. Click ⬇ to save the file to your Downloads folder. Messages saves the file and then displays the Downloads folder.

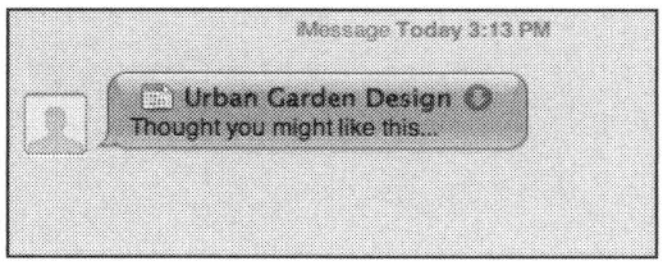

Sign In to FaceTime

FaceTime is a video chat feature that enables you to see and speak to another person over the Internet. To use FaceTime to conduct video chats with your friends, you must each first sign in using your Apple ID. This could be an iCloud account that uses the Apple iCloud.com address, or it could be your existing e-mail address.

After you create your Apple ID, you can use it to sign in to FaceTime. Note that you only have to do this once. In subsequent sessions, FaceTime automatically signs you in.

Sign In to FaceTime

1. In the Dock, click **FaceTime** (icon).

   The FaceTime window appears.

2. Type your Apple ID e-mail address.
3. Type your Apple ID password.

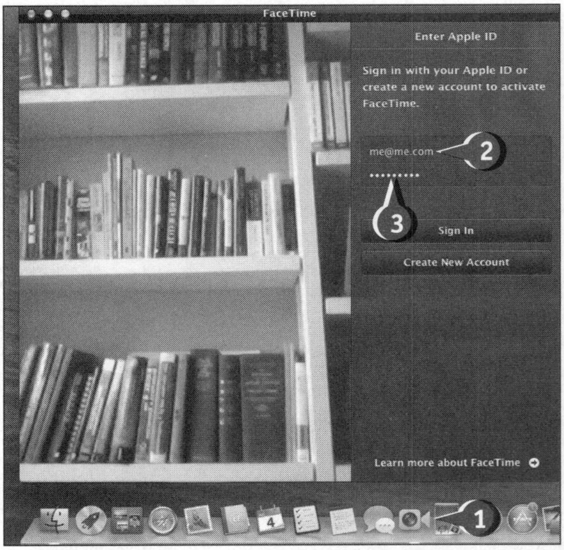

4. Click **Sign In**.

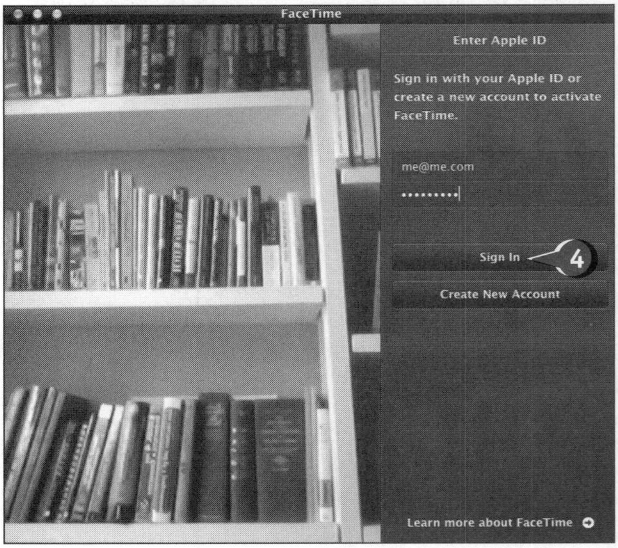

FaceTime prompts you to specify an e-mail address that people can use to contact you via FaceTime.

5 If the address you prefer is different from your Apple ID, type the address you want to use.

6 Click **Next**.

FaceTime verifies your Apple ID and then displays a list of contacts.

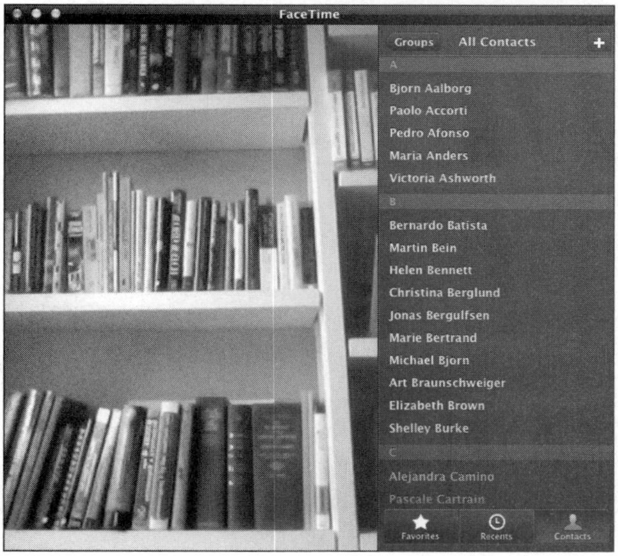

TIPS

What equipment do the person I am calling and I need to use FaceTime?
Your Mac Pro must have an external video camera or webcam, and an external microphone, such as a standalone mic or the built-in microphone that comes with a headset.

Which devices support FaceTime?
You can use FaceTime on any Mac running OS X 10.6.6 or later. For OS X Snow Leopard (10.6.6), FaceTime is available through the App Store for 99 cents. For all later versions of OS X, FaceTime is installed by default. FaceTime is also available as an app that runs on the iPhone 4 and later, the iPad 2 and later, and the iPod touch fourth generation and later.

Connect Through FaceTime

Once you sign in with your Apple ID, you can use the FaceTime application to connect with another person and conduct a video chat. How you connect depends on what device the other person is using for FaceTime. If the person is using a Mac, an iPad, or an iPod touch, you can use whatever e-mail address the person has designated as his or her FaceTime contact address, as described in the previous section, "Sign In to FaceTime." If the person is using an iPhone 4 or later, you can use that person's mobile number to make the connection.

Connect Through FaceTime

1. Click **Contacts**.
2. Click the contact you want to call.

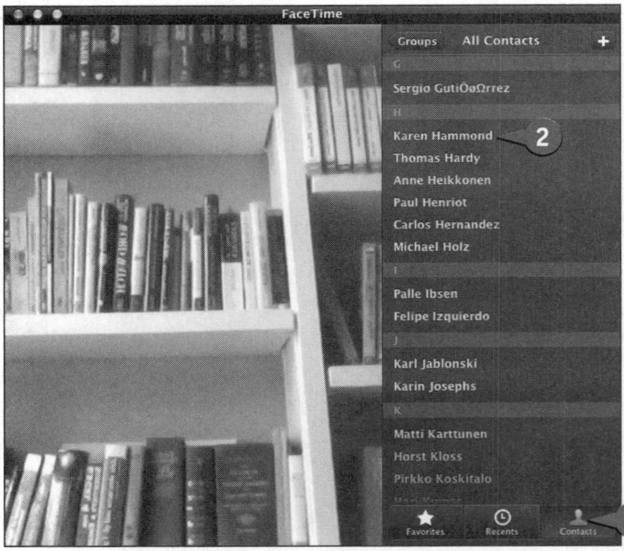

FaceTime displays the contact's data.

3. Click the phone number (for an iPhone) or e-mail address (for a Mac, iPad, or iPod touch) that you want to use to connect to the contact.

FaceTime sends a message to the contact asking if he or she would like a FaceTime connection.

4 The other person must click or tap **Accept** to complete the connection.

FaceTime connects with the other person.

A The other person's video takes up the bulk of the FaceTime screen.

B Your video appears in the picture-in-picture (PiP) window.

Note: You can click and drag the PiP to a different location within the FaceTime window.

5 When you finish your FaceTime call, click **End**.

TIP

Are there easier ways to connect to someone through FaceTime?

Yes, FaceTime offers a couple of methods that you might find faster. If you have connected with a person through FaceTime recently, that person may appear in the FaceTime Recents list. In the FaceTime window, click **Recents** and then click the person you want to contact.

Alternatively, if you connect with someone frequently, you can add that person to the FaceTime Favorites list. Use the Contacts list to click the person, and then click **Add to Favorites**. To connect with a favorite, click **Favorites** and then click the person.

Mute FaceTime

When you are conducting a FaceTime conversation, there may be times when you do not want the other person to hear what you are saying. In a telephone conversation you can cover the microphone or put the other person on hold. In a FaceTime conversation, you must mute your audio, instead.

Muting your FaceTime audio is also useful if you are about to enter a particularly noisy area and you do not want to subject the other person to the noise.

Mute FaceTime

1. Click **Video**.
2. Click **Mute**.

A. You can also click the **Mute** icon (icon) in the FaceTime window.

B. FaceTime displays "Mute" in your PiP window.

C. The Mute icon changes to (icon) with a blue background.

To resume normal audio, either repeats steps **1** and **2** or click the **Mute** icon (icon).

Turn Off FaceTime

If you do not want to be disturbed by incoming FaceTime calls, simply quitting the FaceTime application is not enough. Instead, you must run the FaceTime application and then use it to turn off FaceTime. When other people attempt to call you using FaceTime, they see the message "*Your Name* is not available for FaceTime" (where *Your Name* is the name they use for you in their Contacts list.

Turn Off FaceTime

1. If you are currently on a FaceTime call, end that call.
2. Click **FaceTime**.
3. Click **Turn FaceTime Off**.

   You can also press ⌘+K.

FaceTime turns itself off and displays the Preferences screen.

Ⓐ When you are ready to receive FaceTime calls again, click the **FaceTime** switch to **On**.

CHAPTER 8

Tracking Contacts and Events

You use the Contacts application to store information such as phone numbers, e-mail addresses, street addresses, and more. You use the Calendar application to track events.

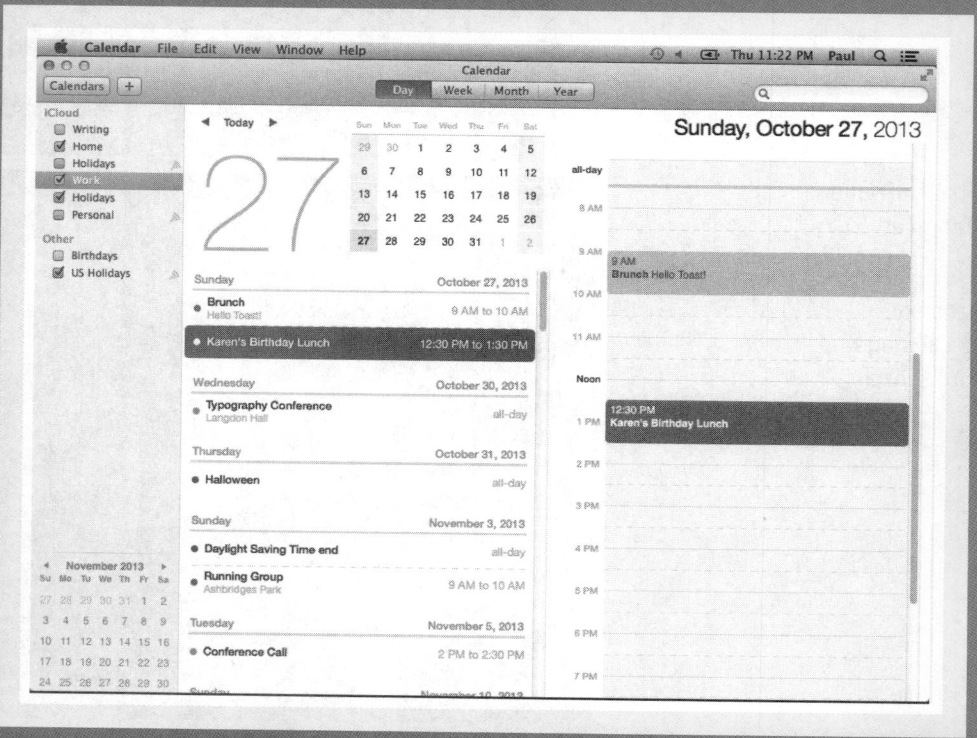

Add a New Contact

Mac Pro includes the Contacts application for managing information about the people you know, whether they are colleagues, friends, or family members. The Contacts app refers to these people as *contacts*, and you store each person's data in an object called a *card*. Each card can store a wide variety of information. For example, you can store a person's name, company name, phone numbers, e-mail address, instant messaging data, street address, notes, and much more. Although you will mostly use Contacts cards to store data about people, you can also use a card to keep information about companies.

Add a New Contact

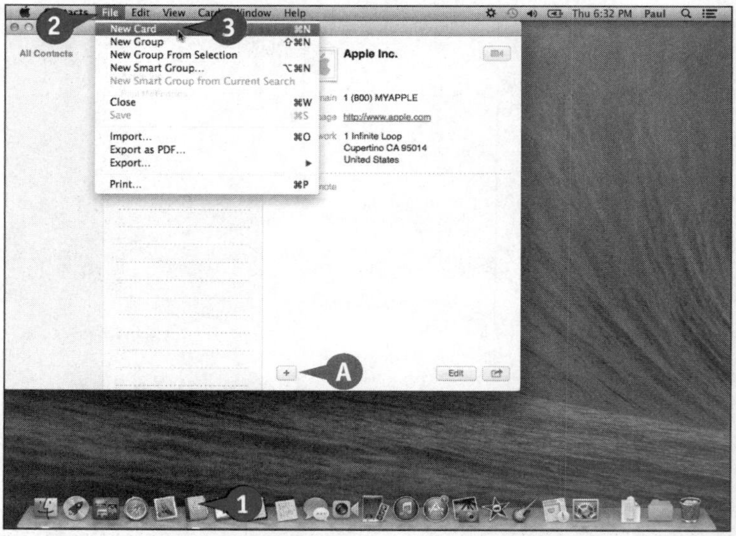

1. In the Dock, click **Contacts** (icon).
2. Click **File**.
3. Click **New Card**.

Ⓐ You can also begin a new contact by clicking **Add** (+) and then clicking **New Contact**.

Note: You can also invoke the New Card command by pressing ⌘+N.

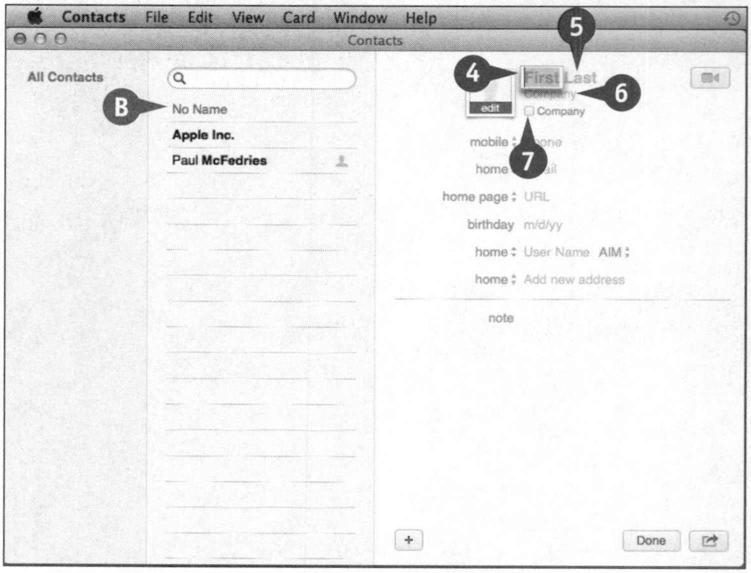

Ⓑ Contacts adds a new card.

4. In the First field, type the contact's first name.
5. In the Last field, type the contact's last name.
6. In the Company field, type the contact's company name.
7. If the contact is a company, select the **Company** option (☐ changes to ☑).

8 In the first Phone field, click and then click the category you want to use.

9 Type the phone number.

10 Repeat steps **8** and **9** to enter data in some or all the other fields.

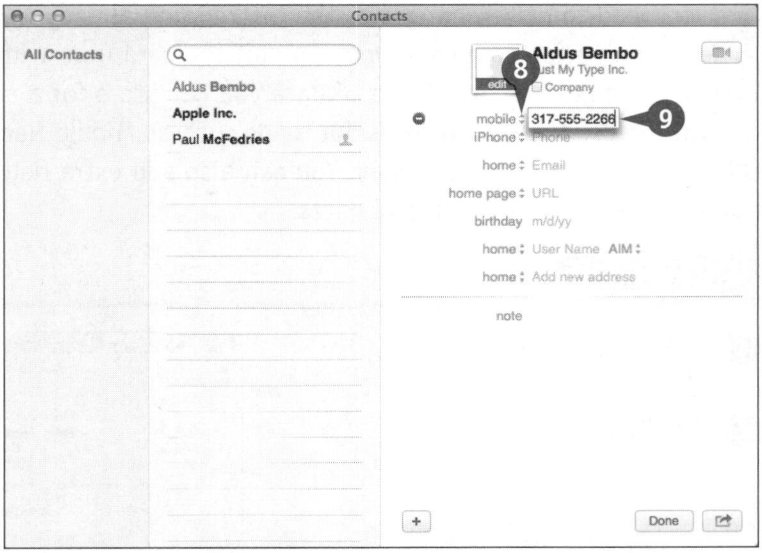

Note: To learn how to add more fields to the card, see the next section, "Edit a Contact."

11 Click **Done**.

Contacts saves the new card.

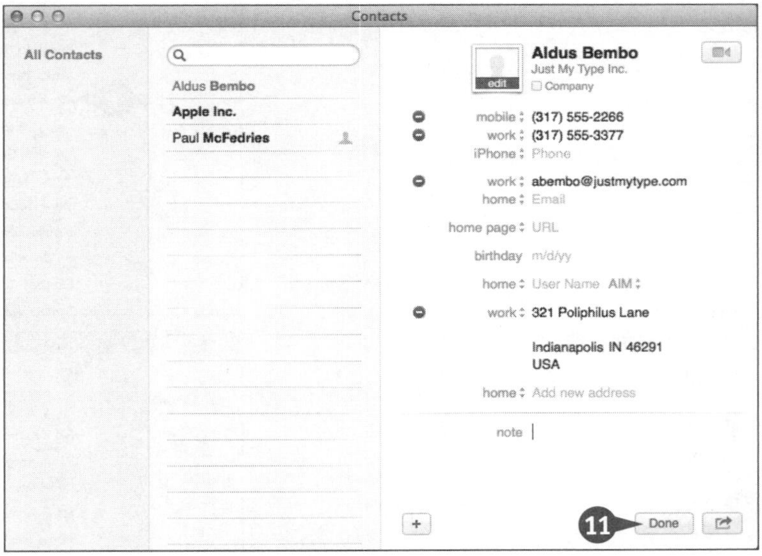

TIP

If I include a contact's e-mail address, is there a way to send that person a message without having to type the address?

Yes. Click the contact's card, click the e-mail address category (such as **work** or **home**), and then click **Send Email.** Mail displays a new e-mail message with the contact already added in the To line. Fill in the rest of the message as required and then click **Send** ( ).

Edit a Contact

If you need to make changes to the information already in a contact's card, or if you need to add new information to a card, you can edit the card from within Contacts. The default fields you see in a card are not the only types of data you can store for a contact. Contacts offers a large number of extra fields. These include useful fields such as Middle Name, Nickname, Job Title, Department, URL (web address), and Birthday. You can also add extra fields for common data items such as phone numbers, e-mail addresses, and dates.

Edit a Contact

1. Click the card you want to edit.
2. Click **Edit**.

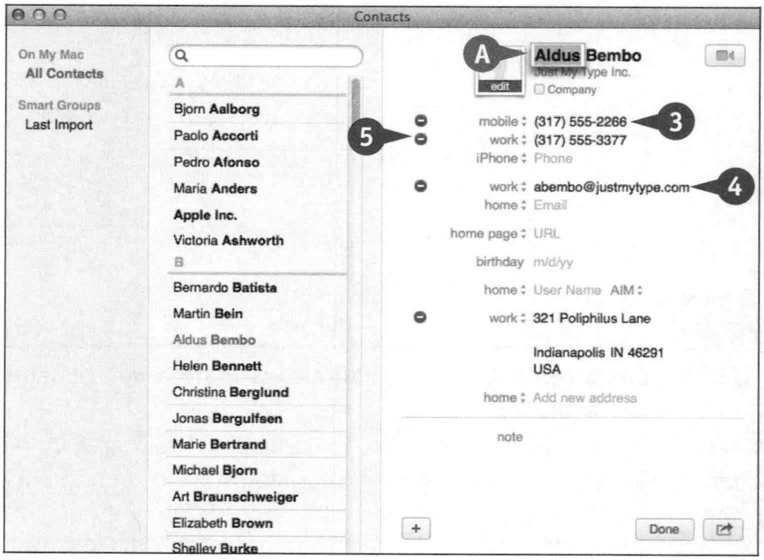

Ⓐ Contacts makes the card's fields available for editing.

3. Edit the existing fields as required.
4. To add a field, click an empty placeholder and then type the field data.
5. To remove a field, click **Delete** (▬).

6. To add a new field type, click **Card**.
7. Click **Add Field**.
8. Click the type of field you want.

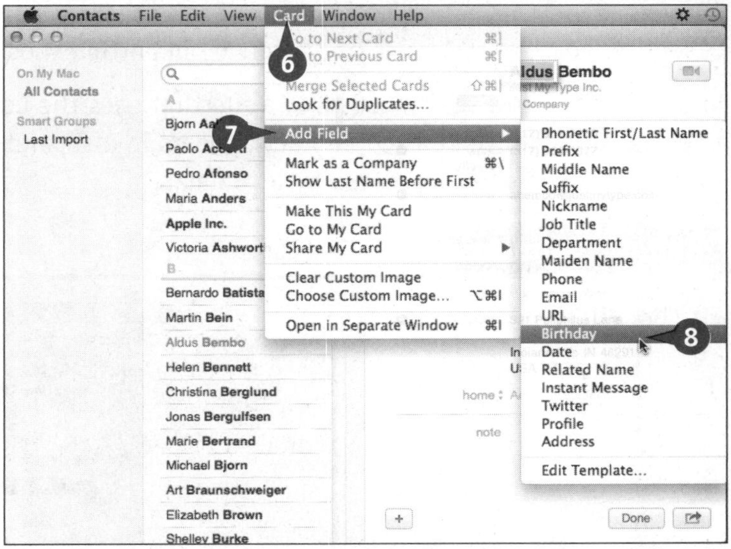

B Contacts adds the field to the card.

9. When you complete your edits, click **Done**.

Contacts saves the edited card.

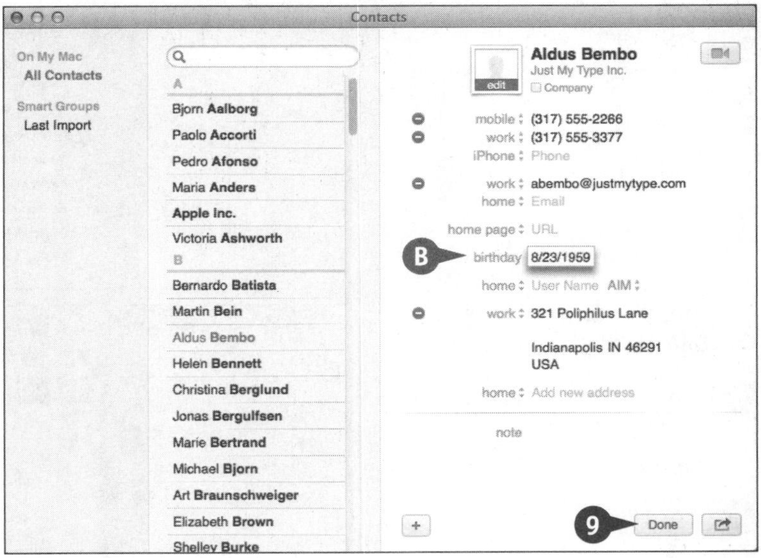

TIP

How do I add a picture for the new contact?

Click the contact's card and then click **Edit**. Double-click the picture box. A dialog of picture options appears. Click the type of picture you want to add: Defaults, iCloud, Faces, or Camera. Click or take the picture and then click **Done** to close the picture dialog. Click **Done** to save the edited card.

Import Contacts

If you already have a collection of contacts that you have created using another application or service, you can save time and effort by importing those contacts into the Contacts app.

To import contacts, they must be in a file that uses the Comma Separated Values (CSV) format. This is a special text file where each contact appears in a separate line, and in each line the various fields of contact data are each separated by a comma.

Import Contacts

1. Click **File**.
2. Click **Import**.

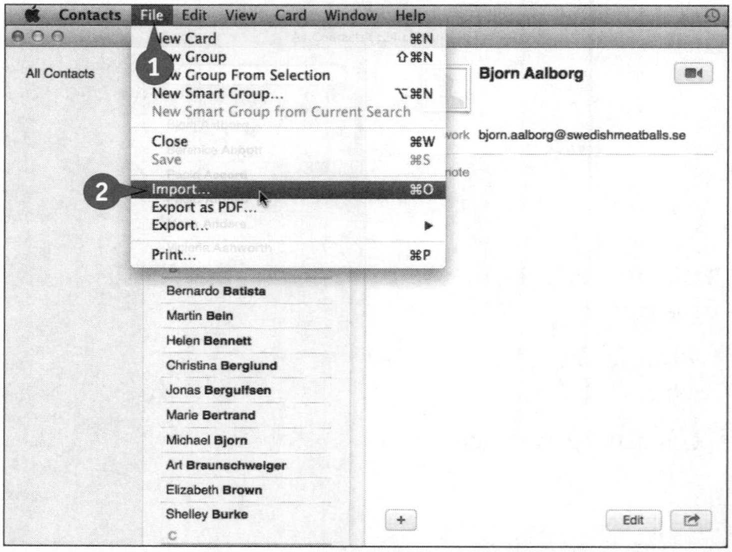

Contacts displays a file selection dialog.

3. Open the folder that contains the CSV file you want to import.
4. Click the CSV file.
5. Click **Open**.

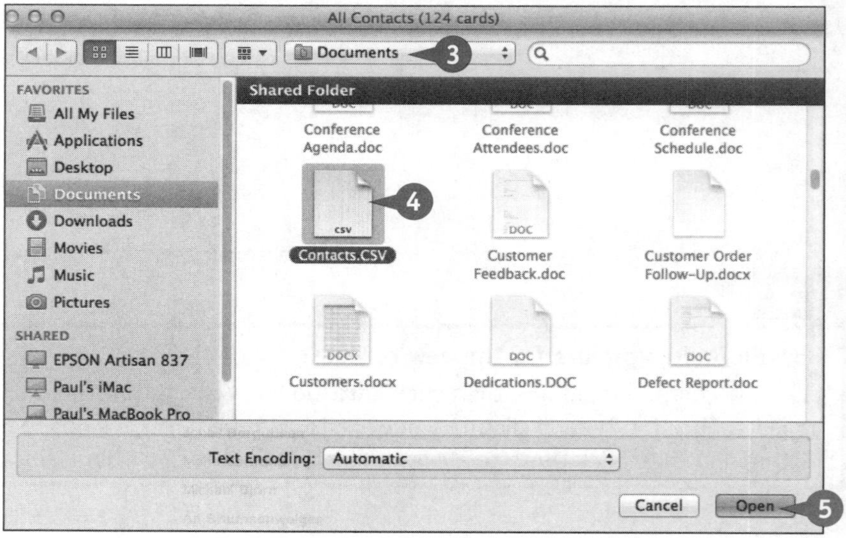

Contacts prompts you to select how the imported fields should be mapped to the Contacts data.

Ⓐ This column represents the existing Contacts fields.

Ⓑ This column represents the names of the fields in the CSV file.

6 Check that each field in the Contacts column corresponds with a field from the imported data.

7 To adjust a mapping, click the Contacts field and then click the imported field you want to use.

8 If the first line of the CSV file contains the names of the fields, select the **Ignore first card** option (☐ changes to ☑).

9 Click **OK**.

Contacts imports the data.

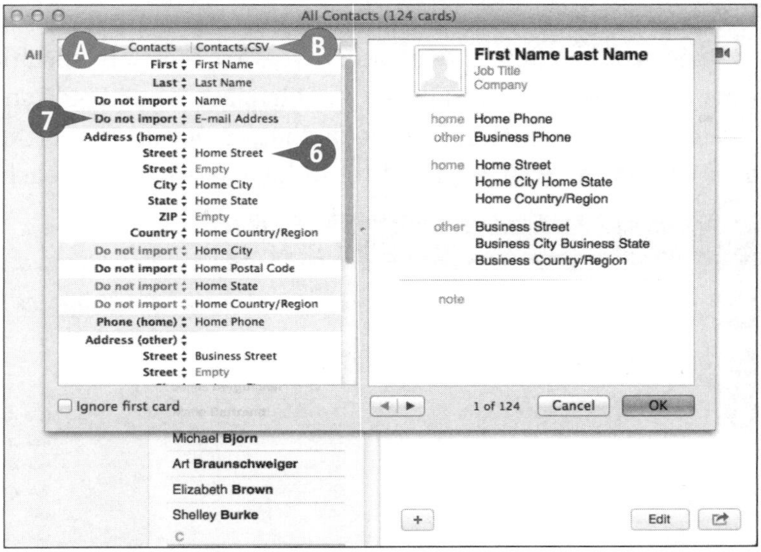

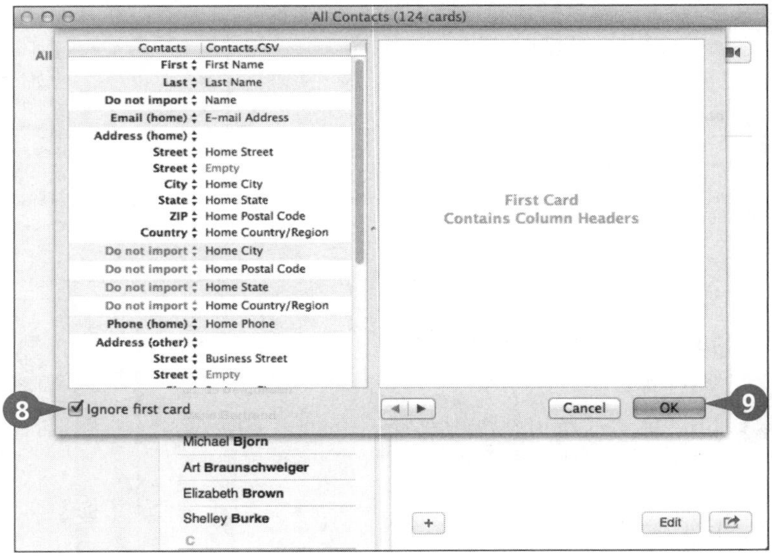

TIPS

Why does Contacts not seem to want to import ZIP codes?

Unfortunately, Contacts does not do a good job of importing postal codes. It usually shows the ZIP field as Empty, and the corresponding postal code field in the CSV file is set to Do Not Import. To fix this, click **ZIP** in the Contacts list and then click the CSV file's postal code field.

How do I import contact data received as an e-mail attachment?

If the file you received uses the vCard format (it should have a .vcf extension in the name), you can import it into Contacts by double-clicking the attachment. See the section "Share Your Contact Info" to learn how to send your own contact data as a vCard.

Create a Custom Contact Template

You can often make the tasks of adding and editing contact data easier and faster by creating your own custom contact template. A contact template specifies what fields appear in each card and in what order. By eliminating from the template those fields you never use, you can make contact cards easier to navigate. By adding fields that do not appear in the default template, you save time by avoiding having to always add those fields manually for each new and existing contact.

Create a Custom Contact Template

1. Click **Card**.
2. Click **Add Field**.
3. Click **Edit Template**.

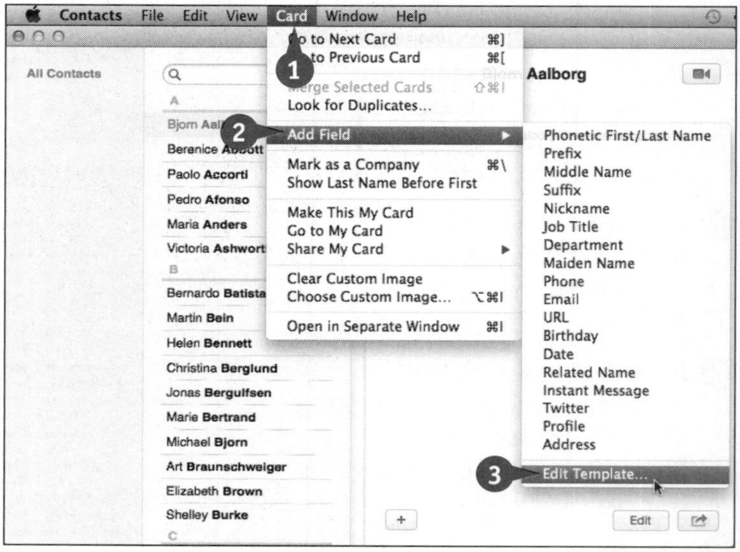

The Contacts preferences appear with the Template tab displayed.

4. To remove a field from the template, click the **Remove Field** icon (⊟) that appears to the left of the field.

Note: Removing a field from the template does not affect the contact data in any way.

5. To add another field of an existing type, click the **Add Field** icon (⊕) that appears to the left of the existing field.

6 To add a new field to the template, click the **Add Field** (▼) and then click a field.

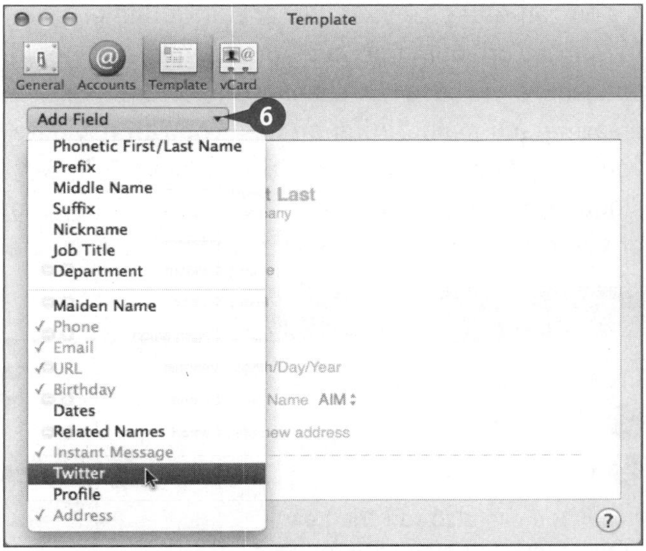

A The new field appears in the template.

7 To change a default field label, click the label's ⬍ and then click the label.

8 Repeat steps **4** to **7** as needed.

9 Click **Close** (■).

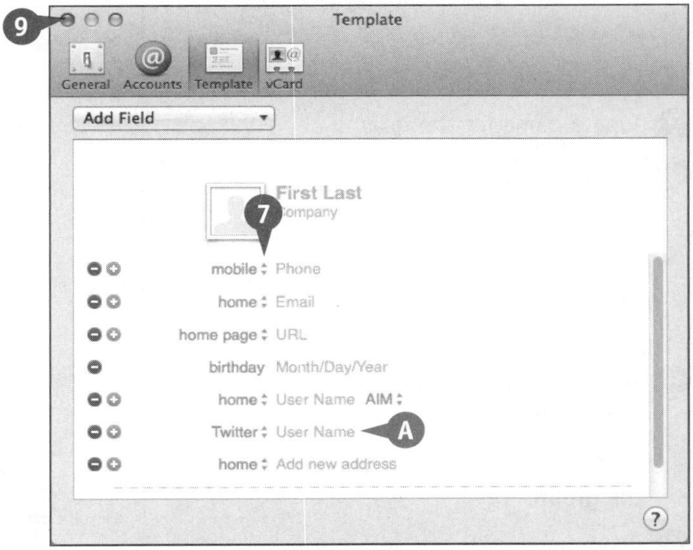

TIPS

How do I remove a field that does not have the Remove Field icon?

Contacts only displays the Remove Field icon (■) for fields in the data section of the template. For extra fields you can add, such as Prefix, Job Title, and Department, you do not see this icon. To remove such fields after you have added them, click the **Add Field** (▼) and then click the field name in the drop-down list.

Can I remove default fields such as First, Last, and Company?

No, you cannot remove those fields. Contacts requires those fields in order to sort the contact data, so they cannot be removed from the template.

Create a Contact Group

You can organize your contacts into one or more groups, which is useful for viewing just a subset of your contacts. For example, you could create separate groups for friends, family, work colleagues, or business clients. Groups are handy if you have many contacts in your address book. By creating and maintaining groups, you can navigate your contacts more easily, particularly because you can add a contact to multiple groups. You can also perform groupwide tasks, such as sending a single e-mail message to everyone in the group. You can create a group first and then add members, or you can select members in advance and then create the group.

Create a Contact Group

Create a Contact Group

1. Click **File**.
2. Click **New Group**.

Note: You can also run the New Group command by pressing Shift + ⌘ + N.

Ⓐ Contacts adds a new group.

3. Type a name for the group.
4. Press Return.

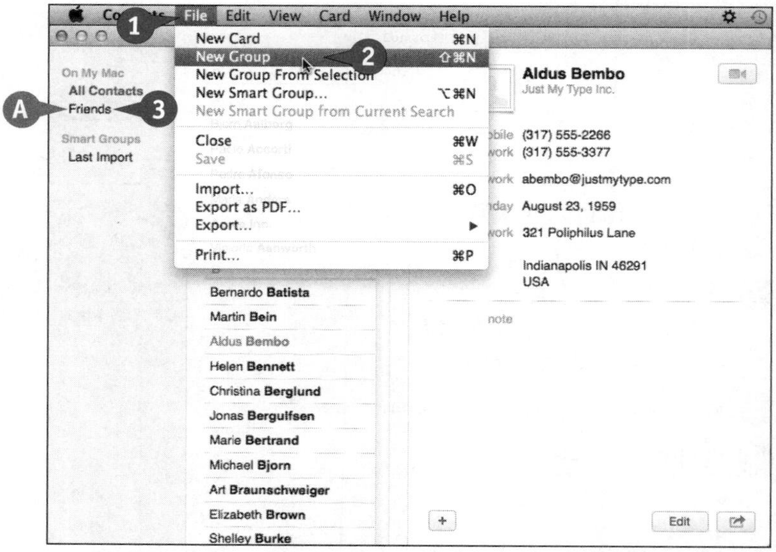

5. Click and drag a contact to the group.

   Contacts adds the contact to the group.

6. Repeat step 5 for the other contacts you want to add to the group.

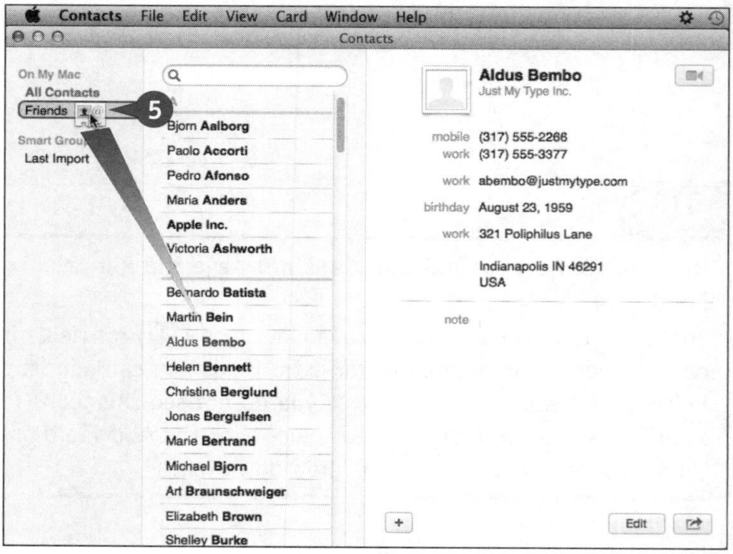

Create a Group of Selected Contacts

1. Select the contacts you want to include in the new group.

Note: To select multiple contacts, press and hold ⌘ and click each card.

2. Click **File**.
3. Click **New Group From Selection**.

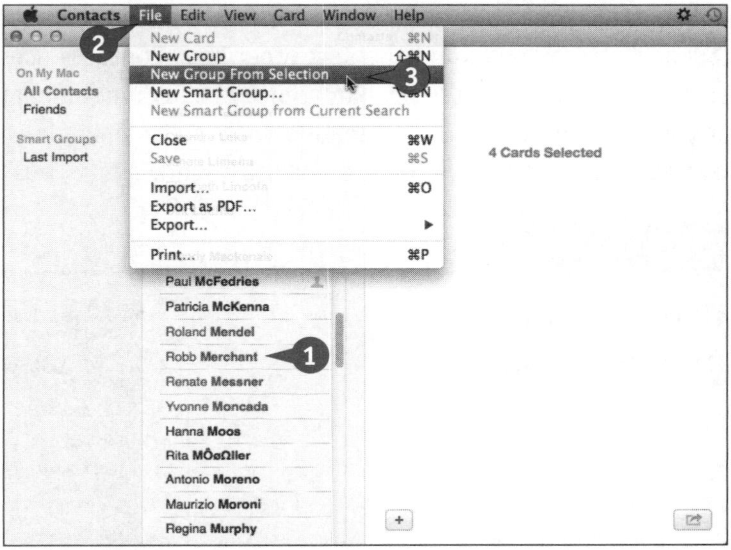

- Ⓑ Contacts adds a new group.
- Ⓒ Contacts adds the selected contacts as group members.

4. Type a name for the group.
5. Press Return.

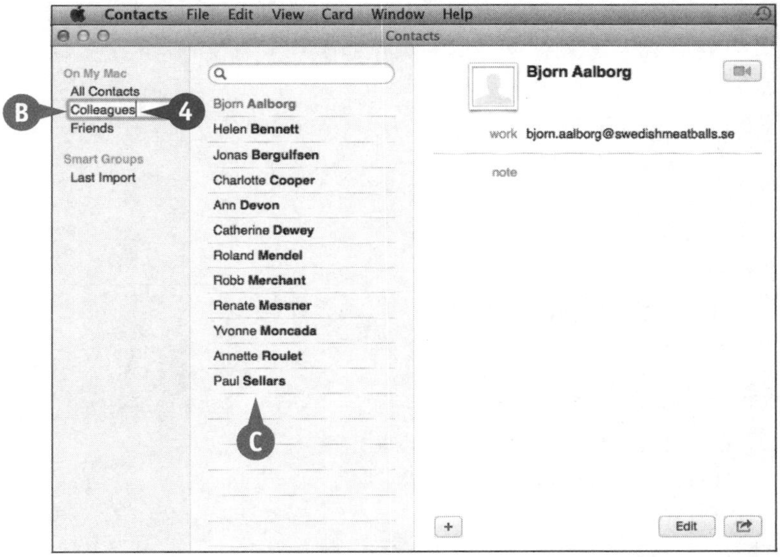

TIPS

Can I send an e-mail message to the group?

Yes. With a group, you send a single message to the group, and Mail automatically sends a copy to each member. Right-click the group and then click **Send Email to *"Group"*** where *Group* is the name of the group.

What is a Smart Group?

A *Smart Group* is a special group where each member has one or more fields in common, such as the company name or city. When you create a Smart Group, you specify one or more criteria, and then Contacts automatically adds members to the group if they meet those criteria. To create a Smart Group, click **File**, click **New Smart Group**, and then enter your group criteria.

Sort Contacts

Depending on how your contact data is entered, you can make the list of contacts easier to navigate by changing the sort order that Contacts uses. By default, Contacts displays the list sorted by each person's last name, or by the company name for those contacts that are companies. If you are more comfortable dealing with first names, however, then you might prefer to sort the contacts based on their first names (although, again, businesses are still sorted by company name).

Sort Contacts

1. Click **Contacts**.
2. Click **Preferences**

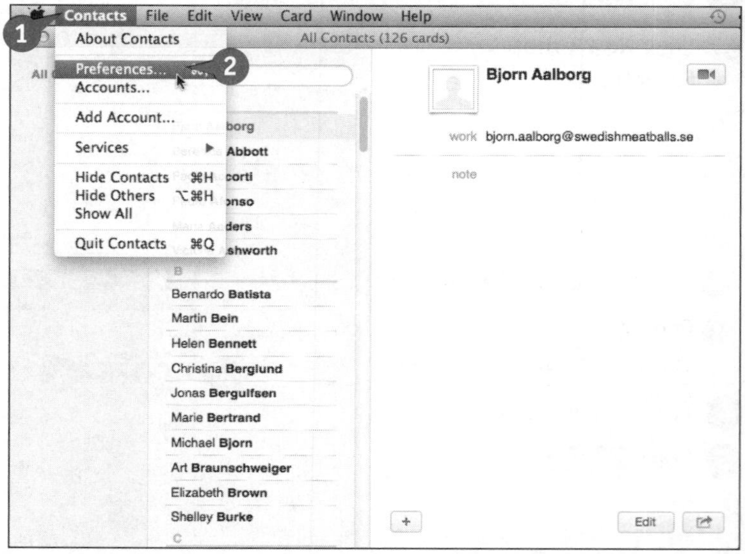

The Contacts preferences appear.

3. Click the **General** tab.
4. Click the **Sort By** ⬍ and then click the sort order you want to use.
5. Click **Close** (■).

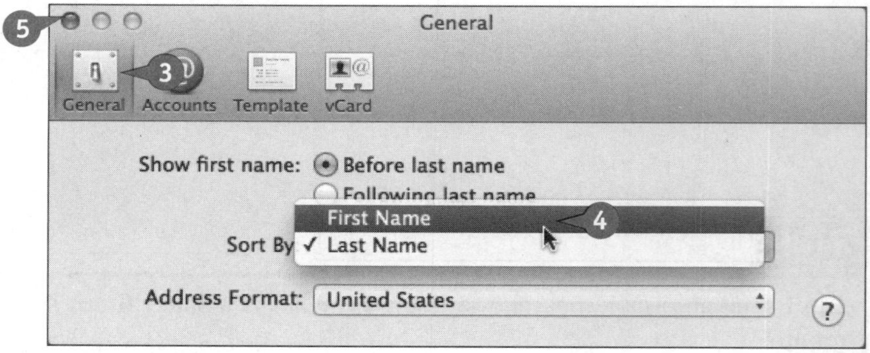

Disable a Contacts Account

If you have added an account to your Mac Pro and are using that account to display the service's contact list, you can make the Contacts app easier to navigate by disabling the account if you do not use it for contacts. Many Internet accounts — particularly iCloud, Google, LinkedIn, Yahoo!, and Exchange — enable you to display their contacts in the Contacts app. This is usually convenient, but if you do not use the contacts list for a particular account, then it clutters the Contacts app.

Disable a Contacts Account

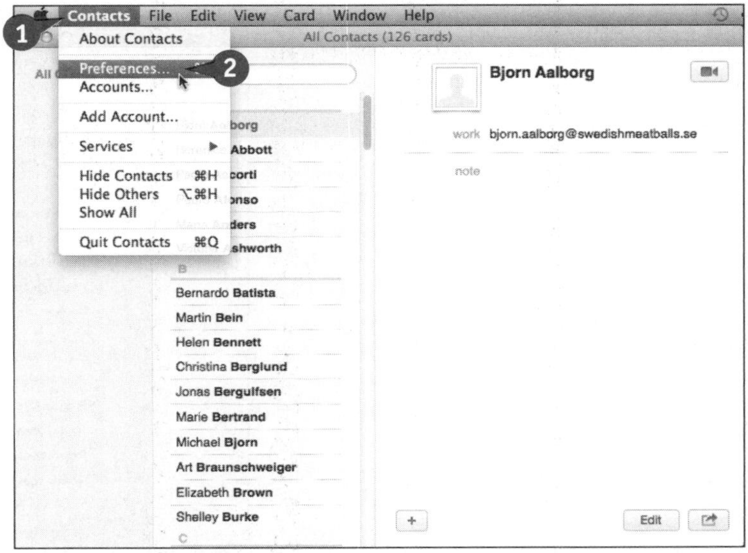

1. Click **Contacts**.
2. Click **Preferences**.

The Contacts preferences appear.

3. Click the **Accounts** tab.
4. Click the account you want to disable.
5. Deselect the **Enable this account** option (☑ changes to ☐).

   Contacts disables the account.
6. Click **Close** (■).

   Contacts returns you to the All Contacts list and no longer displays the contacts from the disabled account.

Share Your Contact Info

You can share your contact data with other people by exporting the data to a vCard and then sending that file as an e-mail attachment. A vCard is a special file format that is the standard format for sharing the data for a single contact.

See the tip in the section "Import Contacts" to learn how to import a contact's data from a vCard that you received as an e-mail attachment.

Share Your Contact Info

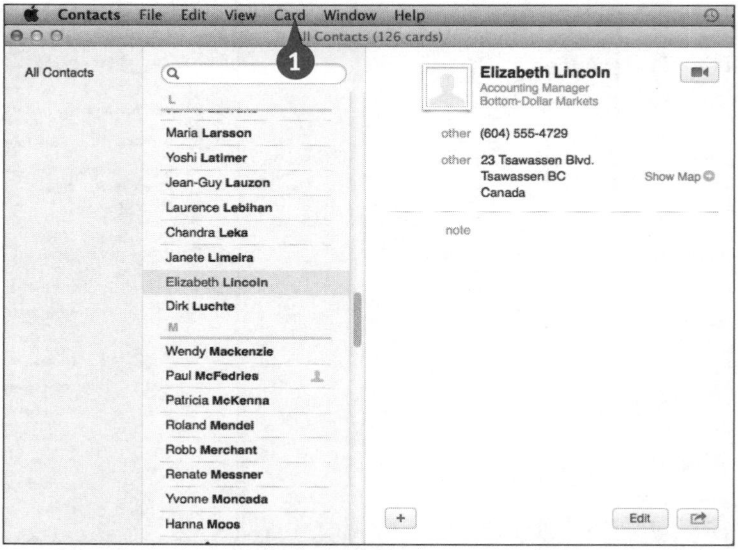

1 Click **Card**.

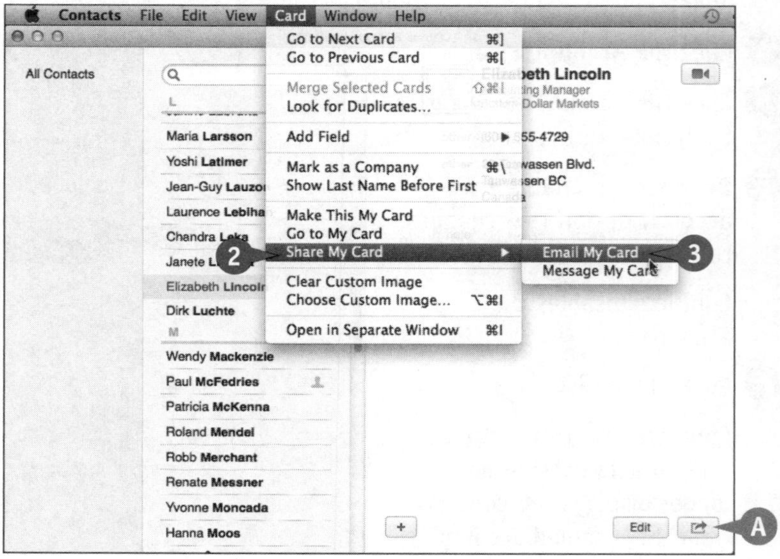

2 Click **Share My Card**.

3 Click **Email My Card**.

A Alternatively, you can select your card, click **Share** ( ), and then click **Email Card**.

Mail creates a new message.

B Your contact data appears as a vCard attachment.

4 Specify a recipient.

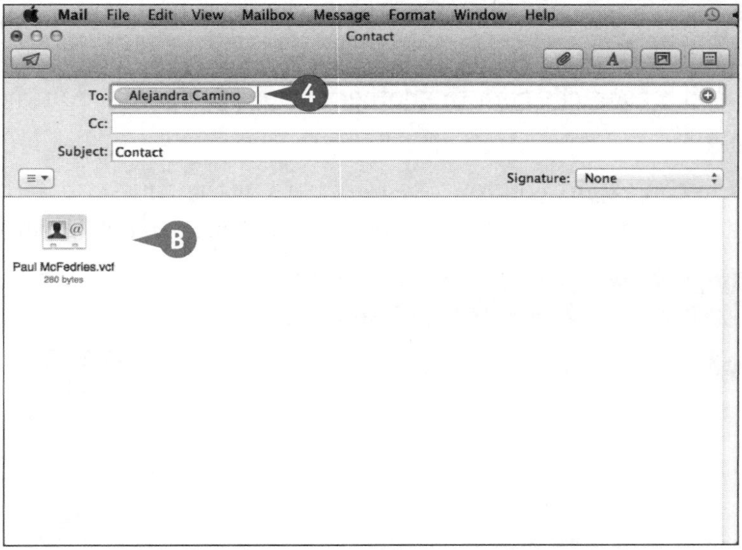

5 Edit the Subject line.

6 Add a message.

7 Click **Send** (![]).

Mail sends your contact data as an attachment.

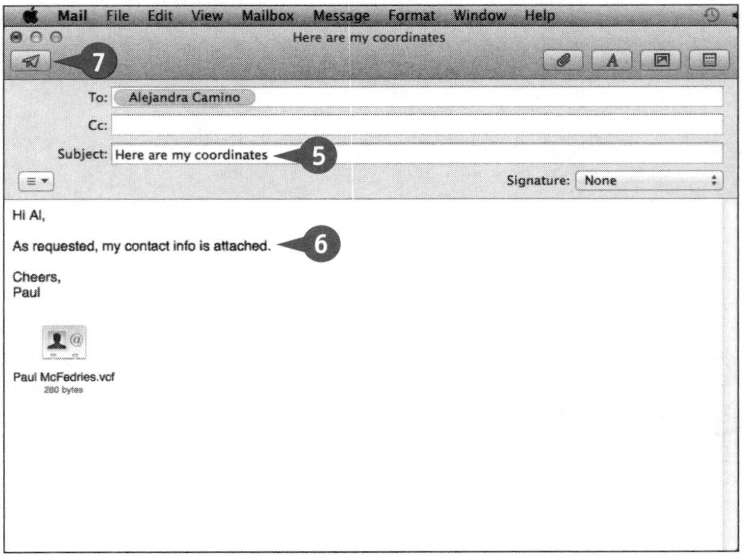

TIPS

I created a different card for my contact data. How do I tell Contacts to use it as my card?

In the Contacts list, click the card that contains your contact data. Click **Card** and then click **Make This My Card**. Contacts adds a silhouette icon (![]) to the right of your name to mark this as your contact data.

Some mail systems block my vCard attachment. How can I get around this?

Create a vCard file for your contact data (see the next section, "Export a Contact as a vCard"). In Finder, right-click the vCard file and then click **Compress**. You can now send the resulting Zip file as an attachment and it will not get blocked.

Export a Contact as a vCard

You can save a contact's information to a file by exporting that data as a vCard. You can use this technique as a simple backup method for contact data, but it is most useful as an easy way to send a contact's data to another person, as described in the previous section, "Share Your Contact Info."

You can export your own contact data or the contact data of another person. If you plan on sharing another person's data, you should seek that person's permission before you do so.

Export a Contact as a vCard

1. Click the contact you want to export.

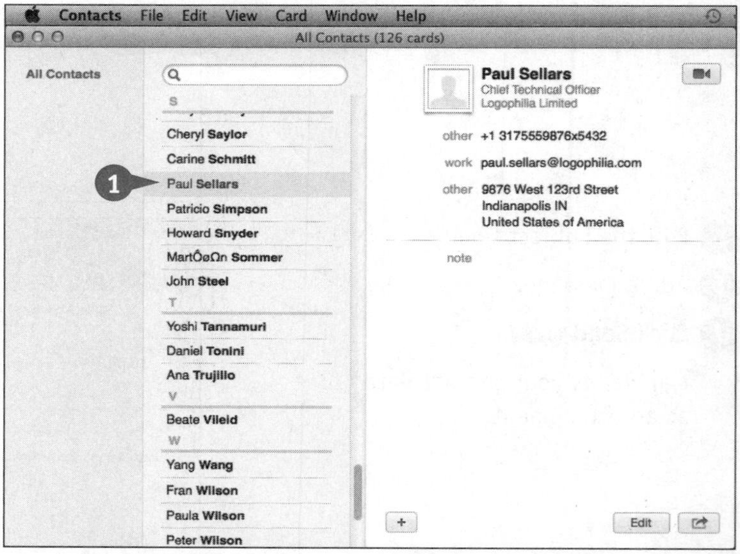

2. Click **File**.
3. Click **Export**.
4. Click **Export vCard**.

   Contacts prompts you to save the file.

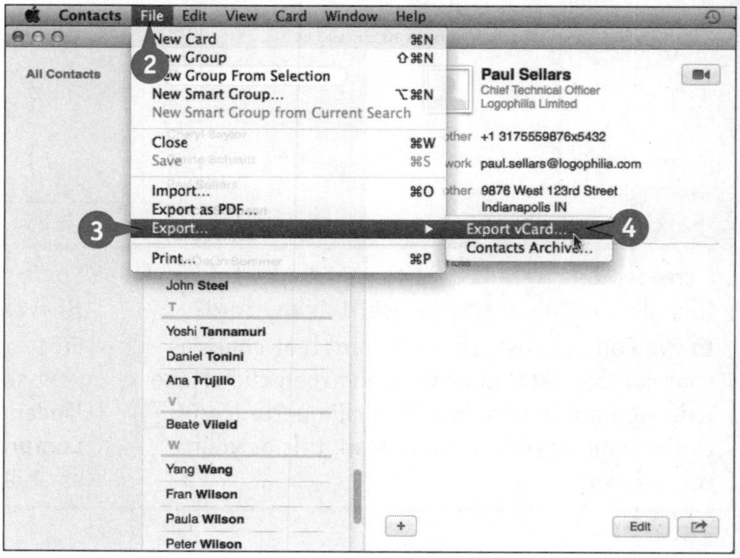

5 Edit the vCard file name, if needed.

6 Click the **Where** ⬍ and then click a location to save the vCard.

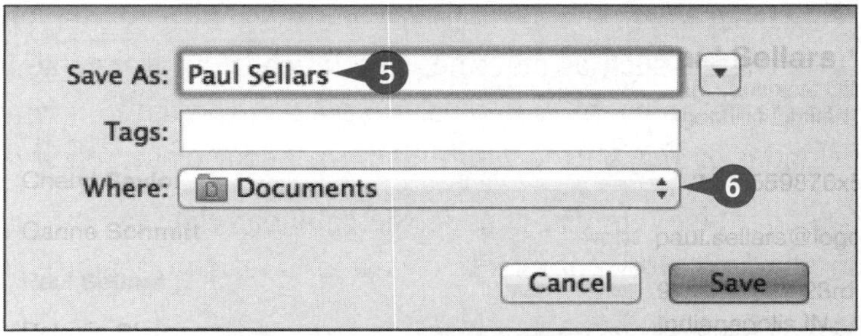

7 Click **Save**.

Contacts exports the contact's data to a vCard file.

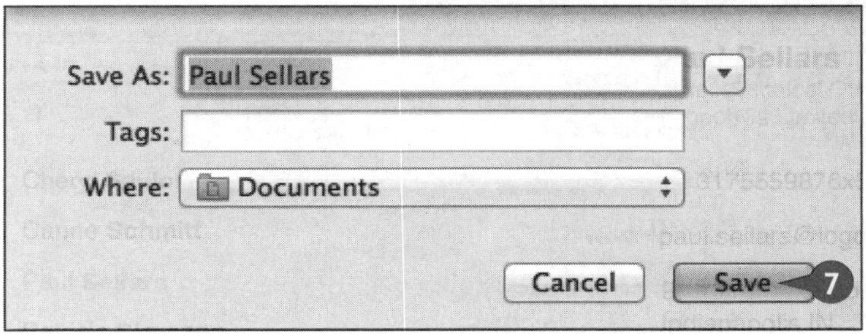

TIPS

Can I export contacts to a readable format?
Yes, you can export one or more contacts to a Portable Document Format (PDF) file. Select the contact or contacts, click **File**, and then click **Export as PDF.** Type a name for the file, select a location, and then click **Save.**

Can I print a contact address on an envelope?
Yes. Select the contact you want to print, click **File**, and then click **Print** (or press ⌘+P). Click the **Style** ⬍, click **Envelopes**, and then click **Print.** To print multiple contacts as mailing labels, select the contacts, click **File**, click **Print**, click the **Style** ⬍, click **Mailing Labels**, and then click **Print.**

Navigate the Calendar

Calendar enables you to create and work with events, which are either scheduled appointments or activities such as meetings and lunches, or all-day activities such as birthdays or vacations. Before you create an event, you must first select the date on which the event occurs. You can do this in Calendar by navigating the built-in calendar or by specifying the date that you want.

Calendar also lets you change the calendar view to suit your needs. For example, you can show just a single day's worth of events or a week's worth of events.

Navigate the Calendar

Using the Calendar

1. In the Dock, click **Calendar** (17).
2. Click **Month.**
3. Click the **Next Month** arrow until the month of your event appears.

A. If you go too far, click the **Previous Month** arrow to move back to the month you want.

B. To see a specific date, click the day and then click **Day** (or press ⌘+1).

C. To see a specific week, click any day within the week and then click **Week** (or press ⌘+2).

D. To return to viewing the entire month, click **Month** (or press ⌘+3).

E. If you want to return to today's date, click **Today** (or press ⌘+T).

Go to a Specific Date

1. Click **View**.
2. Click **Go to Date**.

Note: You can also select the Go to Date command by pressing Shift + ⌘ + T.

The Go to Date dialog appears.

3. In the Date text box, type the date you want using the format mm/dd/yyyy.

F You can also click the month, day, or year and then click ⬍ to increase or decrease the value.

4. Click **Show**.
5. Click **Day**.

G Calendar displays the date.

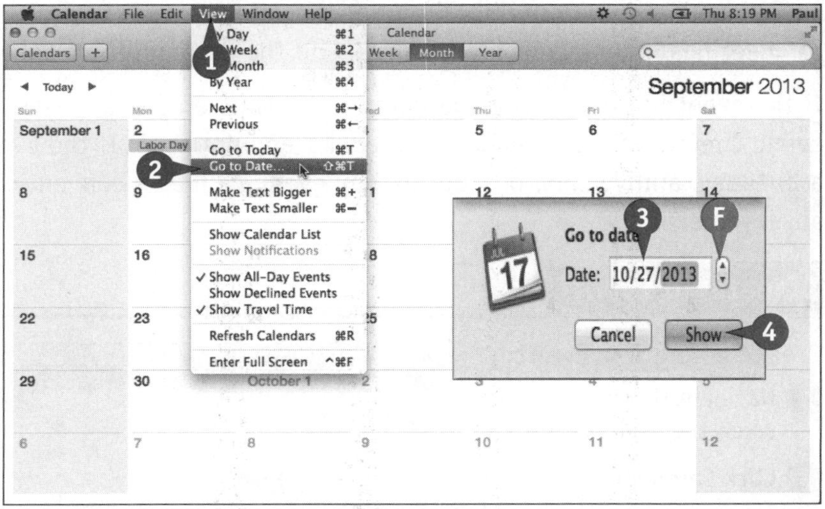

TIP

In the Week view, the week begins on Sunday. How can I change this to Monday?

Calendar's default Week view has Sunday on the left and Saturday on the right. To display the weekend days together, with Monday on the left signaling the start of the week, follow this procedure: Click **Calendar** in the menu bar and then click **Preferences.** The Calendar preferences appear. Click the **General** tab. Click the **Start week on** ⬍, select **Monday** from the pop-up menu, and then click **Close** (■).

Create an Event

You can help organize your life by using Calendar to record your events — such as appointments, meetings, phone calls, and dates — on the date and time they occur.

If the event has a set time and duration — for example, a meeting or a lunch date — you add the event directly to the calendar as a regular appointment. If the event has no set time — for example, a birthday, anniversary, or multiple-day event such as a convention or vacation — you can create an all-day event.

Create an Event

Create a Regular Event

1. Navigate to the date when the event occurs.
2. Click **Calendars**.
3. Select the calendar you want to use (☐ changes to ☑).
4. Double-click the time when the event starts.

Note: If the event is less than or more than an hour, you can also click and drag the mouse over the full event period.

- **A** Calendar adds a one-hour event.

5. Type the name of the event.
6. Press **Return**.

Create an All-Day Event

1. Click **Week**.
2. Navigate to the week that includes the date when the event occurs.
3. Click **Calendars**.
4. Select the calendar you want to use (☐ changes to ☑).
5. Double-click anywhere inside the event date's all-day section.

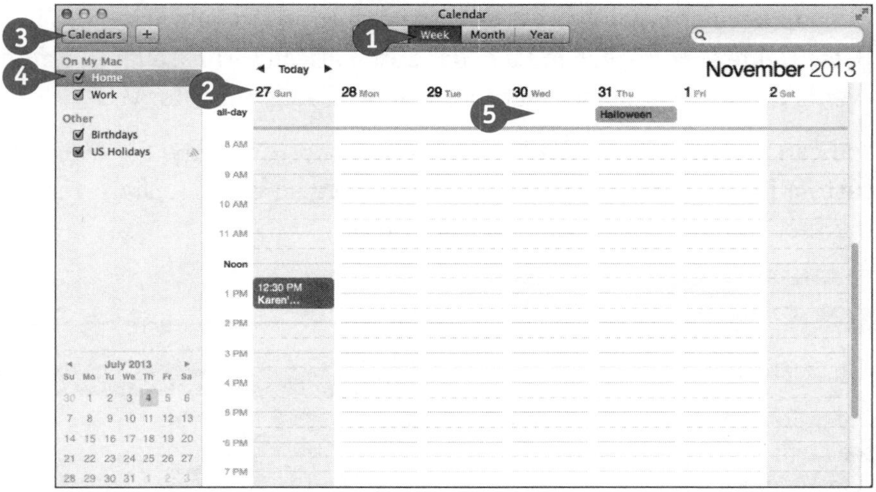

B Calendar adds a new all-day event.

6. Type the name of the event.
7. Press Return.

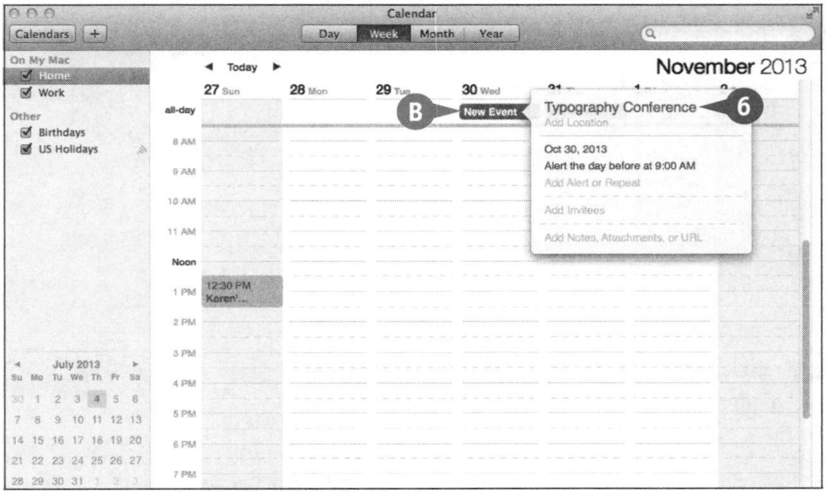

TIP

How can I specify event details such as the location and a reminder message?

Follow the steps in this section to create an event and then double-click the event. Type the location of the event in the Location text box. Click the event's date or time, click **Alert**, and then click the amount of time before the event that you want to receive the reminder. To add notes, attach a file, or add a web address, click **Add Notes, Attachments, or URL** and then click the type of information you want to add. Click the event. Calendar saves the new event configuration.

Create a Repeating Event

If you have an activity or event that recurs at a regular interval, you can create an event and configure it to repeat in Calendar automatically. This saves you from having to add the future events repeatedly yourself because Calendar adds them for you.

You can repeat an event daily, weekly, monthly, or yearly. For even greater flexibility, you can set up a custom interval. For example, you could have an event repeat every five days, every second Friday, on the first Monday of every month, and so on.

Create a Repeating Event

1 Create an event.

Note: To create an event, follow the steps in the previous section, "Create an Event."

2 Double-click the event.

Calendar displays information for the event.

3 Click the event's date and time.

Calendar opens the event for editing.

4 Click the **repeat** ⇕.

5 Click the interval you want to use.

A If you want to specify a custom interval such as every two weeks or the first Monday of every month, click **Custom** and configure your interval in the dialog that appears.

6 Press Return.

B Calendar adds the repeating events to the calendar.

TIPS

How do I configure an event to stop after a certain number of occurrences?

Follow steps **1** to **5** to select a recurrence interval. Click the **end** ⇕ and then select **After** from the pop-up menu. Type the number of occurrences you want. Click **Done**.

Can I delete a single occurrence from a recurring series of events?

Yes, you can delete one occurrence from the calendar without affecting the rest of the series. Click the occurrence you want to delete and then press Delete. Calendar asks whether you want to delete all the occurrences or just the selected occurrence. Click **Delete Only This Event**.

Send or Respond to an Event Invitation

You can include other people in your event by sending them invitations to attend. If you receive an event invitation yourself, you can respond to it to let the person organizing the event know whether you will attend.

If you have an event that requires other people, Calendar has a feature that enables you to send invitations to other people who use a compatible e-mail program. The advantage of this approach is that when other people respond to the invitation, Calendar automatically updates the event. If you receive an event invitation yourself, the e-mail message contains buttons that enable you to respond quickly.

Send or Respond to an Event Invitation

Send an Event Invitation

1. Create an event.

Note: To create an event, follow the steps in the section "Create an Event."

2. Double-click the event.

3. Click **Add invitees**.

4. Begin typing the name of a person you want to invite.
5. Click the person you want to invite.
6. Repeat steps 4 and 5 to add more invitees.
7. Click **Send** (not shown).

Handle an Event Invitation

A. The Invitation button shows the number of pending invitations you have received via iCloud.

B. The event appears tentatively in your calendar.

1. Click the **Invitation** button (📥).
2. Click the button that represents your reply to the invitation:

C. You can click **Accept** if you can attend the event.

D. You can click **Decline** if you cannot attend the event.

E. You can click **Maybe** if you are currently not sure whether you can attend.

TIPS

Is it possible to send a message to all the people who have been invited to an event?

Yes. To send an e-mail message, right-click the event to which you were invited and then click **Email All Invitees**. To send a text message instead, right-click the event and then click **Message All Invitees**.

How do I know when a person has accepted or declined an invitation?

Double-click the event to display its details. In the list of invitees, you see a check mark beside each person who has accepted the invitation; you see a question mark beside each person who has not made a choice or who has selected Maybe; and you see a red "Not" symbol beside each person who has declined the invitation.

Create a Calendar

To gain greater control over your schedule, you can create new calendars to use for your events. By default, the Calendar app comes with two calendars, named Work and Home. These are fine for most needs, but there might be times when you require more specific control over how your events are stored. For example, rather than a general calendar for work, you might prefer separate calendars for specific departments or projects. Similarly, you might want to divide your personal schedule into separate calendars for family, friends, or travel.

Create a Calendar

1. Click **File**.
2. Click **New Calendar**.
3. If you are syncing your calendars with iCloud, click your iCloud account.

Note: If you are not syncing your calendars with iCloud, skip step **3**.

Ⓐ You can also click **Add Calendar** (+).

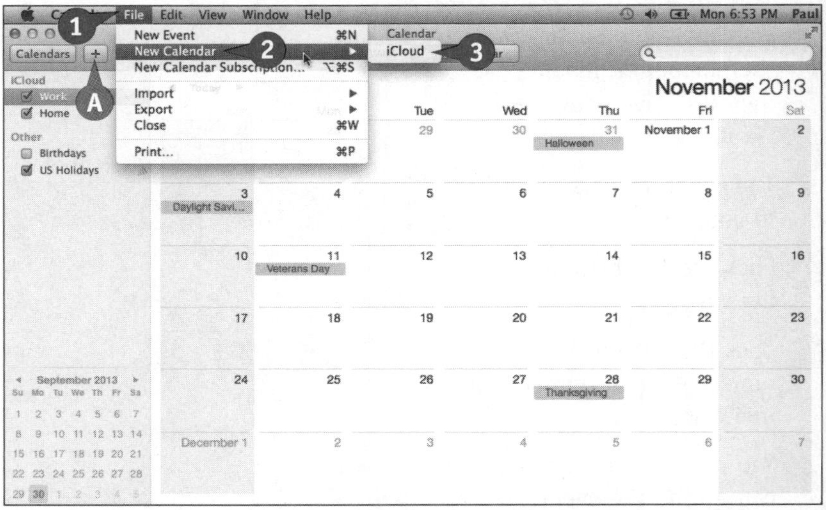

A new calendar appears in the Calendar list.

4. Type the calendar name.
5. Press Return.

Calendar creates the new calendar.

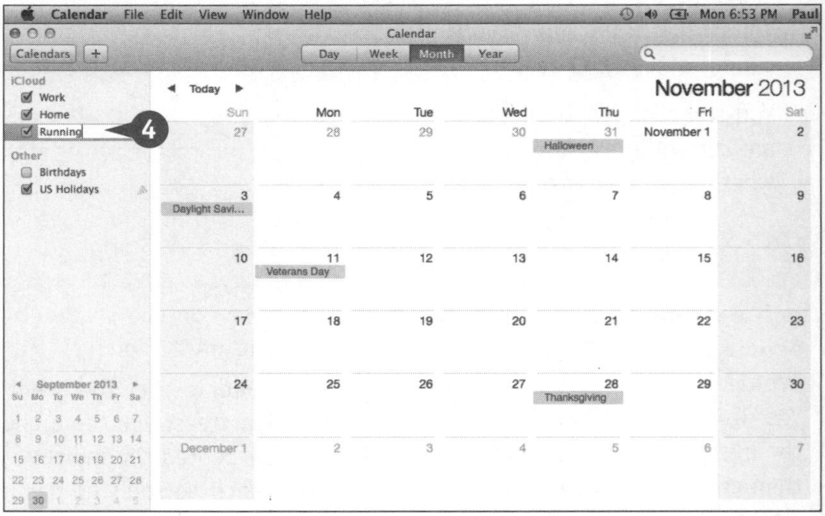

Disable a Calendar

You can make your schedule easier to view and navigate by disabling a calendar to hide its events. This is useful if you have several calendars added to the Calendars app, and you have a number of events in each calendar. If you find the schedule appears crowded and confusing, disabling a calendar can help by temporarily removing that calendar's events from the schedule. Calendar does not delete the calendar's events, and you can display them again at any time by enabling the calendar.

Disable a Calendar

1. If the Calendar list is not currently displayed, click **Calendars**.
2. Deselect the calendar you want to disable (☑ changes to ☐).

Ⓐ Calendar hides the events associated with the disabled calendar.

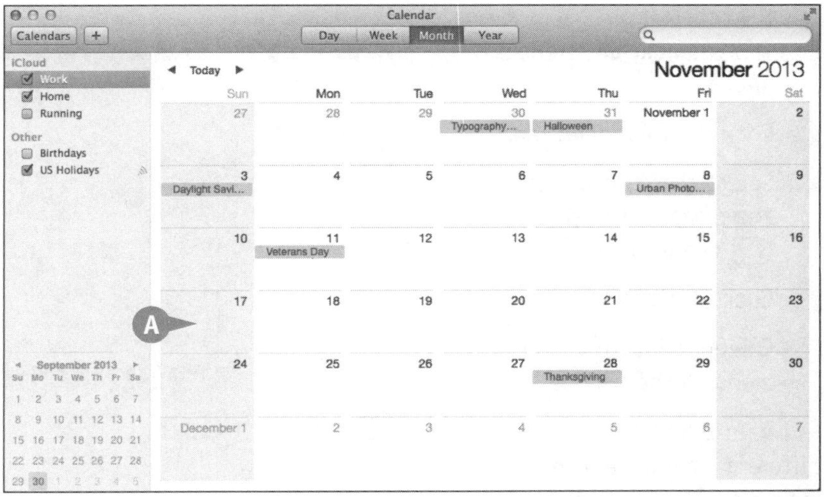

Note: If you are using calendars from multiple accounts, you can also disable an account to reduce calendar clutter. Click **Calendar**, click **Preferences**, click the **Accounts** tab, click the account, and then deselect the **Enable this account** option (☑ changes to ☐).

Enable Time Zones

You can schedule events that occur in a different time zone by enabling Calendar's time zone feature. Calendar assumes that all your events happen in your present time zone. This is a reasonable assumption because for most of us our appointments, meetings, and other events happen locally. If you travel, however, it is quite possible that you might need to schedule events that occur in a different time zone. To do this, you need to configure Calendar to work with different time zones.

Enable Time Zones

1. Click **Calendar**.
2. Click **Preferences**.

The Calendar preferences appear.

3. Click the **Advanced** tab.
4. Select the **Turn on time zone support** option (☐ changes to ☑).
5. Click **Close** (●).

Ⓐ Calendar adds the time zone menu to the window.

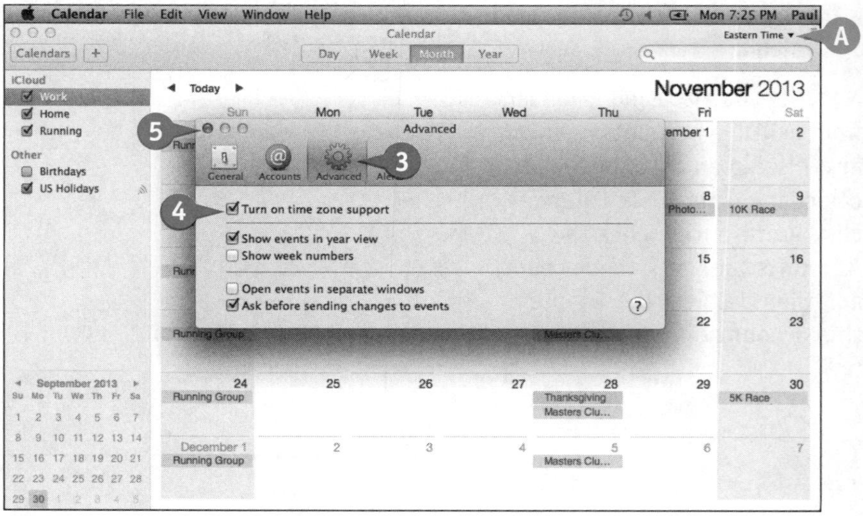

Note: To schedule an event in a different time zone, use the time zone menu to select the new time zone, and then schedule your event using the correct time in that zone.

Set Up a Default Alert

If you set up an alert for all or most of your events, you can save time and effort by configuring Calendar to assign a default alert to the events you create. This means you only have to modify the alert for those events where you do not require an alert or require a different alert.

Note that Calendar *does* use a default alert for both all-day events and birthdays. In both cases, the default alert appears the day before the event at 9 a.m. However, you can change these defaults if they are not suitable.

Set Up a Default Alert

1 Click **Calendar**.

2 Click **Preferences**.

The Calendar preferences appear.

3 Click the **Alerts** tab.

4 If you are using multiple accounts, click the **Account** and then click the account to configure.

5 Click the **Events** and then click the default alert time for your regular events.

6 Use these pop-up menus to modify the default alerts for all-day events and birthdays.

7 Click **Close** ( ).

Each time you create a new event, Calendar automatically sets the default alert.

CHAPTER 9

Connecting to Social Networks

In this age of ubiquitous social connection, your Mac Pro makes everything easier by enabling you to connect and post content to a number of social networks, including Facebook, Twitter, LinkedIn, Flickr, and Vimeo.

Sign In to Your Facebook Account

If you have a Facebook account, you can use it to share information with your friends directly from your Mac Pro because OS X has built-in support for Facebook accounts. This enables you to post status updates and other data directly from many OS X apps. For example, you can send a link to a web page from Safari or post a photo from Photo Booth. Mac Pro also displays notifications when your Facebook friends post to your News Feed. Before you can post or see Facebook notifications, you must sign in to your Facebook account.

Sign In to Your Facebook Account

1 Click **System Preferences** (⚙).

Note: You can also click the **Apple** icon () and then click **System Preferences.**

The System Preferences appear.

2 Click **Internet Accounts.**

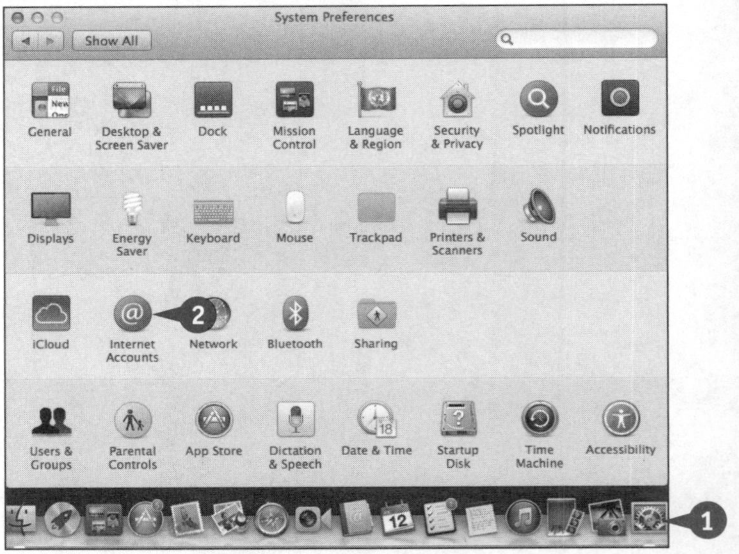

The Internet Accounts preferences appear.

3 Click **Facebook.**

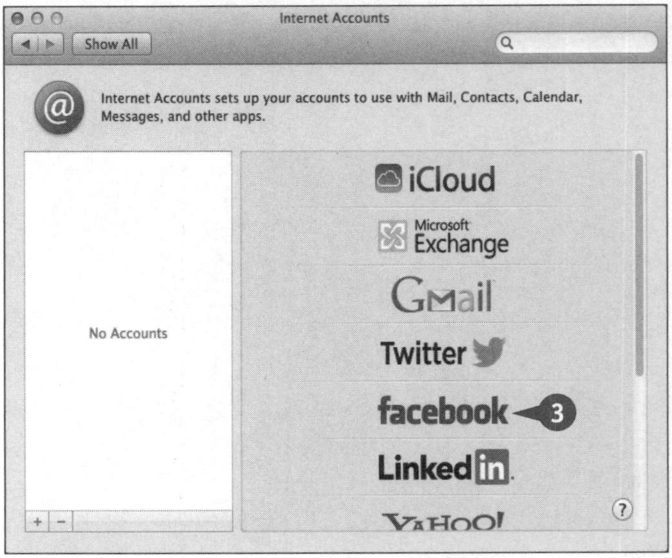

System Preferences prompts you for your Facebook username and password.

4. Type your Facebook username.
5. Type your Facebook password.
6. Click **Next.**

System Preferences displays information detailing what signing in to Facebook entails.

7. Click **Sign In.**

Mac Pro signs in to your Facebook account.

TIPS

Is there an easy way to add my Facebook friends' profile pictures to the Contacts app?

Yes. Follow steps 1 and 2 to open the Internet Accounts window, click your Facebook account, and then click **Get Profile Photos.** When System Preferences asks you to confirm, click **Update Contacts.**

Can I prevent Facebook friends and events from appearing in the Contacts and Calendar apps?

Yes. Follow steps 1 and 2 to open the Internet Accounts window and then click your Facebook account. If you do not want to clutter Contacts with all your Facebook friends, deselect the **Contacts** option (☑ changes to ☐). If you do not want your Facebook events or friends' birthdays to appear in Calendar, deselect the **Calendars** option (☑ changes to ☐).

Post to Facebook

Once you sign in to your Facebook account, you begin seeing notifications whenever your friends post to your News Feed. However, Mac Pro's Facebook support also enables you to use various OS X apps to post information to your Facebook News Feed. For example, if you surf to a web page that you want to share, you can post a link to that page. You can also post a photo to your News Feed.

Post to Facebook

Post a Web Page

1. Use Safari to navigate to the web page you want to share.
2. Click **Share** (icon).
3. Click **Facebook**.

Mac Pro displays the Facebook share sheet.

A. The web page appears as an attachment inside the post.

4. Type your post text.
5. Click **Post**.

Post a Photo

1. In Finder, open the folder that contains the photo you want to share.
2. Click the photo.
3. Click **Share** (📤).
4. Click **Facebook**.

Mac Pro displays the Facebook share sheet.

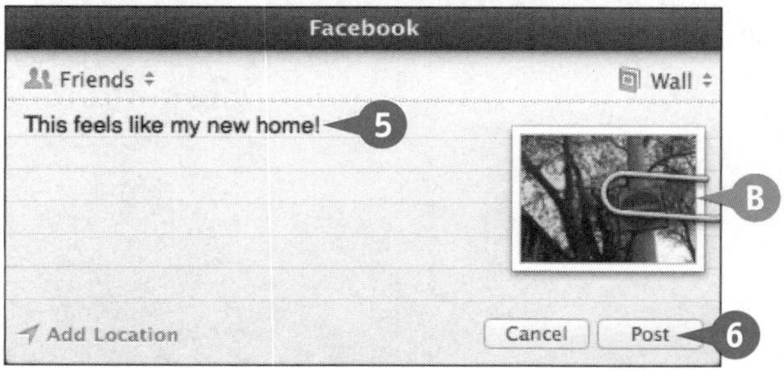

B The photo appears as an attachment inside the post.

5. Type some text to accompany the photo.
6. Click **Post**.

TIPS

How do I control who sees the links and photos that I post to Facebook?
In the Facebook share sheet, click **Friends** to open a pop-up menu that lists your sharing choices. This list includes your Facebook groups and three predefined choices: Public (anyone can view the post), Friends (only your Facebook friends can view the post), and Only Me (only you can view the post).

Can I add a location to my Facebook posts?
Yes, as long as you have location services enabled, as described in Chapter 19. The Facebook share sheet includes an Add Location link which, when clicked, inserts your current location. Note that when you first click **Add Location**, Mac Pro asks if Facebook is allowed to use your location, so be sure to click **OK**.

Publish an iPhoto Album to Facebook

If you have connected Mac Pro to your Facebook account, you can use that connection to publish a collection of iPhoto pictures to a new album in your Facebook profile. The easiest way to do this is to upload an album that you have created in iPhoto. However, you can also upload an iPhoto event, a selection of photos from the iPhoto library, or an item in the Faces or Places categories.

Publish an iPhoto Album to Facebook

1. In iPhoto, click the album you want to publish to Facebook.

   If you want to upload a different collection of photos, select the photos.

2. Click **Share**.
3. Click **Facebook**.

iPhoto displays the Facebook photo sharing options.

4 Click **New Album**.

iPhoto prompts you for the details of the new Facebook album.

5 Edit the album name.

6 Click the **Photos Viewable by** ⬍ and then click with whom you want to share the new album.

7 Click **Publish**.

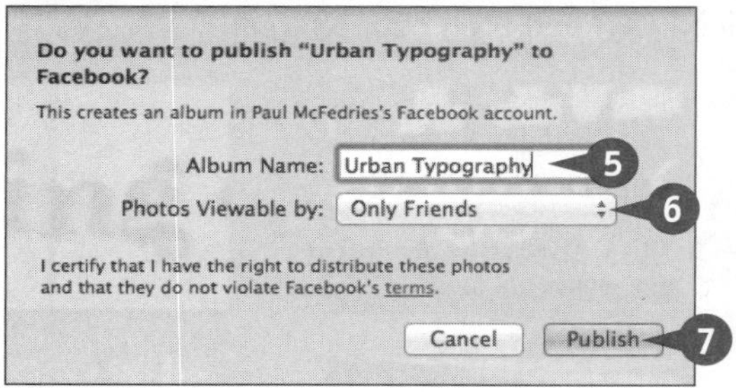

TIP

Can I upload a folder of photos as a Facebook album?

No, not directly. That is, you cannot do this from Finder. Instead, you need to import the folder into iPhoto and then publish the folder from iPhoto. In iPhoto, click **File** and then click **Import to Library** (or press Shift+⌘+I). In the Import Photos dialog, open the folder you want to use and then click **Import**. iPhoto imports the folder and adds it as a new event. Click **Events**, click the imported folder, and then upload the photos as a new Facebook album by following steps **2** to **7**.

Sign In to Your Twitter Account

If you have a Twitter account, you can use it to share information with your followers directly from Mac Pro, which comes with built-in support for Twitter. This enables you to send tweets directly from many OS X apps. For example, you can send a link to a web page from Safari or tweet a photo from Photo Booth. Mac Pro also displays notifications if you are mentioned on Twitter or if a Twitter user sends you a direct message. Before you can tweet or see Twitter notifications, you must sign in to your Twitter account.

Sign In to Your Twitter Account

1. Click **System Preferences** ( ).

Note: You can also click the **Apple** icon ( ) and then click **System Preferences.**

The System Preferences appear.

2. Click **Internet Accounts.**

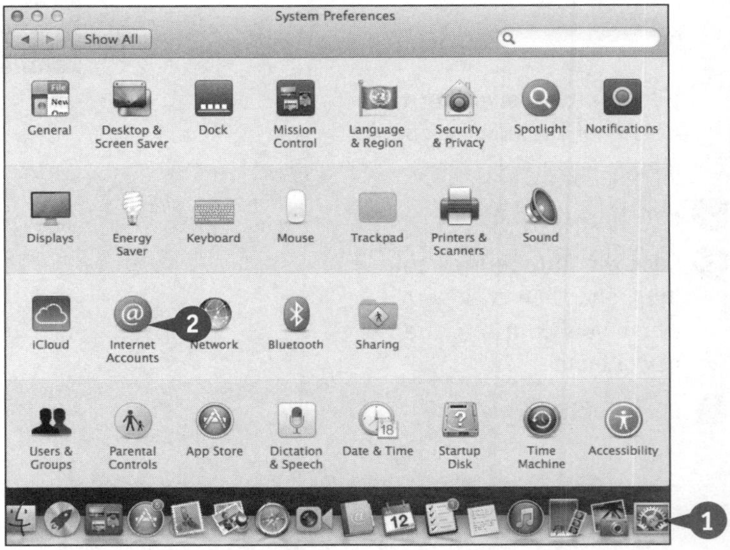

The Internet Accounts preferences appear.

3. Click **Twitter.**

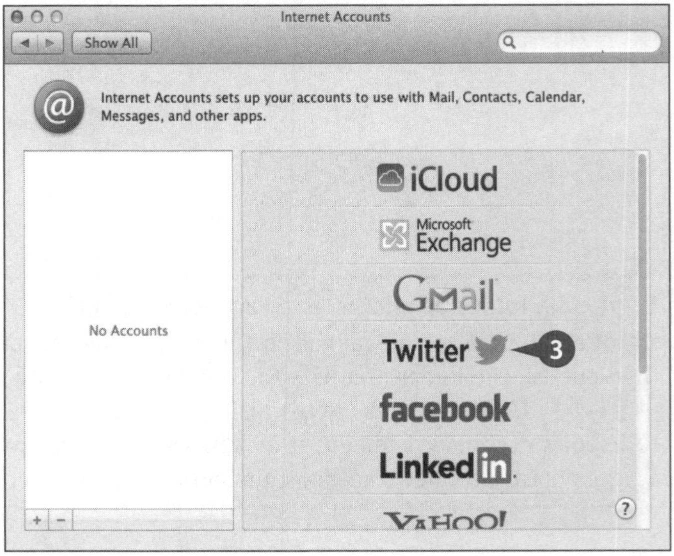

System Preferences prompts you for your Twitter username and password.

4. Type your Twitter username.
5. Type your Twitter password.
6. Click **Next**.

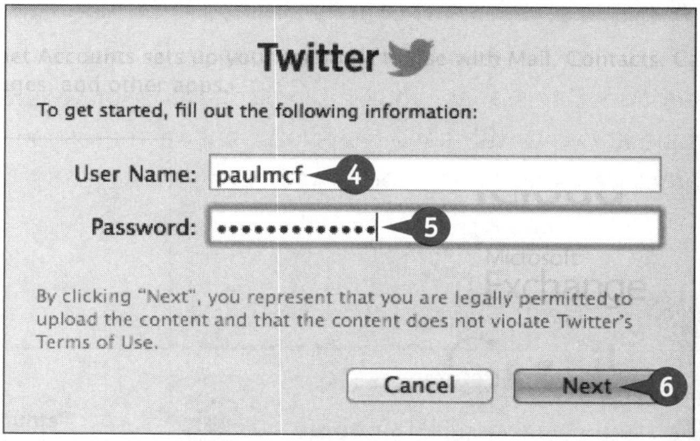

System Preferences displays information detailing what signing in to Twitter entails.

7. Click **Sign In**.

Mac Pro signs in to your Twitter account.

TIP

Some of the people in my contacts list are on Twitter. Is there an easy way to add their Twitter usernames to the Contacts app?

Yes, Mac Pro has a feature that enables you to give permission for Twitter to update your contacts. Twitter examines the e-mail addresses in the Contacts app, and if it finds any that match Twitter users, it updates Contacts with each person's username and account photo.

Follow steps 1 and 2 to open the Internet Accounts window, click your Twitter account, and then click **Update Contacts**. When Mac Pro asks you to confirm, click **Update Contacts**.

Send a Tweet

After you sign in to your Twitter account, you can send tweets from various OS X apps. Although signing in to your Twitter account is useful for seeing notifications that tell you about mentions and direct messages, you will mostly use it for sending tweets to your followers. For example, if you come across a web page that you want to share, you can tweet a link to that page. You can also take a picture using Photo Booth and tweet that picture to your followers.

Send a Tweet

Tweet a Web Page

1. Use Safari to navigate to the web page you want to share.
2. Click **Share** ( ).
3. Click **Twitter**.

Mac Pro displays the Tweet share sheet.

A The attachment appears as a link inside the tweet.

4. Type your tweet text.

B This value tells you how many characters you have remaining.

5. Click **Send**.

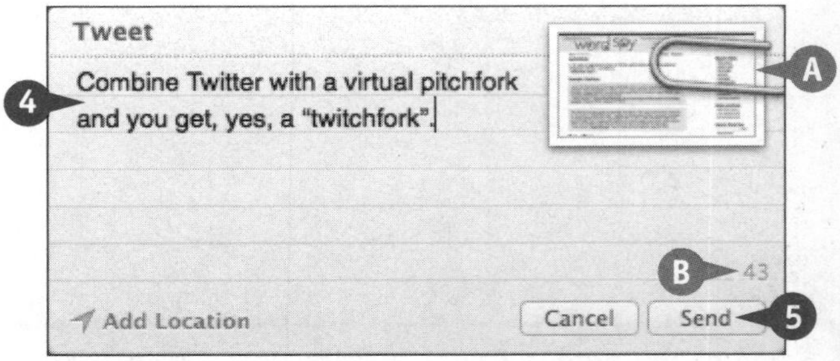

Tweet a Photo Booth Photo

1. Use Photo Booth to take a picture.

Note: For more about taking a picture with Photo Booth, see Chapter 12.

2. Click the picture you want to share.
3. Click **Share** (⎘).
4. Click **Twitter**.

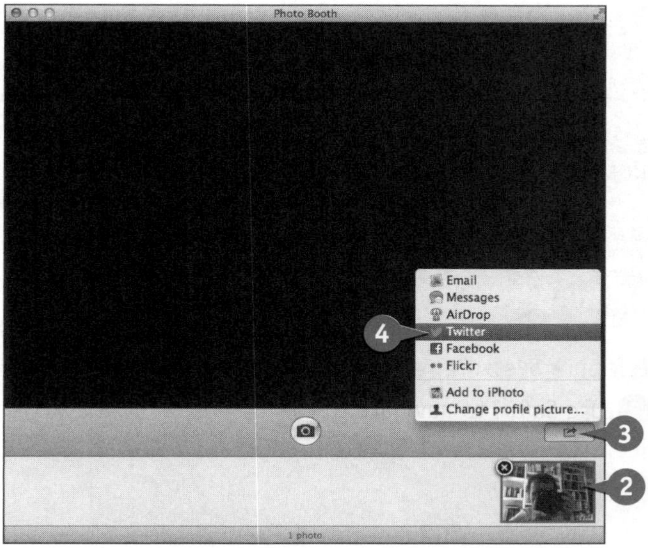

Mac Pro displays the Twitter share sheet.

- **C** The attachment appears as a link inside the tweet.

5. Type your tweet text.

- **D** This value tells you how many characters you have remaining.

6. Click **Send**.

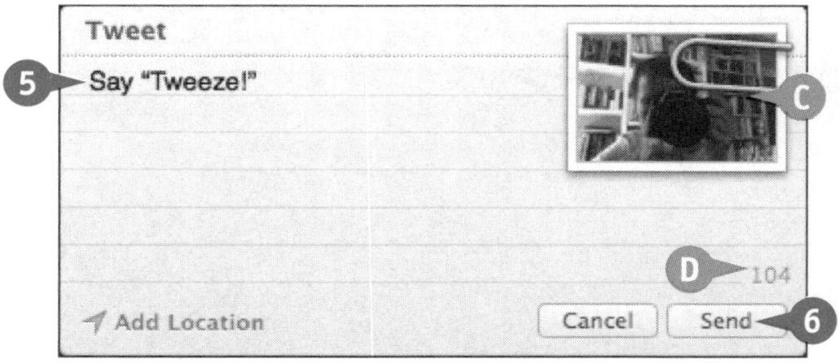

TIPS

Are there other apps I can use to send tweets?
Yes. If you open a photo using Quick Look (click the photo in Finder and then press Spacebar), you can click **Share** (⎘) and then click **Twitter**. Similarly, you can open a photo in Preview, click **Share** (⎘), and then click **Twitter**. Also, with your permission, many third-party apps are able to use your sign-in information to send tweets from the apps without requiring separate Twitter logins for each program.

Can I add a location to my tweets?
Yes, but you must enable location services on Mac Pro, as described in Chapter 19. In the Tweet share sheet, click **Add Location** to insert your current location.

Connect to Your LinkedIn Account

You can use your LinkedIn account to share information with your connections directly from Mac Pro, as OS X comes with built-in support for LinkedIn. This enables you to use Safari to send web page links to your connections and to display the links that your connections share. Mac Pro also displays notifications if one of your connections endorses you or sends you a message. Before you can post updates or see LinkedIn notifications, you must sign in to your LinkedIn account.

Connect to Your LinkedIn Account

1. Click **System Preferences** ( ).

Note: You can also click the **Apple** icon ( ) and then click **System Preferences.**

The System Preferences appear.

2. Click **Internet Accounts.**

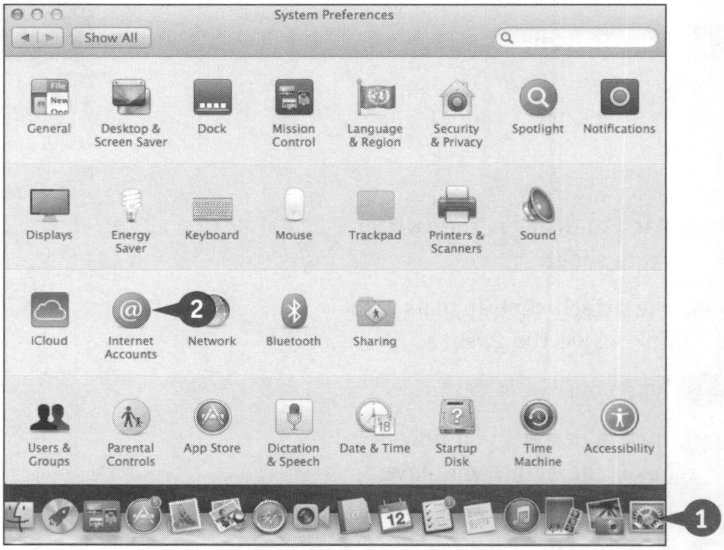

The Internet Accounts preferences appear.

3. Click **LinkedIn.**

System Preferences prompts you for your LinkedIn username and password.

4 Type your LinkedIn username.

5 Type your LinkedIn password.

6 Click **Next**.

System Preferences displays information detailing what signing in to LinkedIn entails.

7 Click **Sign In**.

Mac Pro signs in to your LinkedIn account.

TIPS

Is there an easy way to add my LinkedIn connections' profile pictures to the Contacts app?

Yes. Follow steps **1** and **2** to open the Internet Accounts window, click your LinkedIn account, and then click **Get Profile Photos**. When System Preferences asks you to confirm, click **Update Contacts**.

Can I prevent my LinkedIn connections from appearing in the Contacts app?

Yes. Follow steps **1** and **2** to open the Internet Accounts window and then click your LinkedIn account. To remove your LinkedIn connections from the Contacts app, deselect the **Contacts** option (☑ changes to ☐).

Post to LinkedIn

After you sign in to your LinkedIn account in Mac Pro, you can send updates to your connections. Although signing in to your LinkedIn account is useful for seeing notifications that tell you about endorsements and other messages, you will mostly use it for sending updates to your followers. For example, if you come across a web page that you want to share, you can post a link to that page. You can share the link with just your connections or with the entire LinkedIn community.

Post to LinkedIn

1. Use Safari to navigate to the web page you want to share.

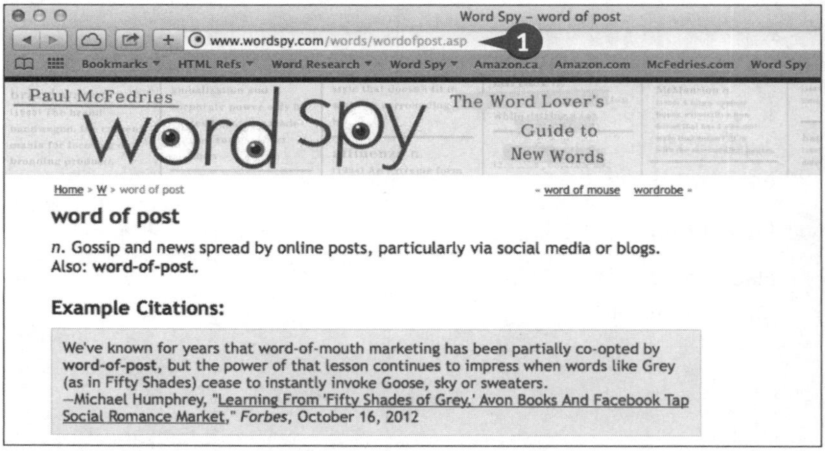

2. Click **Share** (📤).
3. Click **LinkedIn**.

Mac Pro displays the LinkedIn share sheet.

A The attachment appears as a link inside the post.

4 Type your update text.

5 Click **Send**.

Mac Pro sends the update to LinkedIn.

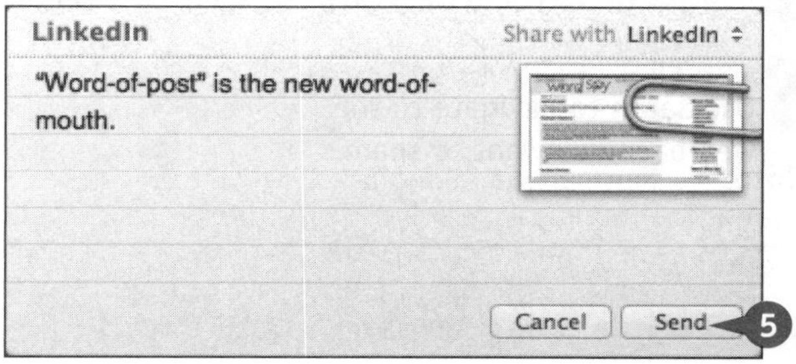

TIPS

How do I control who sees the updates that I post to LinkedIn?
In the LinkedIn share sheet, click the **Share With** ⬍ in the upper right corner and then click either **LinkedIn** (all of LinkedIn can view the update) or **Connections** (only your LinkedIn connections can view the post).

Are there other apps I can use to send updates?
None of the other default OS X apps support LinkedIn. However, with your permission, many third-party apps are able to use your sign-in information to send updates from the apps without requiring separate LinkedIn logins for each program.

Update Your Social Network Profile Picture

You can use your Mac Pro social network connections to easily and quickly update the profile picture for one or more of your accounts. All supported social networks identify you with a photo, which is part of your account profile. Updating this picture for just a single social network is usually a convoluted task, and it is only made worse if you want to use the same photo across multiple social networks. Your Mac Pro enables you to take a single Photo Booth picture and use it to update your profile picture for Facebook, Twitter, and LinkedIn.

Update Your Social Network Profile Picture

1 Use Photo Booth to take a picture.

Note: For more about taking a picture with Photo Booth, see Chapter 12.

2 Click the picture you want to use.

3 Click **Share** (📤).

4 Click **Change profile picture**.

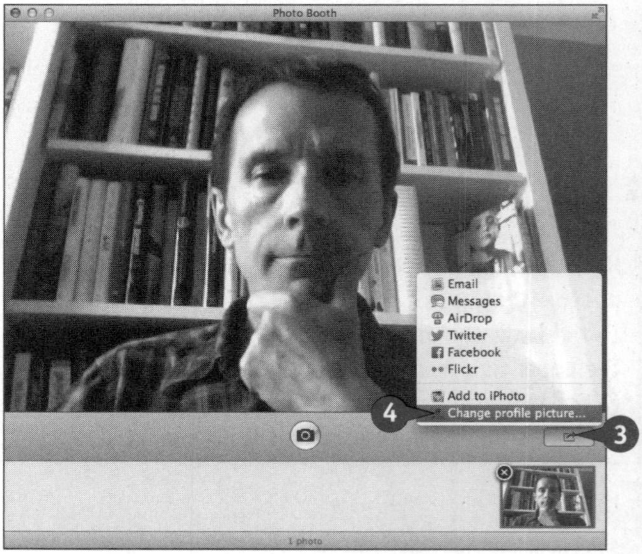

5. Drag the photo to the position you want.
6. Use this slider to set the magnification you want.

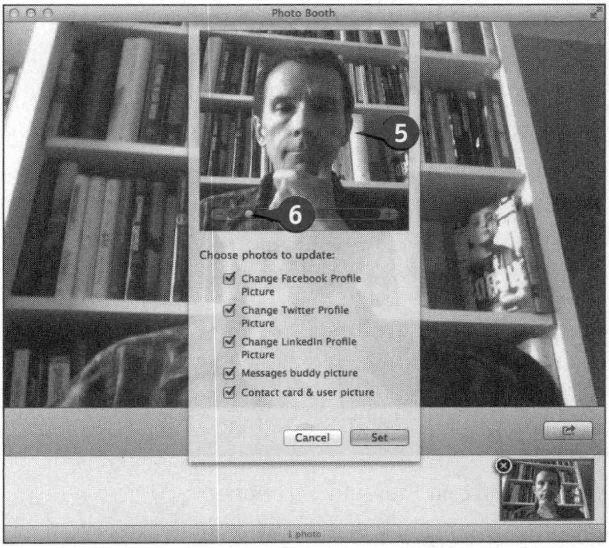

Photo Booth asks which profile you want to update.

7. Deselect the profile pictures you do not want to update (☑ changes to ☐).
8. Click **Set**.

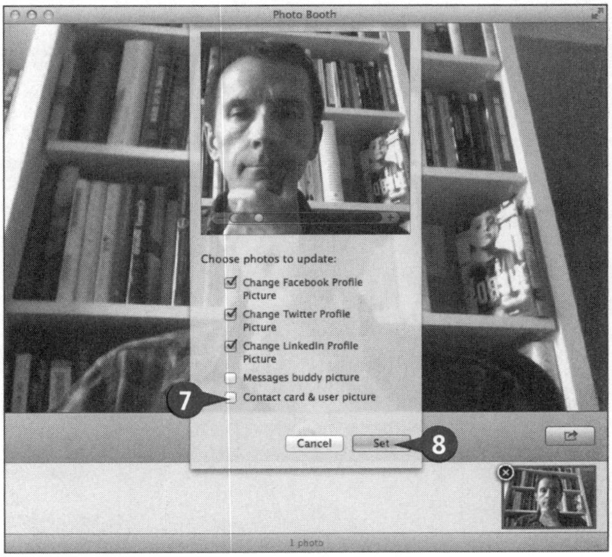

TIP

Can I update my Facebook profile picture from iPhoto?

Yes. In iPhoto, click the photo you want to use for your Facebook profile picture, click **Share**, and then click **Facebook.** The first time you do this, you see the Login to Facebook dialog. Type your Facebook e-mail address and password, select the **I agree to Facebook's terms** option (☐ changes to ☑), and then click **Login**. The Facebook Albums dialog appears. Click **Profile Picture** and when iPhoto asks you to confirm, click **Set.** iPhoto updates your Facebook profile picture.

Connect to Your Flickr Account

Tens of millions of people use Flickr to share their photos with the world. If you have a Flickr account, you can use it to share photos directly from Mac Pro, which comes with built-in support for Flickr. This enables you to send photos from many OS X apps, including Finder, Preview, iPhoto, and Photo Booth. Before you can send photos, you must sign in to your Flickr account.

Connect to Your Flickr Account

1. Click **System Preferences** (⚙).

Note: You can also click the **Apple** icon () and then click **System Preferences**.

The System Preferences appear.

2. Click **Internet Accounts.**

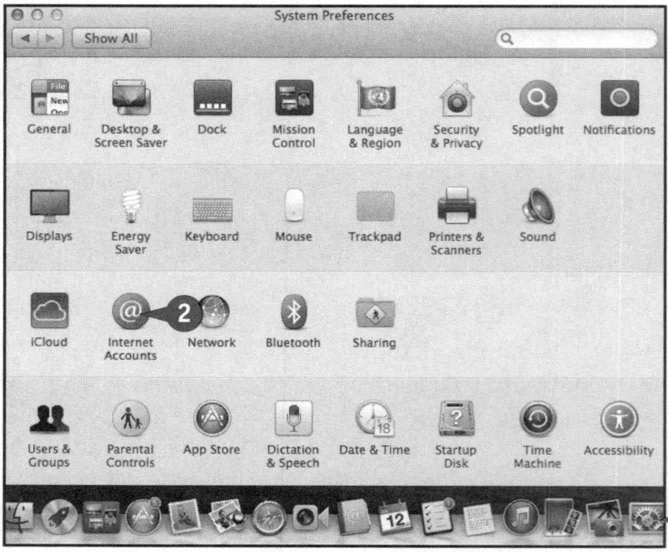

The Internet Accounts preferences appear.

3. Click **Flickr.**

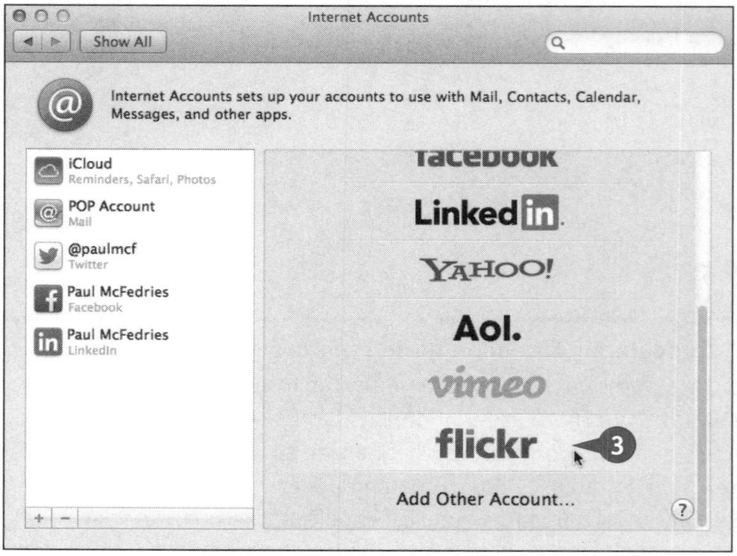

System Preferences prompts you for your Yahoo! ID and password.

4 Type your Yahoo! ID.

Note: Your Yahoo! ID is the e-mail address associated with your Yahoo! account.

5 Type your Flickr password.

6 Click **Sign In**.

Mac Pro signs in to your Flickr account.

TIP

Can I temporarily disable my Flickr account?

Yes. This is a useful technique if you know you will not be using your Flickr account for a while, because it reduces clutter in the Mac Pro sharing menus. To disable Flickr, follow steps 1 and 2 to open the Internet Accounts window. Click your Flickr account and then deselect the **Enable This Account** option (☑ changes to ☐). Note that you can also use this technique to disable your Facebook, LinkedIn, and Vimeo accounts, if needed.

Send Photos to Flickr

Flickr is all about sharing your photos, so once you have connected your Mac Pro to your Flickr account, you can begin using that connection to upload photos. You have two ways to publish photos from Mac Pro to Flickr. First, you can upload individual photos to Flickr, and those photos appear as part of your Flickr Photostream. You can upload single photos using Finder, Preview, or Photo Booth. Second, you can upload an iPhoto event or album to Flickr, and you designate those photos as a new Flickr set.

Send Photos to Flickr

Send One Photo

1. In Finder, Preview, or Photo Booth, select the photo you want to upload.
2. Click **Share** (share icon).
3. Click **Flickr**.

Mac Pro displays the Flickr share sheet.

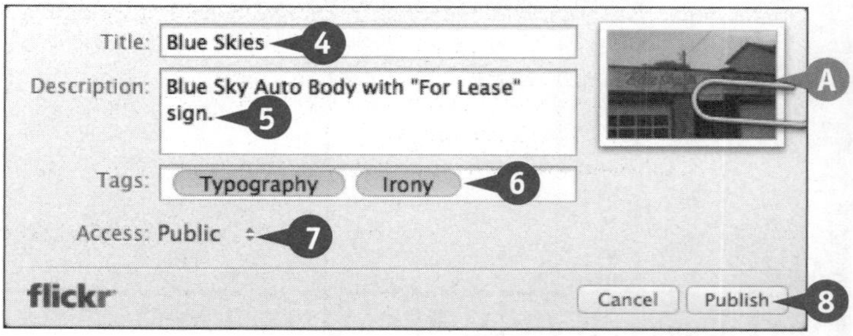

A. The attachment appears as a link inside the post.

4. Type a title.
5. Type a description.
6. Type one or more tags, separating each with a comma.
7. Click the **Access** (pop-up arrows) and then click who can see the photo.
8. Click **Publish**.

Mac Pro sends the photo to your Flickr Photostream.

Send an iPhoto Event or Album

Note: Before uploading, you must give iPhoto permission to access your Flickr account. See the tip in this section.

1. In iPhoto, click the event or album you want to publish to Flickr.
2. Click **Share**.
3. Click **Flickr**.

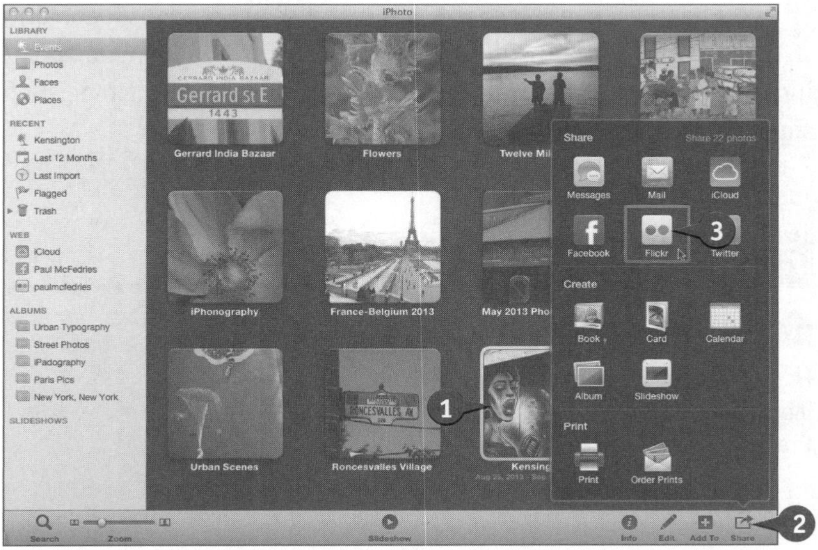

iPhoto displays the Flickr photo sharing options.

4. Click **New Set**.

   iPhoto prompts you for the details of the new Flickr set.

5. Edit the set name.
6. Click the **Photos Viewable by** ⬍ and then click with whom you want to share the new album.
7. Click the **Photo size** ⬍ and then click the size you want to use.
8. Click **Publish**.

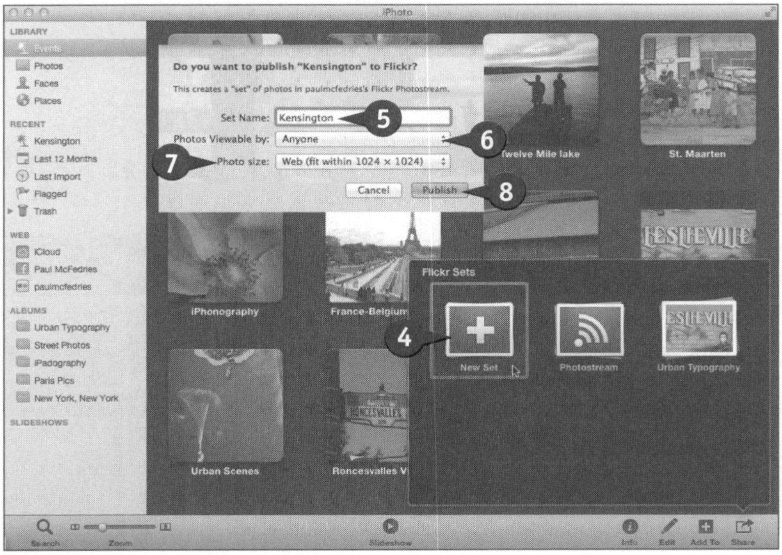

TIP

How do I give iPhoto permission to access my Flickr account?

When you click **Share** and then click **Flickr** for the first time, you run through the following procedure to authorize iPhoto: Click **Set Up** to launch Safari, which prompts you to log in to Flickr. Type your Flickr e-mail address and password and then click **Sign In**. Click **Next** under the text that reads "If you arrived at this page because you specifically asked iPhoto to connect to your Flick account." Click **OK, I'll Authorize It**.

Set Up Your Vimeo Account

If you have a Vimeo account, you can use it to post videos online directly from Mac Pro, which comes with built-in support for Vimeo. This enables you to send videos from many OS X apps, including Finder, QuickTime Player, Photo Booth, and iMovie. Before you can send videos, you must sign in to your Vimeo account.

Set Up Your Vimeo Account

1 Click **System Preferences** ( ).

Note: You can also click the **Apple** icon ( ) and then click **System Preferences.**

The System Preferences appear.

2 Click **Internet Accounts.**

The Internet Accounts preferences appear.

3 Click **Vimeo.**

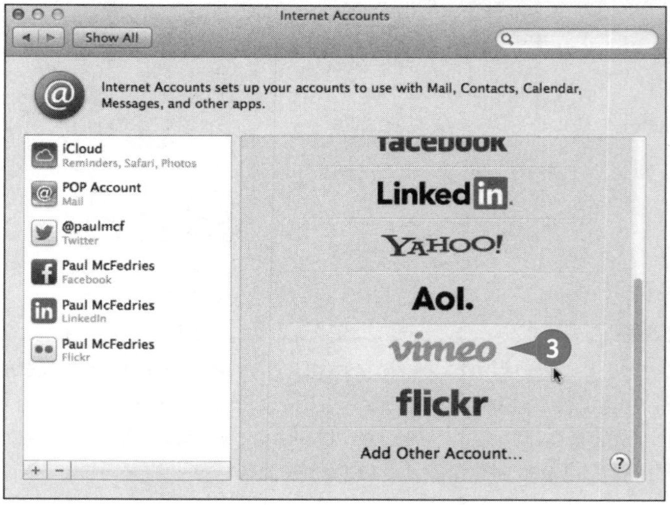

System Preferences prompts you for your Vimeo login data.

4 Type the e-mail address associated with your Vimeo account.

5 Type your Vimeo password.

6 Click **Sign In**.

Mac Pro signs in to your Vimeo account.

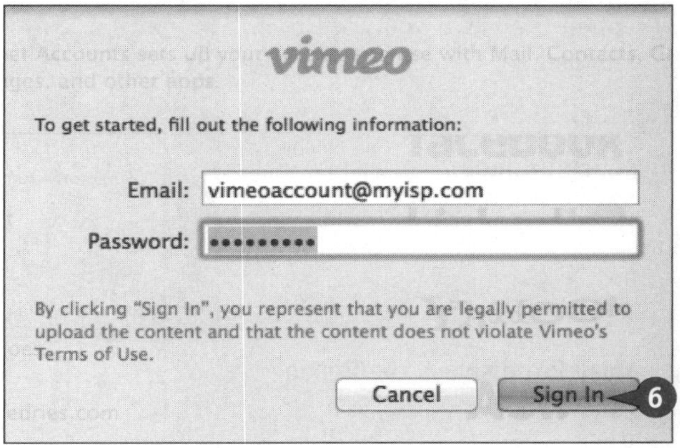

TIP

How do I delete my Vimeo account?

If you no longer use your Vimeo account, you should delete it from Mac Pro. This not only reduces clutter in the OS X sharing menus, but also makes the Internet Accounts window easier to navigate.

To delete your Vimeo account, follow steps **1** and **2** to open the Internet Accounts window. Click your Vimeo account and then click **Remove** (−). When Mac Pro asks you to confirm, click **OK**. Note that you can also use this technique to delete any other account that you no longer use.

Send a Video to Vimeo

Vimeo is one of the web's most popular video-sharing services, so once you have connected your Mac Pro to your Vimeo account, you can begin using that connection to upload videos. You have two ways to publish photos from Mac Pro to Vimeo. First, you can use an OS X share sheet to upload a video to Vimeo using Finder, QuickTime Player, or Photo Booth. Second, you can upload a video to Vimeo from an iMovie project, which gives you many more options for publishing the video.

Send a Video to Vimeo

Send a Video Using a Share Sheet

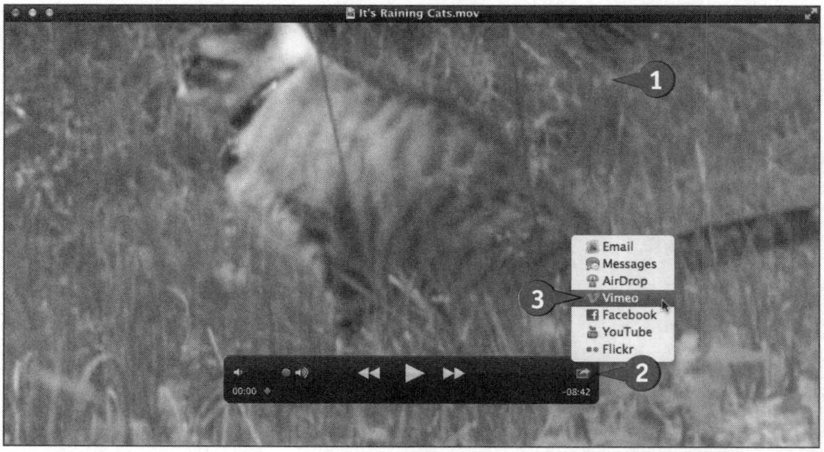

1. In Finder, QuickTime Player, or Photo Booth, select or open the video you want to upload.
2. Click **Share** (📤).
3. Click **Vimeo**.

Mac Pro displays the Vimeo share sheet.

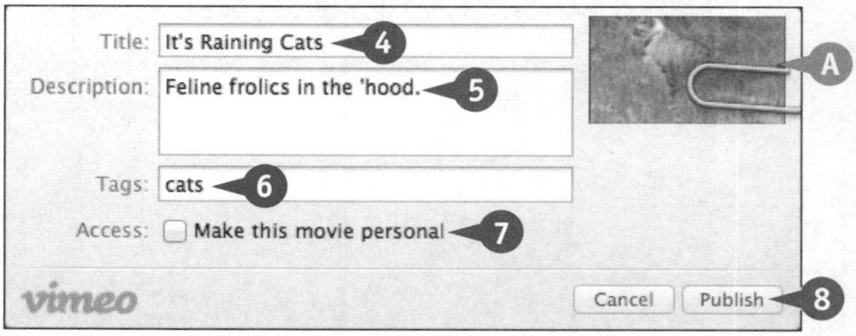

Ⓐ The attachment appears as a link inside the post.

4. Type a title.
5. Type a description.
6. Type one or more tags, separating each with a comma.
7. If you want anyone to be able to view the video, deselect the **Make this movie personal** option (☑ changes to ☐).
8. Click **Publish**.

Mac Pro sends the video to your Vimeo account.

Send a Video from an iMovie Project

Note: Before uploading, you must add your Vimeo account to iMovie. See the tip in this section.

1. In iMovie, open the project you want to publish to Vimeo.
2. Click **Share.**
3. Click **Vimeo.**

iMovie displays the Vimeo dialog.

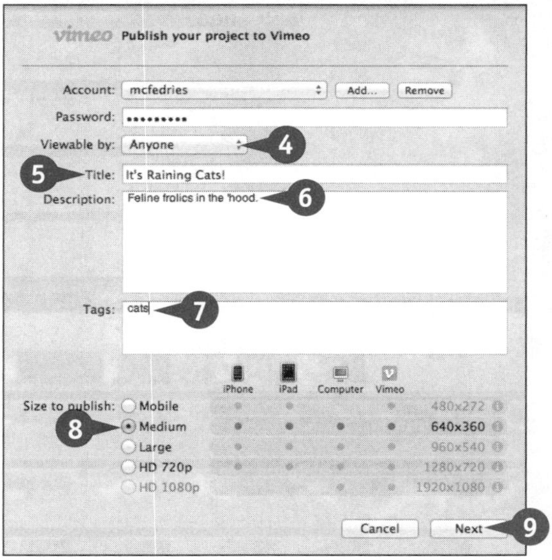

4. Click the **Viewable by** ⬍ and then click with whom you want to share the video.
5. Type a title.
6. Type a description.
7. Type one or more tags, separating each with a comma.
8. Select the movie size you want to use (○ changes to ◉).
9. Click **Next.**

   iMovie displays the Vimeo terms of service.

10. Click **Publish** (not shown).

    iMovie uploads the video.

TIP

How do I add my Vimeo account to iMovie?

In iMovie, when you click **Share** and then click **Vimeo** for the first time, you run through the following procedure to add your Vimeo account: Click **Add** to display the Add Account dialog. Type your Vimeo e-mail address and then click **Done**. iMovie returns you to the Vimeo dialog. Type your Vimeo password. The next time you click **Share** and then **Vimeo**, iMovie enters your Vimeo username and password automatically.

Share Information with Other People

You can use Mac Pro to share information with other people, including web pages, notes, pictures, videos, and photos. OS X Mavericks was built with sharing in mind. In earlier versions of OS X, it was often difficult or tedious to share information such as web pages, images, and videos. OS X Mavericks comes with a feature called the *share sheet*, which makes it easy to share data using multiple methods, such as e-mail and instant messaging, as well as Facebook and Twitter.

Share Information with Other People

Share a Web Page

1. Use Safari to navigate to the web page you want to share.
2. Click **Share** ( ).
3. Click the method you want to use to share the web page.

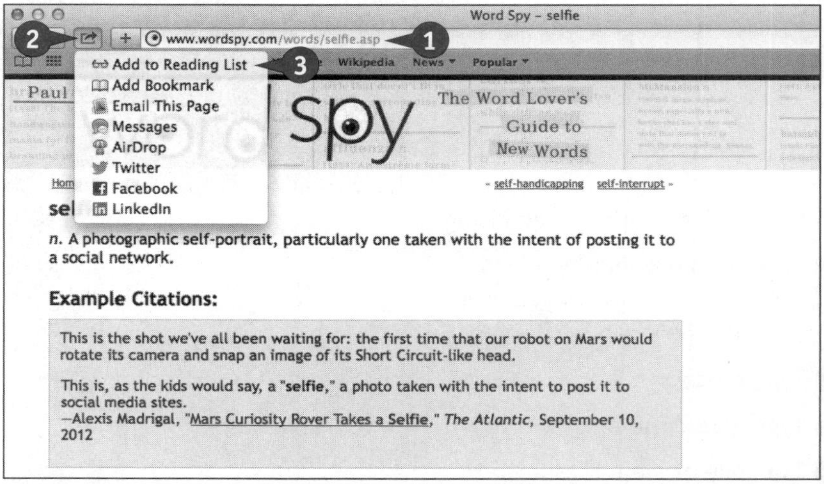

Share a Note

1. In the Notes app, click the note you want to share.
2. Click **Share** ( ).
3. Click the method you want to use to share the note.

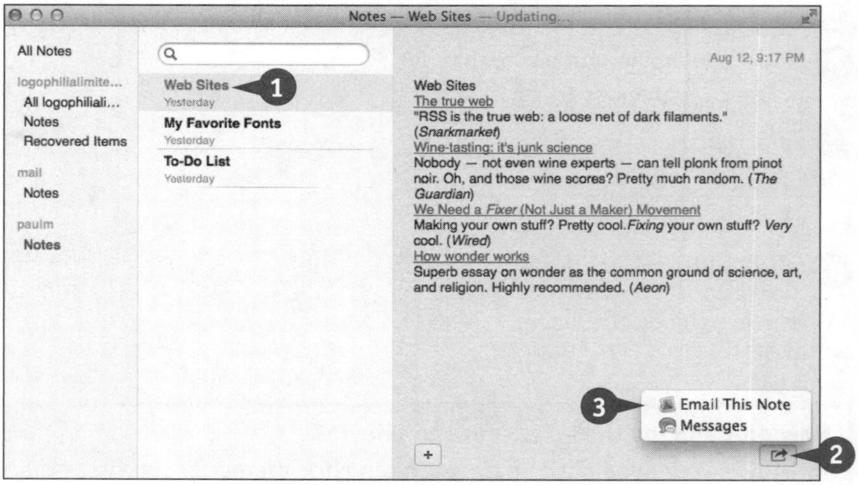

Share an iPhoto Picture

1. In iPhoto, click the picture you want to share.
2. Click **Share**.
3. Click the method you want to use to share the picture.

Share a Video

1. In QuickTime Player, open the video you want to share.
2. Click **Share** ( ).
3. Click the method you want to use to share the video.

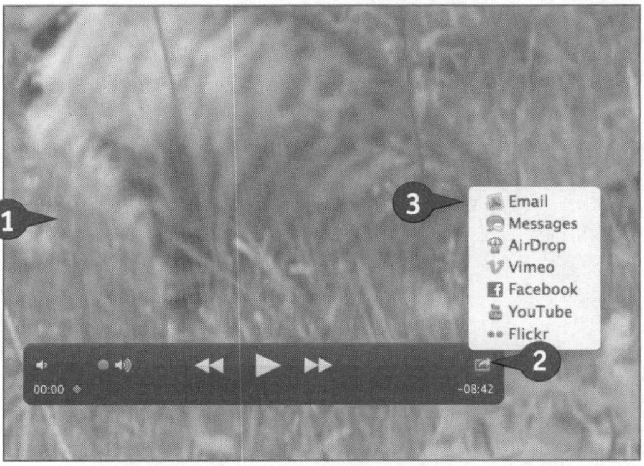

Share a Photo Booth Picture

1. Use Photo Booth to take a picture.

Note: For more about taking a picture with Photo Booth, see Chapter 12.

2. Click the photo.
3. Click **Share** ( ).
4. Click the method you want to use to share the photo.

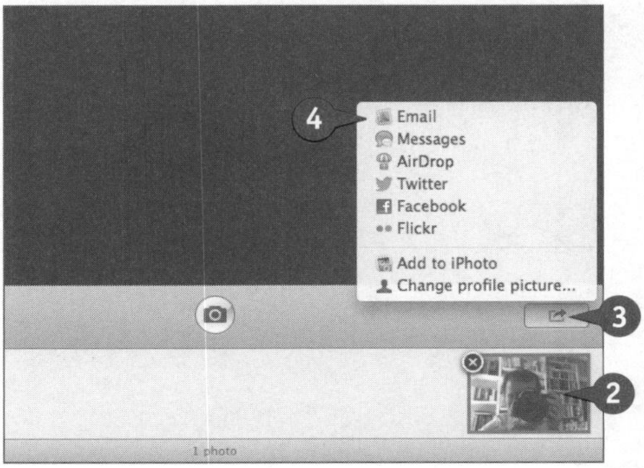

TIP

Do I need to configure Mac Pro to use some of the sharing methods?
Yes. You cannot use the Email method unless you configure Mail with an e-mail account, and you cannot use the Message method until you configure Messages with an account. Social networks must be configured in System Preferences, as described in various sections of this chapter.

CHAPTER 10

Learning Useful Mac Pro Tasks

Mac Pro comes with many tools that help you accomplish everyday tasks. In this chapter, you learn how to synchronize an iPod, iPhone, or iPad; create notes and reminders; and work with notifications, tags, maps, fonts, and e-books.

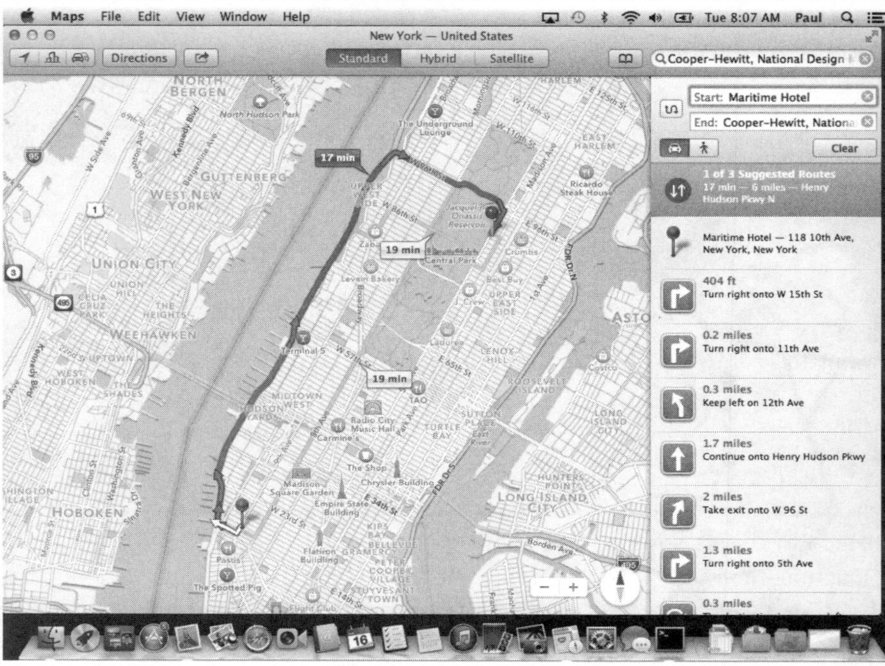

Synchronize an iPod, iPhone, or iPad

You can take your media and other data with you by synchronizing that data from Mac Pro to your iPod touch, iPhone, or iPad. However, you should synchronize movies and TV shows with care. A single half-hour TV episode may be as large as 650MB, and full-length movies can be several gigabytes, so even a modest video collection will consume a lot of storage space on your device.

To synchronize your device, first connect it to your Mac Pro and then click the device when it appears in the iTunes navigation bar, to the left of the iTunes Store button.

Synchronize an iPod, iPhone, or iPad

Synchronize Music

1. Click **Music**.
2. Select the **Sync Music** option (☐ changes to ☑).
3. Select the **Selected playlists, artists, albums, and genres** option (○ changes to ◉).
4. Select each item you want to synchronize (☐ changes to ☑).
5. Click **Apply** to synchronize your music.
6. If you have finished syncing your device, click **Done**.

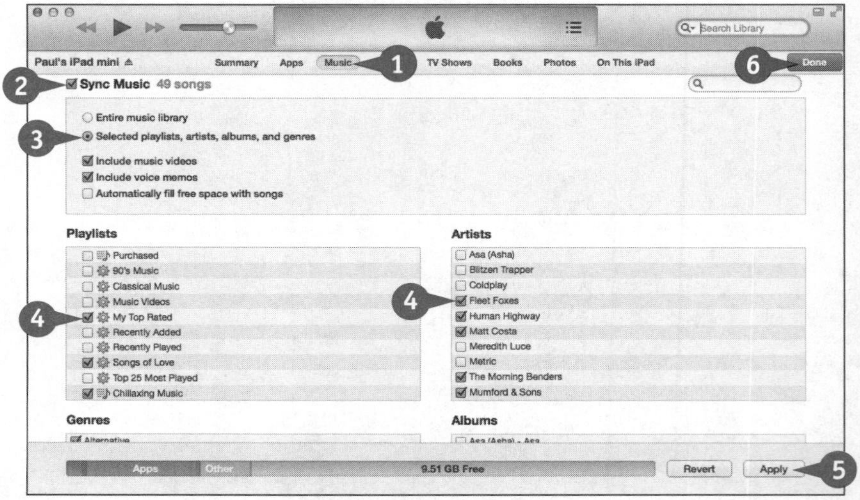

Synchronize Photos

1. Click **Photos**.
2. Select the **Sync Photos from** option (☐ changes to ☑).
3. Select the **Selected albums, Events, and Faces, and automatically include** option (○ changes to ◉).
4. Select each item you want to synchronize (☐ changes to ☑).
5. Click **Apply** to synchronize your photos.
6. If you have finished syncing your device, click **Done**.

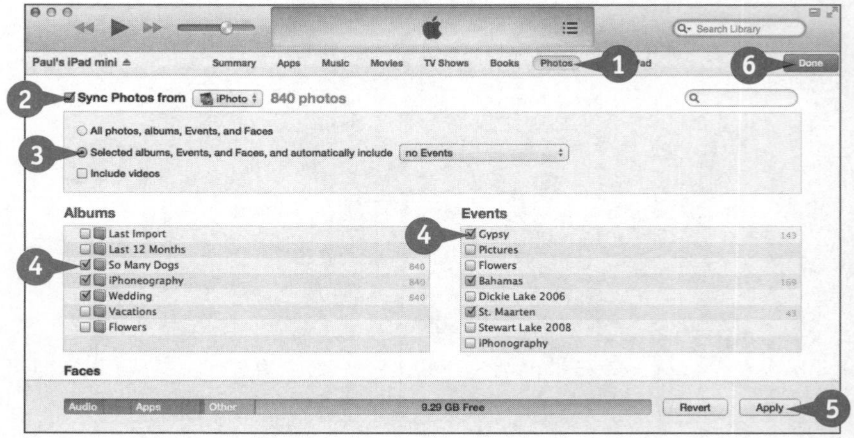

Synchronize Movies

1. Click **Movies.**
2. Select the **Sync Movies** option (☐ changes to ☑).
3. Select each movie you want to synchronize (☐ changes to ☑).
4. Click **Apply** to synchronize your movies.
5. If you have finished syncing your device, click **Done.**

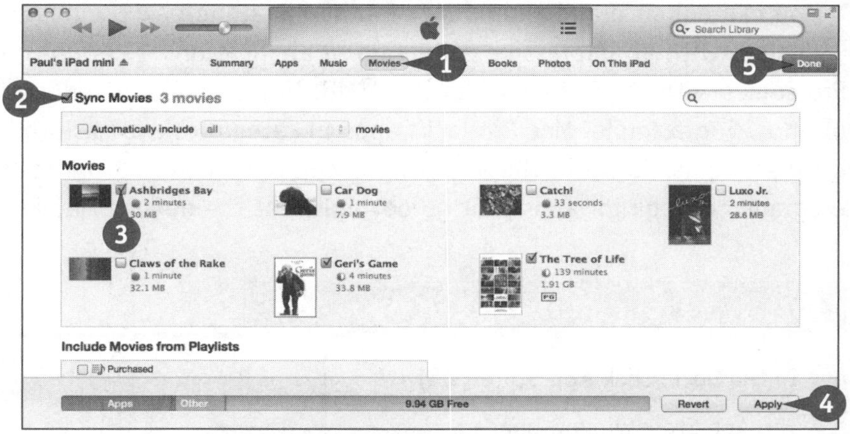

Synchronize TV Shows

1. Click **TV Shows**.
2. Select the **Sync TV Shows** option (☐ changes to ☑).
3. Select each TV show you want to synchronize (☐ changes to ☑).
4. Click **Apply** to synchronize your TV shows.
5. If you have finished syncing your device, click **Done.**

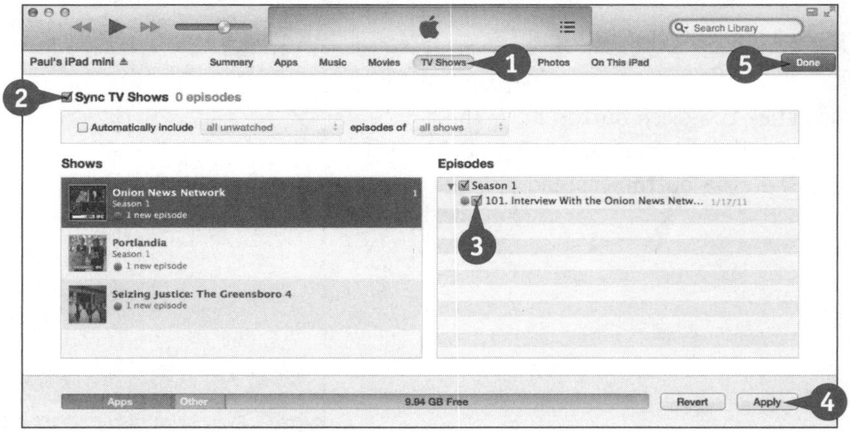

TIPS

Can I sync wirelessly?

Yes. Connect your device and select it in iTunes, click the **Summary** tab, and then select the **Sync with this *device* over Wi-Fi** option, where *device* is iPhone, iPad, or iPod touch (☐ changes to ☑). To sync over Wi-Fi, on your device tap **Settings**, tap **General**, tap **iTunes Wi-Fi Sync**, and then tap **Sync Now**.

How do I get my photos from my device to my Mac Pro?

You can view and work with device pictures on your Mac Pro by importing them into iPhoto. In iPhoto, click your device, press and hold ⌘, and then click each photo you want to import. Use the Event Name text box to type a name for this event and then click **Import Selected**.

Install a Program Using the App Store

You can enhance and extend Mac Pro by installing new programs from the App Store. Mac Pro comes with an impressive collection of applications — or *apps* — particularly because your Mac Pro comes with the iLife suite preinstalled. However, Mac Pro does not offer a complete collection of apps. For example, Mac Pro lacks apps in categories such as productivity, personal finance, and business tools. To fill in these gaps, you can use the App Store to locate, purchase, and install new programs, or look for apps that go beyond what the default Mac Pro programs can do.

Install a Program Using the App Store

1. In the Dock, click **App Store** (App Store icon).

   The App Store window appears.

2. Locate the app you want to install.

3. Click the price button or, if the app is free, as shown here, click the **Free** button instead.

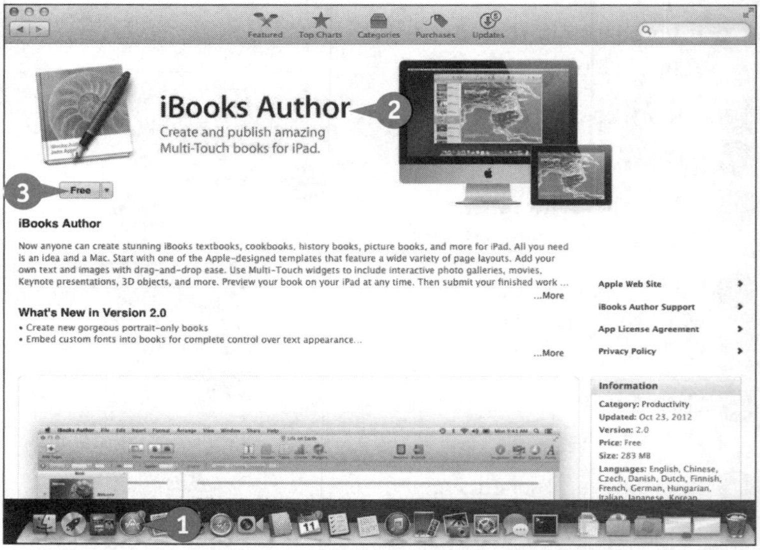

The price button changes to a Buy App button, or the Free button changes to an Install App button.

4. Click **Buy App** (or **Install App**).

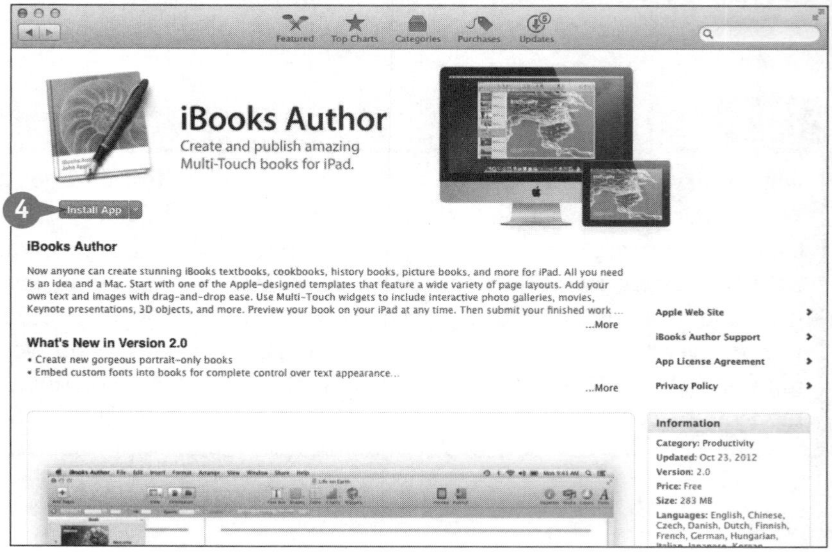

The App Store prompts you to log in with your Apple ID.

5. Type your Apple ID.
6. Type your password.
7. Click **Sign In**.

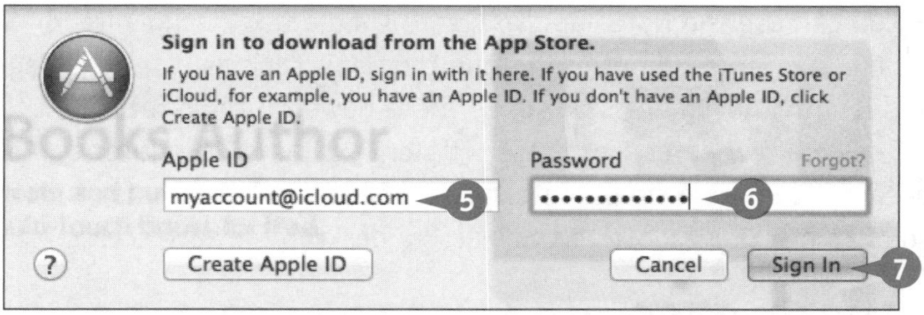

Ⓐ The App Store begins downloading the app.

When the progress meter disappears, your app is installed. Click **Launchpad** (🚀) and then click the app to run it.

TIP

How do I use an App Store gift card to purchase apps?

If you have an App Store or iTunes gift card, you can redeem the card to give yourself store credit in the amount shown on the card. Scratch off the sticker on the back to reveal the code. Click (App Store icon) to open the App Store, click **Featured**, click **Redeem**, type the code, and then click **Redeem**. In the App Store window, the Account item shows your current store credit balance.

Write a Note

You can use the Notes app to create simple text documents for things such as to-do lists and meeting notes. Word processing programs such as Word and Pages are useful for creating complex and lengthy documents. However, these powerful tools feel like overkill when all you want to do is jot down a few notes. For these simpler text tasks, the Notes app that comes with Mac Pro is perfect because it offers a simple interface that keeps all your notes together. As you see in the next section, you can also pin a note to the Mac Pro desktop for easy access.

Write a Note

Create a New Note

1. In the Dock, click **Notes** (icon).

The Notes window appears.

2. Click **New Note** (+).

Note: You can also click **File** and then click **New Note**, or press ⌘+N.

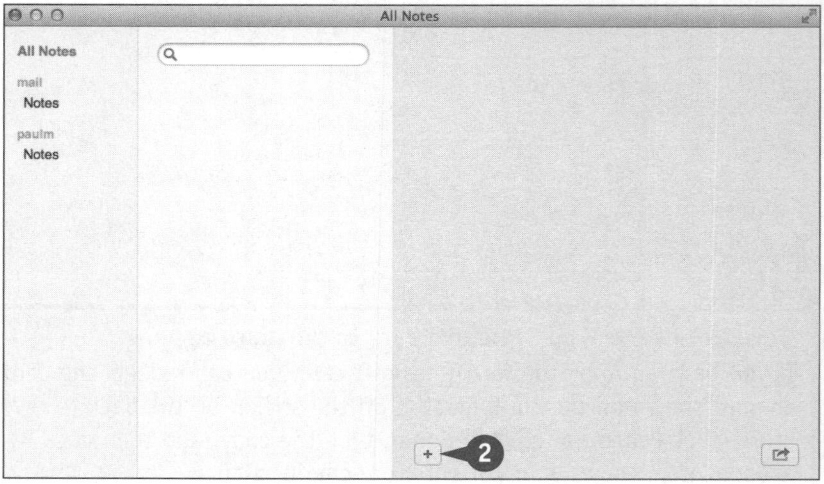

Ⓐ The Notes app creates the new note.

3 Type your note text.

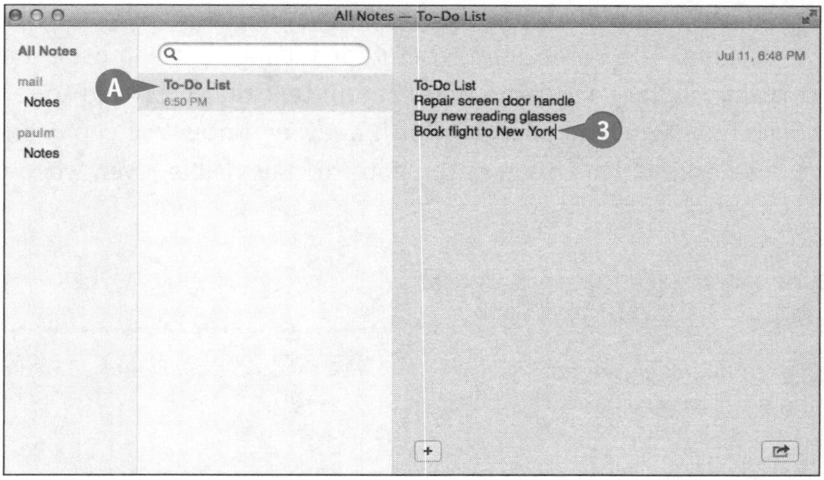

Delete a Note

1 Right-click the note you want to delete.

2 Click **Delete**.

Notes asks you to confirm.

3 Click **Delete Note**.

The Notes app deletes the note.

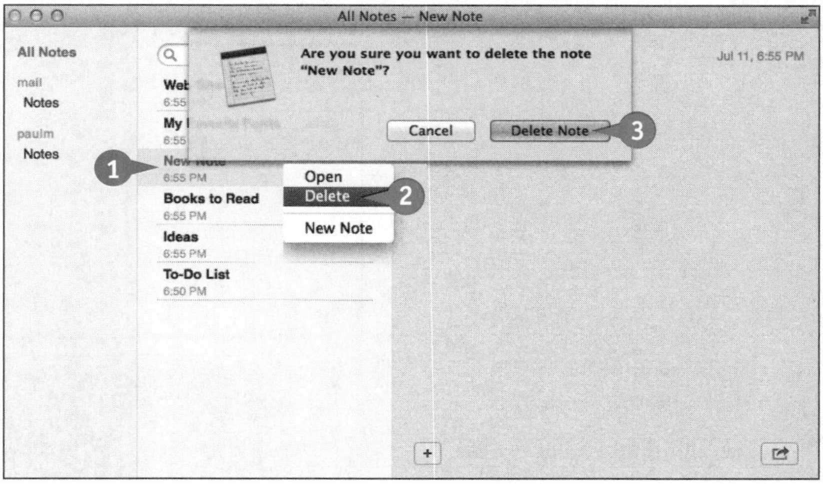

TIPS

Can I synchronize my notes with my iPod touch, iPhone, or iPad?

Yes, as long as you have an iCloud account, you have set up that account in Mac Pro, as described in Chapter 20, and you are syncing notes between your Mac Pro and iCloud. To create a new note using iCloud, click **Notes** under the iCloud folder and then follow the steps in this section.

How do I create a bulleted or numbered list?

Position the cursor where you want the list to begin, click **Format**, and then click **Lists**. In the menu that appears, click **Insert Bulleted List**, **Insert Dashed List**, or **Insert Numbered List**.

Pin a Note to the Desktop

You can ensure that you always see the content of a note by pinning that note to the Mac Pro desktop. The Notes app is useful for setting up to-do lists, jotting down things to remember, and creating similar documents that contain text that you need to refer to while you work. Rather than constantly switching back and forth between Notes and your working application, you can pin a note to the desktop, which forces the note to stay visible, even when you switch to another application.

Pin a Note to the Desktop

1. Double-click the note you want to pin.

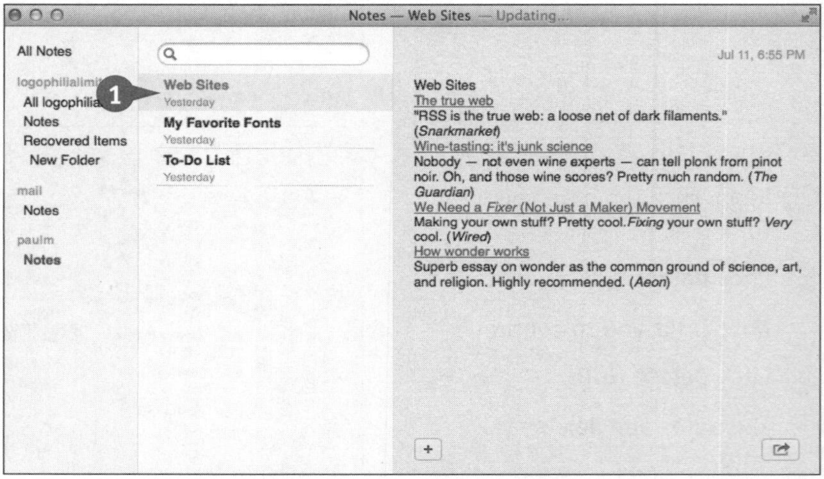

The Notes app opens the note in its own window.

2. Click and drag the note title to the position you want.

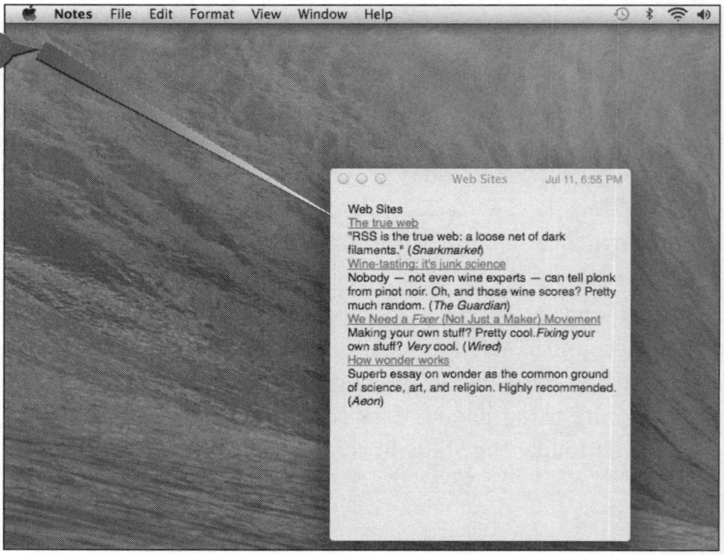

3 Click **Window**.

4 Click **Float on Top**.

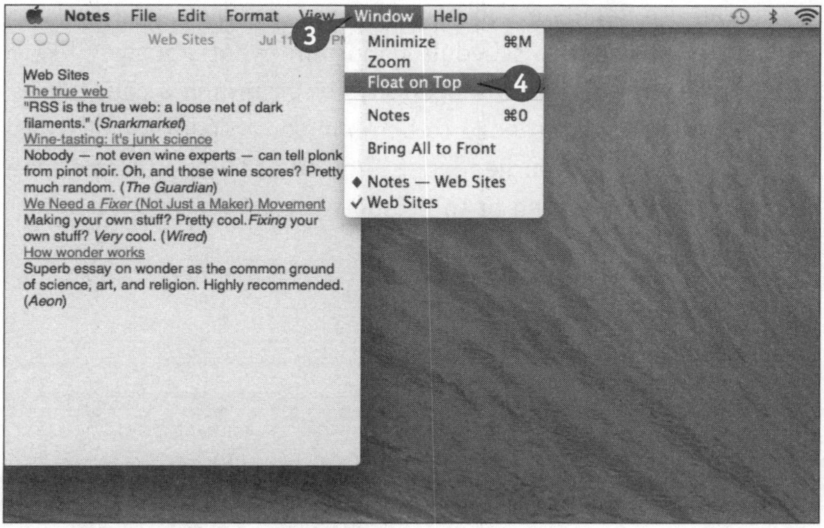

A The Notes app keeps each opened note on top of any other window you open.

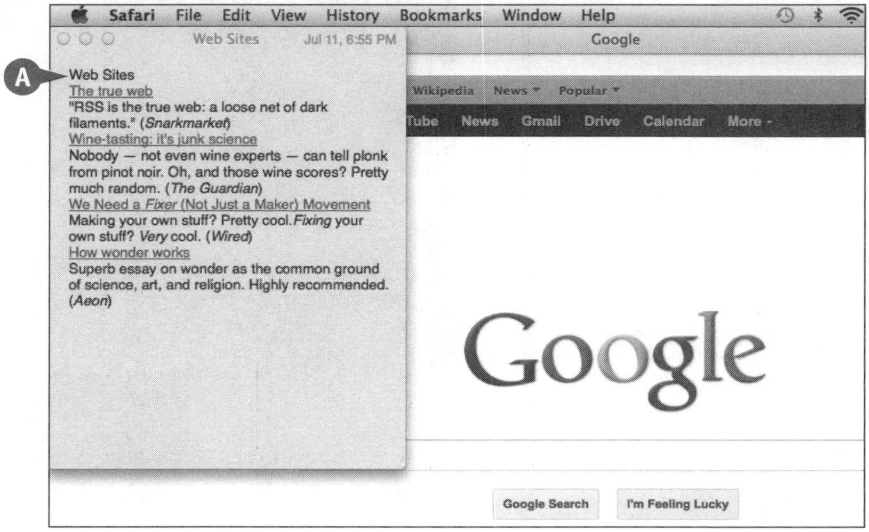

TIPS

Is it possible to pin the Notes app window to the desktop, so that it always remains in view?

No, Mac Pro does not allow you to keep the Notes window on top of other windows on your desktop. The pinning technique in this section applies only to open note windows.

Am I only able to pin one note at a time to the desktop?

No, the Notes app enables you to pin multiple notes to the Mac Pro desktop. This is useful if you have different notes that apply to the same task that you are working on in another application. However, you need to exercise some caution because the pinned notes take up space on the desktop.

Create a Reminder

You can use Reminders to have Mac Pro display a notification when you need to perform a task. You can use Calendar to schedule important events, but you likely have many tasks during the day that cannot be considered full-fledged events: returning a call, taking clothes out of the dryer, turning off the sprinkler. If you need to be reminded to perform such tasks, Calendar is overkill, but Mac Pro offers a better solution: Reminders. You use this app to create reminders, which are notifications that tell you to do something or to be somewhere.

Create a Reminder

1. In the Dock, click **Reminders** (📋).

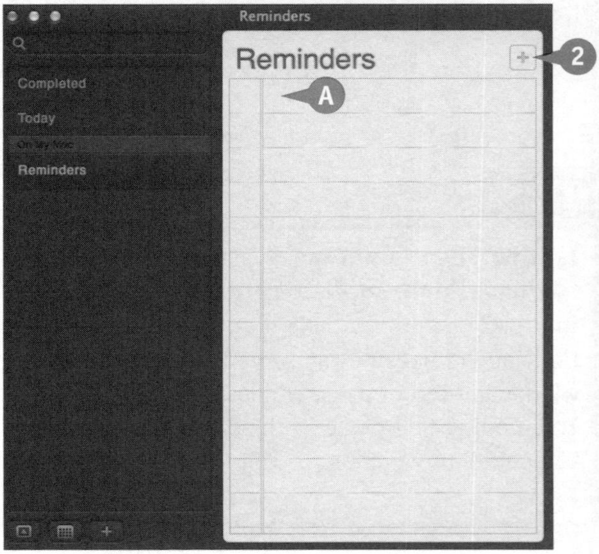

The Reminders app appears.

2. Click **New Reminder** (+).

A. You can also click the next available line in the Reminders list.

Note: You can also click **File** and then click **New Reminder**, or press ⌘+N.

3 Type the reminder title.

4 Click the **Show Info** icon (ⓘ).

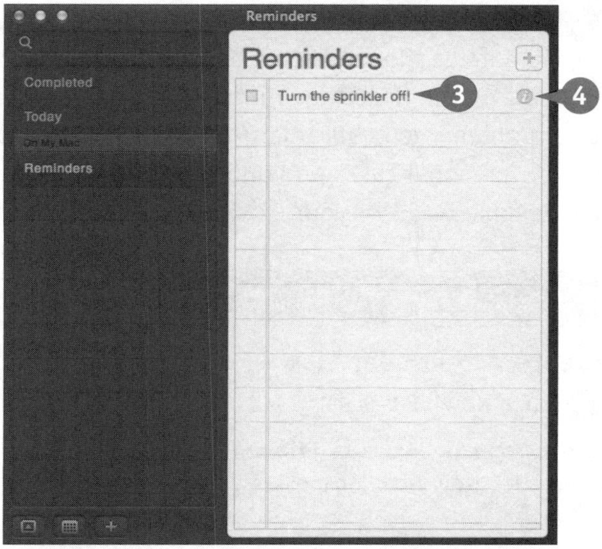

The Reminders app displays the reminder details.

5 Select the **On a Day** option (☐ changes to ☑).

6 Specify the date and time you want to be reminded.

7 Click **Done**.

The Reminders app adds the reminder to the list.

B When you have completed the reminder, select its check box (☐ changes to ☑).

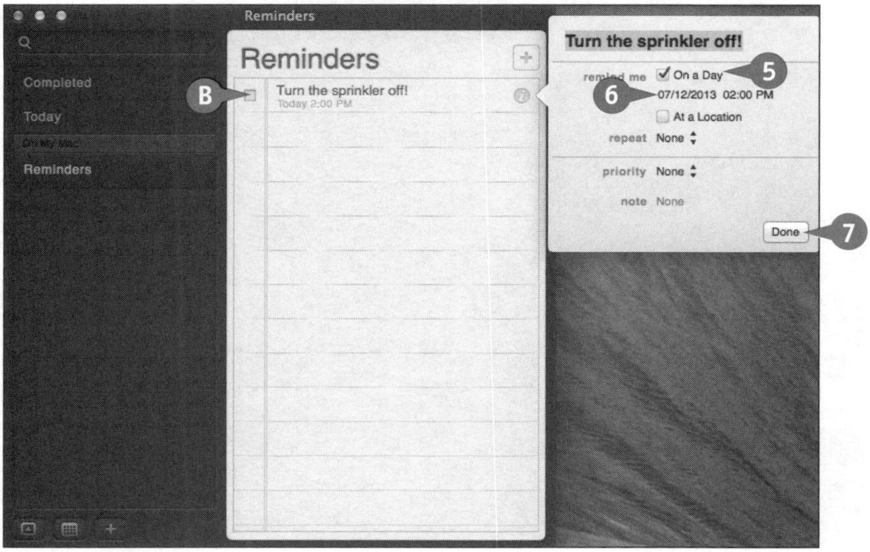

TIP

What does the At a Location option do?

The At a Location option allows the Reminders app to display a notification for a task when you arrive at or leave a location. Of course, you are unlikely to move your Mac Pro from one location to another, but if you use iCloud to sync your reminders to a portable device such as an iPhone or an iPad, that device can use the location-based reminder.

To set this up, follow steps 1 to 4, select the **At a Location** option (☐ changes to ☑), and then type the address or choose a contact that has a defined address. Select either the **Leaving** or **Arriving** option (○ changes to ◉) and then click **Done**.

Create a New Reminder List

You can organize your reminders and make them easier to locate by creating new reminder lists. By default, Reminders comes with a single list called Reminders. However, if you use reminders frequently, the Reminders list can become cluttered, making it difficult to locate reminders. To solve this problem, you can organize your reminders by creating new lists. For example, you could have one list for personal tasks and another for business tasks. After you create one or more new lists, you can move some or all of your existing reminders to the appropriate lists.

Create a New Reminder List

Create a Reminder List

1 Click **New List** (+).

Note: You can also click **File** and then click **New List**, or press ⌘+L.

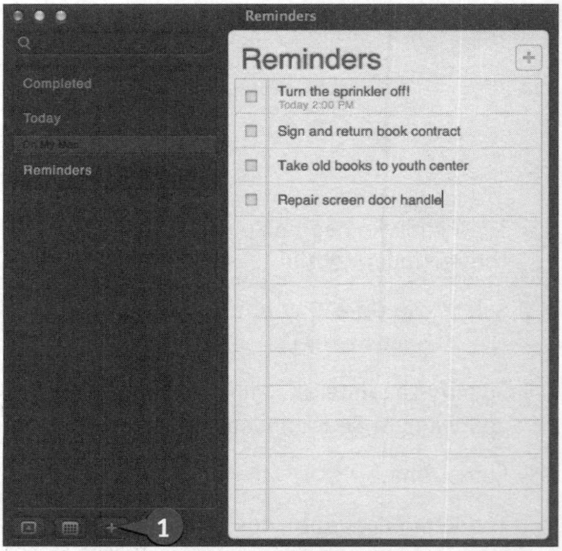

A The Reminders app adds the new list to the sidebar.

2 Type the list name.

3 Press Return.

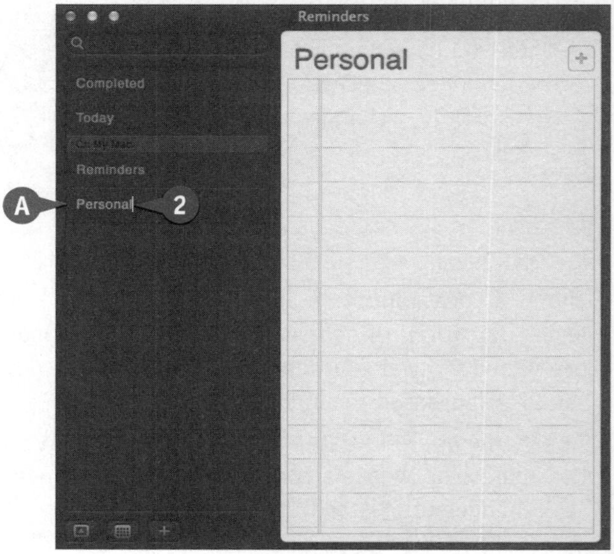

Move a Reminder to a Different List

1. Click the list that contains the reminder you want to move.
2. Click and drag the reminder and drop it on the destination list.

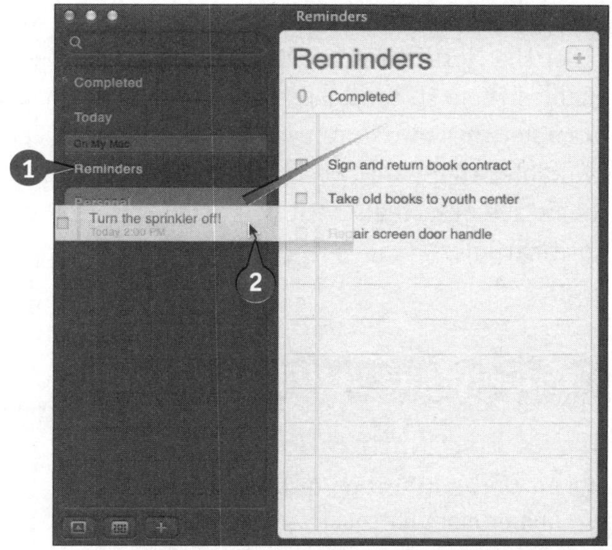

3. Click the destination list.

B The reminder now appears in the destination list.

Note: You can also right-click the reminder, click **Move to List**, and then click the destination list.

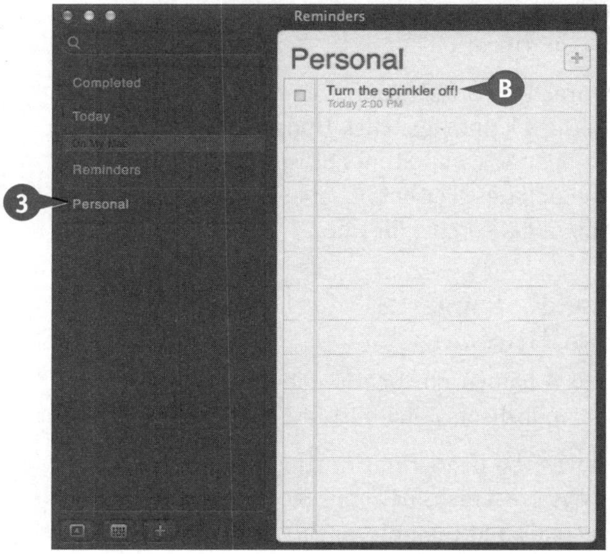

TIPS

Why does my Reminders app not have a Completed list?

The Reminders app does not show the Completed list when you first start using the program. When you mark a reminder as complete by selecting its check box (☐ changes to ☑), Reminders creates the Completed list and moves the task to that list.

Can I change the order of the lists in the sidebar?

Yes. By default, the Reminders app displays the new lists in the order you create them. To move a list to a new position, click and drag the list up or down in the sidebar. When the horizontal blue bar shows the list to be in the position you want, release the mouse button.

Work with the Notification Center

You can keep on top of what is happening while you are using your Mac Pro by taking advantage of the Notification Center. Several apps take advantage of a feature called *notifications*, which enables them to send messages to OS X about events that are happening on your Mac Pro. For example, the App Store uses the Notification Center to let you know when Mac Pro updates are available. There are two types of notifications: a banner that appears temporarily, and an alert that stays on-screen until you dismiss it. You can also open the Notification Center to view recent notifications.

Work with the Notification Center

Handle Alert Notifications

Ⓐ An alert notification displays one or more buttons.

❶ Click a button to dismiss the notification.

Note: In a notification about new OS X updates, click **Update** to open the App Store and see the updates. For details about the updates, click **Details**.

Handle Banner Notifications

Ⓑ A banner notification does not display any buttons.

Note: The banner notification stays on-screen for about 5 seconds and then disappears.

View Recent Notifications

1 Click **Notification Center** (☰).

C Mac Pro displays your recent notifications.

2 Click a notification to view the item in the original application.

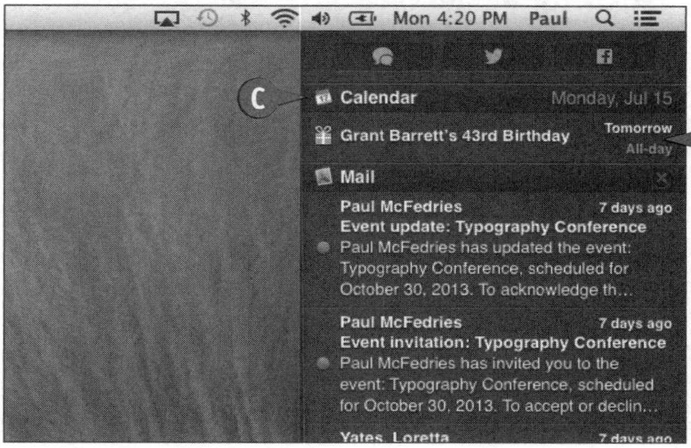

TIP

Can I control what apps use the Notification Center and how they use it?

Yes. Click **System Preferences** (⚙) in the Dock and then click **Notifications.** Click an app on the left side of the window and then click a notification style: **None**, **Banners**, or **Alerts**. To control the number of items the app can display in the Notification Center, click the **Show in Notification Center** option menu and select a number. To remove an app from the Notification Center, deselect the **Show in Notification Center** option (☑ changes to ☐).

Organize Files with Tags

You can describe many of your files to OS X by adding one or more tags that indicate the content or subject matter of the file. A *tag* is a word or short phrase that describes some aspect of a file. You can add as many tags as you need. Adding tags to files makes it easier to search and organize your documents.

For an existing file, you can add one or more tags within Finder. If you are working with a new file, you can add tags when you save the file to your Mac Pro's hard drive.

Organize Files with Tags

Add Tags with Finder

1. Click **Finder** ( ) in the Dock.
2. Open the folder that contains the file you want to tag.
3. Click the file.
4. Click **Edit Tags** ( ).

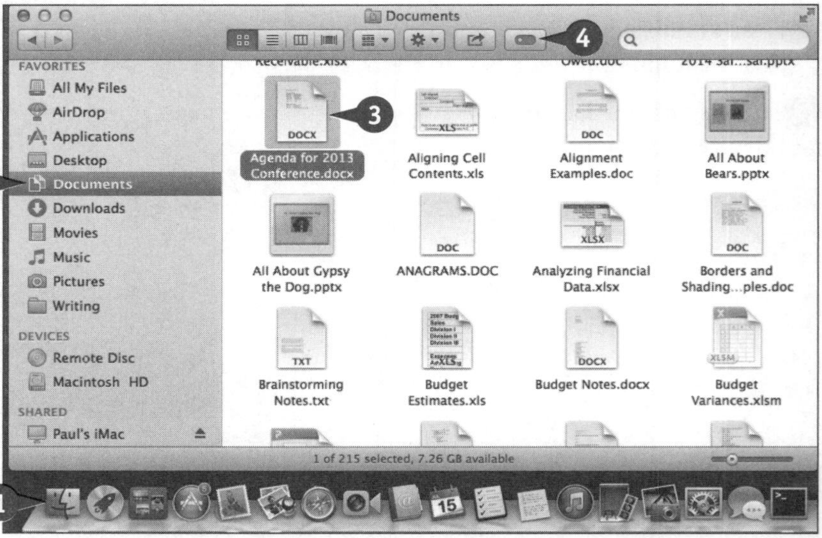

Mac Pro displays the Tags sheet.

5. Type the tag.

Note: To assign multiple tags, separate each one with a comma.

6. Press Return.

Mac Pro assigns the tag or tags.

7. Press Return.

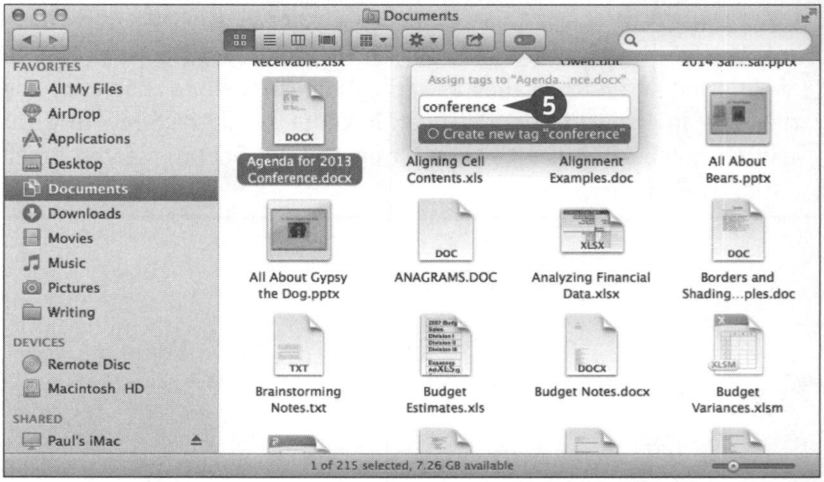

Add Tags When Saving

1. In the application, select the command that saves the new file.

   The application displays the Save sheet.

2. Use the Tags text box to type the tag.

Note: To assign multiple tags, separate each one with a comma.

3. Choose the other save options, such as the filename, as needed.

4. Click **Save**.

   The application saves the file and assigns that tag or tags.

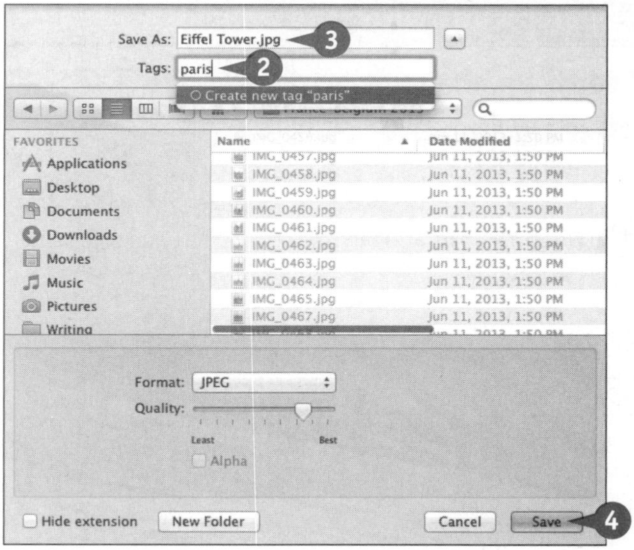

TIPS

Is there an easier method I can use to assign an existing tag to another file?

Yes. Mac Pro keeps a list of your tags, and it displays that list each time you display the Tags sheet. So you can assign the same tag to another file by displaying the Tags sheet and clicking the tag in the list that appears.

Can I assign the same tag or tags to multiple files?

Yes. First, use Finder to select all the files in advance. For example, hold down ⌘ and click each file. Once you select the files, click **Edit Tags** ( ), and then type the tag, Mac Pro automatically assigns the tag to all the selected files.

Search Files with Tags

Once you assign tags to your files, you can take advantage of those tags to make it easier to find and group related files.

Although keeping related files together in the same folder is good practice, that is not always possible. That can make it difficult to locate and work with related files. However, if you assign the same tag or tags to those files, you can use those tags to quickly and easily search for the files. No matter where the files are located, Finder shows them all together in a single window for easy access.

Search Files with Tags

Search for a Tag

1 Use Finder's Search box to type the first few letters of the tag.

2 When the tag appears, click it.

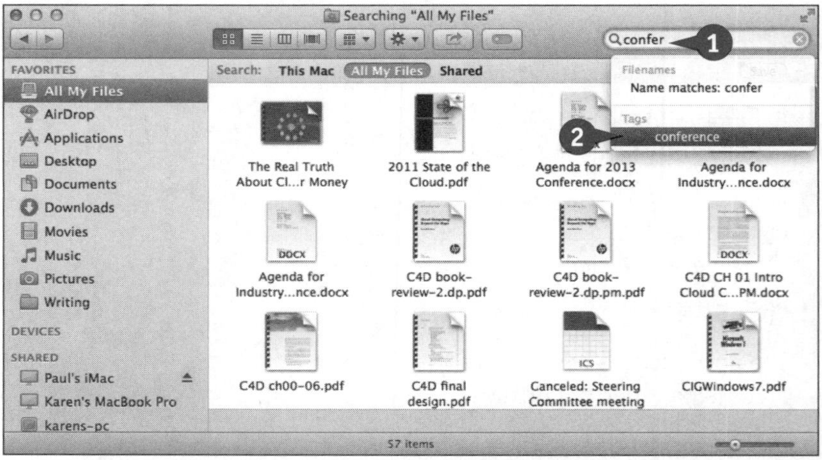

A Finder displays the files assigned that tag.

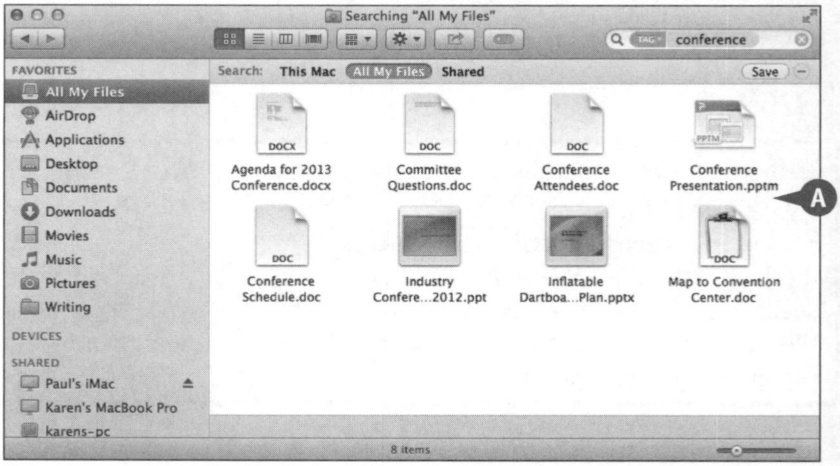

Select a Tag

1 In the Finder sidebar, click the tag.

B If you do not see the tag you want, click **All Tags** to display the complete list.

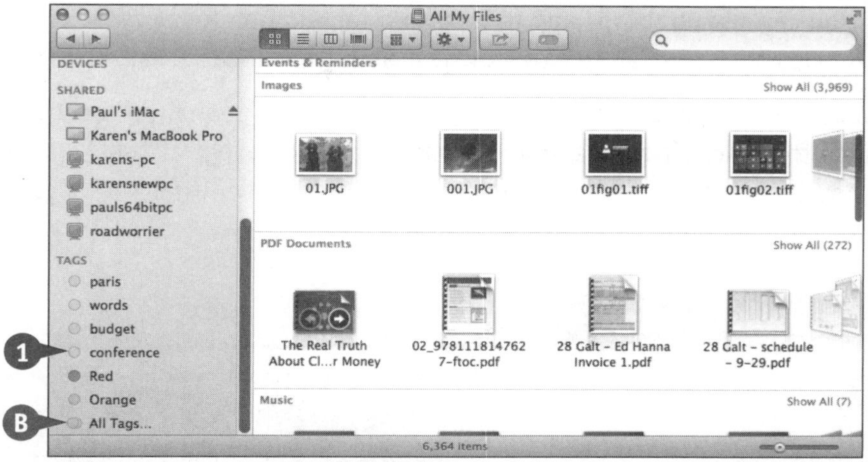

C Finder displays the files to which that tag is assigned.

Note: With the tag folder displayed, you can automatically assign that tag to other files by dragging the files from another Finder window and dropping them within the tag folder.

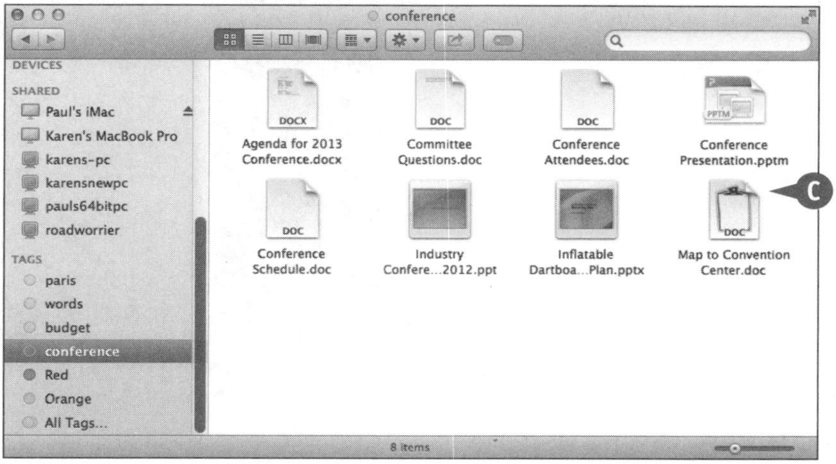

TIP

Can I control what tags appear in Finder's sidebar?

Yes, by following these steps:

1 Open Finder.

2 Click **Finder**.

3 Click **Preferences**.

The Finder preferences appear.

4 Click the **Tags** tab.

5 For each tag you do not want to appear in the sidebar, deselect the check box to the right of the tag (☑ changes to ☐).

6 Click **Close** (■).

Search for a Location

You can use the Maps app to display a location on a map. Maps is an OS X app that displays digital maps that you can use to view just about any location by searching for an address or place name.

Maps comes with a Search box that enables you to search for locations by address or by name. If Maps finds the place, it zooms in and drops a pin on the digital map to show you the exact location. For many public locations, Maps also offers an info screen that shows you the location's address, phone number, and more.

Search for a Location

1 Click **Maps** ( ).

Mac Pro starts the Maps app.

2 Use the Search box to type the address or name of the location.

A If Maps displays the name of the location as you type, click the location.

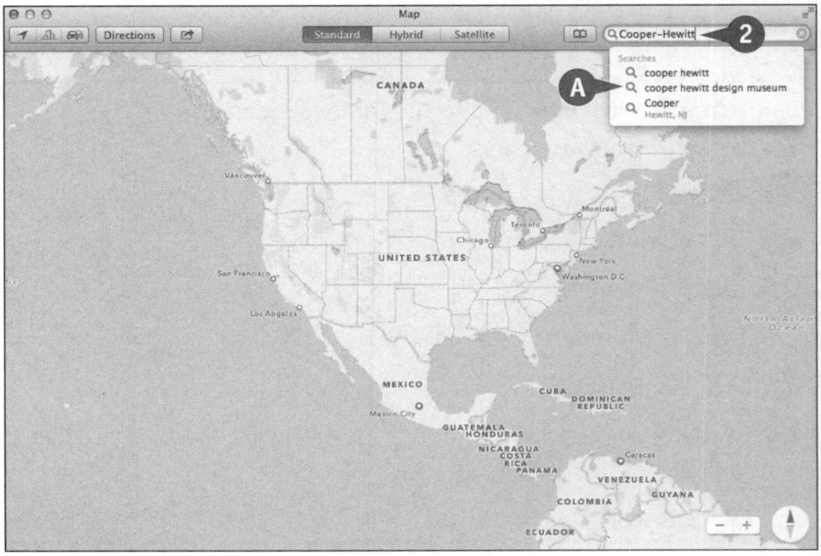

- **B** Maps drops a pin on the location.
- **C** Click **Zoom In** (+) or press ⌘+ + to get a closer look.
- **D** Click **Zoom Out** (−) or press ⌘+ − to see more of the map.
- **3** If Maps offers more data about the location, click **ShowInfo** (i).

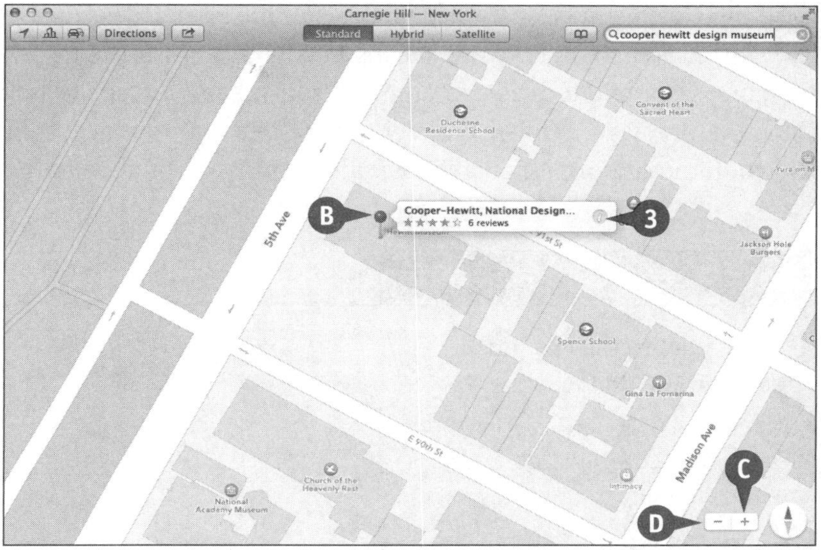

- **E** Maps displays the Info screen for the location.

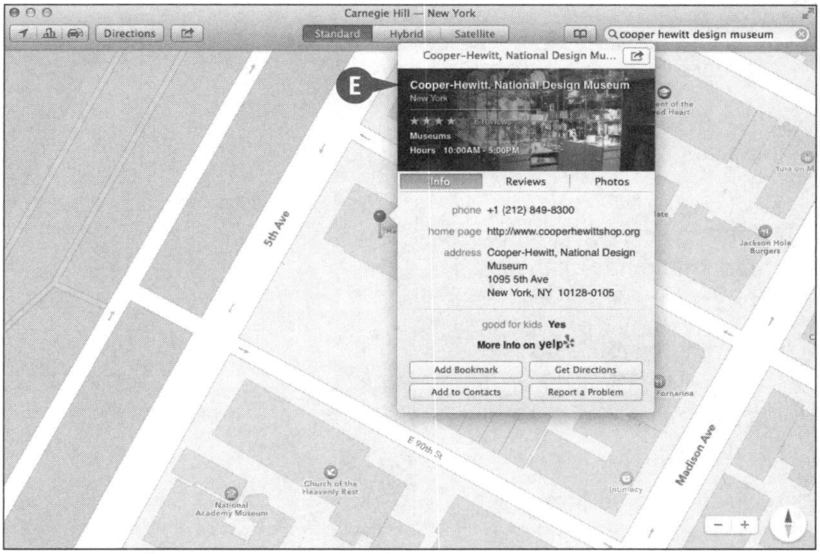

TIPS

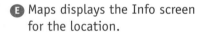

Can I use Maps to show my current location?

Yes. Maps can use surrounding electronic infrastructure, particularly nearby wireless networks, to come up with a reasonably accurate calculation of your current location. Click **Current Location** (➚), or click **View** and then click **Go to Current Location** (or press ⌘+L).

How do I save a location for future use?

You can save a location as a bookmark, which saves you from having to type the location's address or name each time. Display the location on the map, click **ShowInfo** (i), and then click **Add Bookmark.** You can also click **View** and then click **Add Bookmark.** To see a bookmarked location, click **Show Bookmarks** ([book icon]) and then click the location.

Get Directions to a Location

Besides displaying locations, Maps also understands the roads and highways found in most cities, states, and countries. This means that you can use the Maps app to get specific directions for traveling from one location to another. You specify a starting point and destination for a trip, and Maps then provides you with directions for getting from one point to the other. Maps highlights the trip route on a digital map and also gives you specific details for negotiating each leg of the trip.

Get Directions to a Location

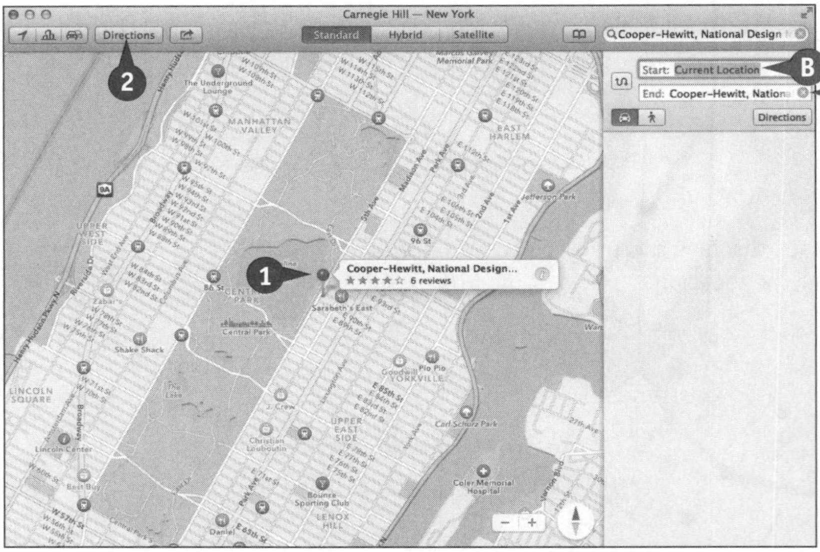

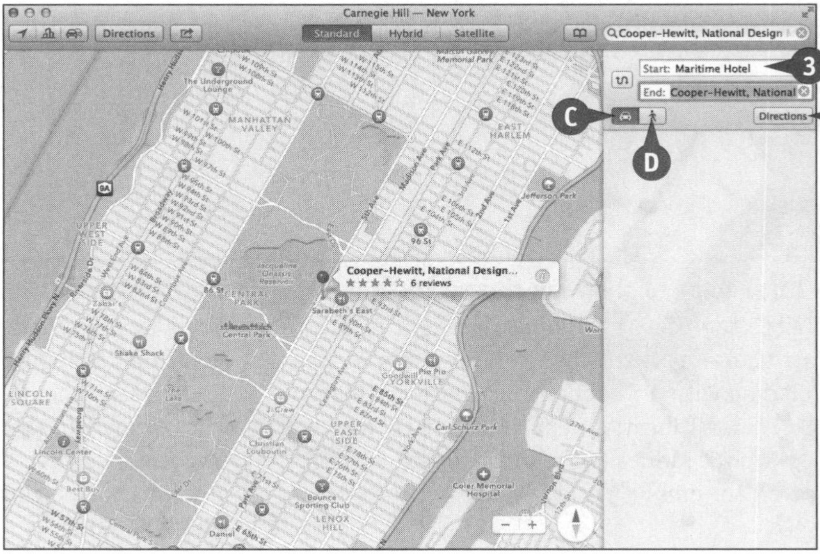

1 Add a pin to the map for your destination.

Note: See the previous section, "Search for a Location," to learn how to add a pin.

2 Click **Directions**.

The Directions pane appears.

A Your pinned location appears in the End text box.

B Maps assumes you want to start the route from your current location.

3 To start the route from another location, type the name or address in the Start text box.

4 Select how you intend to travel to the destination:

C You can click **Car** (car icon) if you plan to drive.

D You can click **Walk** (walk icon) if plan to walk.

5 Click **Directions**.

E Maps displays an overview of your journey.

F This area tells the distance and approximate traveling time.

G This area displays the various legs of the journey.

H If Maps displays alternate routes, you can click these banners to view the routes.

6 Click the first leg of the trip.

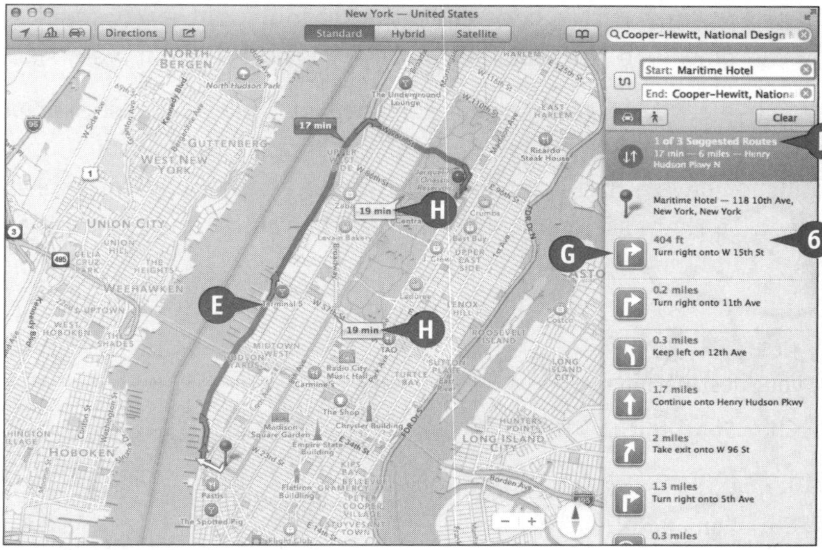

I Maps zooms in to show you just that leg of the trip.

7 As you complete each leg of the trip, click the next leg for further instructions.

TIPS

Can I get traffic information?

Yes, Maps can display current traffic conditions for most major cities. Click **View** and then click **Show Traffic**, or click **Show Traffic** (🚗) in the toolbar. On the map, you see a sequence of red dots where traffic is slow, and a sequence of red dashes where traffic is heavy.

Because I cannot take my Mac Pro with me, how can I use the directions when I am traveling to my destination?

The easiest way to use the directions that Maps provides is to send them to a portable device such as an iPhone or iPad. To do this from Maps, click **Share** (⇪) and then click **Send to *device***, where *device* is the name of your portable device.

Install a Font

Mac Pro ships with a large collection of fonts, but if you require a different font for a project, you can download the font files and then install them on your Mac Pro.

Macs have always placed special emphasis on typography, so it is no surprise that OS X Mavericks ships with nearly 300 fonts. However, typography is a personal, exacting art form, so your Mac Pro might not have a particular font that would be just right for a newsletter, greeting card, or similar project. In that case, you can download the font you need and then install it.

Install a Font

1. Click **Spotlight** ( ).
2. Type **font**.
3. Click **Font Book**.

   You can also open Finder, click **Applications**, and then click **Font Book** ( ).

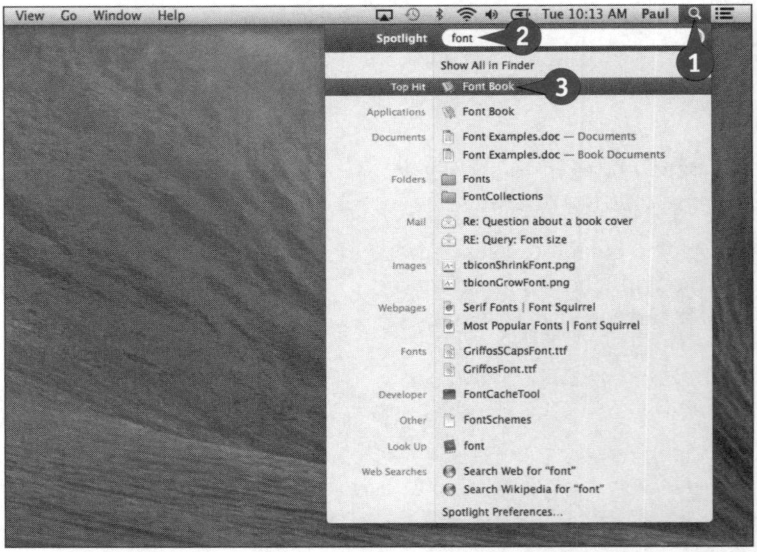

   The Font Book application appears.

4. Click **File**.
5. Click **Add Fonts**.

A. You can also click **Add fonts** ( ) or press ⌘+O.

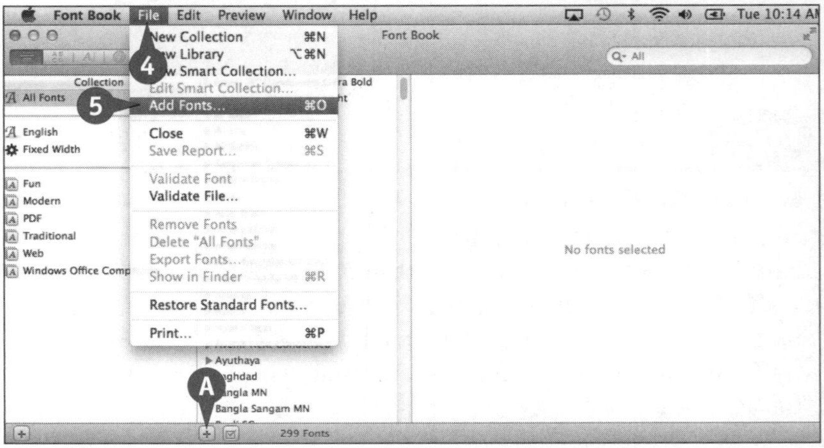

6. Open the location that contains the font you want to install.
7. Click the folder that contains the font files.
8. Click **Open**.

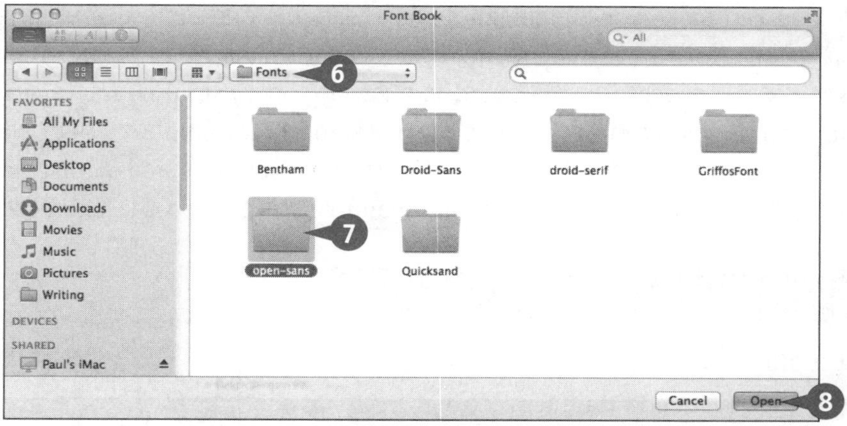

Mac Pro installs the font.

B. The typeface name appears in the Fonts list.

9. Click ▶ to open the typeface and see its individual fonts (▶ changes to ▼).
10. Click a font.

C. A preview of the font appears here.

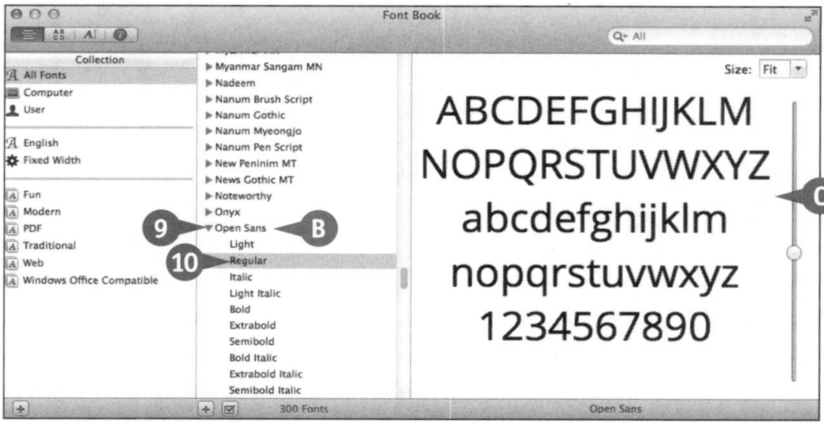

TIPS

What is the difference between a font and a typeface?

A *typeface* is a unique design applied to each letter, number, and symbol. A *font* is a particular style of a typeface, such as regular, bold, or italic. However, in everyday parlance, most people use the terms typeface and font interchangeably.

What is a font collection?

A *collection* is a group of related fonts. For example, the Fun collection contains fonts normally used with informal designs, whereas the Web collection contains fonts that render well on web pages. To add your new font to an existing collection, drag it from the **Fonts** list and drop it on the collection. To create your own collection, click **File** and then click **New Collection** (or press ⌘+N).

Access Non-Keyboard Characters

You can make your documents more readable and more useful by inserting special symbols not available via your keyboard. The keyboard is home to a large number of letters, numbers, and symbols. However, the keyboard is missing some useful characters. For example, it is missing the foreign characters in words such as café and Köln. Similarly, your writing might require mathematical symbols such as ÷ and ½, financial symbols such as ¢ and ¥, or commercial symbols such as © and ®. These and many more symbols are available in OS X via the Character Viewer.

Access Non-Keyboard Characters

Display the Character Viewer

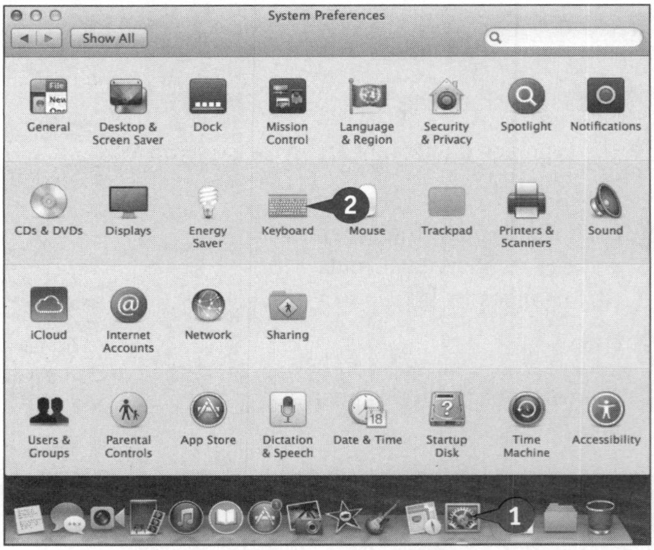

1. Click **System Preferences** ( ).

   The System Preferences appear.

2. Click **Keyboard**.

   The Keyboard preferences appear.

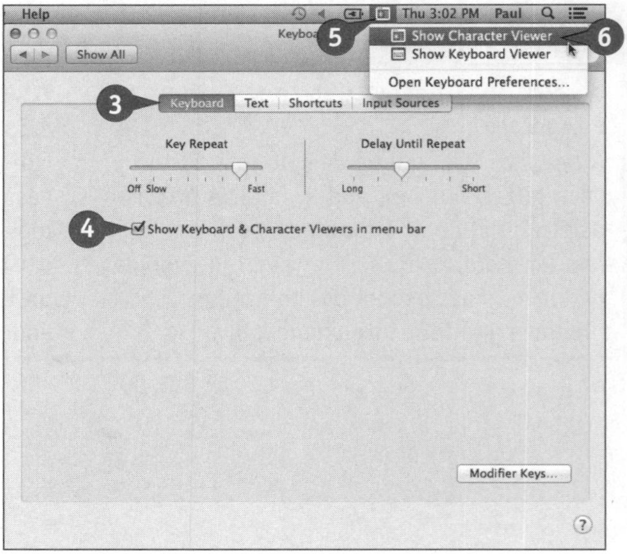

3. Click the **Keyboard** tab.

4. Select the **Show Keyboard & Character Viewers in menu bar** option (☐ changes to ☑).

5. Click **Keyboard & Character Viewers** ( ).

6. Click **Show Character Viewer**.

   The Character Viewer appears.

Insert a Character

1. In the document, position the insertion point where you want the character to appear.
2. In the Character Viewer, select a category.

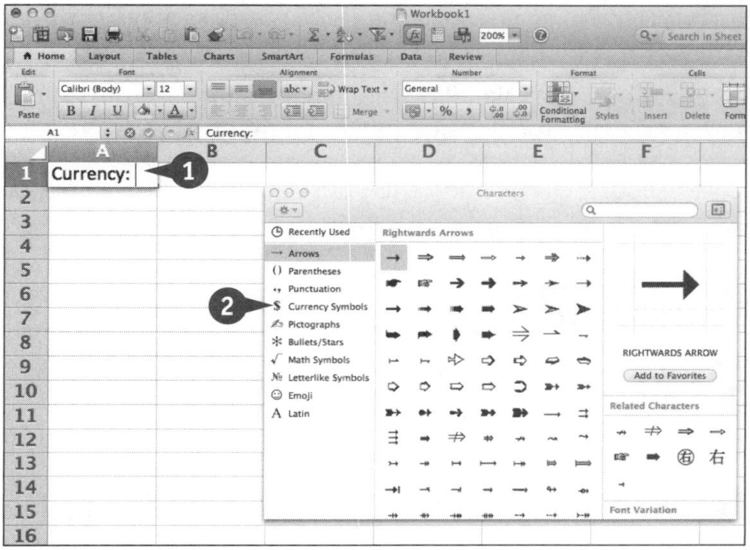

3. Double-click the character you want to use.

Ⓐ The character appears in the document at the insertion point.

4. Click **Close** (■).

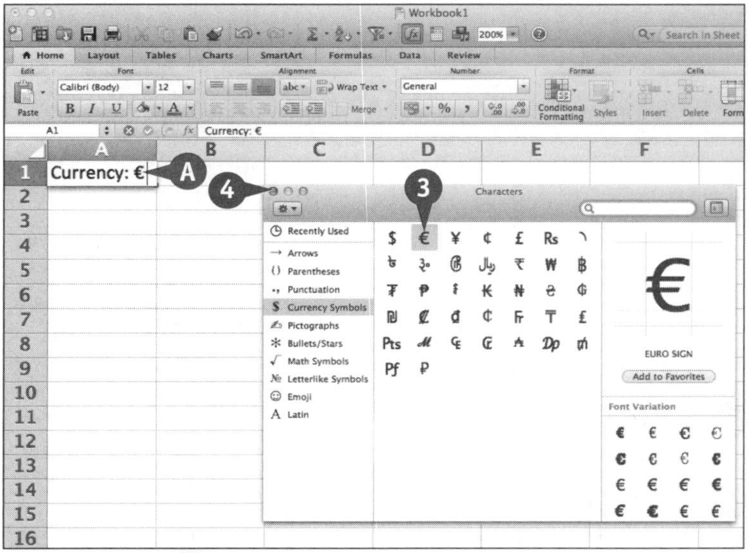

TIPS

Can I access the Character Viewer if I choose not to display the menu bar icon?

Yes, in some applications you can access the Character Viewer directly. For example, in TextEdit, you can click **Edit** and then click **Special Characters**, or you can press Control + ⌘ + Spacebar. This command is also available in Calendar, Contacts, Mail, Messages, and Notes.

Is there an easier way to access characters that I often use?

Yes, you can add those characters to Character Viewer's Favorites section. (Note that this section appears in the Character Viewer only after you have added at least one character to it.) To add a character to the Favorites section, display the Character Viewer, click the character, and then click **Add to Favorites**.

Purchase an E-Book

Your Mac Pro comes with the iBooks application (which is also available as a free download from the App Store), which enables you to read e-books right on your desktop. However, before you can read an e-book on your Mac Pro, you need to purchase the e-book, which you can do using the iBooks Store. You access the iBooks Store using the iBooks app, and your purchases are stored in the iBooks library.

Most e-books, particularly the latest releases, cost money to purchase, but many out-of-copyright e-books are available free of charge at sites such as Project Gutenberg (www.gutenberg.org).

Purchase an E-Book

1. In the Dock, click **iBooks** (icon).

   iBooks appears.

2. Click **iBooks Store**.

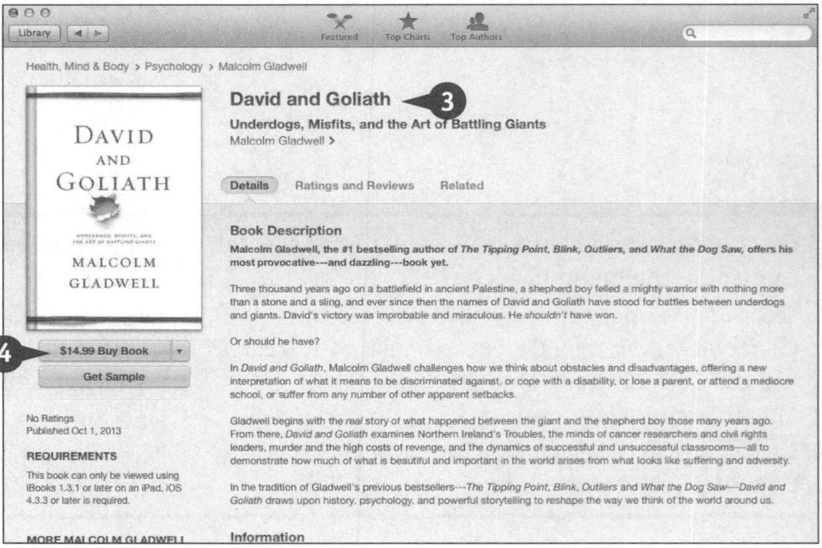

The iBooks Store appears.

3. Locate the e-book you want to purchase.

4. Click the price button or, if the e-book is free, click the **Free** button instead.

The iBooks Store prompts you to log in with your Apple ID.

Note: After you sign in, you can skip steps **5** to **7** for subsequent purchases.

5 Type your Apple ID.

6 Type your password.

7 Click **Buy**.

The iBooks Store asks you to confirm.

8 Click **Buy**.

The iBooks Store adds the e-book to your library.

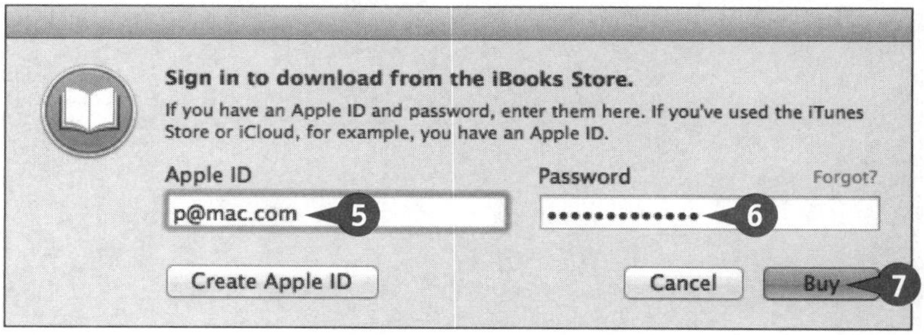

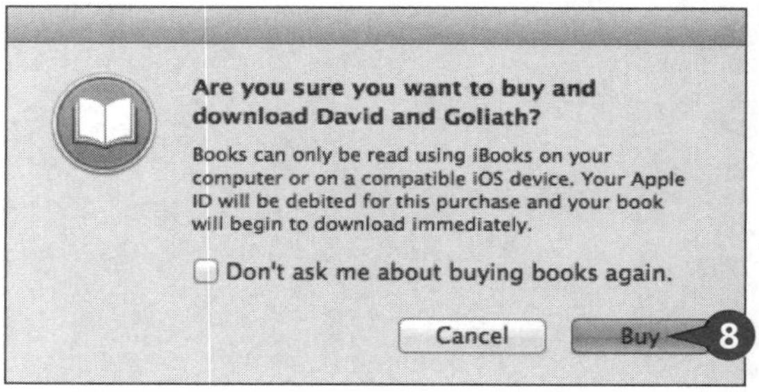

TIP

If I have purchased e-books from the iBooks Store on other devices, how do I get those e-books onto my Mac Pro?

You can configure iBooks to automatically download e-books that you have purchased on, say, an iPhone, iPad, or another Mac. To set this up, click **iBooks**, click **Preferences**, click the **Store** tab, and then select the **Download new purchases automatically** option (☐ changes to ☑). Note, however, that this will work only if you are using the same Apple ID on Mac Pro and the other device.

CHAPTER 11

Playing Mac Pro Audio

You can use iTunes to create a library of music and use that library to play songs, albums, and collections of songs called *playlists*. You can also listen to music CDs and more.

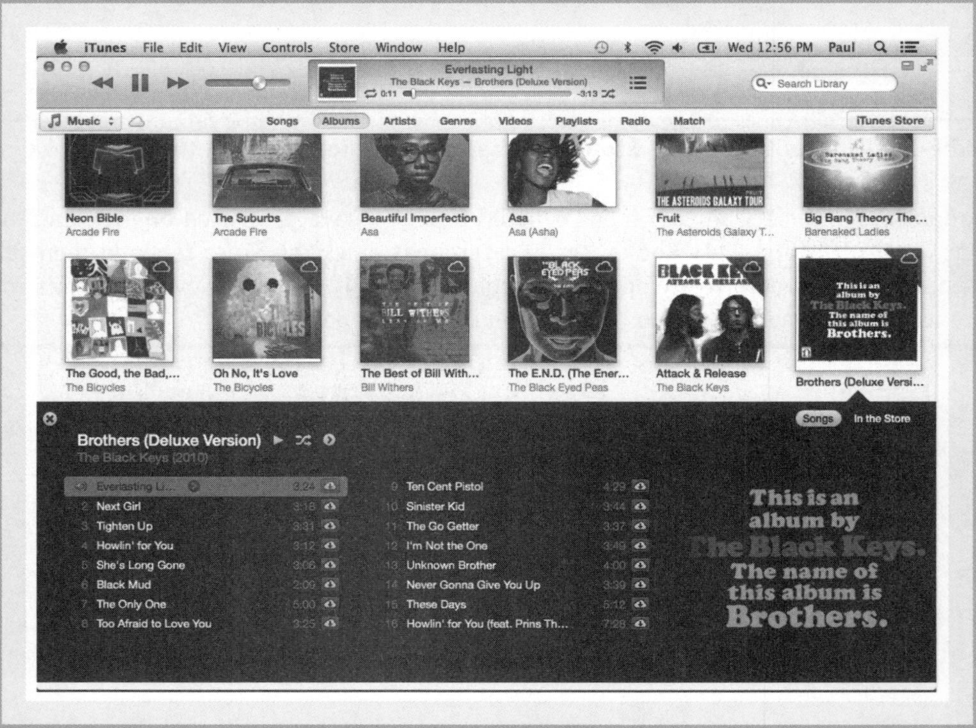

Understanding the iTunes Library

Mac Pro includes iTunes to enable you to play back and manage various types of audio files. iTunes also includes features for organizing and playing videos, watching movies and TV shows, and organizing apps and iOS devices, but iTunes is mostly concerned with audio-related media and content.

Most of your iTunes time will be spent in the library, so you need to understand the various categories — such as music and audiobooks — that iTunes uses to organize the library's audio content. You also need to know how to configure the library to show only the categories with which you will be working.

The iTunes Library

The iTunes library is where your Mac Pro stores the files that you can play and work with in the iTunes application. Although iTunes has some video components, its focus is on audio features, so most of the library sections are audio related. These sections enable you to work with music, podcasts, audiobooks, ringtones, and Internet radio.

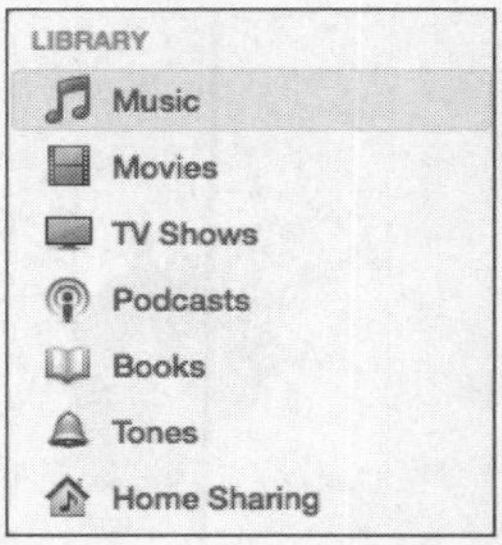

Understanding Library Categories

The Source List button in the upper left corner of the iTunes window displays a menu listing the various categories available in the iTunes library. The audio-related categories include Music, Podcasts, Books (for audiobooks), Ringtones, and Radio. The Store list includes items you have purchased from the iTunes Store. Each category shows you the contents of that category and the different views available. For example, in the Music category, you can view the items by Songs, Albums, Artists, and Genres.

Configure the Library

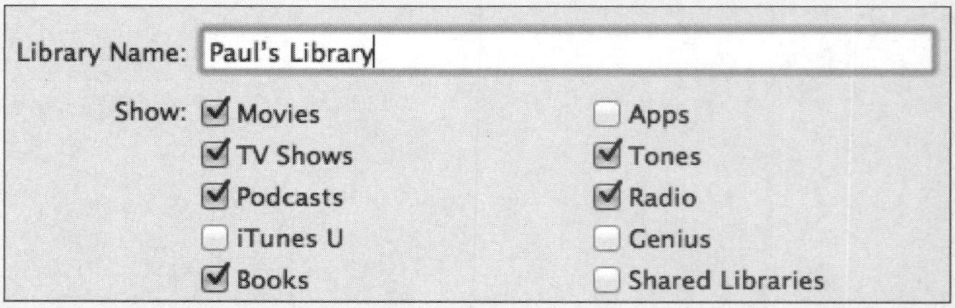

You can configure what categories of the iTunes library appear in the Source List button. Click **iTunes**, click **Preferences** to open the iTunes preferences, and then click the **General** tab. In the Show section, select the check box for each type of content with which you want to work (☐ changes to ☑) and then click **OK**.

CHAPTER 11

Navigate the iTunes Window

Familiarizing yourself with the various elements of the iTunes window is a good idea so that you can easily navigate and activate elements when you are ready to play audio files, music CDs, or podcasts; import and burn audio CDs; create your own playlists; or listen to Internet radio. In particular, you need to learn the iTunes playback controls because you will use them to control the playback of almost all music you work with in iTunes.

Ⓐ Playback Controls

These buttons control media playback and enable you to adjust the volume.

Ⓑ Sort Buttons

These buttons sort the contents of the current iTunes category.

Ⓒ Status Area

This area displays information about the item currently playing or the action that iTunes is currently performing.

Ⓓ iTunes Store

Click this button to access the iTunes Store, which enables you to purchase songs and albums, subscribe to podcasts, and more.

Ⓔ Contents

The contents of the current iTunes library source appear here.

Ⓕ Source List

Click this button to select the type of content you want to view.

Play a Song

You use the Music category of the iTunes library to play a song stored on your computer. Although iTunes offers several methods to locate the song you want to play, the easiest method is to display the albums you have in your iTunes library, and then open the album that contains the song you want to play. While the song is playing, you can control the volume to suit the music or your current location. If you need to leave the room or take a call, you can pause the song currently playing.

Play a Song

1. Click **Music**.
2. Click **Albums**.

   You can also click a sort option such as Songs, Artists, or Genres.
3. Click the album that contains the song you want to play.

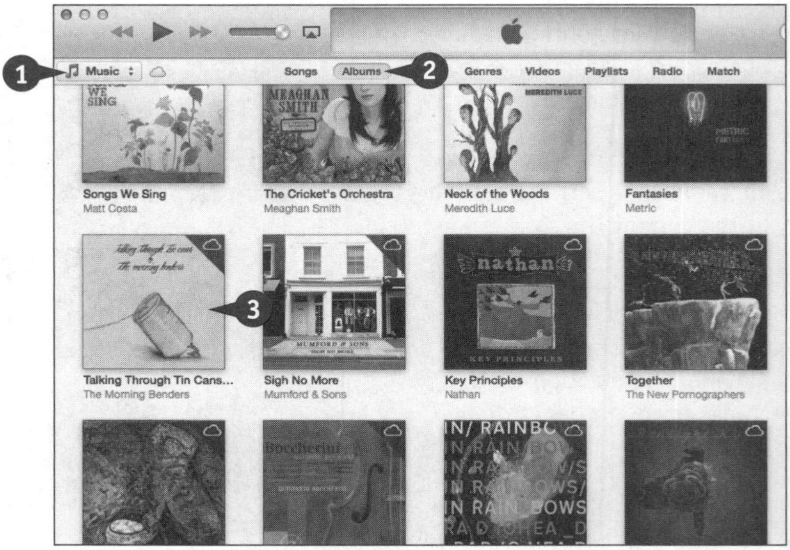

Ⓐ If you want to play the entire album, click **Play** (▶).

4. Double-click the song you want to play.

iTunes begins playing the song.

B Information about the song playback appears here.

C iTunes displays a speaker icon (🔊) beside the currently playing song.

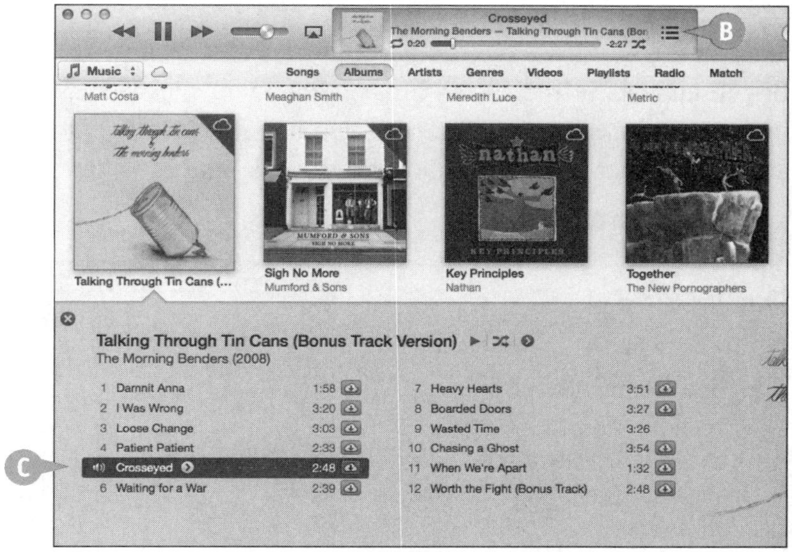

D If you need to stop the song temporarily, click the **Pause** button (⏸).

Note: You can also pause and restart a song by pressing the Spacebar.

E You can use the Volume slider to adjust the volume (see the tip).

Note: See the next section, "Play a Music CD," to learn more about the playback buttons.

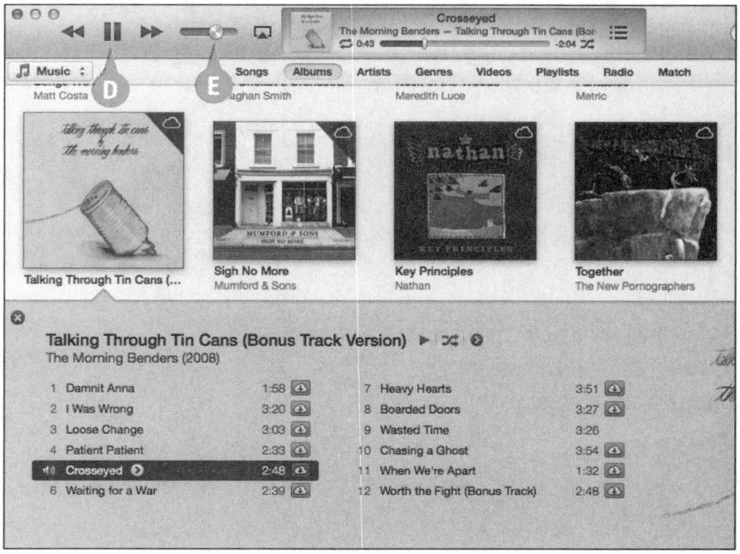

TIP

How do I adjust the volume?

To turn the volume up or down, click and drag the **Volume** slider to the left (to reduce the volume) or to the right (to increase the volume). You can also press ⌘+↓ to reduce the volume, or ⌘+↑ to increase the volume.

To mute the volume, either drag the **Volume** slider all the way to the left, or press Option+⌘+↓. To restore the volume, adjust the **Volume** slider or press Option+⌘+↑.

Play a Music CD

You can play your favorite music CDs in iTunes. If your Mac Pro has an external optical drive (that is, a drive capable of reading CDs and DVDs), then you can insert an audio disc in the drive and the CD appears in the iTunes library. When you click the CD, the iTunes contents area displays the individual tracks on the CD, and if you have an Internet connection, you see the name of each track as well as other track data. During playback, you can skip tracks, pause, and resume play.

Play a Music CD

Play a CD

1. Insert a music CD into your Mac Pro's optical drive.

Ⓐ If you have an Internet connection, after a few moments iTunes shows the contents of the CD.

Note: iTunes shows the contents for most CDs, but it may not show the correct information for some discs, particularly noncommercial mixed CDs.

iTunes asks if you want to import the CD.

2. Click **No**.

Note: To learn how to import a CD, see the next section, "Import Tracks from a Music CD."

3. Click the **Play** button (▶).

iTunes begins playing the CD from the first track.

Skip a Track

1. Click the **Next** button (▶▶) to skip to the next track.

Note: You can also skip to the next track by pressing ⌘+→.

2. Click the **Previous** button (◀◀) to skip to the beginning of the current track; click ◀◀ again to skip to the previous track.

Note: You can also skip to the previous track by pressing ⌘+← twice.

Pause and Resume Play

1. Click the **Pause** button (❚❚) (❚❚ changes to ▶).

   iTunes pauses playback.

2. Click the **Play** button (▶).

   iTunes resumes playback where you left off.

TIPS

Can I change the CD's audio levels?

Yes, iTunes has a graphic equalizer component that you can use to adjust the levels. To display the equalizer, click **Window** and then click **Equalizer** (or press Option+⌘+2). In the Equalizer window, use the sliders to set the audio levels, or click the pop-up menu (⬍) to choose an audio preset.

Can I display visualizations during playback?

Yes. You can click **View** and then click **Show Visualizer** (you can also press ⌘+T). To change the currently displayed visualizer, click **View**, click **Visualizer**, and then click the visualization you want to view.

continued ▶

iTunes gives you more options for controlling the CD playback. For example, you can easily switch from one song to another on the CD. You can also use the Repeat feature to tell iTunes to start the CD over from the beginning after it has finished playing the CD. iTunes also offers the Shuffle feature, which tells iTunes to play the CD's tracks in random order. When the CD is done, you can use iTunes to eject it from the optical drive. If you want to learn how to import music from the CD to iTunes, see the next section, "Import Tracks from a Music CD."

Play a Music CD (continued)

Play Another Song

1. In the list of songs, double-click the song you want to play.

   iTunes begins playing the song.

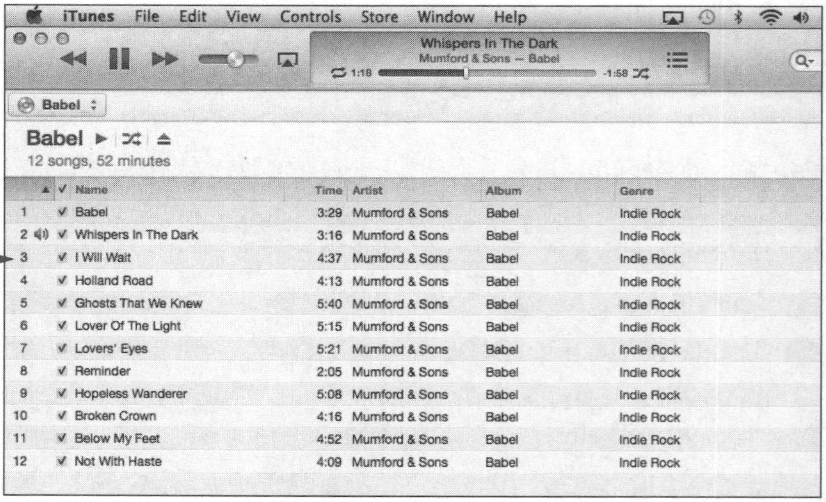

Repeat the CD

1. Click **Controls**.
2. Click **Repeat**.
3. Click **All**.

   iTunes restarts the CD after the last track finishes playing.

A. To repeat just the current song, click **One** instead.

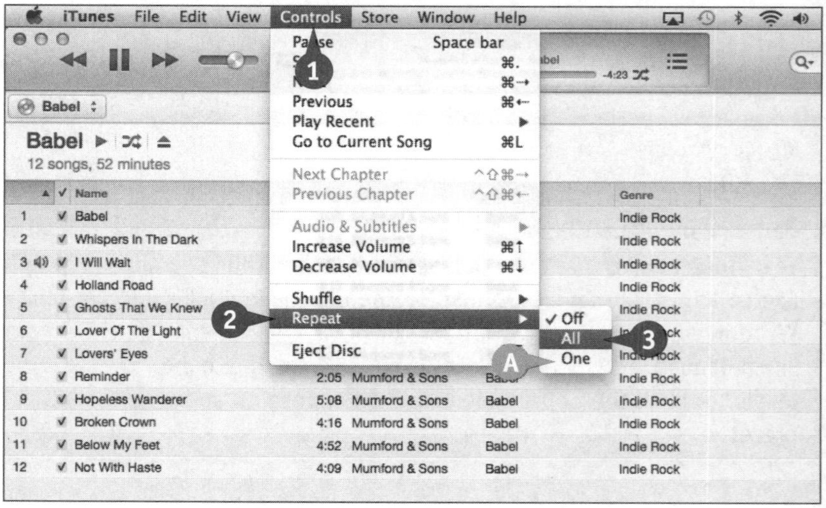

Play Songs Randomly

1. Click **Controls**.
2. Click **Shuffle**.
3. Click **Turn On Shuffle**.

(B) You can also click the **Shuffle** button (shuffle icon).

iTunes shuffles the order of play.

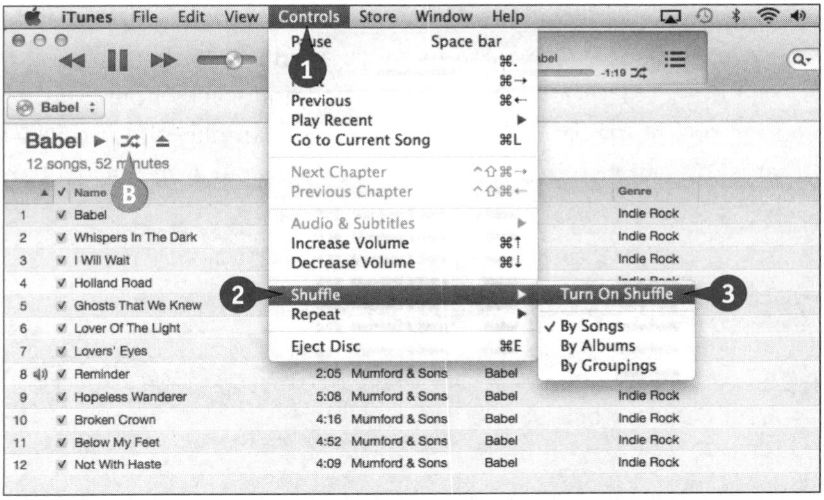

Eject the CD

1. Click the **Eject** button (eject icon) beside the CD.

Note: You can also eject the CD by pressing and holding (eject key).

iTunes ejects the CD from your Mac Pro's optical drive.

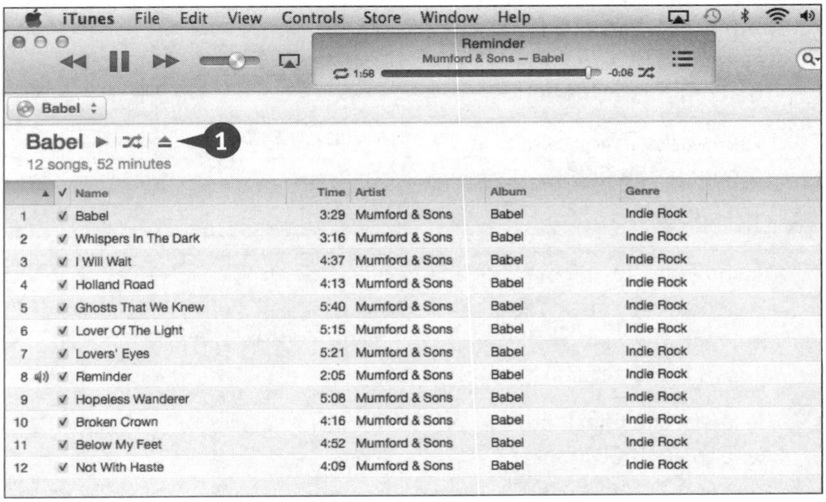

TIP

Why do I not see the song titles after I insert my music CD?

When you play a music CD, iTunes tries to gather information about the album from the Internet. If you still see only track numbers, it may be that you do not have an Internet connection established or that you inserted a noncommercial mixed CD. Connect to the Internet, click **Options**, and then click **Get Track Names**. If iTunes fails to get the track names, it means the CD is not in the database of known discs.

Import Tracks from a Music CD

If you have connected an optical drive to Mac Pro, you can add tracks from a music CD to the iTunes library. This enables you to listen to an album without having to put the CD into your Mac Pro's optical drive each time. The process of adding tracks from a CD is called *importing*, or *ripping*. After you import the tracks from a music CD, you can play those tracks from the Music category of the iTunes library. You can also use the tracks to create your own playlists and to create your own custom CDs.

Import Tracks from a Music CD

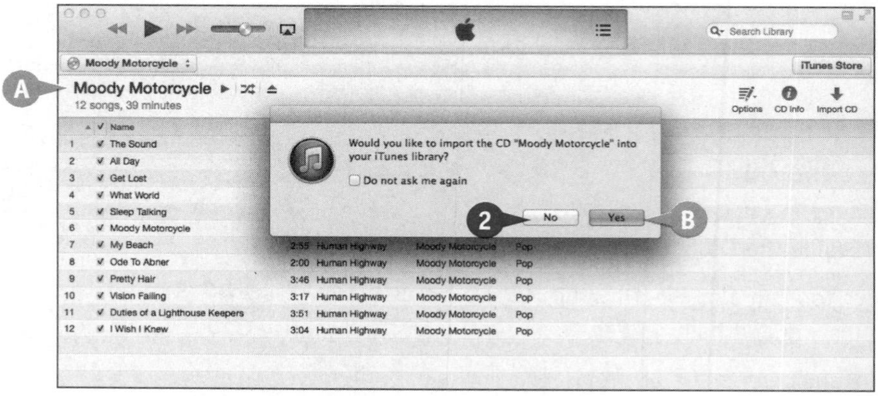

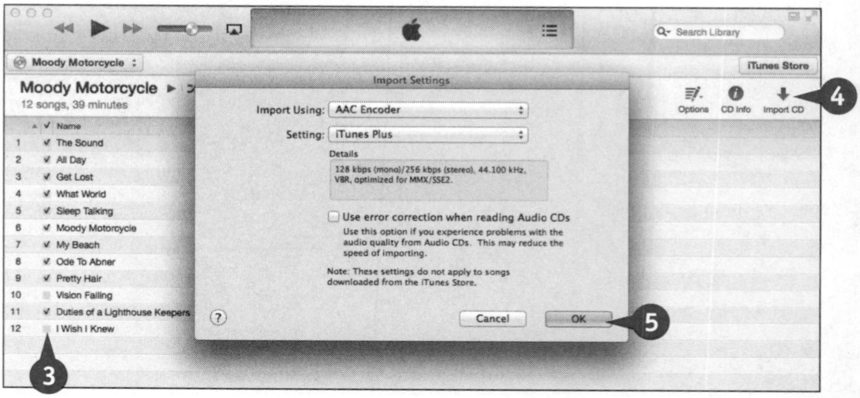

1. Insert a music CD into your Mac Pro's optical drive.

   (A) If you have an Internet connection, after a few moments iTunes shows the contents of the CD.

   iTunes asks if you want to import the CD.

2. Click **No**.

   (B) If you want to import the entire CD, click **Yes** and skip the rest of the steps in this section.

3. Deselect the check box next to each CD track that you do not want to copy (☑ changes to ☐).

4. Click **Import CD**.

   The Import Settings dialog appears.

5. Click **OK**.

Note: If you see a dialog asking if iTunes can send CD info to Gracenote, click **Send**.

iTunes begins importing the selected track or tracks.

C This area displays the copy progress for each track.

D When iTunes is importing a track, it displays beside the track number.

E When iTunes finishes importing a track, it displays beside the track number.

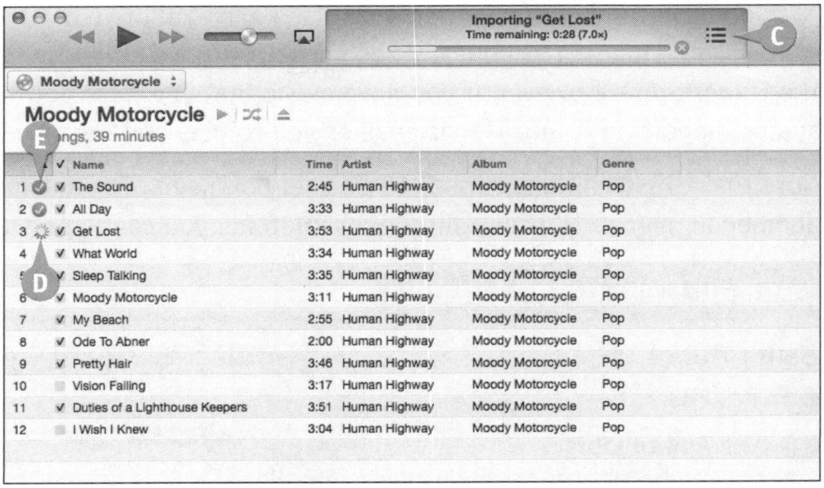

F When iTunes completes the import, you see beside the track numbers of all the tracks you selected.

6 Click the **Eject** button ( ) beside the CD, or press .

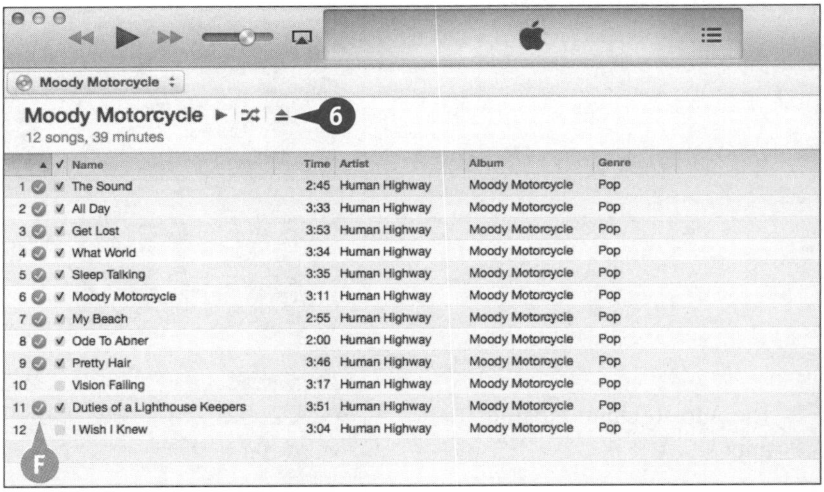

TIPS

I ripped a track by accident. How do I remove it from the library?
Click the **Source List** button, click **Music**, open the album you imported, right-click the track that you want to remove, and then click **Delete** from the shortcut menu. When iTunes asks you to confirm the deletion, click **Delete Song**. When iTunes asks if you want to keep the file, click **Move to Trash**.

Can I specify a different quality when importing?
Yes, you can by changing the *bit rate*, which is a measure of how much of the CD's original data is copied to your computer. In the Import Settings dialog, click the **Setting** , click **Custom**, and then use the Stereo Bit Rate to click the value you want.

Add an Item to the Library

If you have a song or album on your Mac Pro's hard drive or on your network, you can import that item into iTunes. You normally add music to iTunes either by ripping tracks from a CD or by using the iTunes Store. However, if you have music that you have downloaded or purchased from a different source, importing it into iTunes enables you to play and organize the music using the iTunes tools.

Note that this technique applies to a variety of media. For example, if you have downloaded an audiobook, movie, TV show episode, or ringtone, you can import that file into iTunes.

Add an Item to the Library

Using iTunes

1. Click **File**.
2. Click **Add to Library**.

   You can also press ⌘+O.

The Add To Library dialog appears.

3. Navigate to the folder that contains the music you want to import.
4. Click the folder or file you want to import.
5. Click **Open**.

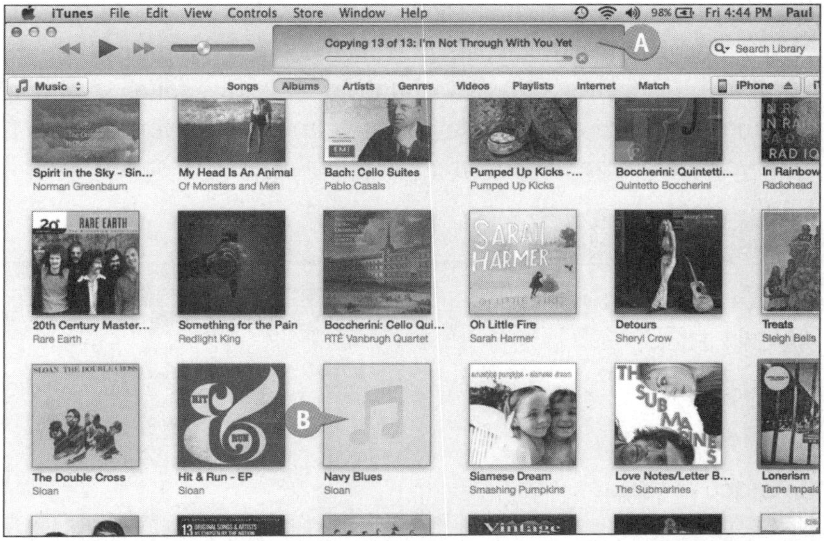

Ⓐ iTunes imports the track or tracks.

Ⓑ The album appears in the iTunes library.

Using Finder

1 Locate the folder or file you want to import.

2 Click and drag the item and drop it on the iTunes icon in the Dock.

iTunes imports the media.

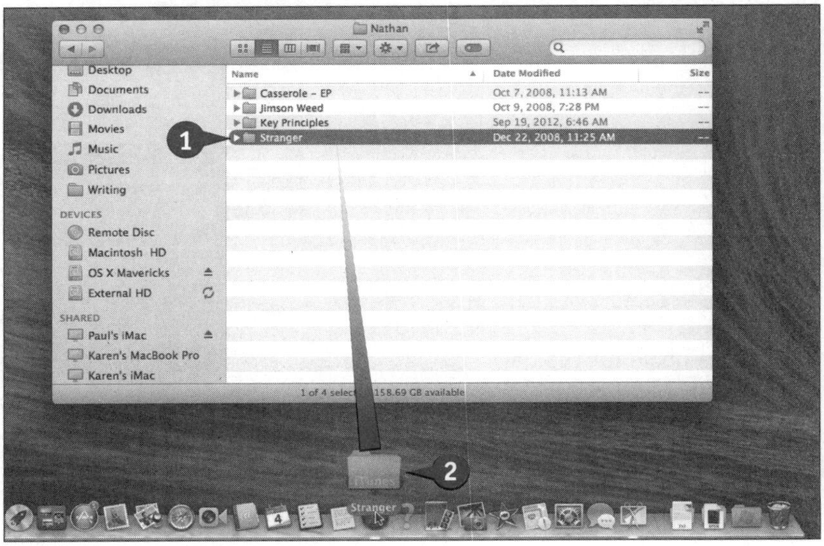

TIP

Does iTunes create a copy of the files I import?

Yes. This is a good idea if the files are located on your network or on an external drive, because it ensures that iTunes always has access to the files. However, if the files reside on your Mac Pro hard drive, creating copies takes up disk space needlessly. In that case, you can prevent iTunes from making copies by clicking **iTunes**, clicking **Preferences**, clicking the **Advanced** tab, and then deselecting the **Copy files to iTunes Media folder when adding to library** option (☑ changes to ☐).

Create a Playlist

A *playlist* is a collection of songs that are related in some way. Using your iTunes library, you can create customized playlists that include only the songs that you want to hear. For example, you might want to create a playlist of upbeat or festive songs to play during a party or celebration. Similarly, you might want to create a playlist of your current favorite songs to burn to a CD. Whatever the reason, once you create the playlist you can populate it with songs using a simple drag-and-drop technique.

Create a Playlist

Create the Playlist

1. Click **File**.
2. Click **New**.
3. Click **Playlist**.

Note: You can create a new playlist by pressing ⌘+N.

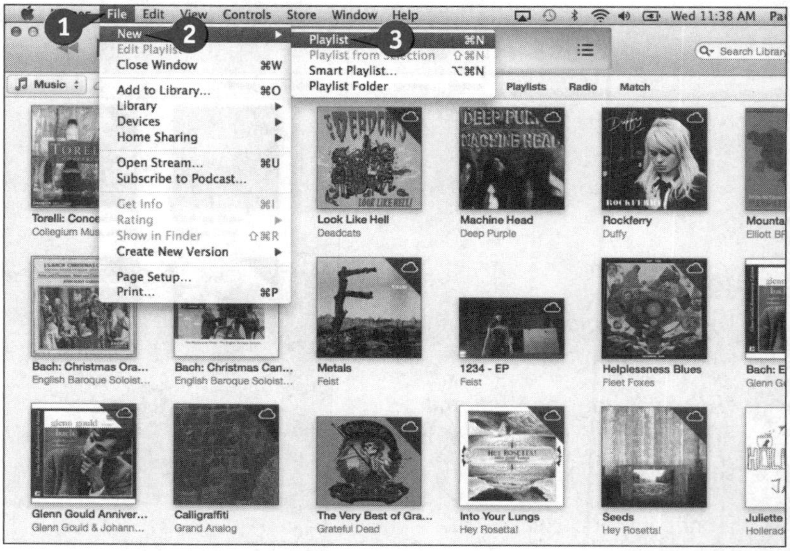

- **A** iTunes creates a new playlist.

4. Type a name for the new playlist.
5. Press Return.

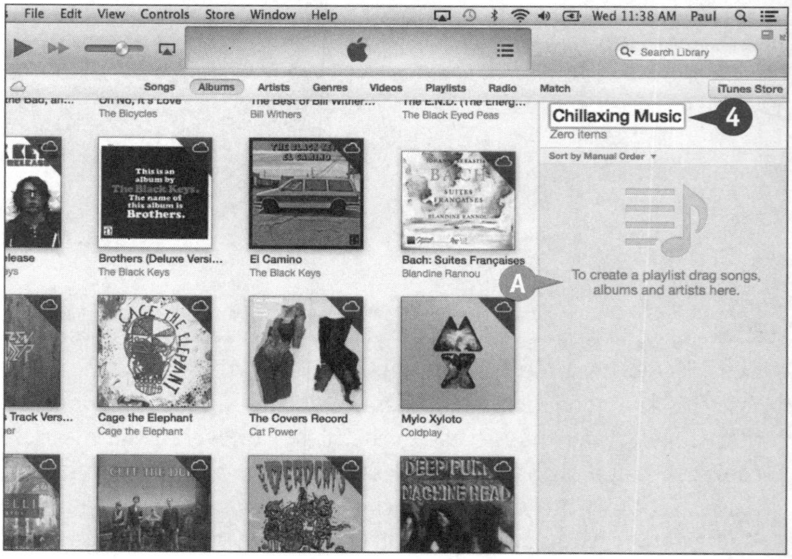

Add Songs to the Playlist

1. In the Source List pop-up, click **Music**.
2. Open an album that has one or more songs you want to add to the playlist.
3. Click a song that you want to add to the playlist.

Note: If you want more than one song from the album's playlist, hold down ⌘ and click each of the songs you want to add.

4. Drag the selected track and drop it on your playlist.
5. Repeat steps **2** to **4** to add more songs to the playlist.
6. Click **Done**.

Ⓑ To access your playlists, click **Playlists**.

TIPS

Is there a faster way to create and populate a playlist?

Yes. Press and hold the ⌘ key and then click each song you want to include in your playlist. Click **File**, click **New**, and then click **Playlist from Selection** (you can also press Shift+⌘+N). Type the playlist name and then press Return.

Can iTunes add songs to a playlist automatically?

Yes, you can create a *Smart Playlist* where the songs have one or more properties in common, such as the genre or text in the song title. Click **File**, click **New**, and then click **Smart Playlist** (you can also press Option+⌘+N). Use the Smart Playlist dialog to create rules that define what songs appear in the playlist.

Burn Music Files to a CD

If your Mac Pro has a recordable optical drive, you can copy, or *burn*, music files onto a CD. Burning CDs is a great way to create customized CDs that you can listen to on the computer or on any device that plays CDs. You can burn music files from within the iTunes window. The easiest way to do this is to create a playlist of the songs you want to burn to the CD. You then organize the playlist by sorting the tracks in the order you want to hear them.

Burn Music Files to a CD

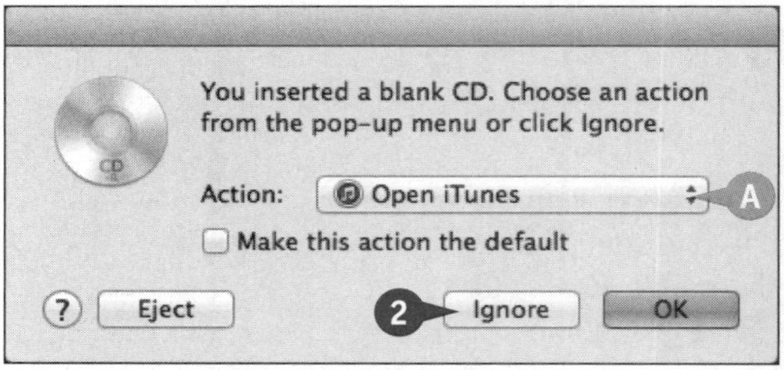

1. Insert a blank CD into your Mac Pro's recordable disc drive.
2. If you already have iTunes running and your Mac Pro asks you to choose an action, click **Ignore**.

(A) If you do not yet have iTunes running, click the **Action** ⬍, click **Open iTunes**, and then click **OK**.

iTunes displays the instructions for burning a playlist to a CD.

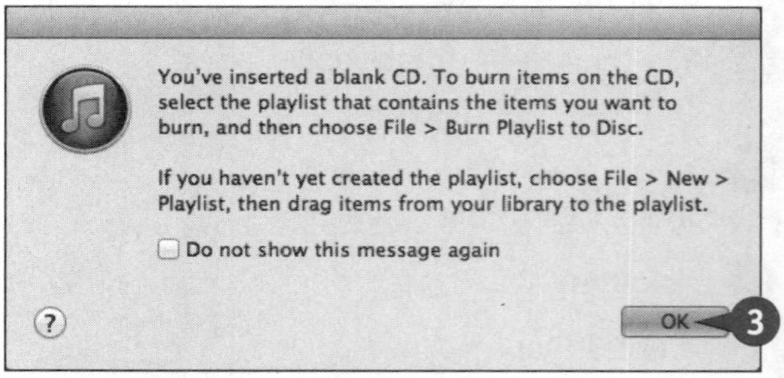

3. Click **OK**.

The iTunes window appears.

4. Click **Playlists**.
5. Click the playlist that you want to burn.
6. To modify the play order, click here.
7. Click and drag songs in the order in which you want them to appear on the CD.

8 Click **File**.

9 Click **Burn Playlist to Disc**.

The Burn Settings dialog appears.

10 Click **Burn**.

iTunes burns the songs to the CD.

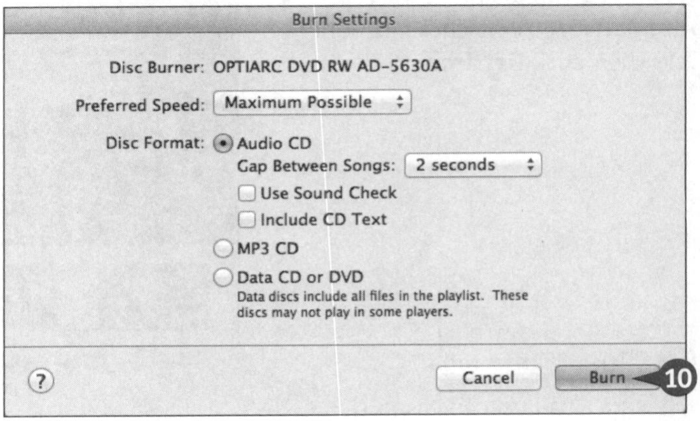

TIPS

Can I control the interval between songs on the CD?

Yes. By default, iTunes adds 2 seconds between each track on the CD. You can change that in the Burn Settings dialog. Click the **Gap between songs** ⬍, and then click the interval you want to use: None, or any time between 1 second and 5 seconds.

What happens if I have more music than can fit on a single disc?

You can still add all the music you want to burn to the playlist. iTunes fills the first disc and then adds the remaining songs to a second disc. After iTunes finishes burning the first disc, it prompts you to insert the next one.

Edit Song Information

For each song in your library or on a music CD, iTunes maintains a collection of information that includes the song title, artist, album title, genre, and more. If a song's information contains errors or omissions, you can edit the data. For example, albums are commonly categorized under the wrong music genre, so you can edit the album to give it the correct genre. You can edit one song at a time, or you can edit multiple songs, such as an entire album or music CD.

Edit Song Information

Edit a Single Song

1. Click the song you want to edit.
2. Click **File**.
3. Click **Get Info**.

Note: You can also press ⌘+I. Alternatively, right-click the song and then click **Get Info**.

4. Click the **Info** tab.
5. Edit or add information to the fields.

Ⓐ If you want to edit another song, click **Previous** or **Next** to display the song you want.

6. Click **OK**.

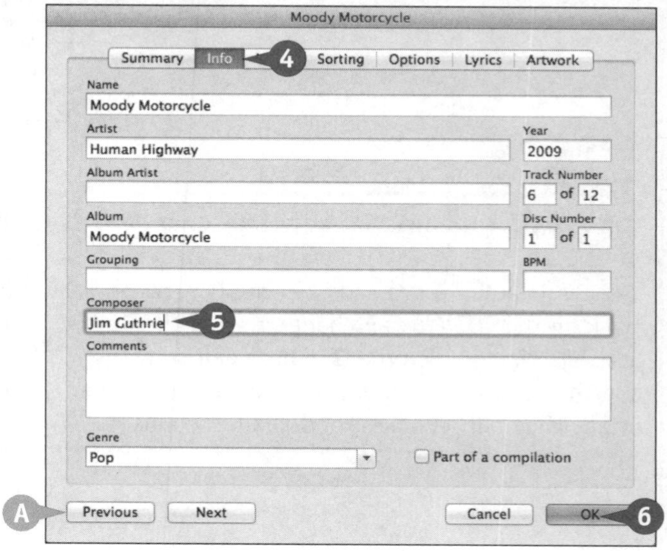

Edit Multiple Songs

1 Select all the songs that you want to edit.

Note: To select individual songs, press and hold ⌘ and click each song; to select all songs (on a music CD, for example), press ⌘+A.

2 Click **File**.

3 Click **Get Info**.

Note: You can also press ⌘+I. Alternatively, right-click any selected song and then click **Get Info**.

iTunes asks you to confirm that you want to edit multiple songs.

4 Click **Yes**.

The Multiple Item Information dialog appears.

5 Edit or add information to the fields.

B iTunes displays ☑ beside each modified field.

6 Click **OK**.

iTunes applies the edits to each selected song.

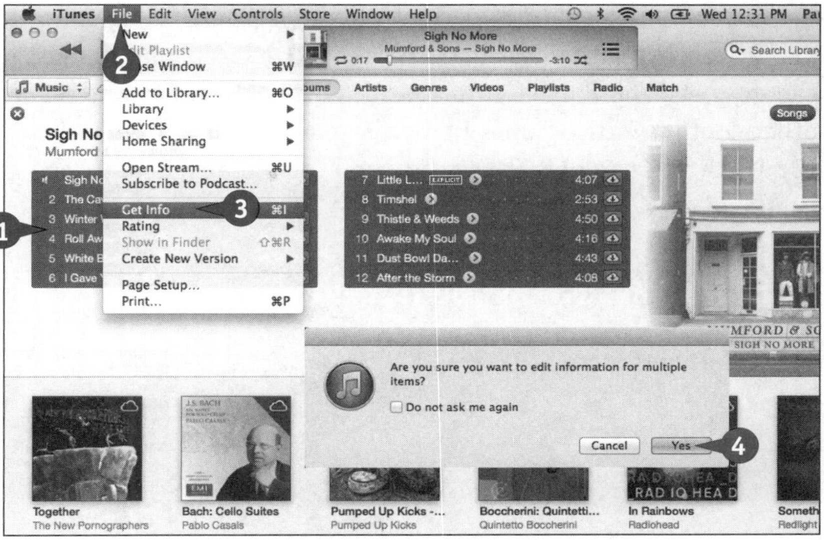

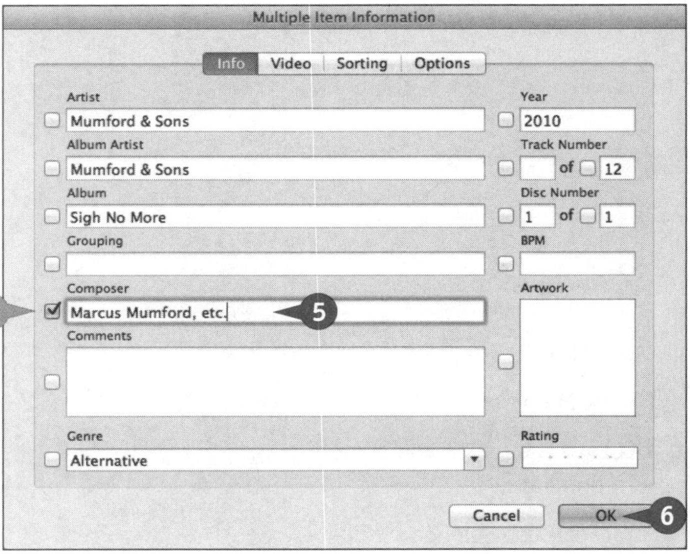

TIP

When I edit multiple songs, why do I not see all the fields in the Multiple Item Information dialog?
When you are editing multiple songs, you can modify only fields containing data common to all the songs, apart from the song title Name field. This makes sense because any changes you make apply to all the selected songs. For example, each song usually has a different title, so you would not want to give every song the same title. You see fields that are common to all the selected songs. For example, on a music CD, data such as the artist, album title, and genre are usually the same for all the songs.

Purchase Music from the iTunes Store

You can add music to your iTunes library by purchasing songs or albums from the iTunes Store. iTunes downloads the song or album to your computer and then adds it to both the Music category and the Purchased playlist. You can then play and manage the song or album just like any other content in the iTunes library. To purchase music from the iTunes Store, you must have an Apple ID, which you can obtain from https://appleid.apple.com. You can also use an AOL account, if you have one.

Purchase Music from the iTunes Store

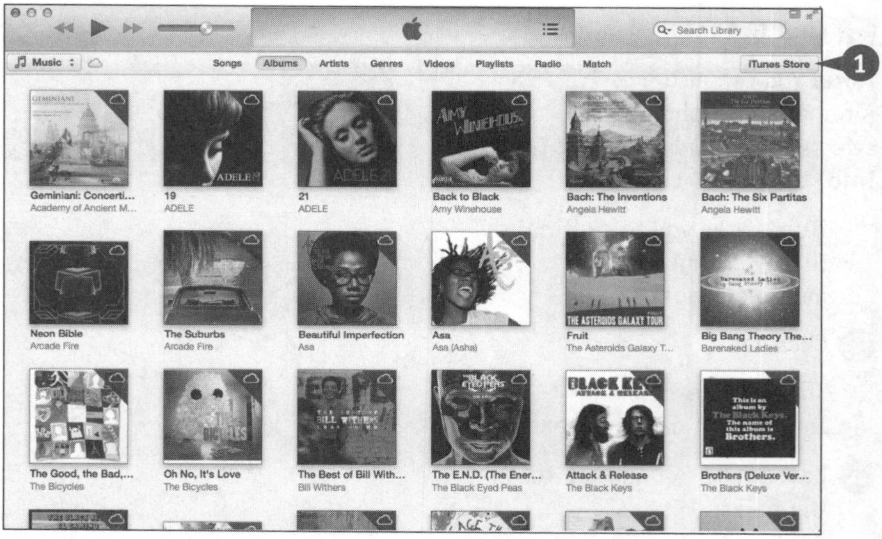

1. Click **iTunes Store**.

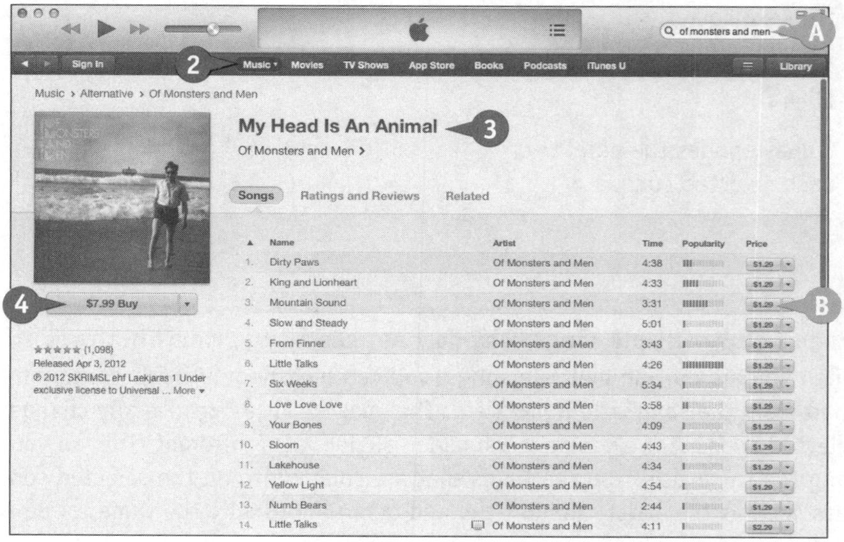

The iTunes Store appears.

2. Click **Music**.
3. Locate the music you want to purchase.

   A. You can use the Search box to search for an artist, album, or song.

4. Click **Buy**.

   B. If you want to purchase just a song, click the song's price button instead.

iTunes asks you to sign in to your iTunes Store account.

5 If you have not signed in to your account, you must type your Apple ID.

6 Type your password.

7 Click **Buy**.

iTunes charges your credit card and begins downloading the music to your Mac Pro.

C The status area displays the progress of the download.

D To return to the iTunes library, click **Library**.

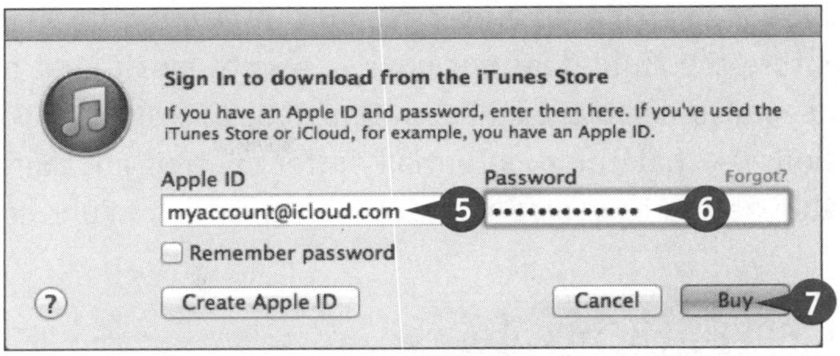

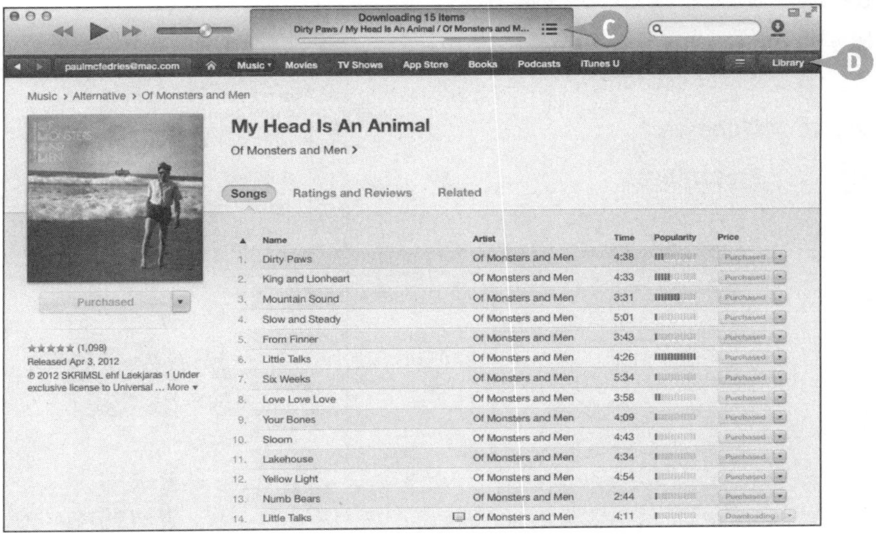

TIPS

Can I use my purchased music on other computers and devices?

Yes. Although many iTunes Store media, particularly movies and TV shows, have digital rights management (DRM) restrictions applied to prevent illegal copying, the songs and albums in the iTunes Store are DRM-free, and so do not have these restrictions. You can play them on multiple devices (such as iPods, iPads, and iPhones), and burn them to multiple CDs.

How do I avoid having many small charges on my credit card bill when purchasing multiple songs?

To avoid many small iTunes charges, purchase an iTunes gift card from an Apple Store or retailer that sells gift cards. On the back of the card, scratch off the sticker that covers the redeem code. Access the iTunes Store, click **Redeem** at the bottom of the store, type the redemption code, and click **Redeem**.

Apply Parental Controls

If you are setting up a user account in Mac Pro for a child, you can use iTunes' parental controls to ensure the child does not have access to music that has been marked as having explicit content. You can also disable certain content types — such as podcasts, the iTunes Store, and Internet radio stations — that could potentially offer content not suitable for the child. Finally, you can also disable access to shared iTunes libraries, which might contain unsuitable music.

Apply Parental Controls

1. Log in to OS X using the child's user account.
2. Click **iTunes**.
3. Click **Preferences**.

The iTunes preferences appear.

4. Click the **Parental** tab.
5. In the Disable section, select the check box beside each type of content you do not want the user to access (☐ changes to ☑).
6. Click the **Ratings for** ⬍ and then click the country ratings you want to use.
7. To ensure the user cannot access explicit musical content, select the **Music with explicit content** option (☐ changes to ☑).

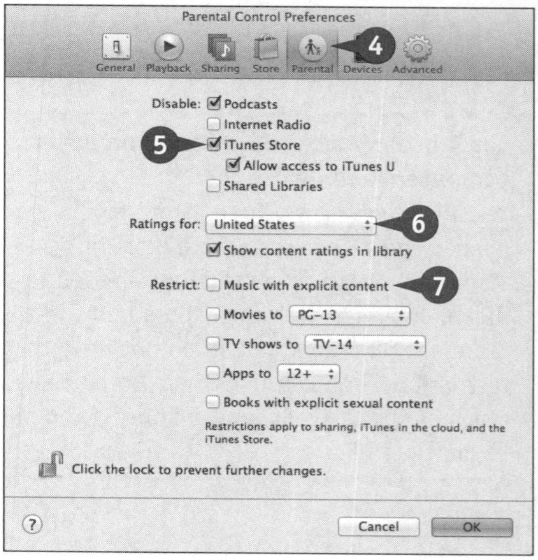

iTunes displays an overview of what it means to restrict explicit content.

8 Click **OK**.

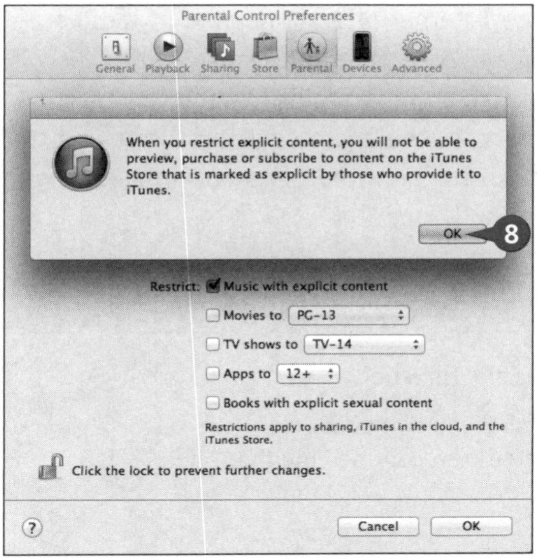

9 Click **OK**.

iTunes puts the parental controls into effect.

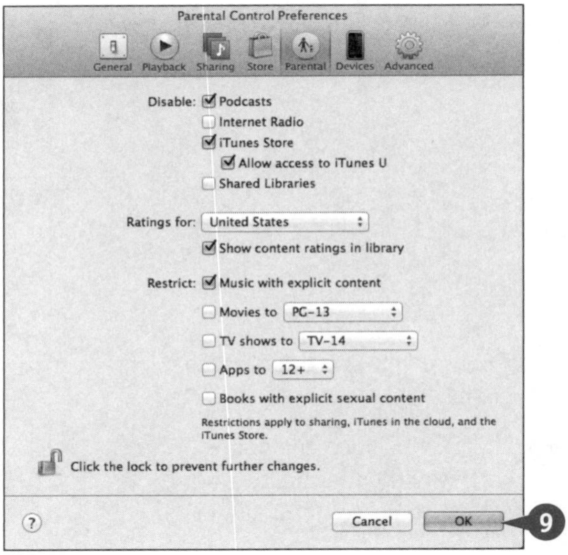

TIP

Is it not possible for the child to open the iTunes preferences and disable the parent controls?
Yes, although this is not likely to be a concern for young children. However, for older children who know their way around OS X, you should lock the parental controls to avoid having them changed. Follow steps 1 to 4 to open the child's user account and display the Parental tab. Click the lock icon (🔓), type your Mac Pro administrator password, and then click **OK**. 🔓 changes to 🔒, indicating that the controls in the Parental tab are now locked and can be unlocked only with your administrator password. Click **OK**.

Listen to an Internet Radio Station

The Internet offers a number of radio stations to which you can listen. iTunes maintains a list of many of these online radio stations, so it is often easier to use iTunes to listen to Internet radio. Just like a regular radio station, an Internet radio station broadcasts a constant audio stream, except you access the audio over the Internet instead of over the air. iTunes offers several radio stations in each of its more than two dozen genres, which include Blues, Classic Rock, Classical, Folk, Hip Hop, Jazz, and Pop.

Listen to an Internet Radio Station

1 Click **Internet**.

Note: If you do not see the Internet category, see the first tip.

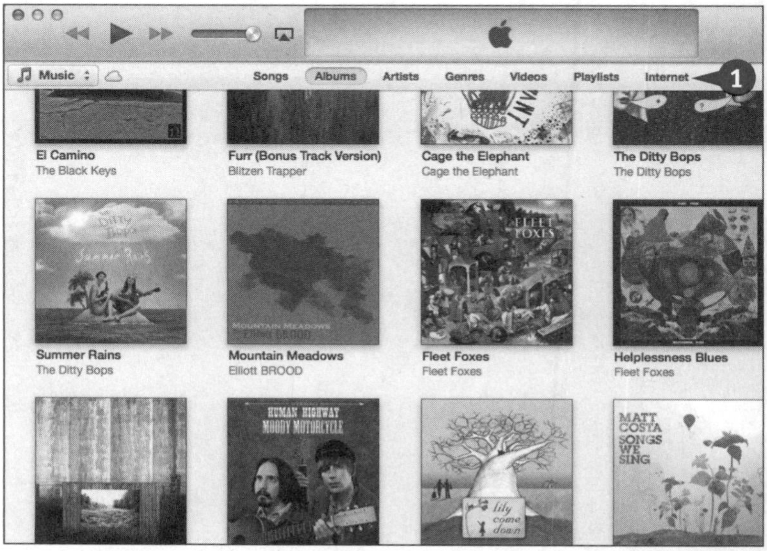

iTunes displays a list of radio genres.

2 Click ▶ to open the genre with which you want to work (▶ changes to ▼).

iTunes displays a list of radio station streams in the genre.

3 Click the radio station stream to which you want to listen.

4 Click **Play** (▶).

iTunes plays the radio station stream.

A The status area displays the name of the station and the name of the currently playing track.

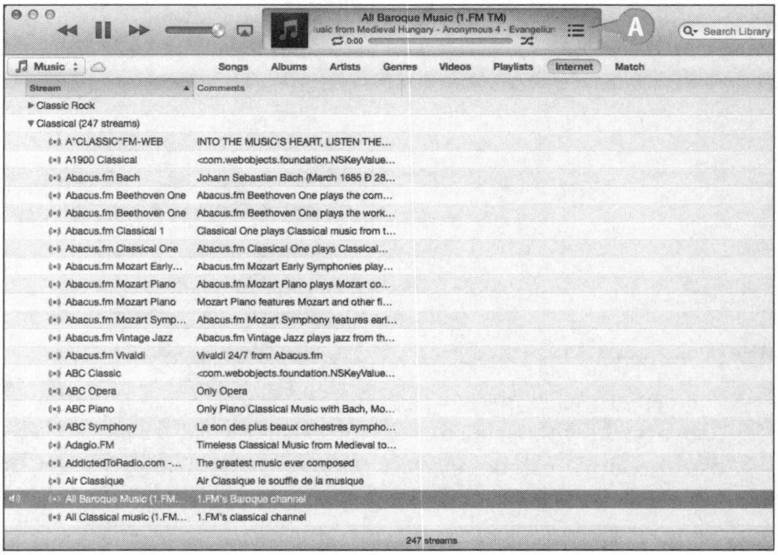

TIPS

The Internet section of the iTunes library does not appear. Can I still listen to Internet radio?

Yes. By default, iTunes does not show all the available library categories and sources. To display the Internet Radio source, click **iTunes** and then click **Preferences** to open the iTunes preferences. Click the **General** tab, select the **Internet Radio** option (☐ changes to ☑), and then click **OK**.

Is it possible to use iTunes to save or record a song from a radio station stream?

No. An Internet radio stream is "listen-only." iTunes does not give you any way to save the stream to your Mac Pro hard drive or to record the stream as it plays.

Subscribe to a Podcast

You can use iTunes to locate, subscribe, manage, and listen to your favorite podcasts. A *podcast* is an audio feed — or sometimes a feed that combines both audio and video — that a publisher updates regularly with new episodes. The easiest way to get each episode is to subscribe to the podcast. This ensures that iTunes automatically downloads each new episode to your iTunes library. You can subscribe to podcasts either via the publisher's website, or via the iTunes Store.

Subscribe to a Podcast

1 Click **iTunes Store**.

2 Click **Podcasts**.

A You can also click the **Podcasts** ▾ to display a list of podcast categories.

3. Locate the podcast to which you want to subscribe.

4. Click **Subscribe**.

B. If you want to listen to just one episode before subscribing, click the episode's **Free** button instead.

iTunes asks you to confirm.

5. Click **Subscribe**.

iTunes begins downloading the podcast.

To listen to the podcast, click the subscription in the Podcasts category of the library.

TIP

How do I subscribe to a podcast via the web?

Use your web browser to navigate to the podcast's home page, click the **iTunes** link to open a preview of the podcast, click **View in iTunes**, and then follow steps 4 and 5.

If the podcast does not have an iTunes link, copy the address of the podcast feed, switch to iTunes, click **File**, and then click **Subscribe to Podcast**. In the Subscribe to Podcast dialog, use the URL text box to paste the address of the podcast feed and then click **OK**.

Share Your iTunes Library

You can make the contents of your iTunes library available to other iTunes users on your network by activating the sharing feature. This is called *home sharing* and it means that as long as another iTunes user on your network is signed in using the same Apple ID, that user can view the contents of your iTunes library and play your media locally.

Home sharing works two ways, meaning that not only can other iTunes users see and play your media, but you can also see and play the content from those users' libraries on your Mac Pro.

Share Your iTunes Library

Share Your Library

1. Authorize your Mac Pro to use your Apple ID, as described in the first tip of this section.
2. Click **File**.
3. Click **Home Sharing**.
4. Click **Turn On Home Sharing**.

iTunes displays the Home Sharing window.

5. Type your Apple ID and password.
6. Click **Turn On Home Sharing**.

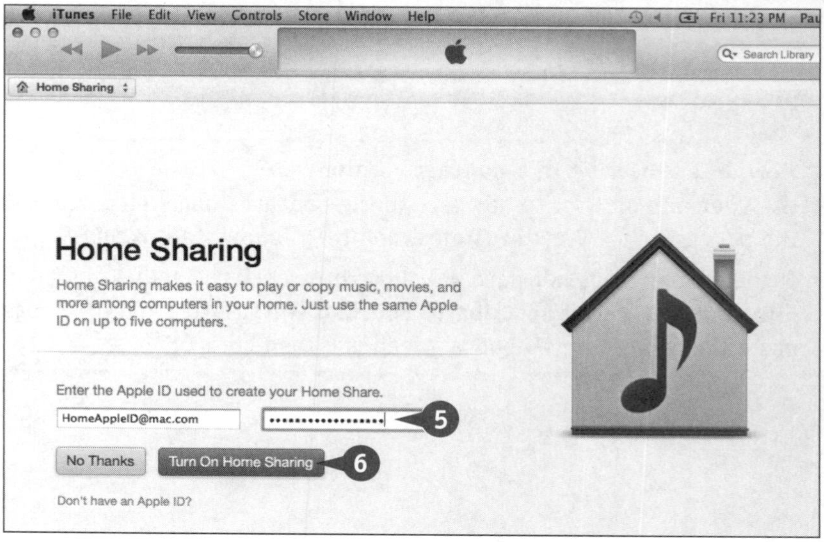

iTunes activates home sharing for your library.

7. Click **Done**.

Other users signed in with the same Apple ID can now see and play your library content.

Display a Shared Library

1. Click the **Source List** ⬍.
2. In the Home Shares section, click the library you want to use.

iTunes displays that library's contents.

TIPS

How do I authorize my Mac Pro?
Click **Store** and then click **Authorize This Computer**. In the Authorize This Computer dialog that appears, type your Apple ID password and then click **Authorize**. iTunes authorizes your Mac Pro and then tells you the authorization was successful. Click **OK**.

Can I change the name of my iTunes library?
Yes. The default name that iTunes assigns to your library is *Name*'s Library, where *Name* is the first name of your Mac Pro user account. To give your library a different name, click **iTunes** and then click **Preferences** to open the iTunes preferences. Click the **General** tab, edit the text in the Library Name text box, and then click **OK**.

Create a Custom Ringtone in iTunes

You can use iTunes to create a custom ringtone from a song in your library. This is useful for Mac Pro FaceTime calls or if you have an iPhone and you want to use something other than its default ringtones. You can also apply a custom ringtone to iOS events such as incoming text and e-mail messages and calendar and reminder alerts, so this technique is also handy for your iPad or iPod touch.

This section shows you how to create a custom ringtone in iTunes. See the next section, "Create a Custom Ringtone in GarageBand," to learn how to also create a ringtone from a song using the GarageBand app.

Create a Custom Ringtone in iTunes

1. In iTunes, play the track you want to use.
2. While the track is playing, watch the playback time and note the start time and end time of the portion of the track you want to use as your ringtone.

3. Click **File**.
4. Click **Get Info**.

   You can also press ⌘+I.

The track's Info dialog appears.

5 Click the **Options** tab.

6 Use the Start Time text box to type the starting point for your ringtone snippet.

7 Use the Stop Time text box to type the ending point for your ringtone.

8 Click **OK**.

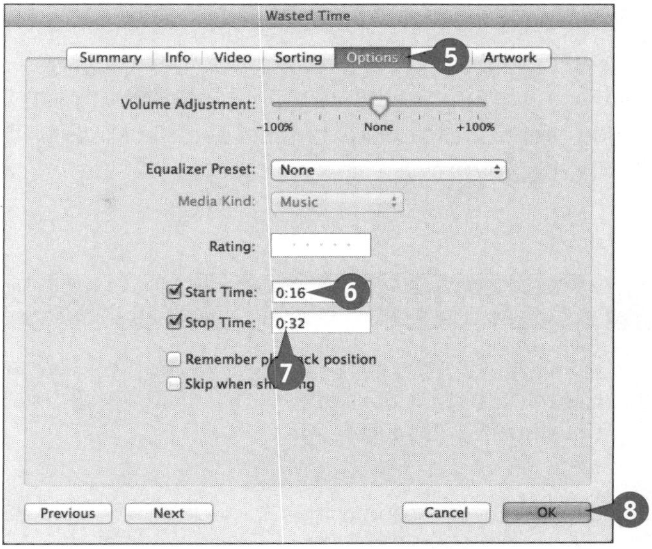

9 Click **File**.

10 Click **Create New Version**.

11 Click **Create AAC Version**.

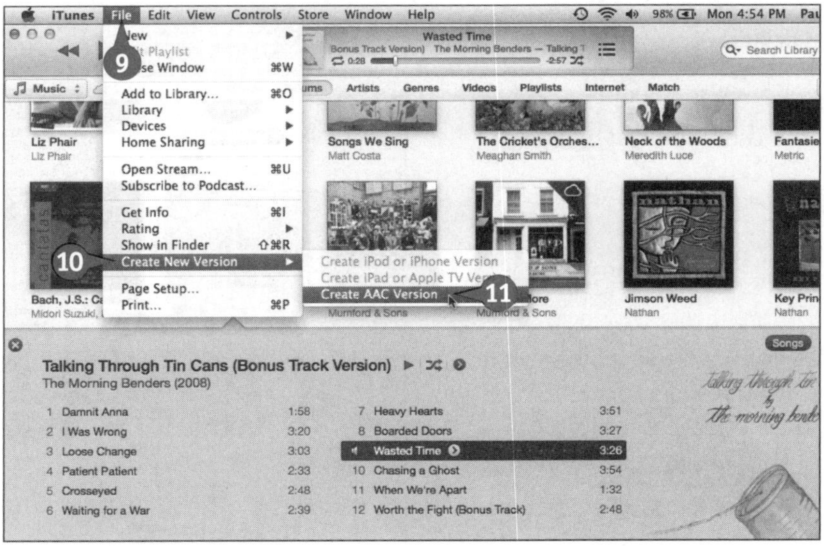

TIPS

Can I make my ringtone as long as I want?

No, iTunes puts a restriction on the length of a ringtone. Specifically, a ringtone can be a maximum of 30 seconds long, so you must select a portion of the track that is no longer than 30 seconds.

What is an AAC file?

AAC stands for *Advanced Audio Coding*, which is a standard file format used for audio content. In the case of iOS used on the iPhone, iPad, and iPod touch, AAC is the file format used as the basis for creating a ringtone, so that is why you must convert the song snippet to AAC.

continued ►

Create a Custom Ringtone in iTunes (continued)

Creating a custom ringtone involves specifying a portion of a song to use as the tone and then converting that snippet to a file that iTunes can recognize as a ringtone. Although programs exist that will perform this process for you, the steps in this section, although long, are not difficult. If you prefer a shorter technique, see the steps in the next section, "Create a Custom Ringtone in GarageBand."

Create a Custom Ringtone in iTunes (continued)

iTunes creates a version of the track that includes only the snippet you specified in steps **6** and **7**.

12 Click the new version of the track.

13 Click **File**.

14 Click **Show in Finder**.

You can also press Shift + ⌘ + R.

A new Finder window appears with the short version of the track selected.

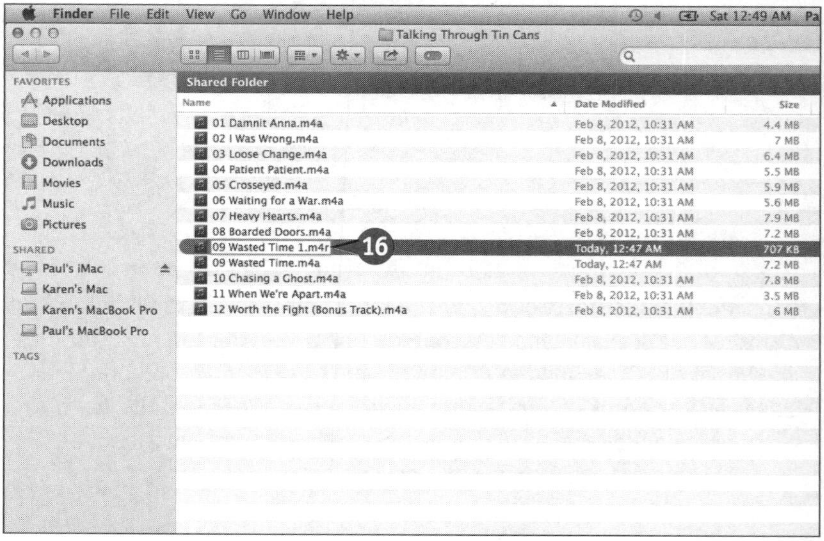

15 Press Return to open the filename for editing.

16 Change the extension from m4a to m4r.

17 Press Return.

Note: The m4r extension designates the file as a ringtone.

Finder asks you to confirm the extension change.

18 Click **Use .m4r**.

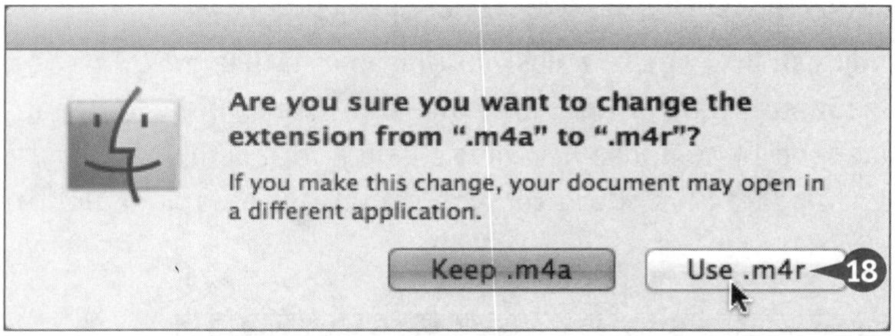

A Finder converts the file to a ringtone.

19 Double-click the file.

iTunes plays the ringtone and adds the file to the Tones section of the library.

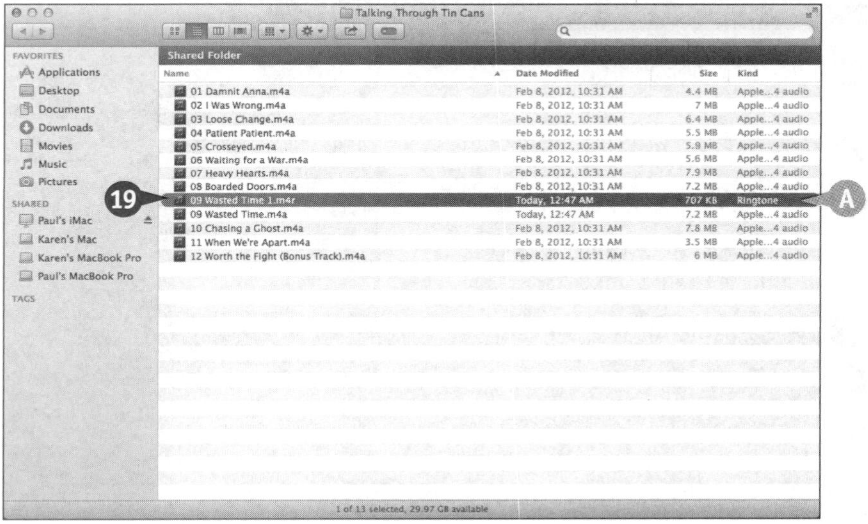

TIP

Do I need to keep the short version of the track?

No, you can delete it by following these steps:

1 In iTunes, click the short version of the track.

2 Click **Edit**.

3 Click **Delete**.

iTunes asks you to confirm.

4 Click **Delete Song**.

iTunes asks if you want to move the file to the Trash.

5 Click **Keep File**.

Create a Custom Ringtone in GarageBand

Besides the iTunes method shown in the previous section, “Create a Custom Ringtone in iTunes,” you can also create a custom ringtone for use in iOS devices using the GarageBand app. GarageBand is part of the iLife suite that comes preinstalled in all new Mac Pros. You normally use GarageBand to compose new music using both computer-generated instruments and real instruments attached to Mac Pro. However, you can also use GarageBand to convert a portion of a song into a ringtone.

Create a Custom Ringtone in GarageBand

1. Click **GarageBand** (🎸) in the Dock.
2. Click **iPhone Ringtone**.
3. Click **Choose**.

   The New Project from Template dialog appears.
4. Type a name for the project.
5. Click **Create**.

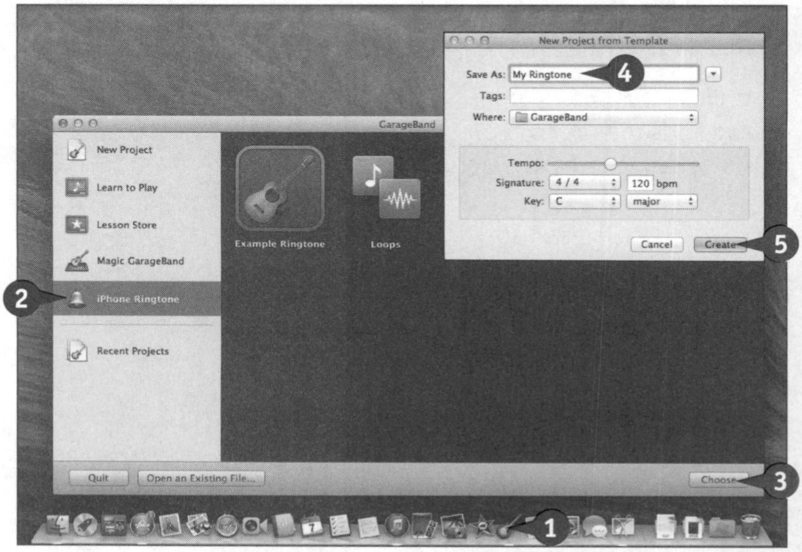

   GarageBand starts a new project.
6. Press ⌘+Delete.

   GarageBand deletes the default track.
7. Switch to iTunes.
8. Click and drag the song you want to use for your ringtone and drop it inside GarageBand.

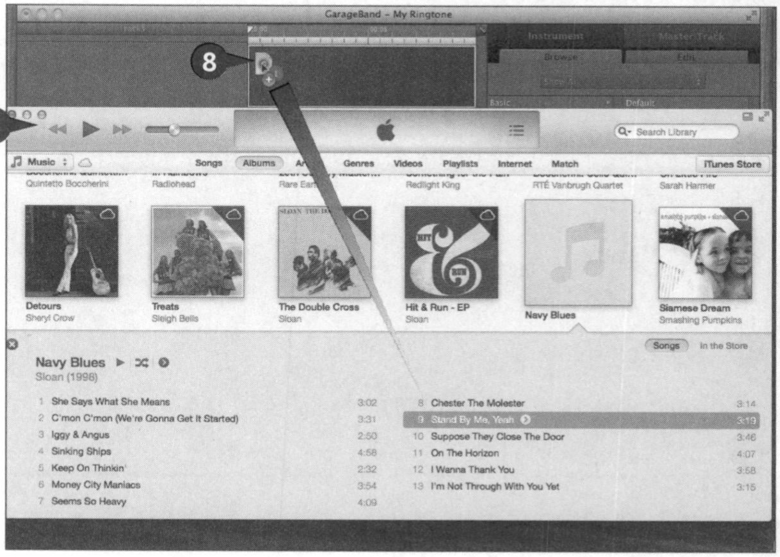

Ⓐ The program creates a new track for the song.

9 Click and drag the left edge of the yellow Cycle Region to define the starting point of the ringtone.

10 Click and drag the right edge to define the ending point.

11 Click **Share**.

12 Click **Send Ringtone to iTunes**.

GarageBand converts the track to a ringtone and then adds it to the Tones category in iTunes.

TIPS

Can I make my ringtone as long as I want?

No, like iTunes, GarageBand puts a restriction on the length of a ringtone. However, with GarageBand a ringtone can be a maximum of 40 seconds long, so you must select a portion of the track that is no longer than 40 seconds.

Can I use any song to create a GarageBand ringtone?

No. Although you can use any song purchased from iTunes as the basis for your ringtone, other songs might be protected by digital rights management (DRM), which is a system that restricts how a song can be used. If a song is protected by DRM, you cannot import it into GarageBand, so you cannot use it to create a ringtone.

CHAPTER 12

Viewing and Editing Photos

Whether you just want to look at your photos, or you want to edit them to crop out unneeded portions or fix problems, Mac Pro comes with a number of useful tools for viewing and editing photos.

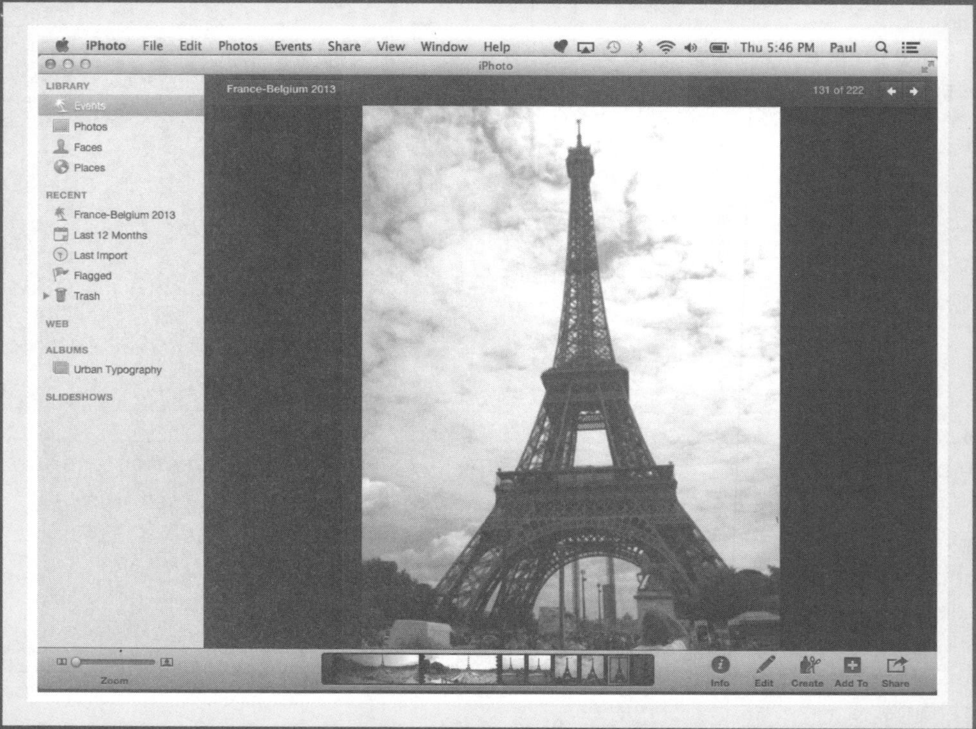

View a Preview of a Photo

OS X offers several tools you can use to see a preview of any photo on your Mac Pro. The Finder application has a number of methods you can use to view your photos, but here you learn about the two easiest methods. First, you can preview any saved image file using the Quick Look feature; second, you can see photo previews by switching to the Cover Flow view. You can also preview photos using the Preview application.

View a Preview of a Photo

View a Preview with Quick Look

1. Click **Finder** () in the Dock.
2. Open the folder that contains the photo you want to preview.
3. Click the photo.
4. Press Spacebar.

A. Finder displays a preview of the photo.

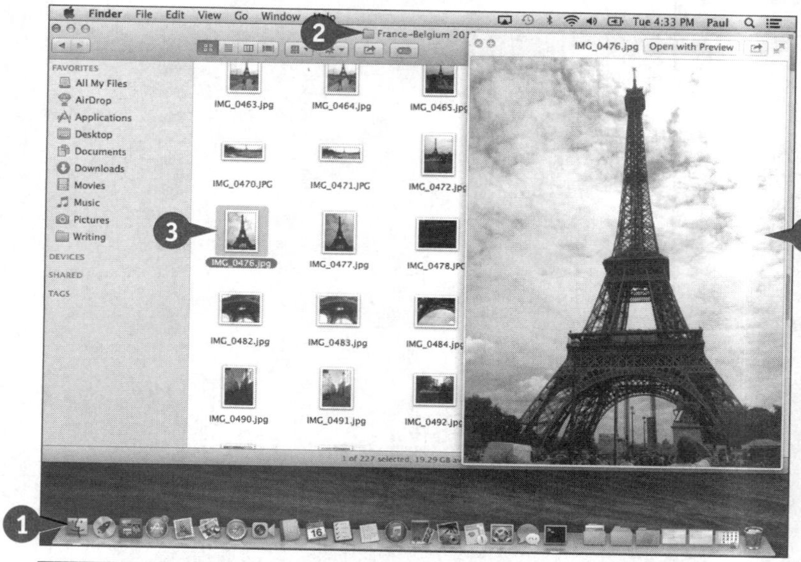

View a Preview with Cover Flow

1. Click **Finder** () in the Dock.
2. Open the folder that contains the photo you want to preview.
3. Click the photo.
4. Click **Cover Flow** ().

B. Finder displays a preview of the photo.

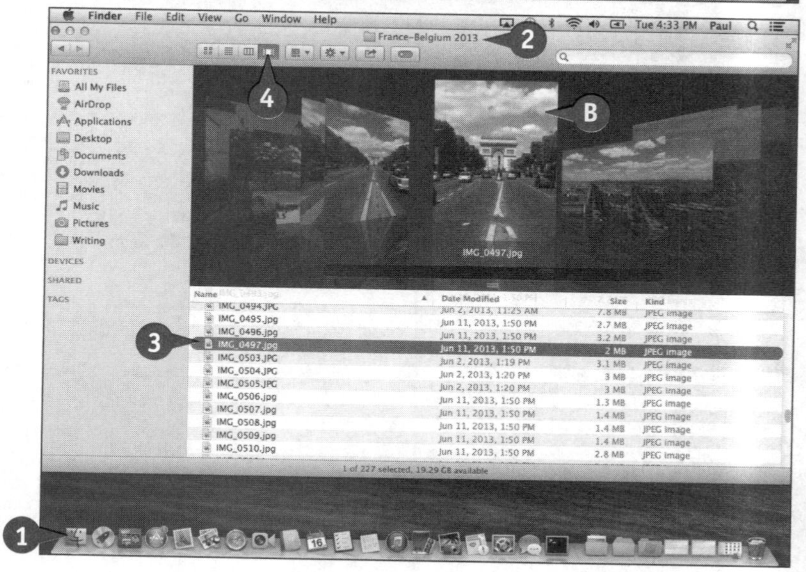

View a Preview in the Preview Application

1. Click **Finder** (icon) in the Dock.
2. Open the folder that contains the photo you want to preview.
3. Click the photo.
4. Click **File**.
5. Click **Open With**.
6. Click **Preview**.

Note: In many cases, you can also simply double-click the photo to open it in the Preview application.

The Preview application opens and displays the photo.

7. Use the toolbar buttons to change how the photo appears in the Preview window.

C More commands are available on the **View** menu.

8. When you finish viewing the photo, click **Close** (icon).

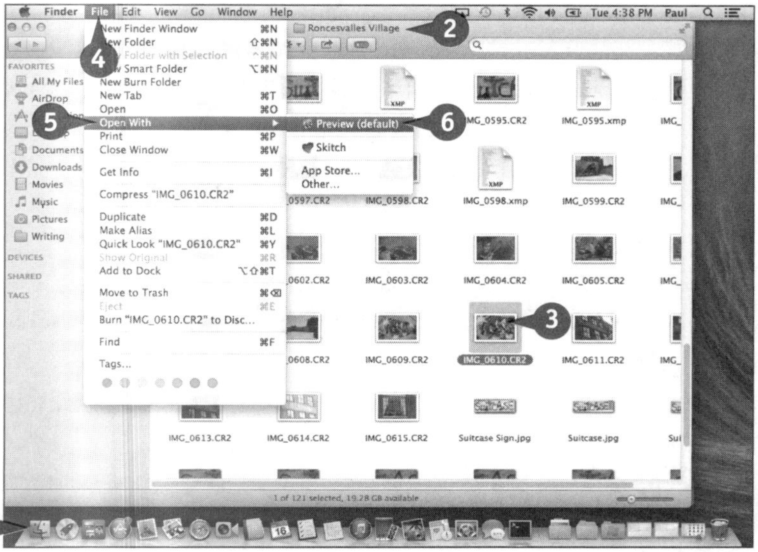

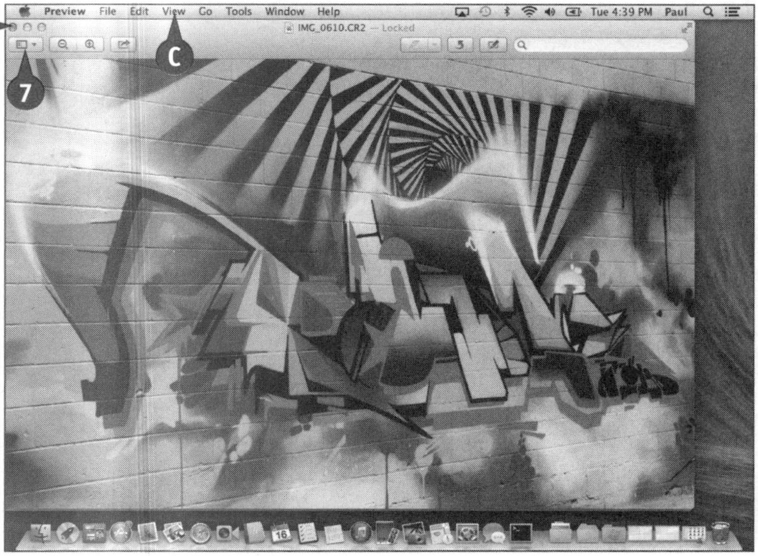

TIPS

Is there an easier way to preview multiple photos using the Preview application?

Yes. In Finder, navigate to the folder that contains the photos and then select each file that you want to preview. Either click and drag the mouse (pointer) over the photos or press and hold ⌘ and click each one. In Preview, click **Next** and **Previous** to navigate the photos.

Is there a way that I can zoom in on just a portion of a photo?

Yes. In Preview, click and drag your mouse (pointer) to select the portion of the photo that you want to magnify. Click **View** and then click **Zoom to Selection** (or press ⌘+*).

View a Slide Show of Your Photos

Instead of viewing your photos one at a time, you can easily view multiple photos by running them in a slide show. You can run the slide show using the Preview application or Quick Look. In Preview, the slide show displays each photo for a few seconds and then automatically displays the next photo. Quick Look also offers several on-screen controls that you can use to control the slide show playback. You can also configure Quick Look to display the images full screen.

View a Slide Show of Your Photos

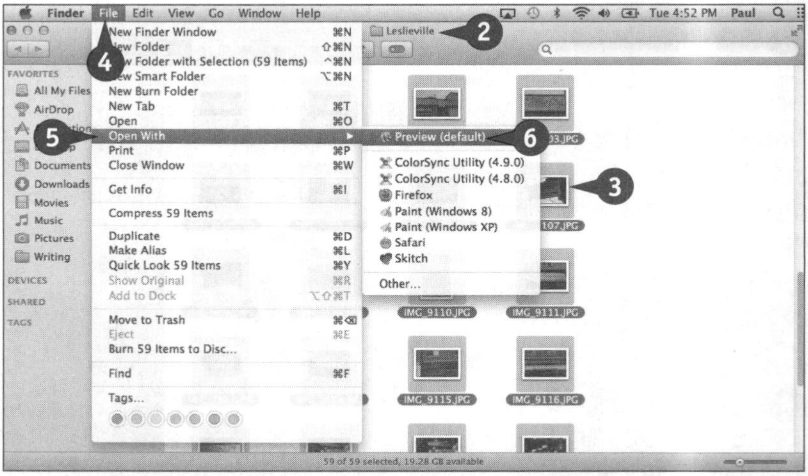

1 Click **Finder** (Finder icon) in the Dock.

2 Open the folder that contains the photos you want to view in the slide show.

3 Select the photos you want to view.

4 Click **File**.

5 Click **Open With**.

6 Click **Preview**.

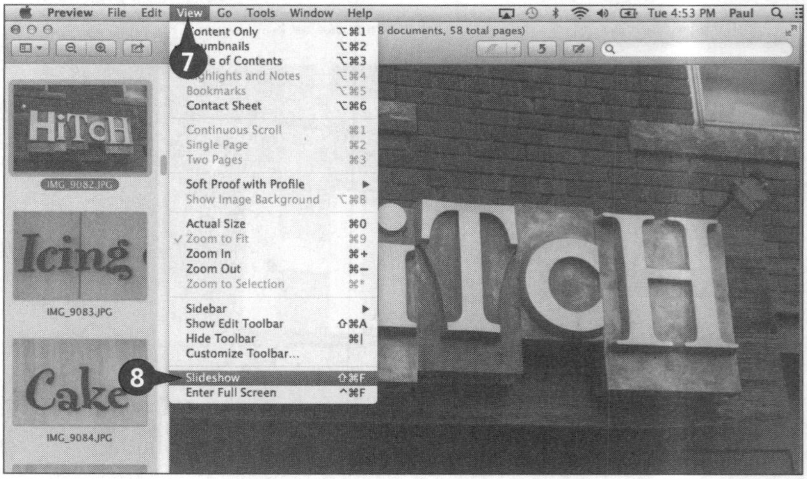

The Preview window appears.

7 Click **View**.

8 Click **Slideshow**.

You can also select Slideshow by pressing Shift + ⌘ + F.

Preview opens the slide show window.

9 Move the mouse (pointer icon).

A Preview displays the slide show controls.

10 Click **Play**.

Preview begins the slide show.

B You can click **Next** to move to the next photo.

C You can click **Back** to move to the previous photo.

D You can click **Pause** to suspend the slide show.

11 When the slide show is over or when you want to return to Finder, click **Close** (☒) or press Esc.

TIPS

Can I jump to a specific photo during the slide show?
Yes. With the slide show running, press Spacebar to stop the show. Use the arrow keys to select the photo that you want to view in the slide show. Click **Play** to resume the slide show.

What keyboard shortcuts can I use when viewing a slide show?
Press → or ↑ to display the next photo, and press ← or ↓ to display the previous photo. Press Esc to end the slide show.

Import Photos from a Digital Camera

You can import photos from a digital camera and save them on your Mac Pro. If you have the iLife suite installed on your Mac Pro, you can use the iPhoto application to handle importing photos. iPhoto is also available separately through the App Store. iPhoto enables you to add a name and a description to each import, which helps you find your photos after the import is complete. To perform the import, you need a cable to connect your digital camera to your Mac Pro. Most digital cameras come with a USB cable.

Import Photos from a Digital Camera

Import Photos from a Digital Camera

1. Connect one end of the cable to the digital camera.
2. Connect the other end of the cable to a free USB port on your Mac Pro.
3. Turn on the camera and put it in either playback or computer mode.

   Your Mac Pro launches the iPhoto application.

Note: You can also launch the application by clicking **iPhoto** ( ) in the Dock.

- A Your digital camera appears in the Devices section.
- B iPhoto displays previews of the camera's photos.

4. Use the Event Name text box to type a name for the group of photos you are going to import.

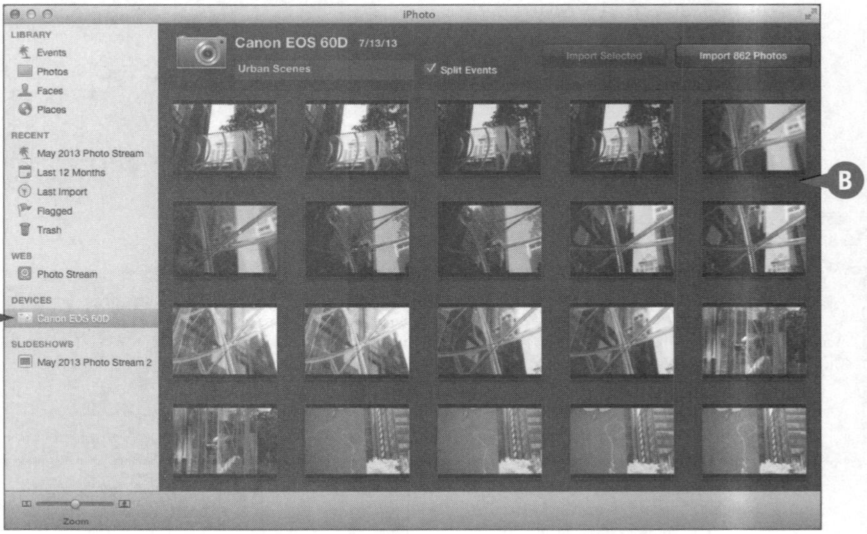

5 Click and drag the mouse around the photos you want, or press and hold ⌘ and click each photo you want to select.

6 Click **Import Selected**.

C To import all the photos from the digital camera, click **Import *X* Photos**, where *X* is the number of photos stored in the camera.

iPhoto imports the photos from the digital camera.

iPhoto asks if you want to delete the original photos from the digital camera.

7 If you no longer need the photos on the camera, click **Delete Photos**.

D To keep the photos on the camera, click **Keep Photos**.

View the Imported Photos

1 Click **Events**.

2 Double-click the event name that you specified in step **4**.

E You can also click **Last Import**.

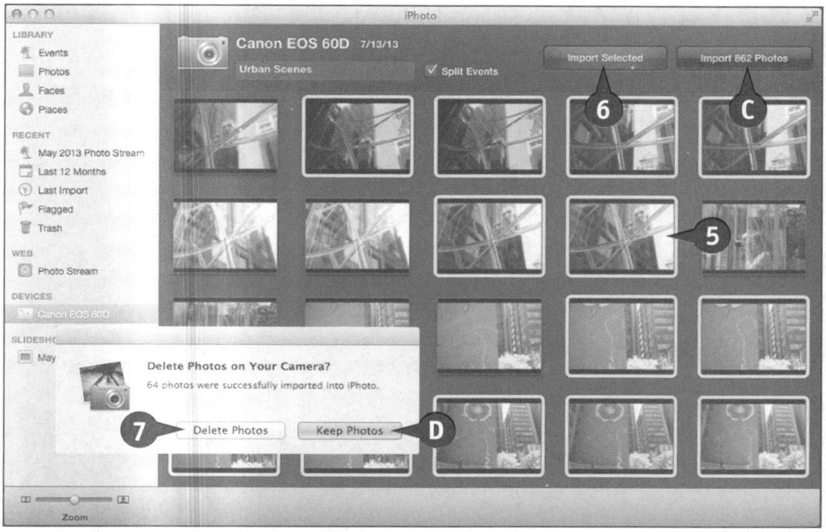

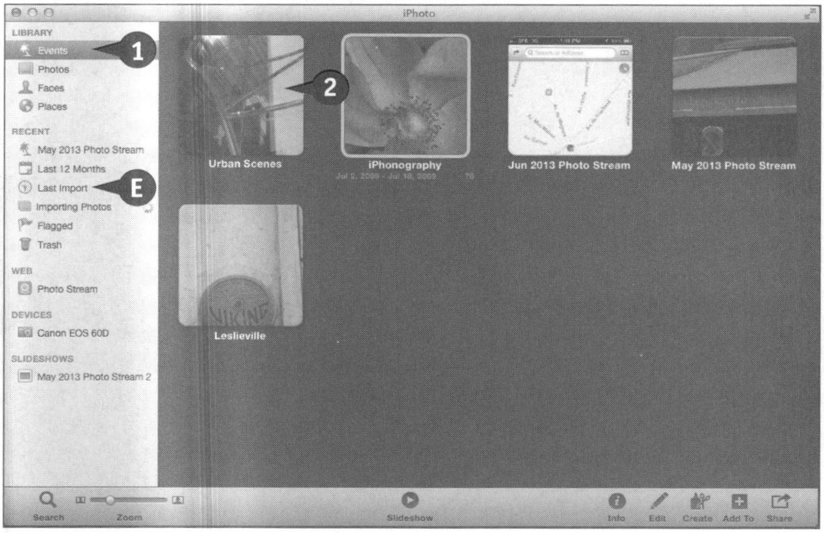

TIP

When I connect my digital camera, why do I see Image Capture instead of iPhoto?

Your Image Capture is not configured to open iPhoto when you connect your camera. To fix this, connect your digital camera to your Mac Pro and the Image Capture application opens. (If you do not see the Image Capture application, click **Finder** in the Dock, click **Applications**, and then double-click **Image Capture**.) Click the **Connecting** and then click **iPhoto**. Click **Image Capture** in the menu bar and then click **Quit Image Capture**.

View Your Photos

If you want to look at several photos, you can use the iPhoto application, which is available with the Apple iLife suite that comes with your Mac Pro. iPhoto offers a feature called full-screen mode, which hides everything else and displays your photos using the entire screen. Once you activate full-screen mode, iPhoto offers several on-screen controls that you can use to navigate backward and forward through the photos. Full-screen mode also shows thumbnail images of each photo, so you can quickly jump to any photo you want to view.

View Your Photos

1. In iPhoto, click **Events**.
2. Double-click the event that contains the photos you want to view.

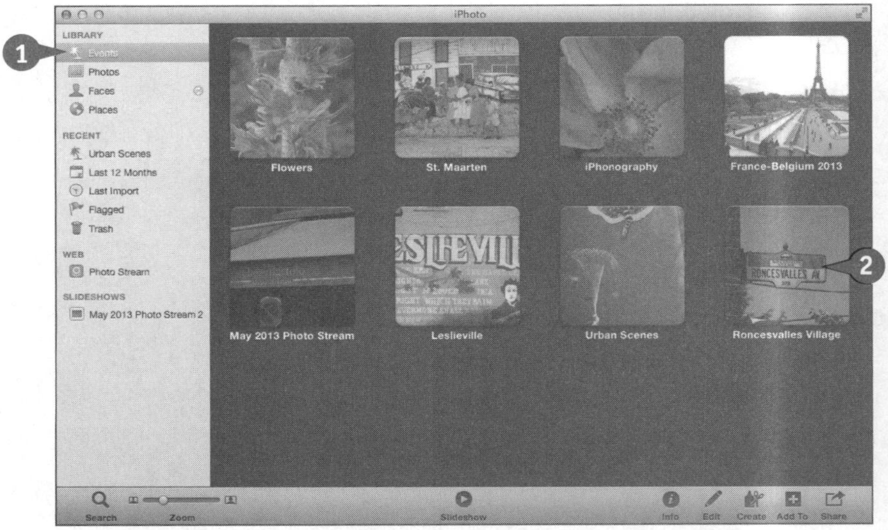

3. Double-click the first photo you want to view.

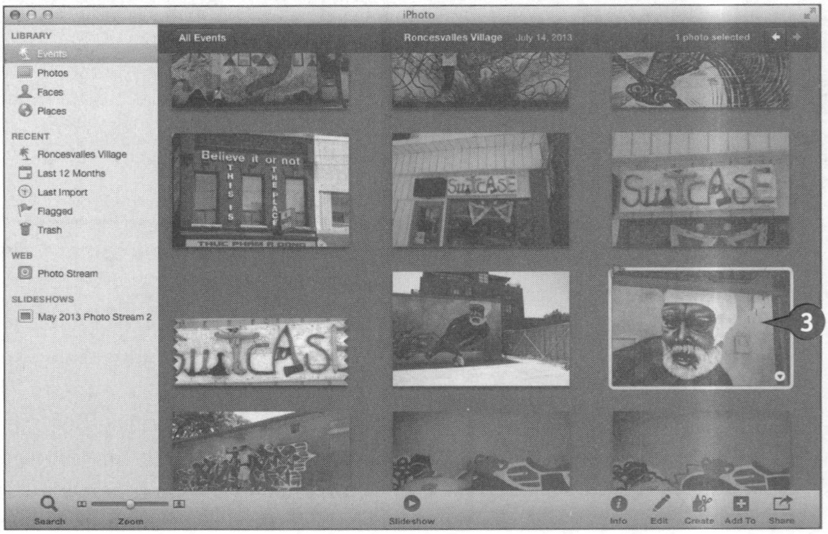

iPhoto displays the photo.

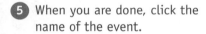

4. Click **Next** ( ) to view the next photo in the event.

A. You can also click **Previous** ( ) to see the previous photo in the event.

Note: You can also navigate photos by pressing and .

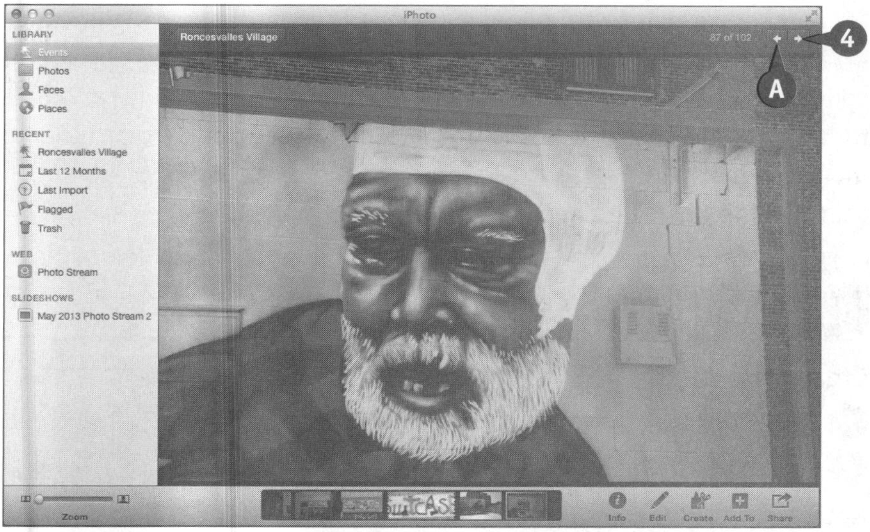

5. When you are done, click the name of the event.

TIP

Is there a way that I can jump quickly to a particular photo in full-screen mode?

Yes. Move the mouse to the thumbnails at the bottom of the iPhoto window and use the horizontal scroll bar to bring the thumbnail of the photo you want into view. Click the photo's thumbnail. iPhoto displays the photo in full-screen mode.

Create an Album

You can use iPhoto to organize your photos into albums. You can get iPhoto either via the iLife suite, which is installed on all new Mac Pros, or via the App Store. In iPhoto, an *album* is a collection of photos that are usually related in some way. For example, you might create an album for a series of vacation photos, for photos taken at a party or other special event, or for photos that include a particular person, pet, or place. Using your iPhoto library, you can create customized albums that include only the photos that you want to view.

Create an Album

Create the Album

1. Click **File**.
2. Click **New Album**.

Note: You can also start a new album by pressing ⌘+N.

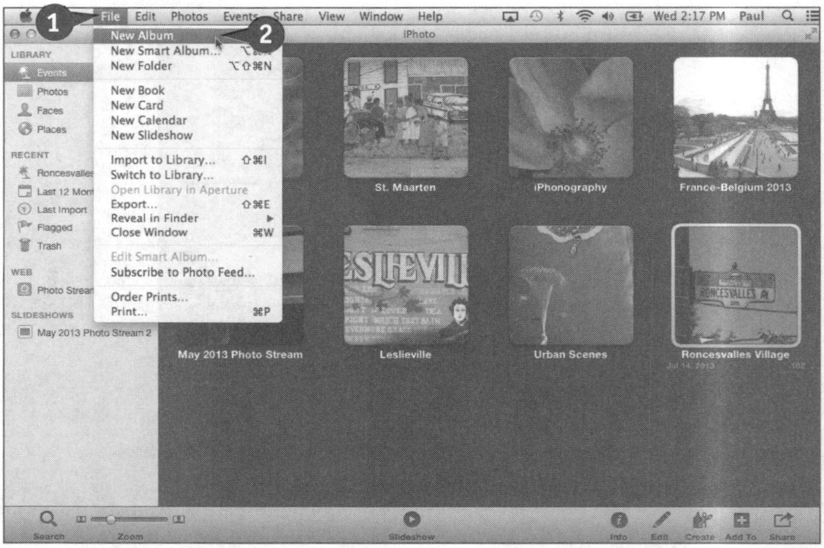

3. Type a name for the new album.
4. Press Return.
5. If you see a dialog asking you to confirm that you want to create an empty album, click **Continue**.

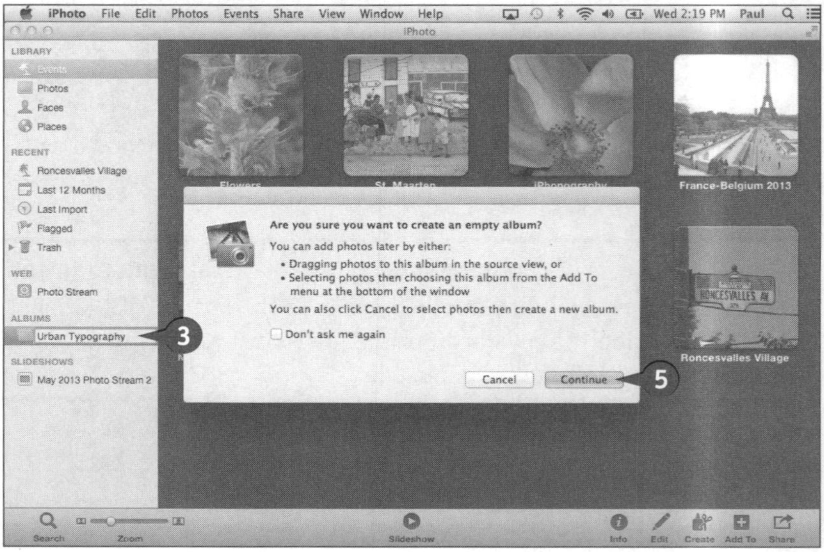

Add Photos to the Album

1. Click **Photos**.
2. Click ▶ beside an event that contains photos with which you want to work (▶ changes to ▼).
3. Click and drag a photo and drop it on the new album.
4. Repeat steps **2** and **3** to add other photos to the album.
5. Click the album.

Ⓐ iPhoto displays the photos you added to the album.

TIP

Is there any way to make iPhoto add photos to an album automatically?

Yes, you can create a *Smart Album* where the photos that appear in the album have one or more properties in common, such as the description, rating, date, or text in the photo title. Click **File** and then click **New Smart Album** (you can also press Option + ⌘ + N). Use the Smart Album dialog to create one or more rules that define which photos you want to appear in the album.

Crop a Photo

If you have a photo containing elements that you do not want to see, you can often cut out those elements. This is called *cropping*, and you can do this with iPhoto, which comes with iLife or via the App Store. When you crop a photo, you specify a rectangular area of the photo that you want to keep. iPhoto discards everything outside of the rectangle. Cropping is a useful skill because it can help give focus to the true subject of a photo. Cropping is also useful for removing extraneous elements that appear near the edges of a photo.

Crop a Photo

1. Click the photo you want to crop.
2. Click **Edit**.

iPhoto displays its editing tools.

3. Click **Crop**.

iPhoto displays a cropping rectangle on the photo.

4 Click and drag a corner or side to define the area you want to keep.

Note: Remember that iPhoto keeps the area inside the rectangle.

5 Click **Done**.

iPhoto saves the cropped photo.

6 Click **Edit**.

iPhoto exits edit mode.

TIP

Is there a quick way to crop a photo to a certain size?

Yes, iPhoto enables you to specify either a specific size, such as 640 × 480, or a specific ratio, such as 4 × 3 or 16 × 9. Follow steps **1** to **3** to display the Crop tool. Select the **Constrain** option (☐ changes to ☑) (A). Click the **Constrain** and then click the size or ratio you want to use (B). Click **Done** and then click **Edit** to exit edit mode.

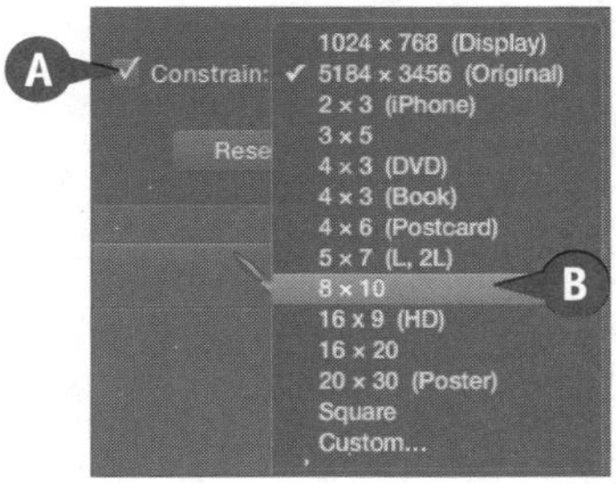

Rotate a Photo

You can rotate a photo using the iPhoto application, which comes with all new Mac Pros as part of iLife, and is also available separately via the App Store. Depending on how you held your camera when you took a shot, the resulting photo might show the subject sideways or upside down. This may be the effect you want, but more likely this is a problem. To fix this problem, you can use iPhoto to rotate the photo so that the subject appears right-side up. You can rotate a photo either clockwise or counterclockwise.

Rotate a Photo

1. Click the photo you want to rotate.

Note: A quick way to rotate a photo is to right-click the photo and then click **Rotate** ().

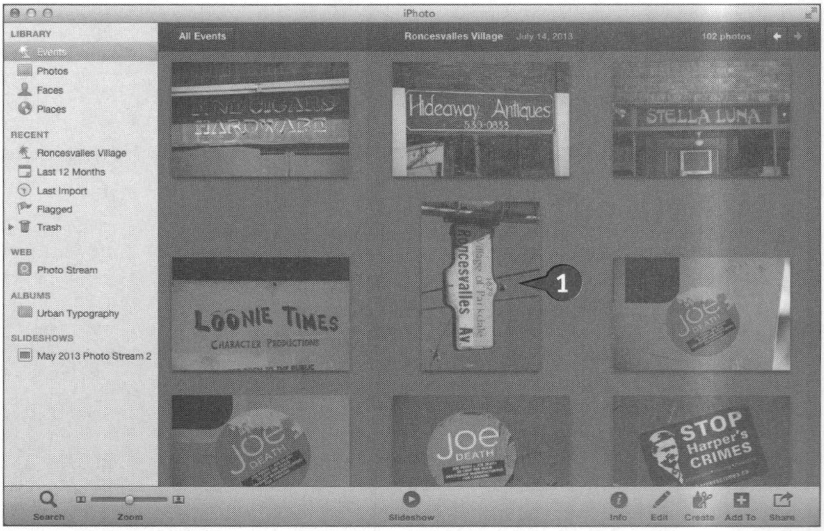

2. Click **Edit**.

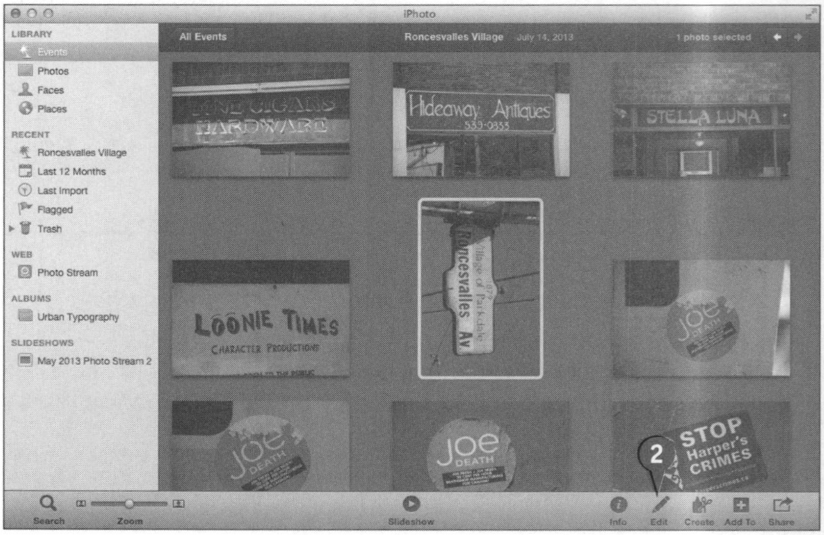

iPhoto displays its editing tools.

3. Click **Rotate** ( ).

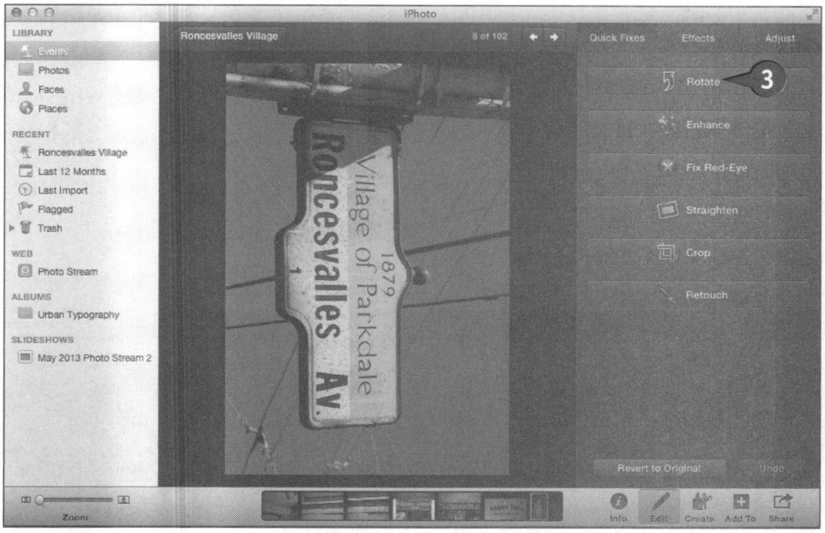

A. iPhoto rotates the photo 90 degrees counterclockwise.

4. Repeat step **3** until the subject of the photo is right-side up.

5. Click **Edit**.

iPhoto exits edit mode.

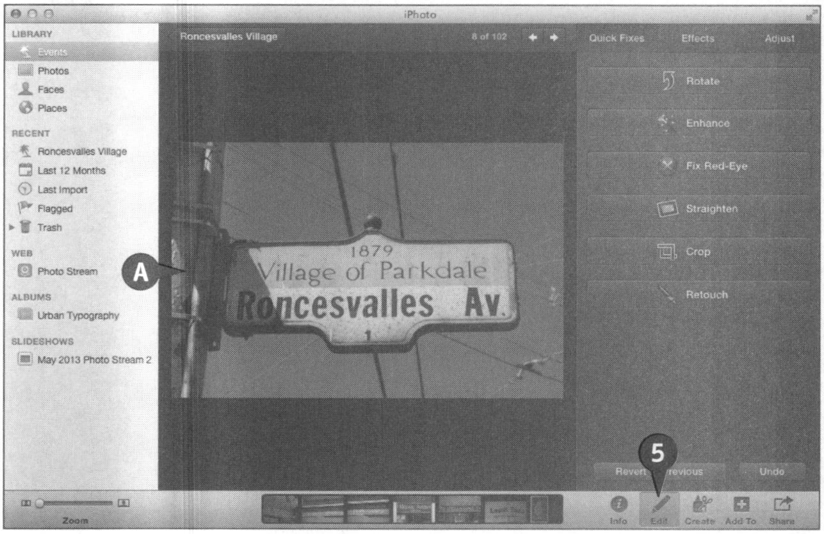

TIP

Can I rotate a photo clockwise instead?

Yes. With the editing tools displayed, press and hold Option. The Rotate icon changes from to . Press and hold Option and then click **Rotate** to rotate the photo clockwise by 90 degrees. You can also right-click the photo and then click **Rotate Clockwise**.

Straighten a Photo

You can straighten a crooked photo using the iPhoto application, which comes with all new Mac Pros as part of iLife, and is also available separately via the App Store. If you do not use a tripod when taking pictures, getting your camera perfectly level when you take a shot is very difficult and requires a lot of practice and a steady hand. Despite your best efforts, you might end up with a photo that is not quite level. To fix this problem, you can use iPhoto to nudge the photo clockwise or counterclockwise so that the subject appears straight.

Straighten a Photo

1. Click the photo you want to straighten.
2. Click **Edit**.

iPhoto displays its editing tools.

3. Click **Straighten**.

iPhoto displays a grid over the photo.

4 Click and drag the **Angle** slider.

Drag the slider to the left to angle the photo counterclockwise.

Drag the slider to the right to angle the photo clockwise.

5 Click **Done**.

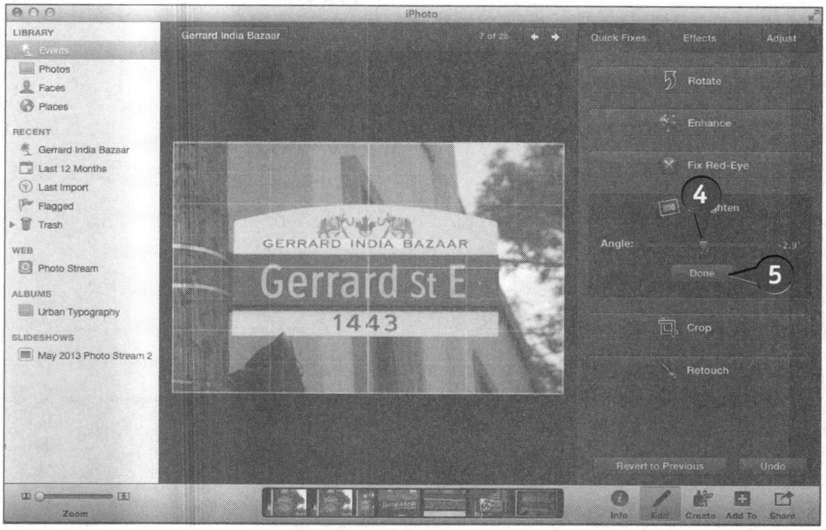

6 Click **Edit**.

iPhoto exits edit mode.

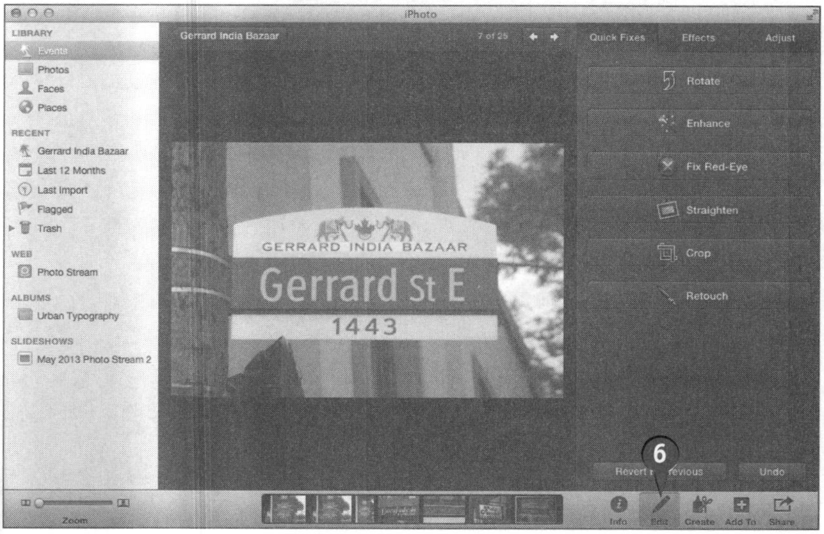

TIP

How do I know when my photo is level?

Use the gridlines that iPhoto places over the photo. Locate a horizontal line in your photo and then rotate the photo so that this line is parallel to the nearest horizontal line in the grid. You can also match a vertical line in the photo with a vertical line in the grid.

Remove Red Eye from a Photo

You can remove red eye from a photo using the iPhoto application, which comes with all new Mac Pros as part of iLife, and is also available separately via the App Store. When you use a flash to take a picture of one or more people, in some cases the flash may reflect off the subjects' retinas. The result is the common phenomenon of *red eye*, where each person's pupils appear red instead of black. If you have a photo where one or more people have red eyes because of the camera flash, you can use iPhoto to remove the red eye and give your subjects a more natural look.

Remove Red Eye from a Photo

1. Click the photo that contains the red eye.
2. Click **Edit**.

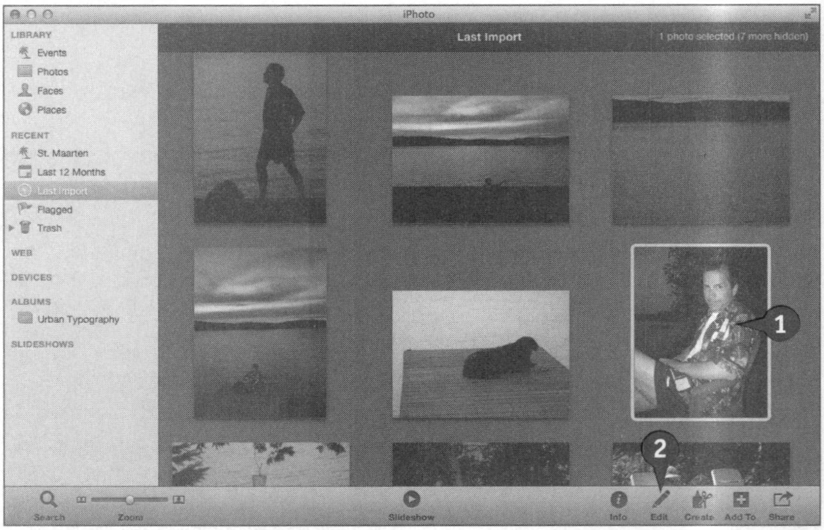

iPhoto displays its editing tools.

- **A** If needed, you can click and drag this slider to the right to zoom in on the picture.
- **B** You can click and drag this rectangle to bring the red eye into view.

3. Click **Fix Red-Eye**.

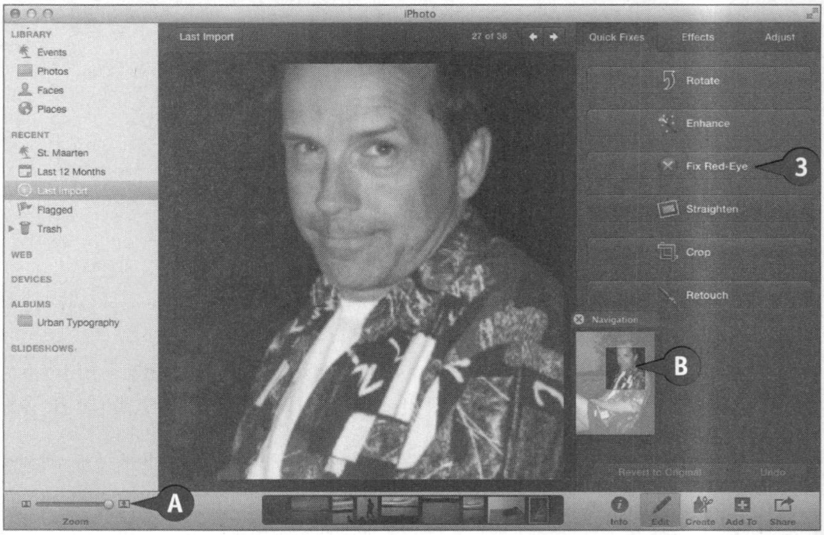

iPhoto displays its Red-Eye controls.

C You may be able to fix the red eye automatically by selecting the **Auto-fix red-eye** option (☐ changes to ☑). If that does not work, continue with the rest of these steps.

4. Move the red eye pointer over a red eye in the photo.
5. Click the red eye.

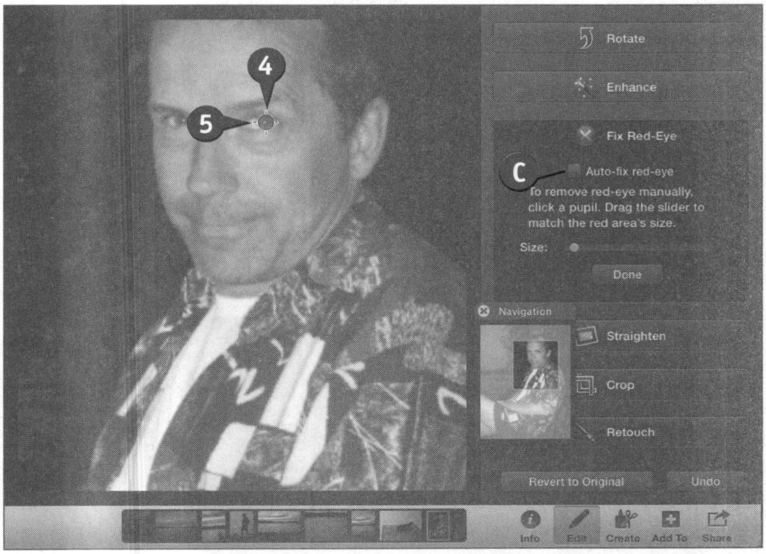

D iPhoto removes the red eye.

6. Repeat steps **4** and **5** to fix any other instances of red eye in the photo.
7. Click **Done**.
8. Click **Edit**.

iPhoto exits edit mode.

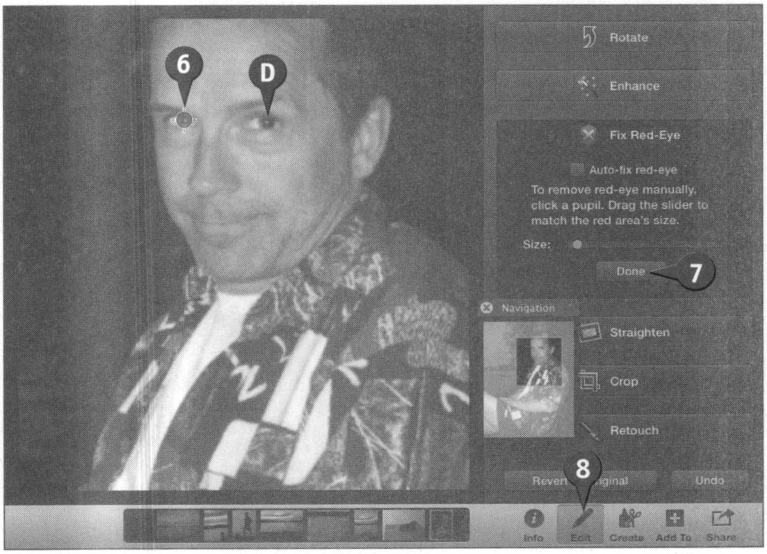

TIP

Why does iPhoto remove only part of the red eye in my photo?
The Red-Eye tool may not be set to a large-enough size. The tool should be approximately the same size as the subject's eye. If it is not, as shown here (**A**), follow steps **1** to **3** to display the Red-Eye controls. Click and drag the **Size** slider until the Red-Eye tool is the size of the red-eye area. Use your mouse to move the circle over the red eye and then click.

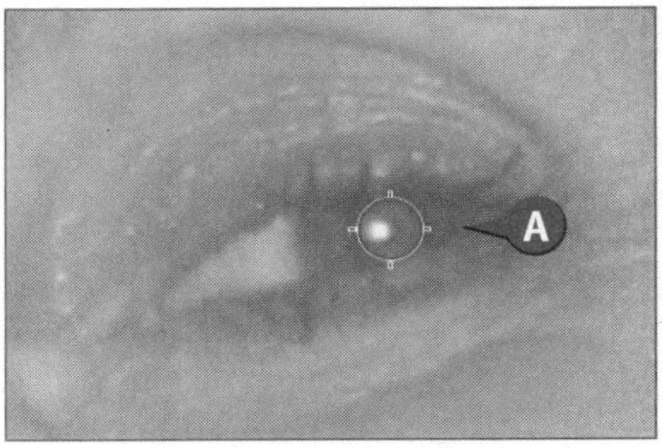

Add Names to Faces in Your Photos

You can make your photos easier to manage and navigate by adding names to the faces that appear in each photo. This is sometimes called *tagging*, and it enables you to navigate your photos by name.

Specifically, iPhoto includes a special Faces section in its library, which organizes your faces according to the names you assign when you tag your photos. This makes it easy to view all your photos in which a certain person appears.

Add Names to Faces in Your Photos

1. Click the photo that you want to tag.
2. Click **Info**.
3. Click ***X* unnamed** (where *X* is the number of faces iPhoto identifies in the photo).

iPhoto displays its naming tools.

4. Click **unnamed**.

5. Type the person's name.
6. Press **Return**.
7. Repeat steps **3** to **5** to name each person in the photo.

(A) If iPhoto did not mark a face in the photo, click **Add a face**, size and position the box over the face, and then type the name in the Click to Name box.

8. Click **Info**.

iPhoto exits naming mode.

TIP

How do I view all the photos that contain a particular person?

You can open a photo, click **Info**, and then click the **Show All** arrow (›) beside the person's name. You can also click **Faces** in the iPhoto sidebar. iPhoto displays the names and sample photos of each person you have named. Double-click the person you want to view. iPhoto displays all the photos that contain the person.

Map Your Photos

You can view your photos by location if you edit each photo to include the location where you took the image. Many modern cameras, particularly smartphone cameras such as those found on the iPhone and iPad, include location information for each photo. If your camera does not add location data automatically, you can tell iPhoto the locations where your photos were taken and then display a map that shows those locations. This enables you to view all your photos taken in a particular place.

Map Your Photos

1. Click the event that you want to map.

   If you want to map a single photo, open the event and then open the photo.

2. Click **Info**.
3. Click **Assign a Place**.

4. Type the location.

   iPhoto displays a list of locations that match what you typed.

5. When you see the place you want to use, click it.

iPhoto displays the location on a Google map.

6 Click and drag the pin to the correct location, if necessary.

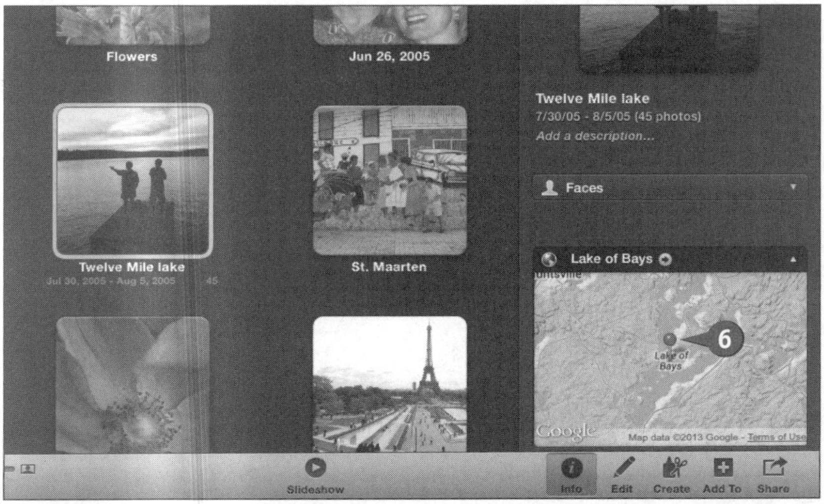

7 Click **Info**.

iPhoto closes the info window.

TIPS

Is there a way to have the location data added automatically?

Yes. To activate this feature, click **iPhoto** in the menu bar, click **Preferences**, and then click the **Advanced** tab. Click the **Look up Places** ⬍ and then click **Automatically**. Note that you may still have to add or edit location names for your photos.

How do I view all the photos that were taken in a particular place?

Click **Places** in the iPhoto sidebar to see a map of the world with pins for each of your photo locations. Position the mouse over the location's pin, and then click the **Show All** arrow (›). iPhoto displays all the photos that were taken in that location.

E-Mail a Photo

If you have a photo that you want to share with someone, and you know that person's e-mail address, you can send the photo in an e-mail message. Using iPhoto, you can specify which photo you want to send, and iPhoto creates a new message. Even if a photo is very large, you can still send it via e-mail because you can use iPhoto to shrink the copy of the photo that appears in the message.

E-Mail a Photo

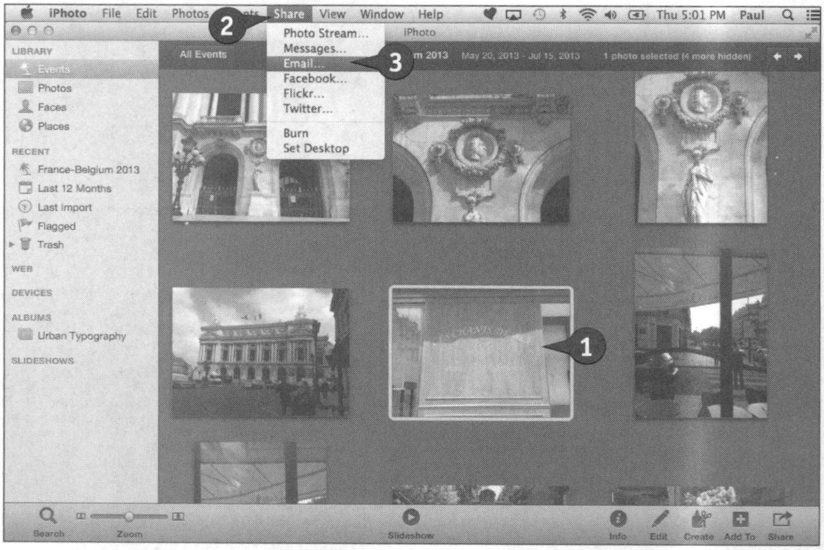

1. Click the photo you want to send.
2. Click **Share**.
3. Click **Email**.

   You can also click **Share** and then click **Email**.

A. iPhoto creates a new message and adds the photo to the message body.

4. Type the address of the message recipient.
5. Type the message subject.

6 Click here and then type your message text.

B You can use these controls to format the text.

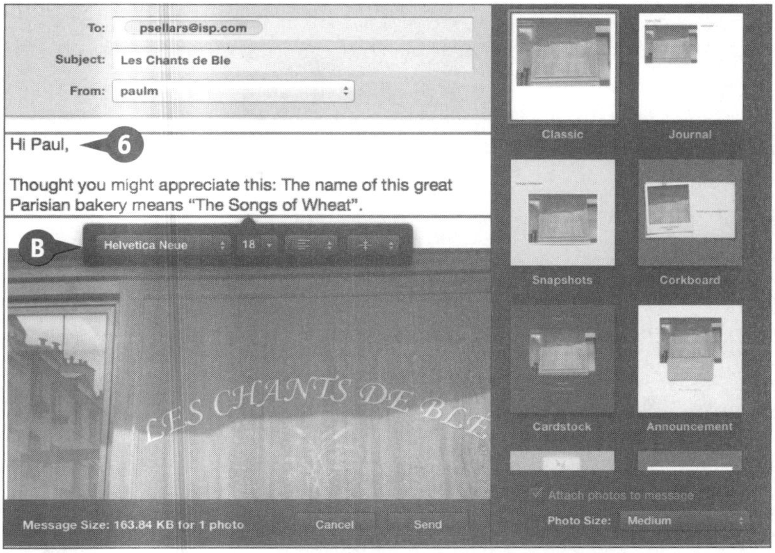

C You can click these thumbnails to apply a special effect to the message.

7 Click **Send**.

iPhoto sends the message with the photo as an attachment.

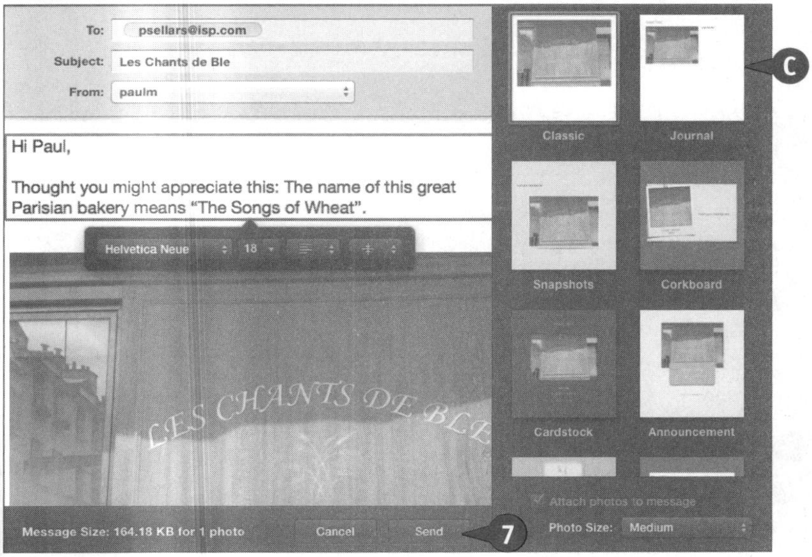

TIP

How do I change the size of the photo?

You need to be careful when sending photos because a single image can be several megabytes in size. If your recipient's e-mail system places restrictions on the size of messages it can receive, your message might not go through.

To change the size of the photo, click the **Photo Size** ⇕ and then click the size you want to use for the sent photo, such as Small or Medium. Note that this does not affect the size of the original photo, just the copy sent with the message.

Take Your Picture

You can use your Mac Pro to take a picture of yourself. If your monitor comes with a built-in video camera, or if you have an external camera attached to your Mac Pro, you can use the camera and the Photo Booth application to take a picture of yourself. After you take your picture, you can e-mail that picture, add it to iPhoto, or set it as your user account or Messages buddy picture.

Take Your Picture

Take Your Picture with Photo Booth

1. In the Dock, click **Photo Booth** ().

   The Photo Booth window appears.

   A. The live feed from the camera appears here.

2. Click **Take a still picture** ().

   B. You can click **Take four quick pictures** () if you want Photo Booth to snap four successive photos, each about 1 second apart.

   C. You can click **Take a movie clip** () if you want Photo Booth to capture the live camera feed as a movie.

3. Click **Take Photo** ().

Note: You can also press ⌘+T or click **File** and then click **Take Photo.**

Photo Booth counts down 3 seconds and then takes the photo.

Note: When the Mac Pro is taking your picture, be sure to look into the camera, not into the screen.

Work with Your Photo Booth Picture

Ⓓ Photo Booth displays the picture.

1 Click the picture.

2 Click **Share** (⎘).

Ⓔ You can click **Add to iPhoto** to add the photo to iPhoto.

Ⓕ You can click **Change profile picture** to set the photo as your user account picture.

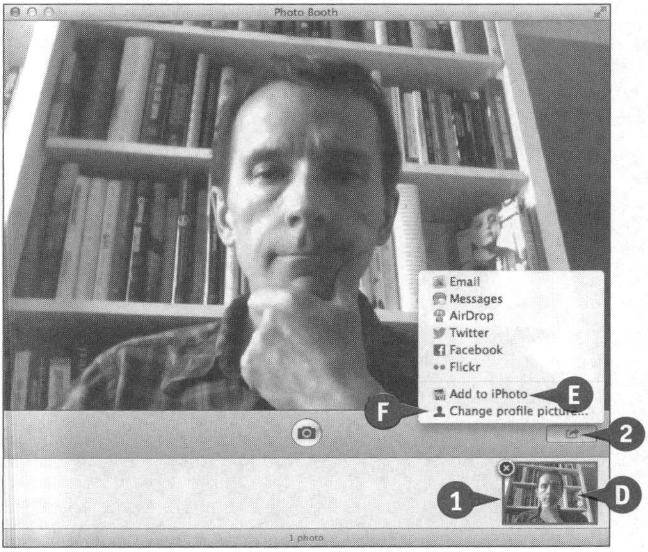

TIP

Can I make my photos more interesting?
Definitely. Photo Booth comes with around two dozen special effects. Follow these steps:

1 Click **Effects**.

2 Click an icon to select a different page of effects.

Ⓐ You can also use the arrow buttons to change pages.

3 Click the effect you want to use.

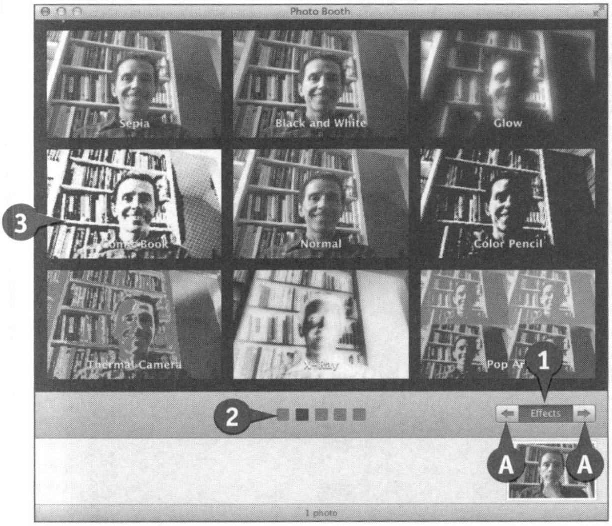

CHAPTER 13

Playing and Creating Videos

Your Mac Pro comes with the tools you need to play movies and digital video, including DVD Player and QuickTime. You can also use iMovie to create your own digital videos.

Play a DVD Using DVD Player

If your Mac Pro has a DVD drive, you can insert a movie DVD into the drive and then use the DVD Player application to play the movie on your Mac Pro. You can either watch the movie in full-screen mode, where the movie takes up the entire Mac Pro screen, or play the DVD in a window while you work on other things. DVD Player has features that enable you to control the movie playback and volume.

Play a DVD Using DVD Player

Play a DVD Full Screen

1. Insert the DVD into your Mac Pro's DVD drive.

   DVD Player runs automatically and starts playing the DVD full screen.

2. If you get to the DVD menu, click **Play** to start the movie.

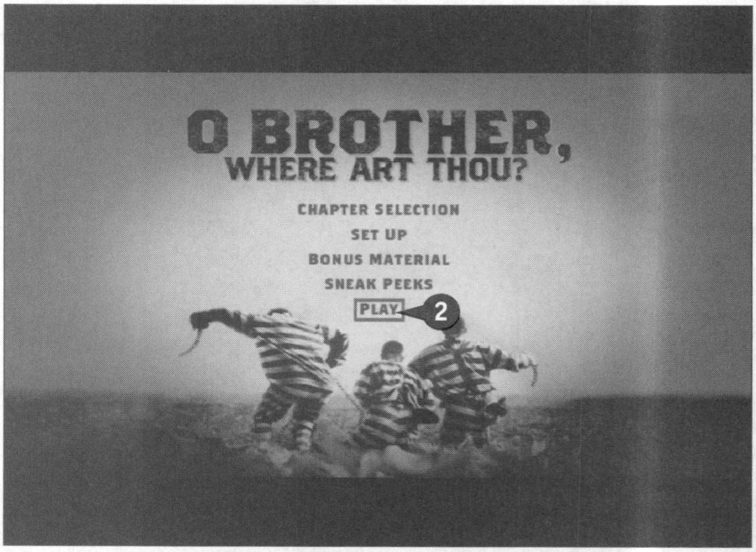

3. Move the mouse to the bottom of the screen.

   The playback controls appear.

- A Click to pause the movie.
- B Click to fast-forward the movie.
- C Click to rewind the movie.
- D Drag the slider to adjust the volume.
- E Click to display the DVD menu.
- F Click to exit full-screen mode.

Play a DVD in a Window

1. Insert the DVD into your Mac Pro's DVD drive.

   DVD Player runs automatically and starts playing the DVD full screen.

2. Press ⌘+F.

Note: You can also press Esc or move the mouse ↖ to the bottom of the screen and then click **Exit full screen**.

DVD Player displays the movie in a window.

- G DVD Player displays the Controller.

3. When you get to the DVD menu, click **Play Movie** to start the movie.

- H Click to pause the movie.
- I Click and hold to fast-forward the movie.
- J Click and hold to rewind the movie.
- K Drag the slider to adjust the volume.
- L Click to display the DVD menu.
- M Click to stop the movie.
- N Click to eject the DVD.

TIP

How can I always start my DVDs in a window?

Press ⌘+F to switch to the window view. Click **DVD Player** in the menu bar, click **Preferences** to open the DVD Player preferences, and then click the **Player** tab. Deselect the **Enter Full Screen mode** option (☑ changes to ☐). To manually control when the playback starts, deselect the **Start playing disc** option (☑ changes to ☐). Click **OK** to put the new settings into effect.

Play Digital Video with QuickTime Player

Your Mac Pro comes with an application called QuickTime Player that can play digital video files in various formats. You will mostly use QuickTime Player to play digital video files stored on your Mac Pro, but you can also use the application to play digital video from the web.

QuickTime Player enables you to open video files, navigate the digital video playback, and control the digital video volume. Although you learn only how to play digital video files in this section, the version of QuickTime that comes with OS X 10.9 (Mavericks) comes with many extra features, including the capability to record movies and audio and to cut and paste scenes.

Play Digital Video with QuickTime Player

1. Click **Finder** ( ).
2. Click **Applications**.
3. Double-click **QuickTime Player** ( ).

Note: If you see the QuickTime Player icon in the Dock, you can also click that icon to launch the program.

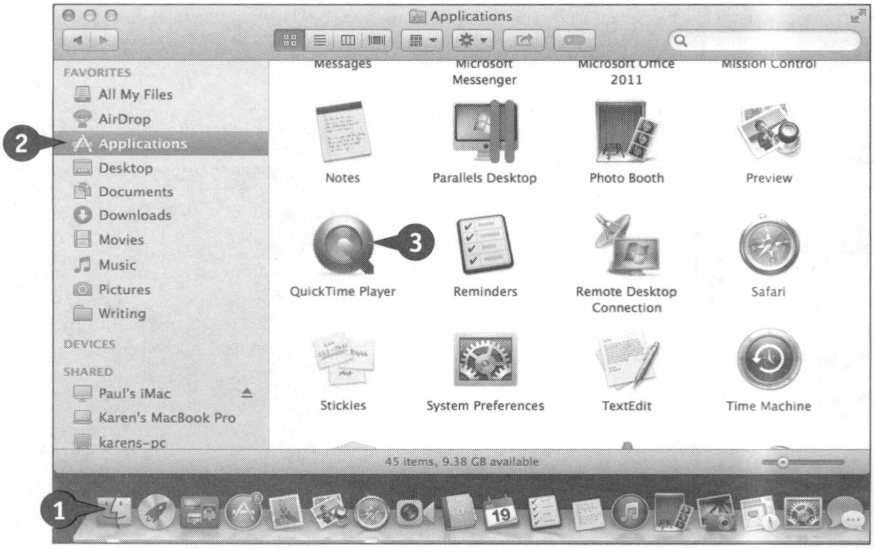

The QuickTime Player application appears.

4. Click **File**.
5. Click **Open File**.

Note: You can also press ⌘+O.

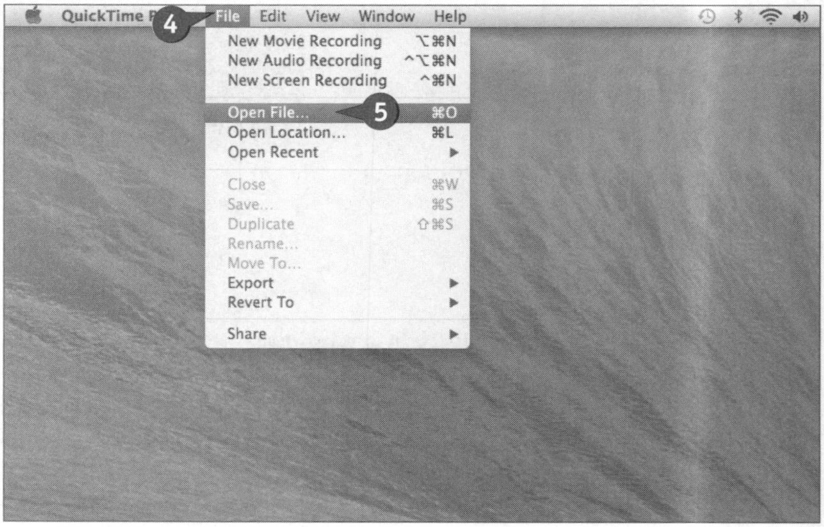

The Open dialog appears.

6 Locate and click the video file you want to play.

7 Click **Open**.

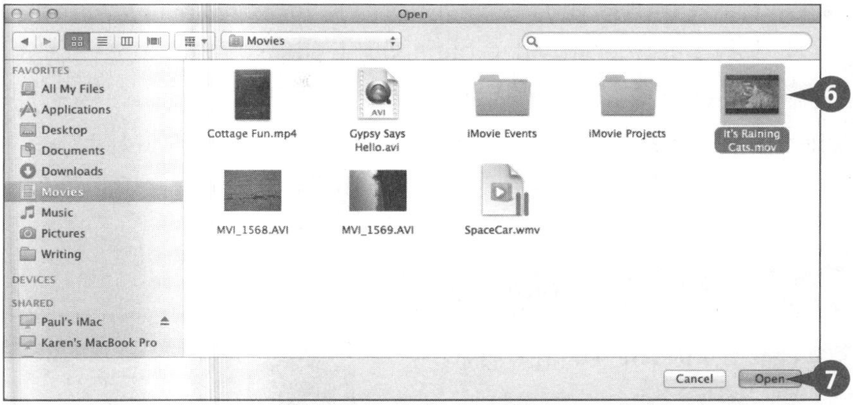

QuickTime opens a new player window.

8 Click **Play** (▶).

A Click to fast-forward the video.

B Click to rewind the video.

C Click and drag the slider to adjust the volume.

If you want to view the video in full-screen mode, press ⌘+F.

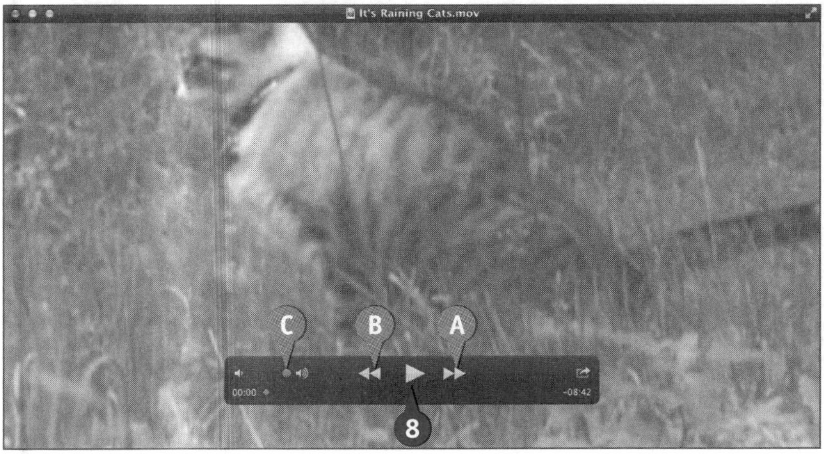

TIP

Can I use QuickTime Player to play a video from the web?

Yes. As long as you know the Internet address of the video, QuickTime Player can play most video formats available on the web. In QuickTime Player, click **File** and then click **Open Location** (or press ⌘+U). In the Open URL dialog, type or paste the video address in the Movie Location text box and then click **Open**.

Create a New Movie Project

The iLife suite installed on your Mac Pro includes iMovie, which enables you to import video from a digital camcorder or video file and use that footage to create your own movies. You do this by first creating a project that holds your video clips, transitions, titles, and other elements of your movie.

When you first start iMovie, the program creates a new project for you automatically. Follow the steps in this section to create subsequent projects. Note, too, that iMovie is also available via the App Store.

Create a New Movie Project

1. Click the **iMovie** icon (★) in the Dock.

The iMovie window appears.

2. Click **File**.
3. Click **New Project**.

Note: You can also press ⌘+N.

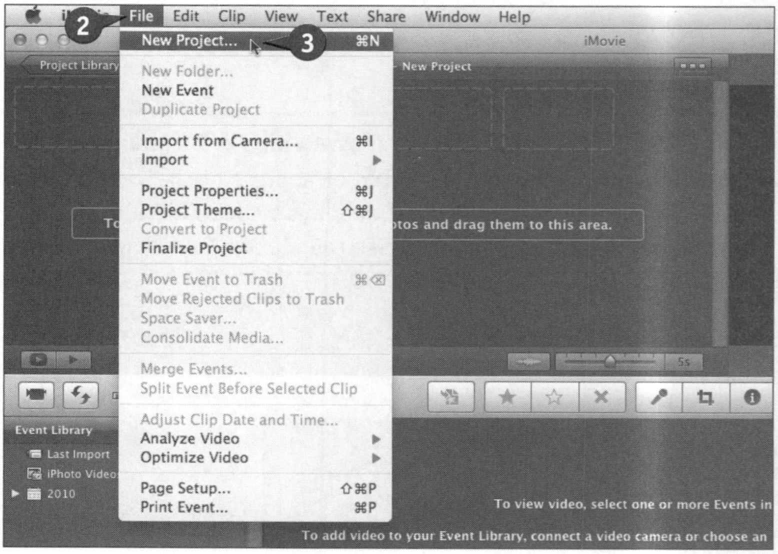

The New Project dialog appears.

4 Type a name.

5 Click the **Aspect Ratio** ⇕ and then click a ratio: Widescreen (16:9) or Standard (4:3).

6 To apply a theme to your project, click one in the Project Themes list.

Note: See the first tip to learn more about themes.

7 To automatically insert transitions between all your clips, select the **Automatically add** option (☐ changes to ☑) and then click ⇕ to choose the type of transition.

If you chose a theme in step 6, the check box changes to **Automatically add transition and titles.**

8 Click **Create**.

iMovie creates your new project.

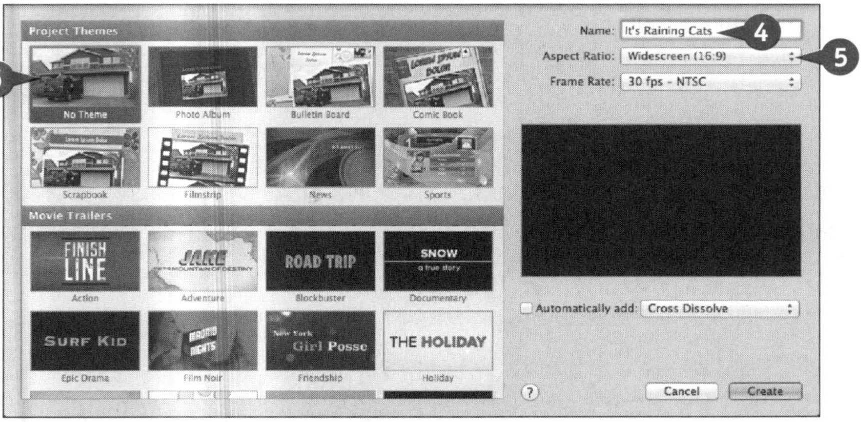

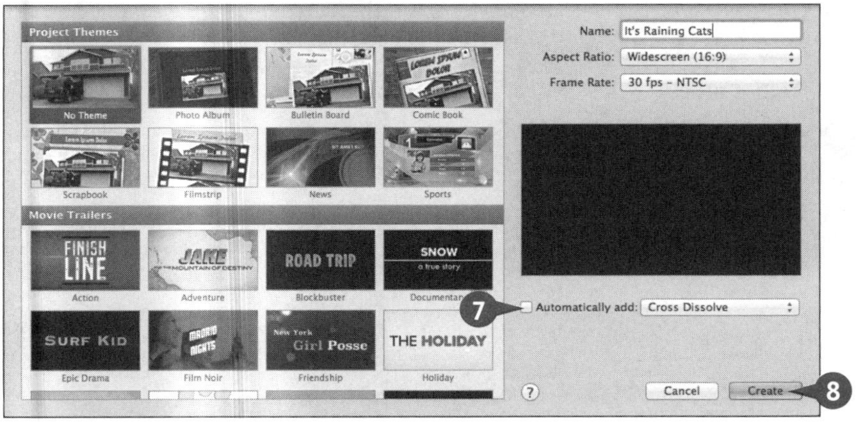

TIPS

What are the iMovie themes?
iMovie offers seven themes that you can apply to a project. Each theme comes with its own set of titles and transitions that are added automatically. Among the themes are Photo Album, Bulletin Board, Comic Book, and Scrapbook. If one of them is suitable for your project, applying it can save you production time.

How do I switch from one project to another?
You use the Project Library, which is a list of your movie projects. To display it, click **Window** and then click **Show Project Library**. You can also click the **Project Library** button in the top left corner of the iMovie window. In the Project Library, double-click the project you want to work with.

Import a Video File

With the iMovie application, you can import digital video from a camera for use in your movie project. If you have video content on a USB digital camcorder, smartphone (such as an iPhone), or tablet (such as an iPad), you can connect the device to your Mac Pro and then import some or all of the video to your iMovie project.

If your monitor has a built-in iSight or FaceTime HD camera, you can also use iMovie to import live images from that camera to use as digital video footage in your movie project.

Import a Video File

Import All Clips

1 Connect the video device to your Mac Pro.

iMovie displays its Import From dialog.

2 Click **Import All**.

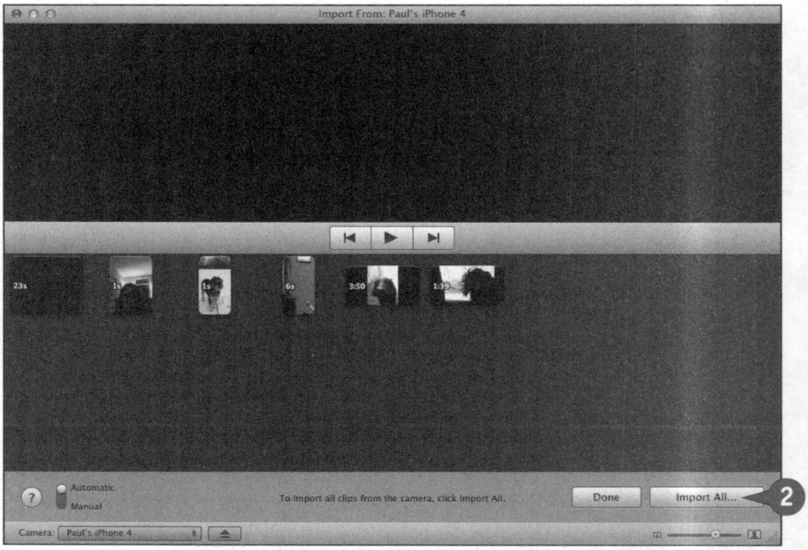

iMovie prompts you to create a new event.

3 Select the **Create new Event** option (☐ changes to ◉).

4 Use the Create New Event text box to type a name for the import event.

Ⓐ If you want to add the video to an existing event, select the **Add to existing Event** option (☐ changes to ◉) and then choose the event from the pop-up menu.

5 Click **Import**.

Import Selected Clips

1. Connect the video device to your Mac Pro and place it in playback mode, if necessary.

   iMovie displays its Import From dialog.

2. Click **Manual**.
3. Deselect the check box under each clip you do not want to import (☑ changes to ☐).
4. Click **Import Checked**.

   iMovie prompts you to create a new event.

5. Select the **Create new Event** option (○ changes to ◉).
6. Use the Create New Event text box to type a name for the import event.
7. Click **Import**.

   iMovie begins importing the clips.

8. Click **OK**.
9. Click **Done** to close the Import From dialog (not shown).

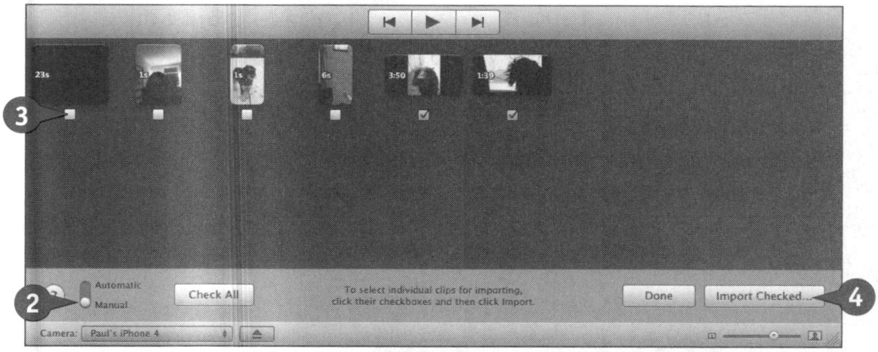

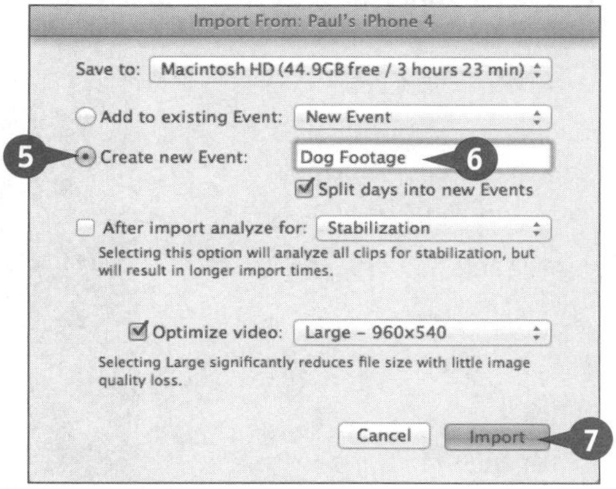

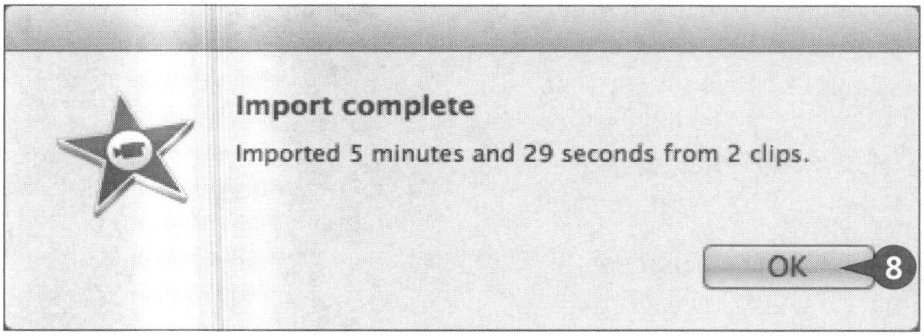

TIP

How do I import digital video from my iSight or FaceTime HD camera?

In iMovie, click **File** and then click **Import from Camera** to open the Import dialog. Click **Capture** and then follow steps 5 and 6 in the subsection "Import Selected Clips." Click **Capture** to begin the video capture. When you are done, click **Stop** and then click **Done** to close the Import dialog.

Add Video Clips to Your Project

To create and work with a movie project in iMovie, you must first add some video clips to that project. A *video clip* is a segment of digital video. You begin building your movie by adding one or more video clips to your project.

When you import digital video as described in the previous section, "Import a Video File," iMovie automatically breaks up the video into separate clips, with each clip being the footage shot during a single recording session. You can then decide which of those clips you want to add to your project, or you can add only part of a clip.

Add Video Clips to Your Project

Add an Entire Clip

1. Click the Event Library item that contains the video clip you want to add.
2. Press and hold Option and click the clip.

A. iMovie selects the entire clip.

3. Click and drag the selected clip and drop it in your project at the spot where you want the clip to appear.

B. iMovie adds the entire video clip to the project.

C. iMovie adds an orange bar to the bottom of the original clip to indicate that it has been added to the project.

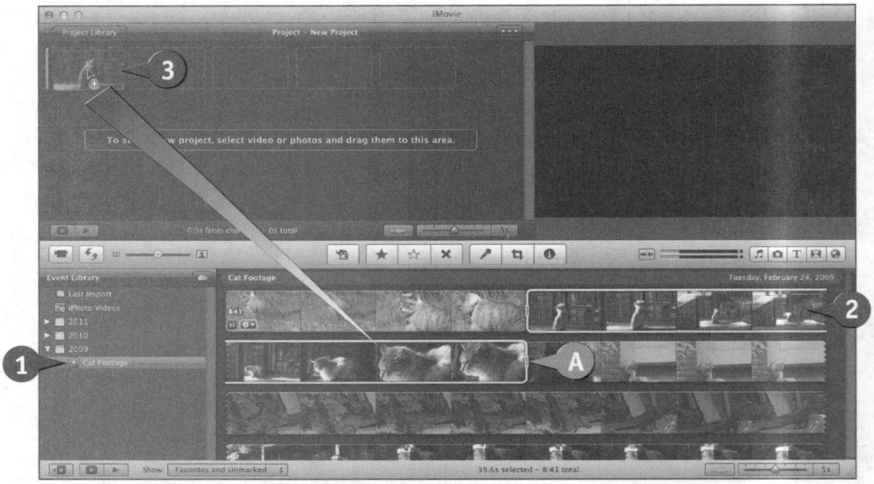

Add a Partial Clip

1. Click the Event Library item that contains the video clip you want to add.
2. Click the clip at the point where you want the selection to begin.
3. Click and drag the right edge of the selection box to the point where you want the selection to end.
4. Click and drag the selected clip and drop it in your project at the spot where you want the clip to appear.

- **D** iMovie adds the selected portion of the video clip to the project.
- **E** iMovie adds an orange bar to the bottom of the original clip to indicate that it has been added to a project.

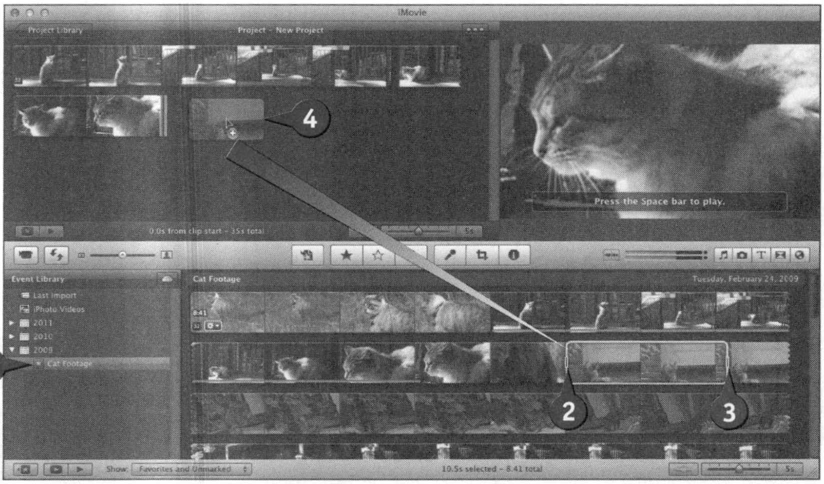

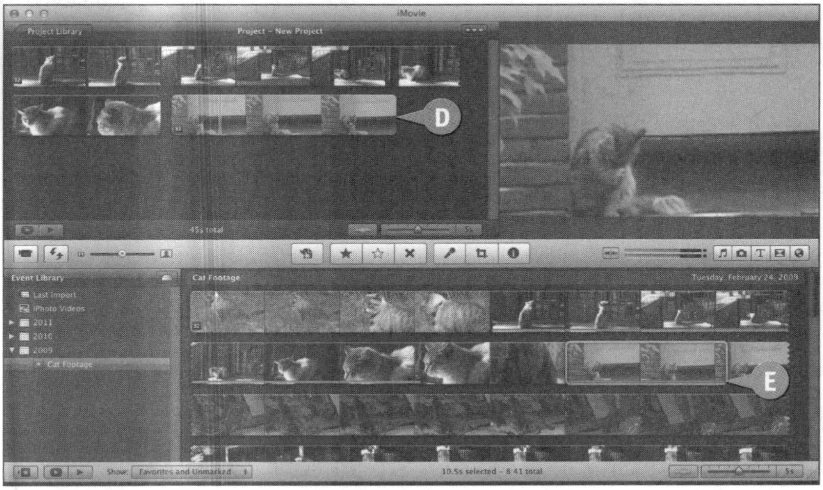

TIPS

Is it possible to play a clip before I add it?
Yes. The easiest way to do this is to click the clip at the point where you want the playback to start and then press Spacebar. iMovie plays the clip in the Viewer in the top right corner of the window. Press Spacebar again to stop the playback.

I added a clip in the wrong place. Can I move it?
Yes. In your project, click the added clip to select it. Use your mouse to click and drag the clip and then drop the clip in the correct location within the project. If you want to delete the clip from the project, click it, click **Edit**, and then click **Delete Entire Clip** (or press Option + Delete).

Trim a Clip

If you have a video clip that is too long or contains footage you do not need, you can shorten the clip or remove the extra footage. Removing parts of a video clip is called *trimming* the clip.

Trimming a clip is particularly useful if you recorded extra, unneeded footage before and after the action you were trying to capture. By trimming this unneeded footage, your movie will include only the material you really require.

Trim a Clip

1. In your project, click the clip you want to trim.

   A. iMovie selects the entire clip.

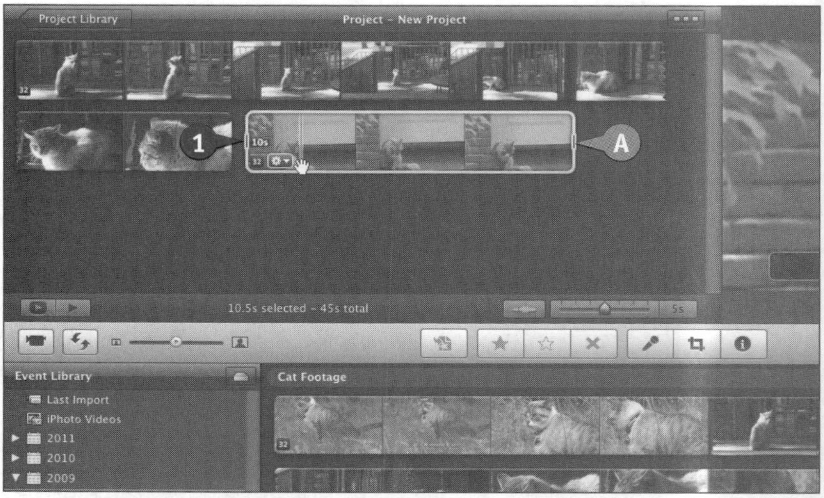

2. Use your mouse to click and drag the left edge of the selection box to the starting position of the part of the clip you want to keep.

3. Use your mouse to click and drag the right edge of the selection box to the ending position of the part of the clip you want to keep.

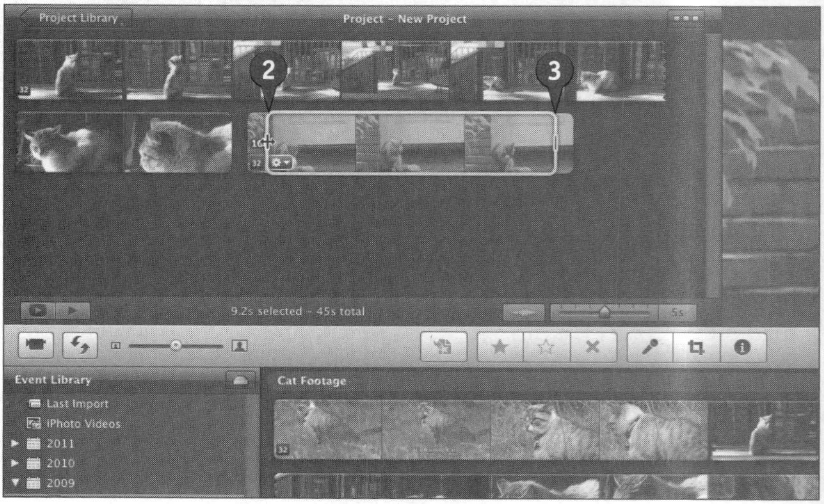

4 Click **Clip**.

5 Click **Trim to Selection**.

Note: You can also press ⌘+B.

B iMovie trims the clip.

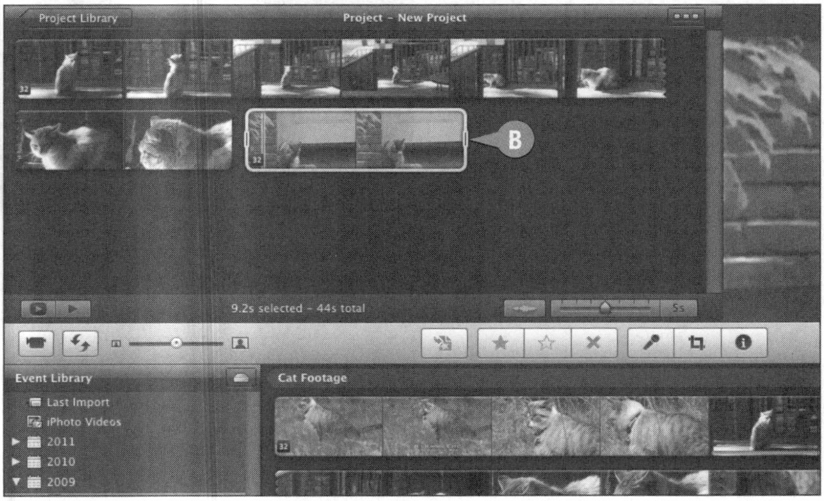

TIP

How can I trim one frame at a time from either the beginning or the end of the clip?

In your project, click the clip you want to trim. Click the **Clip** menu and then click **Trim Clip End**. Select the trim direction by clicking **Move Left** or **Move Right** and repeat until you reach the number of frames that you want to trim.

Add a Transition Between Clips

You can use the iMovie application to enhance the visual appeal of your digital movie by inserting transitions between some or all of the project's video clips. By default, iMovie jumps immediately from the end of one clip to the beginning of the next clip, a transition called a *jump cut*. You can add more visual interest to your movie by adding a transition between the two clips.

iMovie offers 24 different transitions, including various fades, wipes, and dissolves. More transitions are available if you applied a theme to your iMovie project.

Add a Transition Between Clips

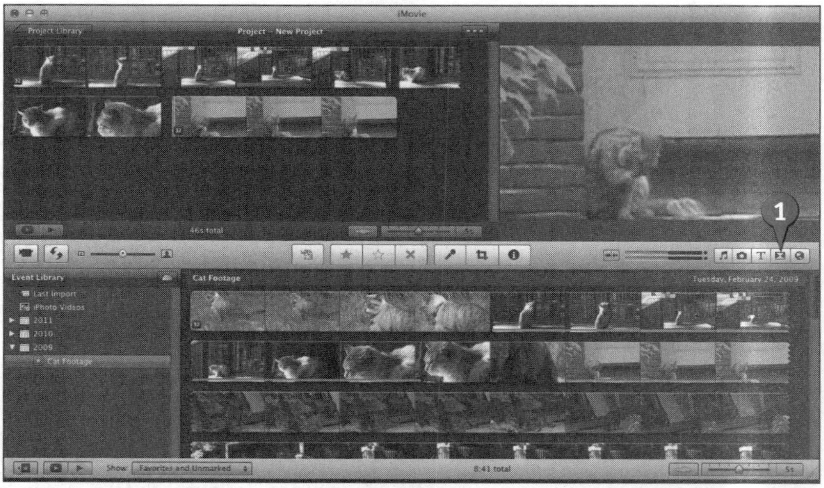

1. Click the **Transitions Browser** button (), or press ⌘+4.

Ⓐ iMovie displays the available transitions.

Note: To see a preview of a transition, position your mouse over the transition thumbnail.

2. Use your mouse to click and drag a transition and drop it between the two clips.

Ⓑ iMovie adds an icon for the transition between the two clips.

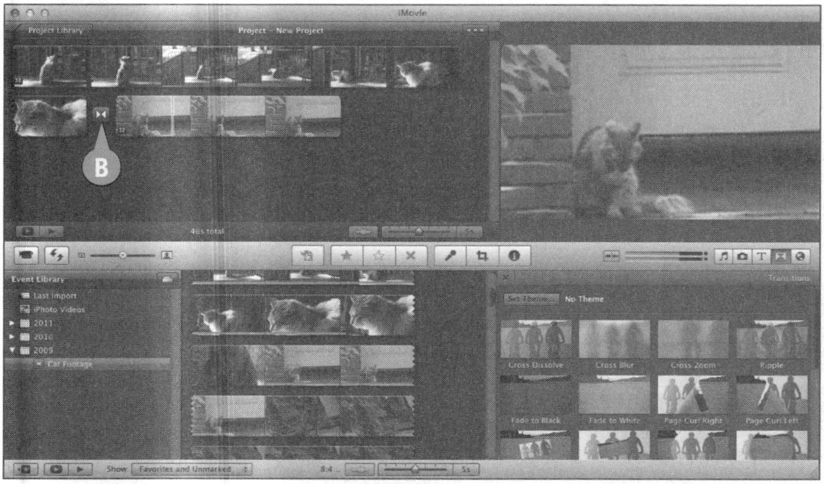

3 Position your mouse over the beginning of the transition and move the mouse to the right.

Ⓒ iMovie displays a preview of the transition.

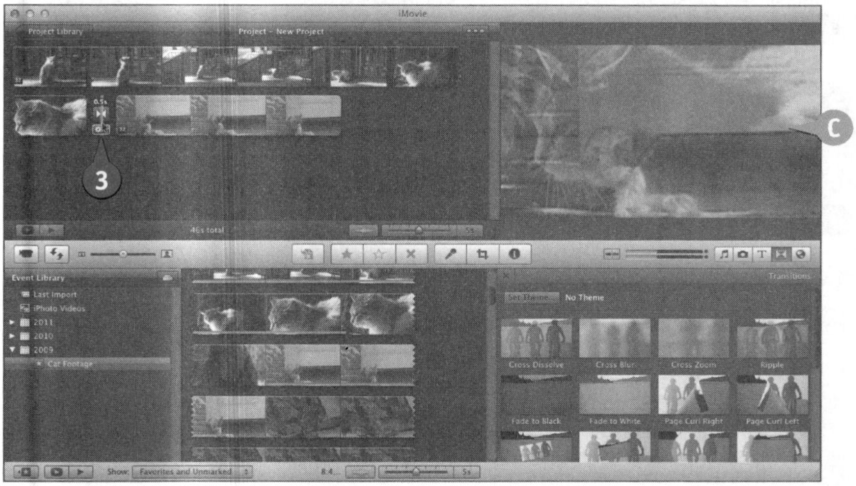

TIP

How can I change the duration of the transition?

Double-click the transition icon in your project. The Inspector appears. Use the Duration text box to set the number of seconds you want the transition to take (Ⓐ). If you want to change only the current transition, deselect the **Applies to all transitions** option (☑ changes to ☐) (Ⓑ). Click **Done** to close the Inspector.

Add a Photo

You can use the iMovie application to enhance your movie projects with still photos. Although most movie projects consist of several video clips, you can also add a photo to your project. By default, iMovie displays the photo for 4 seconds.

You can also specify how the photo fits in the movie frame: You can adjust the size of the photo to fit the frame, you can crop the photo, or you can apply a Ken Burns effect to animate the static photo, which automatically pans and zooms the photo.

Add a Photo

1. Click the **Photos Browser** button ( ), or press ⌘+2.

   A. iMovie displays the available photos.

2. Click the event or album that contains the photo you want to add.
3. Click and drag the photo and drop it inside your project.

   B. iMovie adds the photo to the movie.

4. Click the photo.
5. Click the **Crop** button ( ).

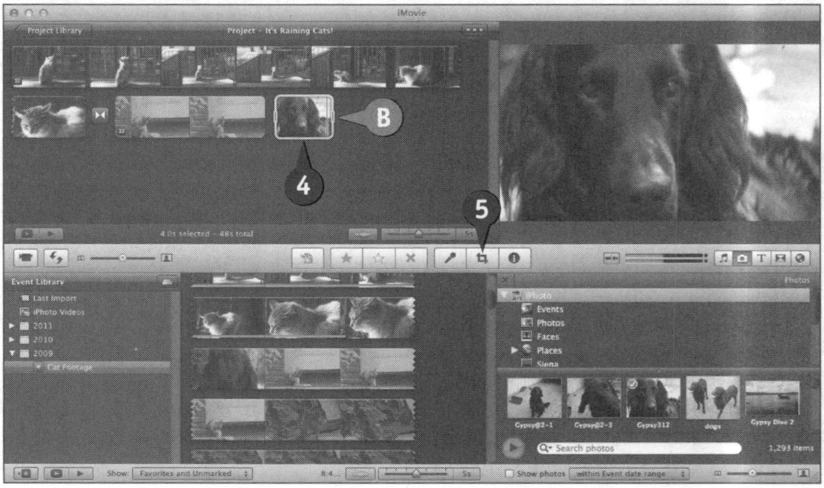

iMovie displays the cropping options for the photo.

6 Click **Ken Burns**.

C You can also click **Fit** to have iMovie adjust the size of the photo to fit the movie frame.

D You can also click **Crop** and then click and drag the cropping rectangle to specify how much of the photo you want to appear in the movie frame.

7 Click and drag the green rectangle to set the start point of the Ken Burns animation.

8 Click and drag the red rectangle to set the end point of the Ken Burns animation.

Note: Click and drag the corners and edges of the rectangle to change the size; click and drag the interior of the rectangles to change the position.

E The arrow shows the direction of motion.

9 Click **Done**.

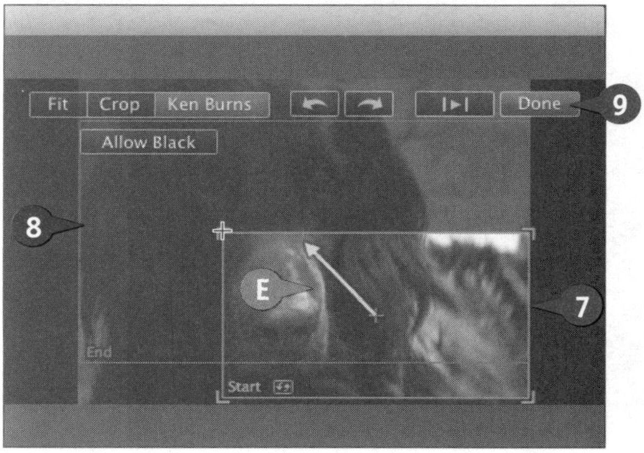

TIP

How can I change the length of time that the photo appears in the movie?
Double-click the photo in your project. The Inspector appears. Click the **Clip** tab (A). Use the Duration text box to set the number of seconds you want the photo to appear (B). To change the duration for all the photos in your project, select the **Applies to all stills** option (☐ changes to ☑) (C). Click **Done** to close the Inspector.

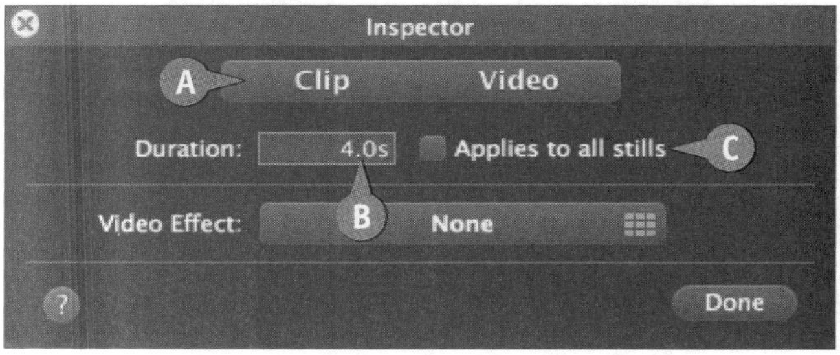

Add a Music Track

Using the iMovie application, you can enhance the audio component of your movie by adding one or more songs that play in the background. With iMovie you can also add sound effects and other audio files that you feel would enhance your project's audio track.

To get the best audio experience, you can adjust various sound properties. For example, you can adjust the volume of the music clip or the volume of the video clip. You can also use iMovie to adjust the time it takes for the song clip to fade in and fade out.

Add a Music Track

1. Click the **Music and Sound Effect Browser** button ( ), or press ⌘+1.

   A. iMovie displays the available audio files.

2. Click the folder, category, or playlist that contains the track you want to add.
3. Use your mouse to click and drag the song and drop it on a video clip.

   B. iMovie adds the song to the movie.

Note: iMovie treats the song like a clip, which means you can trim the song as needed, as described in the section "Trim a Clip."

4. Double-click the music clip.

   iMovie displays the Inspector.

5 Click the **Audio** tab.

6 Use the **Volume** slider to adjust the volume of the music clip.

7 If you want to reduce the video clip volume, select the **Ducking** option (☐ changes to ☑) and then click and drag the slider.

8 To adjust the fade-in time, select the **Fade In: Manual** option (☐ changes to ☑) and then click and drag the slider.

9 To adjust the fade-out time, select the **Fade Out: Manual** option (☐ changes to ☑) and then click and drag the slider.

10 Click **Done**.

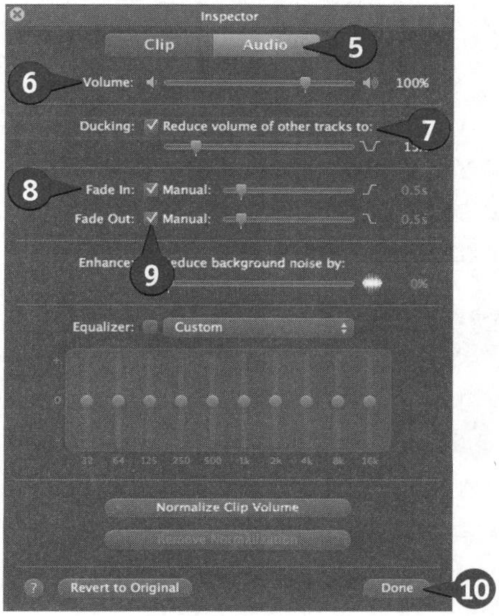

TIP

When I add a video clip before the music clip, the music does not play with the new video clip. How can I work around this?

You need to add your song as a background track instead of as a clip. Follow these steps:

1 Click the **Music and Sound Effect Browser** button (🎵).

2 Click and drag a song onto the project background, not on a clip or between two clips.

A The background turns green when the song is positioned correctly.

Record a Voiceover

You can use the iMovie application to augment the audio portion of your movie with a voiceover. A *voiceover* is a voice recording that you make using audio equipment attached to your Mac Pro.

A voiceover is useful for explaining a video clip, introducing the movie, or giving the viewer background information about the movie. To record a voiceover, your Mac Pro must have either a built-in microphone, such as the one that comes with the iSight or FaceTime HD camera, or an external microphone connected via an audio jack, USB port, or Bluetooth.

Record a Voiceover

1. If your Mac Pro does not have a built-in microphone, attach a microphone.

Note: You may need to configure the microphone as the sound input device. Click **System Preferences** ( ), click **Sound**, click **Input**, and then click your microphone.

2. Click the **Voiceover** button ( ).

The Voiceover dialog appears.

3. Click the spot in the movie at which you want the voiceover to begin.

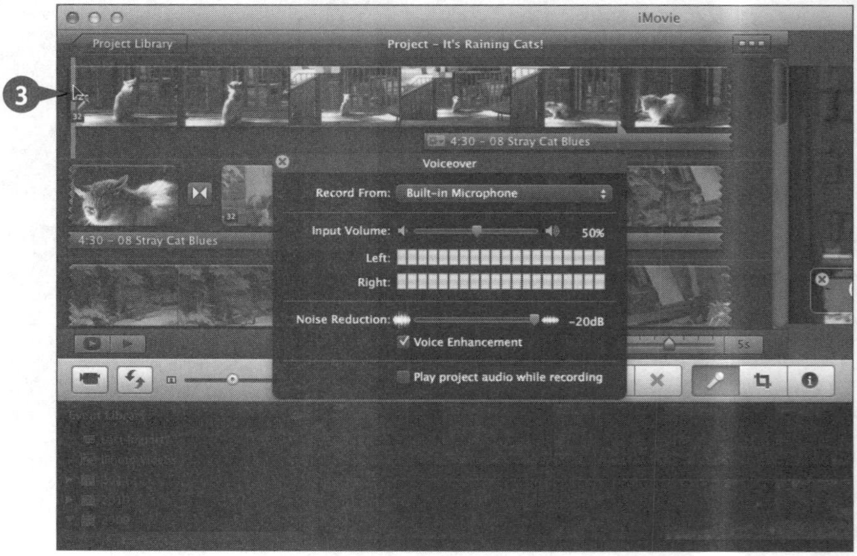

iMovie counts down and then begins the recording.

4 Speak your voiceover text into the microphone.

A The progress of the recording appears here.

5 When you finish, click **Recording**.

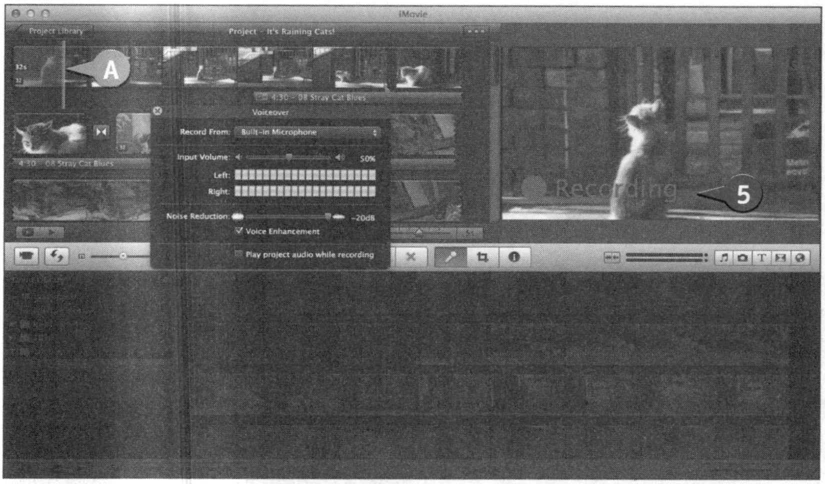

B iMovie adds the voiceover to the clip.

6 Click **Close** (☒).

You can double-click the voiceover to adjust the audio, as described in the previous section, "Add a Music Track."

TIP

Is there a way to tell if my voice is too loud or too soft?

Yes. You can use the controls in the Voiceover dialog to check your voice level by talking into the microphone and then watching the Left and Right volume meters. No green bars or just a few green bars indicate the voice level is too low (A). Yellow or red bars indicate the voice level is too high (B). Use the Input Volume slider to adjust the voice level up or down, as needed.

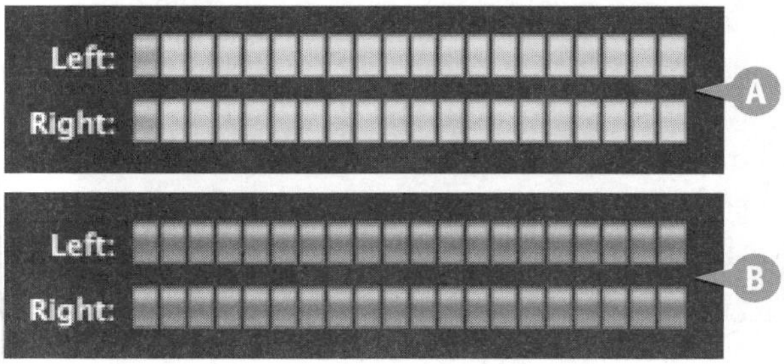

Add Titles and Credits

You can use the iMovie application to enhance your movie project with titles and scrolling credits. You can get your movie off to a proper start by adding a title and a subtitle at or near the beginning of the movie. iMovie offers a number of title styles from which you can choose, and you can also change the title font.

You can also enhance your movie with *scrolling credits*. This is a special type of title that you place at the end of the movie and that scrolls the names of the people responsible for the project.

Add Titles and Credits

1. Click the **Titles browser** button (T).

A. iMovie displays the available title types.

2. Use your mouse to click and drag a title and drop it where you want the titles to appear.

Note: To see just the titles, drop the title thumbnail at the beginning of the movie or between two clips. To superimpose the titles on a video clip, drop the title thumbnail on the clip.

B. If you want to add credits, click and drag the **Scrolling Credits** thumbnail and drop it at the end of the movie.

Ⓒ iMovie adds a clip for the title.

❸ Replace this text with the movie title.

❹ Replace this text with the movie subtitle.

❺ Click **Done**.

Note: iMovie treats the title like a clip, which means you can lengthen or shorten the title duration by clicking and dragging the beginning or end, as described in the section "Trim a Clip."

TIP

How do I change the font of the titles?

The Text menu offers several font-related commands, including Bold, Italic, Bigger, and Smaller. You can also click **Text** and then **Show Fonts** to display the Choose Font dialog. You can switch to iMovie's predefined fonts by clicking **iMovie Font Panel**. You can then click a typeface, font color, and type size; click **Done** to close the dialog.

Play the Movie

The iMovie application offers the Viewer pane, which you can use to play your movie. While you are building your iMovie project, it is a good idea to occasionally play some or all of the movie to check your progress. For example, you can play the entire movie to make sure the video and audio are working properly and are synchronized correctly. You can also play parts of the movie to ensure that your transitions appear when you want them to.

Play the Movie

Play from the Beginning

1. Click **View**.
2. Click **Play from Beginning**.

Note: You can also press \ or click the **Play Project from beginning** button ( ).

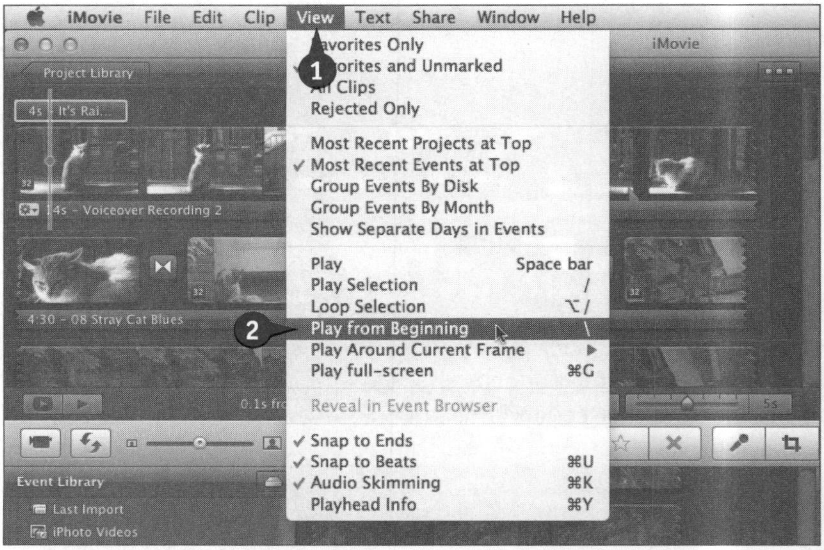

Play from a Specific Location

1. Position the mouse over the spot where you want to start playing the movie.
2. Press Spacebar.

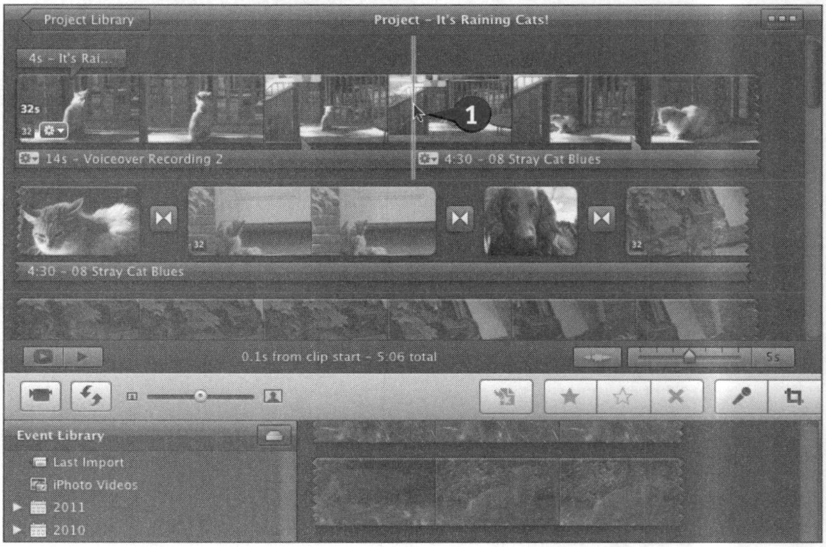

Play a Selection

1. Select the video clips you want to play.

Note: See the first tip to learn how to select multiple video clips.

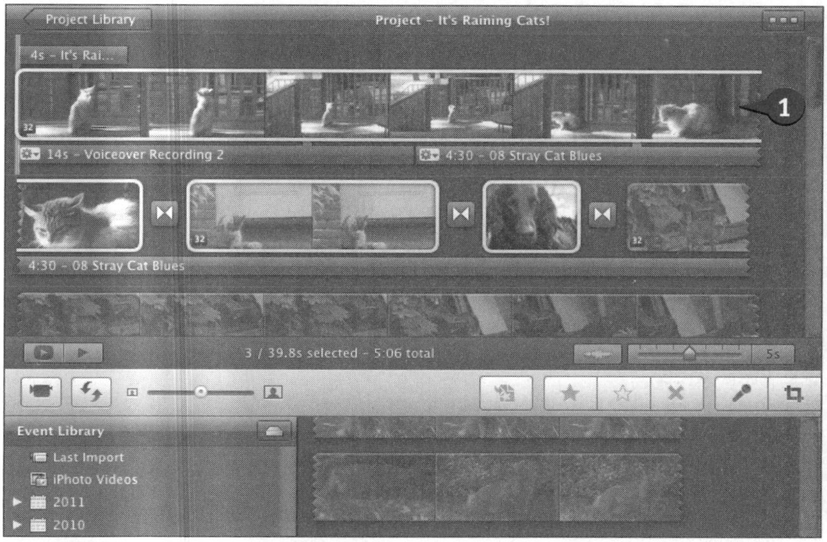

2. Click **View**.
3. Click **Play Selection**.

Note: You can also press /.

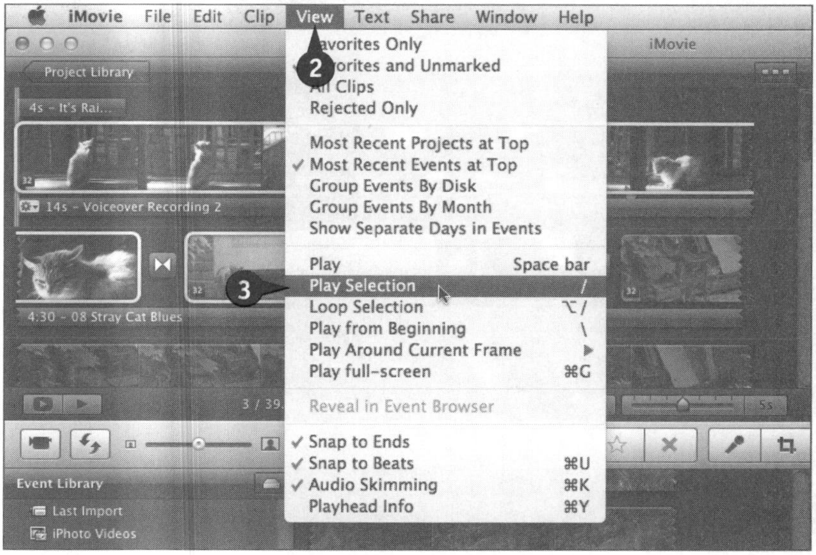

TIPS

How do I select multiple video clips?
To select multiple video clips, press and hold ⌘ and then click anywhere inside each clip you want to select. If you select a clip by accident, ⌘+click it again to deselect it. If you want to skip just a few clips, first press ⌘+A to select all the clips, press and hold ⌘, and then click the clips you do not want in the selection.

Can I enlarge the size of the playback pane?
Yes, you can play your movie in full-screen mode. To do this, click **View** and then click **Play full-screen**. You can also press ⌘+G or click the **Play Project full screen** button (▶).

Publish Your Movie to YouTube

When your movie project is complete, you can send it to YouTube for viewing on the web. To publish your movie to YouTube, you must have a YouTube account, available from www.youtube.com. You must also know your YouTube username, which you can see by clicking your account icon on YouTube and then clicking Settings. Your movie must be no more than 15 minutes long. Before you can publish your movie, you must select a YouTube category, such as Entertainment or Pets and Animals, provide a title and description, and enter at least one tag, which is a word or short phrase that describes some aspect of the movie's content.

Publish Your Movie to YouTube

1. Click **Share**.
2. Click **YouTube**.

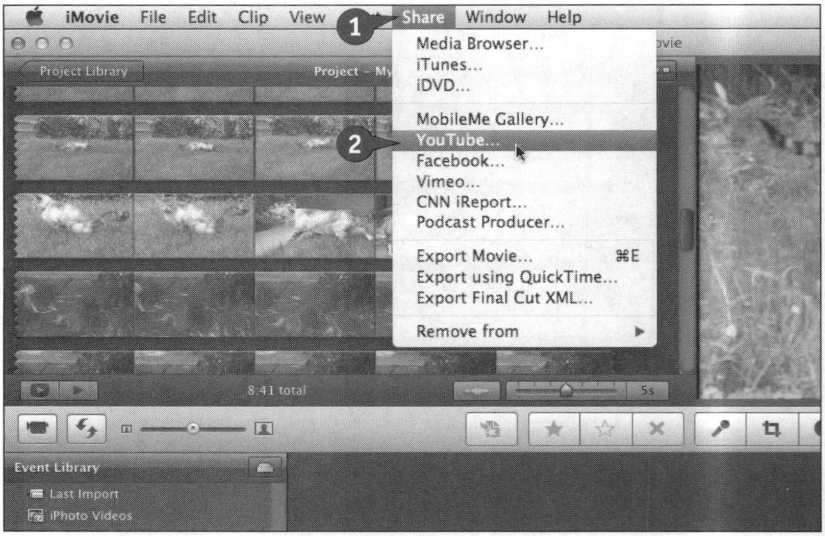

3. Click **Add**.

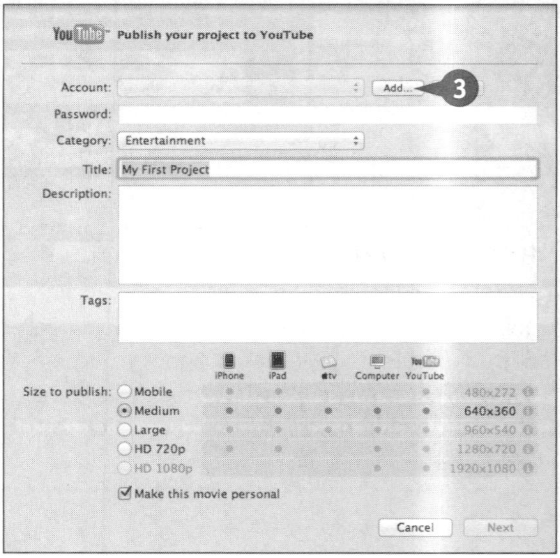

iMovie prompts you for your YouTube username.

4 Type your username.

5 Click **Done**.

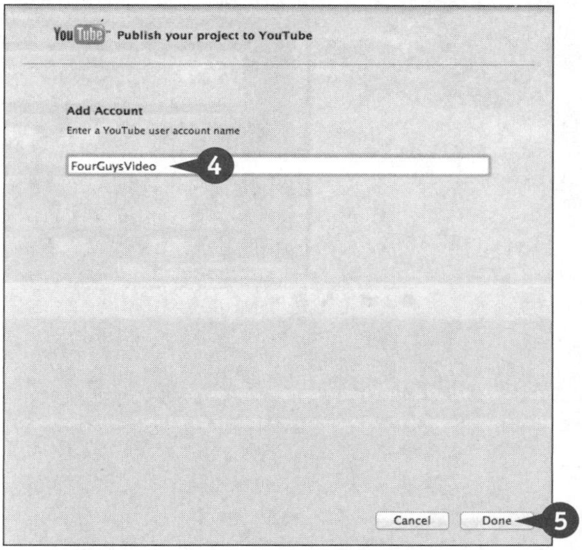

6 Type your YouTube password.

7 Select a category.

8 Type a title.

9 Type a description.

10 Type one or more tags for the video.

11 If you do not want to allow anyone to view the movie, select the **Make this movie personal** option (☐ changes to ☑).

12 Click **Next**.

iMovie displays the YouTube terms of service.

13 Click **Publish** (not shown).

iMovie prepares the movie and then publishes it to YouTube.

14 Click **OK** (not shown).

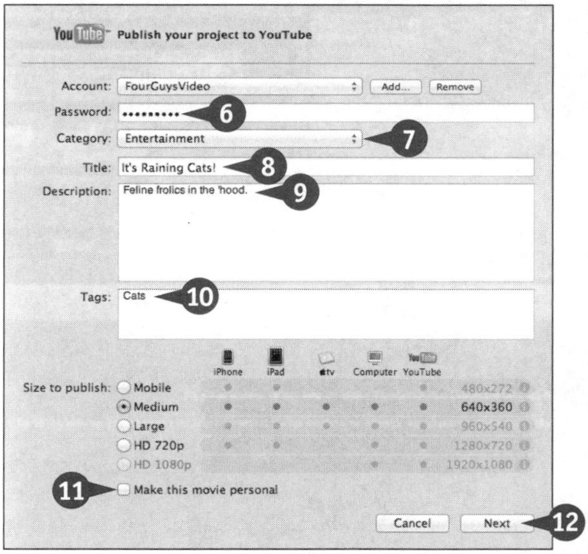

TIPS

How do I publish my movie to Facebook?
If you have a Facebook account, click **Share** and then click **Facebook**. Click **Add**, type your Facebook e-mail address, and then click **Done**. Type your Facebook password. Use the **Viewable by** pop-up menu to choose who can see the video. Type a title and description, select a size, click **Next**, and then click **Publish**.

How do I view my movie outside of iMovie?
Beyond viewing it on YouTube or Facebook, you need to export the movie to a digital video file. Click **Share** and then click **Export Movie** (or press ⌘+E). Type a title for the movie, and then select a **Size to Export** option, such as **Large** or **HD 720p** (◯ changes to ◉). Click **Export**.

CHAPTER 14

Customizing Mac Pro

OS X comes with a number of features that enable you to customize your Mac Pro. For example, you might not like the default desktop background or the layout of the Dock. Not only can you change the appearance of Mac Pro to suit your taste, but you can also change the way Mac Pro works to make it easier and more efficient for you to use.

Display System Preferences

You can find many of the Mac Pro customization features in System Preferences, a collection of settings and options that controls the overall look and operation of Mac Pro. You can use System Preferences to change the desktop background, specify a screen saver, set your Mac Pro's sleep options, add user accounts, and customize the Dock, to name some of the tasks that you learn about in this chapter. To use these settings, you must know how to display the System Preferences window.

Display System Preferences

Open System Preferences

1. In the Dock, click **System Preferences** ( ).

The System Preferences appear.

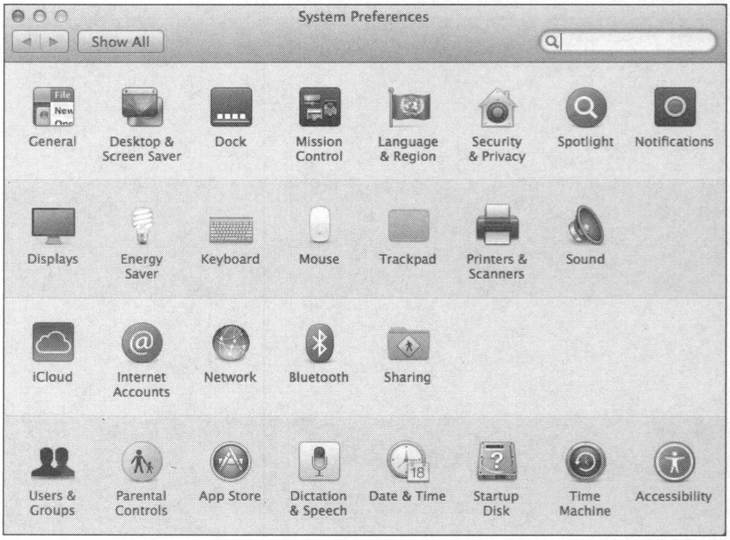

Close System Preferences

1 Click **System Preferences.**

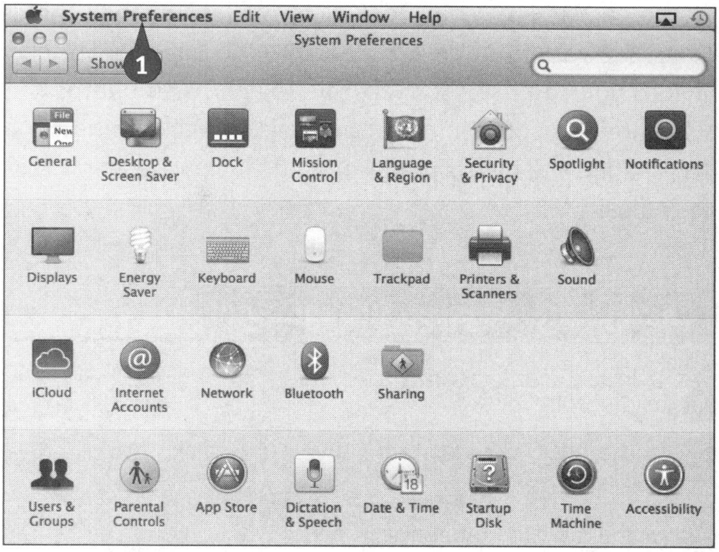

2 Click **Quit System Preferences.**

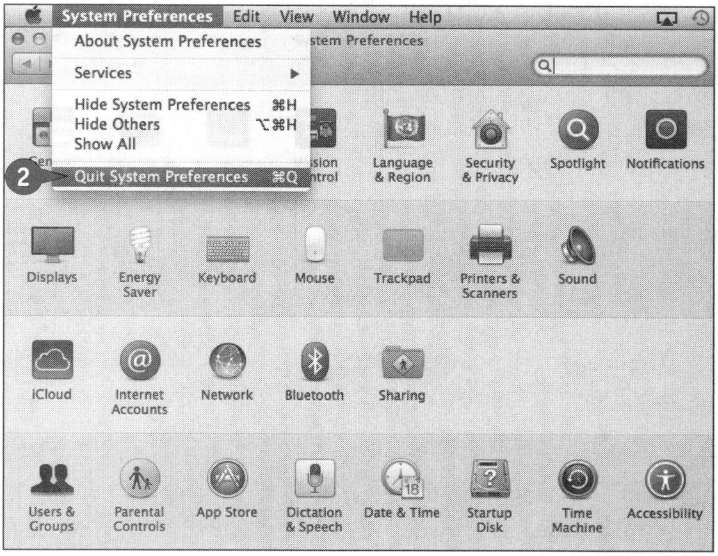

TIPS

Are there other methods I can use to open System Preferences?

If you have hidden the Dock (as described in the section "Hide the Dock") or removed the System Preferences icon from the Dock, you can click the **Apple** icon () and then click **System Preferences.**

Sometimes when I open System Preferences, I do not see all the icons. How can I restore the original icons?

When you click an icon in System Preferences, the window changes to show just the options and settings associated with that icon. To return to the main System Preferences window, click **View** and then click **Show All Preferences** (or press ⌘+L). You can also click ◀ until the main window appears, or click **Show All.**

Change the Desktop Background

To give Mac Pro a different look, you can change the default desktop background. Mac Pro offers a wide variety of desktop background options. For example, Mac Pro comes with several dozen images you can use, from abstract patterns to photos of plants and other natural images. You can also choose a solid color as the desktop background, or you can use one of your own photos. You can change the desktop background to show either a fixed image or a series of images that change periodically.

Change the Desktop Background

Set a Fixed Background Image

1. In the Dock, click **System Preferences** ( ).
2. In the System Preferences, click **Desktop & Screen Saver**.

Note: You can also right-click the desktop and then click **Change Desktop Background**.

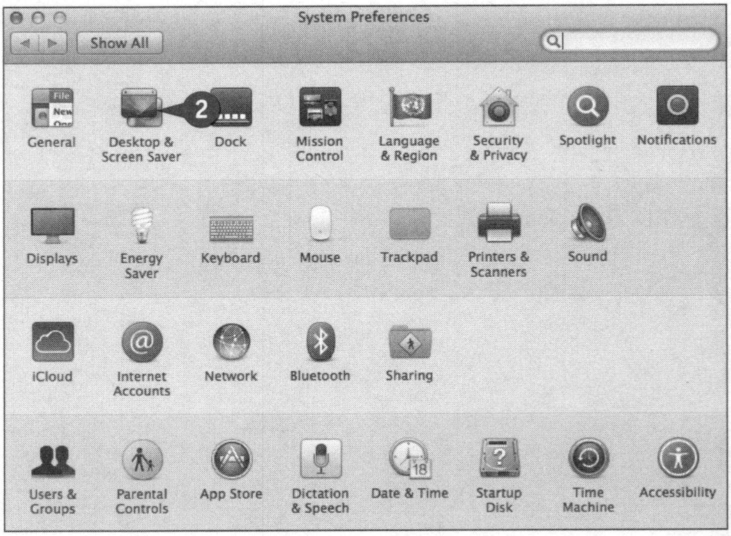

The Desktop & Screen Saver preferences appear.

3. Click the **Desktop** tab.
4. Click the image category you want to use.

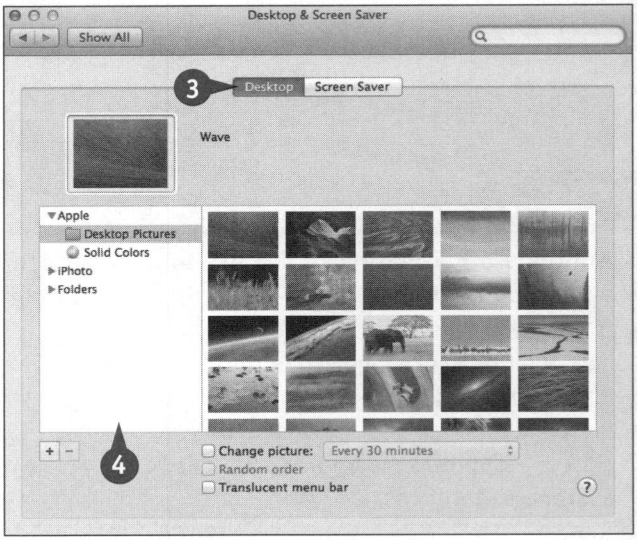

5 Click the image you want to use as the desktop background.

Your Mac Pro changes the desktop background.

6 If you chose a photo in step **5**, click ⇕ and then click an option to determine how your Mac Pro displays the photo.

Note: Another way to set a fixed background image is to select a photo in iPhoto, click **Share**, and then click **Set Desktop**.

Set a Changing Background Image

1 Select the **Change picture** option (☐ changes to ☑).

2 Click ⇕ and then click how often you want the background image to change.

3 If you want your Mac Pro to choose the periodic image randomly, select the **Random order** option (☐ changes to ☑).

Your Mac Pro changes the desktop background periodically based on your chosen interval.

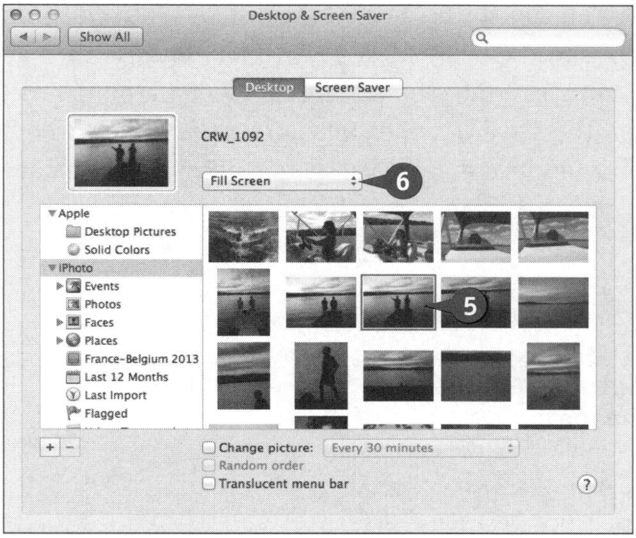

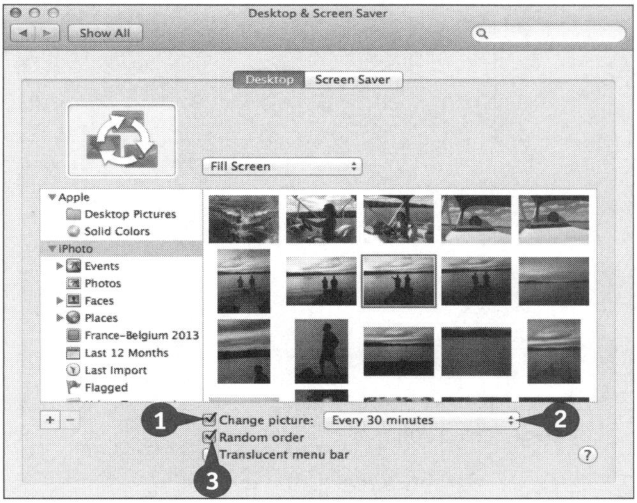

TIP

When I choose a photo, how do the various options differ for displaying the photo?

Your Mac Pro gives you five options for displaying the photo:

- **Fill Screen**. Expands the photo in all four directions until it fills the entire desktop.
- **Fit to Screen**. Expands the photo in all four directions until the photo is either the same height as the desktop or the same width as the desktop.
- **Stretch to Fill Screen**. Expands the photo in all four directions until it fills the entire desktop.
- **Center**. Displays the photo at its actual size and places the photo in the center of the desktop.
- **Tile**. Repeats your photo multiple times to fill the entire desktop.

Activate the Screen Saver

You can set up Mac Pro to display a *screen saver*, a moving pattern or series of pictures. The screen saver appears after your computer has been idle for a while. If you leave your monitor on for long stretches while your computer is idle, a faint version of the unmoving image can endure for a while on the screen, a phenomenon known as *persistence*. A screen saver prevents this by displaying a moving image. However, persistence is not a major problem for modern screens, so for the most part, you use a screen saver for visual interest.

Activate the Screen Saver

1. In the Dock, click **System Preferences** ( ).
2. In the System Preferences, click **Desktop & Screen Saver**.

The Desktop & Screen Saver preferences appear.

3. Click the **Screen Saver** tab.

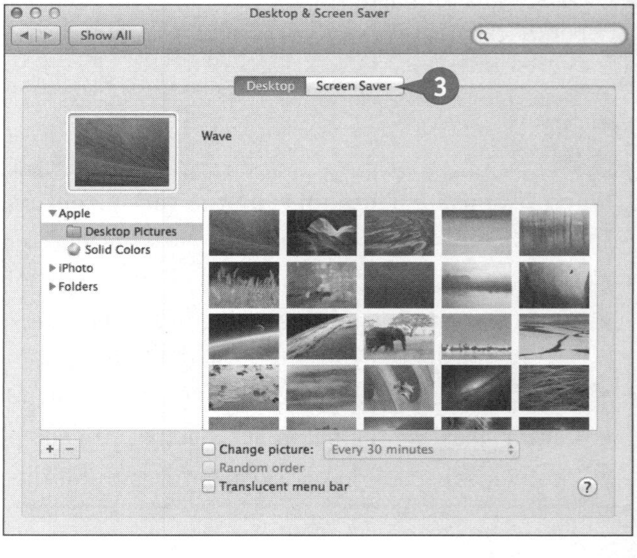

4 Click the screen saver you want to use.

A A preview of the screen saver appears here.

5 Click the **Start after** ⬍ and then click a time delay until the screen saver begins.

Note: The interval you choose is the number of minutes or hours that your Mac Pro must be idle before the screen saver starts.

B If the screen saver is customizable, click **Screen Saver Options** to configure it.

C If you chose a slide show instead of a screen saver, click the **Source** ⬍ to select an image collection.

D If you also want to see the current time when the screen saver is active, select the **Show with clock** option (☐ changes to ☑).

Note: To learn how to set up hot corners on Mac Pro, see the section "Configure Hot Corners."

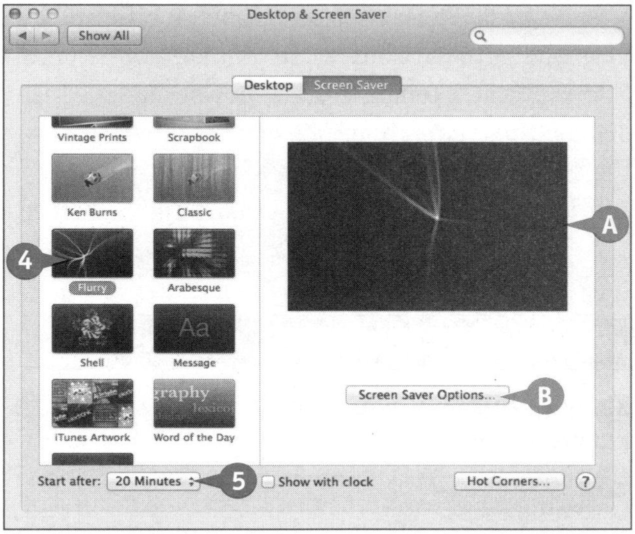

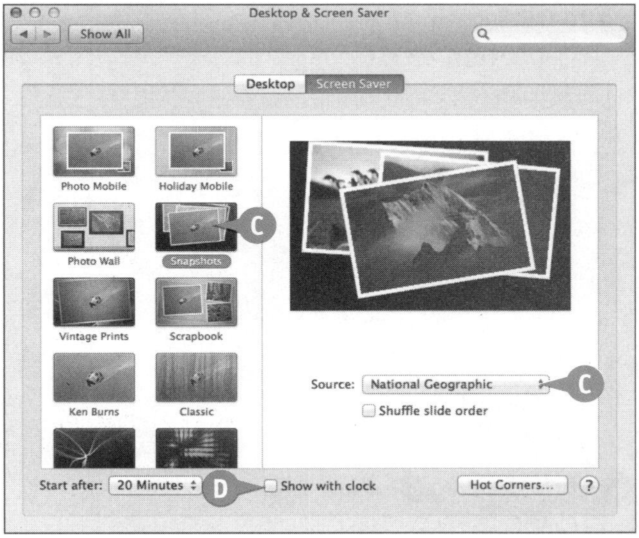

TIP

Can I just display a black screen as a screen saver?

No, Mac Pro does not come with a screen saver that displays a completely black screen. However, you can come close to this by selecting the **Message** screen saver. Click **Screen Saver Options**, use the Message text box to type a space, and then click **OK**. In this case, when the screen saver kicks in you only see the gray Apple logo, which changes position on the screen every few seconds.

If you want to display a blank screen after a period of inactivity, do not set a screen saver. Instead, configure your Mac Pro display to sleep automatically, as described in the next section.

Set Your Mac Pro's Sleep Options

You can make Mac Pro more energy efficient by configuring parts of the computer to go into sleep mode automatically when you are not using them. *Sleep mode* means that your display or your Mac Pro is in a temporary low-power mode, which saves energy. You can set up Mac Pro to put the display to sleep automatically after a period of inactivity. Similarly, you can configure Mac Pro to put the entire computer to sleep after you have not used it for a specified amount of time. You can also configure Mac Pro to sleep automatically at a certain time.

Set Your Mac Pro's Sleep Options

Set Mac Pro to Sleep after a Period of Inactivity

1. In the Dock, click **System Preferences** ( ).
2. In the System Preferences, click **Energy Saver**.

The Energy Saver preferences appear.

3. Click and drag the slider to set the computer sleep timer.

   This specifies the period of inactivity after which your computer goes to sleep.

4. Click and drag the slider to set the display sleep timer.

   This specifies the period of inactivity after which your display goes to sleep.

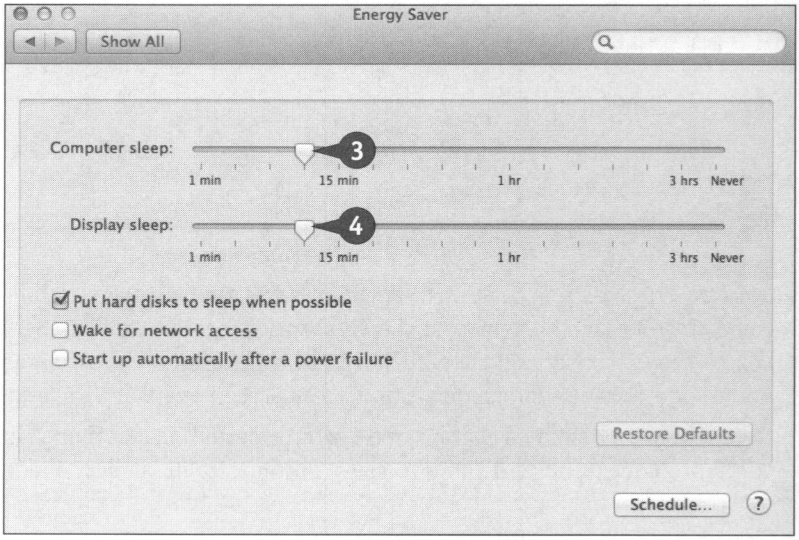

Schedule Mac Pro to Sleep at a Set Time

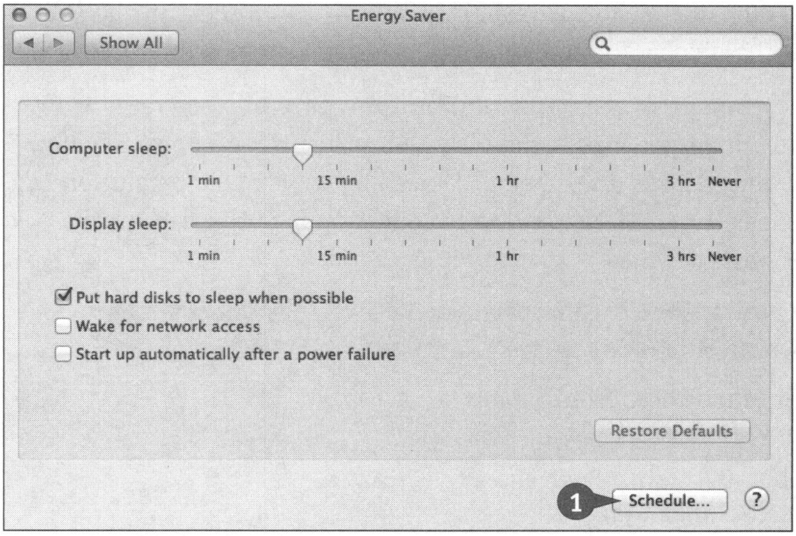

1. In the Energy Saver dialog, click **Schedule**.

2. Select this check box (☐ changes to ☑).
3. Click ⬍ and then click when you want Mac Pro to sleep.
4. Click ⬍ and then click the time you want Mac Pro to go to sleep.
5. Click **OK**.

System Preferences puts the new setting into effect.

TIPS

How do I wake a sleeping display or computer?
If your Mac Pro's display is in sleep mode, you can wake it by moving your mouse or sliding your finger on a trackpad, if you have one connected to your Mac Pro. You can also wake up the display or your entire Mac Pro by pressing any key.

I changed the display sleep timer, now I never see my screen saver. Why?
You set the display sleep timer to a time that is less than your screen saver timer. Suppose you configured Mac Pro to switch on the screen saver after 15 minutes. If you set the display sleep timer to a shorter interval, such as 10 minutes, Mac Pro always puts the display to sleep before the screen saver appears.

Change the Display Resolution and Brightness

You can change the resolution and the brightness of the Mac Pro display. This enables you to adjust the display for best viewing or for maximum compatibility with whatever application you are using.

Increasing the display resolution is an easy way to create more space on the screen for applications and windows because the objects on the screen appear smaller. Conversely, if you have trouble reading text on the screen, decreasing the display resolution can help because the screen objects appear larger. If you find that your display is too dark or too bright, you can adjust the brightness for best viewing.

Change the Display Resolution and Brightness

1. In the Dock, click **System Preferences** ( ).
2. In the System Preferences, click **Displays**.

The Displays preferences appear.

3. Click the **Display** tab.

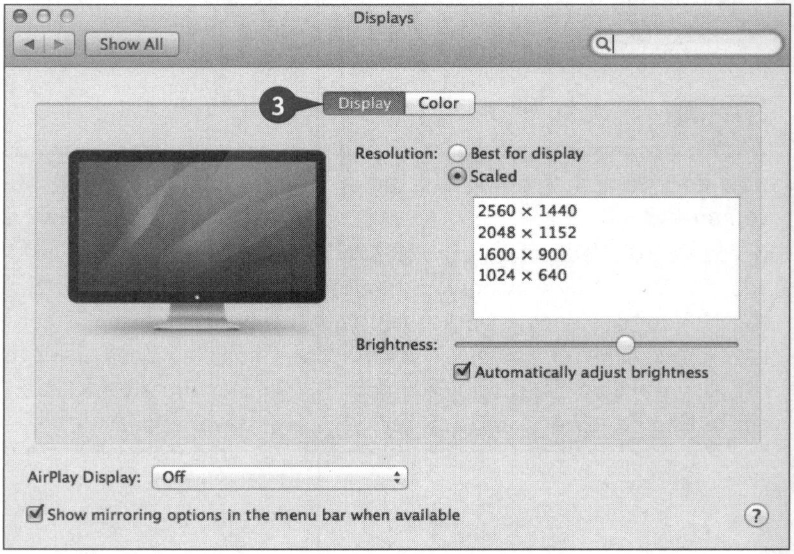

4 Select the resolution:

A To have Mac Pro set the resolution based on your display, select the **Best for display** option (changes to).

B To set the resolution yourself, select the **Scaled** option (changes to) and then click the resolution you want to use.

Mac Pro adjusts the screen to the new resolution.

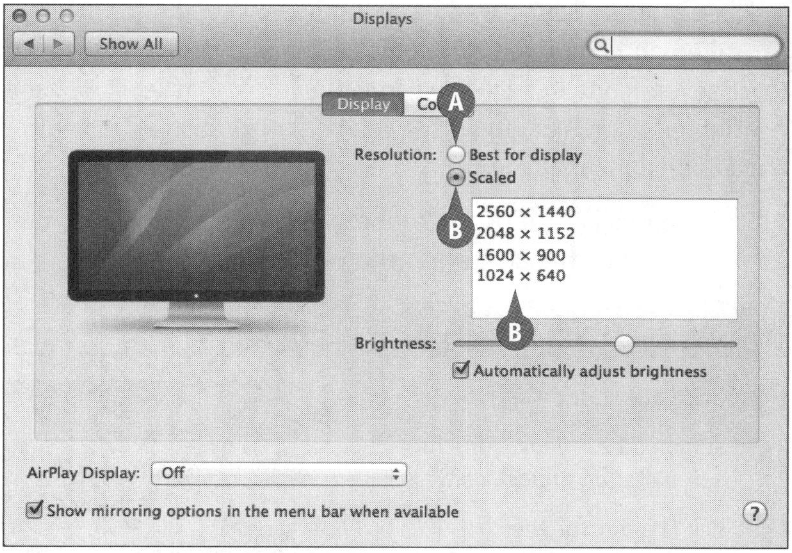

5 Click and drag the **Brightness** slider to set the display brightness.

Mac Pro adjusts the screen to the new brightness.

C If you do not want Mac Pro to adjust the brightness based on the ambient light, deselect the **Automatically adjust brightness** option (changes to).

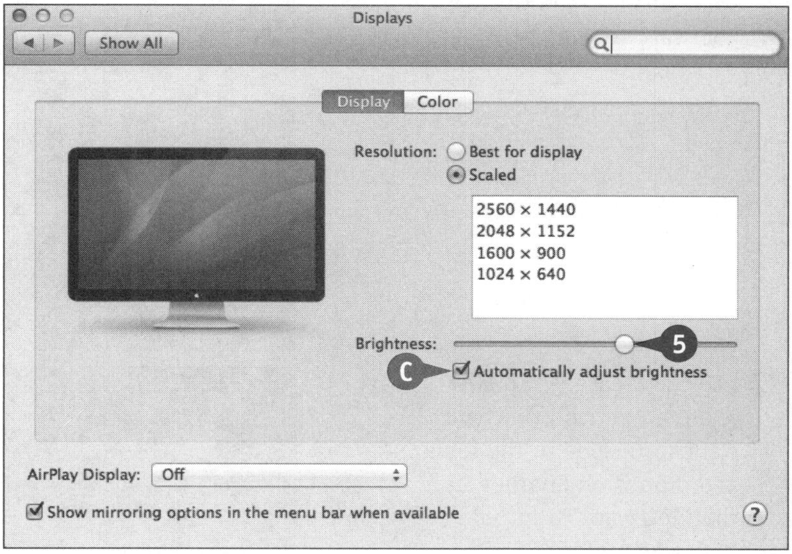

TIPS

What do the resolution numbers mean?
The resolution numbers are expressed in *pixels*, short for picture elements, which are the individual dots that make up what you see on your Mac Pro's screen, arranged in rows and columns. So a resolution of 1440 × 900 means that the display is using 1,440-pixel rows and 900-pixel columns.

Why do some resolutions also include the word stretched?
Most older displays use an aspect ratio (width to the height) of 4:3. However, most new Mac Pro displays use an aspect ratio of 16:10, which is called *widescreen*. Resolutions designed for 4:3 displays take up only part of a widescreen display. To make them take up the entire display, choose the *stretched* version of the resolution.

Create an App Folder in Launchpad

You can make Launchpad easier to use by combining multiple icons into a single storage area called an *app folder*. Normally, Launchpad displays icons in up to five rows per screen, with at least seven icons in each row, so you can have at least 35 icons in each screen. Also, if you have configured your Mac Pro with a relatively low display resolution, you might see only partial app names in Launchpad.

All this can make it difficult to locate your apps. However, app folders can help you organize similar apps and reduce the clutter on the Launchpad screens.

Create an App Folder in Launchpad

1. Click **Launchpad** ( ).

   A. Launchpad displays icons for each installed application.

2. Click the dot for the Launchpad screen with which you want to work.

3. Use the mouse ( ) to click and drag an icon that you want to include in the folder, and drop it on another icon that you want to include in the same folder.

- **B** Launchpad creates the app folder.
- **C** Launchpad applies a name to the folder based on the type of applications in the folder.
- **D** Launchpad adds the icons to the app folder.

4 To specify a different name, click the name and then type the one you prefer.

5 Click outside of the app folder.

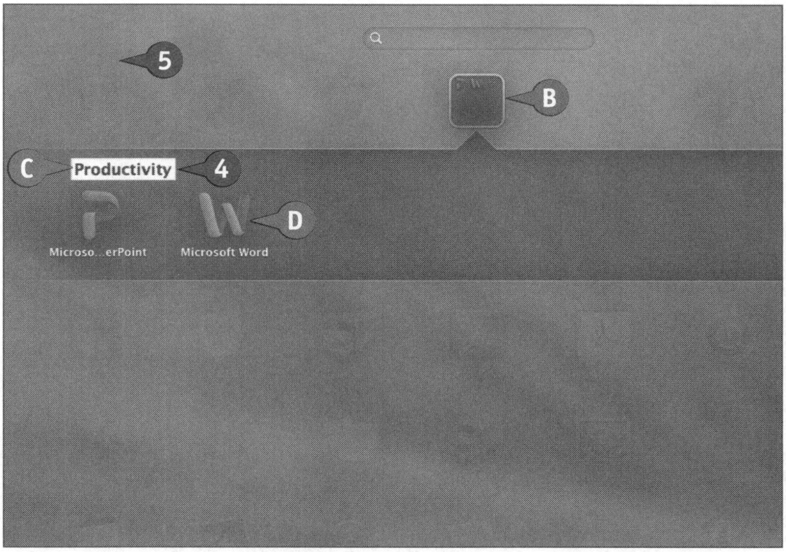

- **E** Launchpad displays the app folder.

6 To add more icons to the new app folder, use the mouse to click and drag each icon and drop it on the folder.

Note: To launch a program from an app folder, click **Launchpad** ( ), click the app folder to open it, and then click the program's icon.

TIPS

How do I make changes to an app folder?
Click to open Launchpad and then click the app folder. To rename the app folder, click the current name, type the new name, and then press Return. To rearrange the icons, use the mouse to drag and drop the apps within the folder. When you are done, click outside the app folder to close it.

How do I remove an icon from an app folder?
Click to open Launchpad and then click the app folder. To remove an app from a folder, use the mouse to click and drag the app out of the folder. Launchpad closes the folder, and you can then drop the icon within the Launchpad screen.

Add a User Account

You can share your Mac Pro with another person by creating a user account for that person. This enables the person to log in to Mac Pro and use the system. The new user account is completely separate from your own account. This means that the other person can change settings, create documents, and perform other Mac Pro tasks without interfering with your settings or data. For maximum privacy for all users, you should set up each user account with a password.

Add a User Account

1 In the Dock, click **System Preferences** ( ).

2 In the System Preferences window, click **Users & Groups**.

A In most Mac Pro systems, to modify accounts you must click the lock icon ( ) and then type your administrator password (changes to).

3 Click **Add** (+).

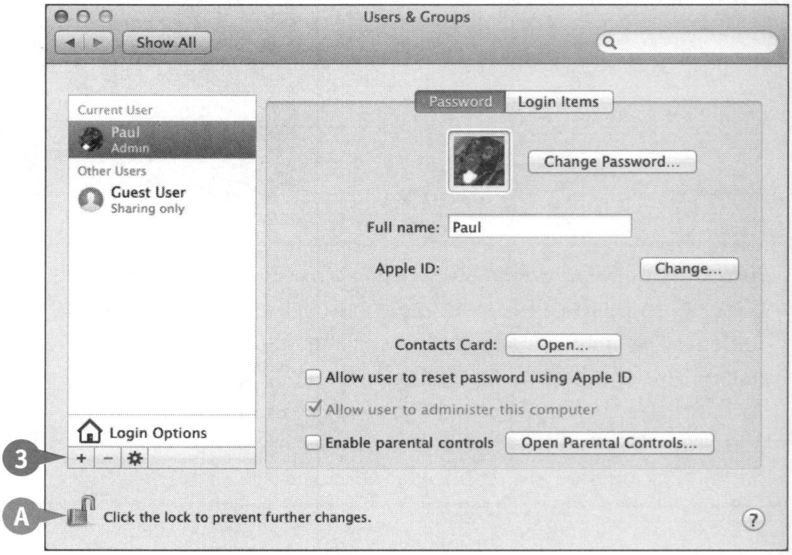

The New Account dialog appears.

4 Click ⬍ and then click an account type.

5 Type the user's name.

6 Edit the short username that Mac Pro creates.

7 Type a password for the user.

8 Retype the user's password.

9 Type a hint that Mac Pro will display if the user forgets the password.

10 Click **Create User**.

B Mac Pro adds the user account to the Users & Groups preferences.

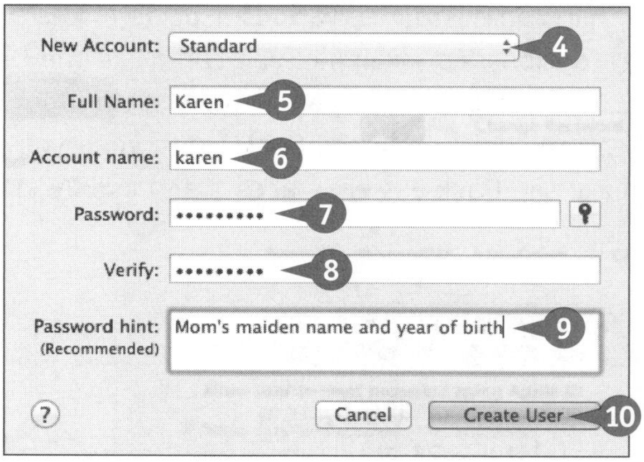

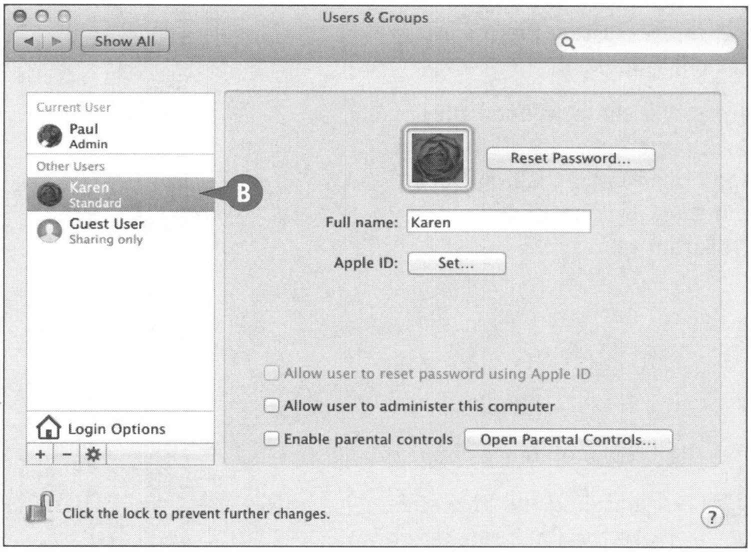

TIPS

Which account type should I use for the new account?

The Standard account type is a good choice because it can make changes only to its own account settings. Avoid the Administrator option because it is a powerful account type that enables the user to make major changes to the system. If the user is a child, consider the Managed with Parental Controls account type.

How do I change the user's picture?

In the Users & Groups preferences, click the user and then click the picture. Mac Pro displays a list of the available images. If you see one you like, click it. If your Mac Pro has a camera attached and the user is nearby, you can click **Camera** and then click the **Camera** icon to take the user's picture. Click **Done** to set the picture.

Customize the Dock

You can customize various aspects of the Dock by using System Preferences to modify a few Dock options. For example, you can make the Dock take up less room on the screen by adjusting the size of the Dock. You can also make the Dock a bit easier to use by turning on the Magnification feature, which enlarges Dock icons when you position the mouse pointer over them. You can also make the Dock easier to access and use by moving it to either side of the screen.

Customize the Dock

1. In the Dock, click **System Preferences** ( ).
2. In the System Preferences, click **Dock**.

Note: You can also open the Dock preferences by clicking the Apple icon ( ), clicking **Dock**, and then clicking **Dock Preferences**.

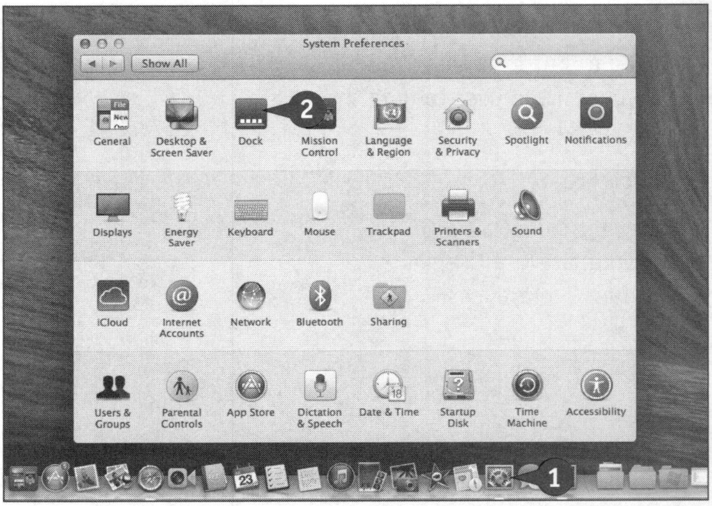

The Dock preferences appear.

3. Click and drag the **Size** slider to make the Dock smaller or larger.

A. You can also click and drag the Dock divider: Drag up to increase the Dock size, and drag down to decrease the Dock size.

B. System Preferences adjusts the size of the Dock.

Note: If your Dock is already as wide as the screen, dragging the Size slider to the right (toward the Large value) has no effect.

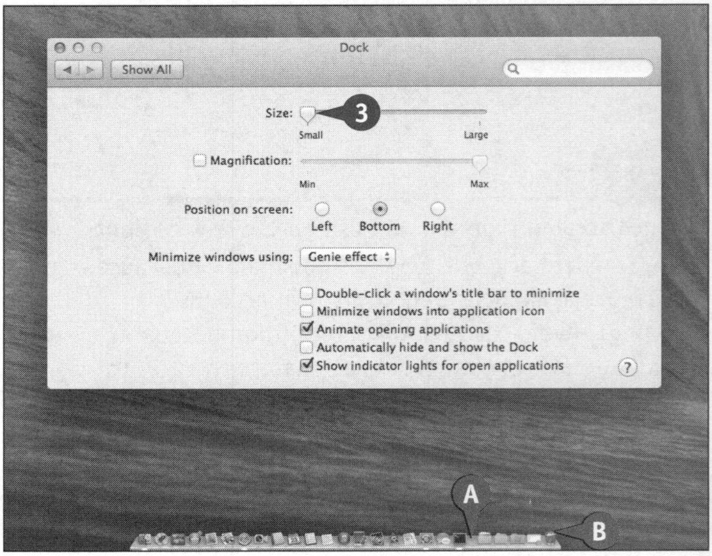

4 Select the **Magnification** option (☐ changes to ☑).

5 Click and drag the **Magnification** slider to set the magnification level.

C When you position the mouse over a Dock icon, your Mac Pro magnifies the icon.

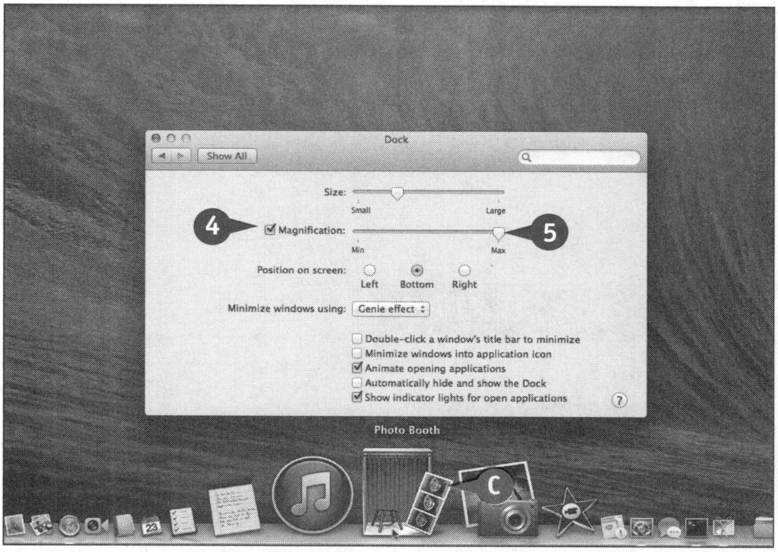

6 Use the **Position on screen** options to select where you want the Dock to appear, such as the **Left** side of the screen (◯ changes to ◉).

D Your Mac Pro moves the Dock to the new position.

7 Click the **Minimize windows using** and then click the effect you want your Mac Pro to use when you minimize a window: **Genie effect** or **Scale effect**.

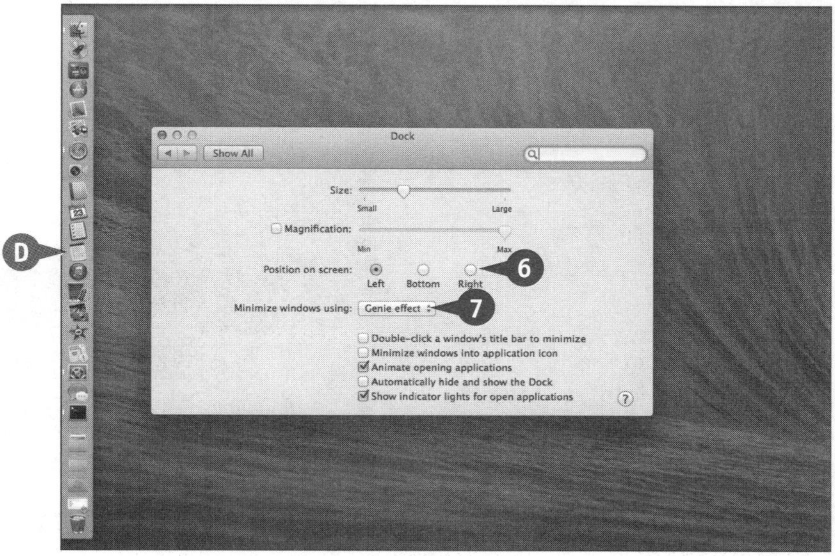

TIP

Is there an easier method I can use to control some of these preferences?

Yes, you can control these preferences directly from the Dock. To set the Dock size, click and drag the Dock divider left or right. For the other preferences, right-click the Dock divider. Click **Turn Magnification On** to enable the magnification feature; click **Turn Magnification Off** to disable this feature. To change the Dock position, click **Position on Screen** and then click **Left**, **Bottom**, or **Right**. To set the minimize effect, click **Minimize Using** and then click either **Genie Effect** or **Scale Effect**. Finally, you can also click **Dock Preferences** to open the Dock pane in System Preferences.

Add an Icon to the Dock

The icons on the Dock are convenient because you can open them with just a single click. You can enhance the convenience of the Dock by adding an icon for an application you use frequently.

The icon remains in the Dock even when the application is closed, so you can always open the application with a single click. You can add an icon to the Dock even if the program is not currently running.

Add an Icon to the Dock

Add an Icon for a Nonrunning Application

1. Click **Finder** ( ).
2. Click **Applications**.

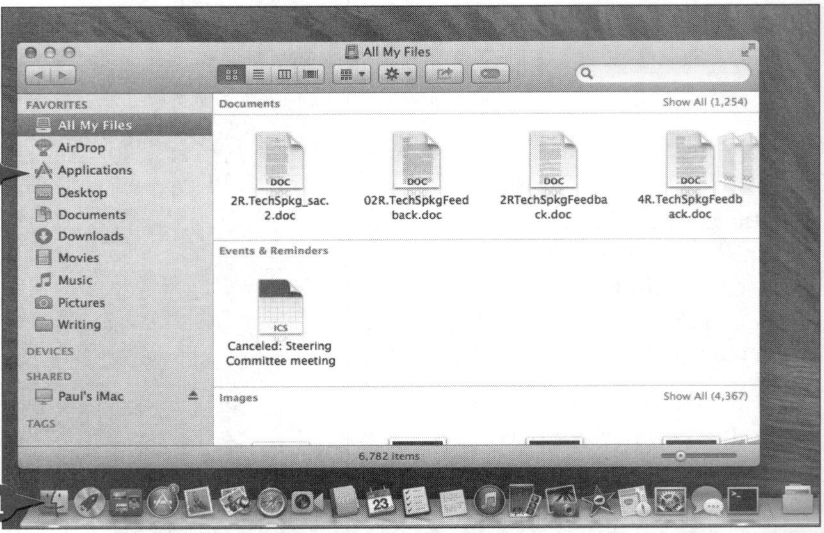

3. Click and drag the application icon and then drop it inside the Dock.

A. Be sure to drop the icon anywhere to the left of the Dock divider.

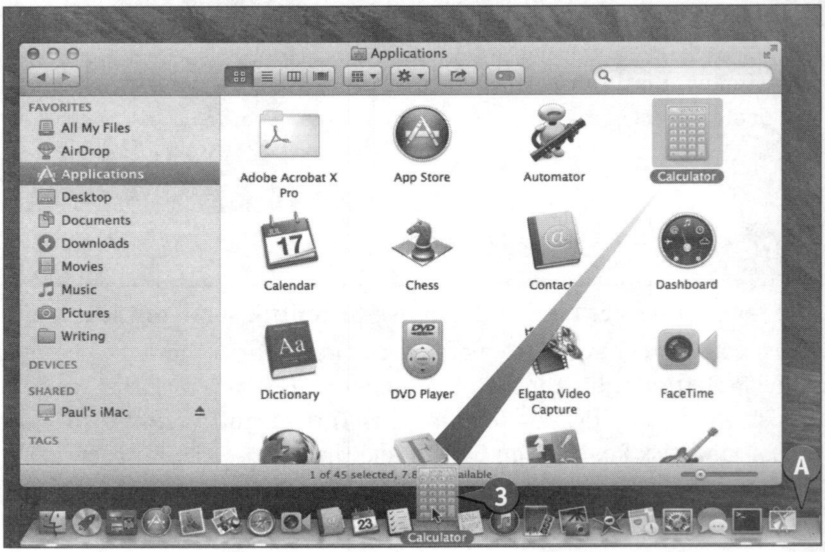

B Mac Pro adds the application's icon to the Dock.

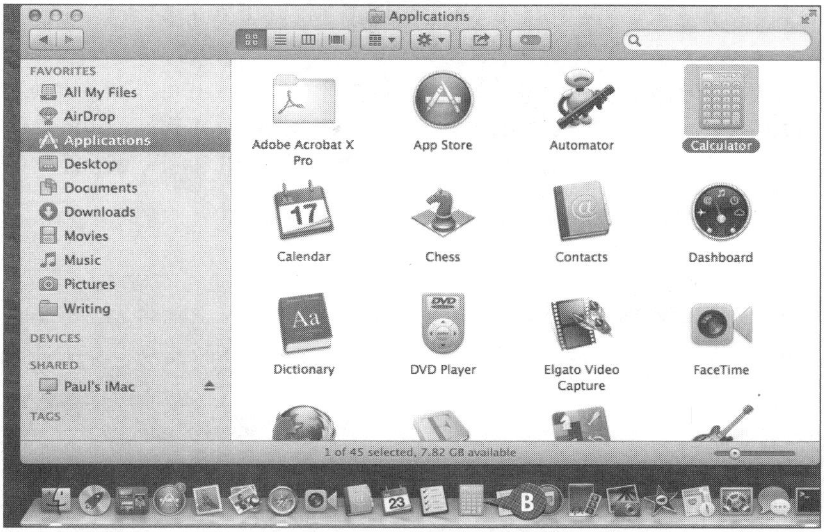

Add an Icon for a Running Application

1 Right-click the application icon in the Dock.

2 Click **Options**.

3 Click **Keep in Dock**.

The application's icon remains in the Dock even after you close the program.

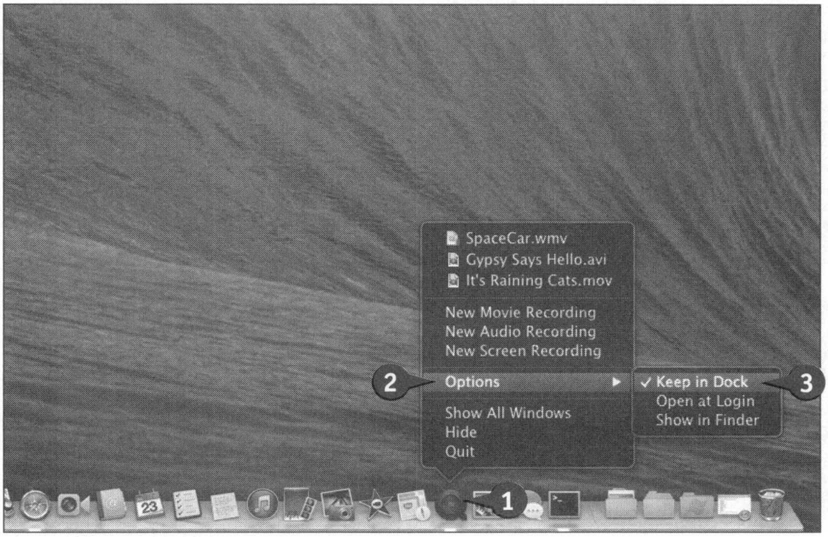

TIPS

Can my Mac Pro start the application automatically each time I log in?
Yes. Your Mac Pro maintains a list of *login items*, which are applications that run automatically after you log in. You can configure your application as a login item, and your Mac Pro opens it automatically each time you log in. Right-click the application's Dock icon, click **Options**, and then click **Open at Login**.

How do I remove an icon from the Dock?
Right-click the application's Dock icon, click **Options**, and then click **Remove from Dock.** If the application is currently running, Mac Pro removes the icon from the Dock when you quit the program. Note that you can remove any application icon except Finder () and Launchpad ().

Hide the Dock

When you are working in an application, you might find that you need to maximize the amount of vertical space the application window takes up on-screen. This might come up, for example, when you are reading or editing a long document or viewing a large photo. In such cases, you can size the window to maximum height, but Mac Pro will not let you go past the Dock. You can work around this by hiding the Dock. When hidden, the Dock is still easily accessible whenever you need to use it.

Hide the Dock

Turn On Dock Hiding

1 Click the **Apple** icon ().

2 Click **Dock**.

3 Click **Turn Hiding On**.

A You can also right-click the Dock divider and then click **Turn Hiding On**.

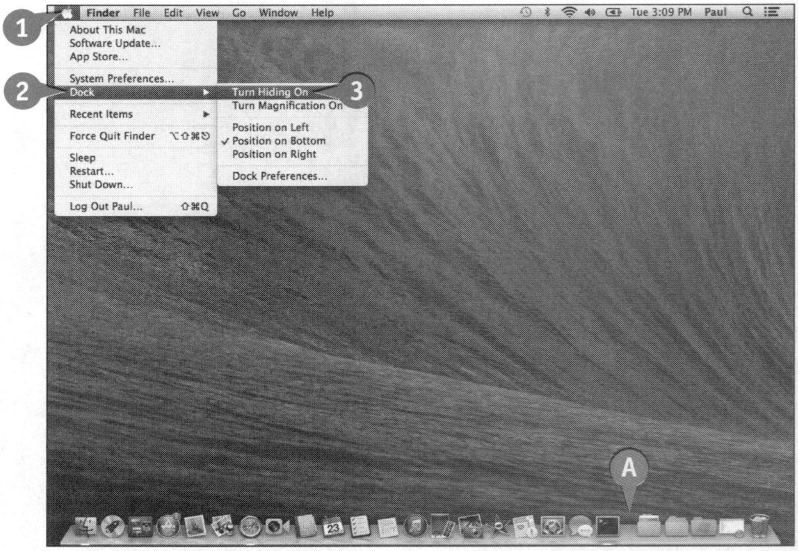

B Mac Pro removes the Dock from the desktop.

Display the Dock Temporarily

1. Move the mouse to the bottom of the screen.

C Mac Pro temporarily displays the Dock.

Note: To hide the Dock again, move the mouse away from the bottom of the screen.

TIPS

Is there a faster way to hide the Dock?

Yes. You can quickly hide the Dock by pressing Option+⌘+D. This keyboard shortcut is a toggle, which means that you can also turn off Dock hiding by pressing Option+⌘+D. When the Dock is hidden, you can display it temporarily by pressing Control+F3 (on some keyboards you must press Fn+Control+F3).

How do I bring the Dock back into view?

When you no longer need the extra screen space for your applications, you can turn off Dock hiding to bring the Dock back into view. Click the **Apple** icon ( ), click **Dock**, and then click **Turn Hiding Off**. Alternatively, display the Dock, right-click the Dock divider, and then click **Turn Hiding Off**.

Add a Widget to the Dashboard

The Dashboard is a Mac Pro application that you use to display widgets. You can customize the Dashboard to include any widgets that you find useful or informative. A widget is a mini-application, particularly one designed to perform a single task, such as displaying the weather, showing stock data, or providing sports scores. Mac Pro comes with 16 widgets, which include a clock, a calculator, a tile game, and a unit converter. There are also many widgets available online.

Add a Widget to the Dashboard

1. Click **Finder** ( ).
2. Click **Applications**.
3. Double-click **Dashboard** ( ).

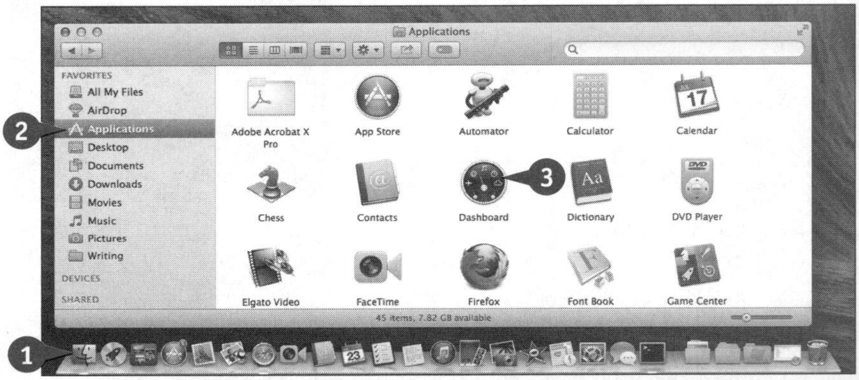

Your Mac Pro displays the Dashboard and its current set of open widgets.

4. Click **Add** ( ).

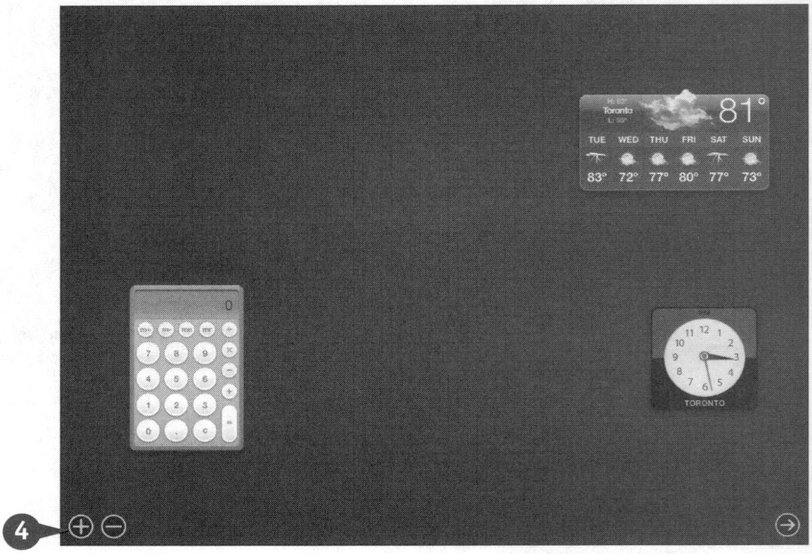

Mac Pro displays its collection of widgets.

5 Click the widget you want to add.

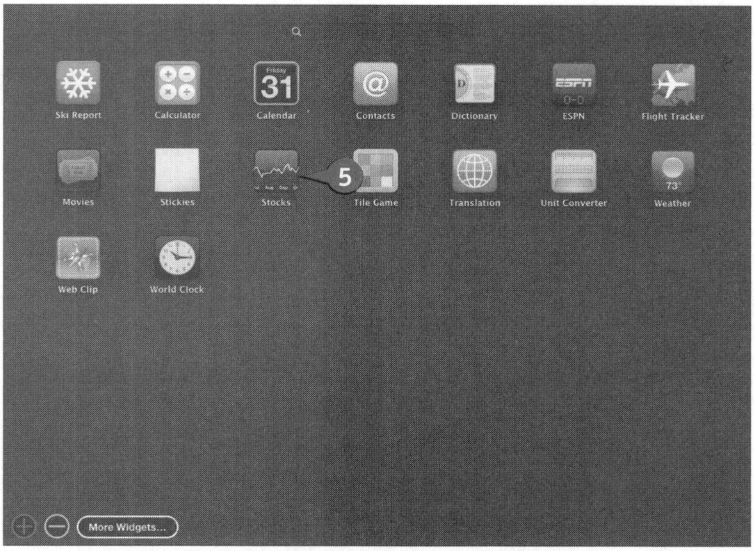

A Your Mac Pro adds the widget to the Dashboard.

6 Use the mouse (pointer) to click and drag the widget to the position you prefer.

B If the widget is configurable, it displays an *i* when you position the mouse (pointer) over it.

7 Click the ***i***.

8 Configure the widget as needed. For example, you can choose the companies to display in the Stocks widget.

9 Click **Done** to close the widget configuration options (not shown).

10 Click **Exit** (Exit icon).

Your Mac Pro closes the Dashboard.

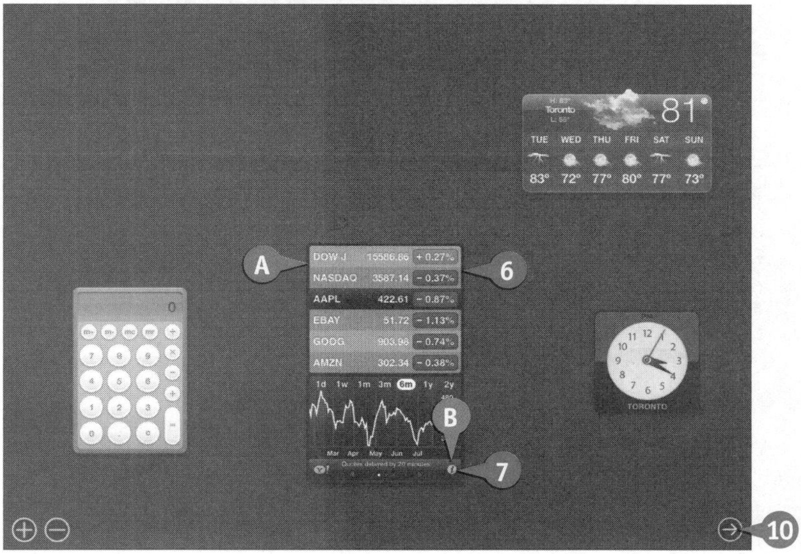

TIPS

Are there other methods I can use to open the Dashboard?

Yes. You can open and close the Dashboard quickly on most Mac Pros by pressing F12 (or Fn+F12). On most Apple keyboards, you can also press F4 to open and close the Dashboard.

How do I remove a widget from the Dashboard?

To remove a single widget, press and hold Option, position the mouse (pointer) over the widget, and then click the **Close** button (Close icon) that the Dashboard displays in the upper left corner of the widget. To remove more than one widget, click **Remove** (Remove icon) and then click the **Close** button (Close icon) in each widget that you want to remove.

Configure Hot Corners

A *hot corner* is a corner of your Mac Pro's screen that you have configured to perform an action when you move the mouse (pointer) to that specific corner. Mac Pro offers a wide variety of actions you can assign to each hot corner. For example, you can put the Mac Pro display to sleep; you can display Launchpad, the Dashboard, the Notification Center, Mission Control, or the desktop; and you can start or stop the screen saver.

Configure Hot Corners

1 Click the **Apple** icon ( ).

2 Click **System Preferences.**

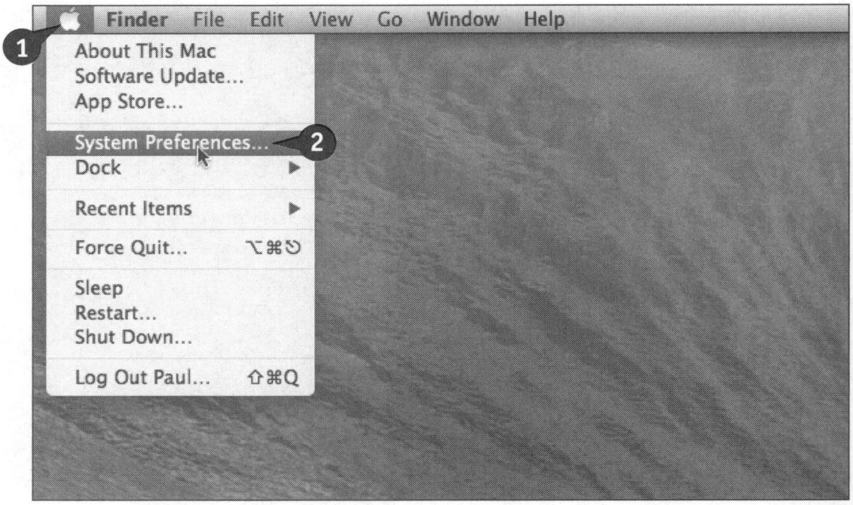

The System Preferences appear.

3 Click **Desktop & Screen Saver.**

The Desktop & Screen Saver preferences appear.

4. Click the **Screen Saver** tab.
5. Click **Hot Corners**.

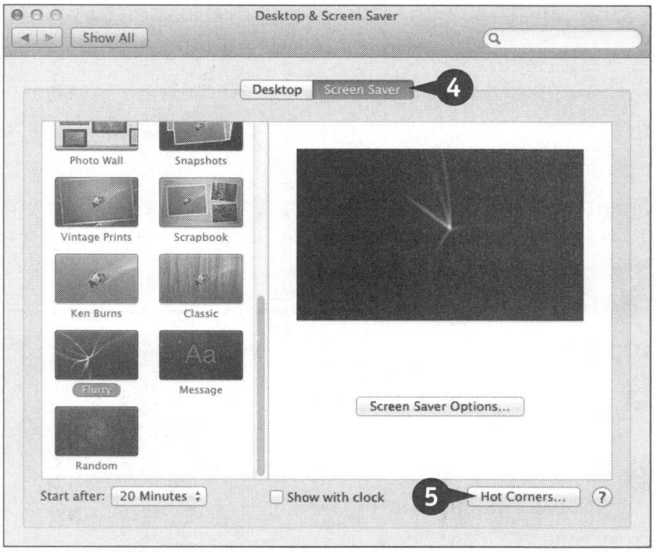

The Active Screen Corners dialog appears.

6. For each hot corner you want to configure, click and then click the action you want Mac Pro to perform when you move the mouse to that corner of the screen.
7. Click **OK**.

Mac Pro puts the new hot corners into effect.

TIPS

How do I know which menu to use for each hot corner?
In the Active Screen Corners dialog, the relative position of each pop-up menu corresponds to the hot corner that it configures. For example, the upper left pop-up menu configures the upper left hot corner, the lower left pop-up menu configures the lower left hot corner, and so on.

What does the Application Windows action do?
When you configure a hot corner with the Application Windows action, moving the mouse to that corner gathers all your open application windows to the center of the screen. You can then switch between applications either by clicking the Dock icons or by pressing ⌘+Tab.

Set Up Spaces

You can make your Mac Pro screen easier to manage and less cluttered by organizing your running apps into two or more spaces. A *space* is a version of the desktop that includes only the windows of the apps that you have assigned to that space. For example, you might have a work space that includes only a word processor, a spreadsheet, and Safari for research; a social space that includes only Mail, Messages, Contacts, and Calendar; and a media space that includes only iTunes, iPhoto, and iMovie. You can quickly switch from one space to another.

Set Up Spaces

Add a New Space

1. In the Dock, click **Mission Control** ( ).
2. Move the mouse ( ) toward the top right corner of the screen.
3. Click **Add**.

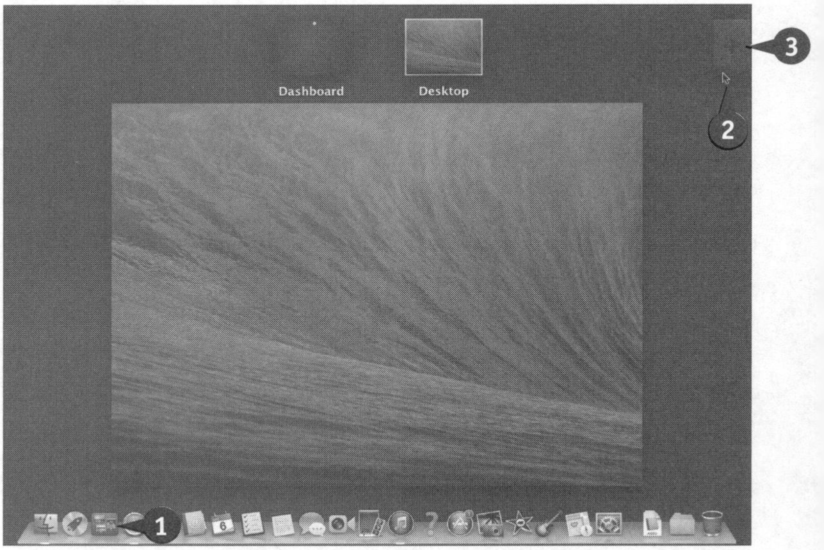

A Mission Control creates a new space.

B Your original desktop is shown as a space named Desktop 1.

C The Dashboard is also considered a space.

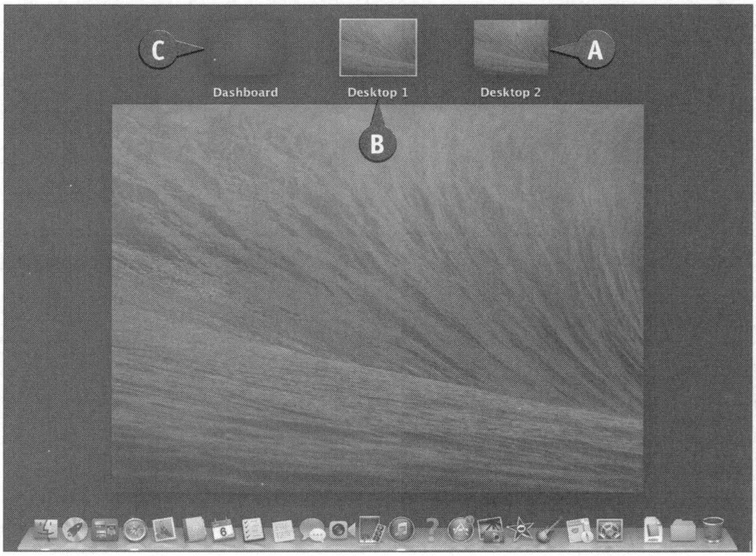

Switch to a Another Space

1. In the Dock, click **Mission Control** ( ).
2. Click the space you want to use.

   Mac Pro switches to that desktop and displays its open windows.

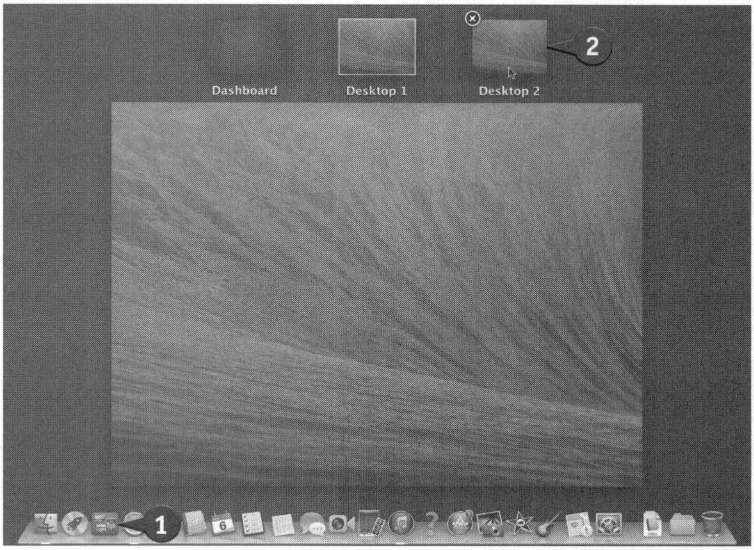

Assign an App to a Space

1. Switch to the space to which you want to assign the app.
2. Right-click the app's Dock icon.
3. Click **Options**.
4. Click **This Desktop**.

   Mac Pro assigns the app to the current space.

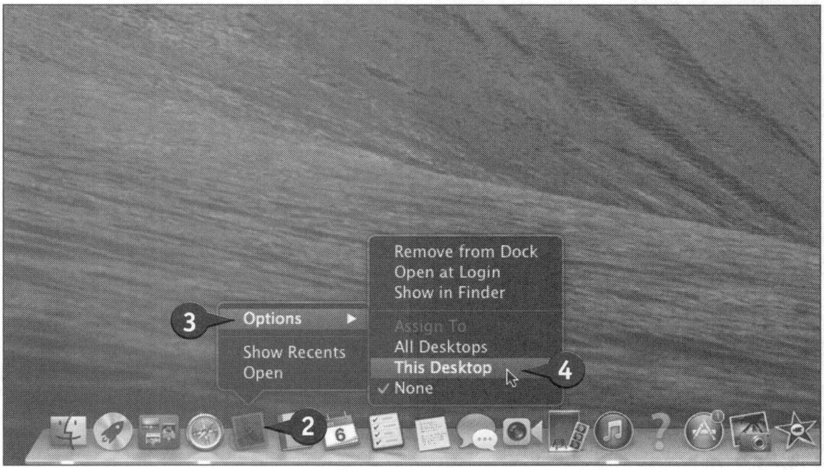

TIPS

Are there shortcut methods I can use?
Display Mission Control quickly either by pressing the Mission Control key (F3), or by pressing Control+↑. To switch between spaces, press and hold Control and tap ← or →. If you have a trackpad connected to Mac Pro, display Mission Control by swiping up with four fingers. You can switch between spaces by swiping left or right with four fingers.

How do I delete a space?
Display Mission Control, move the mouse over the space you want to delete, and then click the **Delete** icon ( ) that appears in the upper left corner of the space thumbnail. Mac Pro deletes the space. If the space contained running apps, those windows are assigned to the Desktop 1 space.

CHAPTER 15

Working with Disks

Your Mac Pro comes with an internal hard drive, but you can also attach external drives, including hard drives, flash drives, and optical drives. This chapter introduces you to Mac Pro's powerful and useful disk drive tools.

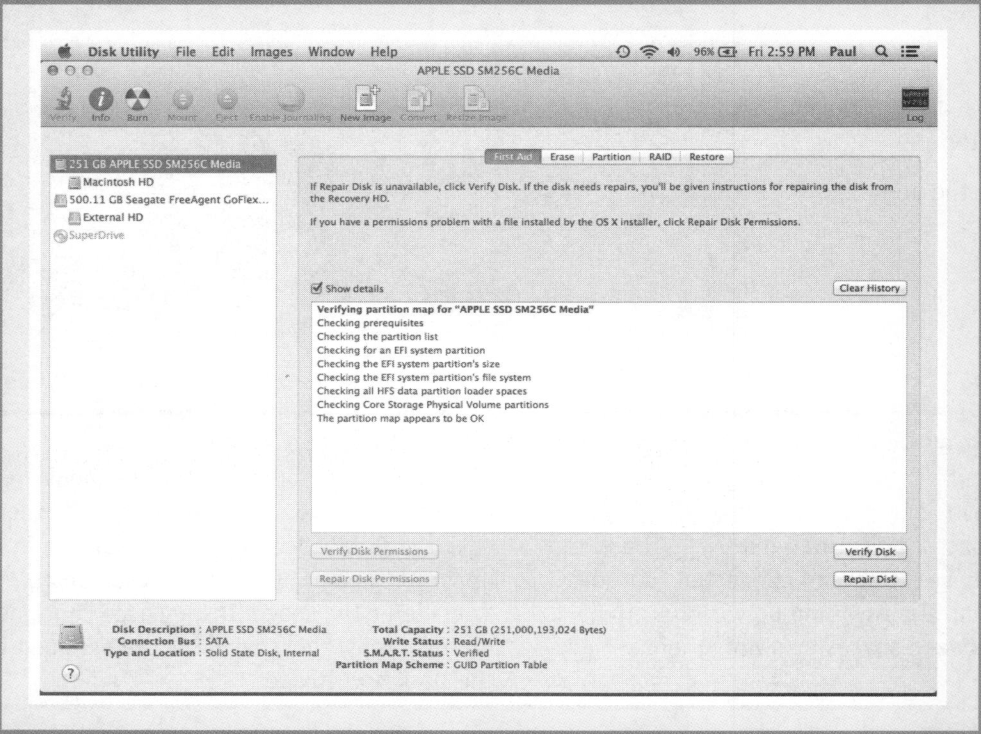

View Hard Drive Free Space

To ensure that your Mac Pro's hard drive does not become full, you should periodically check how much free space it has left. If you run out of room on your Mac Pro's hard drive, you will not be able to install more applications or create more documents, and your Mac Pro's performance will suffer. To ensure your free space does not become too low — say, less than about 20GB or 25GB — you can check how much free space your hard drive has left.

You should check your Mac Pro's hard drive free space about once a month.

View Hard Drive Free Space

Check Free Space Using Finder

1. Click **Finder** ().
2. Click **Desktop**.

Note: You can also click any folder on your Mac Pro's hard drive.

3. In the status bar, read the available value, which tells you the amount of free space left on the hard drive.

   If you do not see the status bar, press ⌘+/.

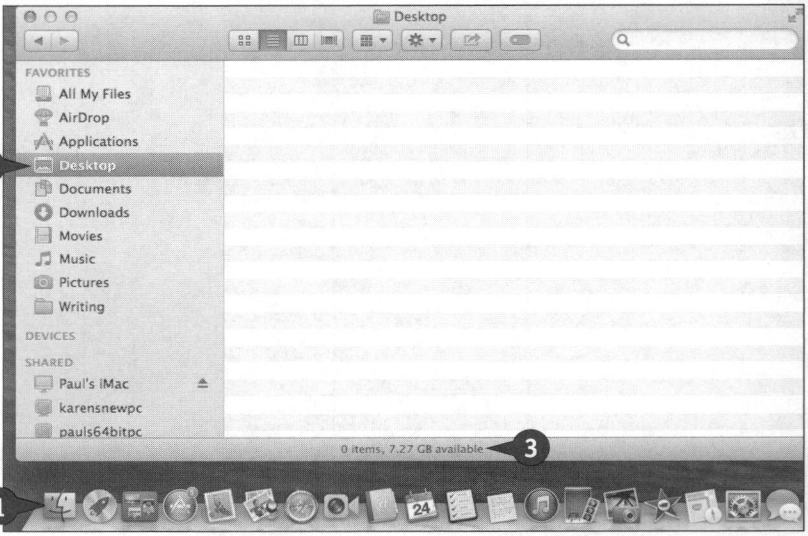

Display Free Space on the Desktop

1. Display your Mac Pro's HD (hard drive) icon on the desktop, as described in the first tip.
2. Click the desktop.
3. Click **View**.
4. Click **Show View Options**.

Note: You can also run the Show View Options command by pressing ⌘+J.

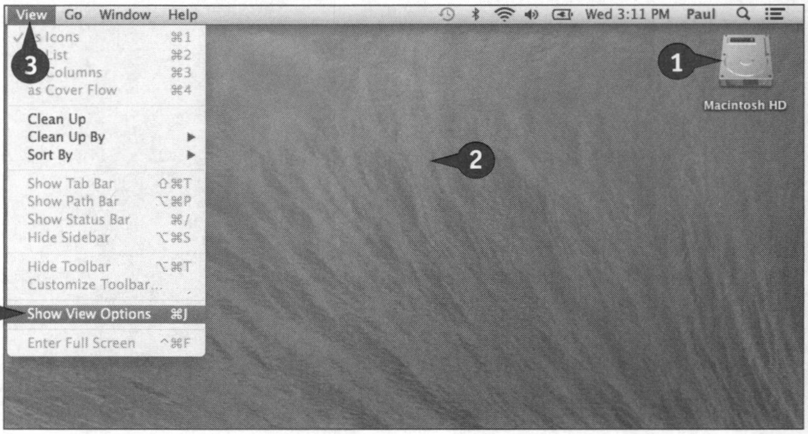

The Desktop dialog appears.

5. Select the **Show item info** option (☐ changes to ☑).

A. Your Mac Pro displays the amount of free hard drive space under the Macintosh HD icon.

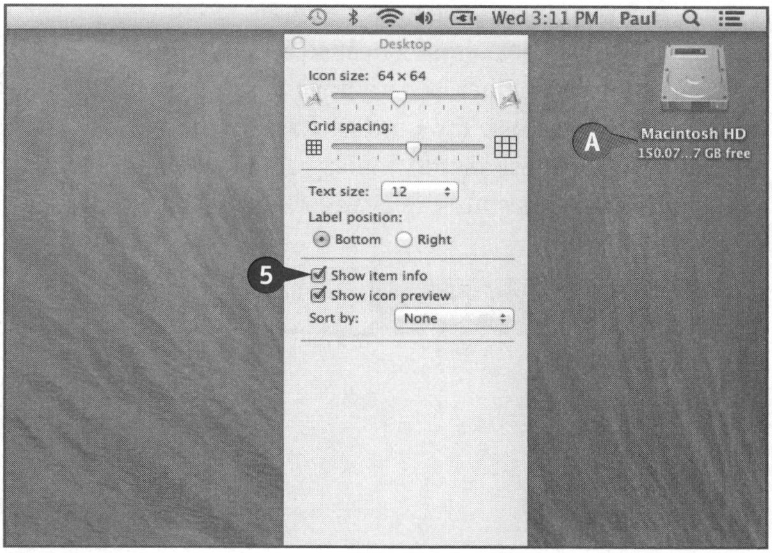

6. Drag the **Icon size** slider until you can read all the icon text.

7. If you still cannot read all the text, click the **Text size** ⬍ and then click a larger size.

8. Click **Close** (■).

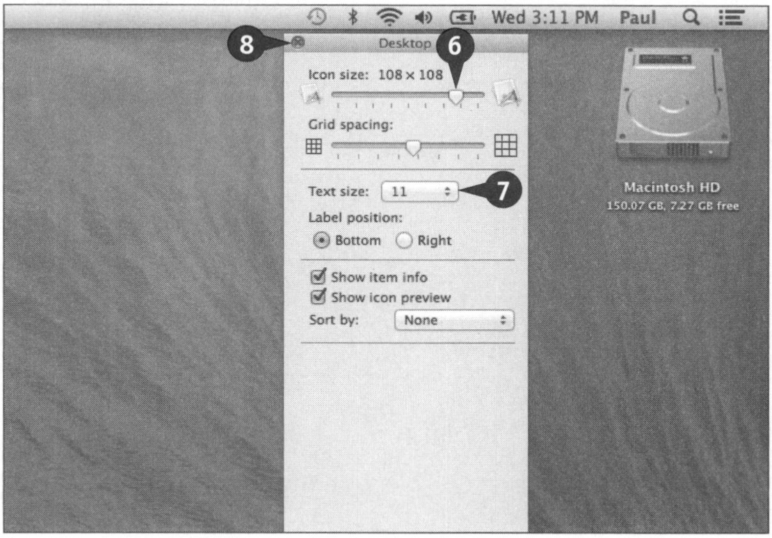

TIPS

My Mac's hard drive icon does not appear on the desktop. How do I display it?

If you do not see the Macintosh HD icon on your desktop, click the desktop, click **Finder** in the menu bar, and then click **Preferences**. Click the **General** tab, select the **Hard disks** option (☐ changes to ☑), and then click **Close** (■).

What should I do if my Mac's hard drive space is getting low?

First, empty the Trash, as described in Chapter 16. Next, uninstall applications you no longer use, which is also covered in Chapter 16. If you have large documents you no longer need, either move them to an external hard drive or flash drive, or delete them and then empty the Trash.

Check Hard Drive Status

You can watch for an impending hard drive failure by checking your Mac Pro's hard drive status. The hard drive includes a system called Self-Monitoring Analysis and Reporting Technology (S.M.A.R.T.), which monitors a number of hard drive parameters, including spin-up time, drive temperature, drive errors, and bad sectors. It monitors these factors over time and looks for signs of impending hard drive failure. If any of these factors indicates a potential drive failure, the S.M.A.R.T. status changes, so it pays to monitor this status so that you can save your data if a failure is imminent.

Check Hard Drive Status

Check the Status

1. Click **Spotlight** (🔍).
2. Type **disk**.
3. Click **Disk Utility**.

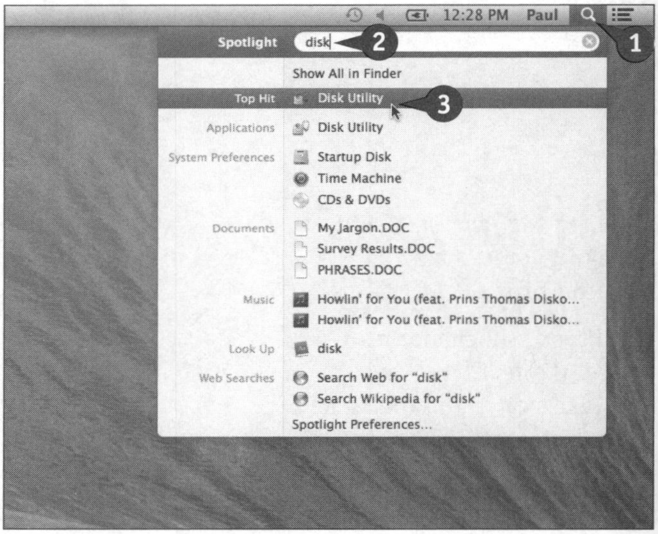

The Disk Utility window appears.

4. Click the Mac Pro hard drive.

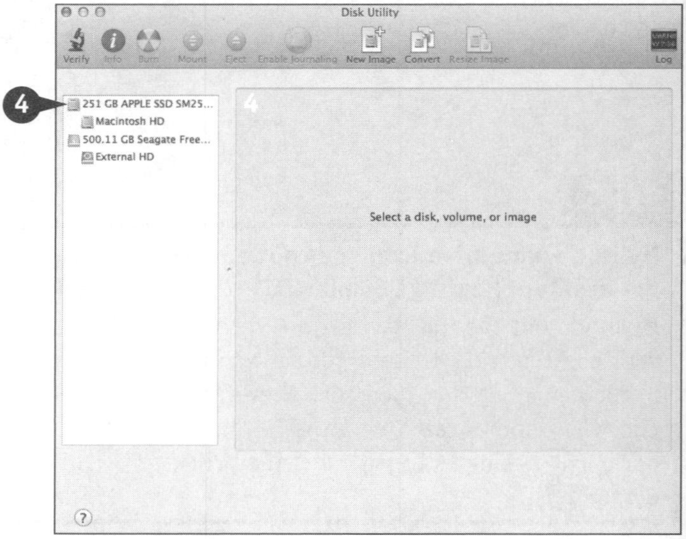

Healthy Drive Status

A You see this status if the hard drive is healthy.

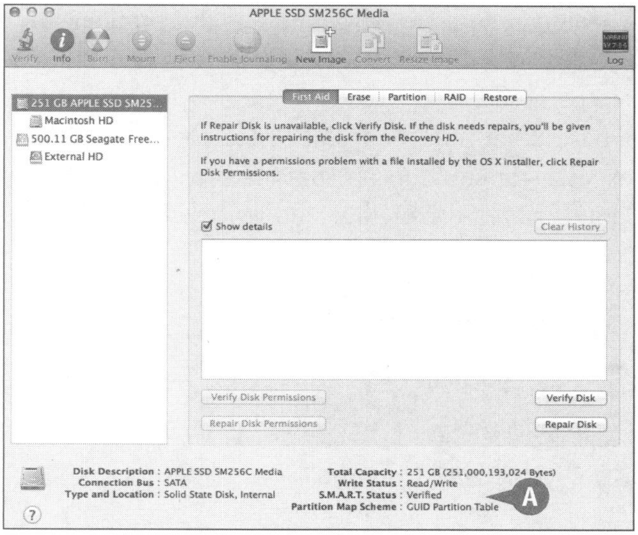

Failing Drive Status

B You see this status (or *About to Fail*) if S.M.A.R.T. detects a problem.

Note: In this case, perform an immediate backup of your files. You will need to replace the Mac Pro hard drive, as described in Chapter 18.

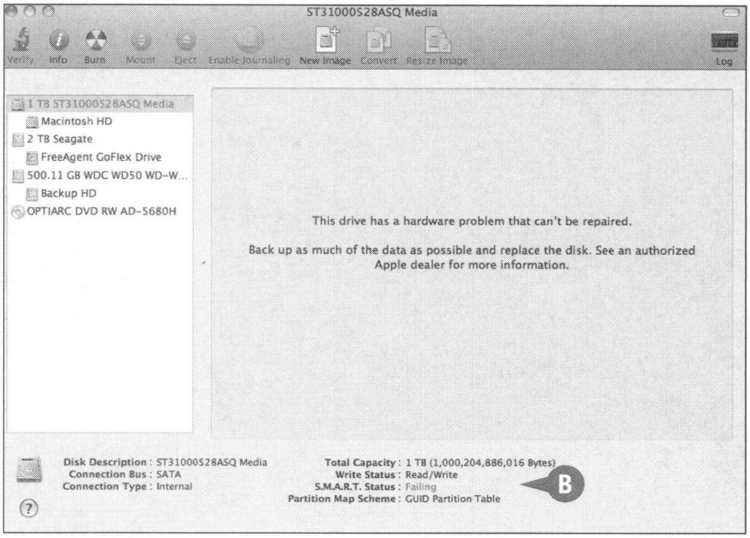

TIP

What factors does the S.M.A.R.T. system monitor?

S.M.A.R.T. monitors the number of times that the hard drive has been powered up, the number of hours it has been in use, and the number of times the drive has started and stopped spinning. More technical factors include a slowing spin-up time and increases in the drive temperature, error rate, and bad sector count. (A *sector* is a small storage location on your hard drive. A *bad sector* is one that, through physical damage or some other cause, can no longer be used to reliably store data.) S.M.A.R.T. uses a sophisticated algorithm to combine these attributes into a value that represents the overall health of the drive.

Monitor Hard Drive Usage

You can help troubleshoot Mac Pro problems by monitoring the hard drive activity. With respect to the hard drive, OS X basically does two things: It reads data from the hard drive, and it writes data to the hard drive. If your Mac Pro is running slowly, the hard drive could be the culprit. For example, a hard drive that reads data excessively could be fragmented, while a hard drive that writes data excessively could mean that Mac Pro does not have enough memory. You can use Activity Monitor to monitor hard drive reads and writes.

Monitor Hard Drive Usage

1. Click **Spotlight** (🔍).
2. Type **activity**.
3. Click **Activity Monitor**.

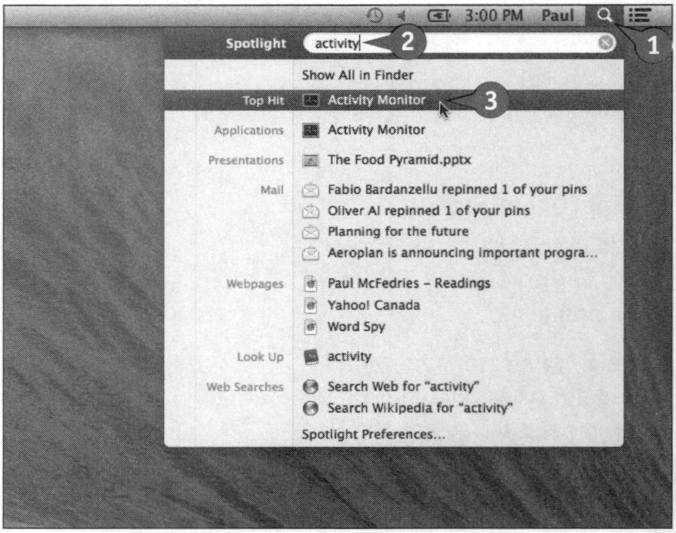

The Activity Monitor window appears.

4. Click the **Disk** tab.

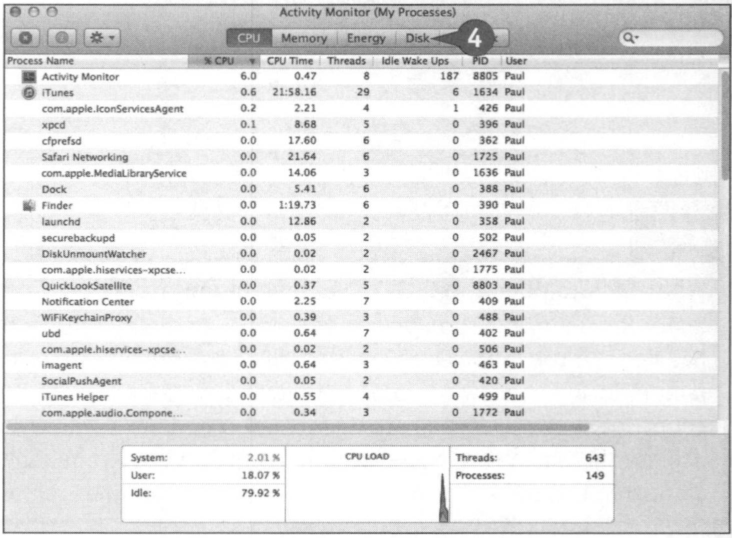

5 To monitor data read from the hard drive, examine the Reads In/Sec value.

A Read activity appears as blue spikes in the graph.

Note: The Reads In/Sec value should be 0 most of the time. A value that stays above 0 for an extended period indicates a hard disk read problem.

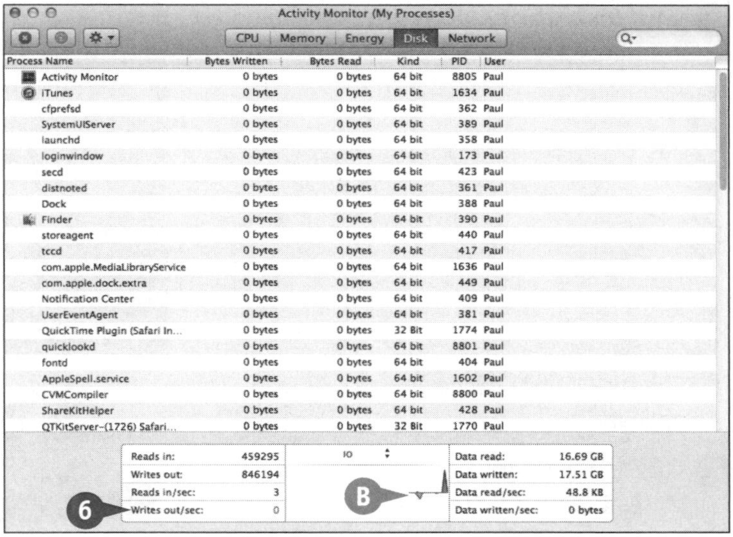

6 To monitor data written to the hard drive, examine the Writes Out/Sec value.

B Write activity appears as red spikes in the graph.

Note: The Writes Out/Sec value should be 0 most of the time. A value that stays above 0 for an extended period indicates a hard disk write problem.

TIP

What is hard drive fragmentation?

It means that many or most of the files are stored in chunks scattered all over the hard drive, instead of being stored together. Fortunately, Mac Pro's files do not easily get fragmented. This is probably why your Mac Pro does not come with a disk optimization utility to fix fragmentation. Fragmentation can happen, however, so to fix it you need a program such as iDefrag from Coriolis Systems (www.coriolis-systems.com), which costs $30.95, but there is a demo version that will defragment up to 100MB.

Verify or Repair Disk Permissions

The permissions associated with files determine what specific users or groups can do with those files. This is particularly important for the Mac Pro system files, so you should periodically verify that the permissions on your Mac Pro's hard drive are working properly.

If the permissions on one or more of the OS X system files become corrupted, your Mac Pro may freeze, run slowly, or become unstable. You can sometimes solve these problems by repairing your Mac Pro's disk permissions.

Verify or Repair Disk Permissions

Open the Hard Drive in Disk Utility

1. Click **Spotlight** (🔍).
2. Type **disk**.
3. Click **Disk Utility**.

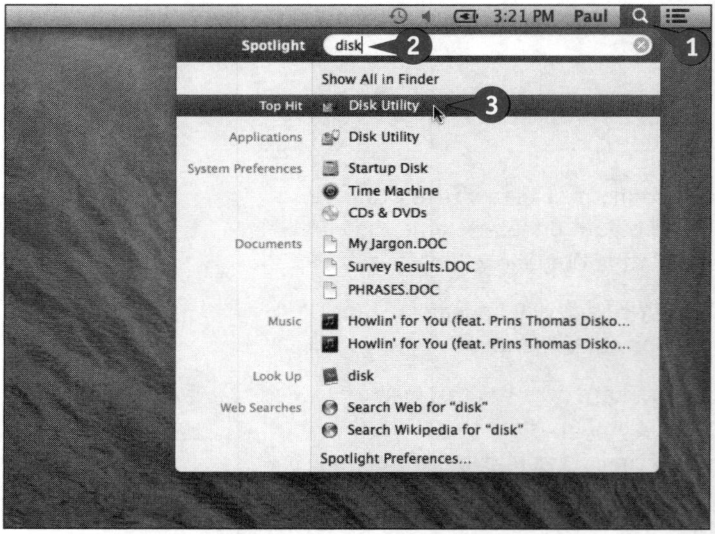

The Disk Utility window appears.

4. Click the hard drive that stores the OS X system files.

Note: The OS X system files are usually found on the hard drive partition named Macintosh HD.

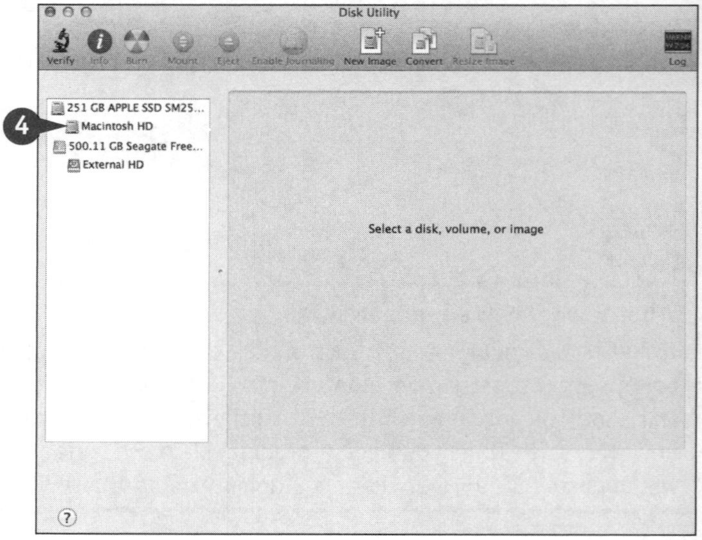

Verify Disk Permissions

5 Click the **First Aid** tab.

6 Click **Verify Disk Permissions.**

Ⓐ Disk Utility verifies the permissions and displays the progress of the operation.

Ⓑ If permission problem exist, they appear here.

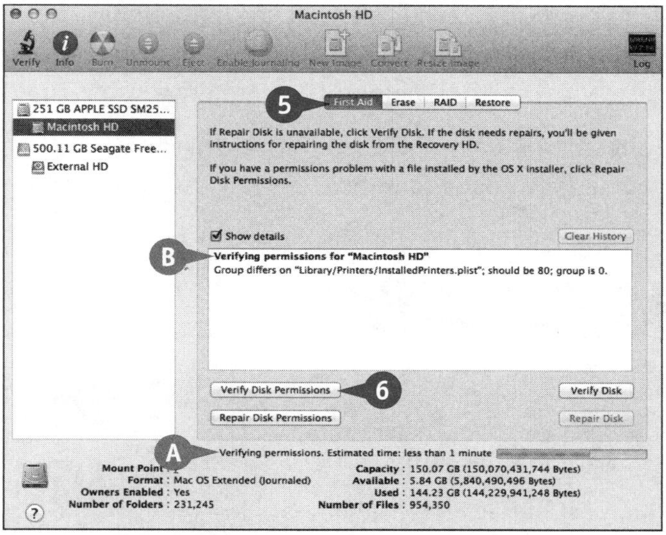

Repair Disk Permissions

7 To correct disk permission problems, click **Repair Disk Permissions.**

Ⓒ Disk Utility repairs the disk permissions and displays the progress of the operation.

Ⓓ A list of the repair tasks completed appears here.

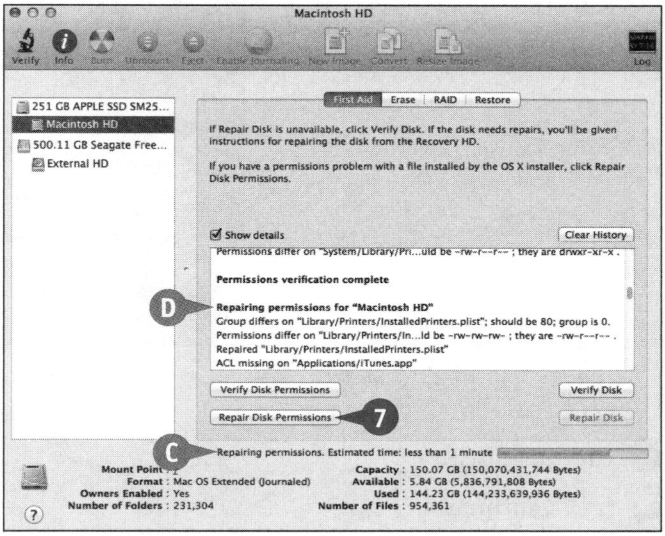

TIPS

What are disk permissions?

All the files on your Mac Pro have *permissions* associated with them. Permissions are a collection of settings that determines what users or groups of users can do with each file. For example, if read-only permissions apply to a file, it means that all users can only read the contents of the file and cannot make any changes to the file or delete it. If the permissions for your Mac Pro's system files change or get corrupted, it can cause problems, including program lock-ups and unstable system behavior.

How do I repair permissions if I cannot start my Mac?

Corrupt disk permissions might prevent your Mac Pro from booting. In this case, follow steps **1** to **6** in the next section, "Repair the Hard Drive," click the **Disk Utility** tab, and then follow steps **5** to **7** in this section.

Repair the Hard Drive

If your Mac Pro will not start, or if an application freezes, an error on the main hard drive — that is, the hard drive on which OS X is installed — is possibly causing the problem. To see if this is the case, you can try repairing the hard drive using the Disk Utility program.

To repair your Mac Pro's main hard drive, you must boot to the Recovery HD. If you cannot do that, you can also boot to a recovery disk, as described in Chapter 16.

Repair the Hard Drive

1. Restart Mac Pro.
2. Press and hold Option while Mac Pro is restarting.

   A list of Mac Pro's hard drives appears.
3. Click **Recovery HD**.

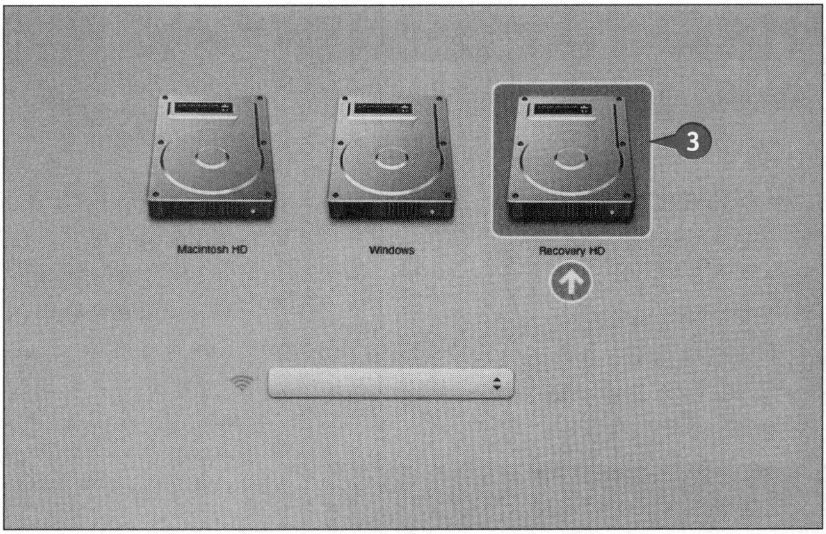

The OS X Utilities window appears.

4. Click **Disk Utility**.
5. Click **Continue**.

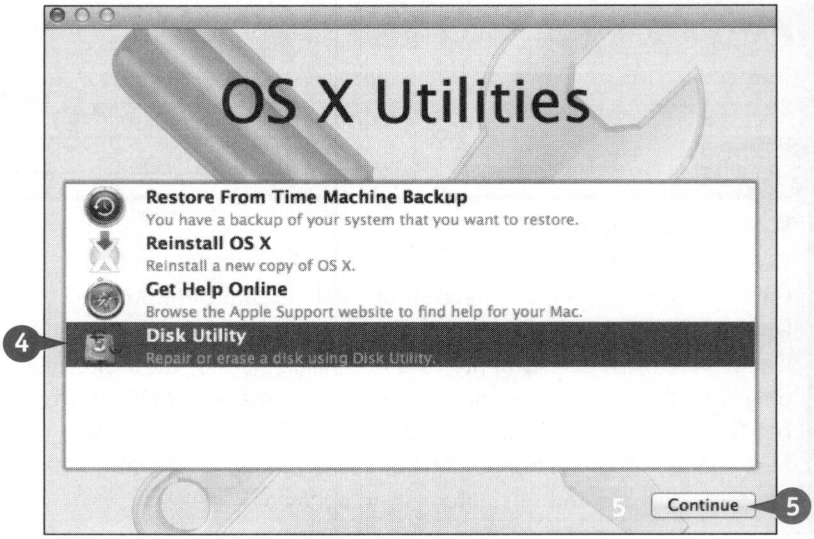

The Disk Utility window appears.

6 Click your Mac Pro's hard drive.

7 Click the **First Aid** tab.

8 Click **Repair Disk.**

Disk Utility verifies the hard disk and attempts to repair any errors it finds.

A Information on the disk checks appears here.

B The result of the checks appears here.

9 Press ⌘+Q.

Disk Utility quits and returns you to OS X Utilities.

10 Press ⌘+Q.

OS X Utilities asks you to confirm.

11 Click **Restart**.

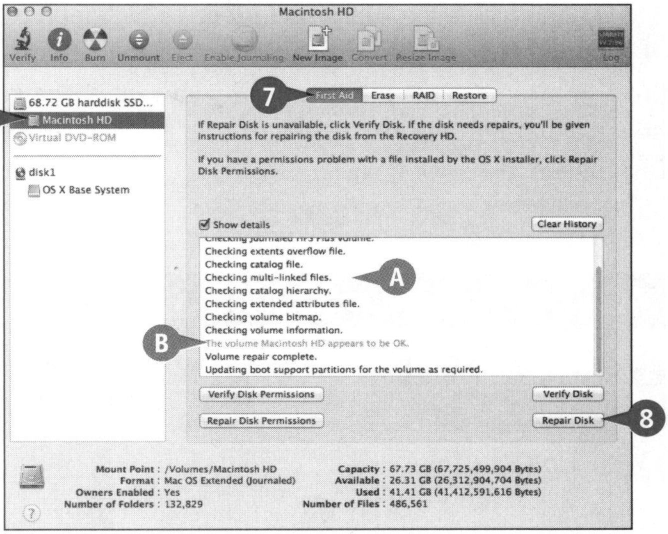

TIPS

How do I repair errors on a secondary hard drive?

If you are working with Mac Pro's startup hard drive, you must boot to the OS X Recovery HD to repair that drive. If that does not work, you can boot to a recovery disk, as described in Chapter 16. For all other hard drives, you can perform the repair without rebooting. Open Disk Utility, click the drive you want to repair, click the **First Aid** tab, and then click **Repair Disk**.

What happens if Disk Utility finds a problem?

Disk Utility attempts to fix any errors it finds. If Disk Utility cannot fix the errors, you must turn to a third-party disk repair application. Two useful tools are DiskWarrior (www.alsoft.com) and Techtool Pro (www.micromat.com).

Copy a Hard Drive to a Disk Image

You can make a backup of a hard drive by copying the contents of the drive to a disk image. A *disk image* is a special file that contains the contents — the structure, folders, and files — of a hard drive. A disk image is also useful if you want a straightforward way to send the contents of a hard drive to another person. You learn how to view a disk image in OS X in the next section, "Mount a Disk Image."

Copy a Hard Drive to a Disk Image

1. Click **Spotlight** (🔍).
2. Type **disk**.
3. Click **Disk Utility**.

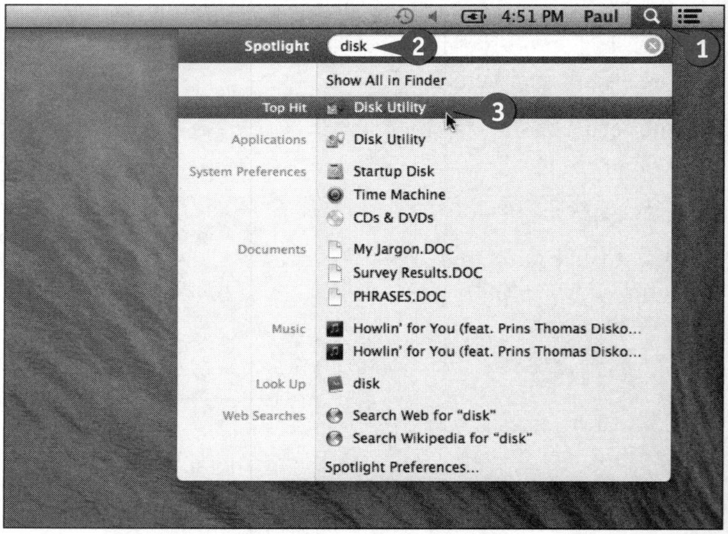

The Disk Utility window appears.

4. Click the hard drive you want to copy.
5. Click the **New Image** tab.

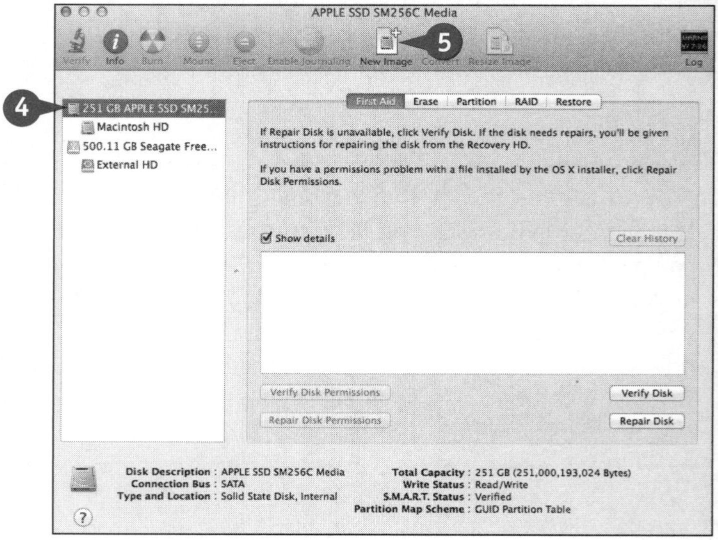

The New Image dialog appears.

6 Use the Save As text box to type a name for the disk image.

7 Choose the location where you want the disk image saved.

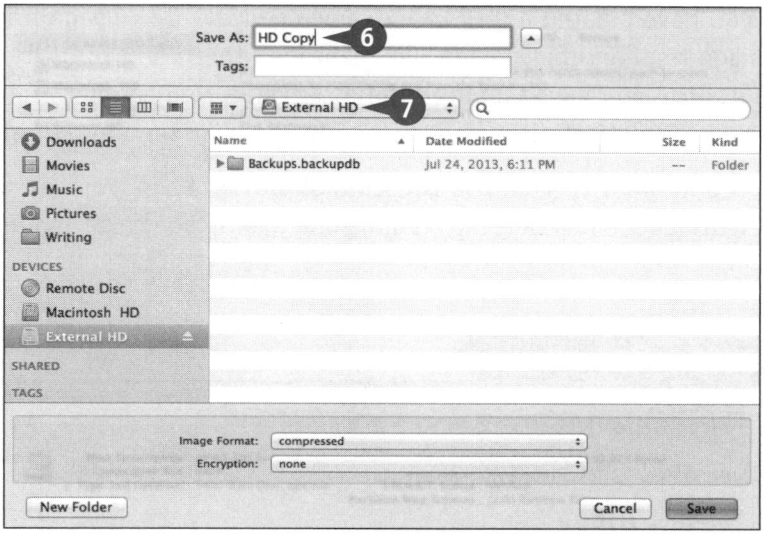

8 Click **Save**.

Disk Utility creates the disk image.

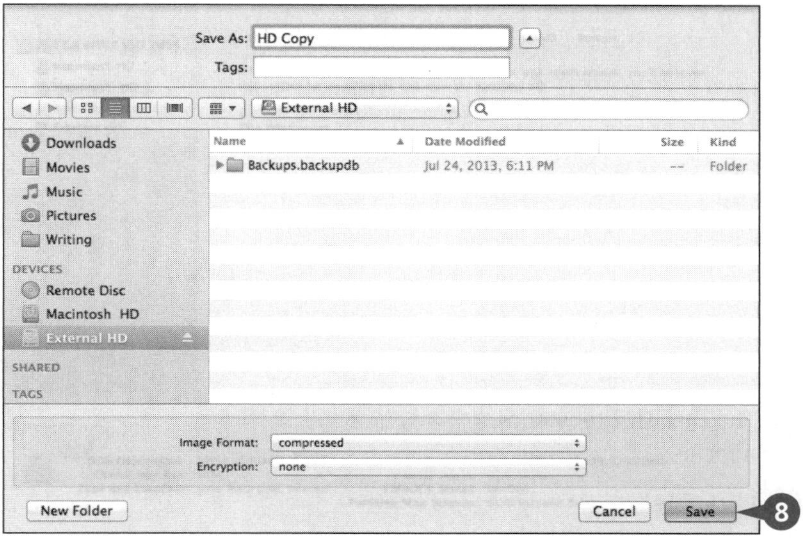

TIP

Can I create a disk image from a folder instead of an entire hard drive?

Yes. This is a faster method if you want to back up or share a particular folder instead of the entire drive. It also creates a much smaller disk image, depending on the original size of the folder. To create a disk image from a folder, follow steps 1 to 3 to open Disk Utility, click **File**, click **New**, and then click **Disk Image from Folder**. Use the Select Folder to Image dialog to select the folder and then click **Image**. In the New Image from Folder dialog, type a name for the disk image, select a location, and then click **Save**.

Mount a Disk Image

If you have created a disk image, downloaded a disk image from the Internet, or received a disk image from another person, you can open the file in Disk Utility. This is called *mounting* the disk image. Once you have mounted the disk image, you can perform other tasks, such as burning the image to an optical disc, as described in the next section, "Burn a Disk Image to a CD or DVD."

If you only want to view the contents of a disk image, you can usually just double-click the file. Other tasks (such as burning) require the disk image to be mounted in Disk Utility.

Mount a Disk Image

1. Click **Spotlight** (🔍).
2. Type **disk**.
3. Click **Disk Utility**.

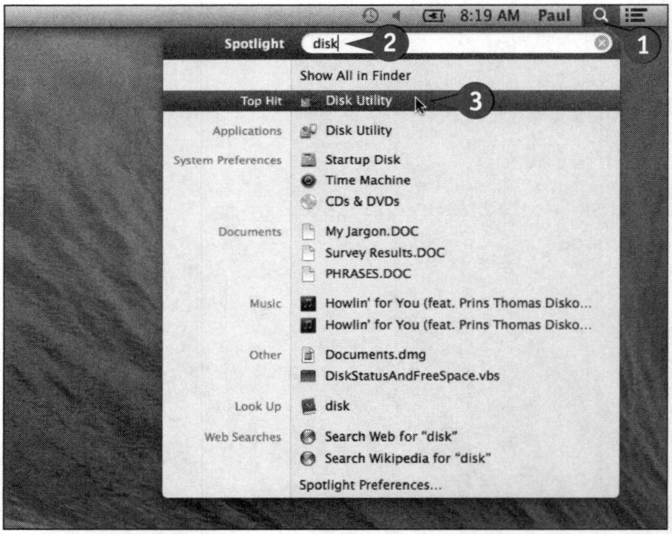

The Disk Utility window appears.

4. Click **File**.
5. Click **Open Disk Image.**

You can also press Option + ⌘ + O.

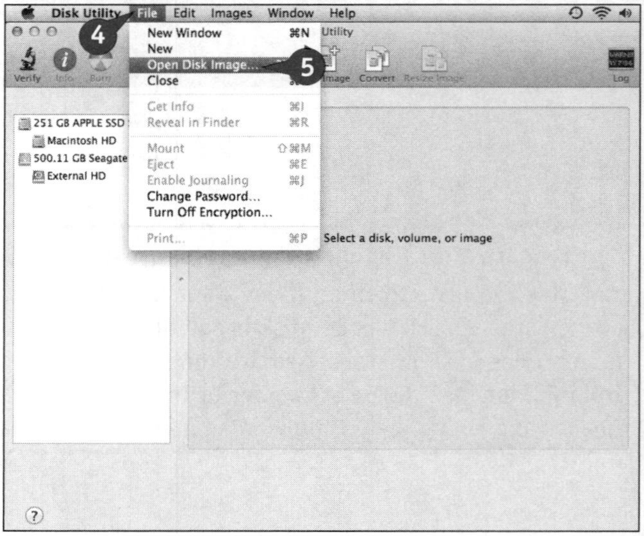

The Select Image to Attach dialog appears.

6 Select the location of the disk image.

7 Click the disk image.

8 Click **Open**.

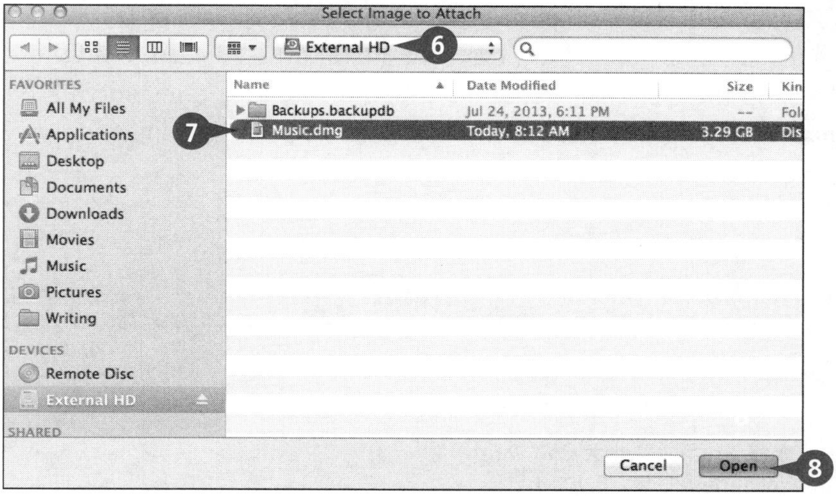

A Disk Utility opens a Finder window to show the contents of the disk image.

B The disk image appears in the Disk Utility window.

C This item represents the contents of the disk image.

Note: It might take a minute or two for the disk image to open, depending on its size.

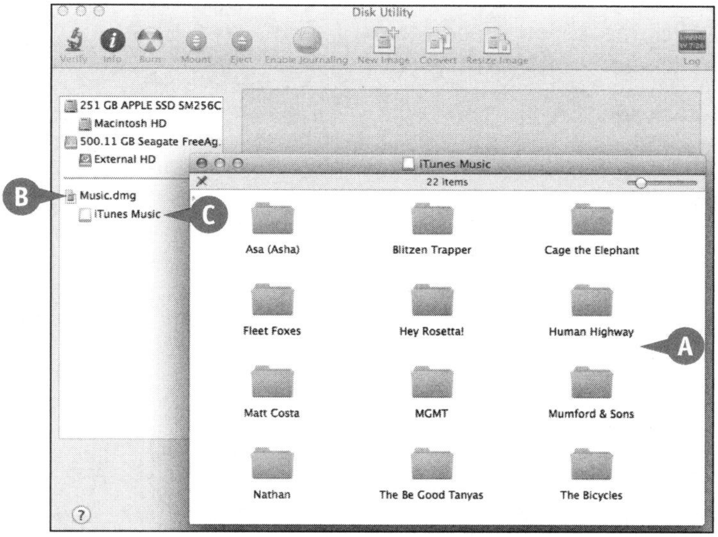

TIPS

How do I unmount a disk image's contents?

It is a good idea to unmount the contents of a disk image to avoid making accidental changes. In Disk Utility, click the contents of the disk image and then click **Unmount**. To hide the disk image contents, click the disk image and then click **Eject**.

Why does the disk image still appear in Disk Utility after I have ejected it?

Disk Utility assumes you will want to reopen the disk image in the future. Instead of doing this by repeating steps 4 to 8, you can simply click the disk image and then click **Open**. If you know that you will not open the disk image again, right-click the disk image and then click **Remove**.

Burn a Disk Image to a CD or DVD

If your Mac Pro has an optical drive capable of writing — also known as *burning* — data, you can use Disk Utility to burn the contents of a disk image to a CD or DVD. This is useful if you want to back up the disk image to a disc. Also, in some rare instances a program's installation files will come packaged as a disk image, and you need to burn that image to a disc in order to run the installation program.

Burn a Disk Image to a CD or DVD

1. Insert a blank CD or DVD in your Mac Pro optical drive.

   Mac Pro asks what you want to do with the blank disc.

2. Click the **Action** ⬍ and then click **Open Disk Utility**.

3. Click **OK**.

   Disk Utility appears.

4. Mount the disk image you want to burn.

Note: See the previous section, "Mount a Disk Image," to learn how to mount an image file.

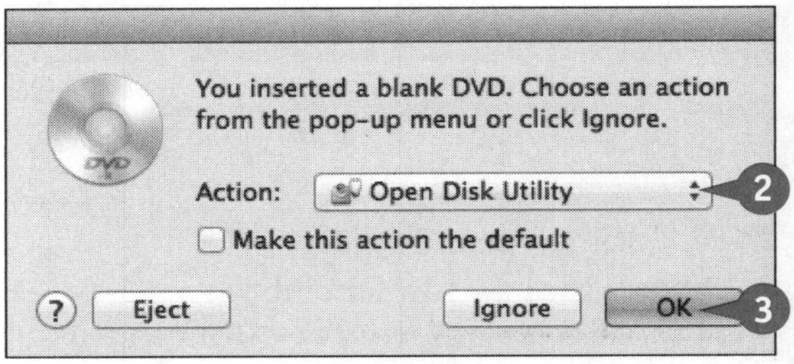

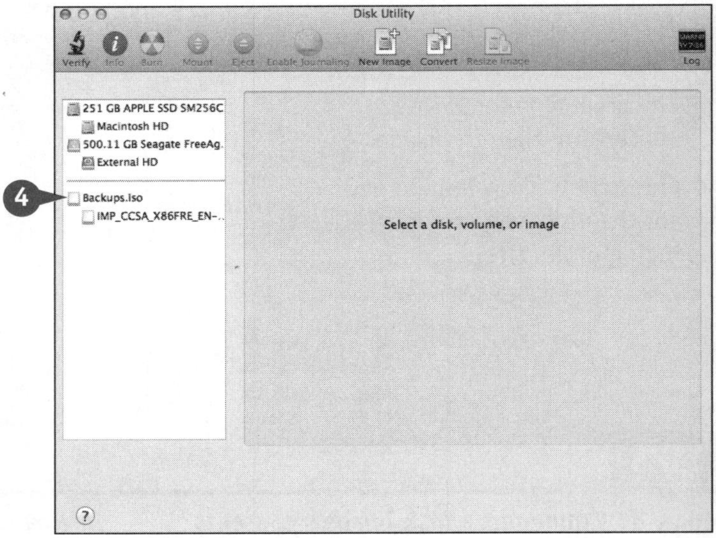

5. Click the disk image.
6. Click the **Burn** tab.

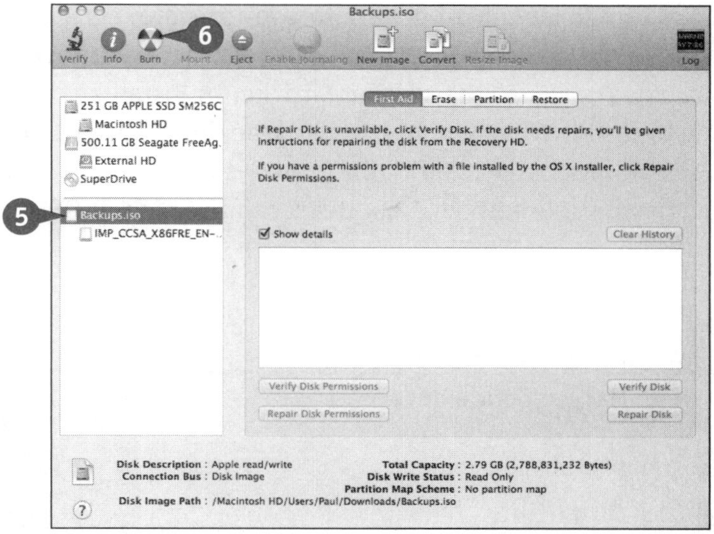

Disk Utility tells you it is ready to burn the disc.

7. Click **Burn**.

Disk Utility burns the disk image to the disc.

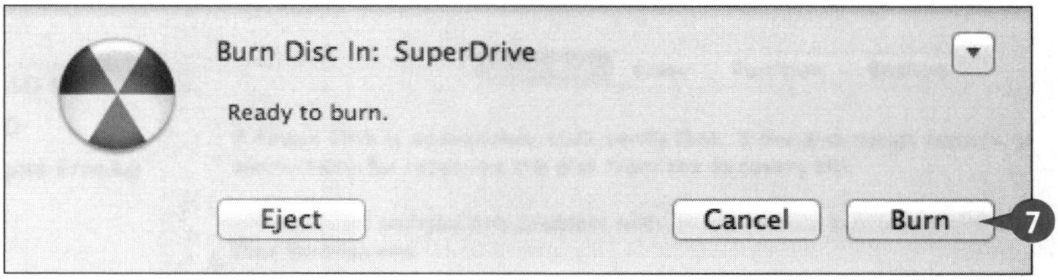

TIPS

Does it matter whether I use a CD or DVD?

The type of disc you use depends on how much data is in the disk image. Most CDs can hold a maximum of about 700MB of data. If your disk image contains more than 700MB, you need to use a DVD. Single-layer DVDs hold up to 4.7GB (single-sided) or 9.4GB (double-sided); double-layer DVDs hold up to 8.5GB (single-sided) or 17GB (double-sided).

How do I know how much data is in my disk image?

The easiest way to find out how much data is stored in a disk image is to mount it in Disk Utility, select it, and then read the Total Capacity value near the bottom of the Disk Utility window.

Partition a Hard Drive

You can divide a hard drive into two (or more) separate areas called *partitions*, which effectively turns the device into two logically distinct hard drives. The most common reason to partition a hard drive is to use the second partition to install another operating system. In Chapter 22 you learn how to install Windows on a second Mac Pro partition. However, you can also use a second partition to install another version of OS X. This is often a good idea because if your main version of OS X fails, you may be able to boot from the second version of OS X to troubleshoot.

Partition a Hard Drive

1. Click **Spotlight** (🔍).
2. Type **disk**.
3. Click **Disk Utility**.

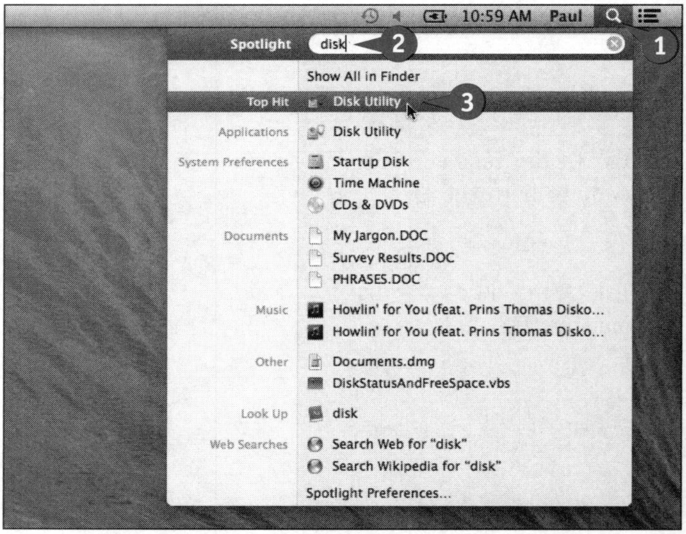

The Disk Utility window appears.

4. Click the hard drive you want to partition.
5. Click the **Partition** tab.
6. Click **Add** (+).

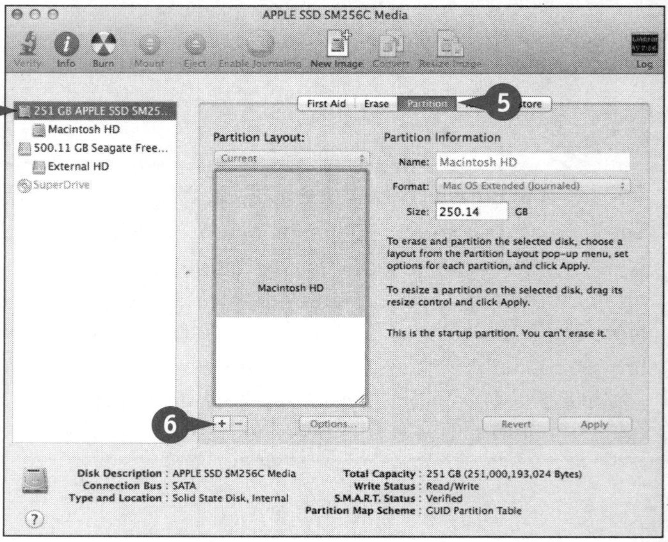

Disk Utility adds a partition to the drive layout.

7 Click the new partition.

8 Click and drag the separator until the drive is the size you want.

A The size of the new partition appears here.

9 Type a name for the new partition.

10 Click **Apply**.

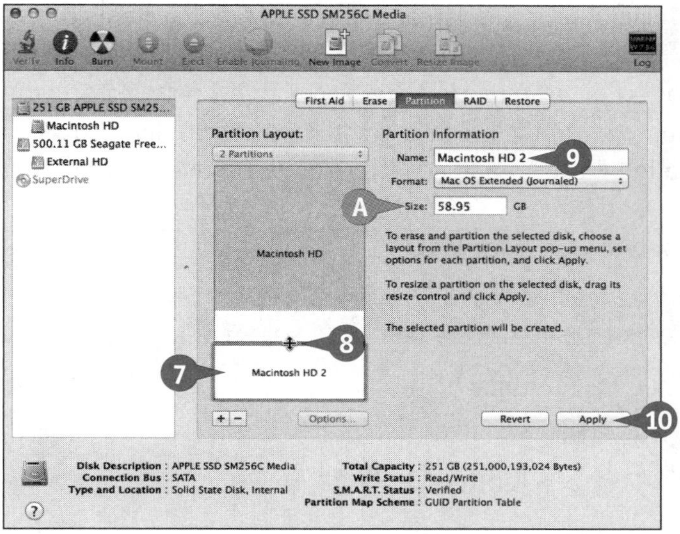

Disk Utility asks you to confirm.

11 Click **Partition**.

Disk Utility partitions the hard drive.

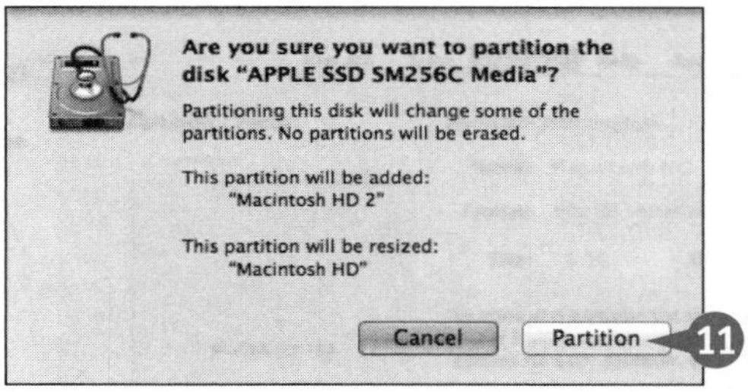

TIP

Which format should I use for the new partition?

In most cases, you should choose the Mac OS Extended (journaled) format. The journaled option improves OS X's capability to recover from unexpected shutdowns that arise from power losses, system crashes, and similar circumstances. The Mac OS Extended (Case-sensitive, journaled) format is similar, except that filenames are case sensitive. This means that OS X treats a document named, say, BudgetNotes2014.doc as a different file from one named budgetnotes2014.doc.

If you will be using the new partition to install Windows, use the MS-DOS (FAT) format.

Erase a Hard Drive's Free Space

If you use an external or secondary hard drive to deal with files that contain private, sensitive, or secure data, even if you delete those files and then empty the Trash, the files remain on the drive for an indeterminate time. A person who steals or gains physical access to your Mac Pro and has the appropriate disk recovery software can easily recover those files. To prevent this, Mac Pro has a tool called Erase Free Space that can write over deleted files multiple times, thus ensuring that they can never be recovered. You should run this tool periodically to ensure the security of deleted files that contain important data.

Erase a Hard Drive's Free Space

1. Click **Spotlight** (🔍).
2. Type **disk**.
3. Click **Disk Utility**.

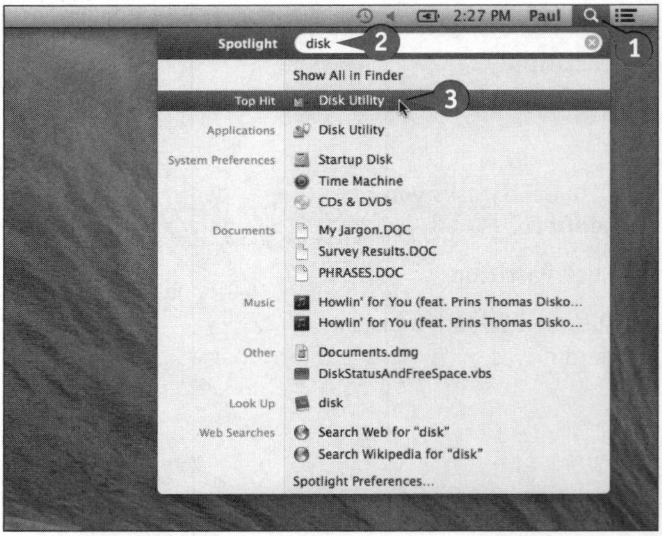

The Disk Utility window appears.

4. Click the hard drive partition with the free space you want to erase.
5. Click the **Erase** tab.
6. Click **Erase Free Space**.

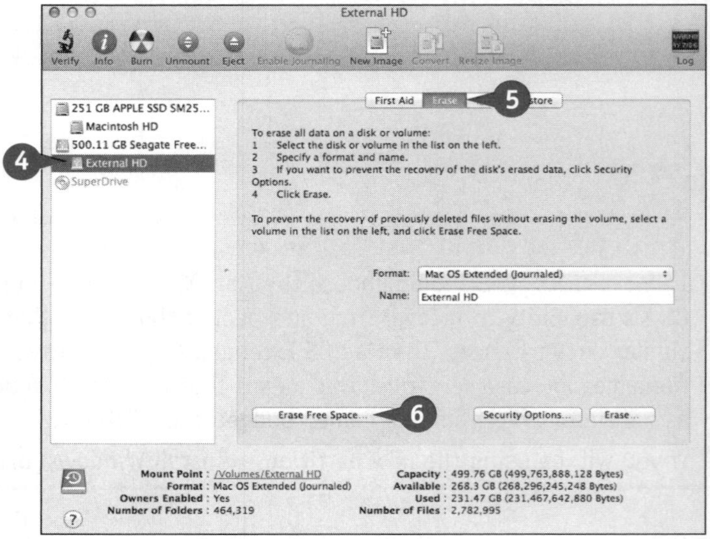

The Erase Free Space Options dialog appears.

7 Use this slider to specify how you want the free space erased:

A This option writes over the free space once. This is the quickest option, but it provides the least security.

B This option writes over the free space three times. The erasure takes three times as long, but it gives you a medium level of security.

C This option writes over the free space seven times. This takes the longest, but gives the highest security.

8 Click **Erase Free Space**.

Disk Utility erases the free space on the hard drive.

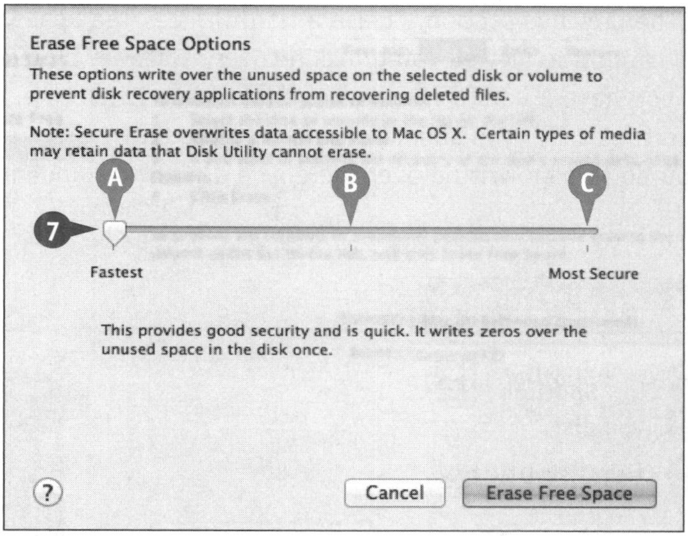

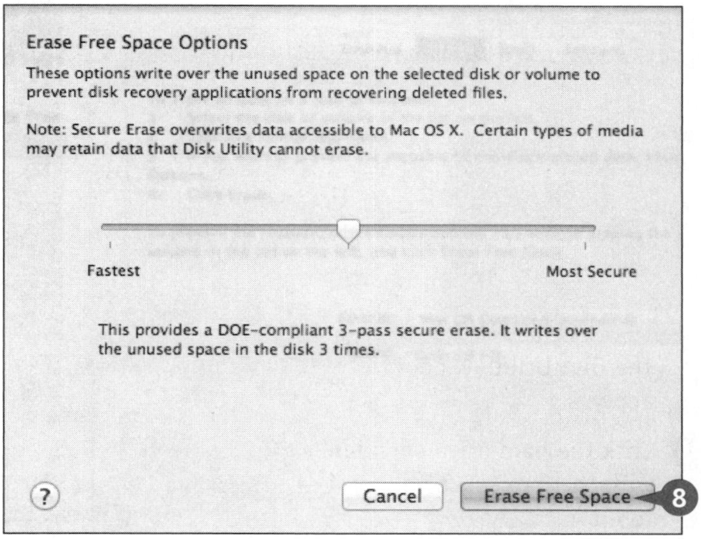

TIPS

Why do files remain in the drive after I empty the Trash?
When you empty the Trash, OS X does not do anything to the data stored on the drive (unless the drive is solid-state; see the next tip). Instead, it just marks the drive location as available for new data.

Why is Erase Free Space disabled for my main hard drive?
The main hard drive is a solid-state drive (SSD) that supports a command called Trim. OS X uses Trim to alert the drive when a datum is no longer being used (for example, when you delete a file from the Trash). The SSD then automatically writes over the data so that it cannot be recovered. Therefore, the Erase Free Space tool is not needed.

Erase a Hard Drive

The previous section, "Erase a Hard Drive's Free Space," discussed how to ensure that deleted files cannot be viewed using disk recovery software by overwriting the deleted file location with zeroes. If you have a hard drive that contains personal, secure, or sensitive data and you no longer want to use that drive, you should ensure that the entire drive cannot be viewed with disk recovery software. You do this by writing over the entire drive with random or gibberish data.

Erase a Hard Drive

1. Click **Spotlight** (🔍).
2. Type **disk**.
3. Click **Disk Utility**.

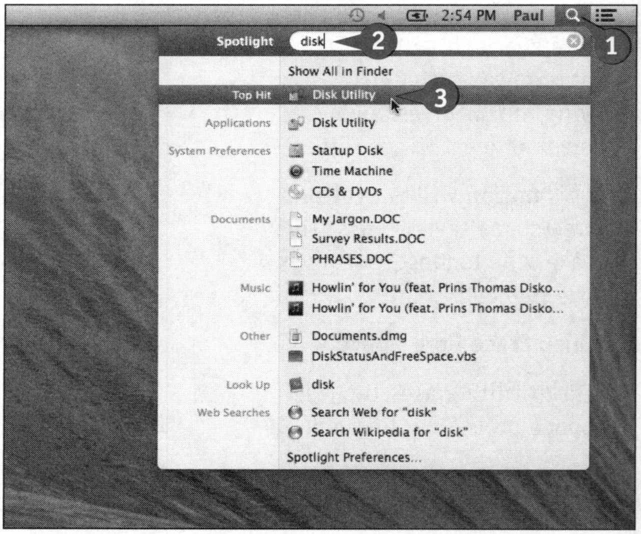

The Disk Utility window appears.

4. Click the hard drive partition with the free space you want to erase.
5. Click the **Erase** tab.
6. Click **Security Options**.

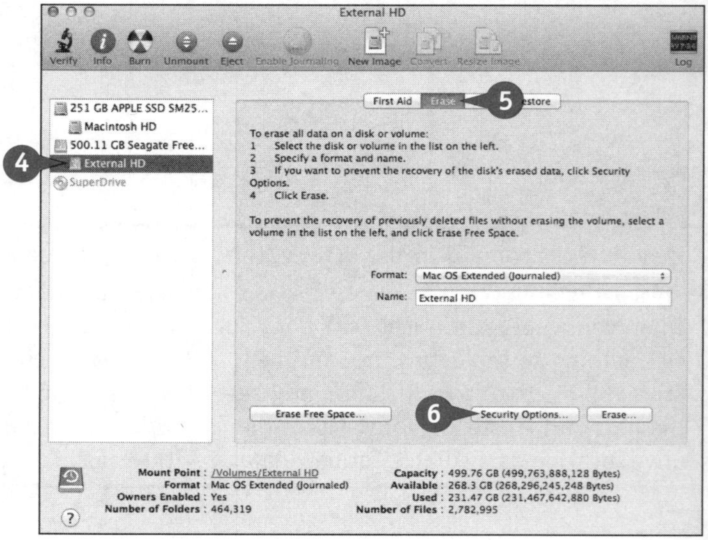

The Secure Erase Options dialog appears.

7 Use this slider to specify how you want the drive erased.

Note: With the exception of the Fastest option, which does not securely erase the drive data, the other three options are similar to the ones discussed in the previous section, "Erase a Hard Drive's Free Space." See also the tip that follows.

8 Click **OK**.

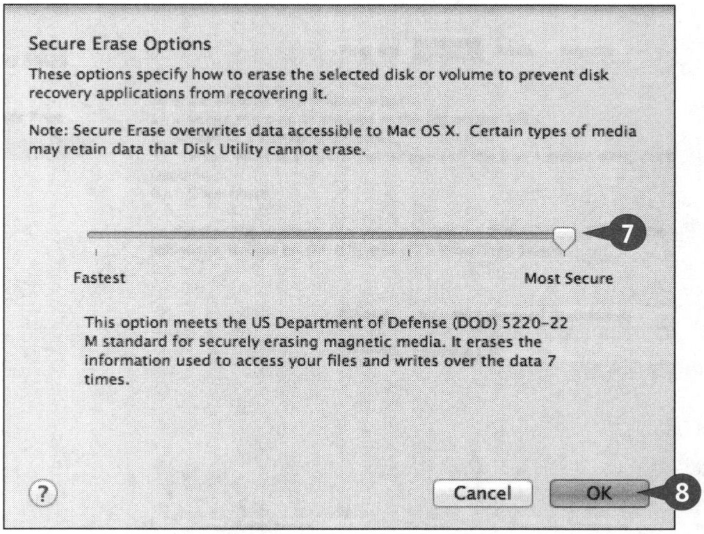

9 Click **Erase**.

Disk Utility asks you to confirm.

10 Click **Erase**.

Disk Utility erases the hard drive.

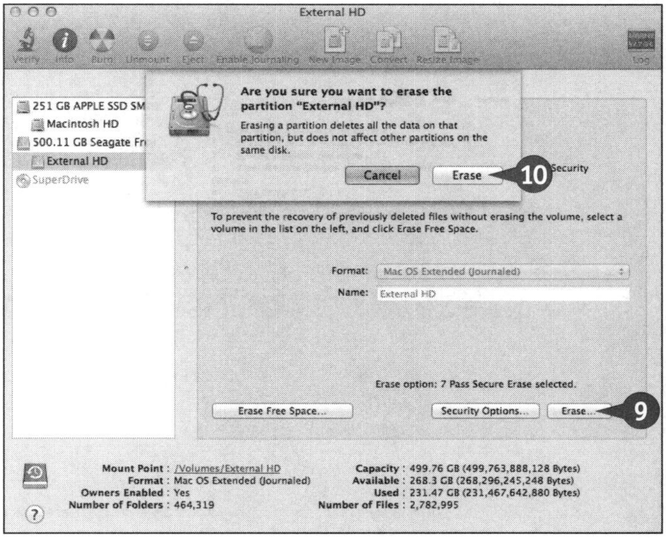

TIP

What specifically does each of the three secure erase options do to the data on the hard drive?

The first secure option is a *zero-out* operation, which means that Disk Utility overwrites the entire drive once with a series of 0s.

The second secure option is a *DOE (Department of Energy)-compliant 3-pass secure erase*, which means that Disk Utility overwrites the entire drive twice with random data and then a third time with a known data pattern.

The third secure option is a *DOD (Department of Defense) 5220-22 M secure erase*, which means that Disk Utility overwrites the entire drive seven times with random data.

CHAPTER 16

Maintaining Mac Pro

To keep Mac Pro running smoothly, maintain top performance, and reduce the risk of computer problems, you need to perform some routine maintenance chores. This chapter shows you how to empty the Trash, monitor CPU and memory usage, uninstall applications, back up your files, and more.

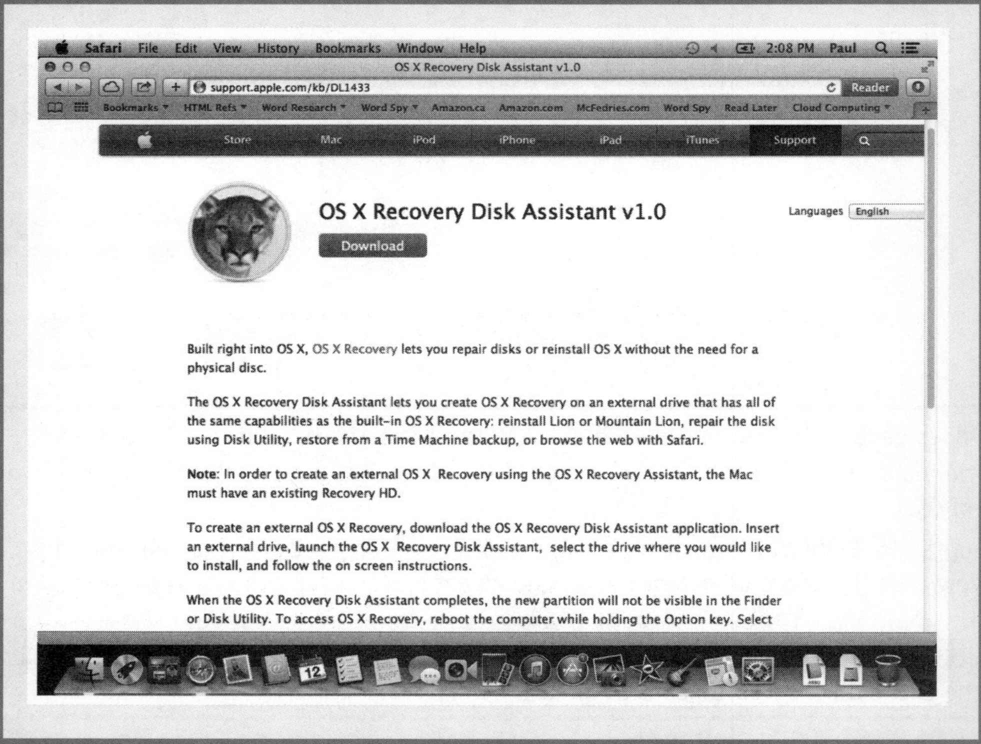

Empty the Trash

You can free up disk space on your Mac Pro by periodically emptying the Trash. When you delete a file or folder, OS X does not immediately remove the file from your Mac Pro's hard drive. Instead, OS X moves the file or folder to the Trash. This is useful if you accidentally delete an item, because it means you can open the Trash and restore the item. However, all those deleted files and folders take up disk space, so you need to empty the Trash periodically to regain that space. You should empty the Trash at least once a week.

Empty the Trash

1. Click the desktop.
2. Click **Finder** from the menu.
3. Click **Empty Trash**.

A. You can also right-click the **Trash** icon () and then click **Empty Trash**.

Note: Another way to select the Empty Trash command is to press Shift + ⌘ + Delete.

Mac Pro asks you to confirm the deletion.

4. Click **Empty Trash**.

Mac Pro empties the Trash (changes to).

Organize Your Desktop

You can make your Mac Pro desktop easier to scan and navigate by organizing the icons. The Mac Pro desktop automatically displays icons for objects such as your external hard drives, inserted CDs and DVDs, disk images, and attached iPods. The desktop is also a handy place to store files, file aliases, copies of documents, and more. However, the more you use your desktop as a storage area, the more the desktop can become disarrayed, making it hard to find the icon you want. You can fix this by organizing the icons.

Organize Your Desktop

1. Click the desktop.
2. Click **View.**
3. Click **Clean Up By.**
4. Click **Name.**

   You can also right-click the desktop, click **Clean Up By**, and then click **Name**, or press Option + ⌘ + 1.

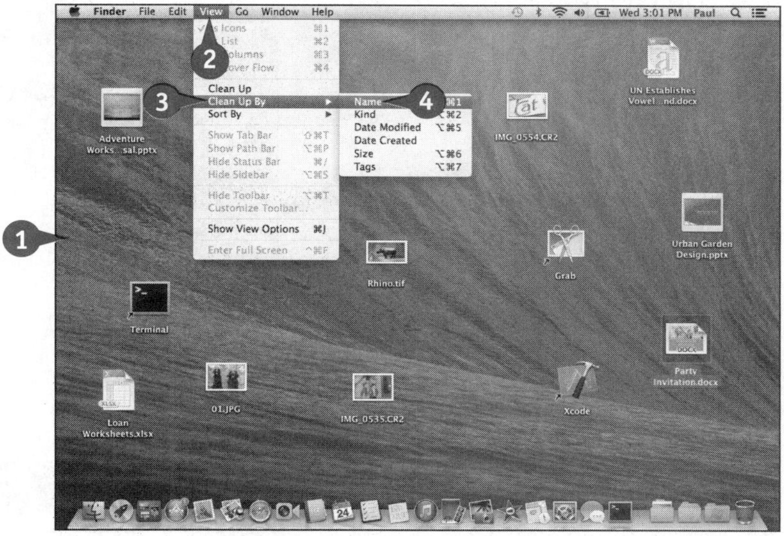

Ⓐ Mac Pro organizes the icons alphabetically and arranges them in columns from right to left.

Monitor CPU Usage

The *CPU* (*central processing unit*) is the chip inside Mac Pro that acts as the control and command center. Almost everything you do on Mac Pro and almost everything that happens within Mac Pro goes through the CPU, so it pays to keep an eye on how much the system is taxing it. If Mac Pro feels sluggish, or if a program has become very slow, it could be because the CPU is running at or near full capacity. To check, you can use Activity Monitor, which tells you what is running on Mac Pro and what percentage of the CPU's resources is being used.

Monitor CPU Usage

1. Click **Spotlight** (🔍).
2. Type **activity**.
3. Click **Activity Monitor.**

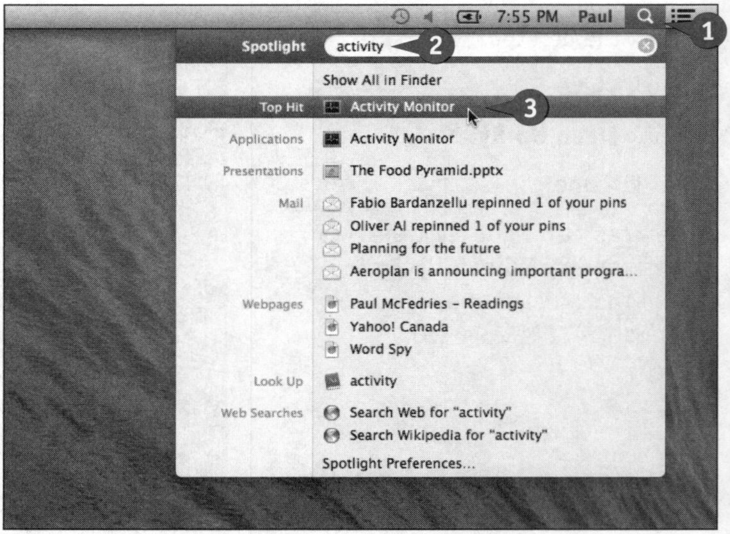

The Activity Monitor window appears.

4. Click the **CPU** tab.

5 Use the % CPU column to track the percentage of CPU resources each running process uses.

Note: A *process* is a running instance of an executable program or background service.

A For easiest monitoring, click the % **CPU** column header until the processes are displayed in descending order of CPU usage, as shown here.

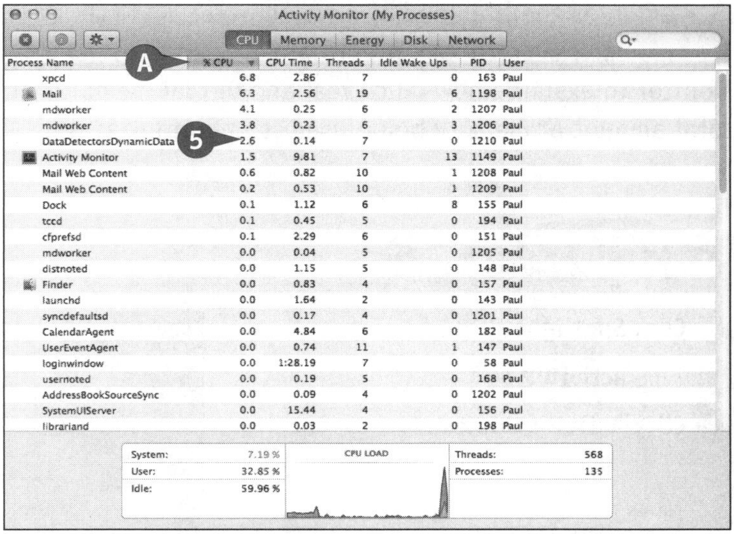

6 Monitor the System value to track the percentage of the CPU that OS X is using.

7 Monitor the User value to track what percentage of the CPU your running programs are using.

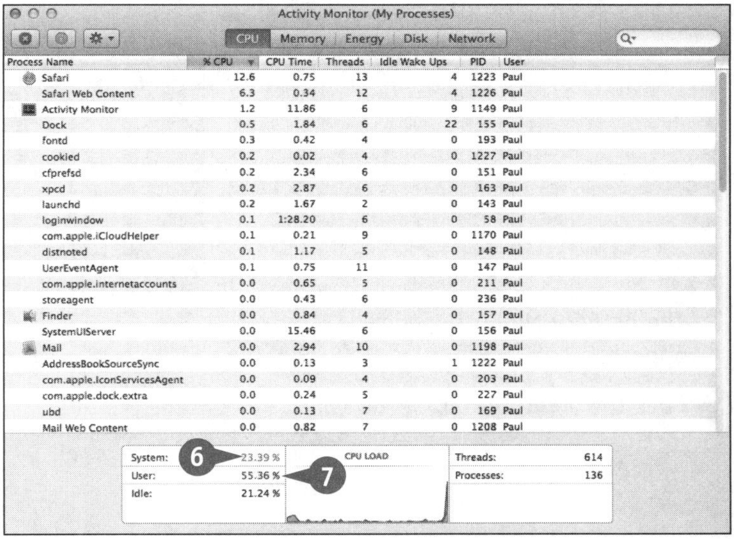

TIPS

What do I do if a program is stuck at 100 percent CPU usage for a long time?

Although rare, a program can stay at 100 percent usage for a few minutes while it completes a CPU-intensive task. If after 5 minutes or so the program is still showing 100 percent usage, you should shut it down. Click the program and then click **Force a process to quit** (⊗). When Activity Monitor asks you to confirm, click **Force Quit**.

Is there a way to monitor CPU usage without having to switch to the Activity Monitor window?

Yes, you can convert the Activity Monitor Dock icon into a CPU usage graph. Click **View**, click **Dock Icon**, and then click **Show CPU Usage**.

Track Memory Usage

Memory is the lifeblood of any computer, and Mac Pro is no different. If your system runs low on memory, everything slows to a crawl, and programs may mysteriously fail. You can use Activity Monitor to examine how much real and virtual memory each running process is using. However, the total amount of memory being used is important as well.

Track Memory Usage

1. Click **Spotlight** (🔍).
2. Type **activity**.
3. Click **Activity Monitor**.

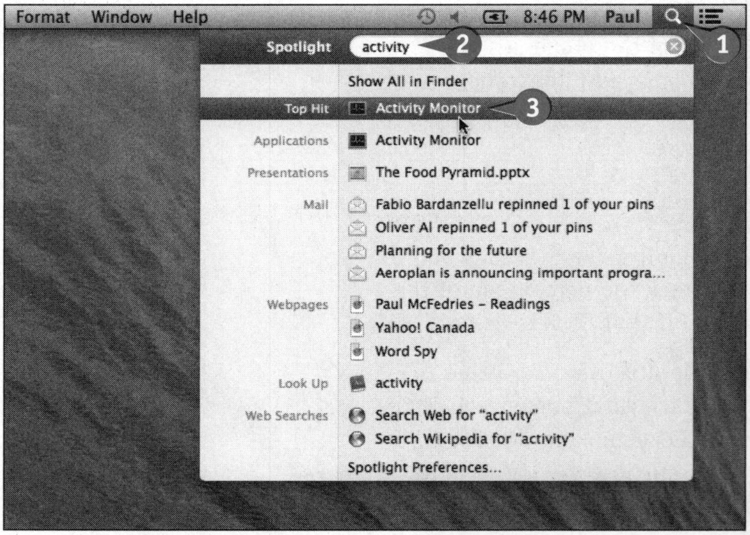

The Activity Monitor window appears.

4. Click the **Memory** tab.

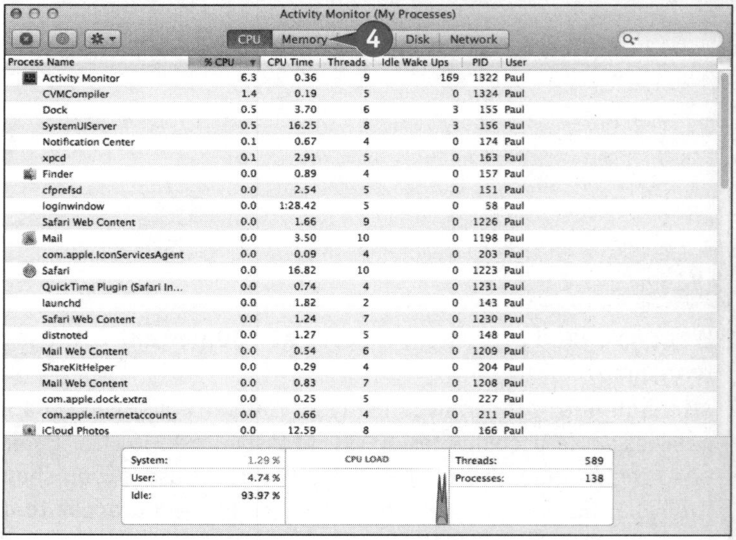

5. Monitor the Memory Used value to track how much of Mac Pro's memory is currently being used.

A. The Total Memory value tells you how much physical memory is installed in Mac Pro.

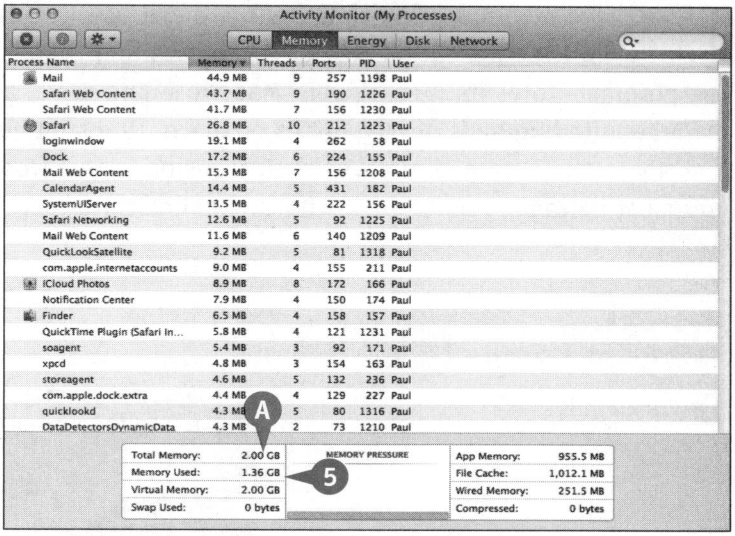

6. Monitor the Virtual Memory value to track the overall amount of virtual memory that the system has reserved.

7. Monitor the Swap Used value to track how much of the virtual memory OS X and your apps are using.

Note: Swap Used should be 0 most of the time, but it may grow to a few megabytes. If you see that it grows to hundreds of megabytes over a short period, Mac Pro likely does not have enough memory for the programs you are running.

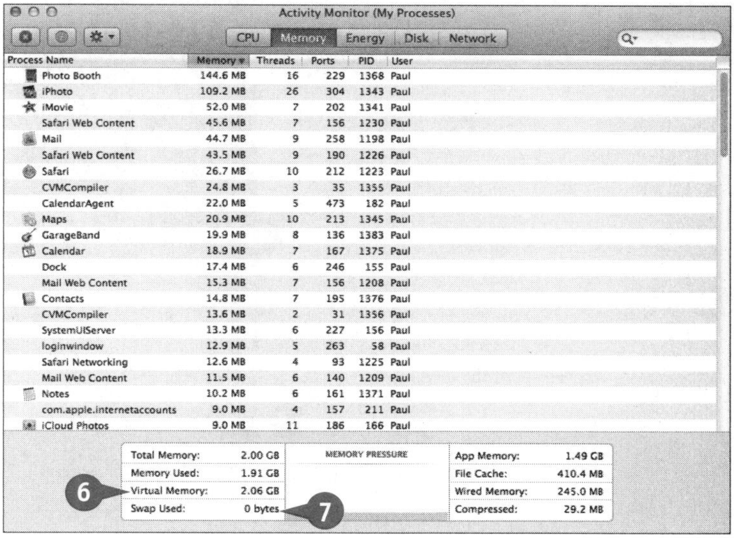

TIP

What is virtual memory?

Mac Pro can address memory beyond what is physically installed on the system. This nonphysical memory, called *virtual memory*, is set up as an extension of the Mac Pro's physical memory. Although the size of the virtual memory can be several gigabytes or more, only a small part of that is usually in use at any time, and that part is called the *swap file*. It is implemented by using a piece of the Mac Pro hard drive that OS X has set aside and configured to emulate physical memory.

Uninstall Unused Applications

If you have an application that you no longer use, you can free up some disk space and reduce clutter in the Applications folder by uninstalling that application. When you install an application, the program stores its files on your Mac Pro's hard drive, and although most programs are quite small, many require hundreds of megabytes of space. Uninstalling applications you do not need frees up the disk space they use and removes their icons or folders from the Applications folder. In most cases, you must be logged on to OS X with an administrator account to uninstall applications.

Uninstall Unused Applications

1 Click **Finder** (![]).

2 Click **Applications**.

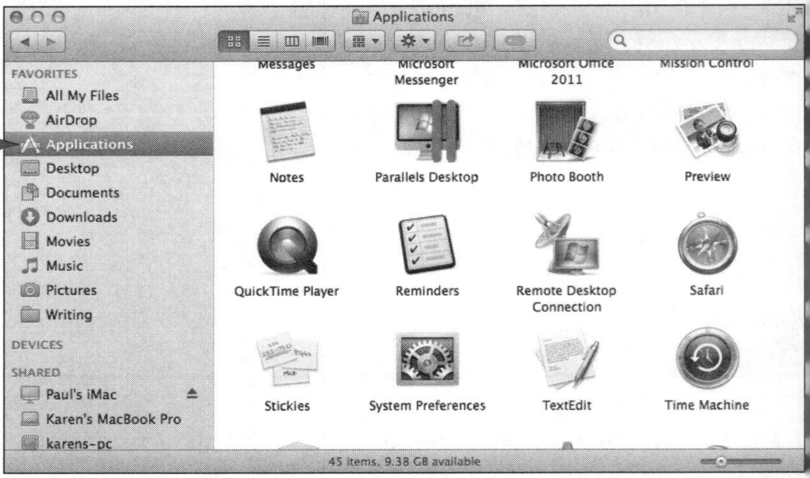

3 Click and drag the application or its folder and drop it on the **Trash** icon (🗑).

If your Mac Pro prompts you for an administrator password, type the password and then click **OK**.

A Your Mac Pro uninstalls the application.

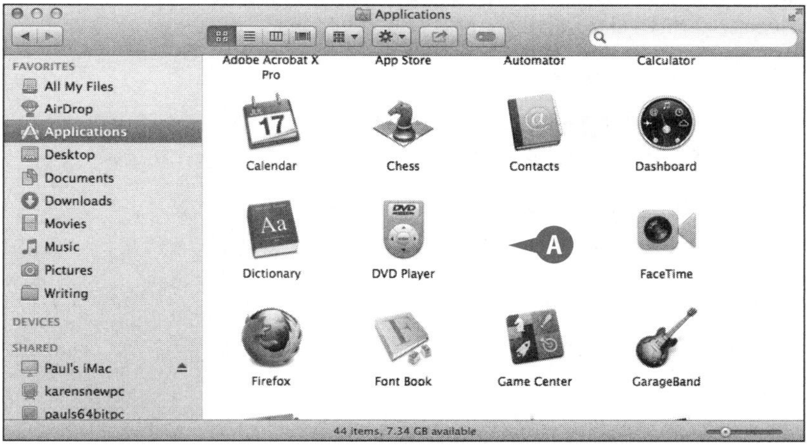

TIP

Is there another way to uninstall an application?

Yes, in some cases. A few Mac applications come with a separate program for uninstalling the application. Follow steps 1 and 2. Open the application's folder, if it has one (A). Double-click the Uninstaller icon and then follow the instructions on-screen (B).

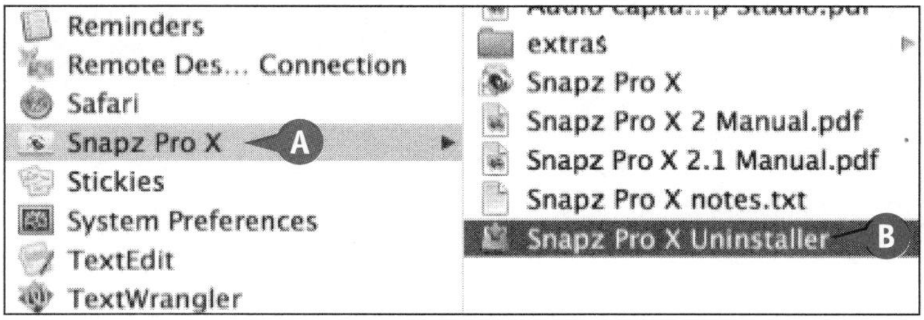

Configure Time Machine Backups

One of the most crucial Mac Pro maintenance chores is to configure your system to make regular backups of your files. Mac Pros are reliable machines, but they can crash; and all hard drives eventually die, so at some point your data will be at risk. To avoid losing that data forever, you need to configure Time Machine to perform regular backups.

To use Time Machine, your Mac Pro requires a second hard drive.

Configure Time Machine Backups

Configure Backups Automatically

1. Connect an external USB or Thunderbolt hard drive to your Mac Pro.

   OS X asks if you want to use the hard drive as your backup disk.

2. Click **Use as Backup Disk**.

Note: If OS X does not ask to use the hard drive, continue with the following steps.

Configure Backups Manually

1. Click **System Preferences** ().

   The System Preferences appear.

2. Click **Time Machine**.

The Time Machine preferences appear.

3 Click **Select Backup Disk**.

Time Machine displays a list of available backup devices.

4 Click the external hard drive.

5 Click **Use Disk**.

Time Machine enables backups and prepares to run the first backup automatically in 2 minutes.

6 Click **Close** ( ) to close the Time Machine preferences.

TIP

How do Time Machine backups work?

Time Machine makes backing up your Mac Pro easy because backups are handled automatically as follows:

- The initial backup occurs 2 minutes after you configure Time Machine for the first time. This backup includes your entire Mac Pro.
- Another backup runs every hour. These hourly backups include files and folders you have changed or created since the most recent hourly backup.
- Time Machine runs a daily backup that includes only those files and folders that you have changed or created since the most recent daily backup.
- Time Machine runs a weekly backup that includes only those files and folders that you have changed or created since the most recent weekly backup.

Create a Secondary User Account

Although Mac Pro lets you define multiple accounts, if you are the sole user of the computer, you might think you do not need another account. However, having a secondary account is a useful troubleshooting tool, as long as you do not customize or tweak OS X using that account so that it always uses only the default settings. That way, if Mac Pro starts acting up, you can log in to the secondary account and see if the problem persists. If it does not, you know the problem is likely related to user-specific settings you applied in your main account.

Create a Secondary User Account

1. In the Dock, click **System Preferences** ( ).

   The System Preferences appear.

2. Click **Users & Groups**.

   The Users & Groups preferences appear.

3. Click the lock icon ( ).

   System Preferences asks for your Mac Pro administrator password.

4. Type the password.

5. Click **Unlock**.

    changes to and System Preferences unlocks Users & Groups.

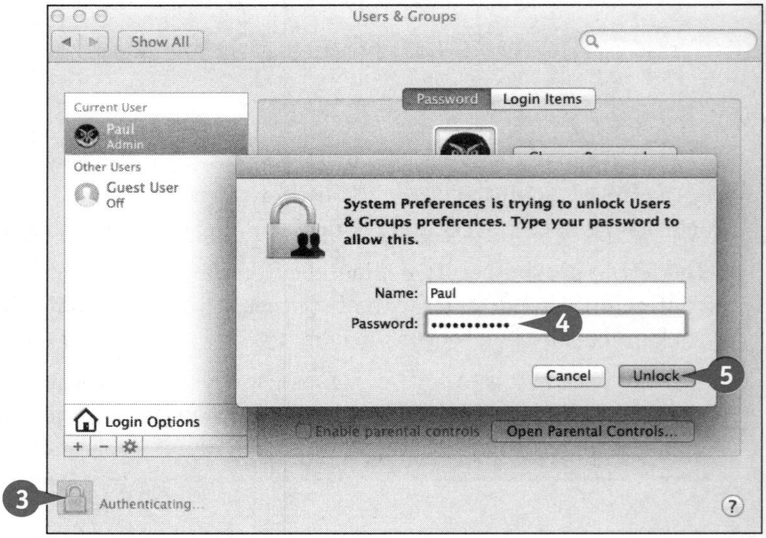

6 Click **Add a user account** (+).

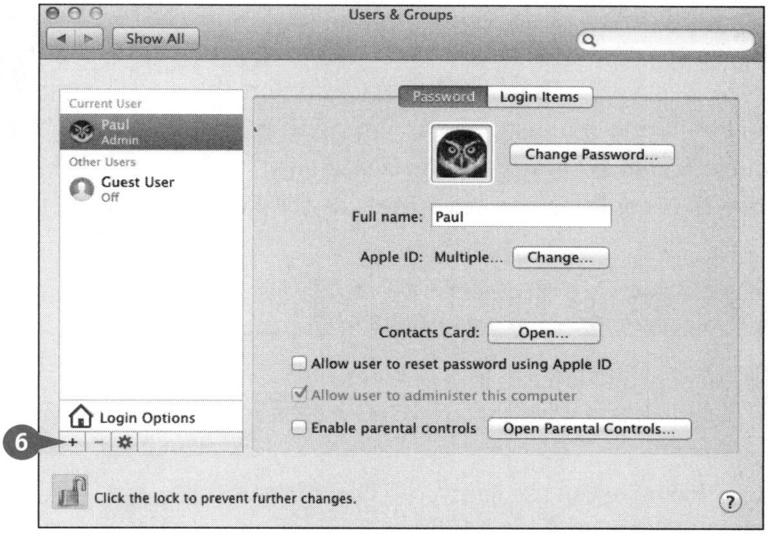

7 Click the **New Account** ⇕ and then click **Administrator**.

8 Type a name for the account.

A System Preferences generates the account name automatically.

9 Type a password in the Password text box and again in the Verify text box.

10 Use the Password Hint text box to type a hint about your password.

11 Click **Create User**.

System Preferences creates the secondary account.

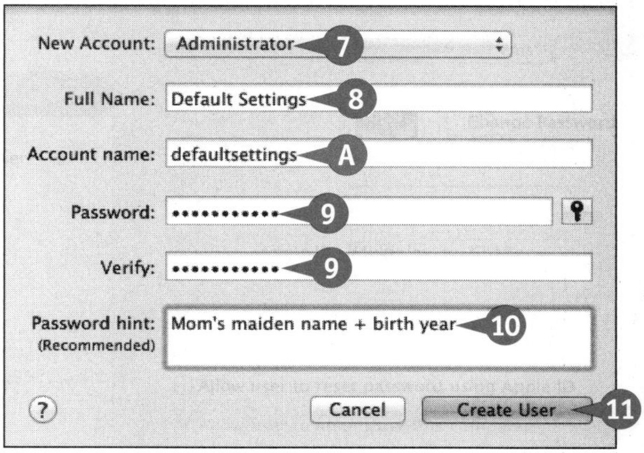

TIP

Do I need to use a password for this account?

No, System Preferences allows you to create the account without a password. However, because you are creating an all-powerful administrator account, it is really important that you give this account a secure password. The password should be at least eight characters long, and it should include at least one character from at least three of the following sets: lowercase letters, uppercase letters, numbers, and symbols.

To check your password strength, click the **Password Assistant** icon (🔑) to open the Password Assistant dialog. Type your password in the Suggestion text box and watch the Quality bar. You have a strong password when this bar turns green.

Create an OS X Recovery Disk

You can use an external hard drive or USB flash drive to create an OS X Recovery disk that can help you troubleshoot problems. As described in Chapter 17, you can troubleshoot Mac Pro by booting to the Recovery HD, which is a partition on the Mac Pro hard drive. This is a useful tool, but it suffers from a glaring problem: If Mac Pro's entire hard drive fails, the Recovery HD also fails. To protect yourself from such a scenario, create an OS X Recovery disk, which is an external hard drive or flash drive that contains the same tools as the Recovery HD.

Create an OS X Recovery Disk

1. Connect a USB flash drive or external hard drive to Mac Pro.

Note: The drive you use must have a capacity of at least 1GB.

2. Download and then open the Recovery Disk Assistant, as described in the first tip of this section.

3. Double-click **Recovery Disk Assistant.**

   The first time you open this program, Mac Pro asks you to confirm.

4. Click **Open**.

   The Recovery Disk Assistant license agreement appears.

5. Click **Agree** (not shown).

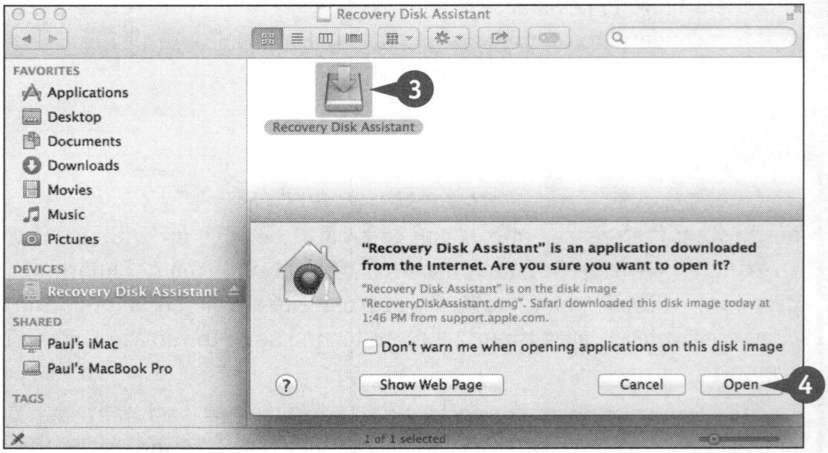

Recovery Disk Assistant appears and displays an icon for the external drive.

Note: Recovery Disk Assistant erases the existing contents of the disk. Therefore, if the disk contains any files you want to preserve, be sure to copy the files to a safe location before proceeding.

6. Click the drive icon.
7. Click **Continue**.

Mac Pro prompts you for your administrator password.

8. Type your password.
9. Click **OK**.

The Recovery Disk Assistant creates the disk.

10. Click **Quit**.
11. Eject the disk, label it, and then store it in a safe place.

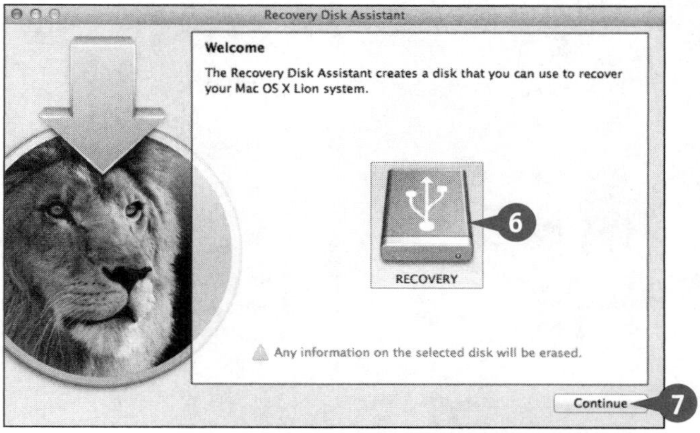

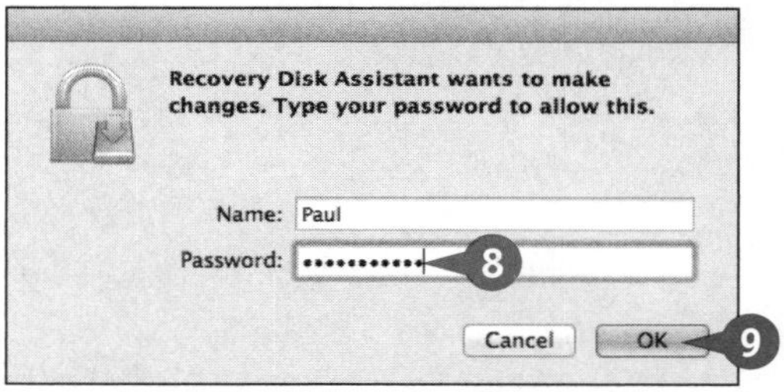

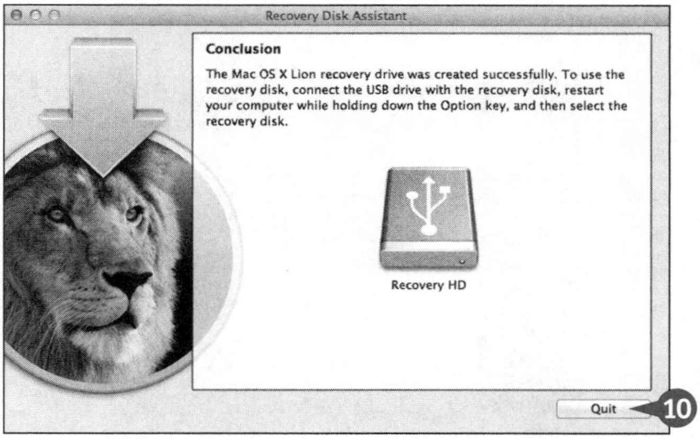

TIPS

How do I get the Recovery Disk Assistant?

Use Safari to navigate to http://support.apple.com/kb/DL1433 and then click **Download**. When the download is complete, click **View**, click **Show Downloads**, and then double-click **RecoveryDiskAssistant.dmg**.

How do I troubleshoot Mac Pro if I did not create a Recovery disk and I cannot access the Recovery HD?

You might still be able to troubleshoot Mac Pro if you have another Mac. You need to restart Mac Pro in target disk mode, as described in Chapter 17. Mac Pro's hard drive then appears as a drive on the other Mac. This enables you to use Disk Utility on the other Mac to verify or repair your Mac Pro's hard drive.

CHAPTER 17

Troubleshooting Mac Pro

Your Mac Pro is a solid computer, and it should give you many years of dependable performance. However, *all* computers eventually run into problems, and your Mac Pro will likely be no exception. To help you get through these inevitable rough patches, this chapter offers a few tried-and-true troubleshooting techniques.

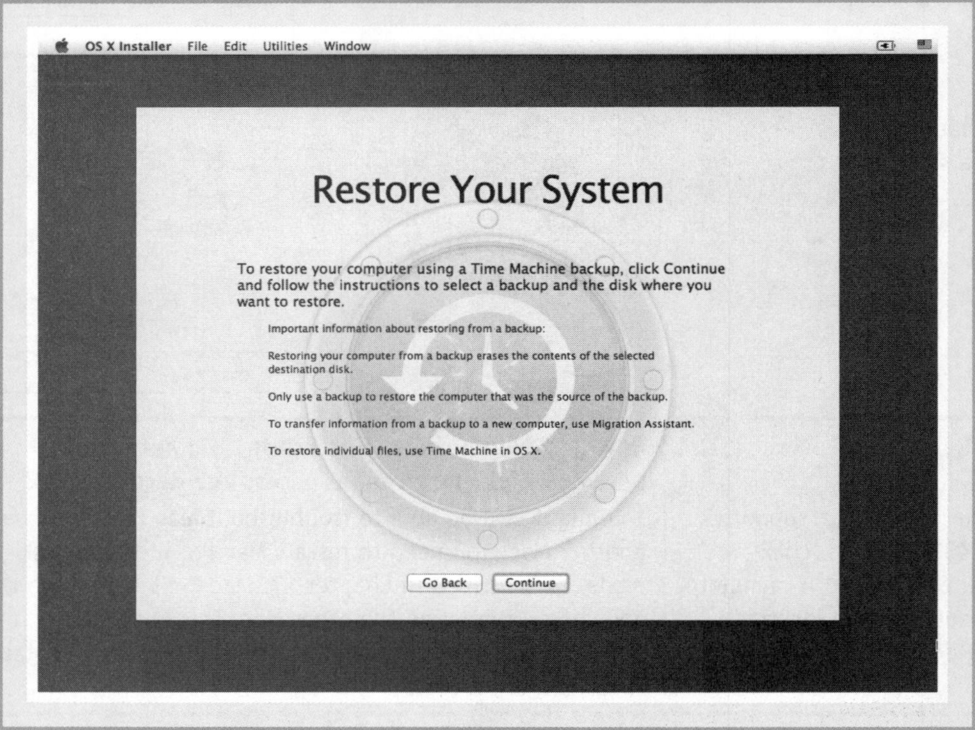

Review General Troubleshooting Techniques

One of the mysteries that you have no doubt experienced is the computer glitch that plagues you for a while and then simply vanishes without any intervention on your part. Unfortunately, most computer ills do not just disappear. There is no easy or set way to solve these more intractable problems, but it can be done if you take a systematic approach. This involves first trying a few generic troubleshooting techniques and, if these do not work, asking a series of questions designed to gather the required information or to narrow down the cause.

Troubleshoot Hardware

Check Connections

Some of the most common causes of hardware problems are the simple physical things, such as devices being unplugged or disconnected. So your first troubleshooting steps should concentrate on the obvious: making sure that a device is turned on, checking that cable connections are secure, and ensuring that external devices (such as those using a Thunderbolt or USB cable) are properly connected.

Replace the Batteries

Wireless devices, such as keyboards and mice, use up batteries very quickly. If a wireless device is working intermittently or not at all, always try replacing the batteries to see if that solves the problem.

Power Cycle the Device

You *power cycle* a device by turning it off, waiting a few seconds, and then turning it back on. This simple procedure is often enough to get a device back up and running. Many wireless mice have a reset button, and some keyboards have an on/off switch. Thunderbolt and USB devices often get their power directly from the corresponding port. Power cycle these devices by unplugging them and then plugging them back in.

Troubleshoot Software

Basic Troubleshooting Steps

First, you can often fix a problem by shutting down all your open programs and starting again. This is a particularly useful fix for problems caused by low memory or low system resources. Next, log out of your user account, which clears the memory and gives you a slightly cleaner slate than merely closing all your programs. Finally, restart Mac Pro to reload the entire system, which is often enough to solve many problems.

Did You Get an Error Message?

Unfortunately, most computer error messages are obscure and do little to help you resolve a problem directly. However, error codes and error text can help you down the road, either by giving you something to search for in an online database or by providing information to a tech support person. Therefore, you should always write down the full text of any error message that appears, or press Shift+⌘+3 to place an image of the screen on the desktop.

Did You Recently Change Any Settings?

If the problem started after you changed an application preference or an OS X preference via System Preferences, try reversing the change to see if that solves the problem. Even something as seemingly innocent as activating a screen saver can cause problems, so do not rule anything out. If you determine that changing a program's setting causes the problem, check with the software developer to see if an update to the program is available.

Did You Recently Install a New Program?

If you suspect a new program is causing system instability, restart Mac Pro and try operating the system for a while without using the new program. If the program has any login items that load at startup, be sure to deactivate them (see the section "Bypass Login Items"). If the problem does not reoccur, the new program is likely the culprit. Try using the program without any other programs running. Also check that the program is compatible with OS X Mavericks.

Check Console Messages

The section "Review General Troubleshooting Techniques" recommended that you write down any error messages that appear on-screen. However, if an error occurs behind the scenes, you do not see anything on-screen to tell you that a problem exists. However, Mac Pro likely made a note of the error as a Console message. This message is probably very technical, but it will likely make sense to someone in tech support. You can also Google the message text to see if a solution appears online.

Check Console Messages

1. Click **Spotlight** (🔍).
2. Type **console**.
3. Click **Console**.

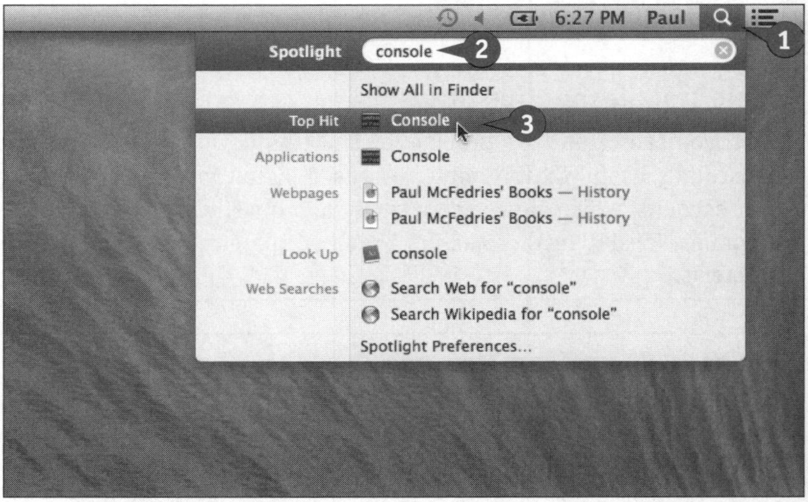

The Console window appears.

4. Click **system.log**.
5. Examine the system log for errors.

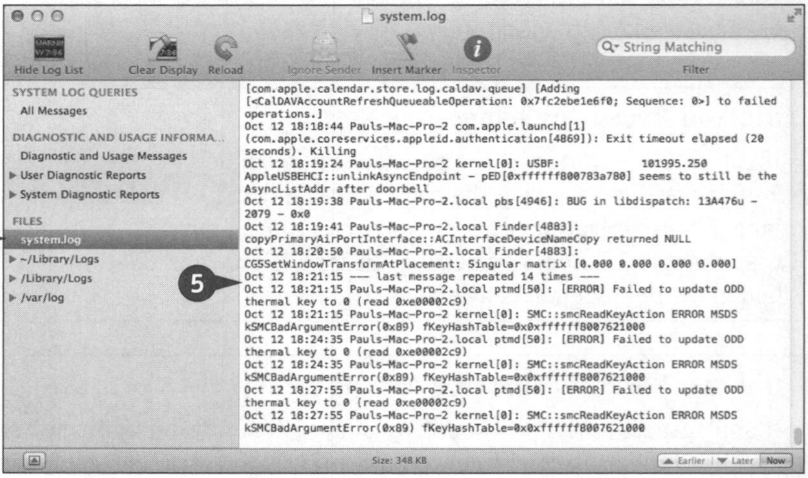

CHAPTER 17

Get System Information

When you are trying to solve a problem, it helps to know what components your Mac Pro is using. You might also require system data, such as how much memory is installed. Mac Pro comes with a System Information utility that can provide you with this data and much more. System Information breaks down this data into three categories: Hardware, such as memory, graphics, and storage; Network, such as the firewall and Wi-Fi; and Software, such as applications, startup items, and logs for various components.

Get System Information

1. Click **Spotlight** (🔍).
2. Type **system**.
3. Click **System Information**.

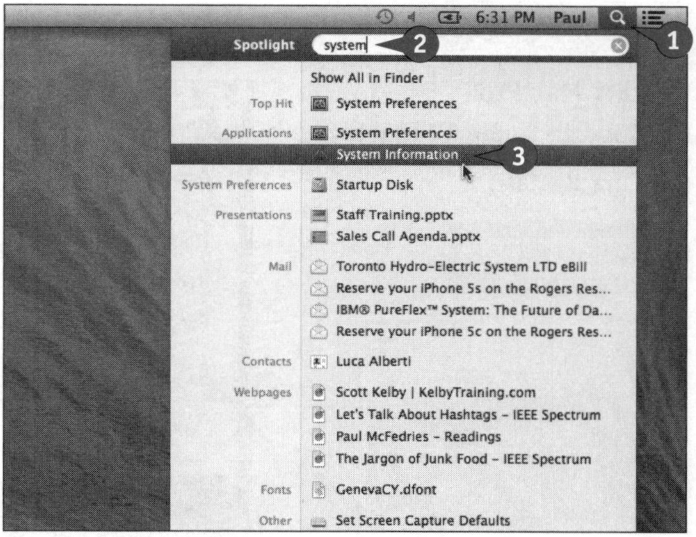

The System Information window appears.

4. Click a category.
5. Examine the category information.

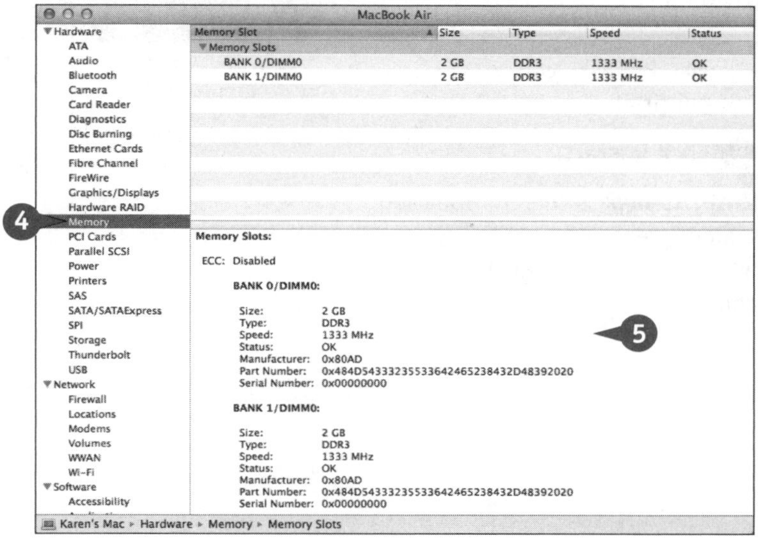

Restart Mac Pro

If a hardware device is having a problem with some system files, it often helps to restart Mac Pro. By rebooting the computer, you reload the entire system, which is often enough to solve many computer problems.

For a problem device that does not have its own power switch, restarting Mac Pro might not resolve the problem because the device remains powered up the whole time. You can *power cycle* — shut down and then restart — such devices as a group by power cycling Mac Pro.

Restart Mac Pro

Restart Mac Pro

1. Click the **Apple** icon ().
2. Click **Restart**.

Mac Pro asks you to confirm.

3. Click **Restart**.

Note: To bypass the confirmation dialog, press and hold Option when you click the **Restart** command.

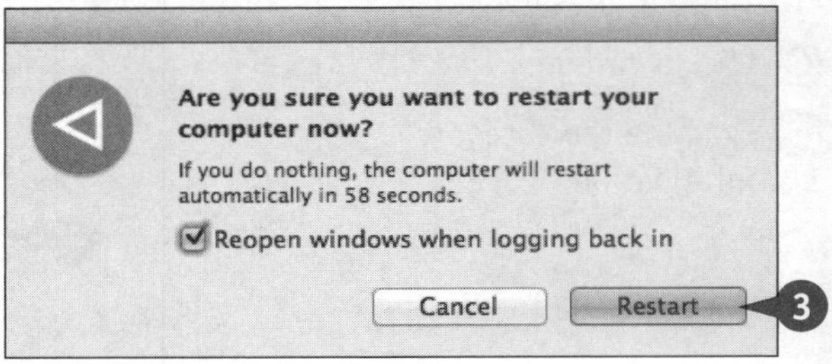

Power Cycle Mac Pro

1. Click the **Apple** icon (🍎).
2. Click **Shut Down**.

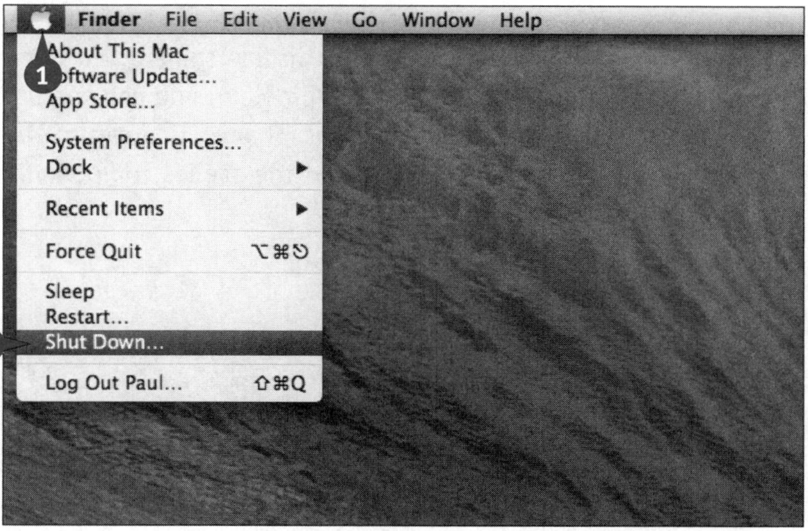

Mac Pro asks you to confirm.

Note: To bypass the confirmation dialog, press and hold Option when you click **Shut Down**.

3. Click **Shut Down**.
4. Wait for 30 seconds to give all devices time to spin down.
5. Turn Mac Pro back on.

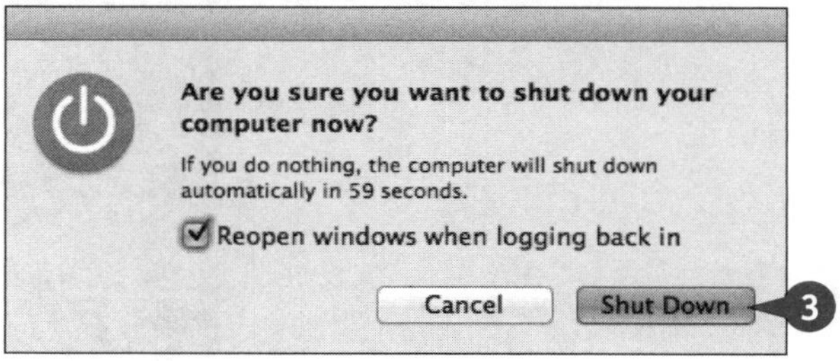

TIP

What do I do if Mac Pro is locked up and I cannot select the Shut Down command?

Your have to force Mac Pro to restart or shut down. To force Mac Pro to restart, press and hold Control and then press the power button. To force Mac Pro to shut down, press and hold the power button until Mac Pro shuts off.

This does not give you any way to close your running applications, so you might lose unsaved document changes. Therefore, wait for a few minutes to make sure Mac Pro really is locked up and not just in a temporary state of suspended animation while it is waiting for some lengthy process to finish.

Restart Mac Pro in Safe Mode

Behind-the-scenes processes that Mac Pro and your applications use can run amok and cause trouble. You learn how to temporarily disable some of these processes in the section "Bypass Login Items." If that does not solve your problem, you can see if some other process is at the root of your problem by performing a Safe Boot. That is, you can start Mac Pro in Safe Mode, which means that it does not load most of those behind-the-scenes components.

Restart Mac Pro in Safe Mode

1. Click the **Apple** icon (🍎).
2. Click **Restart**.

   Mac Pro asks you to confirm.

3. Click **Restart**.

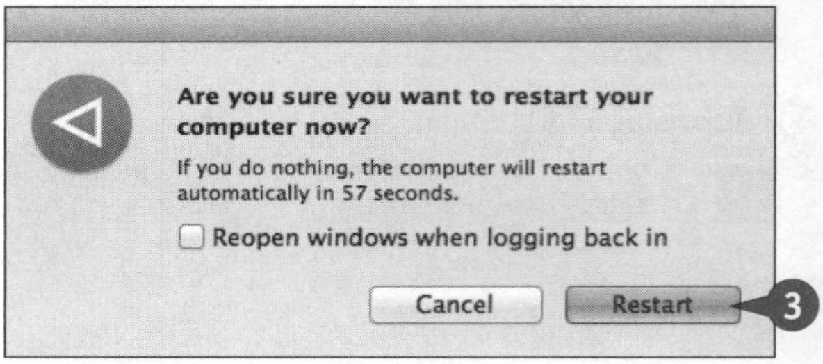

Mac Pro logs you out and then restarts.

4 Press and hold Shift until you see the Apple logo.

Mac Pro loads with only a minimal set of components.

A When you get to the login screen, you see the words "Safe Boot."

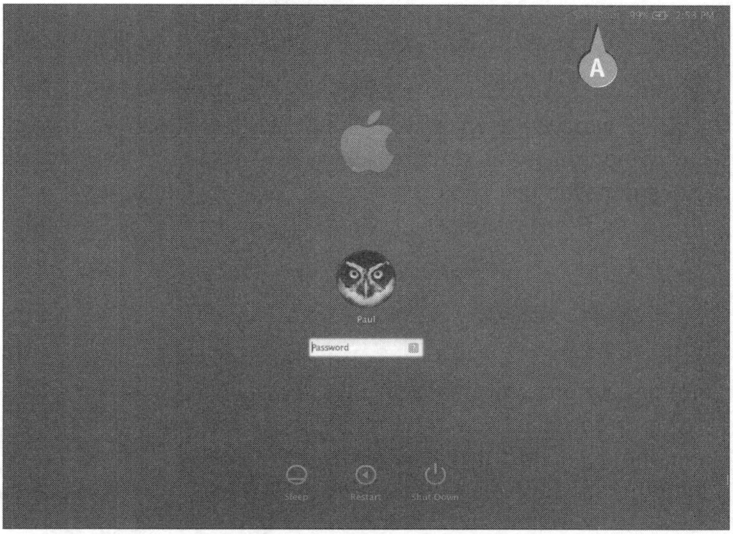

5 If you have multiple user accounts, click your user account icon.

6 Type your password and then press Return.

7 Check to see if the problem is still present.

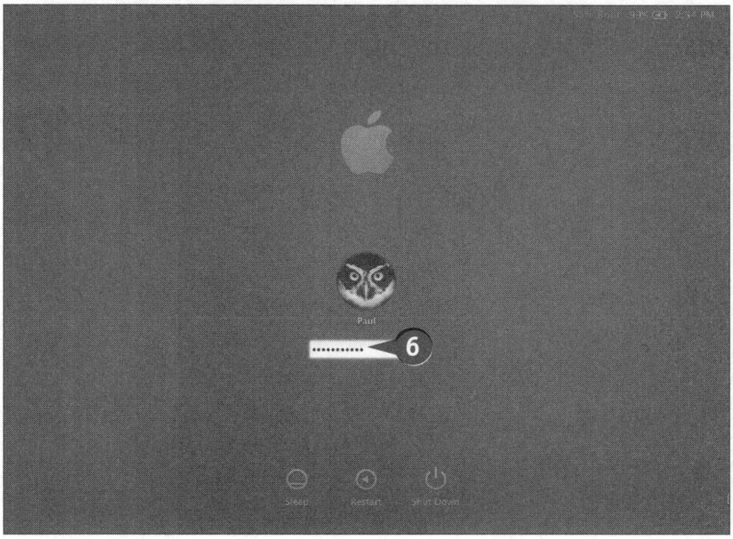

TIPS

Does it take longer to boot in Safe Mode?
You might think it would take Mac Pro less time to load without those extra components, but Mac Pro actually takes longer to start in Safe Mode. If you want to know why, see the following: http://support.apple.com/kb/HT1564.

What benefit do I get from booting Mac Pro in Safe Mode?
Safe Mode is mostly a technique of elimination. That is, if the problem still persists in Safe Mode, you know a hidden process is not causing it. If the problem does go away, it is a bit harder to deal with because Mac Pro offers no method for disabling individual components. You may need to reinstall OS X, as described in the section "Reinstall OS X."

Restart Mac Pro in Target Disk Mode

You can use target disk mode to help troubleshoot Mac Pro. If you are having trouble starting Mac Pro, a problem with the main hard drive might be the culprit. You normally troubleshot such a problem by booting either to the Recovery HD or to a Recovery drive, as described in the section "Boot to the Recovery HD." If you cannot access the Recovery HD and you do not have a Recovery drive, then you can still troubleshoot the problem by connecting Mac Pro to another Mac using a Thunderbolt cable and booting Mac Pro in target disk mode.

Restart Mac Pro in Target Disk Mode

1. Connect Mac Pro and the other Mac using a Thunderbolt cable.

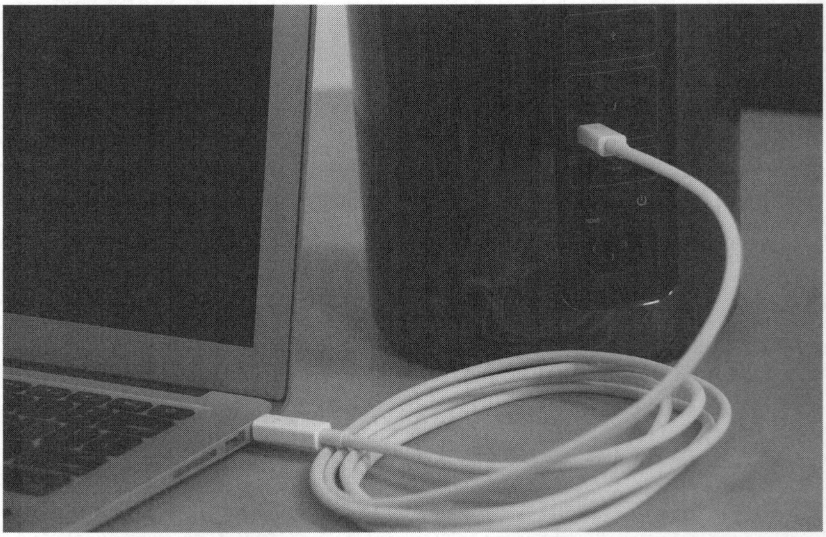

2. Restart Mac Pro.
3. During the restart, press and hold T until you see the Thunderbolt icon.

Mac Pro is now in target disk mode.

4. Restart the other Mac.

(A) When the other Mac's desktop appears, the Mac Pro's hard drive appears as a drive on the other Mac.

5. Click **Spotlight** (🔍).

6. Type **disk**.

7. Click **Disk Utility**.

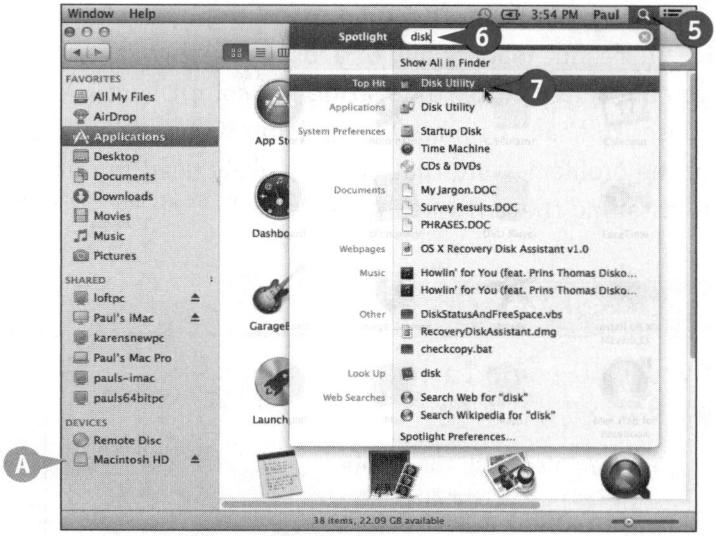

The Disk Utility window appears.

8. Click the Mac Pro hard drive.

9. Click the **First Aid** tab.

10. Verify or repair the Mac Pro hard drive, as described in Chapter 15.

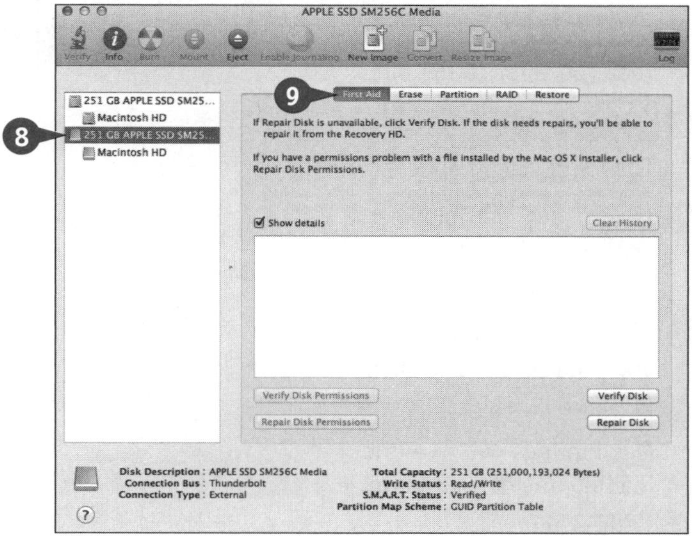

TIP

Mac Pro will not start in target disk mode. Why?

This can happen if you use a wireless keyboard because Mac Pro does not recognize that you are holding down T. The best way to work around this problem is to connect a wired keyboard and try again.

If that is not an option, the only other possibility is to configure target disk mode as the startup disk, although this requires access to the OS X desktop. If you have such access, open System Preferences, click **Startup Disk**, click **Target Disk Mode**, and then click **Restart**.

Bypass Login Items

Flaky system behavior could be caused by one of your login items. To find out, it is possible to log in without loading any of your login items (this is called a *safe login*). If the problem goes away, you are a step closer to locating the culprit because you can be fairly certain that a login item is the cause. You can then remove the login items one at a time until you find the one that is the source of the problem. Note that you will likely need to reinstate the previously removed login items by reinstalling the software.

Bypass Login Items

Bypass All Login Items

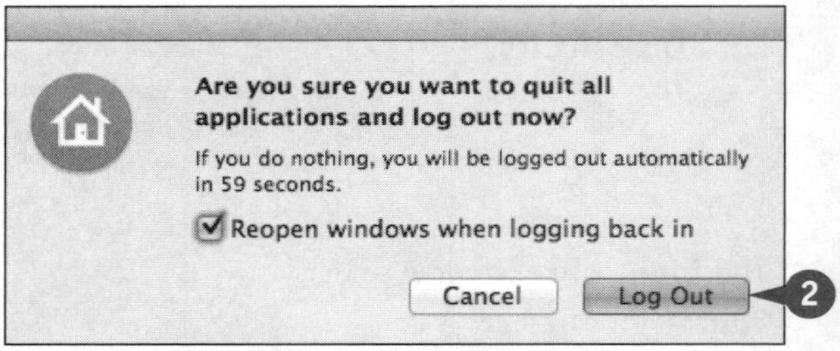

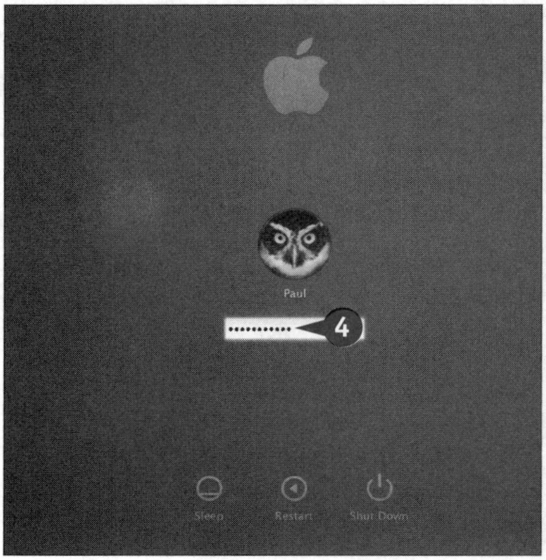

1. Press Shift+⌘+⌘.

   You can also click the **Apple** icon () and then click **Log Out**.

   Mac Pro asks you to confirm that you want to log out.

2. Click **Log Out**.

   The login screen appears.

3. If you have multiple user accounts, click your user account icon.

4. Type your password, press and hold Shift, and then press Return.

   Mac Pro logs you in without loading any of your login items.

   When you see the desktop, release Shift.

Remove a Login Item

1. In the Dock, click **System Preferences** ( ).

   The System Preferences appear.

2. Click **Users & Groups**.

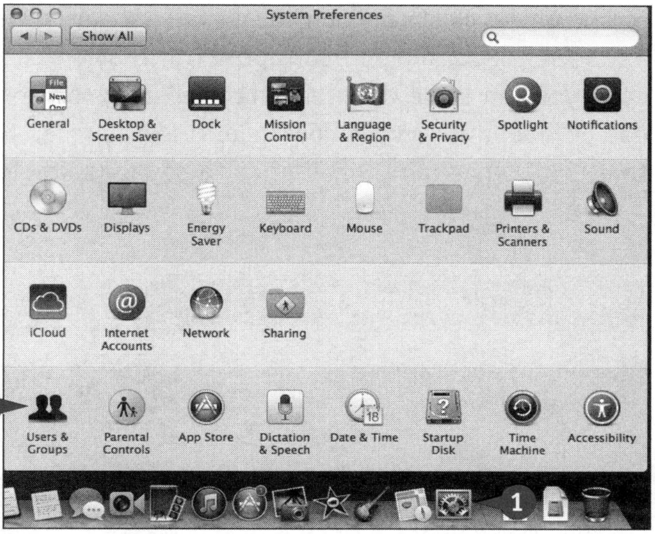

   The Users & Groups preferences appear.

3. Click your user account.
4. Click the **Login Items** tab.
5. Deselect the check box beside the item you want to remove (changes to).
6. Click **Remove** ( ).

   Mac Pro removes the login item.

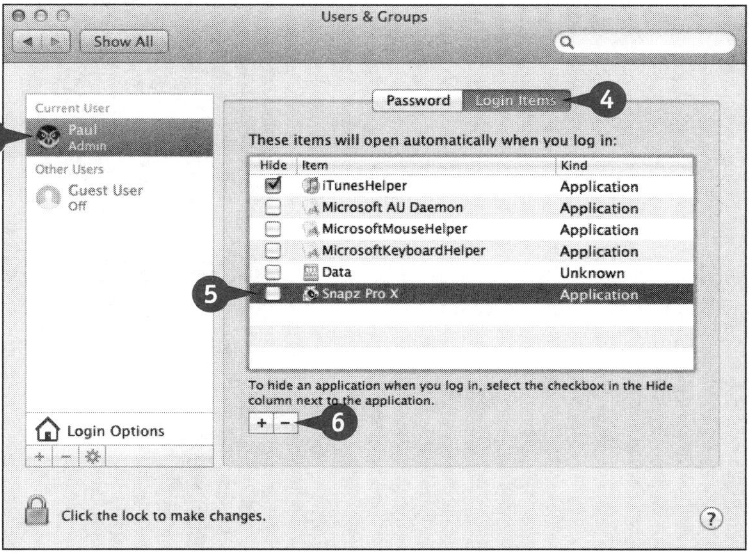

TIPS

What is a login item?

At startup, Mac Pro performs many behind-the-scenes setup tasks. One of these tasks is that Mac Pro checks the list of items supposed to open automatically when you log in to your user account. These items are usually applications, but they can also be files, folders, and shared network locations. These are called *login items*.

Can you give me an example of a problem related to a login item?

If you uninstall an application, the application may leave behind one or more login items, and these will cause an error each time you log in. Similarly, if a login item refers to a network resource that no longer exists, you will see an error.

Delete a Program's Preferences

One of the most common causes of application flakiness is a preferences file that somehow becomes damaged or corrupted (for example, its data is written with the wrong syntax). In that case, you can solve the problem by deleting (or moving) the preferences file so that the application has to rebuild it. On the downside, this may mean that you have to reenter some preferences, but that is usually a fairly small price to pay for a stable application.

Delete a Program's Preferences

1. Quit the application if it is currently running.
2. In Finder, click **Go**.
3. Press and hold Option and then click **Library**.

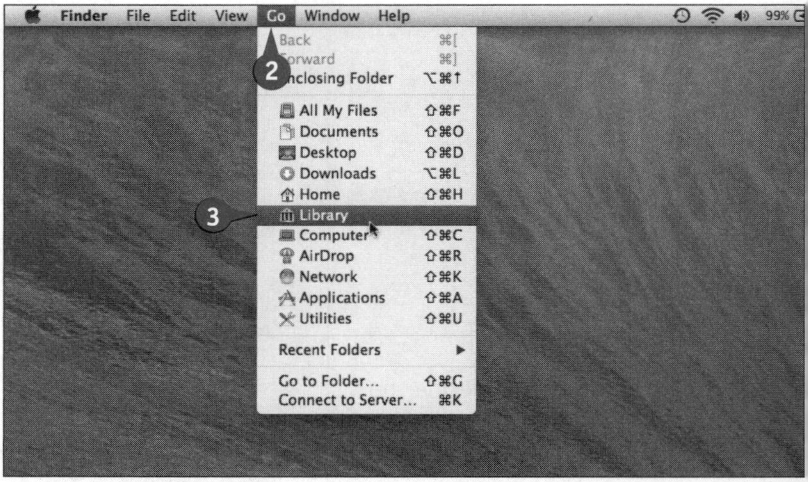

Mac Pro opens the Library folder.

4. Double-click **Preferences**.

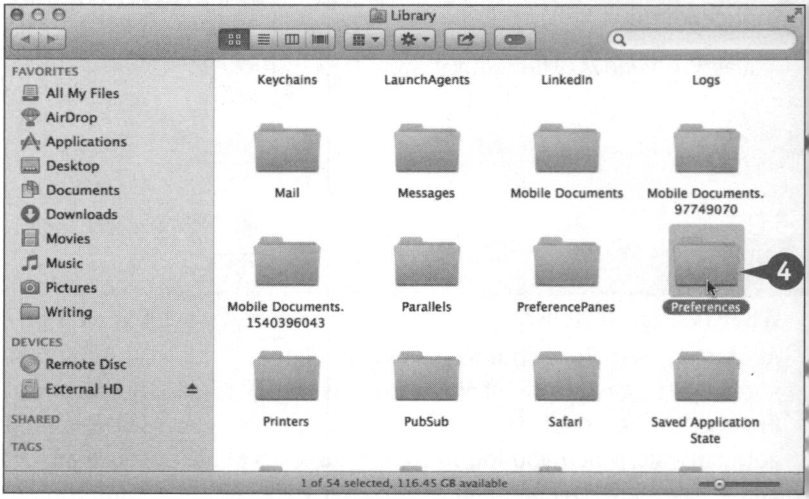

5 Locate the application's preferences file.

Note: If you cannot find the preferences file, click **Go**, click **Computer**, double-click **Macintosh HD**, double-click **Library**, and then double-click **Preferences** to see if it appears in that folder.

6 Click and drag the preferences file to the desktop.

Note: If the application has multiple preferences files, move all of them to the desktop.

7 Run the application and see if the problem persists:

A If the problem is resolved, then the preferences file was the source after all, so move it to the Trash.

B If the problem remains, then the preferences file was not the source. Quit the application and move the preferences file back to the Preferences folder.

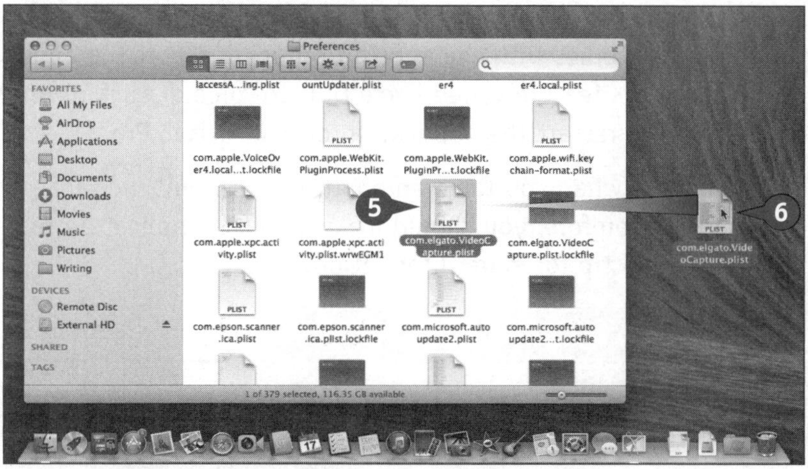

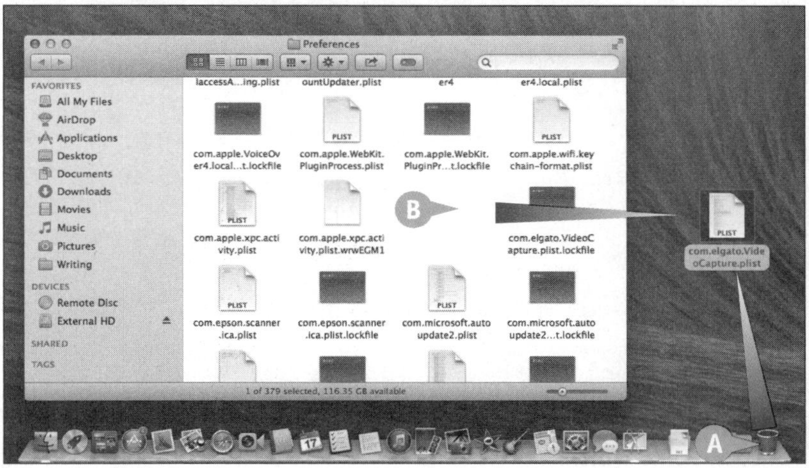

TIP

What is a preferences file?

A preferences file is a document that stores options and other data that you have entered using the application's Preferences command. Preferences files use the PLIST filename extension. In most cases, the filename uses the following general format: com.*company*.*application*.plist.

Here, *company* is the name of the software company that makes the application, and *application* is the name of the program. Here are some examples:

- com.apple.iTunes.plist
- com.microsoft.Word.plist
- com.adobe.PhotoshopElements.plist

Unfortunately, not every preferences file uses the com.*company*.*application*.plist format. If you cannot find the preferences file you are looking for, type either the company name or the program name in Finder's Search box.

Force a Stuck Application to Close

When you are working with an application, you may find that it becomes unresponsive and you cannot interact with the application or even quit the application normally. In that case, you can use an OS X feature called Force Quit to force a stuck or unresponsive application to close, which enables you to restart the application or restart Mac Pro.

Unfortunately, when you force an application to quit, you lose any unsaved changes in your open documents. Therefore, you should make sure the application really is stuck before forcing it to quit. See the second tip for more information.

Force a Stuck Application to Close

1 Click the **Apple** icon ( ).

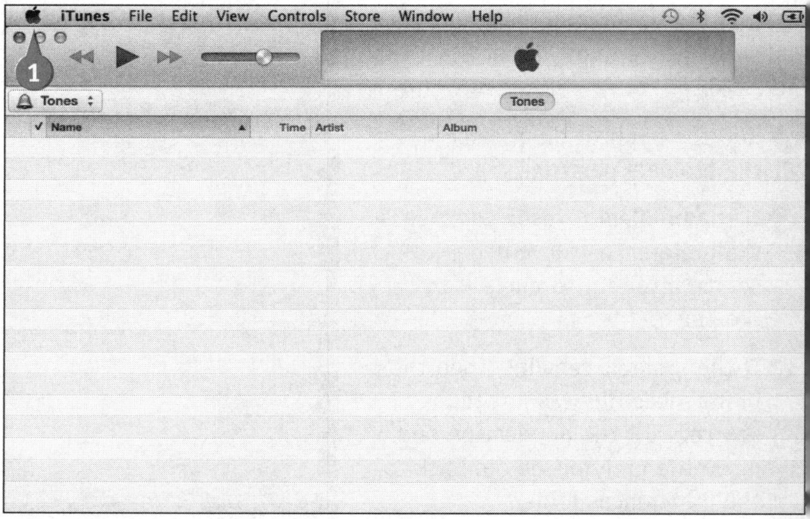

2 Click **Force Quit**.

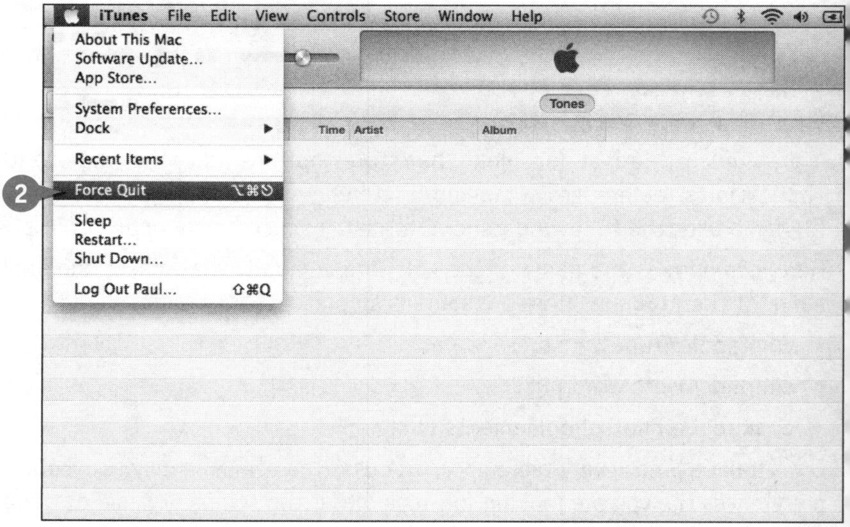

The Force Quit Applications window appears.

3 Click the application you want to shut down.

4 Click **Force Quit**.

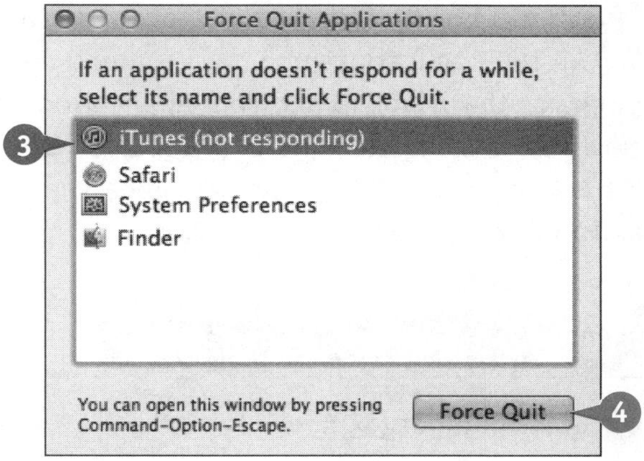

Mac Pro asks you to confirm that you want to force the application to quit.

5 Click **Force Quit**.

Mac Pro shuts down the application.

6 Click **Close** (■) to close the Force Quit Applications window.

TIPS

Are there easier ways to run the Force Quit command?

Yes. From the keyboard, you can run the Force Quit command by pressing Option + ⌘ + Esc. If the application has a Dock icon, press and hold Control + Option and then click the application's Dock icon. In the menu that appears, click **Force Quit**.

If an application is not responding, does that always mean the application is stuck?

Not necessarily. Some operations — such as recalculating a large spreadsheet or rendering a 3-D image — can take a few minutes, and during that time the application can appear stuck. If Mac Pro is low on memory, it can also cause an application to seem stuck. In this case, try shutting down some other applications to free up some memory.

Force a Stuck Process to Close

A *process* is a running instance of an executable program or an execution thread within a program. All the applications you have running are processes, but so are all the behind-the-scenes programs that Mac Pro and your applications require to function properly. If Mac Pro is running very slowly or is using all of its CPU resources (see Chapter 16) but the Force Quit command does not show a stuck application, then a stuck process may be at fault. You can use Activity Monitor to check this and to force a stuck process to close.

Force a Stuck Process to Close

1. Click **Spotlight** (🔍).
2. Type **activity**.
3. Click **Activity Monitor**.

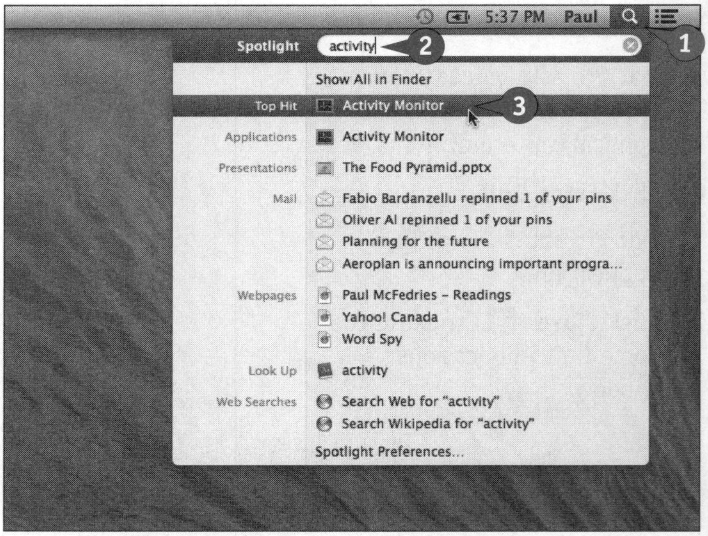

The Activity Monitor window appears.

4. Click the **CPU** tab.

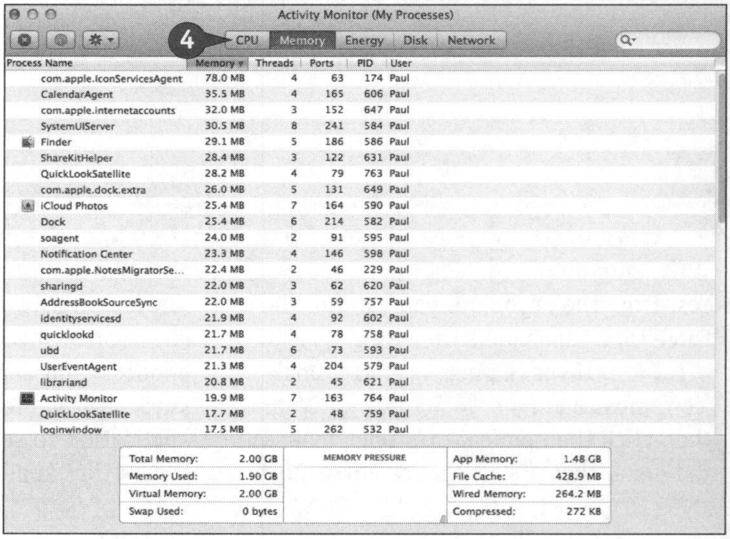

5 Click the process you want to close.

6 Click **Force a process to quit** (⊗).

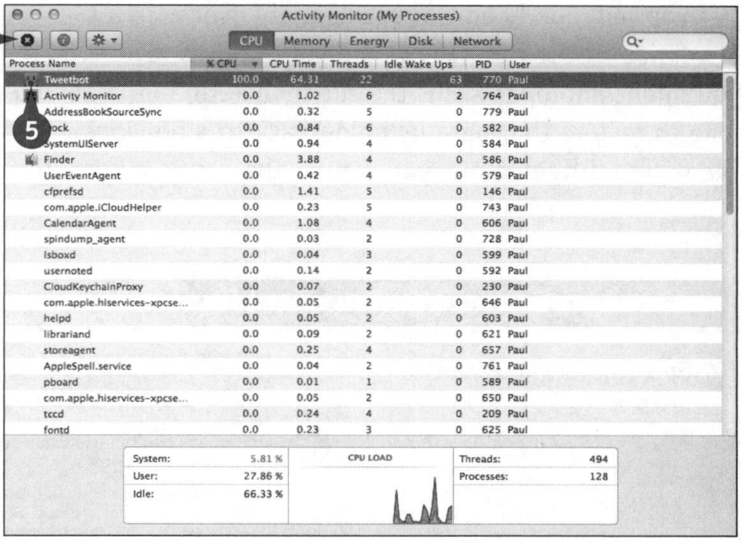

Activity Monitor asks you to confirm.

7 Click **Force Quit**.

Activity Monitor closes the process.

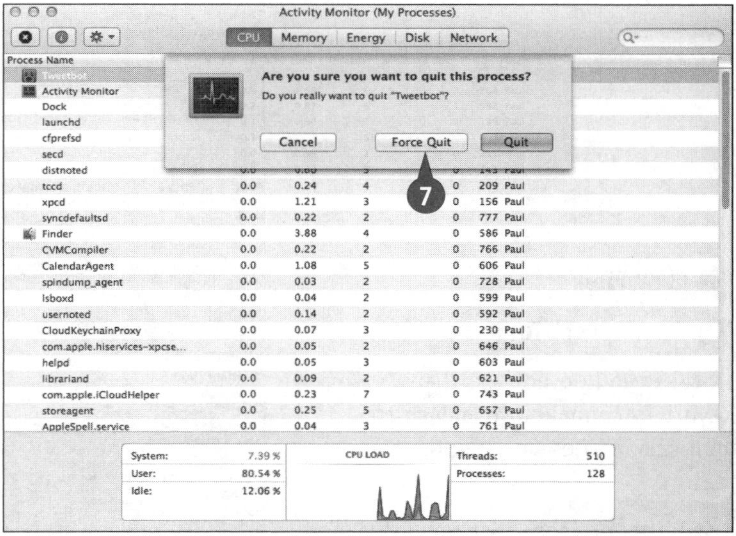

TIP

What happens if I do not see a stuck process in Activity Monitor?

By default, Activity Monitor shows you just the list of processes running under your user account. You can see more processes by clicking **View** and then clicking one of the following:

- **All Processes**. Displays all the running processes.
- **System Processes**. Displays processes started by OS X.
- **Other User Processes**. Displays processes running under an account other than yours and OS X.
- **Active Processes**. Displays processes currently using or that have recently used the CPU.

Restore an Earlier Version of a File

If you improperly edit or accidentally overwrite a file, some apps enable you to revert to an earlier version of the file. Why would you want to revert to an earlier version of a file? One reason is that you might improperly edit the file by deleting or changing important data. In some cases you may be able to restore that data by going back to a previous version of the file. Similarly, if you overwrite the file with a different file, you can fix the problem by restoring an earlier version of the file.

Restore an Earlier Version of a File

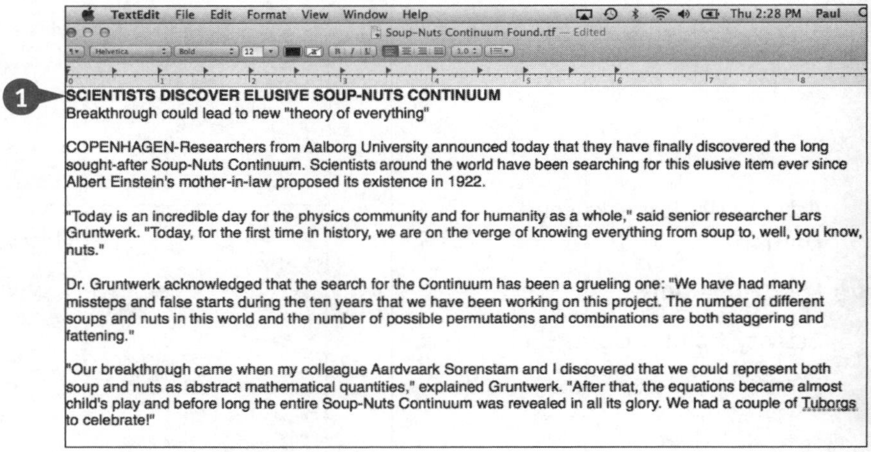

1 Open the file you want to restore.

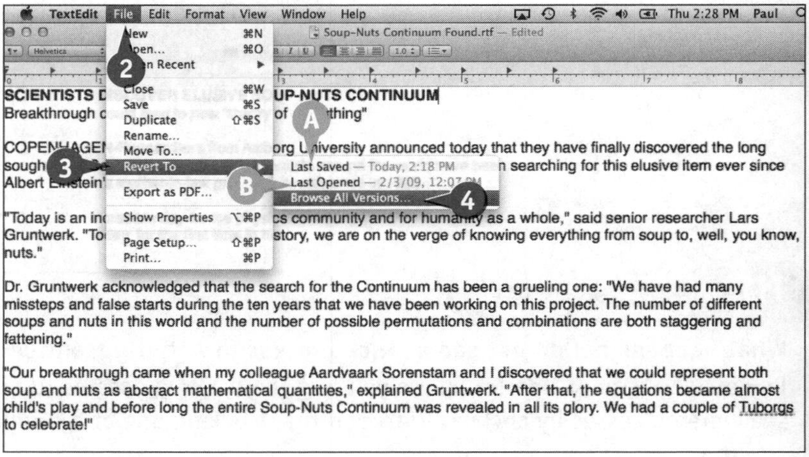

2 Click **File**.

3 Click **Revert To**.

Note: If you do not see the Revert To command, it means the application does not support this feature.

A To restore the most recently saved version, you can click **Last Saved**.

B To restore the most recently opened version, you can click **Last Opened**.

4 Click **Browse All Versions**.

The restore interface appears.

C This window represents the current version of the file.

D Each of these windows represents an earlier version of the file.

E This area tells you when the displayed version of the file was saved.

F You can use this timeline to navigate the earlier versions.

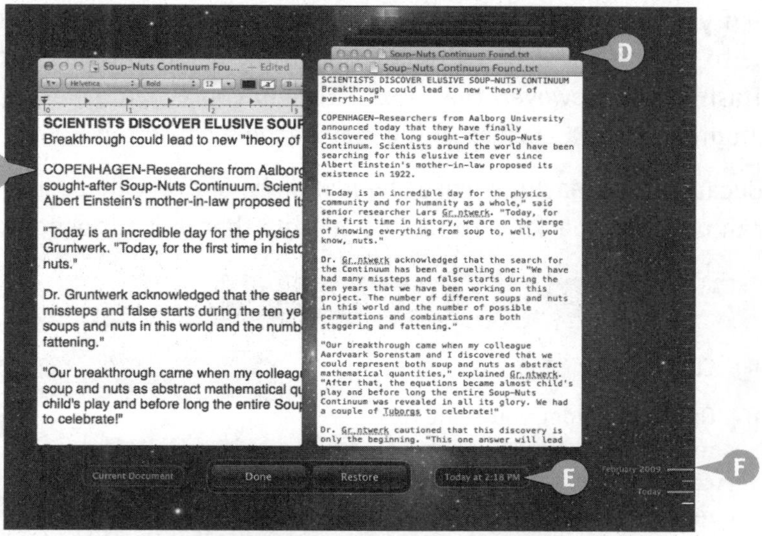

5 Navigate to the date that contains the version of the file you want to restore.

Note: See the tip to learn how to navigate the previous versions.

6 Click **Restore**.

Mac Pro reverts the file to the earlier version.

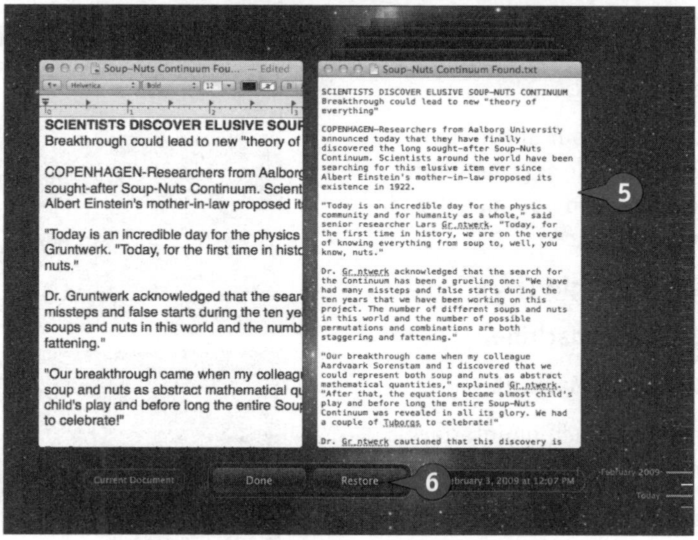

TIPS

How do I navigate the previous versions?

There are two methods you can use:

- Use the timeline on the right side of the window to click a specific version.
- Click the title bars of the version windows.

Can I restore a previous version without overwriting the current version of the file?

Yes, you can restore a copy of the file. This is useful if the current version has data you want to preserve, or if you want to compare the current version with the earlier version. Follow steps **1** to **5** to navigate to the version of the file that you want to restore. Press and hold Option and then click **Restore a Copy**.

Restore Files Using Time Machine

If you have configured Mac Pro to make regular Time Machine backups, you can use those backups to restore a lost file. If you accidentally delete a file, you can quickly restore it by opening the Trash folder. However, that does not help you if you have emptied the Trash folder. Similarly, if the program or OS X crashes, a file may become corrupted.

Because Time Machine makes hourly, daily, and weekly backups, it stores older copies of your data. You can use these backups to restore any file that you accidentally delete or that has become corrupted.

Restore Files Using Time Machine

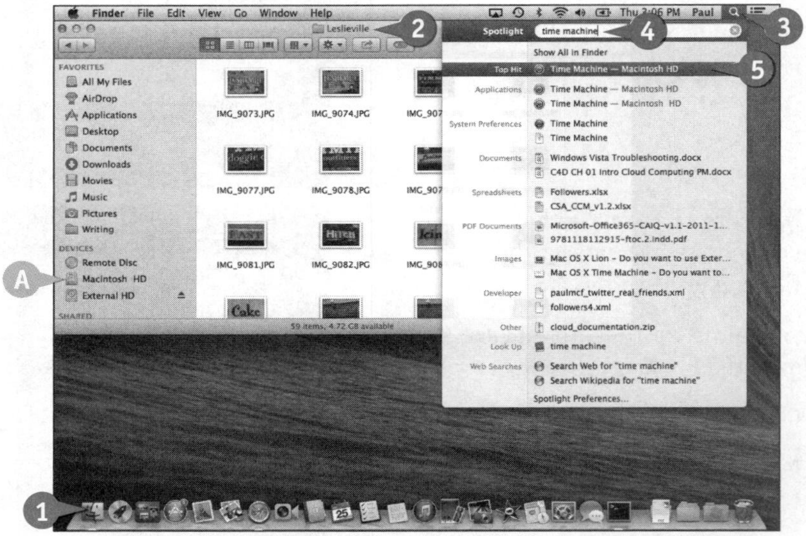

1. Click **Finder** ( ).
2. Open the folder you want to restore, or the folder that contains the file you want to restore.

   A To restore your entire hard drive, choose **Macintosh HD** in the sidebar.

Note: Restore your entire hard drive only if your original hard drive crashed and you have had it repaired or replaced.

3. Click **Spotlight** ( ).
4. Type **time machine**.
5. Click **Time Machine**.

   The Time Machine interface appears.

   B Each window represents a backed-up version of the folder.

   C This area tells you when the displayed version of the folder was backed up.

   D You can use this timeline to navigate the backed-up versions.

6 Navigate to the date that contains the backed-up version of the folder or file.

Note: See the tip to learn how to navigate the Time Machine backups.

7 If you are restoring a file, click the file.

8 Click **Restore**.

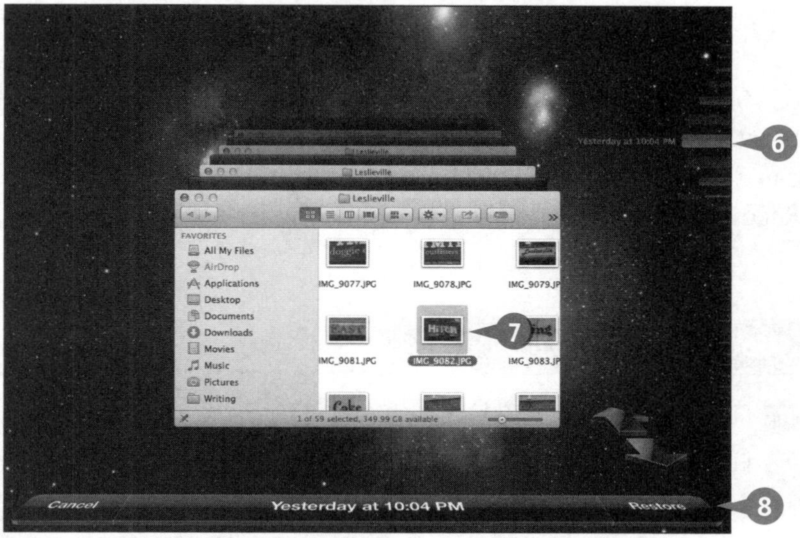

If another version of the folder or file already exists, Time Machine asks if you want to keep it or replace it.

9 Click **Replace**.

Time Machine restores the folder or file.

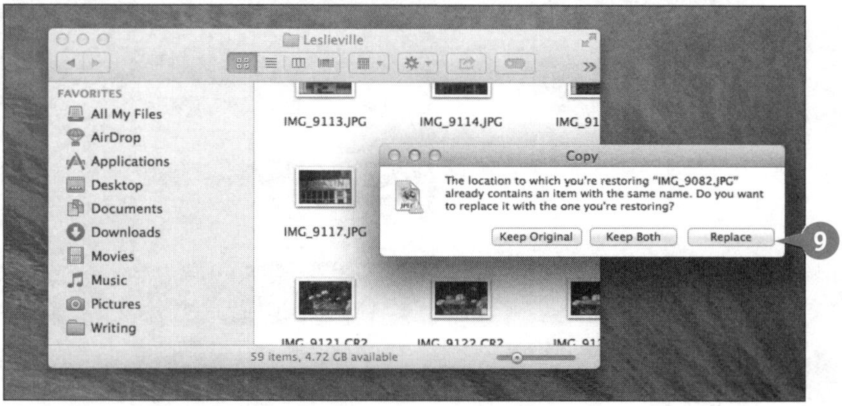

TIP

How do I navigate the backups in the Time Machine interface?

Here are the most useful techniques:

- Click the top arrow to jump to the earliest version; click the bottom arrow to return to the most recent version.
- Press and hold ⌘ and click the arrows to navigate through the backups one version at a time.
- Use the timeline to click a specific version.
- Click the version windows.

Boot to the Recovery HD

You can recover from some problems by accessing the recovery tools that come with Mac Pro. OS X creates a hidden area of the hard drive called Recovery HD, which contains a program called *OS X Utilities*. This program offers various tools that you can use to troubleshoot and recover from problems. For example, if you suspect that your Mac Pro's main hard drive is causing a problem, you can access Recovery HD and use Disk Utility to verify or repair the drive. Similarly, you can also use Recovery HD to restore Mac Pro from a Time Machine backup and to reinstall OS X.

Boot to the Recovery HD

1. Click the **Apple** icon (🍎).
2. Click **Restart**.

Mac Pro asks you to confirm.

3. Click **Restart**.

4 Press and hold Option while Mac Pro is restarting.

A list of Mac Pro's hard drives appears.

5 Click **Recovery HD**.

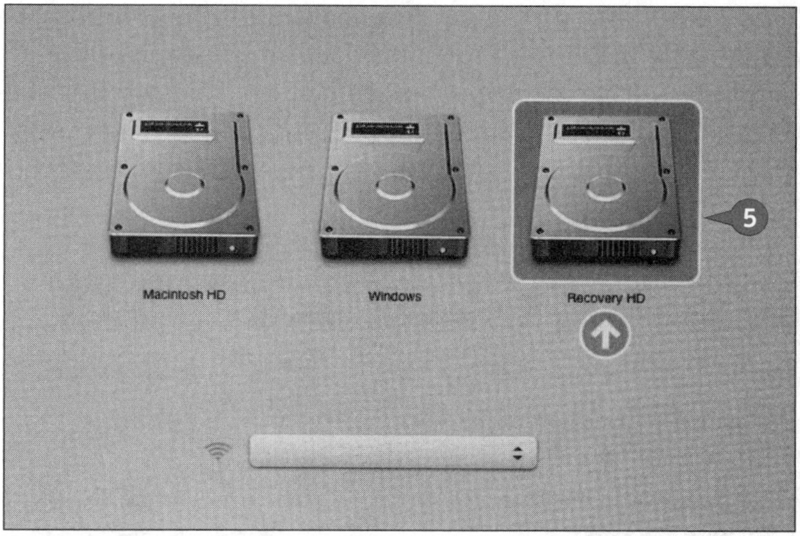

The OS X Utilities window appears.

A To use a utility, click it and then click **Continue**.

Note: See the sections that follow to learn how to restore a backup and reinstall OS X.

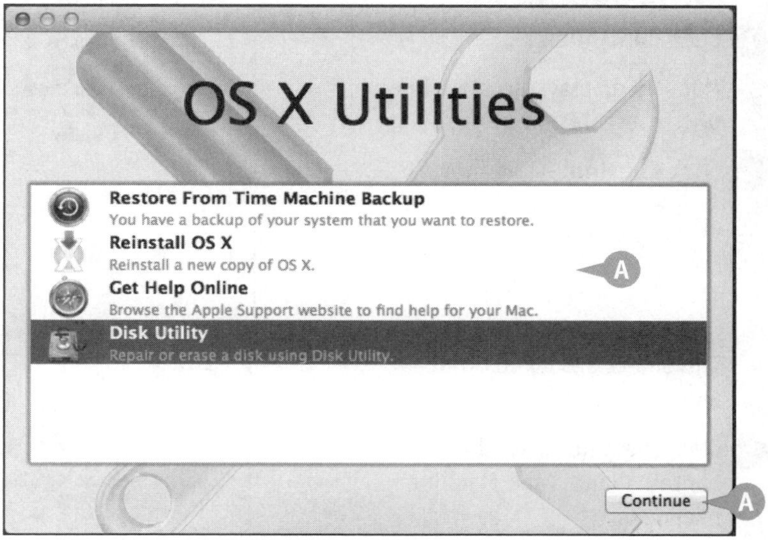

TIPS

Can I use the Recovery HD to get online?
Yes. If you cannot start Mac Pro and have no other device for Internet access, access troubleshooting information on the web by booting to the Recovery HD. Click the **Wi-Fi Status** icon (), click your Wi-Fi network, and then type your Wi-Fi password. In the OS X Utilities window, click **Get Help Online** and then **Continue**. OS X Utilities loads Safari and displays troubleshooting steps. You can also use Safari to surf to any site that has the information you seek.

How do I boot to the main Mac Pro hard drive?
To restart Mac Pro and boot to the main drive, click **OS X Utilities**, click **Quit OS X Utilities**, and then click **Restart**.

Restore the System from a Time Machine Backup

If you cannot start Mac Pro and you have tried other troubleshooting techniques to no avail, you may be able to get Mac Pro running again by restoring the entire system from a Time Machine backup. If you have tried repairing the hard drive permissions and the hard drive itself, as described in Chapter 15, but Mac Pro still will not start, one or more corrupt system files might be to blame. By restoring the system from a backup, you are essentially reverting Mac Pro to an earlier, working state.

Restore the System from a Time Machine Backup

1. Boot to the Recovery HD.

Note: See the previous section, "Boot to the Recovery HD."

2. Click **Restore From Time Machine Backup**.
3. Click **Continue**.

   Mac Pro displays an overview of the restoration process.

4. Click **Continue** (not shown).

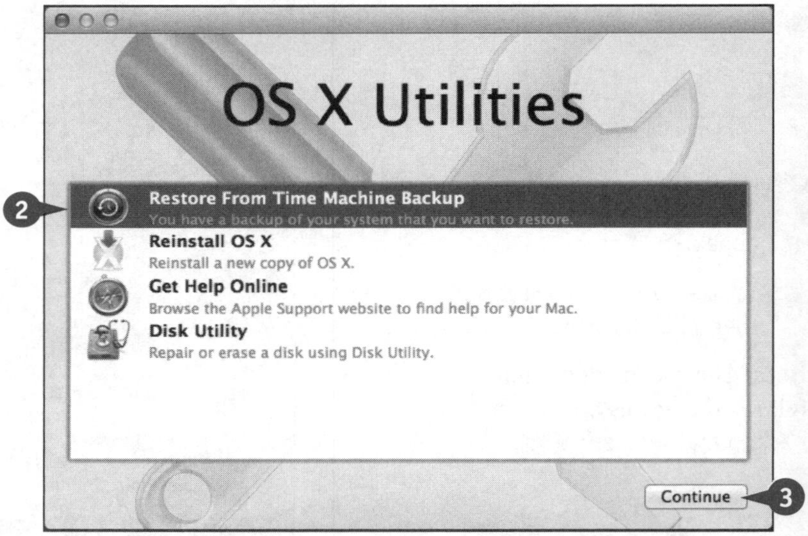

   The Select a Backup Source window appears.

5. Click the hard drive that contains your Time Machine backups.
6. Click **Continue**.

The Select a Backup window appears.

7 Click the backup you want to use for the restore.

8 Click **Continue**.

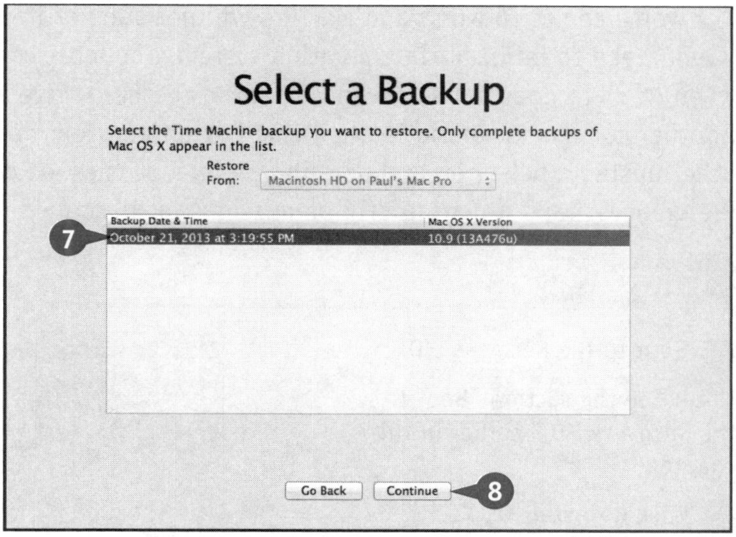

The Select a Destination window appears.

9 Click **Macintosh HD**.

10 Click **Restore**.

Mac Pro restores your system.

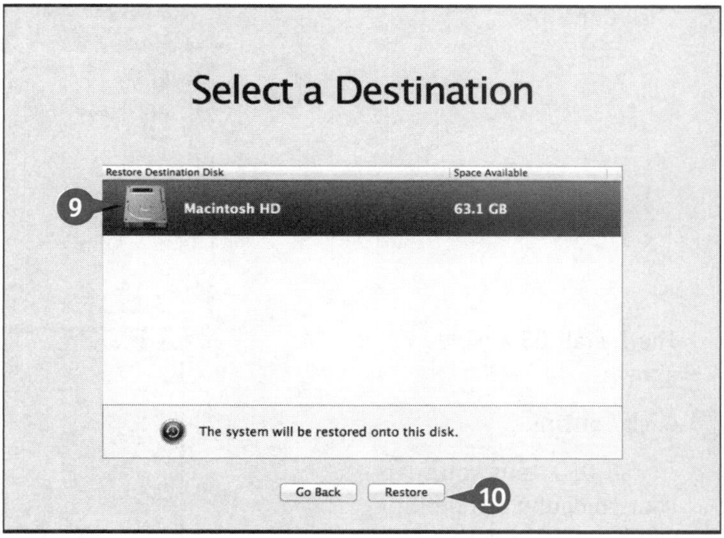

TIP

I cannot access the Recovery HD. Is it still possible to restore my system from a backup?

Yes, as long as you created an OS X Recovery Disk, as described in Chapter 16. In this case, you can boot to the OS X Recovery Disk to access the recovery tools and then follow steps 2 to 9 to restore your system.

Note, however, that not being able to access the Recovery HD is a sign that your Mac Pro hard drive might be having problems. After you restore your computer, you should use Disk Utility to repair the hard drive, as described in Chapter 15.

Reinstall OS X

If worse comes to worst and Mac Pro will not start or if your system is completely unstable, then you need to reinstall the operating system. The most common scenario for reinstalling OS X is when Mac Pro does not start, and repairing the hard drive as described in Chapter 15 has no effect. Another common scenario is when Mac Pro suffers from frequent lockups, application crashes, and other unstable behavior, and deleting preference files, as described in the section "Delete a Program's Preferences," and repairing disk permissions, as described in Chapter 15, have no effect.

Reinstall OS X

1. Boot to the Recovery HD.

Note: See the section "Boot to the Recovery HD," earlier in this chapter.

2. Click **Reinstall OS X**.
3. Click **Continue**.

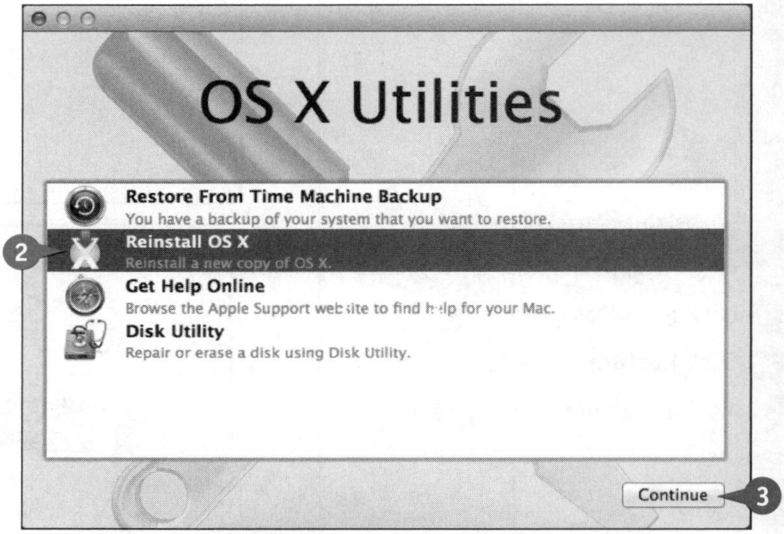

The Install OS X window appears.

4. Click **Continue**.

Install OS X tells you that your computer's eligibility will be verified with Apple.

5. Click **Continue**.

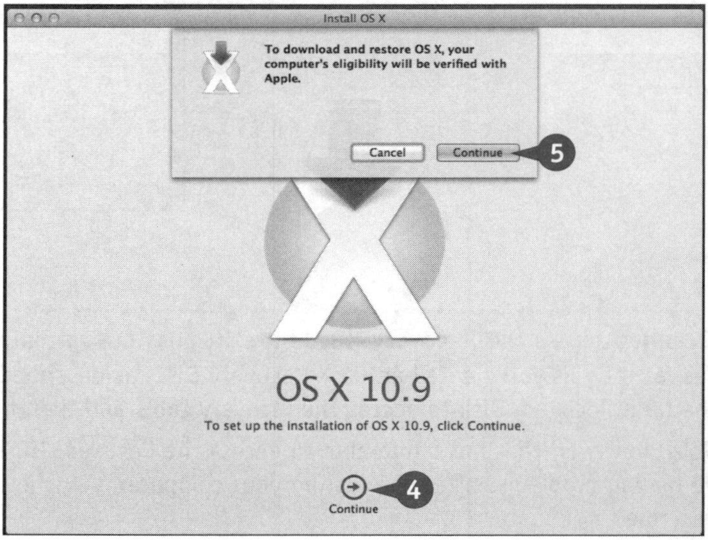

The OS X license terms appear.

6 Click **Agree**.

Install OS X asks you to confirm.

7 Click **Agree**.

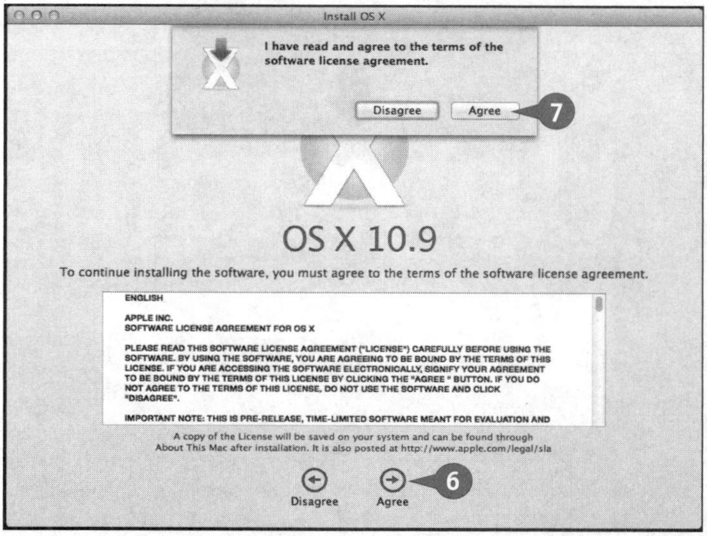

Install OS X asks you to select where you want OS X installed.

8 Click **Macintosh HD**.

9 Click **Install**.

OS X Install reinstalls OS X on Mac Pro.

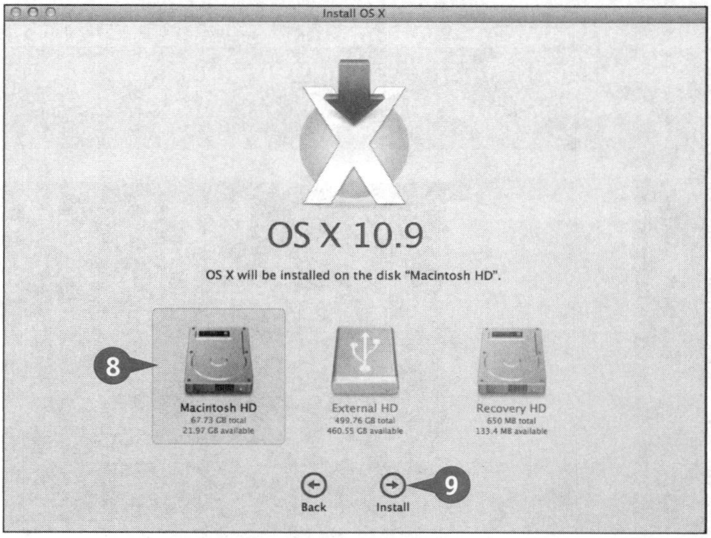

TIPS

Do I need to back up my data before reinstalling?
No, this is not usually necessary. The OS X Installer preserves your user accounts, settings, and data. However, it is a good general rule to back up your data before any major computer operation, so if you have access to Mac Pro, run a backup before reinstalling OS X.

Can I still access the Recovery HD if I replaced my Mac Pro hard drive?
No, when you are dealing with a brand new hard drive, the Recovery HD is available only after OS X has been reinstalled. However, if you created an OS X Recovery Disk, as described in Chapter 16, you can boot to that disk and install OS X from there.

CHAPTER 18

Upgrading Mac Pro

Your Mac Pro is a near-perfect machine right out of the box, but it might become less than perfect over time. On the hardware side, you might want to add more memory or put in a bigger hard drive. On the software side, you might want to install the newest versions of OS X and your apps. This chapter shows you how to upgrade your Mac Pro hardware and software.

Remove the Mac Pro Case

You can upgrade the Mac Pro memory and hard drive by removing the case to access Mac Pro's internal components. Unlike Mac notebooks such as the MacBook Pro and the MacBook Air, and unlike Mac desktops such as the iMac and Mac mini, the Mac Pro comes with an external case designed to allow for easy removal. You do not require any special tools or expertise, and it takes only a few seconds to open the case and close it again when you have finished working with Mac Pro's components.

Remove the Mac Pro Case

Remove the Case

1. Shut down Mac Pro if it is currently running.
2. Disconnect the Mac Pro power cord.
3. Turn Mac Pro so that you can see the back.
4. Slide the case latch to the right to release the case.

5. Lift the case straight up until it clears the top of the unit.

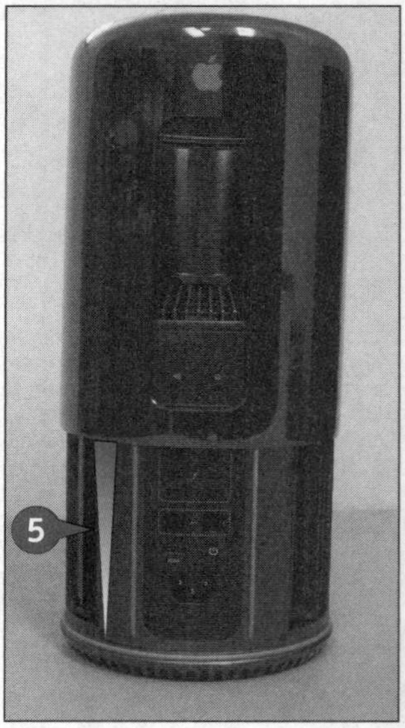

Close the Case

1. Position the case over the top of Mac Pro.
2. Line up the port openings on the case with the ports in back of Mac Pro.

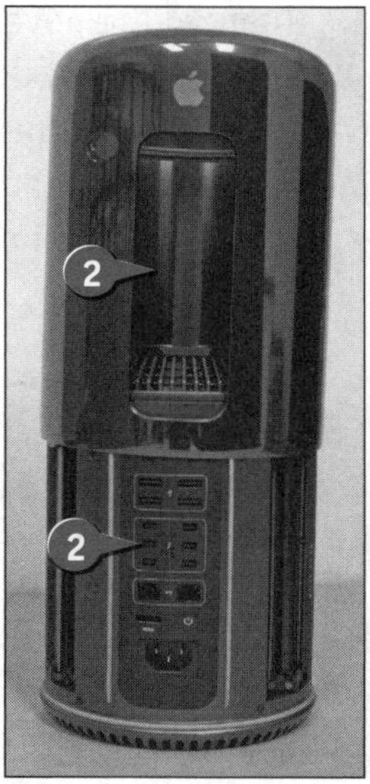

3. Carefully slide the case over Mac Pro until you hear the latch click into place.

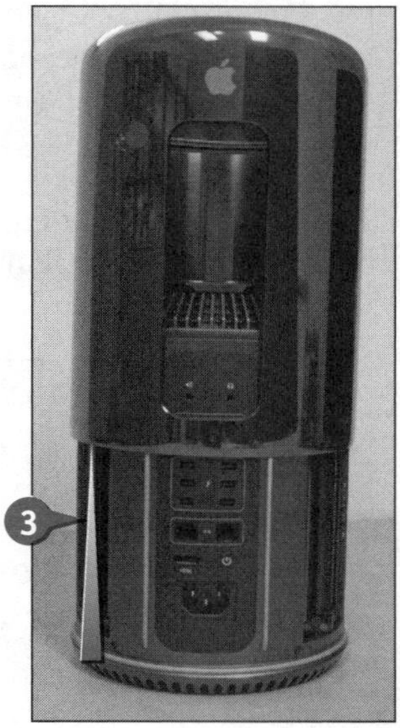

TIPS

Are there any safety issues associated with working inside my Mac Pro?
As long as you disconnect the power cable before opening the case, working inside Mac Pro presents no major safety issues. However, it is a good idea to wait for a couple of minutes after opening the case before beginning work to give hot internal components time to cool down.

Should I take any precautions to avoid damaging Mac Pro's internal components?
Before you touch anything inside Mac Pro, you should discharge your built-up static electricity by touching something metal to ground yourself. Also, do not have drinks or any other liquids nearby to avoid the danger of spillage. Finally, handle all components with care to avoid damaging them.

Review the Mac Pro's Internal Components

When you remove the Mac Pro case, you expose several of the machine's internal components. Although you do not need to know the name and purpose of every visible component to work with Mac Pro internally, you do need to know the location of those components you can change: the memory modules and the hard drive. Beyond that, Mac Pro is a marvel of engineering, so it is worthwhile to see how Apple managed to fit so much inside such a small package.

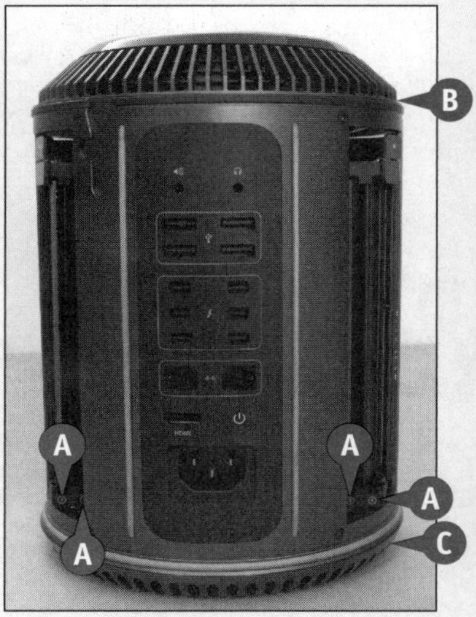

Ⓐ Memory

This component is the internal *random access memory* (*RAM*) that the Mac Pro processor uses to manipulate and store data from OS X and your applications. There are four memory slots, each of which contains a memory module. You can replace these memory modules, as described in the next section, "Upgrade the Memory."

Ⓑ Fan

Mac Pro is kept cool by a single fan at the top, which pulls air vertically through the machine, with the hot air generated by the components expelled through the top.

Ⓒ Intake

The Mac Pro fan not only expels hot air through the top, but it also brings in cool external air through a bottom intake grate.

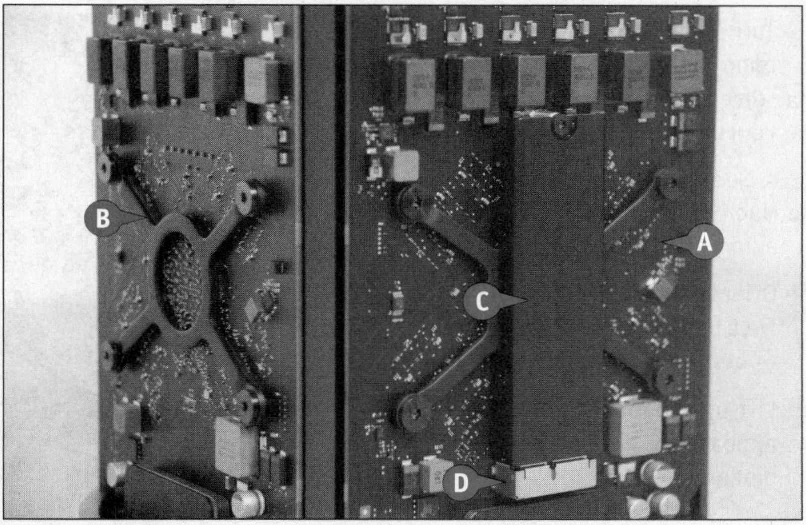

Ⓐ Graphics Card

This component contains the *graphics processing unit* (*GPU*), which is a dedicated processor for handling Mac Pro graphics. The graphics card also includes onboard *video random access memory* (*VRAM*) that enables the GPU to keep data in memory without using up system memory.

Ⓑ Second Graphics Card

Your Mac Pro comes with a second graphics card identical to the first and so offers twice the graphics performance.

Ⓒ Hard Drive

This is the solid-state drive (SSD) that Mac Pro uses as internal storage for OS X, your applications, and your data. You can replace this drive with another, as described in the section "Upgrade the Hard Drive."

Ⓓ Hard Drive Connector

This component connects the hard drive to the Mac Pro's input/output system, which the processor uses to move data to and from the hard drive.

Upgrade the Memory

The Mac Pro has four memory module sockets, two on one side of the rear ports and two on the other side of the ports. You need to upgrade your memory by using identical modules. The module sockets are numbered from 1 to 4, and you need to use up the module sockets in numeric order. For example, if you want to use only two sockets, then you must insert the memory modules in sockets 1 and 2. See the first tip in this section to learn what type of memory to use.

Upgrade the Memory

1. Turn off and unplug Mac Pro, remove the case, and touch something metal to ground yourself.

Note: See the section "Remove the Mac Pro Case" for the details on taking off the case.

2. Orient Mac Pro so that the first bank of memory modules (slots 1 and 2) is facing you.
3. Lift up the ejector tab that appears above the memory modules.

4. Carefully slide the memory module out of its socket.

5. Orient the new memory module over the memory socket so that the module's notch lines up with the socket's ridge.

6. Slide the memory module into the thin horizontal channels on the ends of the socket and then carefully press the module into place.
7. Repeat steps 4 to 6 to replace the other memory module.
8. Press the lever at the top of the modules to pivot the modules back into the locked position.
9. Repeat steps 3 to 8 to upgrade the other bank of memory modules, if needed.

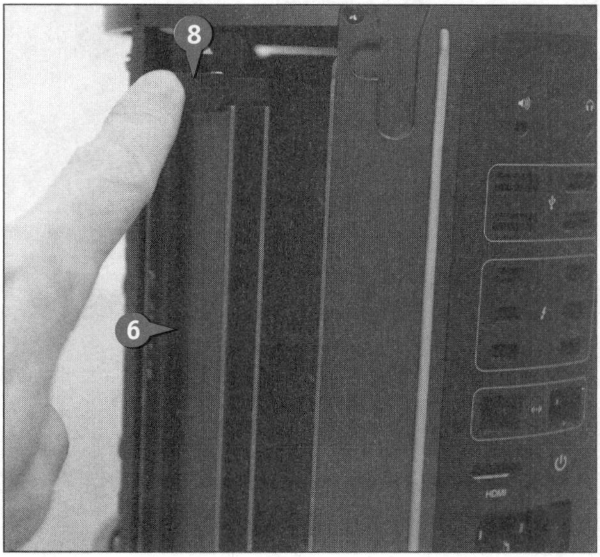

TIPS

What type of memory do I use for Mac Pro?
Your Mac Pro uses *double data rate 3* (*DDR3*) *error-correcting code* (ECC) memory that runs at 1866 megahertz (MHz). This type of memory is also sometimes advertised as PC3-15000 memory.

How much memory can I add to Mac Pro?
Your Mac Pro can store a maximum of 64GB of memory, which you implement by adding four memory modules of 16GB each. Other configurations that use all four memory module sockets are 32GB, which uses four 8GB memory modules, and 16GB, which uses four 4GB modules.

Upgrade the Hard Drive

Your Mac Pro comes with a single internal hard drive, which is mounted over one of the graphics cards. The hard drive is held in place by a single screw, so you can easily replace it with another drive if you require more capacity. See the tip in this section to learn what type of drive you should purchase. Remember that you will need to restore your system from a backup after installing the new drive; see Chapter 17.

Upgrade the Hard Drive

1. Turn off and unplug Mac Pro, remove the case, and touch something metal to ground yourself.

Note: See the section "Remove the Mac Pro Case" for the details on taking off the case.

2. Orient Mac Pro so that the hard drive is facing you.
3. Using a T8 Torx driver, remove the screw that holds the hard drive in place.

4. Remove the hard drive by carefully pulling it out of the connector.

5 Insert the new hard drive into the connector.

6 Insert the screw to hold the new hard drive in place.

TIP

What type of hard drive do I need to use in Mac Pro?

Your Mac Pro requires a solid-state drive (SSD) that uses flash memory for storage. This differs from a regular hard drive in that it has no moving parts and is faster than a traditional hard drive. The interface connection the flash drive uses is based on *Peripheral Component Interconnect Express*, which is often abbreviated either as *PCI Express* or as *PCIe*. Mac Pro flash drives are stored on a special card, so be sure to purchase a drive advertised as being compatible with Mac Pro.

Update OS X

To make sure that OS X is currently up to date with the latest features and fixes, you can update the software. Apple makes OS X updates available from time to time. These updates fix problems, add new features, and resolve security issues. You can reduce computer problems and maximize online safety by installing these updates as they become available. OS X displays a notification when new updates are ready, and you can initiate the update either by using that notification or by using the App Store.

Update OS X

Install All Available Updates

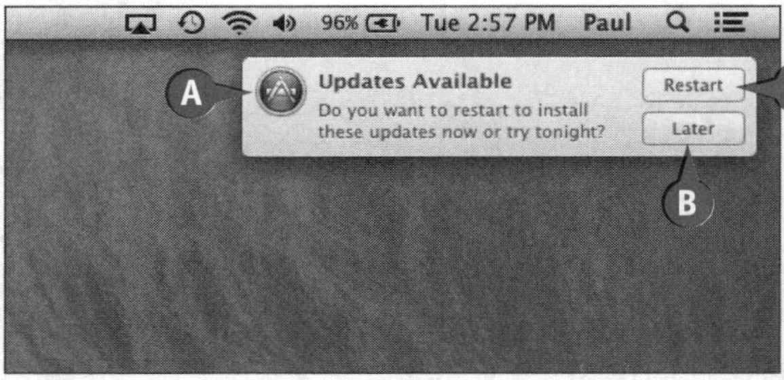

Ⓐ This notification appears when updates become available.

❶ Click **Restart**.

Mac Pro restarts and then installs the OS X updates.

Ⓑ If you do not want to perform the update now, you can click **Later** and then click when you want to be reminded.

Install Selected Updates

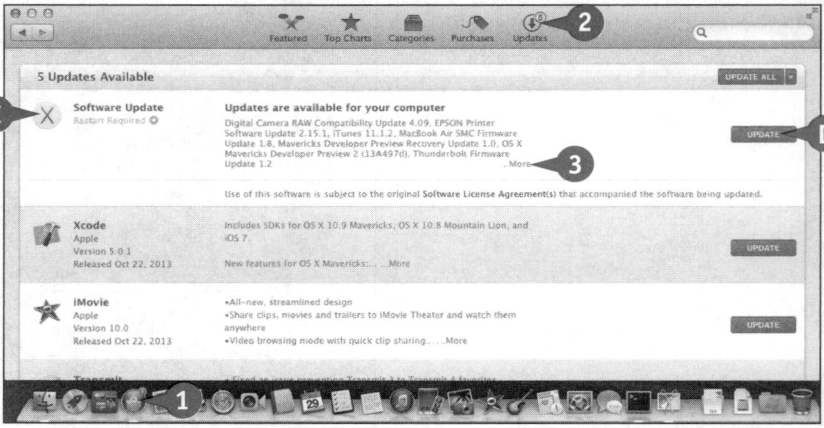

❶ Click **App Store** (App Store icon).

The App Store appears.

❷ Click **Updates**.

The App Store connects with the Apple servers and checks for new updates.

Ⓒ OS X updates appear here.

Ⓓ If you want to install all the available OS X updates, click this **Update** button. Skip to step 5.

❸ Click **More**.

The App Store displays the list of available OS X updates.

E If you install any updates that say Restart Required, Mac Pro will restart automatically to complete the installation.

4 Click **Update** beside the update you want to install.

F The App Store displays the update download and install progress.

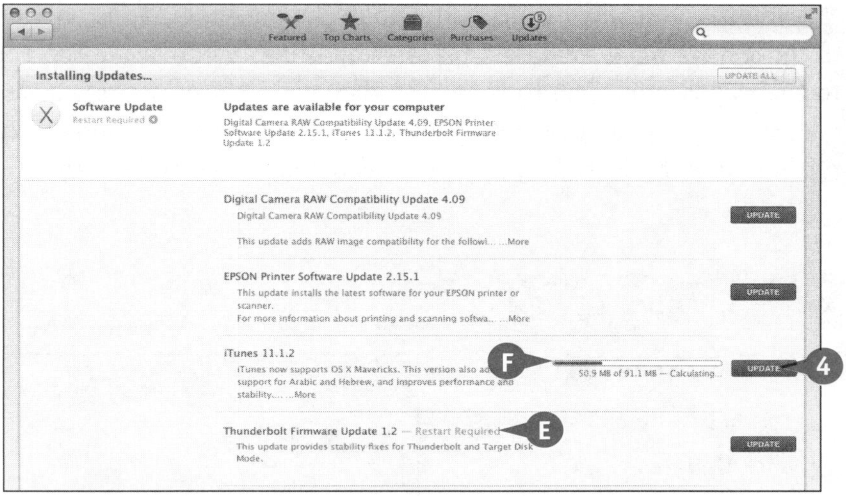

For some updates, your Mac Pro prompts you to restart the computer.

5 If you have any unsaved work, save and close those documents.

6 Click **Restart**.

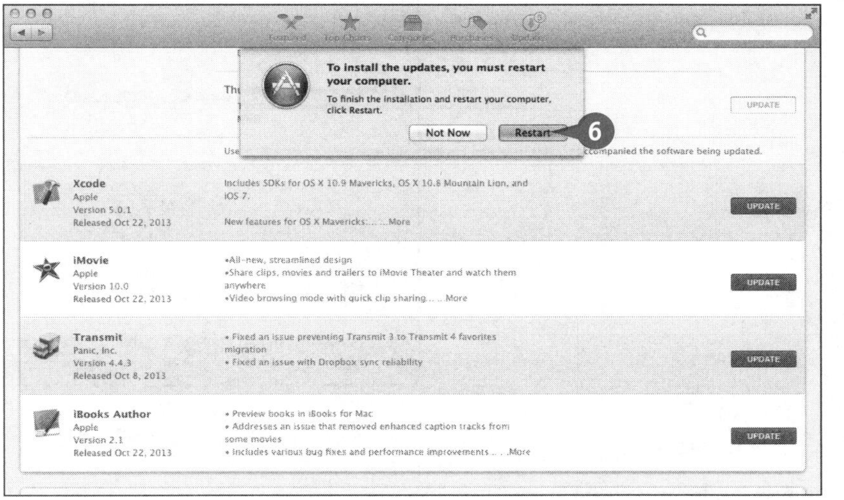

TIPS

Should I always install every available update?

As a general rule, yes. However, some exceptions exist. For example, if an update is available for a device that you no longer use, you can safely skip that update. Also, if your Internet connection is slow, you may prefer to install the updates one at a time.

Is the Mavericks Update important?

Yes, any update named Mavericks Update is very important. These are major updates to your Mac Pro's operating system, and they generally improve system stability and security. Because such an update affects your entire Mac and is usually quite large — often several hundred megabytes — it is best to install this update on its own.

Update Third-Party Apps

If you have installed third-party (that is, non-Apple) apps on your Mac Pro, you can ensure that those apps have the latest features and fixes by updating the apps. Most developers create updates to their apps from time to time, and they make those updates available via the App Store. These updates fix bugs, implement new features, and more, so you can ensure that your apps continue to run smoothly by installing app updates as they become available.

Update Third-Party Apps

1. Click **App Store** (![App Store icon]).

   The App Store appears.

2. Click **Updates**.

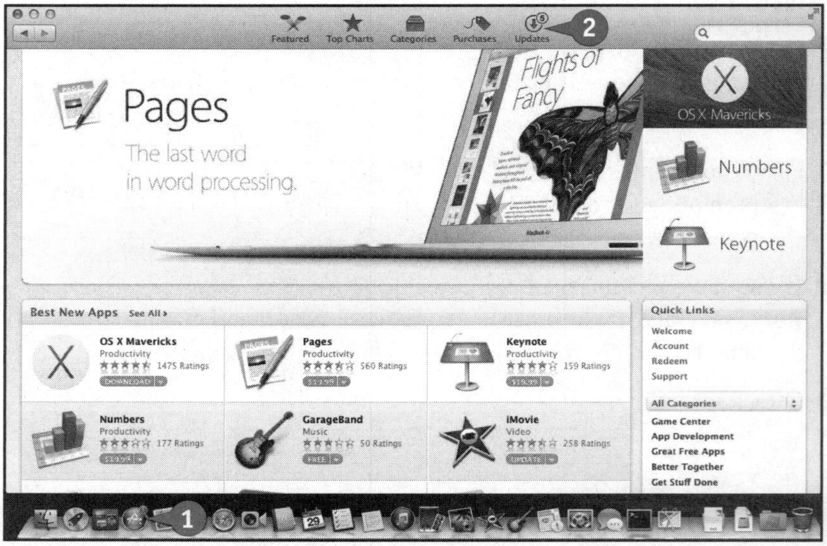

The App Store checks for new updates.

A App updates appear here.

B If you want to install all the available updates, click **Update All**. Skip to step **4**.

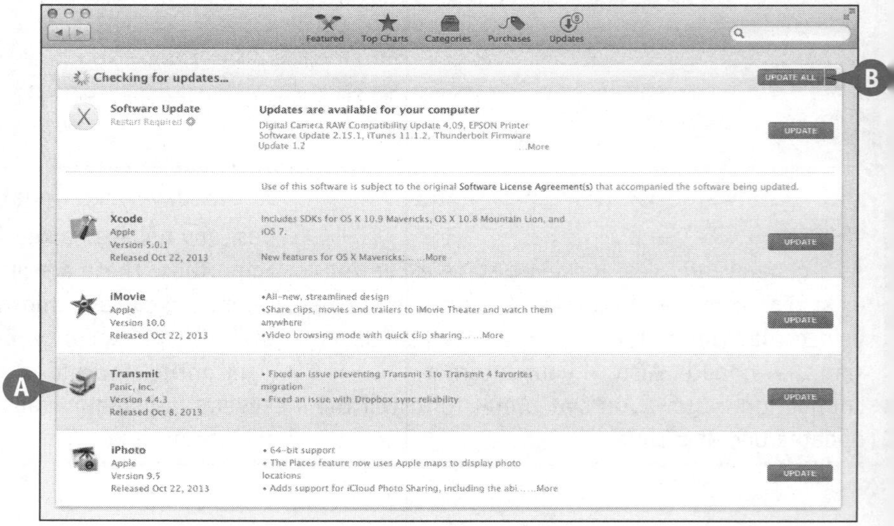

App Store displays the list of available app updates.

C To find out more information about an update, click **More**.

3 Click **Update** beside the app update you want to install.

4 If the App Store asks you to sign in, type your App Store password.

5 Click **Accept**.

D The App Store displays the update download and install progress.

6 Repeat step **3** for each app you want to update.

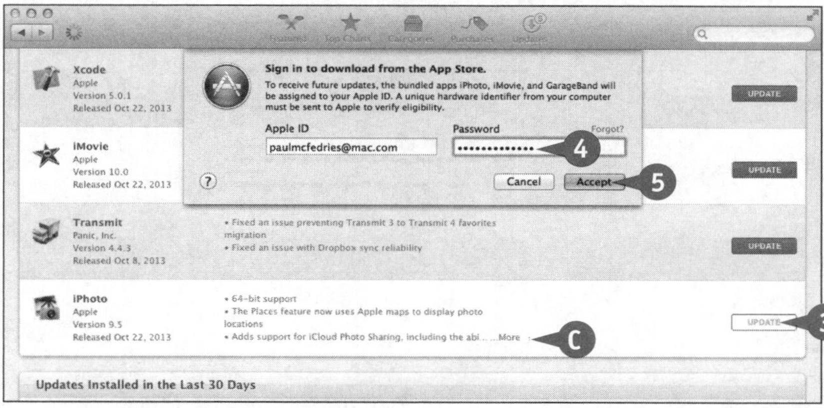

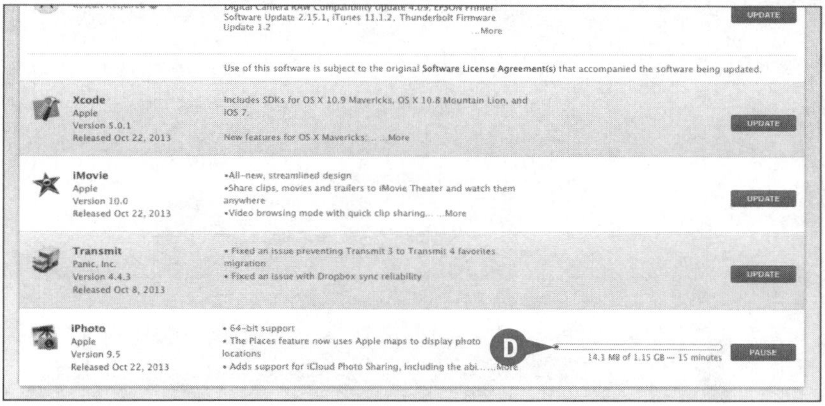

TIPS

Is there a way to have apps updated automatically?

Yes, you can configure Mac Pro to download and install app updates automatically. This is useful if you have many apps installed and do not want to check constantly for updates. In the Dock, click **System Preferences** (), click **App Store**, and then select the **Install app updates** option (☐ changes to ☑).

Are all third-party apps updated via the App Store?

No, some apps come with their own updating mechanisms. For example, most versions of the Microsoft Office productivity suite and most software Adobe makes come with their own software updating tools. These normally run on an automatic schedule, such as once per week.

CHAPTER 19

Securing Mac Pro

Threats to your computing-related security and privacy often come from the Internet and from someone simply using your Mac Pro while you are not around. To protect yourself and your family, you need to understand these threats and know what you can do to thwart them.

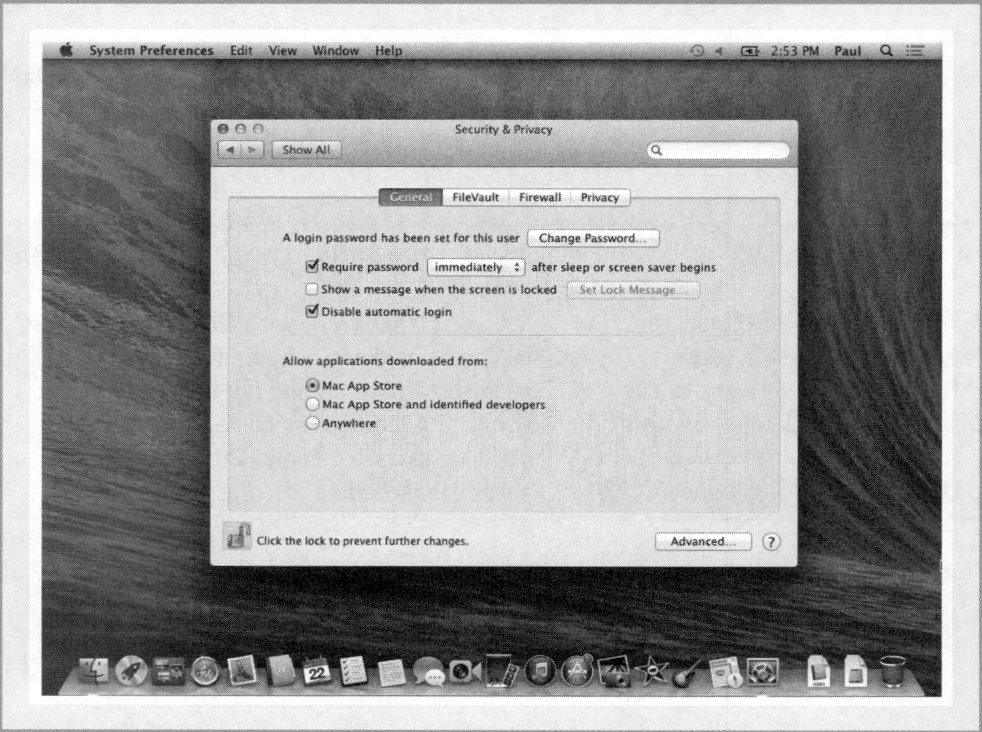

Change Your Password

You can make Mac Pro more secure by changing your password. For example, if you turn on file sharing, as described in Chapter 21, you can configure each shared folder so that only someone who knows your password can get full access to that folder. Similarly, you should change your password if other network users know your current password and you no longer want them to have access to your shared folders. Finally, you should also change your password if you feel that your current password is not secure enough. See the tip to learn how to create a secure password.

Change Your Password

1. Click **System Preferences** (⚙).

   The System Preferences appear.

2. Click **Users & Groups**.

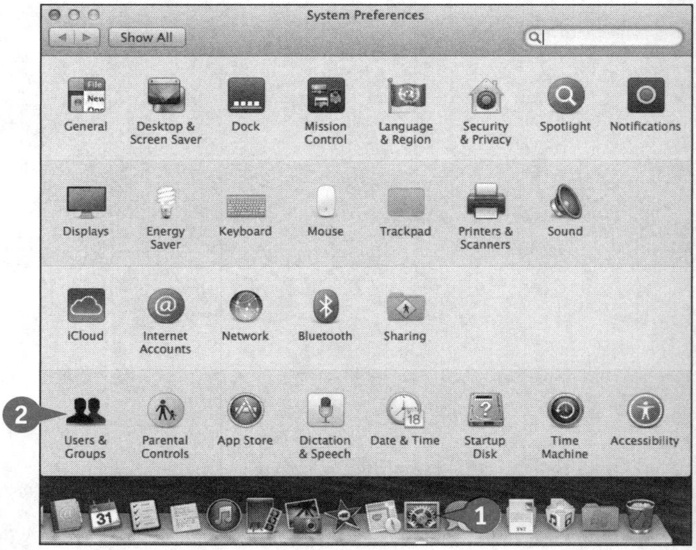

The Users & Groups preferences appear.

A. Your user account is selected automatically.

B. If you want to work with a different user account, you must click the lock icon (🔒), type your administrator password (🔒 changes to 🔓), and then click the account.

3. Click **Change Password**.

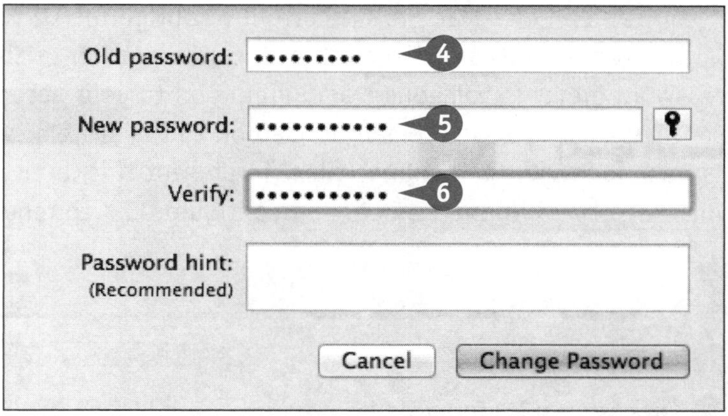

The Change Password dialog appears.

4 Type your current password.

5 Type your new password.

6 Retype the new password.

7 Type a hint that Mac Pro will display if you forget the password.

Note: Construct the hint in such a way that it makes the password easy for you to recall, but hard for a potential snoop to guess.

8 Click **Change Password**.

Mac Pro changes your password.

TIP

How do I create a secure password?

Follow these steps:

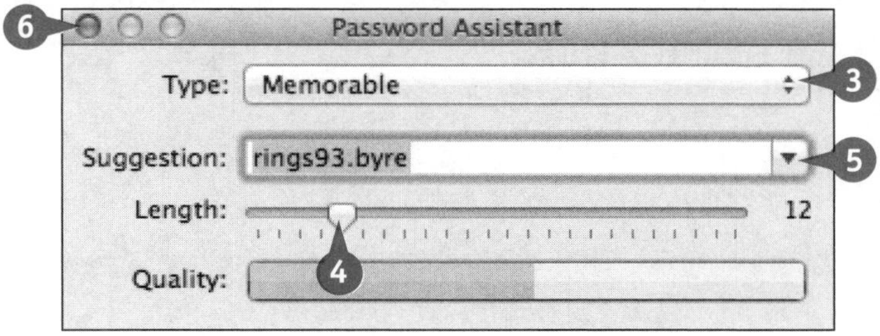

1 Follow steps 1 to 4 in this section.

2 Click the **Password Assistant** icon ( ).

The Password Assistant dialog appears.

3 Click the **Type** and then click a password type.

4 Click and drag the **Length** slider to set the password length you want to use.

5 Click the **Suggestion** and then click the password you want to use.

6 Click **Close** ( ).

Require a Password on Waking

You can enhance Mac Pro's security by configuring OS X to ask for your user account password when the system wakes up from either the screen saver or sleep mode. Protecting your account with a password prevents someone from logging on to your account, but what happens when you leave Mac Pro unattended? If you remain logged on to the system, any person who sits down at your computer can use it to view and change files. To prevent this, activate the screen saver or sleep mode before you leave Mac Pro unattended, and configure OS X to require a password on waking.

Require a Password on Waking

1. Click the **Apple** icon (■).
2. Click **System Preferences**.

   You can also click **System Preferences** (■) in the Dock.

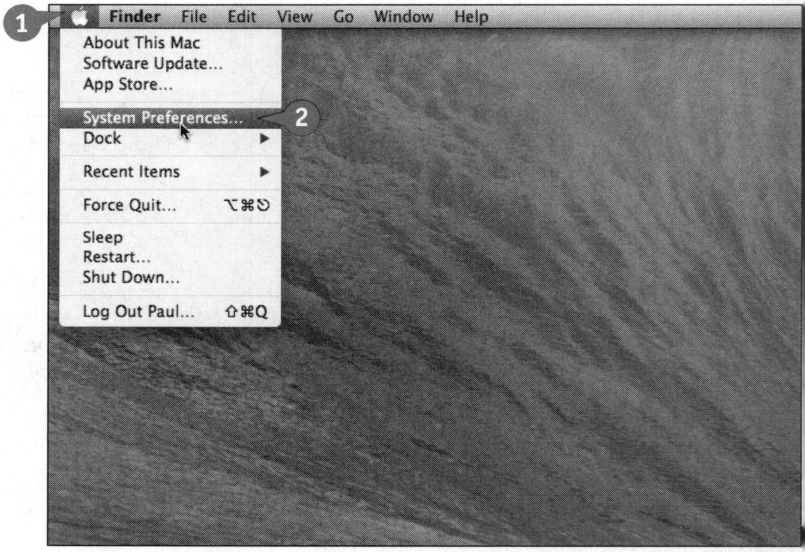

The System Preferences appear.

3. Click **Security & Privacy**.

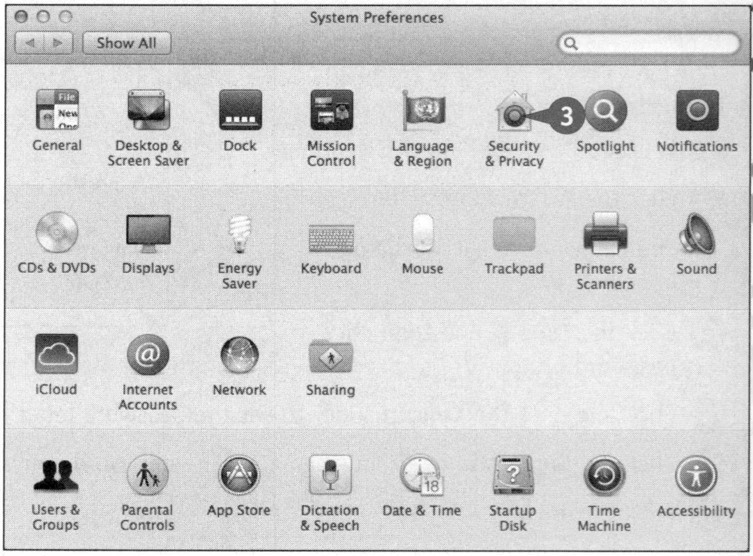

The Security & Privacy preferences appear.

4 Click the **General** tab.

5 Select the **Require password** option (☐ changes to ☑).

6 Click **Close** (■).

Mac Pro puts the new setting into effect.

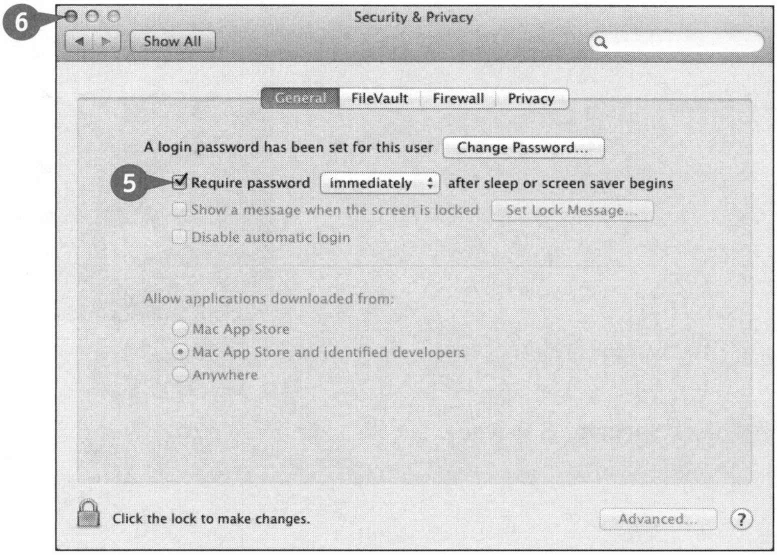

TIPS

How do I activate the screen saver or sleep mode before I leave Mac Pro unattended?
Configure a hot corner to automatically enable the screen saver, as described Chapter 14. To put your Mac Pro display to sleep, press Control + Shift + ⏏. To engage full sleep mode, click the **Apple** icon (■) and then click **Sleep**.

If I engage the screen saver or sleep mode accidentally, entering my password is a hassle. Is there a workaround for this?
Yes, you can tell Mac Pro to not require the password as soon as the screen saver or sleep mode is activated. Follow steps 1 to 5, click the **Require password** ⬍, and then click the amount of time you want Mac Pro to wait.

Disable Automatic Logins

You can enhance Mac Pro security by preventing OS X from logging in your user account automatically. If you are the only person who uses your Mac Pro, you can configure OS X to automatically log in your account. This saves time at startup by avoiding the login screen, but it opens a security hole. If a snoop or other malicious user has access to your Mac Pro, that person can start the computer and gain access to your documents, settings, web browsing history, and network. To prevent this, configure OS X to disable the automatic login.

Disable Automatic Logins

1. Click the **Apple** icon (■).
2. Click **System Preferences**.

   You can also click **System Preferences** (⚙) in the Dock.

   The System Preferences appear.

3. Click **Security & Privacy**.

The Security & Privacy preferences appear.

4. Click the lock icon (🔒).

   Mac Pro prompts you for your administrator password.

5. Type the administrator password.

6. Click **Unlock**.

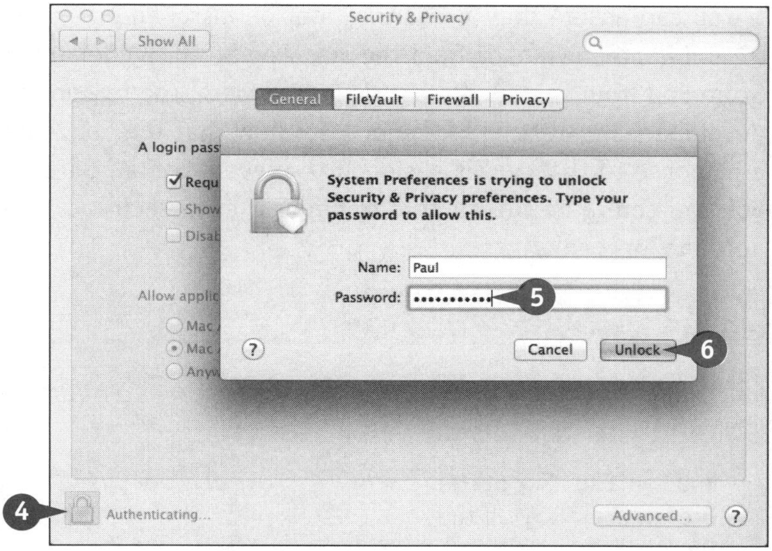

Mac Pro unlocks the preferences (🔒 changes to 🔓).

7. Click the **General** tab.

8. Select the **Disable automatic login** option (☐ changes to ☑).

9. Click **Close** (●).

   Mac Pro puts the new setting into effect.

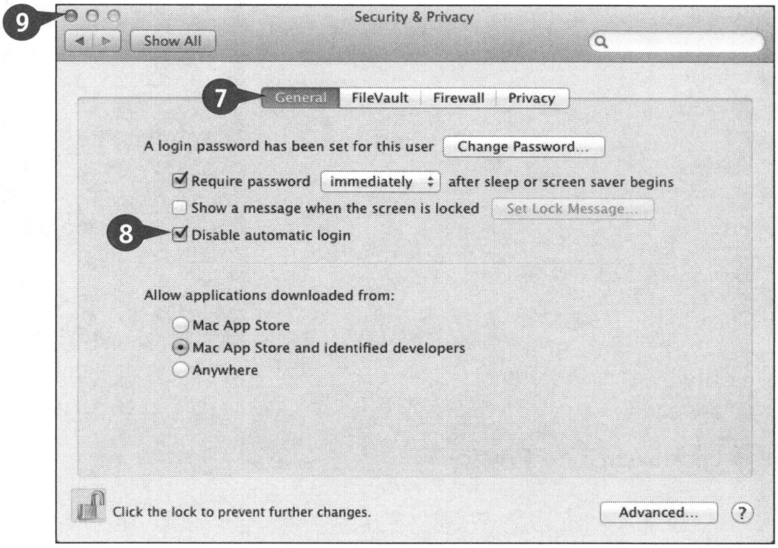

TIP

Is there a way to get Mac Pro to log out my account automatically?

Yes, you can configure the system to log you out of your account when Mac Pro has been idle for a specified amount of time. Follow steps **1** to **7** to unlock and display the General tab and then click **Advanced.** In the dialog that appears, select the **Log out after *X* minutes of inactivity** option (☐ changes to ☑) and then use the spin box to set the amount of idle time after which Mac Pro logs you out automatically. You can select a time as short as 5 minutes and as long as 960 minutes. Click **OK** to put the setting into effect.

Configure App Downloads

You can ensure that malware cannot be installed on Mac Pro by configuring the system to allow only app downloads from the Mac App Store. By default, Mac Pro allows downloads from the App Store and from so-called *identified developers*. The reason for this heightened security is that malware developers are starting to target Macs now that they have become so popular. The extra security is a response to that and is designed to prevent users from accidentally installing malware. However, you can configure this feature to be even more secure, which is useful if you are setting up a user account for a child.

Configure App Downloads

1. Click the **Apple** icon (🍎).
2. Click **System Preferences**.

   You can also click **System Preferences** (⚙) in the Dock.

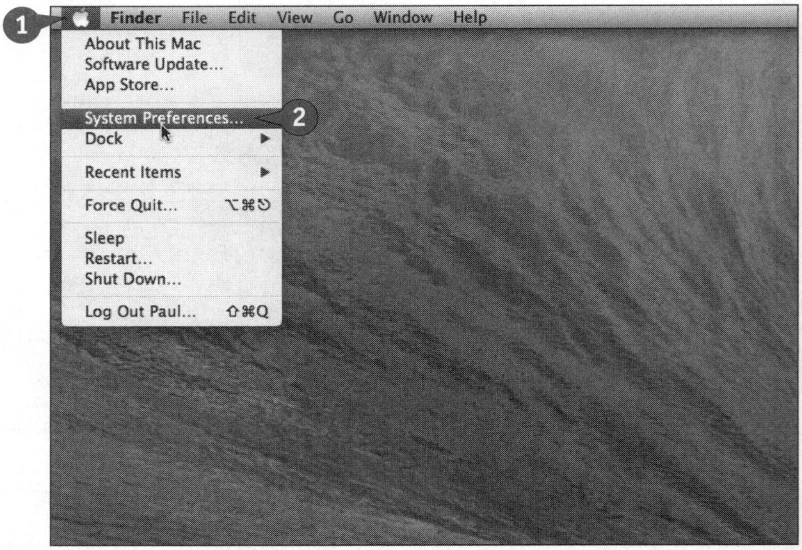

The System Preferences appear.

3. Click **Security & Privacy**.

The Security & Privacy preferences appear.

4 Click the lock icon ().

Mac Pro prompts you for your administrator password.

5 Type the administrator password.

6 Click **Unlock**.

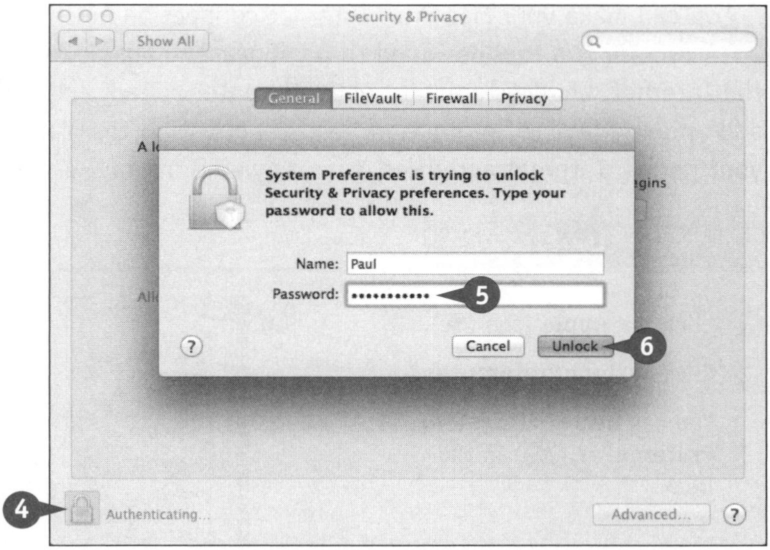

Mac Pro unlocks the preferences (changes to).

7 Click the **General** tab.

8 Select the **Mac App Store** option (changes to).

9 Click **Close** ().

Mac Pro puts the new setting into effect.

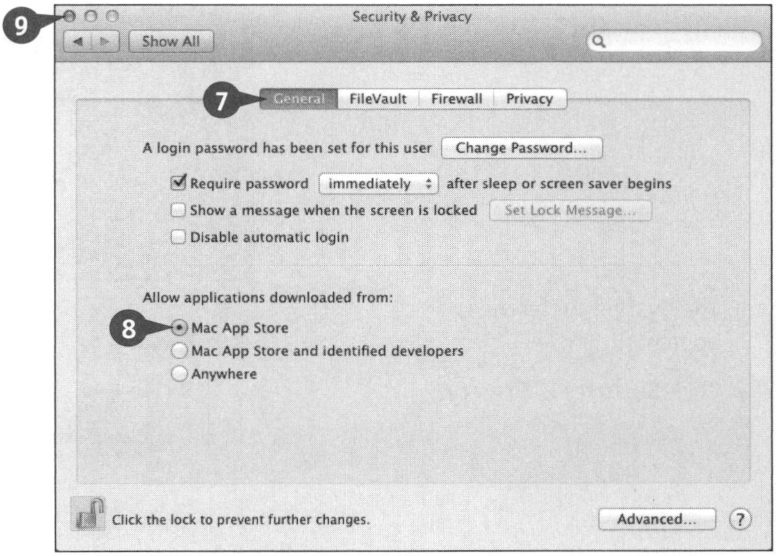

TIPS

What is an identified developer?
An identified developer is one who has registered with Apple and has been given a security certificate for digitally signing apps, thus certifying where the apps came from. There is a possibility that a malicious developer could spoof a digitally signed app, so allowing only App Store apps is the safest option.

How can I install an app that I downloaded from the web?
If you are absolutely certain the app is legitimate — that is, it was created by a reputable developer and you purchased it from a reputable dealer — you can temporarily allow it to be installed. Follow steps **1** to **7**, select the **Anywhere** option (changes to), and then install your app. Then follow steps **1** to **9** to restore the secure setting.

Turn On the Firewall

You can make your Mac Pro's Internet connection much more secure by turning on the OS X firewall. A *firewall* is a tool designed to prevent malicious users from accessing a computer connected to the Internet. Chances are your network router already implements a hardware firewall, but you can add an extra layer of protection by also activating the Mac Pro software firewall. This will not affect your normal Internet activities, such as web browsing, e-mailing, and instant messaging.

Turn On the Firewall

1. Click the **Apple** icon (🍎).
2. Click **System Preferences.**

   You can also click **System Preferences** (⚙) in the Dock.

The System Preferences appear.

3. Click **Security & Privacy.**

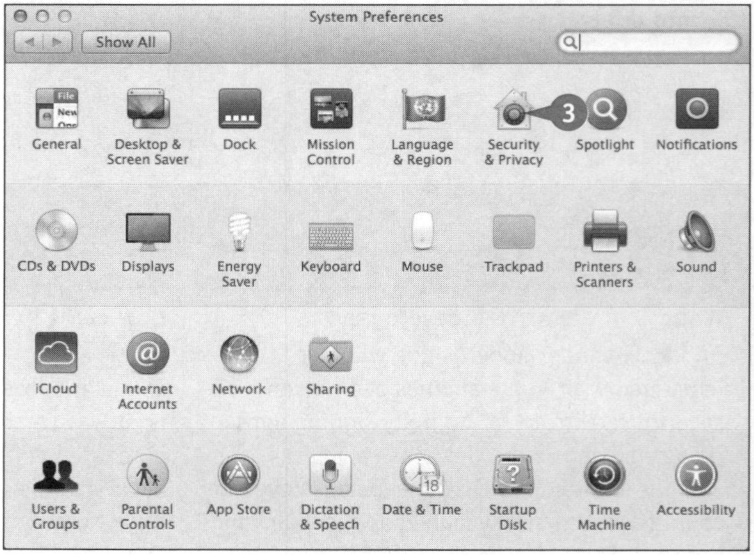

The Security & Privacy preferences appear.

4 Click the lock icon ( ).

Mac Pro prompts you for your administrator password.

5 Type the administrator password.

6 Click **Unlock**.

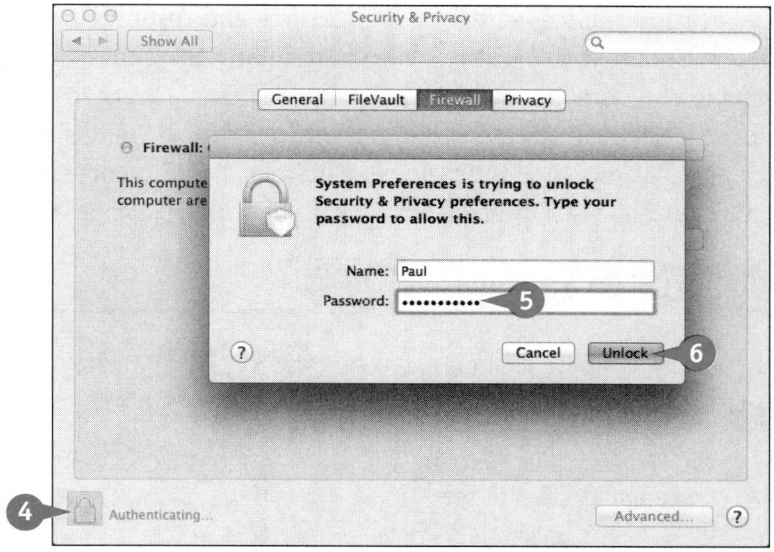

Mac Pro unlocks the preferences (changes to).

7 Click the **Firewall** tab.

8 Click **Turn On Firewall**.

9 Click **Close** ( ).

Mac Pro puts the new setting into effect.

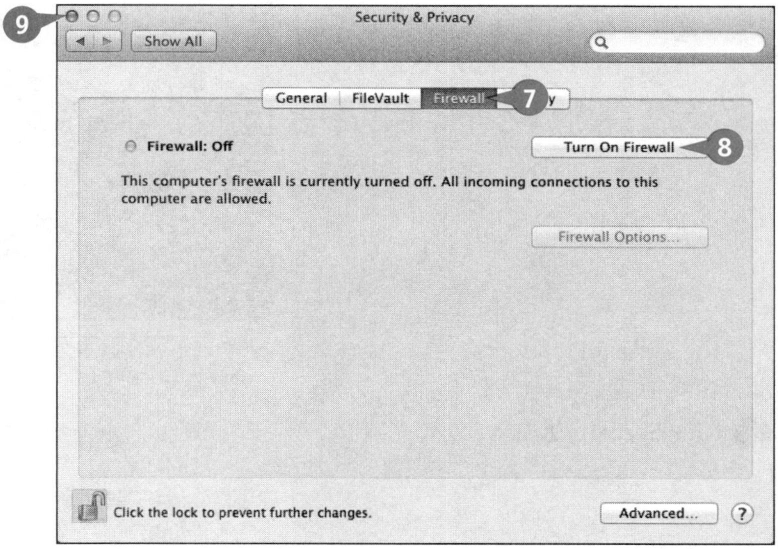

TIPS

Can I prevent malicious users from finding my computer over the Internet?

Yes. Malicious users often probe for connected machines, which they then test for vulnerabilities. You can put Mac Pro into *stealth mode*, which hides it from these probes. Follow steps 1 to 7, click **Firewall Options**, select the **Enable stealth mode** option (changes to), and then click **OK**.

With the Firewall on, can I still use Internet applications such as my FTP program?

Mac Pro allows digitally signed apps to receive connections, but if you want to use an Internet app that is not digitally signed, you must add it as an exception. Follow steps 1 to 7, click **Firewall Options**, click **Add** ( ), click the application you want to use, and then click **Add**.

Configure Location Services

Location services refers to the features and technologies that provide apps and system tools with access to location data, particularly the current location of your Mac Pro. This is a handy and useful thing, but it is also something that you need to keep under your control because your location data, especially your current location, is fundamentally private and should not be given to applications thoughtlessly. Fortunately, Mac Pro comes with a few tools for controlling and configuring location services.

Configure Location Services

1. Click the **Apple** icon ( ).
2. Click **System Preferences**.

   You can also click **System Preferences** ( ) in the Dock.

   The System Preferences appear.

3. Click **Security & Privacy**.

The Security & Privacy preferences appear.

4 Click the lock icon ( ).

Mac Pro prompts you for your administrator password.

5 Type the administrator password.

6 Click **Unlock**.

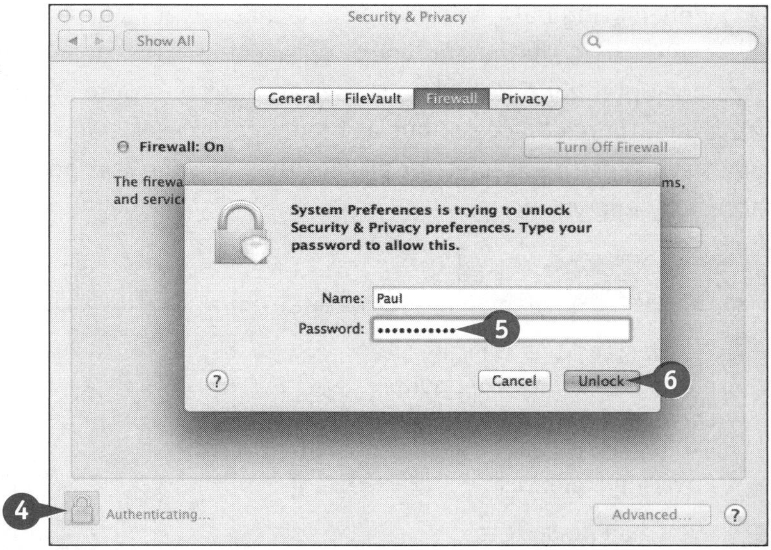

Mac Pro unlocks the preferences (changes to).

7 Click the **Privacy** tab.

8 Click **Location Services.**

9 Deselect the check box beside each app that you do not want to determine your location (changes to).

10 Click **Close** ( ).

Mac Pro puts the new setting into effect.

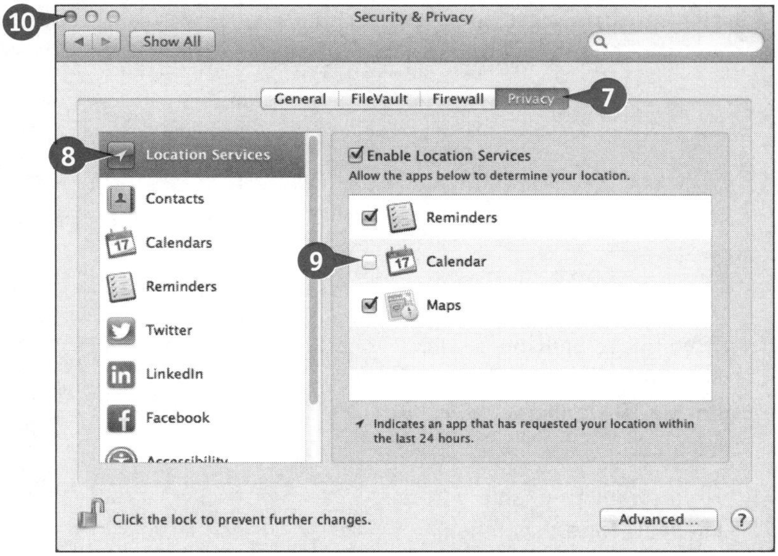

TIPS

How does the location services feature know my location?

Location services uses several bits of data to determine your location. First, it looks for known Wi-Fi networks that are near your location. Second, if you are connected to the Internet, it uses the location information embedded in your unique Internet Protocol (IP) address.

Can I turn off location services?

Yes. Follow steps 1 to 7 to unlock and display the Privacy tab. Click **Location Services** and then deselect the **Enable Location Services** option (changes to). Note, however, that by turning off location services, you disable many features in apps such as Reminders and Maps.

Encrypt Your Data

By encrypting data, you can ensure that a malicious user who has physical access to your Mac Pro cannot read the files in your user account. This means that your data appears as gibberish until it is decrypted by entering your user account password. Your password protects your user account from unauthorized access, but a sophisticated user can still access your data by using special tools. If you have sensitive, secret, or private files in your user account, you can protect that data from such access by encrypting it.

Encrypt Your Data

1. Follow steps **1** to **6** in the previous section, "Configure Location Services," to display and unlock the Security & Privacy preferences.
2. Click the **FileVault** tab.
3. Click **Turn On FileVault**.

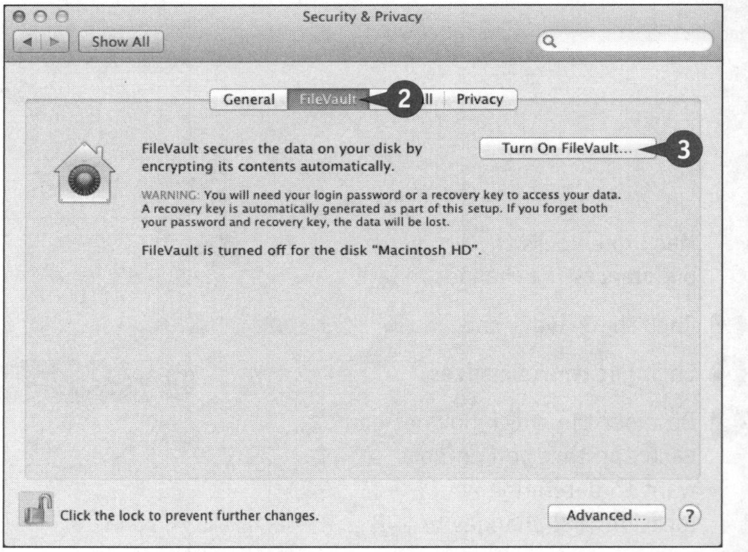

If you have multiple users, Mac Pro prompts you to enable FileVault for the other accounts.

- **A** If you want to enable FileVault for a user, click **Enable User**, type the account password, and then click **OK**.

4. Click **Continue**.

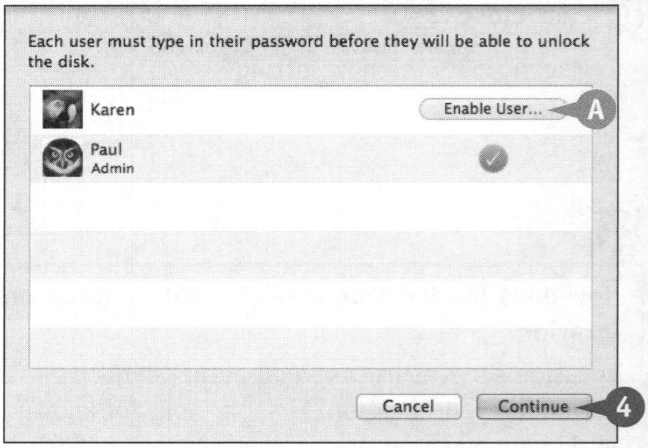

Mac Pro displays a recovery key.

5 Click **Continue**.

The recovery key is a "safety net" which can be used to unlock the disk if you forget your password.
Make a copy and store it in a safe place. If you forget your password and lose the recovery key, all the data on your disk will be lost.
CX43-V4H6-LUXD-Z4EC-B4JW-G8WV
?
Cancel
What is the middle name of your oldest sibling?
Griselda
*Apple can only decrypt the recovery key using exact answers. If you cannot provide these answers, then Apple will be unable to access the key. Answer attempts may be restricted. Apple is not responsible for failing to provide the recovery key. Fees may apply, subject to support eligibility.
Back
Continue
5

6 Select the **Store the recovery key with Apple** option (changes to).

7 For each of the three security questions, click to select a question and then type the answer.

8 Click **Continue**.

Mac Pro prompts you to restart the computer.

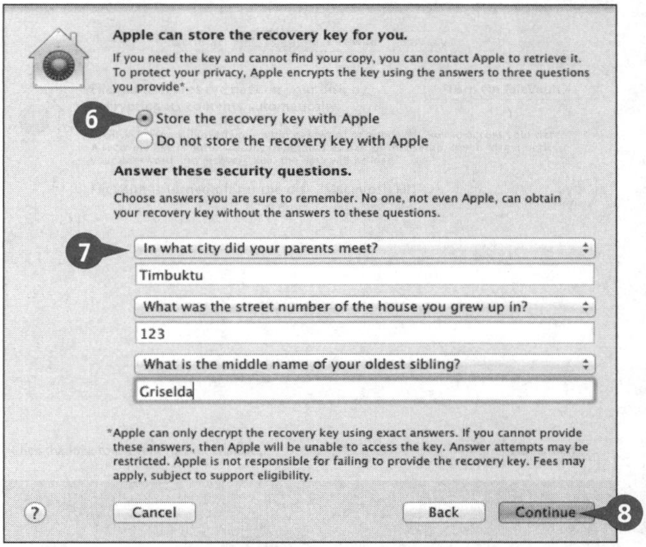

If you need the key and cannot find your copy, you can contact Apple to retrieve it. To protect your privacy, Apple encrypts the key using the answers to three questions you provide*.

Choose answers you are sure to remember. No one, not even Apple, can obtain your recovery key without the answers to these questions.

In what city did your parents meet?
Timbuktu
What was the street number of the house you grew up in?

9 Click **Restart**.

Mac Pro restarts and begins encrypting your user account data.

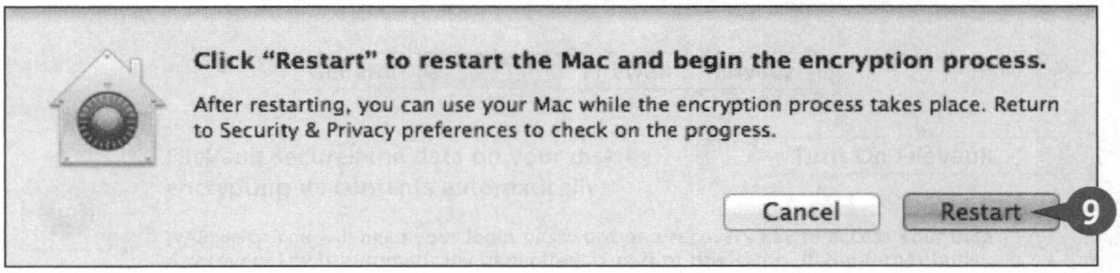
Click "Restart" to restart the Mac and begin the encryption process.
After restarting, you can use your Mac while the encryption process takes place. Return to Security & Privacy preferences to check on the progress.
Cancel
Restart
9

TIPS

Do I have to store the recovery key with Apple?
No, this is not necessary. Instead, you can write down the recovery key and then, in step **6**, select the **Do not store the recovery key with Apple** option (changes to). Continue with steps **8** and **9** to begin the encryption. Be sure to store the recovery key in a secure, offsite location, such as a safety deposit box. If you lose the recovery key, you will lose access to your data.

Does encryption change how I work with my files?
No. After Mac Pro has finished encrypting your user account files, you will not notice any differences. Mac Pro also decrypts your files extremely quickly, so you will not see a performance drop after encryption.

CHAPTER 20

Working with iCloud

You can get a free iCloud account, which is a web-based service that gives you e-mail, an address book, and a calendar. You can also use iCloud to automatically synchronize data between iCloud and your Mac Pro (as well as your iPhone, iPad, iPod touch, and other iCloud-synced computers).

Create an Apple ID

To use iCloud, you need to create a free Apple ID, which you use to sign in to iCloud on the web and to synchronize your Mac Pro and other devices. An Apple ID is an e-mail address. You can use an existing e-mail address for your Apple ID, or you can sign up for a new iCloud e-mail address, which uses the icloud.com domain name. If you use an existing e-mail address, you are required to verify via e-mail that the address is legitimate.

Create an Apple ID

1. Click **System Preferences** (⚙).

   The System Preferences appear.

2. Click **iCloud**.

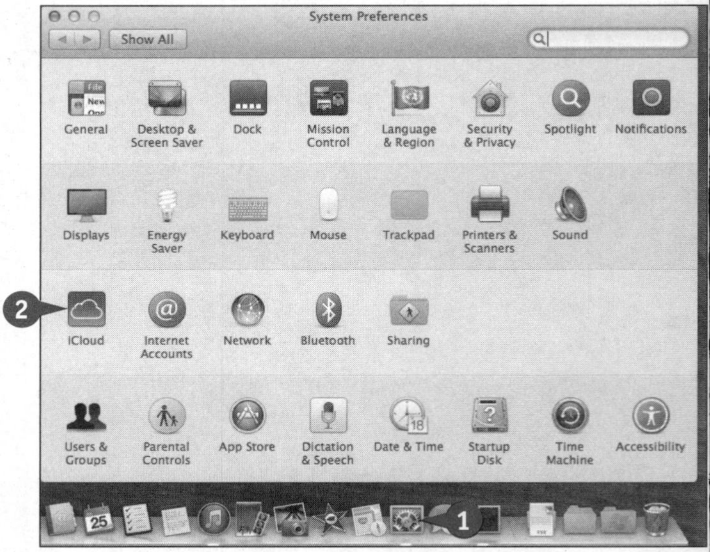

The iCloud preferences appear.

3. Click **Create an Apple ID**.

The Create an Apple ID dialog appears.

4 Click and use the **Location** pop-up menu to choose your country.

5 Click and use the three **Birthday** pop-up menus to choose your month, day, and year of birth.

6 Click **Next**.

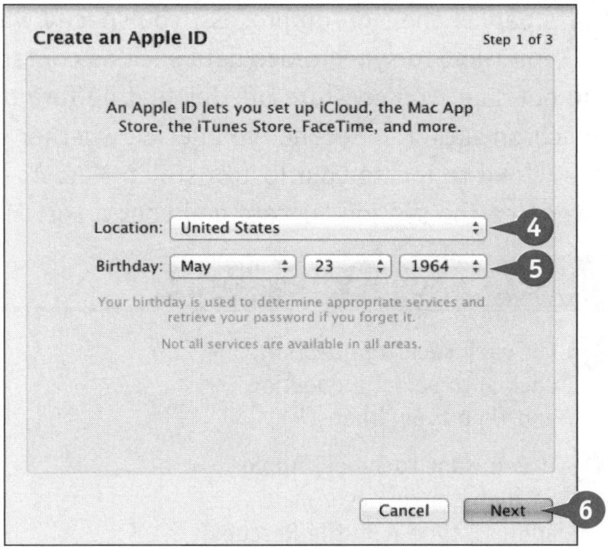

7 Select the **Get a free iCloud email address** option (○ changes to ◉).

A If you prefer to use an existing address, select the **Use an existing email address** option (○ changes to ◉) instead.

8 Type the address.

9 Type your name.

10 Type the password.

11 Click **Next**.

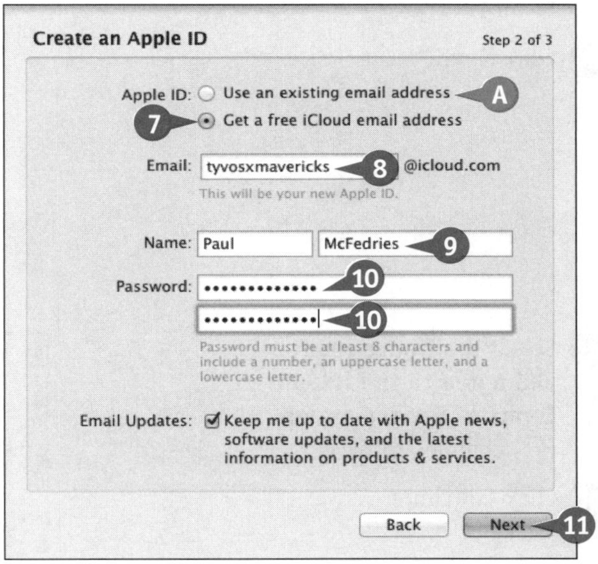

TIP

If I do not want to create a new iCloud address, can I use any e-mail address?
Yes, as long as the address belongs to you. Also, you need to be able to retrieve and read messages sent to that address, because this is part of the verification process. To learn how to verify an existing address that you entered in step 8, see the tip at the end of the section "Create an Apple ID."

continued ►

As part of the sign-up process, you specify which iCloud services to use. First, you decide whether you want to synchronize data such as contacts, calendars, and bookmarks with iCloud. If you are not sure, you can turn off this feature for now and decide later (see the section "Set Up iCloud Synchronization"). Second, you decide whether you want to use Find My Mac, which enables you to use iCloud to locate your lost or stolen Mac. Again, if you are not sure what to do, you can decide later (see the section "Locate and Lock a Lost Mac, iPod, iPhone, or iPad").

Create an Apple ID (continued)

12. For each security question, click to select a question and then type an answer.
13. If you want to supply Apple with an emergency e-mail address, type it in the Rescue Email text box.
14. Click **Next**.

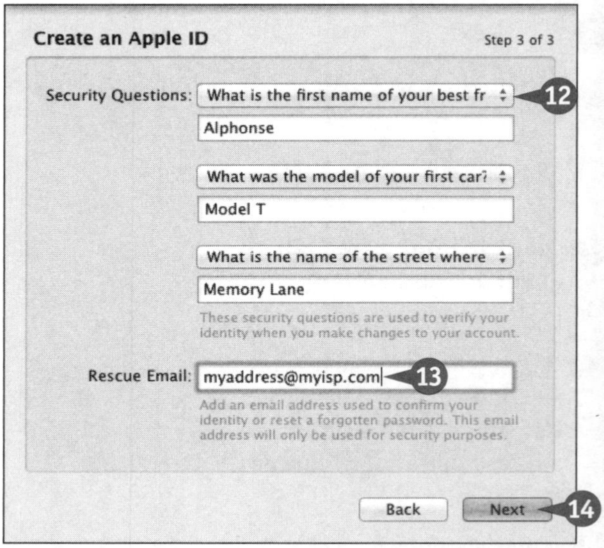

15. Select the **I have read and agree to the iCloud Terms of Service** option (changes to).
16. Click **Continue**.

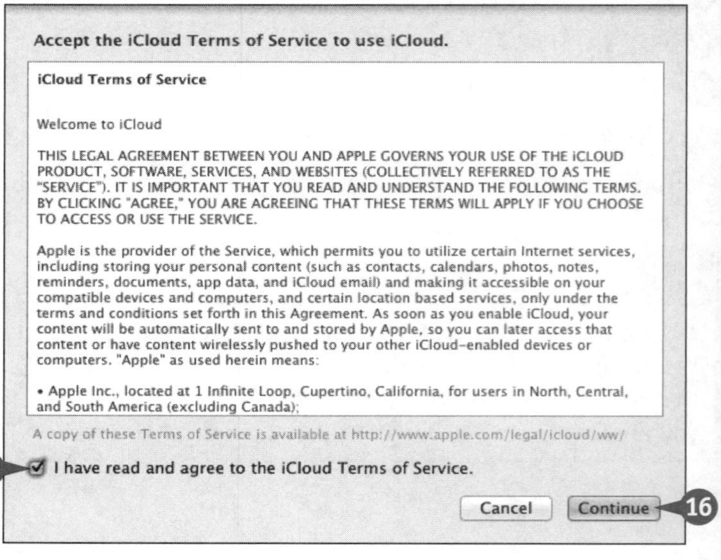

Mac Pro prompts you to choose which iCloud services you want to use.

17 If you do not want to sync your data to iCloud, deselect the **Use iCloud for contacts, calendars, reminders, notes, and Safari** option (☑ changes to ☐).

18 If you do not want to use iCloud to locate your Mac Pro, deselect the **Use Find My Mac** option (☑ changes to ☐).

19 Click **Next**.

If you elected to use Find My Mac, Mac Pro asks you to confirm.

20 Click **Allow**.

Mac Pro sets up your iCloud account.

Note: If you have trouble enabling Find My Mac, see the tip in the section "Locate and Lock a Lost Mac, iPod, iPhone, or iPad."

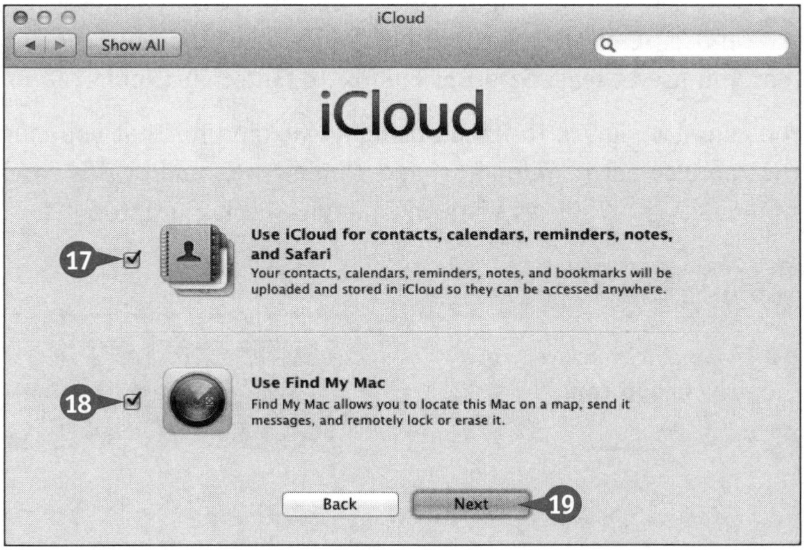

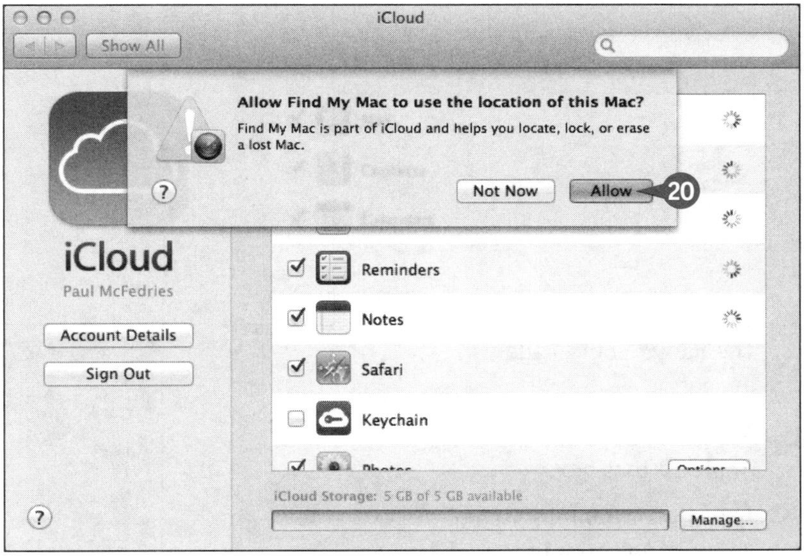

TIP

What happens after I create my Apple ID from an existing address?

After you agree to the terms of service, Apple sends an e-mail message to the address you typed in step 8. When that message arrives, open it and click the verification link. In the web page that appears, type your Apple ID (that is, the e-mail address from step 8), type your password, and then click **Verify Address**. Return to the iCloud preferences, click **Next**, and then follow steps 15 to 20.

Sign In to iCloud

Before you can use the features associated with your iCloud account, you must sign in to the service. iCloud is a web-based service, so you access it using a web browser. Apple recommends that you use at least Safari 6, Firefox 16, Internet Explorer 9, or Chrome 23.

You can also sign in to iCloud using a Mac, and for that you must be using OS X Lion 10.7.5 or later. You can also access iCloud using a Windows PC, and in this case the PC must be running Windows 8, Windows 7, or Windows Vista with Service Pack 2 or later.

Sign In to iCloud

1. In your web browser, type **www.icloud.com**.
2. Press Return.

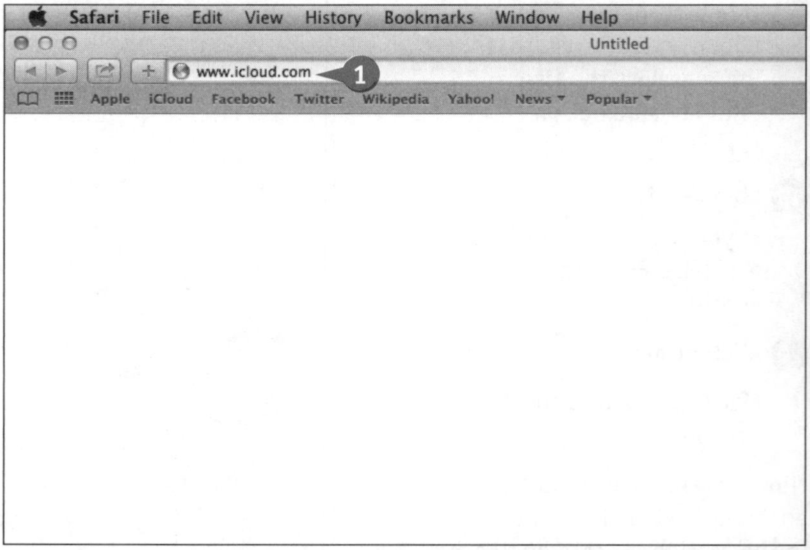

The iCloud Login page appears.

3. Type your Apple ID into the Apple ID text box.
4. Type the password for your Apple ID into the Password text box.

A If you want iCloud to sign you in automatically in the future, select the **Remember me** option (☐ changes to ☑).

5 Click **Sign In** (➔).

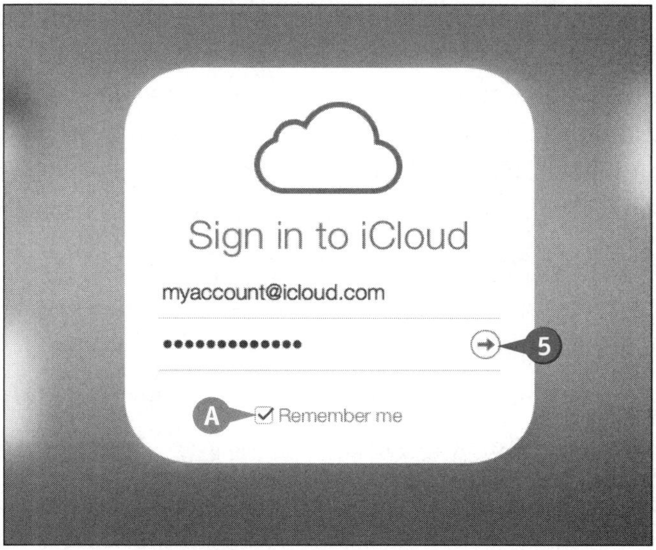

The first time you sign in, iCloud prompts you to configure some settings.

6 Click **Add Photo**, drop a photo on the dialog that appears, and then click **Done**.

7 Click **Done**.

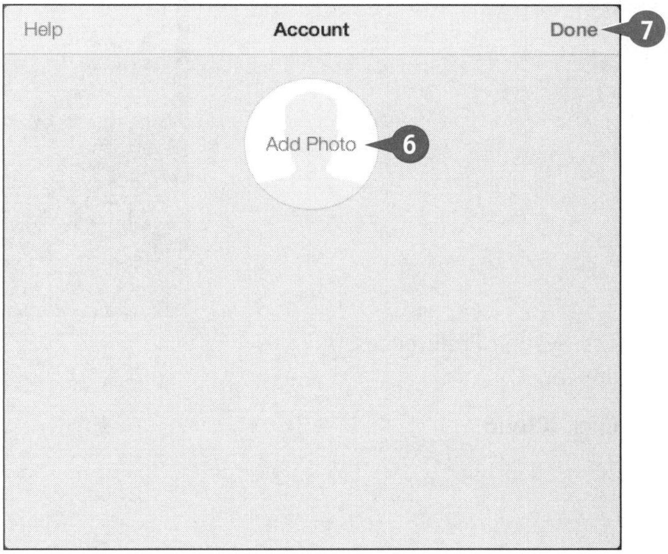

TIPS

Can I sign in from my Mac Pro?

Yes. Click **System Preferences** (⚙) in the Dock (or click and then click **System Preferences**) and then click **iCloud**. Type your Apple ID and password and then click **Sign In**.

How do I sign out from iCloud?

When you are done working with your iCloud account, if you prefer not to remain signed in to your account, click the **Sign Out** link beside your account name in the upper right corner of the iCloud page.

Set Up iCloud Synchronization

You can ensure that your Mac Pro and your iCloud account have the same data by synchronizing the two. The main items you will want to synchronize are Mail e-mail accounts, contacts, calendars, reminders, and notes. However, there are many other types of data you may want to synchronize to iCloud, including Safari bookmarks, photos, and documents. If you have a second Mac, a Windows PC, or an iPhone, iPad, or iPod touch, you can also synchronize it with the same iCloud account, which ensures that your Mac Pro and the device use the same data.

Set Up iCloud Synchronization

1. Click the **Apple** icon (■).
2. Click **System Preferences.**

Note: You can also open System Preferences by clicking its icon (■) on the Dock.

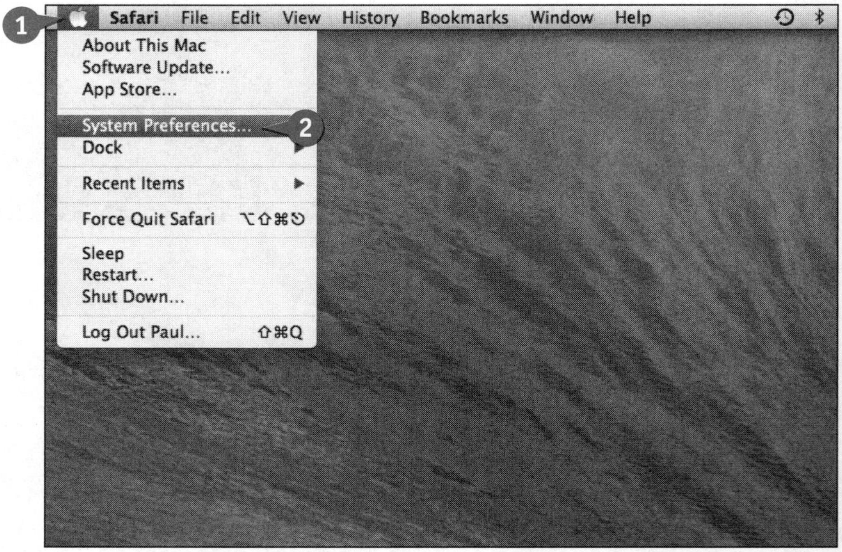

The System Preferences appear.

3. Click **iCloud**.

The iCloud preferences appear.

4 Select the check box beside a type of data you want to sync (☐ changes to ☑).

A OS X sets up the sync.

5 Repeat step 4 for each type of data you want to sync.

6 If you do not want to sync a type of data, deselect its check box (☑ changes to ☐).

Mac Pro asks if you want to keep or delete the iCloud data that you are no longer syncing.

7 Click here to keep the data on Mac Pro.

B If you do not want to keep the data, click **Delete from Mac**.

Mac Pro synchronizes the data with your iCloud account.

TIPS

What happens if I modify an appointment, contact, bookmark, or other data in iCloud?

The synchronization process works both ways. That is, all the Mac Pro data you selected to synchronize is sent to your iCloud account. However, the data on your iCloud account is also sent to Mac Pro. This means that if you modify, add, or delete data on your iCloud account, those changes are also reflected in your Mac Pro data.

When I connect an iPhone, iPad, or iPod touch to Mac Pro, how do I sync contacts, calendars, and e-mail accounts?

You cannot use iTunes to sync contacts, calendars, and e-mail accounts. Instead, you must sync those items between Mac Pro and iCloud and then sync them between iCloud and the device.

Generate a Website Password

You can make it easier and faster to navigate many websites by using Safari to generate, and iCloud to store, passwords for those sites that require you to log in. Many websites require you to set up an account, which means you must log in with a username and password. Good security practices dictate using a unique and hard-to-guess password for each site, but this requires memorizing a large number of passwords. To enhance security and ease web navigation, you can use Safari to automatically generate for each site a unique and secure password stored safely with your iCloud account.

Generate a Website Password

Turn On iCloud Keychain

1. Open System Preferences.
2. Click **iCloud**.

The iCloud preferences appear.

3. Select the **Keychain** option (☐ changes to ☑).

   OS X prompts you for your Apple ID password.

4. Type your password.
5. Click **OK**.

   OS X activates iCloud Keychain.

Generate a Website Password

1. In Safari, navigate to a web page that requires a new password.
2. Click inside the password field.
   - A. Safari displays its suggested password.
3. Click the password.

   OS X asks if you want to keep or delete the iCloud data that you are no longer syncing.

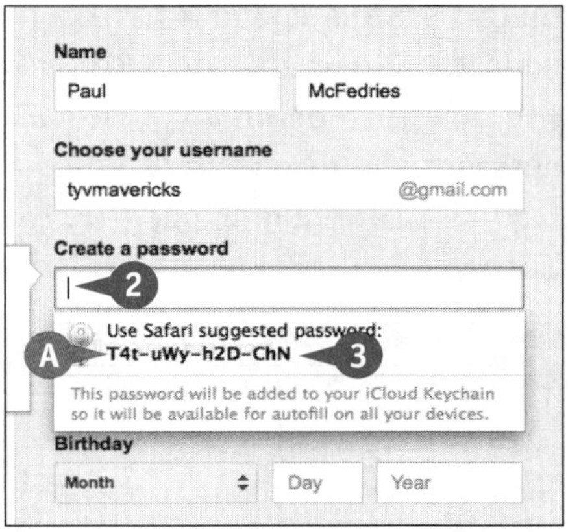

Using a Generated Website Password

1. In Safari, navigate to a web page that requires you to log in using a previously generated password.
2. Begin typing the username.
   - B. Safari displays the full username.
3. Click **Use password from *website***, where *website* is the name of the site.

   Safari fills in the website password.

TIP

What is iCloud Keychain?

A *keychain* is a master list of usernames and passwords that a system stores for easy access by an authorized user. iCloud Keychain is a special type of keychain that stores website passwords auto-generated by Safari. This means that you do not have to remember these passwords because Safari can automatically retrieve them from your iCloud account. Even better, any Mac or iOS device such as an iPhone or iPad that uses the same iCloud account has access to the same keychain, so your website passwords also work on those devices.

On the downside, this sets up a possible security problem should you lose your iPhone or iPad. Therefore, be sure to configure your device with a passcode lock to prevent unauthorized access to your iCloud Keychain.

Send and Receive iCloud Mail

You can use the iCloud Mail feature to work with your iCloud e-mail account online. Using either your Mac Pro or any computer or device with web access, you can access iCloud using a web browser and then perform your e-mail tasks. These include checking for incoming messages, replying to messages you receive, forwarding a received message, and composing and sending a new message. You can also configure iCloud Mail to send blind courtesy copies and to automatically send vacation messages.

Send and Receive iCloud Mail

Display iCloud Mail

1. Sign in to your iCloud account.

Note: See the section "Sign In to iCloud" earlier in this chapter.

2. If you are using another section of iCloud, click **iCloud** (not shown).
3. Click **Mail** ( ).

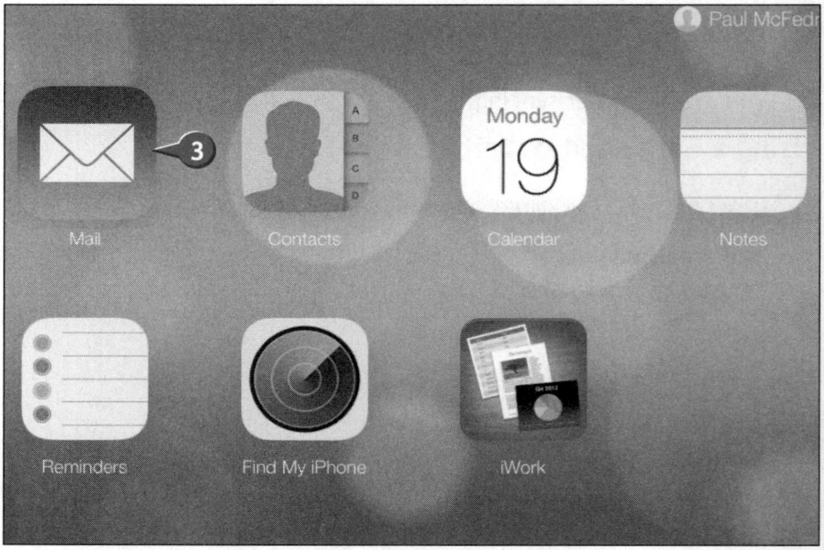

Get Incoming Messages

1. Click **Get Mail** ( ).

A. iCloud Mail checks for incoming messages and, if there are any, displays them in the Inbox folder.

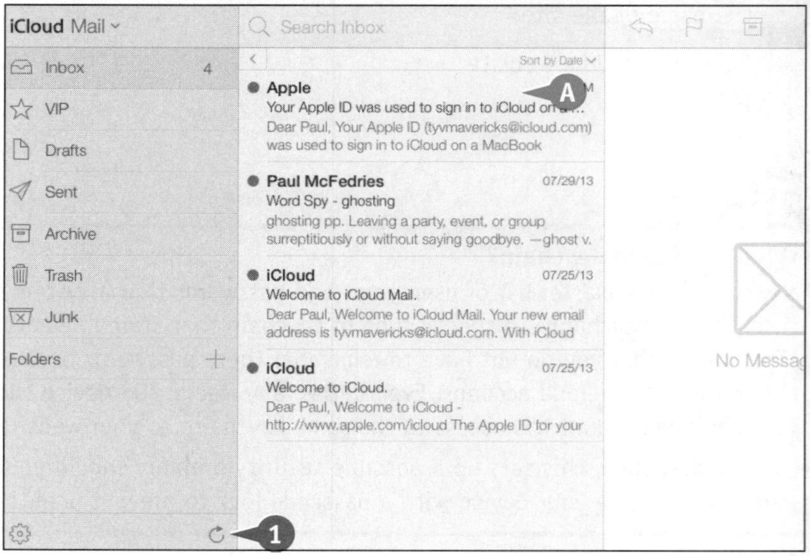

Reply to a Message

1. Click the message.
2. Click **Reply, Reply All, Forward** ( ).
3. Click **Reply**.
4. In the message window that appears (not shown), type your message and then click **Send**.

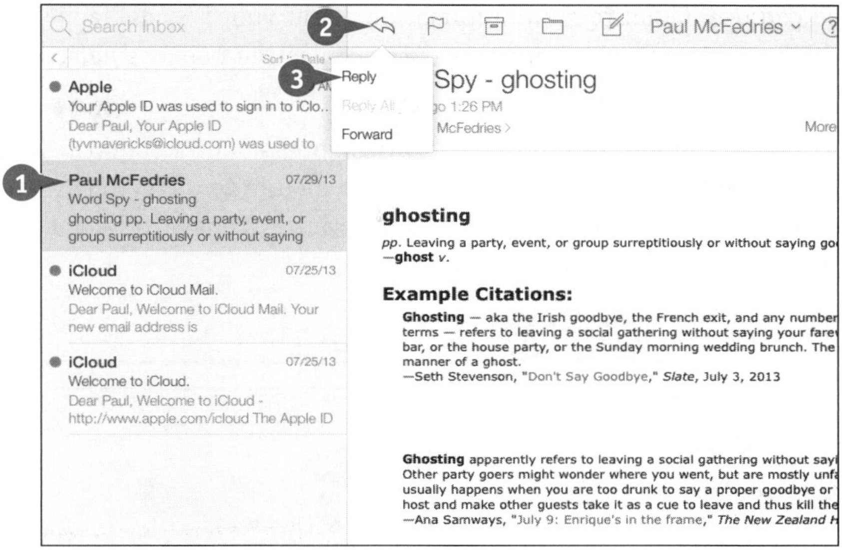

Send a New Message

1. Click **Compose new message** ( ).

   The New Message window appears.
2. Click the To text box and type the recipient's name or e-mail address.
3. Click the Subject text box and type the subject of the message.
4. Type your message.
5. Click **Send**.

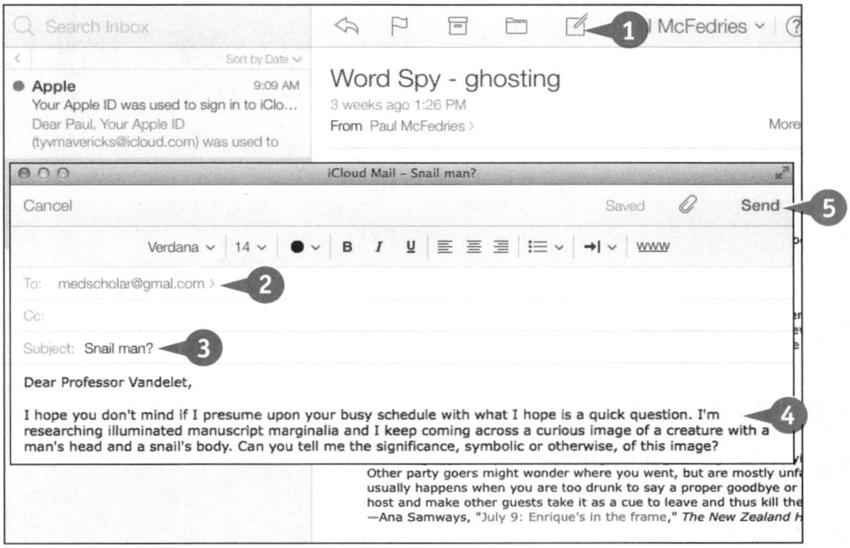

TIP

Can I use iCloud to send a message to a person without other recipients knowing?

Yes, you can send that person a blind courtesy copy (Bcc), which means that he or she receives a copy of the message, but the other message recipients do not see that person's name or address in the recipient fields. To activate this feature, open iCloud Mail, click **Actions** ( ), click **Preferences**, and then click the **Composing** tab. Select the **Show Bcc field** option (changes to) and then click **Done**.

Work with iCloud Contacts

You can use iCloud to store information about your friends, family, colleagues, and clients. Using the Contacts app, you can store data such as the person's name, company name, phone numbers, e-mail address, and street address.

The Contacts app also enables you to write notes about a contact, store extra data such as the person's job title and birthday, and assign a picture to a contact. If you already have contacts in your Mac Pro's Contacts app, you can synchronize them with iCloud. See the section "Set Up iCloud Synchronization" earlier in this chapter.

Work with iCloud Contacts

Display iCloud Contacts

1. Click **iCloud**.
2. Click **Contacts** ( ).

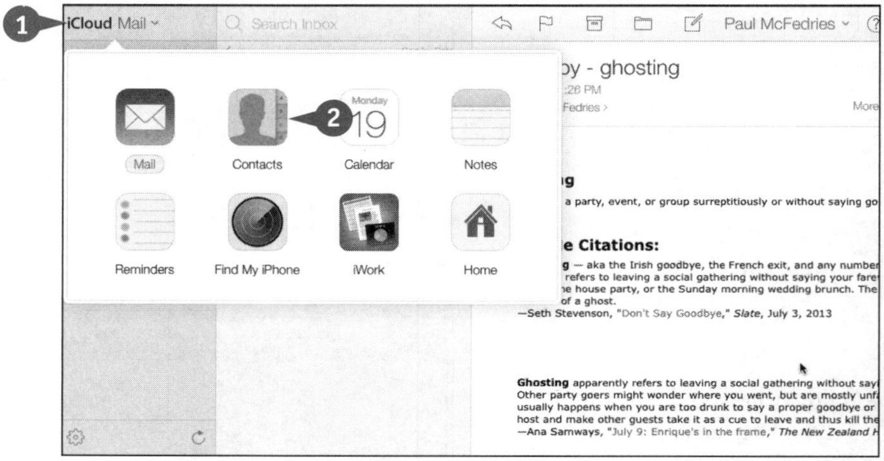

Create a Contact

1. Click **Create a new contact** ( ).
2. Click **New Contact**.
3. Type the person's first name and last name.
4. Type the person's company's name.
5. Click here and then click a phone number category.
6. Type the phone number.
7. Click an e-mail category.
8. Type the person's e-mail address.

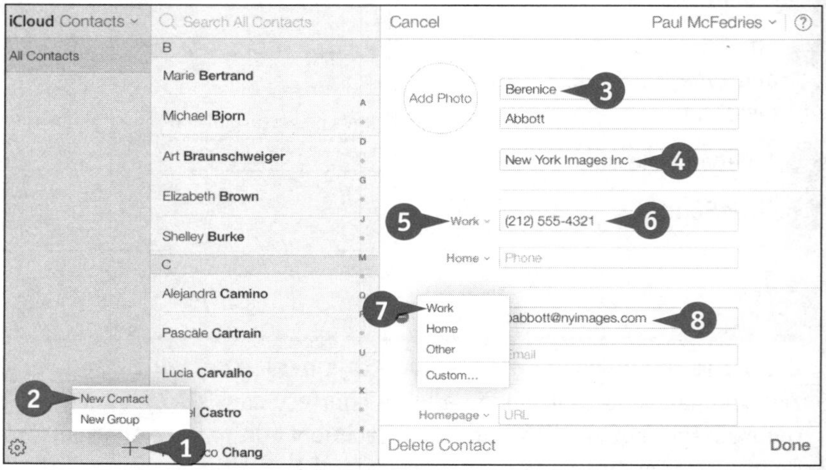

9. Click **Add new address** (not shown).
10. Click a street address category.
11. Use the text boxes in this section to type the person's street address.
12. Click **Done**.

iCloud saves the contact.

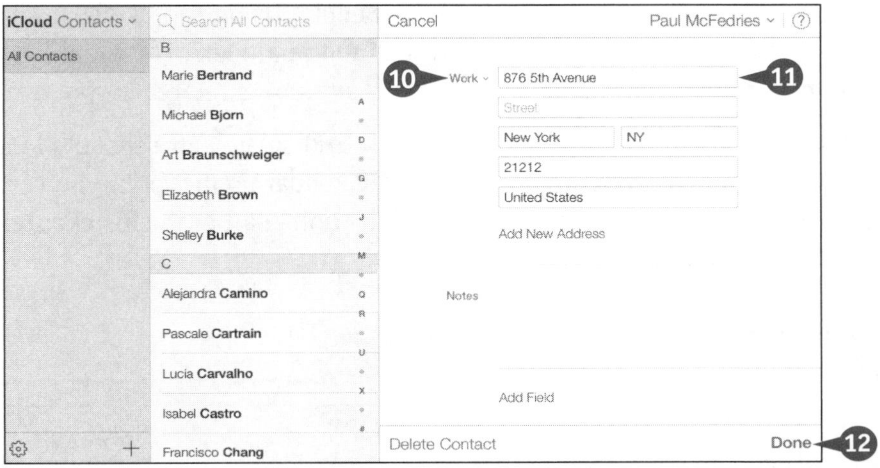

Display a Contact

1. Use the scroll bar to locate the contact.
2. Click the contact.

A. iCloud displays the contact's details.

B. You can also type part of the contact's name in the Search box.

C. To e-mail the contact, you can click the address.

D. To make changes to the contact, you can click **Edit**.

To remove the contact, you can click **Edit** and then click **Delete Contact**.

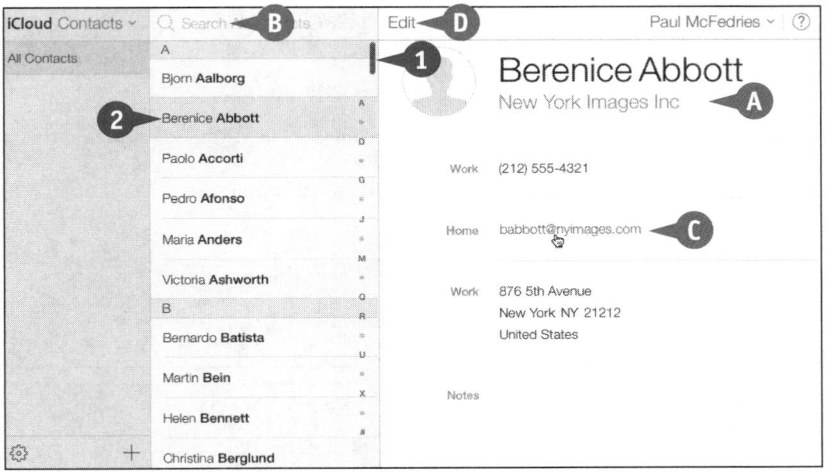

TIPS

How do I add a photo for a contact?
Click the contact, click **Edit**, click **Add Photo**, and then drag a photo to the dialog that appears. Alternatively, click **Choose Photo**, click the photo you want to use, and then click **Choose**. Click **Done**. Note that you can use only GIF, JPEG, or PNG files that are no larger than 1MB.

Is there any way to store data such as the person's birthday or job title?
Yes. To add a field to an existing contact, click the contact and then click **Edit**. Click **Add Field**, click the field you want, and then enter the field data.

Manage Your Schedule with iCloud

You can use iCloud to manage your schedule. Using the Calendar application, you can add events (appointments and all-day activities) and reminders. For events, you can specify the date and time they occur, the event name and location, and notes related to the event.

You can also use the Calendar application to display your schedule by day, by week, or by month. If you already have events in your Mac Pro Calendar application, you can synchronize them with iCloud. See the section "Set Up iCloud Synchronization" earlier in this chapter.

Manage Your Schedule with iCloud

Display iCloud Calendar

1. Click **iCloud**.
2. Click **Calendar** (19).

Navigate Calendar

1. Click **Month**.
2. Click **Next Month** (>) and **Previous Month** (<) to select the month you want.
3. Click the date.

- A. To see just that date, click **Day**.
- B. To see the date in the context of its week, click **Week**.
- C. To return to today's date, click **Go to today**.

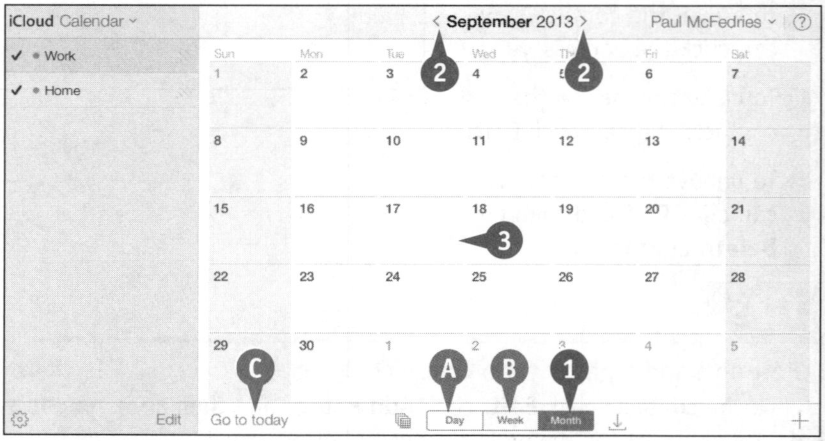

Create an Event

1. Navigate to the date when the event occurs.
2. Click the calendar you want to use.
3. Click **Week**.
4. Position the mouse at the time when the event starts.
5. Click and drag the mouse down to the time when the event ends.

(D) Calendar adds the event.

6. Type the event name.
7. Type the event location.

(E) If the event lasts all day, select the **all-day** option (☐ changes to ☑).

8. Adjust the start time.
9. Adjust the end time.
10. Fill in the other event details.
11. Click **OK**.

Note: To edit the event, double-click it.

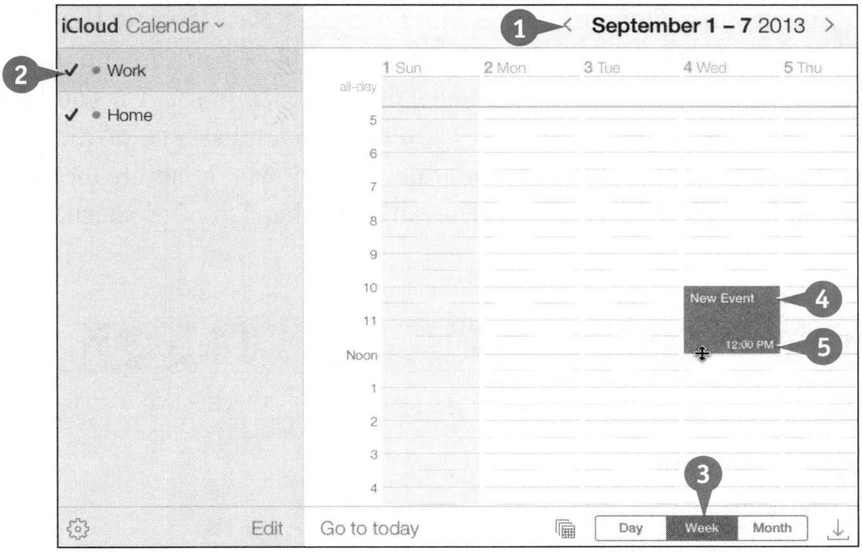

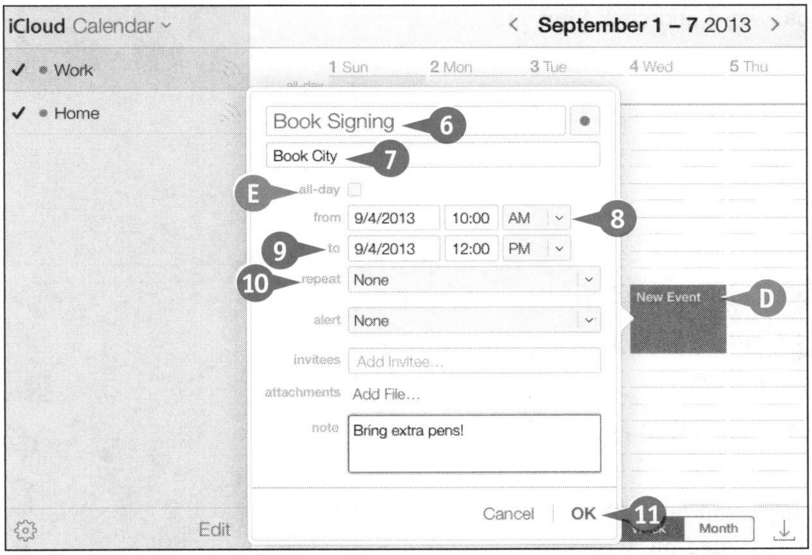

TIP

How do I create a reminder?

Click **iCloud** and then click **Reminders** ( ) to open the iCloud Reminders window. Click the list you want to use for the new reminder. Click **New Item** and then type the reminder name (A). If you also want to add extra data such as the reminder date or notes, click **Details**, use the Details dialog to fill in the reminder details as needed, and then click **Done**.

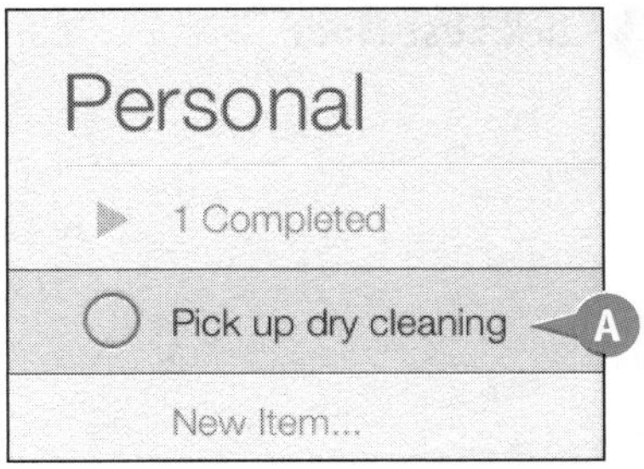

Locate and Lock a Lost Mac, iPod, iPhone, or iPad

You can use iCloud to locate a lost or stolen Mac, iPod touch, iPhone, or iPad. Depending on how you use your Mac, iPod touch, iPhone, or iPad, you can end up with many details of your life residing on the device. That is generally a good thing, but if you happen to lose your device, you have also lost those details, plus you have created a large privacy problem because anyone can now see your data. You can locate your device and even remotely lock the device using an iCloud feature called Find My iPhone, which also works for the Mac, iPod touch, and iPad.

Locate and Lock a Lost Mac, iPod, iPhone, or iPad

1. Click **iCloud**.
2. Click **Find My iPhone** ( ).

Note: If iCloud asks you to sign in to your account, type your password and click **Sign In**.

3. Click **All Devices**.
4. Click the device you want to locate.

Ⓐ iCloud displays the device location on a map.

Note: You only see the device if it is turned on.

5. Click **Lost Mode**.

The Lost Mode dialog appears.

6 Click a four-digit lock code.

7 Enter the lock code again to confirm (not shown).

iCloud prompts you to enter a phone number where you can be contacted.

8 Type the phone number.

9 Click **Next**.

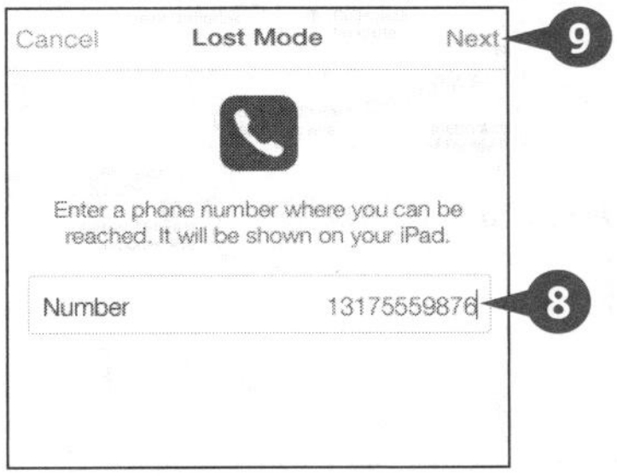

iCloud prompts you to enter a message to display on the device.

10 Type your message.

11 Click **Done**.

iCloud locks the device and sends the message, which then appears on the device screen.

TIP

I tried to enable Find My Mac, but OS X would not allow it. How can I enable Find My Mac?

You first need to enable location services. To do this, click **System Preferences** ( ) in the Dock. Click **Security & Privacy**, click the lock icon ( ), type your OS X administrator password, and then click **OK** (changes to). Click **Privacy**, click **Location Services**, and then select the **Enable Location Services** option (changes to).

Access Mac Pro over the Internet

You can ensure you always have access to your Mac Pro documents and applications by using the Back to My Mac feature to access your Mac Pro via iCloud over an Internet connection. This way, if you are away from Mac Pro and are using a portable Mac such as a MacBook Air or a Mac at work, you can access any document you might have forgotten, or any application not available on the Mac you are using. To use Back to My Mac, both Macs must be using a broadband Internet connection and must be signed in to the same iCloud account.

Access Mac Pro over the Internet

Activate Back to My Mac

1. On Mac Pro, click **System Preferences** ( ).

   The System Preferences appear.

2. Click **iCloud**.

   The iCloud preferences appear.

3. Select the **Back to My Mac** option (changes to).

4. Repeat steps 1 to 3 on the other Mac (that is, the Mac you will be using remotely).

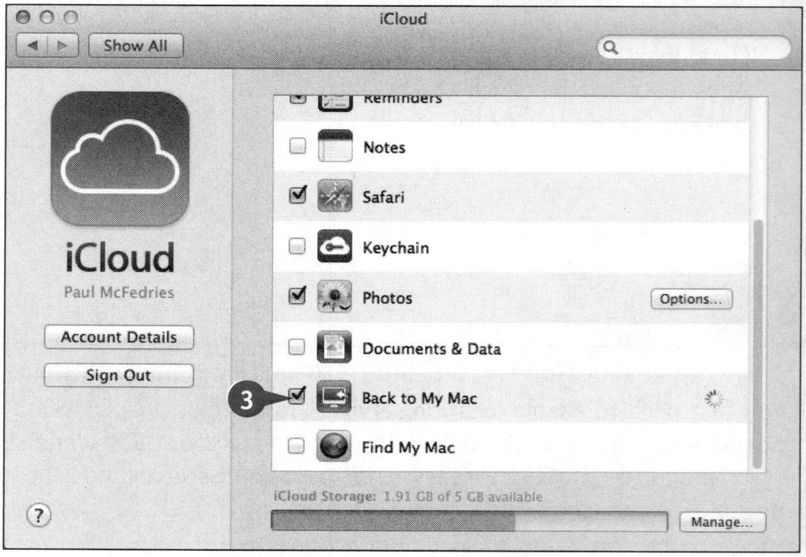

Activate Screen and File Sharing

1. On Mac Pro, open the Sharing preferences.
2. Activate Screen Sharing.
3. Allow your user account to access screen sharing.
4. Activate File Sharing.

Note: See Chapter 21 to learn more about screen sharing and file sharing.

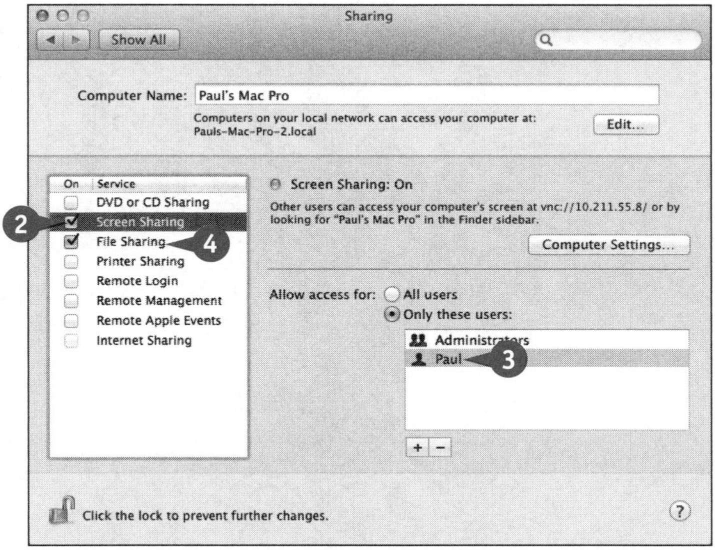

Access Mac Pro Remotely

1. On the other Mac, open Finder.
2. Click the name of your Mac Pro in the Shared section of the sidebar.

   Finder connects to Mac Pro over the Internet using the shared iCloud account.
3. To control the Mac Pro remotely, click **Share Screen**.
4. When you are done, click **Disconnect**.

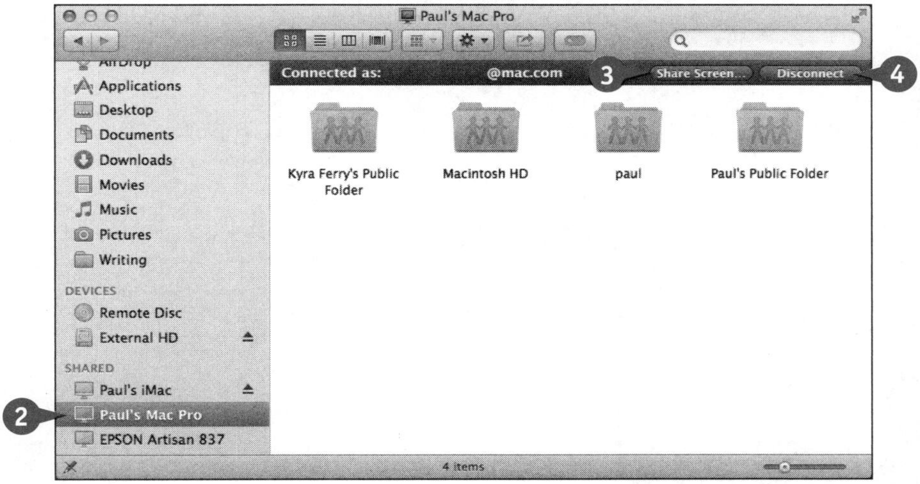

TIPS

Why does my remote Mac not connect to my Mac Pro?

The most likely reason is that your Mac Pro is on a network with a router that does not support Universal Plug and Play (UPnP). Most modern routers support UPnP, so this is not normally a problem. You should check the manual that came with your router to see how to enable UPnP.

Can I copy data from Mac Pro to my other Mac?

When you use the screen sharing feature, you have access to the Mac Pro clipboard, which is the area of memory that Mac Pro uses when you cut or copy data. To retrieve the contents on the Mac Pro clipboard, click **Edit** and then click **Get Clipboard**.

CHAPTER 21

Networking with Mac Pro

If you have multiple computers in your home or office, you can set up these computers as a network to share information and equipment. This chapter gives an overview of networking concepts and shows you how to connect to a network, how to work with the other computers on your network, and how to share your Mac Pro's resources with other network users.

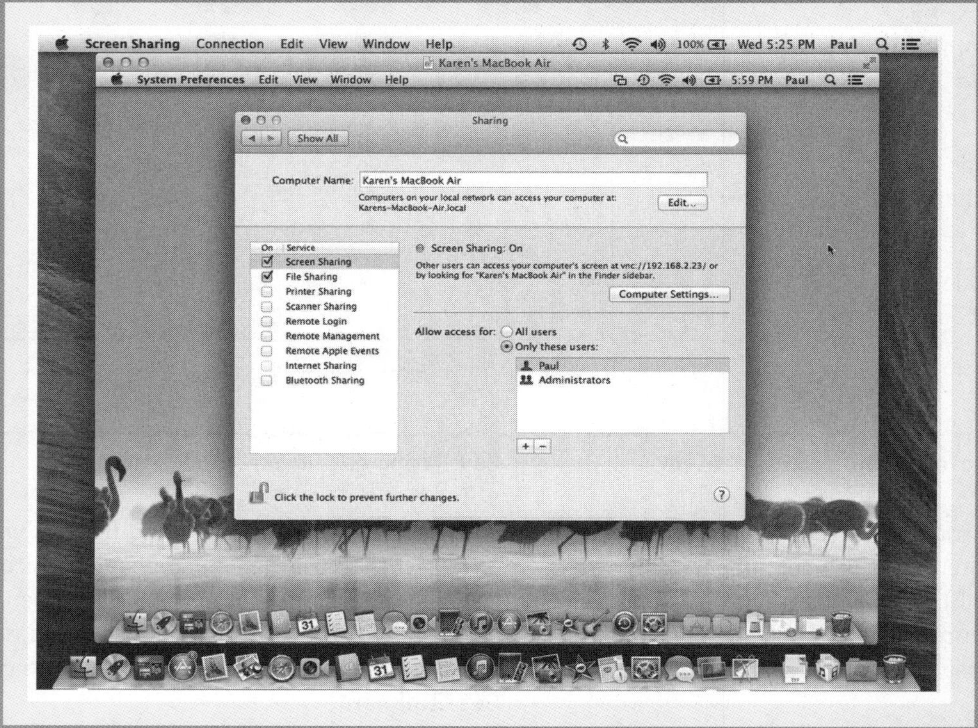

Understanding Networking

A *network* is a collection of computers and other devices that are connected. You can create a network using cable hookups, wireless hookups, or a combination of the two. In both cases, you need special networking equipment to make the connections.

A network gives you a number of advantages. For example, once you have two or more computers connected on a network, those computers can share documents, photos, and other files. You can also use a network to share equipment, such as printers and optical drives.

Shared Resources

Share Files

Networked computers are connected to each other, and so they can exchange files with each other along the connection. This enables people to share information and to collaborate on projects. Mac Pro includes built-in security, so that you can control what files you share with other people.

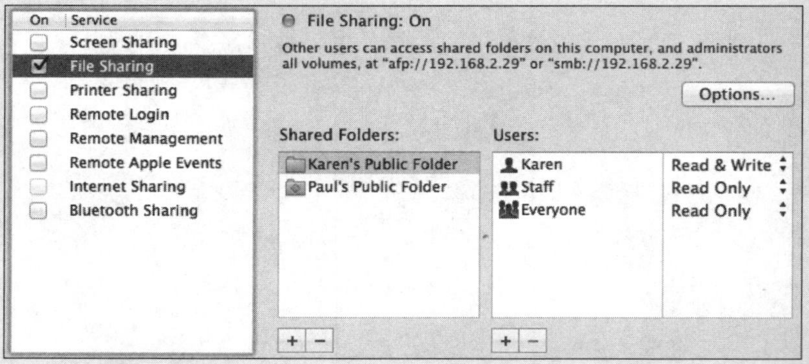

Share Equipment

Computers connected over a network can share some types of equipment. For example, one computer can share its printer, which enables other network users to send their documents to that printer. Networked computers can also share hard drives, optical drives, and document scanners.

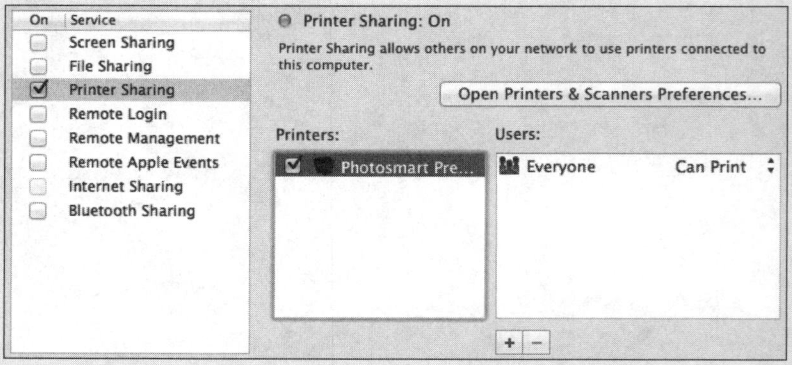

Wired Networking

Network Cable

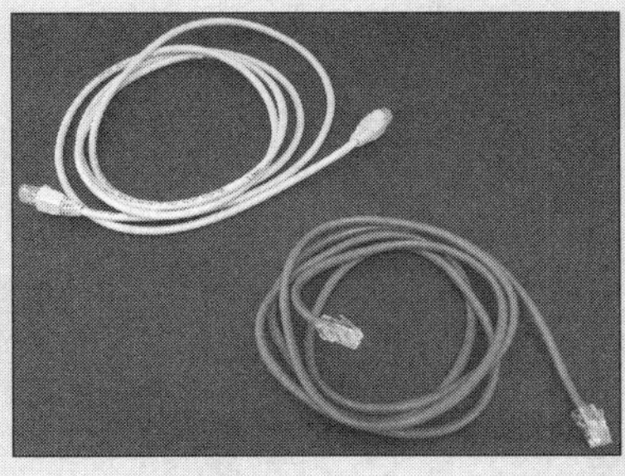

A *network cable* is a special cable designed for exchanging information. One end of the cable plugs into one of the Mac Pro's network ports. The other end plugs into a network connection point, which is usually the network's router (discussed next), but it could also be a switch, hub, or even another Mac. Information, shared files, and other network data travel through the network cables.

Router

A *router* is a central connection point for all the computers on the wired portion of the network. For each computer, you run a network cable from one of the Mac Pro's network ports to a port in the router. When network data travels from computer A to computer B, it first goes out through computer A's network port, along its network cable, and into the router. Then the router passes the data along computer B's network cable and into its network port.

Wireless Networking

Wireless Connections

A *wireless network* is a collection of two or more computers that communicate with one another using radio signals instead of cable. The most common wireless technology is Wi-Fi (rhymes with hi-fi) or 802.11. Each of the five main types (802.11a, 802.11b, 802.11g, 802.11n, and 802.11ac) has its own range and speed limits. The other common wireless technology is Bluetooth, which enables devices to communicate directly with one another.

Wireless Access Point

A *wireless access point* (WAP) is a device that receives and transmits signals from wireless computers to form a wireless network. Many WAPs also accept wired connections, which enables both wired and wireless computers to form a network. If your network has a broadband modem, you can connect the modem to a type of WAP called a *wireless gateway*, which includes a built-in router that extends Internet access to all the computers on the network.

Connect to a Wireless Network

Your Mac Pro has built-in wireless networking capability that you can use to connect to a wireless network within range. This could be a network in your home, your office, or a public location such as a hotel. In most cases, this gives you access to the wireless network's Internet connection.

Most wireless networks have security turned on, which means you must know the correct password to connect to the network. However, after you connect to the network once, your Mac Pro remembers the password and connects automatically the next time the network comes within range.

Connect to a Wireless Network

1 Click the **Wi-Fi status** icon (📶) in the menu bar.

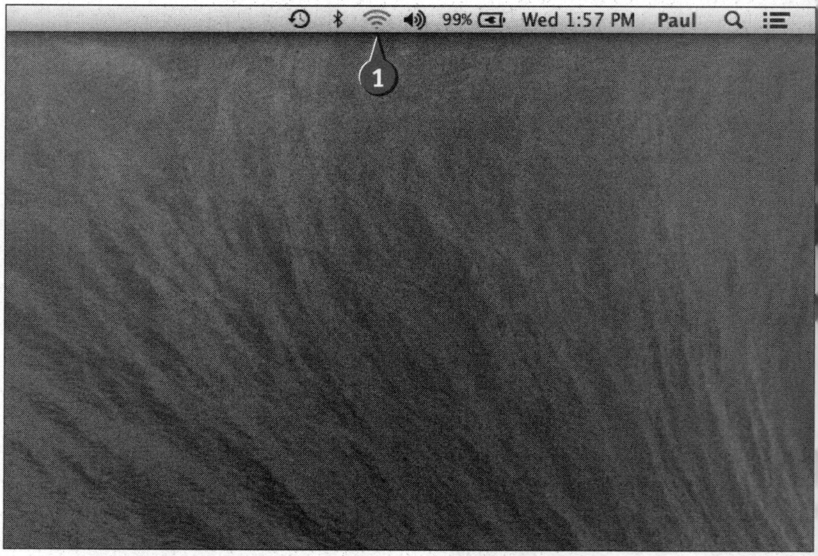

Mac Pro locates the wireless networks that are within range.

A The available networks appear in the menu.

Note: If the network you want does not appear, it might be hidden. See the first tip for more information.

B Networks with a lock icon (🔒) require a password to join.

2 Click the wireless network you want to join.

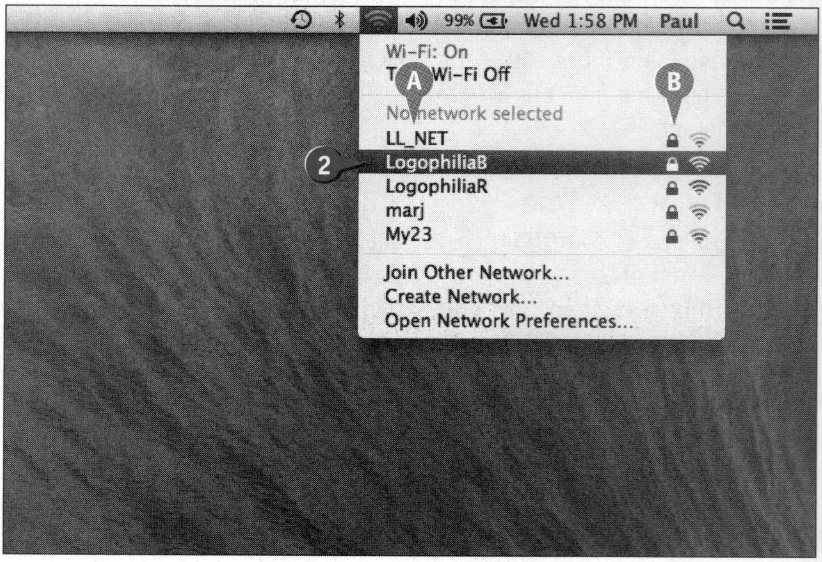

If the wireless network is secure, Mac Pro prompts you for the password.

3. Type the network password into the Password text box.

C. If the password is very long and you are sure no one can see your screen, you can select the **Show password** option (☐ changes to ☑) to see the actual characters instead of dots. This helps to ensure you type the password correctly.

4. Click **Join**.

Mac Pro connects to the wireless network.

D. The Wi-Fi status icon changes from [icon] to [icon] to indicate the connection.

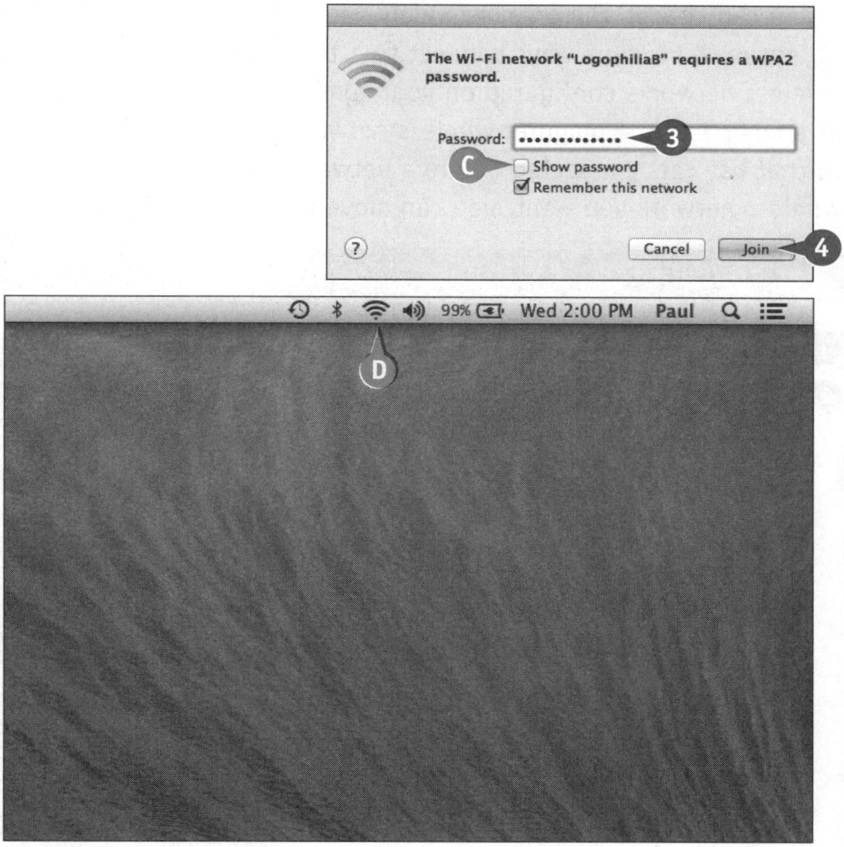

TIPS

I know a particular network is within range, but I do not see it in the list. Why not?

As a security precaution, some wireless networks do not broadcast their availability. However, you can still connect to such a network, assuming you know its name and the password. Click the **Wi-Fi status** icon ([icon]) and then click **Join Other Network**.

I do not see the Wi-Fi status icon on my menu bar. How do I display the icon?

Click **System Preferences** ([icon]) in the Dock (or click [icon] and then click **System Preferences**) to open the System Preferences. Click **Network**, click **Wi-Fi**, and then select the **Show Wi-Fi status in menu bar** option (☐ changes to ☑).

Set Your Preferred Wireless Network

You can change the order in which Mac Pro connects automatically to your wireless networks to ensure that you always connect first to the network you want. It is not unusual to have multiple wireless networks configured on your computer. For example, you may have a wireless gateway as well as a computer-to-computer wireless network. Mac Pro maintains a priority list, and a network higher in that list gets connected before a network lower in the list. If you are not getting connected to the wireless network you want, you can move the network higher in the list.

Set Your Preferred Wireless Network

1. Click the **Apple** icon ().
2. Click **System Preferences.**

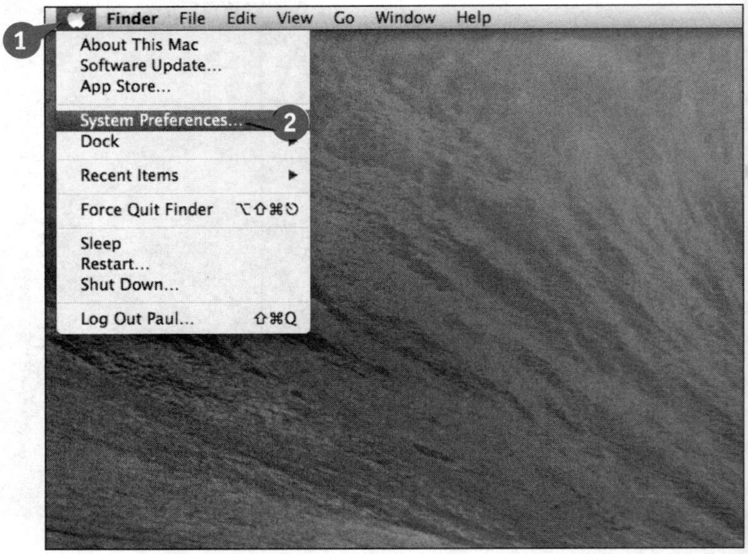

The System Preferences appear.

3. Click **Network.**

The Network preferences appear.

4. Click the **Wi-Fi** connection.
5. Click **Advanced**.

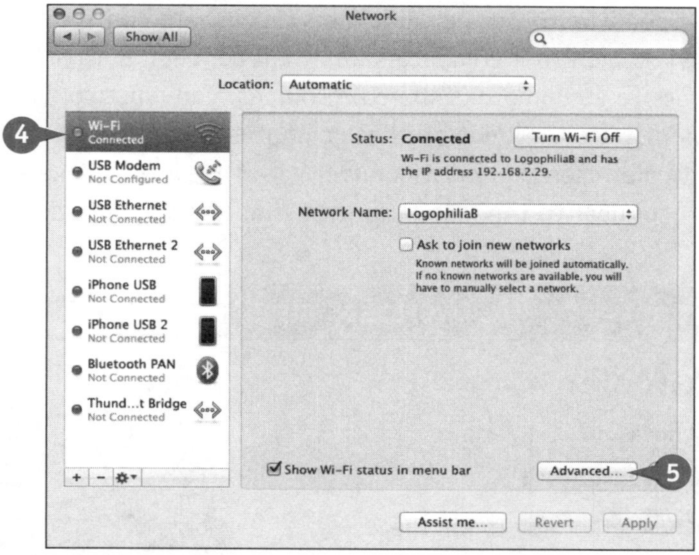

A. The Wi-Fi dialog appears with the Wi-Fi tab displayed.

6. Click and drag your preferred wireless network to the top of the list.
7. Click **OK**.

Mac Pro will now first connect to your preferred network each time the network comes within range.

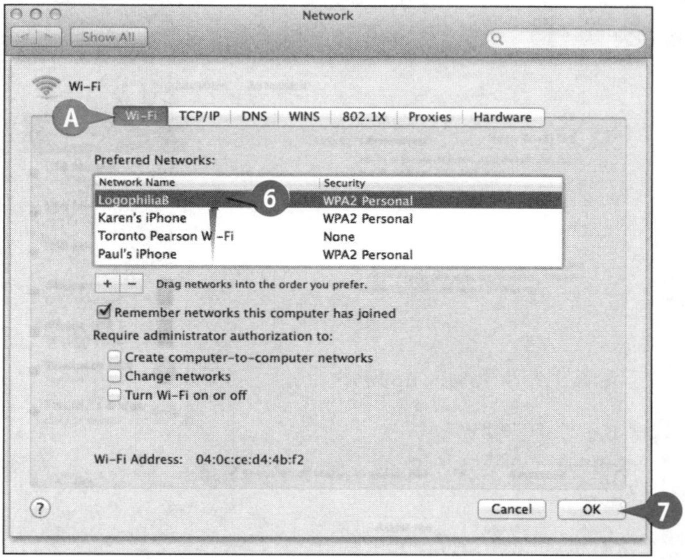

TIPS

How do I create a computer-computer wireless network?

Click the **Wi-Fi status** icon () and then click **Create Network**. Type a name for the network, click the **Security**, and then click **128-bit WEP**. Type a 13-character password in the Password and Confirm Password text boxes and then click **Create**.

Can I remove a wireless network?

Yes, you can also use the Wi-Fi dialog to remove any wireless networks that you no longer need. Follow steps 1 to 3 to open the Wi-Fi dialog and display the Wi-Fi tab. Click the network you want to delete and then click **Remove** (). Mac Pro deletes the wireless network from the list. Click **OK**.

Connect to a Network Resource

To see what other network users have shared on the network, you can use the Network folder to view the other computers and then connect to them to see their shared resources. To get full access to a computer's shared resources, you must connect with a username and password for an administrator account on that computer. To get access to the resources that have been shared by a particular user, you must connect with that user's name and password. Note, too, that Mac Pro can also connect to the resources that Windows computers share.

Connect to a Network Resource

1. Click the desktop.
2. Click **Go**.
3. Click **Network**.

Note: Another way to run the Network command is to press Shift + ⌘ + K.

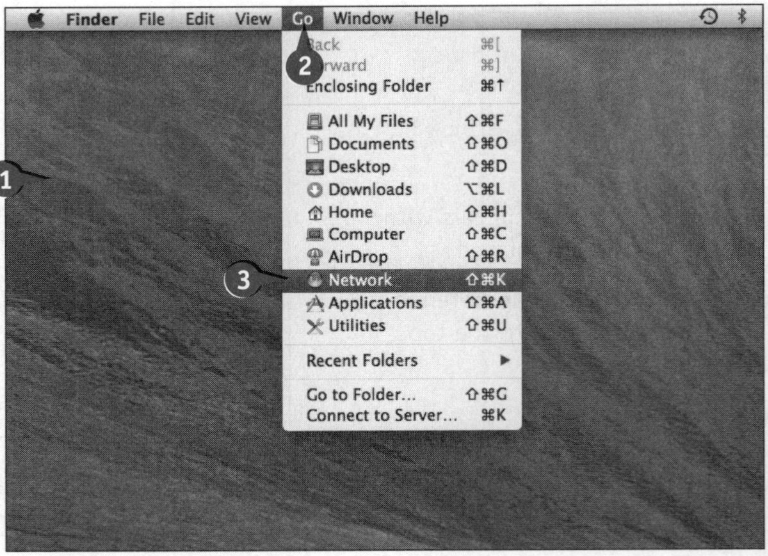

The Network folder appears.

A Each icon represents a computer on your local network.

4. Double-click the computer to which you want to connect.

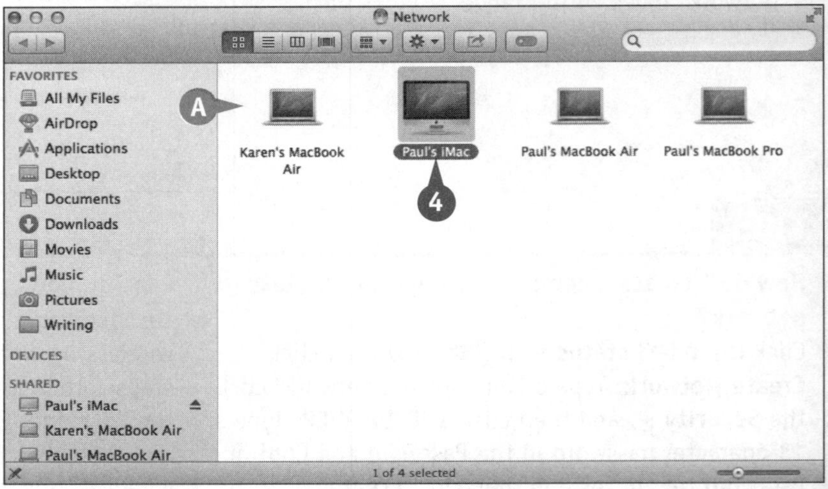

Mac Pro connects to the network computer using the Guest account.

Note: The Guest account has only limited access to the network computer.

5 Click **Connect As.**

Mac Pro prompts you to connect to the network computer.

6 Select the **Registered User** option (◯ changes to ◉).

7 Use the Name text box to type the username of an account on the network computer.

8 Type the password of the account in the Password text box.

9 To store the account data, select the **Remember this password in my keychain** option (☐ changes to ☑).

10 Click **Connect.**

Mac Pro connects to the computer and shows the shared resources that you can access.

11 When you are done, click **Disconnect.**

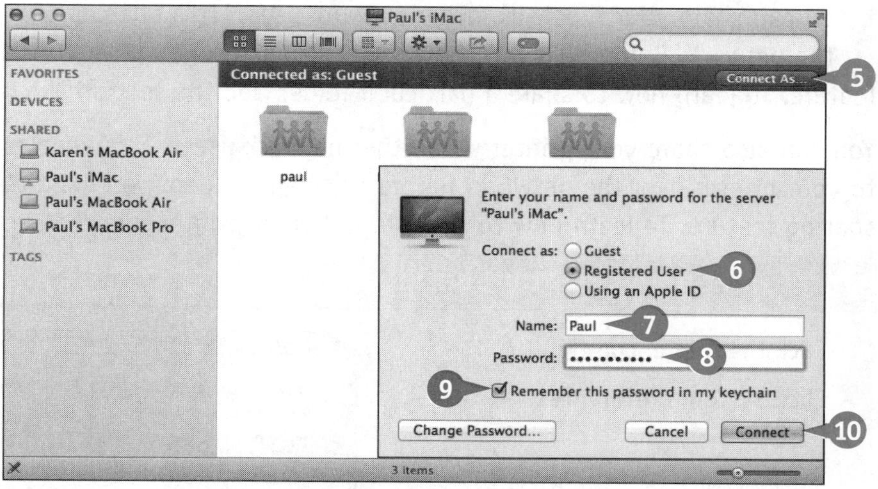

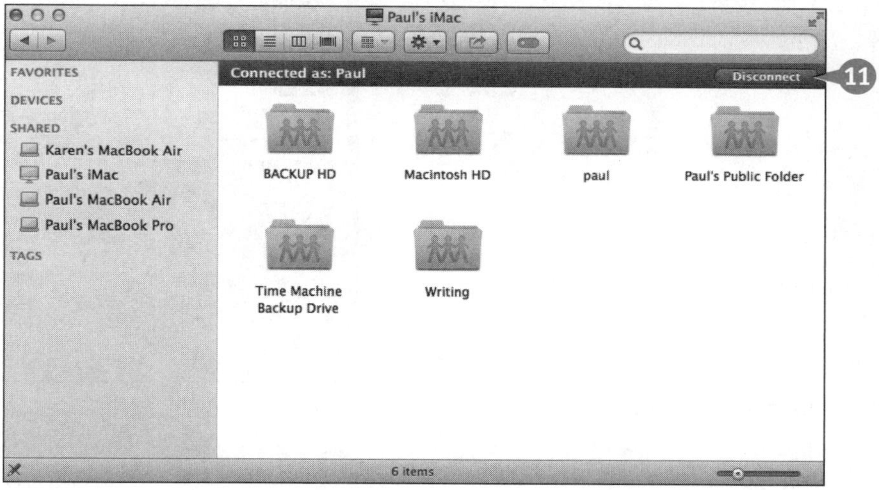

TIP

Is there a faster way to connect to a network computer?

Yes. In the Shared section of Finder's sidebar area, click the computer with which you want to connect (A) and then follow steps 5 to 10 to connect as a registered user.

Turn On File and Printer Sharing

You can share your files with other network users. This enables those users to access your files over the network. Before you can share these resources, you must turn on your Mac Pro's file sharing feature. To learn how to share a particular folder, see the section "Share a Folder."

You can also share your printer with other network users. This enables those users to send print jobs to your printer over the network. Before this can happen, you must turn on your Mac Pro's printer sharing feature. To learn how to share a particular printer, see the section "Share a Printer."

Turn On File and Printer Sharing

1. Click the **Apple** icon ().
2. Click **System Preferences**.

The System Preferences appear.

3. Click **Sharing**.

The Sharing preferences appear.

4 Select the **File Sharing** option (☐ changes to ☑).

You can now share your folders, as described in the section "Share a Folder."

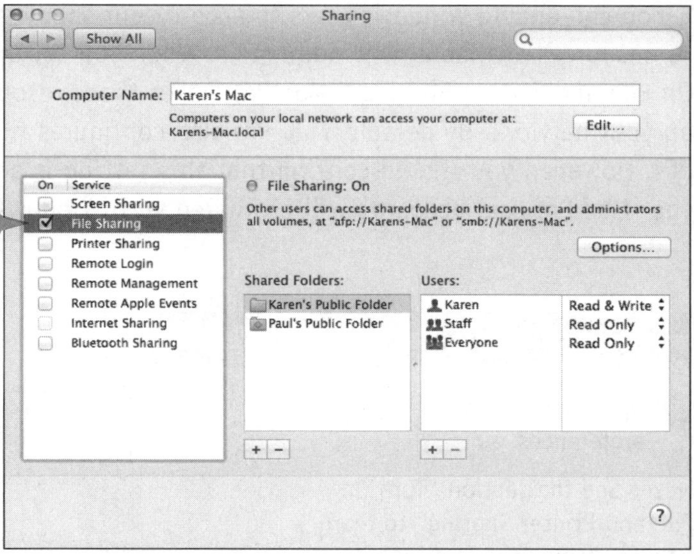

5 Select the **Printer Sharing** option (☐ changes to ☑).

You can now share your printers, as described in the section "Share a Printer."

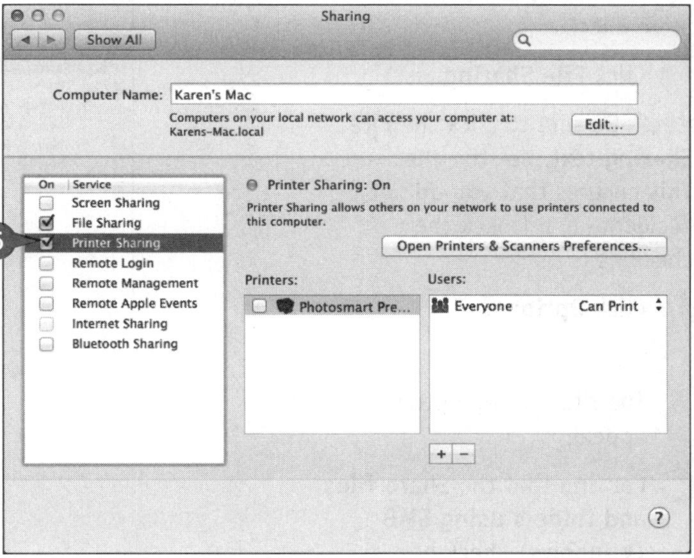

TIPS

How do I look up my Mac Pro IP address?

In System Preferences, click ◀ to return to the main window and then click **Network.** Click **Wi-Fi** if you have a wireless network connection, or click **Ethernet** if you have a wired connection. In the Status section, read the IP address value.

What is the Public folder and how do I access it?

The Public folder is a special folder for sharing files. Anyone who connects to your Mac Pro using your username and password has full access to the Public folder. To access the folder, click **Finder** ( ), click **Go**, click **Home**, and then open the **Public** folder.

Set Up Sharing for Windows Users

You can enable Windows users to access your shared files by configuring Mac Pro to make those resources available to Windows PCs. When you set up file sharing as described in the section "Turn On File and Printer Sharing," Mac Pro makes those resources immediately available to the other Macs on your network. By default, Mac Pro also configures file sharing to allow connections from Windows PCs. However, you should confirm that this setting is activated, and you need to specify which of your Mac Pro user accounts will be shared with Windows users.

Set Up Sharing for Windows Users

1. Open the Sharing preferences.

Note: See the section "Turn On File and Printer Sharing" to learn how to display the Sharing preferences.

2. Click **File Sharing**.

Note: Be sure to click the **File Sharing** text, not the check box. This ensures that you do not accidentally uncheck the check box.

3. Click **Options**.

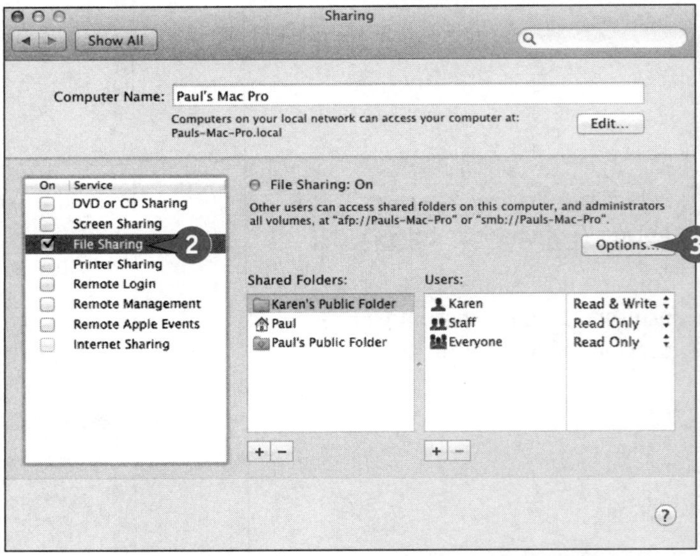

The file sharing options appear.

4. Confirm that the **Share files and folders using SMB (Windows)** check box is selected (☑).

5. Select the check box for the user account you want to share with Windows (☐ changes to ☑).

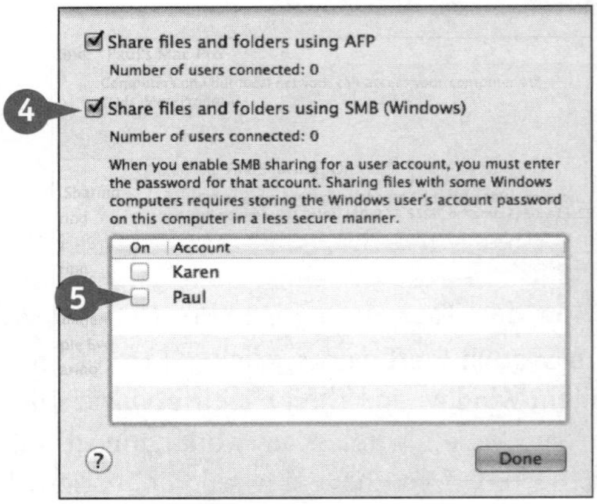

Mac Pro prompts you for the user account password.

6 Type the user account password.

7 Click **OK**.

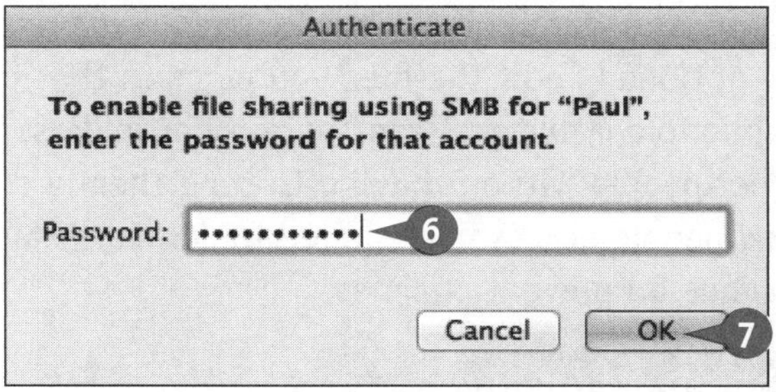

8 Click **Done**.

Mac Pro now allows Windows users to connect to your Mac Pro's shared resources.

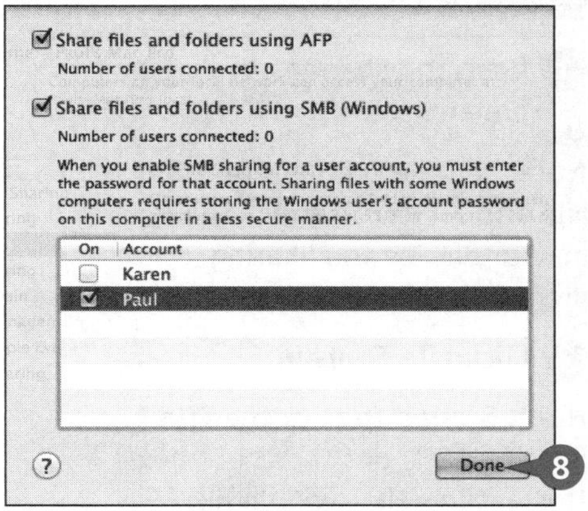

TIP

How do I access a shared Mac Pro folder from a Windows PC?

In many cases, you can open Windows Explorer (File Explorer in Windows 8 or 8.1), click **Network**, and then double-click the icon for Mac Pro. If you do not see that icon, then you can type the share address directly using either the Run dialog box (press ⊞+R) or Windows Explorer's address bar. You have two choices:

- *IP**user*
- *Computer**user*

Here *IP* is the IP address shown in Mac Pro's Sharing preferences, *Computer* is the Mac Pro's computer name, and in both cases *user* is the username of the account enabled for Windows sharing.

Share a Folder

You can share one of your folders on the network, enabling other network users to view and optionally edit the files you place in that folder. Mac Pro automatically shares your user account's Public folder, but you can share other folders. Sharing a folder enables you to work on a file with other people without having to send them a copy of the file. Mac Pro gives you complete control over how people access your shared folder. For example, you can allow users to make changes to the folder, or you can prevent changes.

Share a Folder

1. Open the Sharing preferences.

Note: See the section "Turn On File and Printer Sharing" to learn how to display the Sharing preferences.

2. Click **File Sharing**.

Note: Be sure to click the **File Sharing** text, not the check box. This ensures that you do not accidentally uncheck the check box.

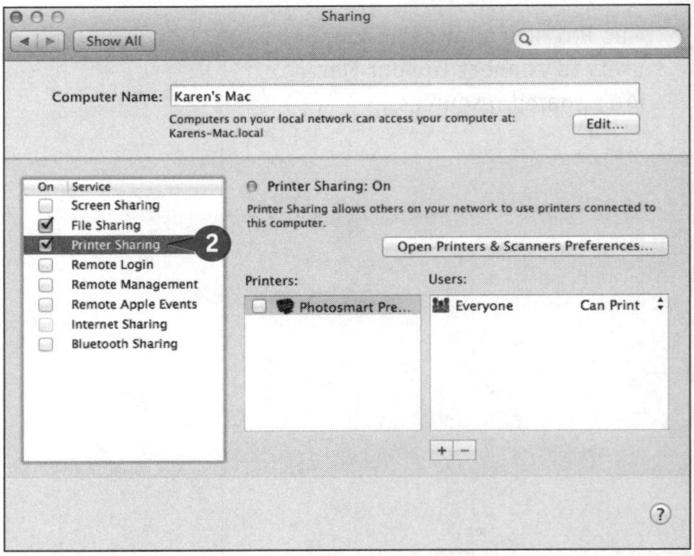

3. Under Shared Folders, click **Add** (+).

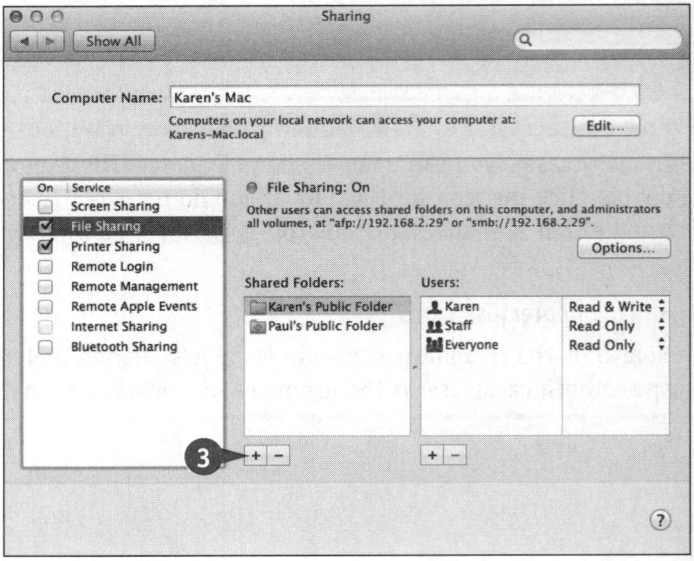

An Open dialog appears.

4 Click the folder you want to share.

5 Click **Add**.

Mac Pro begins sharing the folder.

Note: You can also click and drag a folder from a Finder window and drop it on the list of shared folders.

A The folder appears in the Shared Folders list.

6 Click the folder.

7 For the Everyone user, click the current permission and then click the permission you want to assign.

B The current permission is indicated with a check mark (☑).

Mac Pro assigns the permission to the user.

C You can also click **Add** (+) under the Users list to add more users.

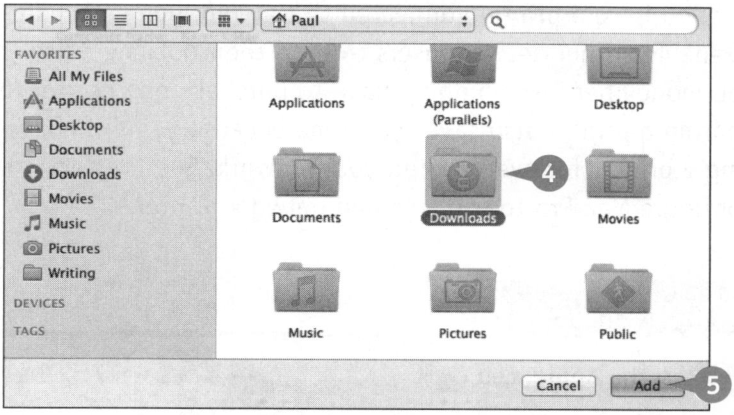

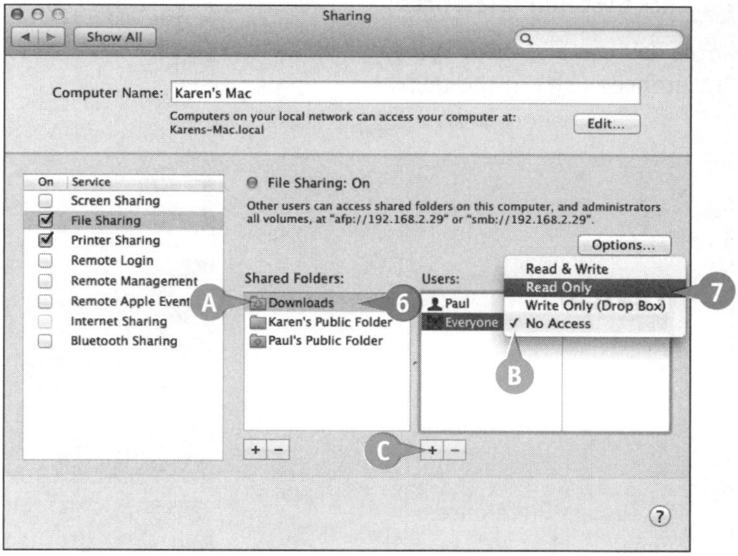

TIP

What are the differences among the permission types?

Read & Write means users can open files, add new files, rename or delete existing files, and edit file contents. Read Only means users can only open and read files, but cannot add, delete, rename, or edit files. Write Only (Drop Box) means users can add files to the folder as a Drop Box, but cannot open the folder. No Access means users cannot open the folder.

Share a Printer

If you have a printer connected to Mac Pro, you can share the printer with the network. This enables other network users to send their documents to your printer. Sharing a printer saves you money because you only have to purchase one printer for all the computers on your network. Sharing a printer also saves you time because you only have to install, configure, and maintain a single printer for everyone on your network. See the section "Add a Shared Printer" to learn how to configure Mac Pro to use a shared network printer.

Share a Printer

1. Click the **Apple** icon ( ).
2. Click **System Preferences**.

Note: You can also click **System Preferences** ( ) in the Dock.

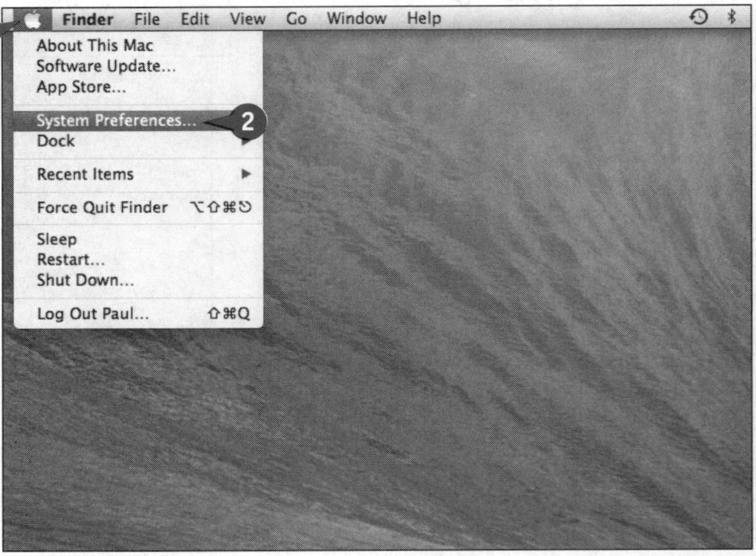

The System Preferences appear.

3. Click **Sharing**.

The Sharing preferences appear.

4 Click **Printer Sharing**.

Note: Be sure to click the **Printer Sharing** text, not the check box. This ensures that you do not accidentally uncheck the check box.

5 Select the check box beside the printer you want to share (☐ changes to ☑).

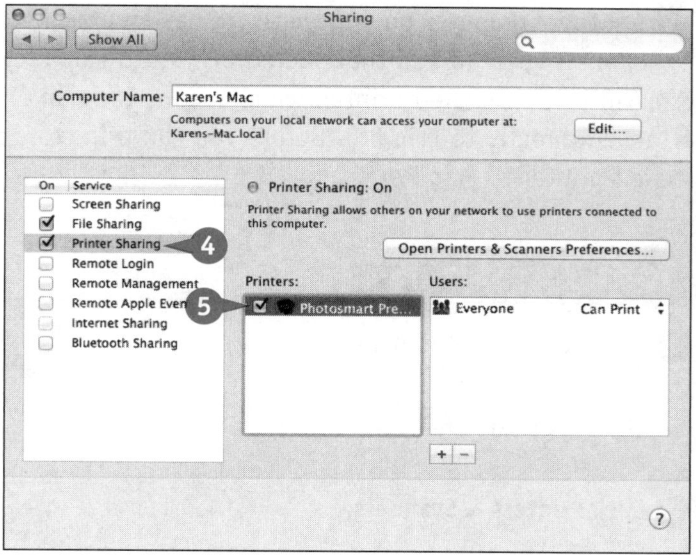

TIP

Is there another method I can use to share a printer?

Yes, you can follow these steps:

1 Click the **Apple** icon ().

2 Click **System Preferences**.

The System Preferences appear.

3 Click **Printers & Scanners**.

The Printers & Scanners preferences appear.

4 Click the printer you want to share.

5 Select the **Share this printer on the network** option (☐ changes to ☑).

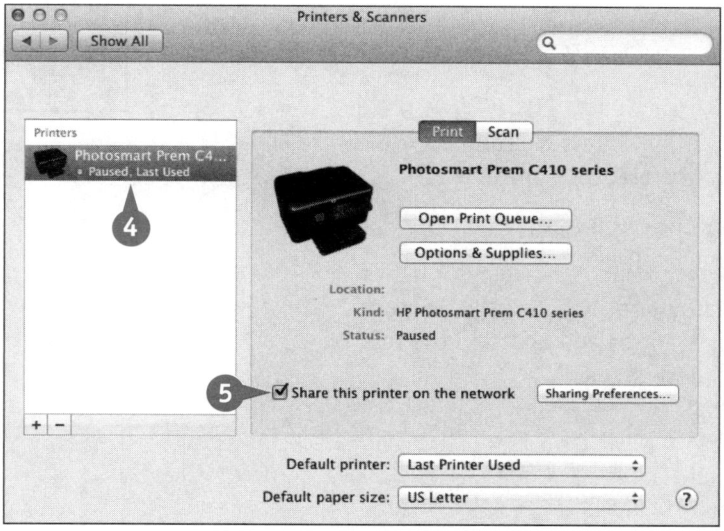

Add a Shared Printer

If another computer on your network has an attached printer that has been shared with the network, you can add that shared printer to Mac Pro. This enables you to send a document from Mac Pro to that shared printer, which means you can print your documents without having a printer attached directly to Mac Pro. Before you can print to a shared network printer, you must add the shared printer to Mac Pro.

Add a Shared Printer

1. Click **System Preferences** (⚙) in the Dock.

   The System Preferences appear.

2. Click **Printers & Scanners.**

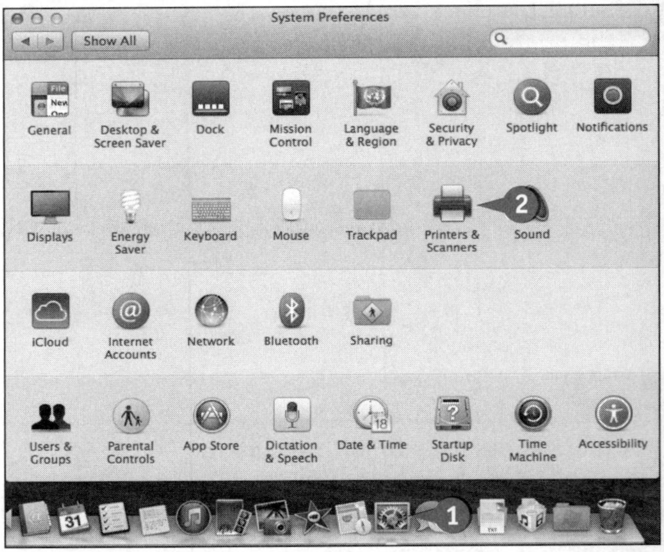

   The Printers & Scanners preferences appear.

3. Click **Add** (+).

Note: If Mac Pro displays a list of nearby printers, click the printer you want to add and skip the rest of these steps.

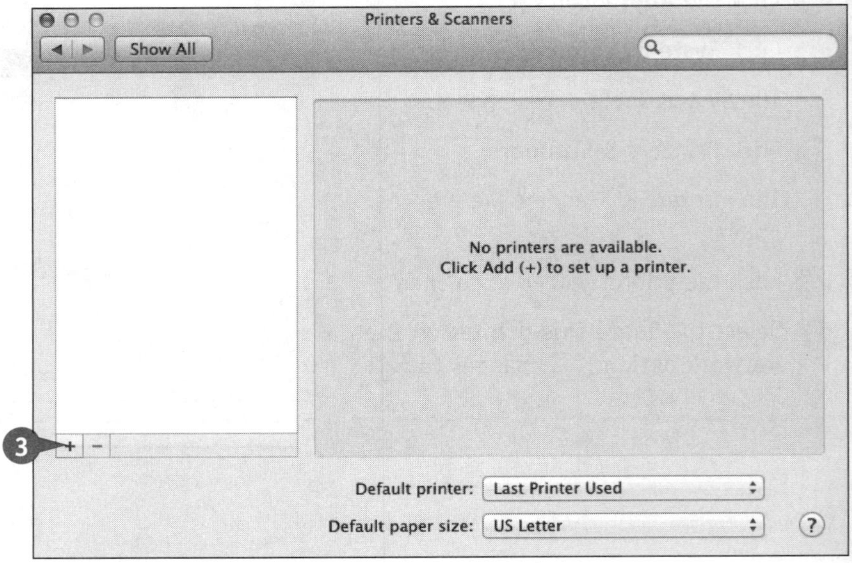

4 Click the **Default** tab.

5 Click the shared printer.

A Look for the word *Shared* in the printer description.

6 Click **Add**.

Note: If Mac Pro alerts you that it must install software for the printer, click **Download & Install**.

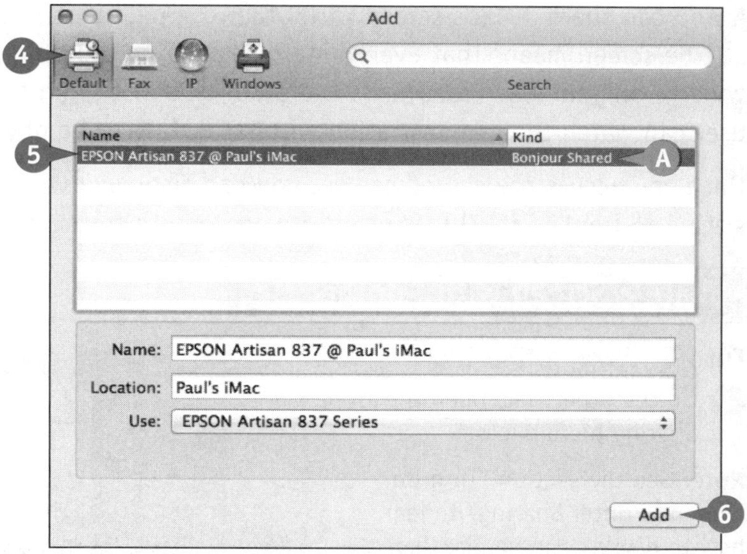

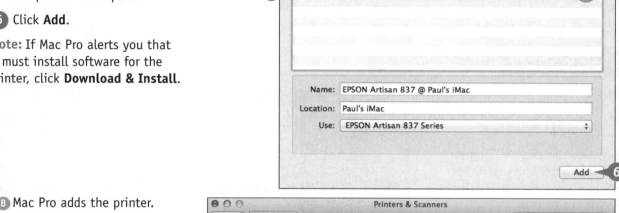

B Mac Pro adds the printer.

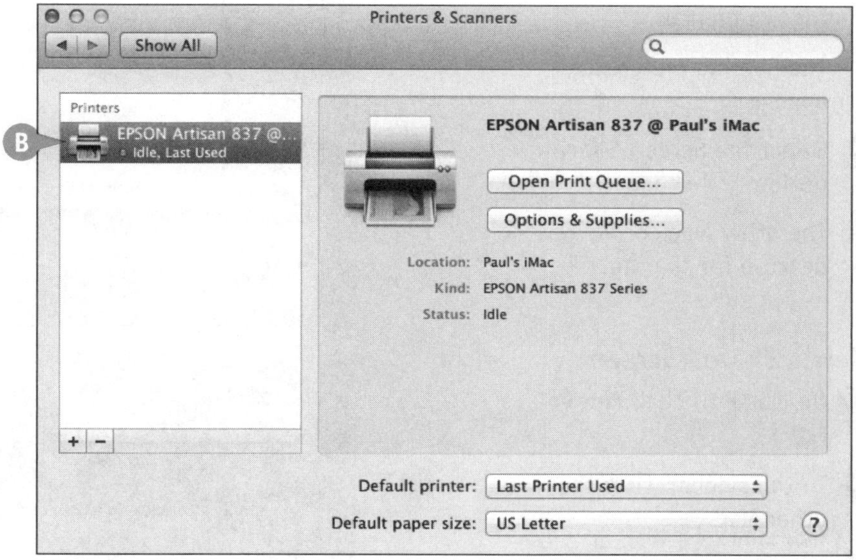

TIPS

Can I add a shared Windows printer?

Yes. Follow steps 1 to 3 and then click the **Windows** tab. Click the Windows workgroup, click the computer with the shared printer, log on to the Windows computer, and then click the shared printer you want to use. In the Print Using list, click **Add** (+), click **Other**, and then click the printer in the list that appears. Click **Add**.

How do I print to the shared network printer that I added?

In any application that supports printing, click **File** and then click **Print**. In the Print dialog, click the **Printer** ⇕, click **Add** (+), and then click the shared printer. Choose any other printing options you require, and then click **Print**.

Share a Screen with Another Mac

You can share a Mac's screen with other computers on your network, including your Mac Pro. Sharing the screen means that everything displayed on the other Mac's desktop also appears inside a window on your Mac Pro. This is useful for demonstrating something on the screen, because the other user can watch the demonstration without having to be physically present in front of your Mac Pro.

Once you access the shared screen, you can also work with the other Mac just as though you were sitting in front of it. This is useful if you need to troubleshoot a problem on the other Mac.

Share a Screen with Another Mac

Turn On Screen Sharing

1. On the other Mac, open the Sharing preferences.

Note: See the section "Turn On File and Printer Sharing" to learn how to display and unlock the Sharing preferences.

   The Sharing preferences appear.

2. Select the **Screen Sharing** option (☐ changes to ☑).

   The other Mac configures the desktop for sharing.

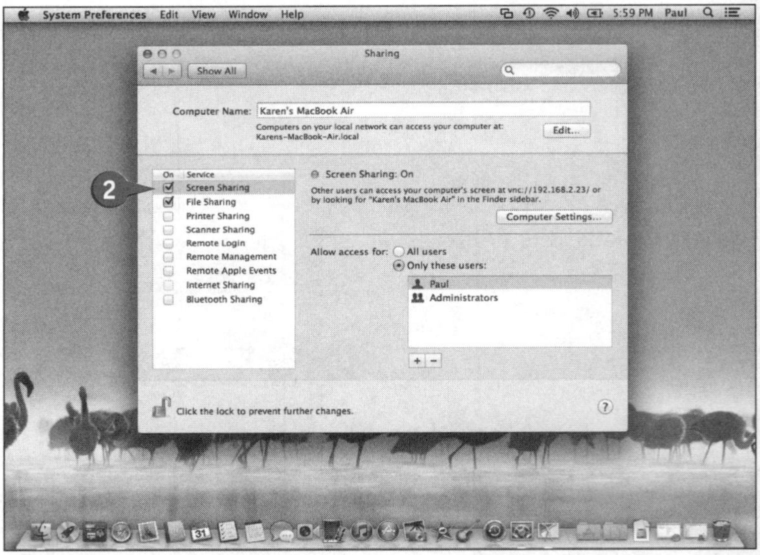

View a Shared Screen

1. On Mac Pro, click **Finder** (Finder icon).
2. In the sidebar, click the other Mac.
3. Click **Share Screen**.

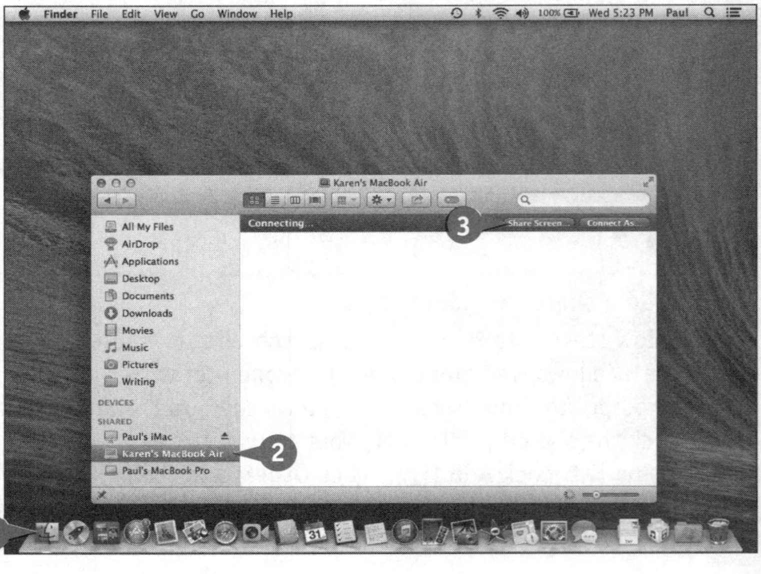

OS X prompts you to log in to the remote computer.

4 Type the password for an administrative account on the other Mac.

5 Click **Connect**.

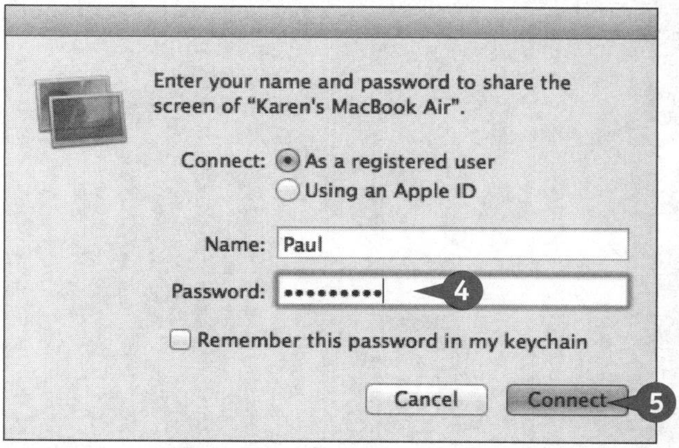

A OS X displays the shared screen in a window.

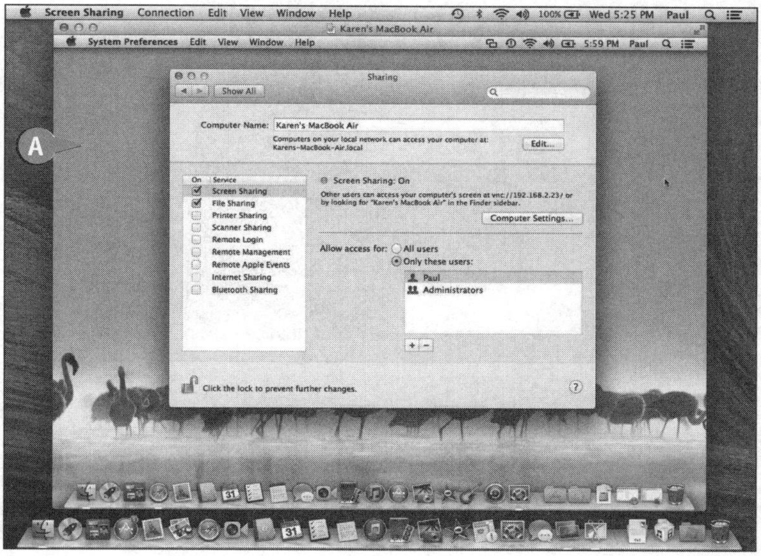

TIP

The other Mac's screen is scaled to fit inside the Screen Sharing window. Can I see the screen at regular size?

Yes. To see the other Mac's screen without scaling, you have two choices. The first option is to display the other Mac's screen at regular size within the Screen Sharing window: Click **View** and then click **Turn Scaling Off**. Alternatively, switch Screen Sharing to full screen mode by clicking **View** and then clicking **Enter Full Screen**. Note that this works only if the other Mac's screen resolution is the same as or lower than the Mac Pro's. To exit full screen mode, move the mouse [pointer icon] to the top of the screen, click **View**, and then click **Exit Full Screen**.

CHAPTER 22

Running Windows on Mac Pro

If there is a Windows application or game that does not have a Mac equivalent, one solution is to create a Boot Camp partition on Mac Pro and use it to install Windows. This enables you to dual-boot between OS X and Windows.

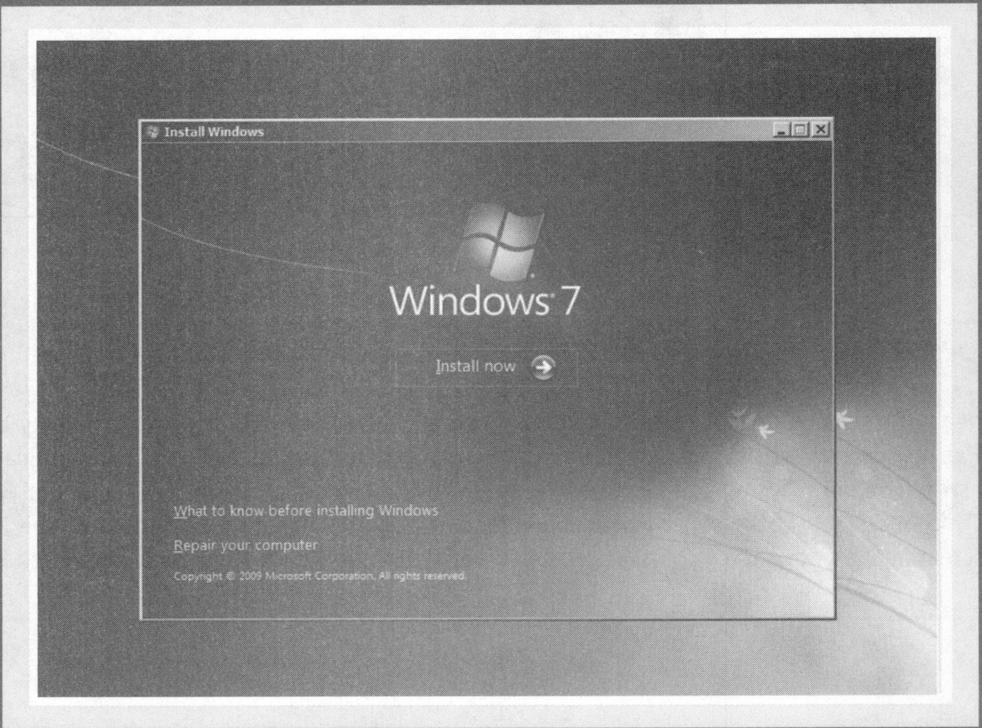

Review Windows Options

There are many reasons to run Windows on Mac Pro. For example, there might not be a Mac version of a software program that you need to use for work or for a hobby. Or if there is a Mac version, you might not like it as much as the Windows version. Whatever the reason, you need to understand the various options available for running Windows on Mac Pro, as well as how to prepare for the Windows installation technique discussed later in this chapter.

Dual-Boot

To *dual-boot* Mac Pro means to configure it with two different operating systems — OS X and Windows — running on two separate hard drive partitions. When you start Mac Pro, you can boot into OS X or into Windows. If you choose OS X, Mac Pro runs exactly as it does now. If you boot into Windows instead, Mac Pro turns into a Windows PC. You use Apple's Boot Camp software to set up a dual-boot configuration with Windows.

Virtualization

Virtualization refers to running Windows on your Mac Pro in a virtual machine: A software environment that simulates a physical computer. In this scenario, you boot into OS X as usual and then you run Windows essentially as an application in its own window. This virtual machine is configured in such a way that fools Windows into thinking that it controls an actual PC. Several virtualization applications are available, including Parallels Desktop (www.parallels.com), VMware Fusion (www.vmware.com/mac), and VirtualBox (www.virtualbox.org). This chapter does not cover virtualization.

Dual Boot vs. Virtualization

You should dual-boot OS X and Windows if your budget is tight because Boot Camp comes free with Mac Pro, and most third-party virtualization programs are commercial products that you have to pay for. Dual-booting also gives you maximum performance because Windows gets to use all the Mac Pro's hardware resources. On the other hand, you should use virtualization to run Windows if you want to access Windows without the hassle of rebooting, or if you want to run older versions of Windows (because Boot Camp supports only Windows 7 and Windows 8).

Boot Camp Requirements

Boot Camp comes with Mac Pro, but you can only use it to dual-boot with Windows if you have a copy of Windows to install. Specifically, you need the full installation version (the upgrade version does not work) for Windows 8 or one of the following versions of Windows 7: Home Premium, Professional, or Ultimate version. You must install the 64-bit version of Windows. The Windows installation can be either be a DVD (in which case you must connect a DVD drive to Mac Pro) or an ISO disk image.

Boot Camp Preparation

Mac Pro needs to have enough room on its hard drive to create a partition big enough to hold Windows and whatever Windows applications you plan on using. At a bare minimum, your Mac Pro hard drive needs about 20GB free to install a 64-bit version of Windows 7 or Windows 8. Before beginning the process of installing Windows on Mac Pro, check your hard drive free space and clear some space, if necessary. Also, it is a good idea to run a Time Machine backup before you install Windows.

Guard Against Malware

Although writers of viruses and other malware do not often target Macs, they regularly target Windows, so after you have completed the installation of Windows you should install a top-of-the-line antivirus program. Some examples are Norton Internet Security (www.symantec.com), McAfee Internet Security Suite (http://mcafee.com), Microsoft Security Essentials (www.microsoft.com/security/pc-security/mse.aspx), and avast! antivirus (http://avast.com). If you do catch a virus or other form of malware on Windows, note that it is not possible for the malware to also infect your Mac, although it could delete data from your hard drive.

Create a Windows Partition

You begin the process of running Windows on Mac Pro by using Boot Camp to create a partition in which to install Windows. Recall from Chapter 15 that a partition is a separate section of the hard drive. By dividing the Mac Pro hard drive into two partitions, you can continue to run OS X on one partition, while running Windows on the second partition. As described in the section "Review Windows Options," you switch between OS X and Windows by booting into one or the other at startup.

Create a Windows Partition

1. Click **Spotlight** (🔍).
2. Type **boot**.
3. Click **Boot Camp Assistant**.

   Boot Camp Assistant appears.

4. Click **Continue**.

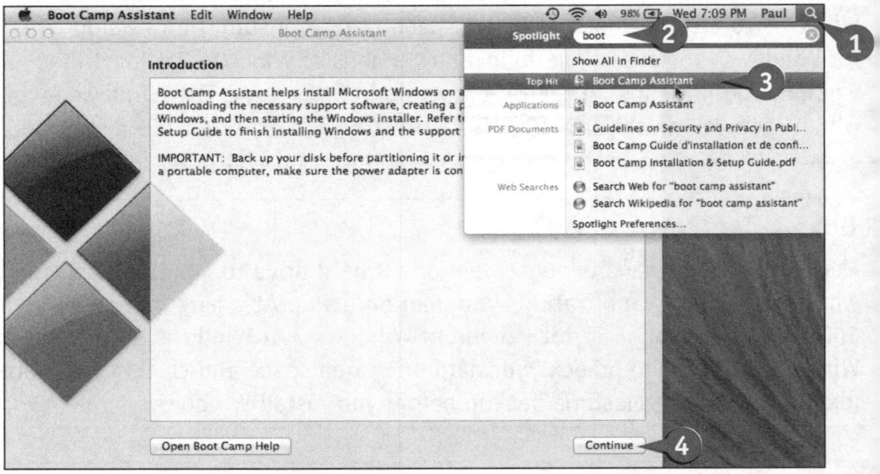

Boot Camp Assistant displays the Select Tasks dialog.

5. If you are using a Windows install DVD, deselect the **Create a Windows 7 or later version install disk** option (☑ changes to ☐).
6. Insert the install disk:

   If you have a Windows DVD, insert the disc.

   If you have a Windows ISO image, insert a USB drive.

7. Click **Continue**.

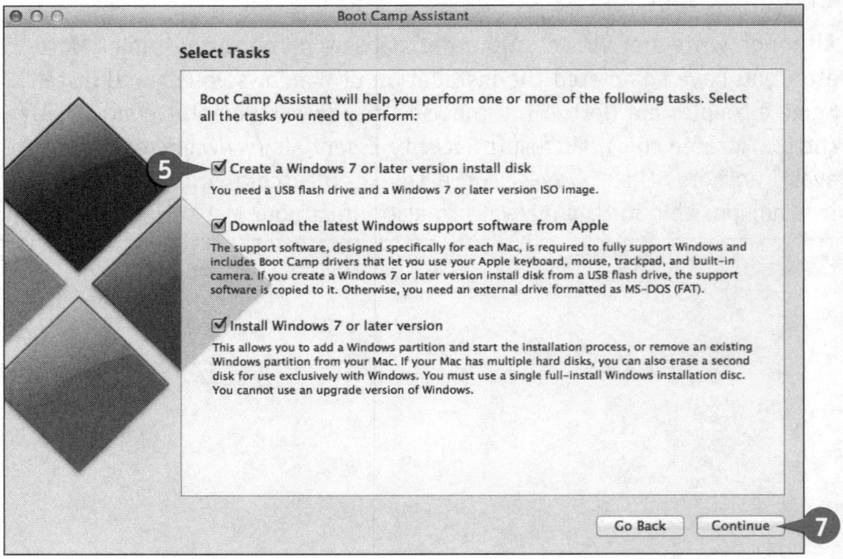

If you are using a Windows ISO image, the Create Bootable USB Drive for Windows Installation dialog appears.

8 Click **Choose**.

9 In the Open dialog, click the ISO file.

10 Click **Open**.

11 Click the disk to which you want the Windows installation files copied.

12 Click **Continue**.

13 When Boot Camp Assistant warns you that the drive will be erased, click **Continue** (not shown).

Boot Camp Assistant creates the installation drive. If OS X displays a message about allowing a new helper tool, type your password and click **Add Helper**.

14 In the Create a Partition for Windows dialog, click and drag the dot separating the two partitions until the Windows partition is the size you want.

Note: Continue with the next section, "Install Windows."

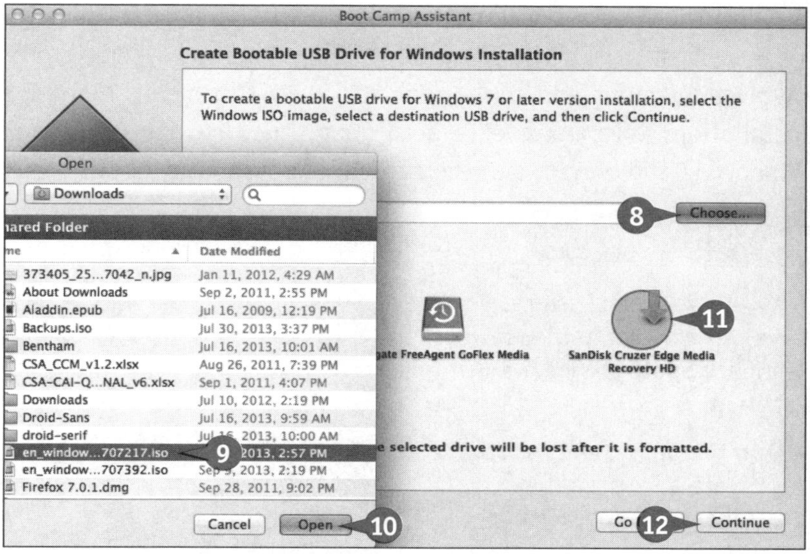

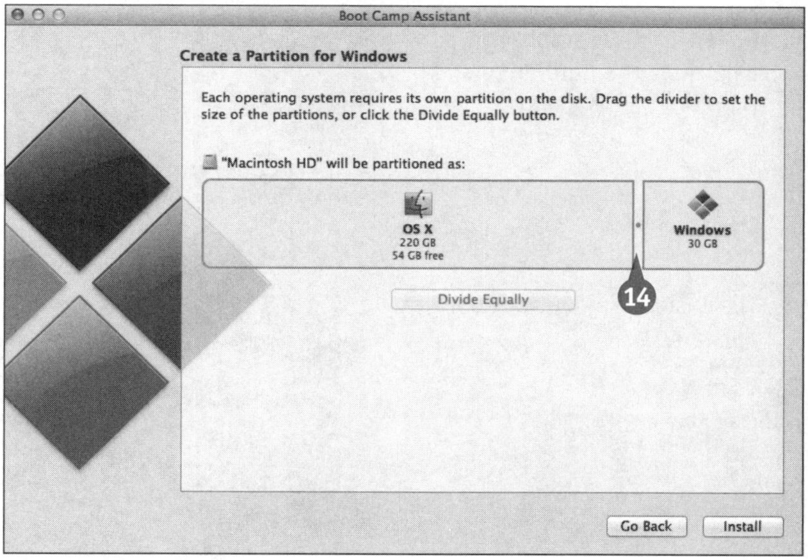

TIP

How do I decide how big to make the Windows partition?

The more applications you want to use in Windows, the more space you need, particularly if you will be installing large programs such as Microsoft Office. Similarly, if you have lots of huge video files and thousands of audio files and photos, you need a great deal of storage space to handle everything. If you will not be installing many Windows applications and your data files are not massive, use a 30GB partition for 64-bit Windows 7 or Windows 8. Otherwise, if you have enough room on your Mac Pro hard drive, go with a 50GB partition for either Windows 7 or Windows 8.

Install Windows

With the Windows installation drive created and a second partition added to the Mac Pro hard drive, the first part of the setup for running Windows on Mac Pro is complete. The next part of the setup involves installing and configuring Windows. This means running through the steps of the Windows installation. Note, however, that although the first part of the installation is the same for both Windows 7 and Windows 8, the subsequent steps vary, so they are not covered in detail in this section.

Install Windows

Note: This section assumes you have just completed the previous section, "Create a Windows Partition."

1. In the Boot Camp Assistant's Create a Partition for Windows dialog, click **Install**.

   Boot Camp Assistant partitions the hard drive and then reboots Mac Pro.

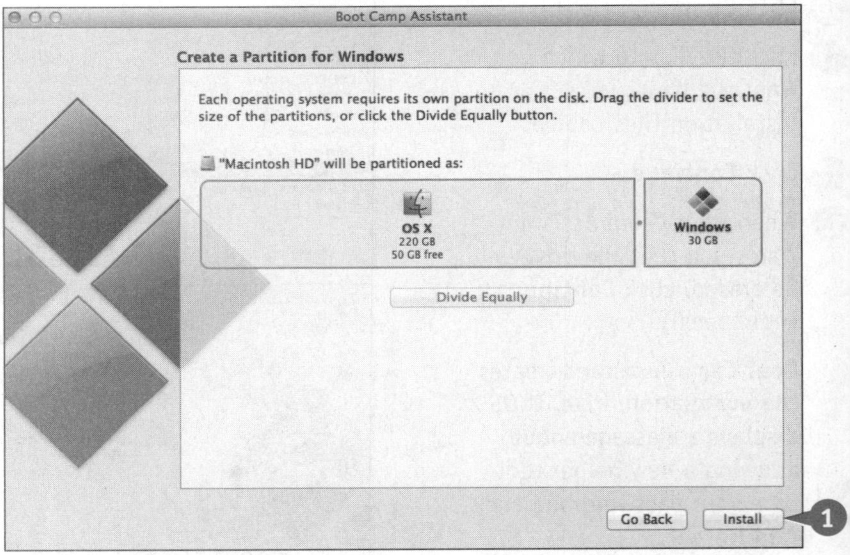

   The Install Windows window appears.

2. Click **Next**.

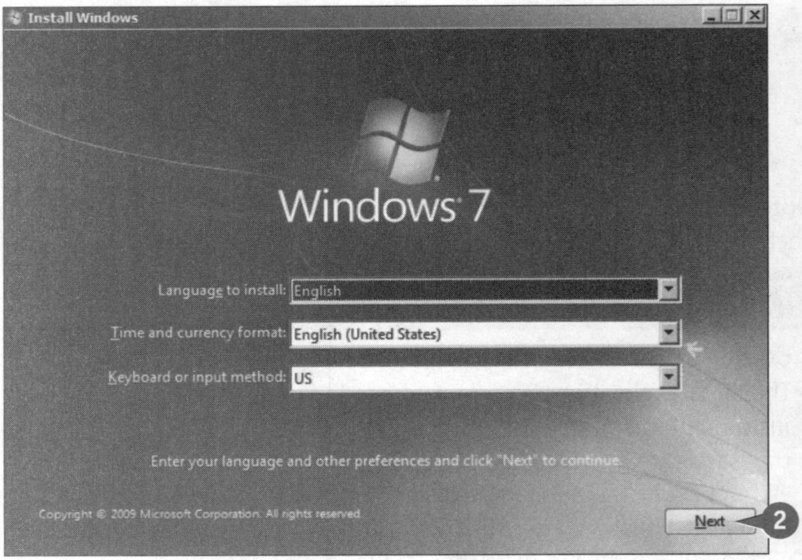

3 Click **Install now**.

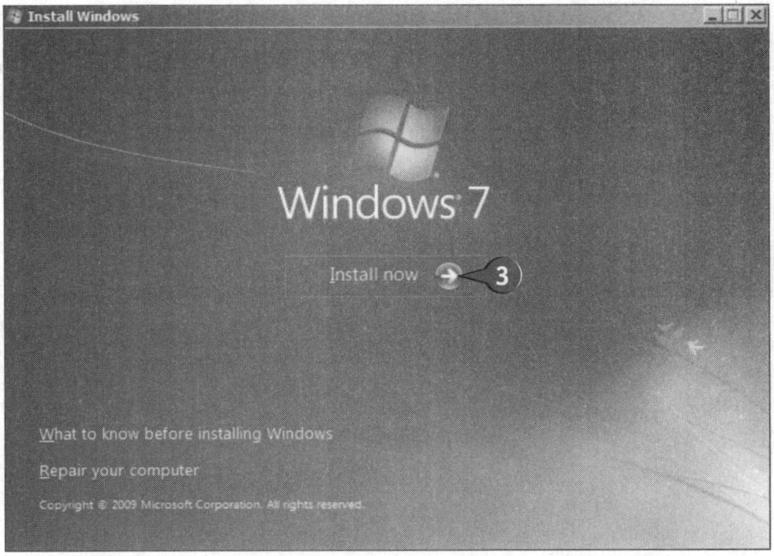

The Windows license agreement appears.

4 Select the **I accept the license terms** option (☐ changes to ☑).

5 Click **Next**.

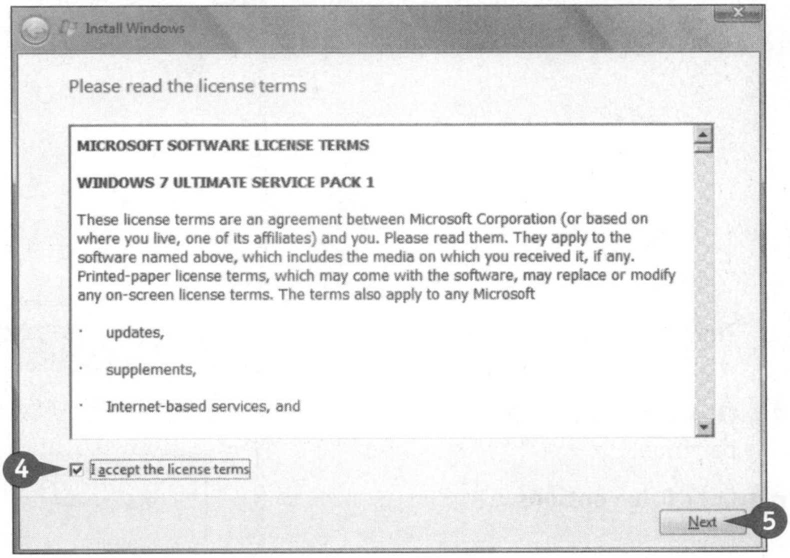

TIP

What information do I require to install Windows?

In addition to the Windows product key, you may need to provide:

- A user account name and password.
- A name for the Windows PC that Boot Camp creates. This name can be up to 14 characters with no spaces.
- How you want Windows protected. In this case, it is best to select the Use Recommended Settings option.
- The type of network you are using. In most cases, you click Home Network.

continued ►

Install Windows (continued)

As part of the installation process, you must format the partition that Boot Camp Assistant created. You need to do this because Boot Camp Assistant originally formats the partition using the FAT32 file system, but you cannot install Windows 7 or Windows 8 on a FAT32 partition. Instead, Windows 7 and Windows 8 require a partition that uses the NTFS file system. When you format the partition during the installation, it automatically changes the partition from FAT32 to NTFS.

Install Windows (continued)

Windows asks you to choose the type of installation.

6 Click **Custom**.

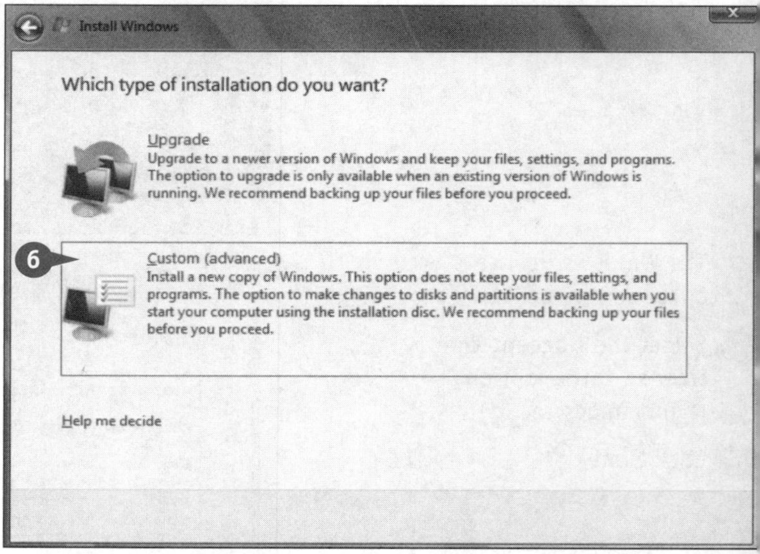

The installer asks where you want to install Windows.

7 Click the **BOOTCAMP** partition.

8 Click **Drive options**.

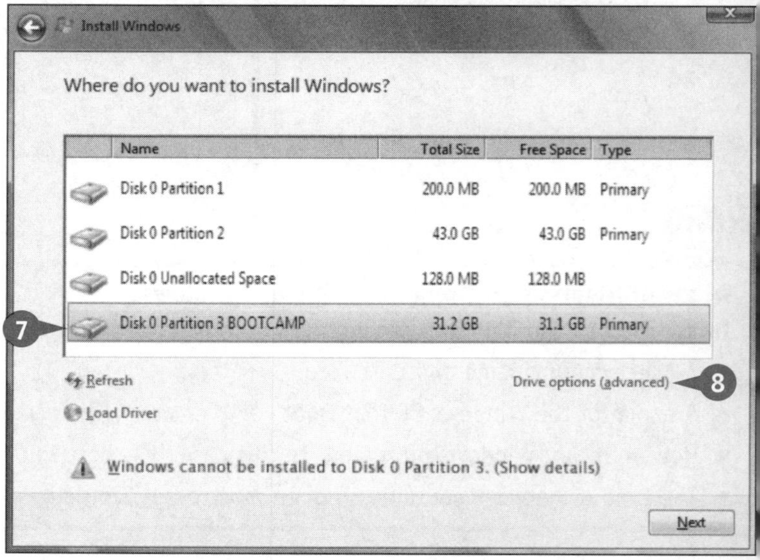

9 Click **Format**.

If the installer displays a warning, click **OK**.

The installer formats the partition.

10 Click **Next**.

The installer begins the Windows installation.

Note: If you are installing from a DVD, ignore the "Press any key to boot from CD/DVD" message you see each time Mac Pro restarts.

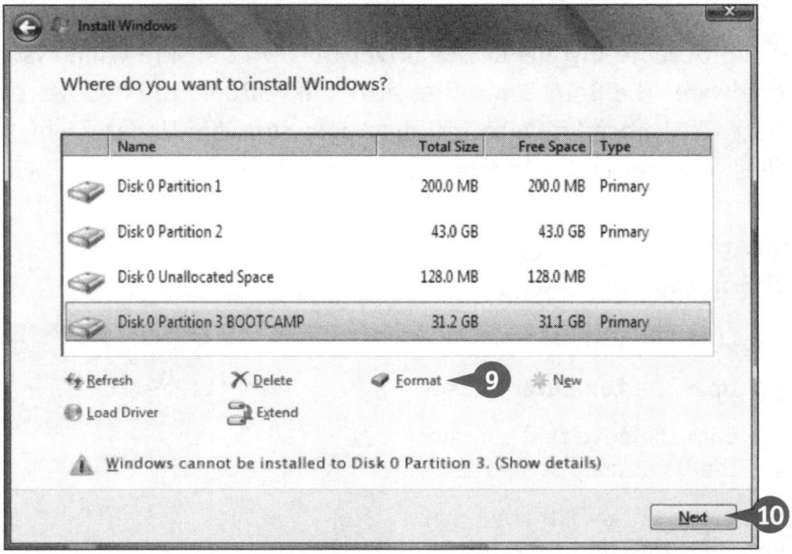

The Set Up Windows dialog appears.

11 Type the name you want to use for your main Windows user account.

12 Type a name for the Boot Camp PC.

13 Click **Next**.

From here, the steps you follow to complete the installation vary depending on the Windows version.

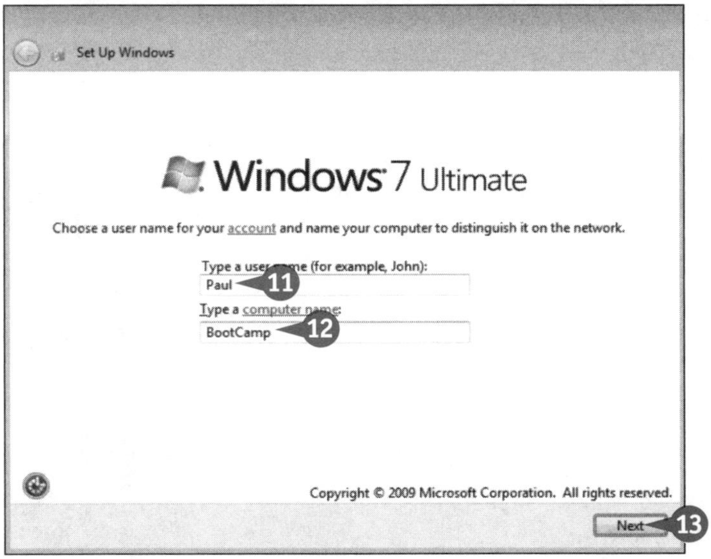

TIP

What is a file system?

It is a technology the operating system uses to keep track of the files stored on a drive, such as a hard drive. FAT32 (The FAT part is short for File Allocation Table) is a relatively simple file system used by some versions of Windows, whereas NTFS (New Technology File System) is a more sophisticated file system used by Windows 7/8 and other higher-end versions of Windows (such as Windows Server 2012). For the record, your Mac Pro uses a file system called HFS+ (where HFS is short for Hierarchical File System).

Install Boot Camp

After you have completed the Windows installation, you must install the Boot Camp files. This procedure installs device driver files that ensure Windows can work successfully with the Mac Pro hardware. The Boot Camp files also add features to Windows that make it easier to reboot back into OS X. The procedure also installs Apple Software Update, which enables you to keep the Boot Camp files updated as Apple releases new versions.

Install Boot Camp

1. Click **File Explorer**.
2. Open the **Computer** folder.
3. Click the drive that contains the Boot Camp setup files.

Note: This is the USB drive that Boot Camp Assistant created in the section "Create a Windows Partition."

4. Double-click **setup**.
5. If you see the Use Account Control dialog, click **Yes** (not shown).

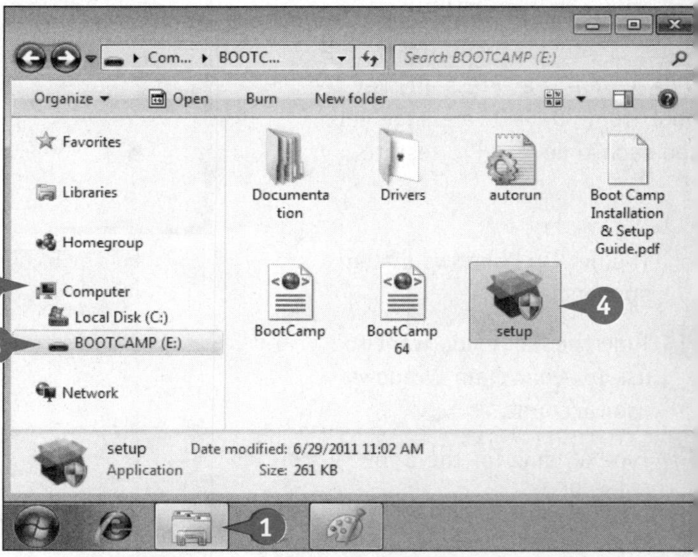

The Boot Camp installer appears.

6. Click **Next.**

The Boot Camp license agreement appears (not shown).

7. Select the **I accept the terms in the license agreement** option (changes to).
8. Click **Next.**

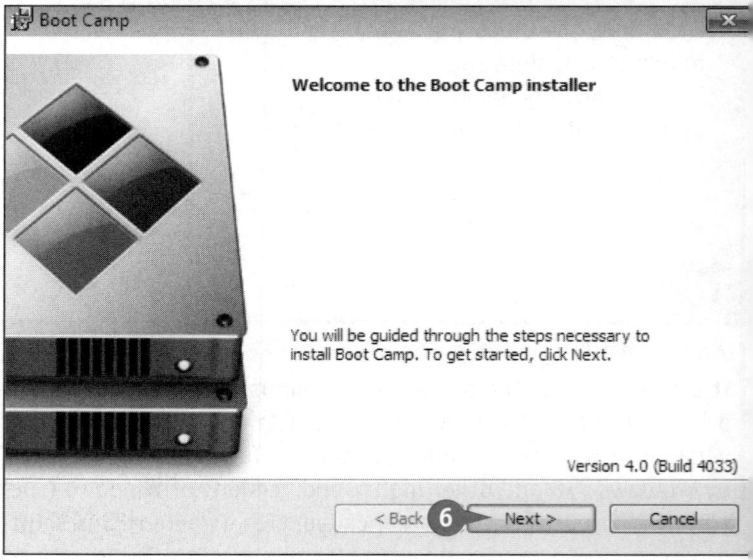

9 Click **Install**.

The Boot Camp installer runs the installation.

10 Click **Finish** (not shown).

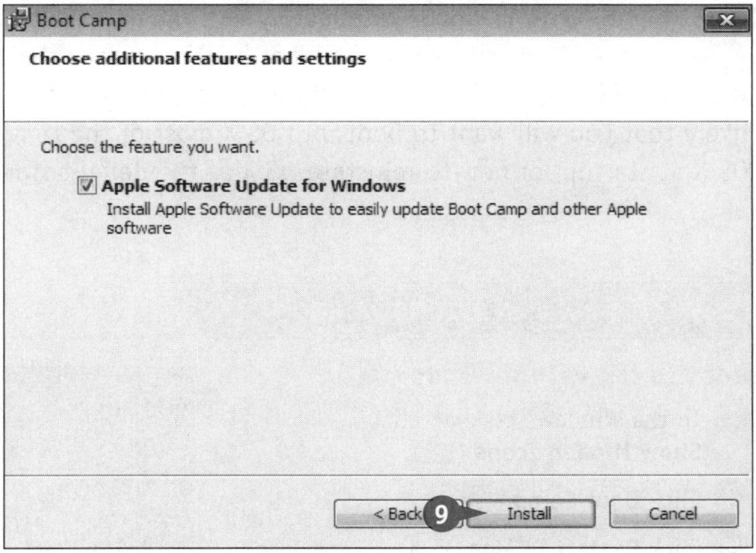

Boot Camp prompts you to restart the PC.

11 Click **Yes**.

Boot Camp restarts the PC.

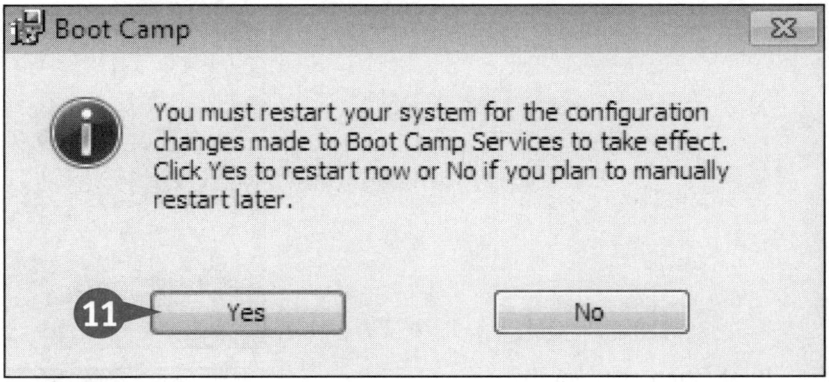

TIP

What is a device driver?

A *device driver* is a small software program that acts as an intermediary between an operating system and a device. This means that the operating system does not need to know the specific commands that make a device perform particular operations. Instead, the operating system tells the device driver what action it wants to perform — such as displaying something on the monitor or printing a document — and the device driver translates that instruction into a series of commands that the device understands. In the case of Boot Camp, Windows requires device drivers that enable it to work successfully with the Mac Pro graphics system, audio system, processor, memory, hard drive, networking, input/output ports, and more.

Switch Between Windows and OS X

After you have Windows installed on Mac Pro, you need to know how to switch between Windows and OS X. As discussed earlier, dual-booting means that you boot Mac Pro into either OS X or Windows. After the Windows installation, Mac Pro automatically boots to Windows. Because it is more likely that you will want to boot into OS X most of the time, you need to know either how to boot to OS X at startup, or how to reinstate OS X as the default startup choice.

Switch Between Windows and OS X

Boot to OS X from Windows

1. In the Windows taskbar, click **Show Hidden Icons** (▲).
2. Click **Boot Camp** (◆).
3. Click **Restart in Mac OS X.**

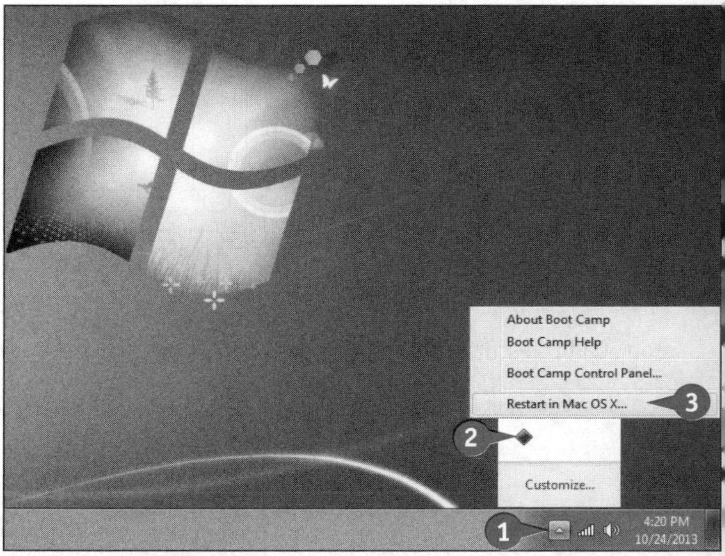

Boot Camp asks you to confirm the restart.

4. Click **OK.**

Mac Pro restarts and loads OS X.

Reinstate OS X as the Default Start OS

1. In OS X, click **System Preferences** (⚙).

   The System Preferences appear.

2. Click **Startup Disk**.

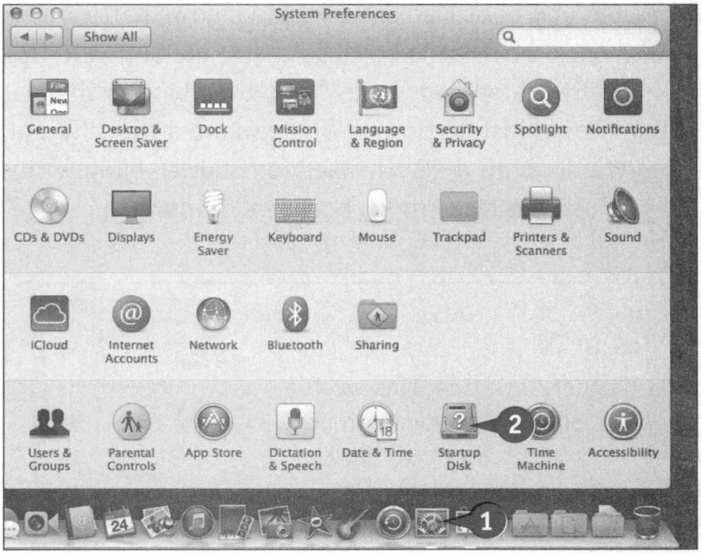

   The Startup Disk preferences appear.

3. Click your OS X startup disk.

Note: The default name of the OS X startup disk is Macintosh HD OS X, 10.9.

   Mac Pro now boots directly to OS X each time you start the system.

TIPS

Can I boot to OS X without first booting to Windows?

Yes. If Windows is still the default operating system, it is inefficient to first boot to Windows when you want to use OS X. Instead, press and hold Option when you start Mac Pro. You can release Option when you see the Startup Manager, which displays icons for Macintosh HD and Windows (as well as the Recovery HD). Click the Macintosh HD icon to boot to OS X.

If I reinstate OS X as the default operating system, how do I boot to Windows?

Follow the steps in the previous tip to restart Mac Pro and display the Startup Manager. Click the Windows hard drive icon to boot to Windows.

Work with Windows

When you boot Mac Pro to the Windows partition, you can work with Windows normally, for the most part. That is because the Apple Software Update loads device drivers and other support files that enable Windows to work directly with the Mac Pro hardware. However, a few elements of a Boot Camp installation of Windows are a bit different than what you might be used to if you have used Windows on a PC. This section shows you how to share data between Windows and OS X and how to use the Mac Pro keyboard in Windows.

Work with Windows Files in OS X

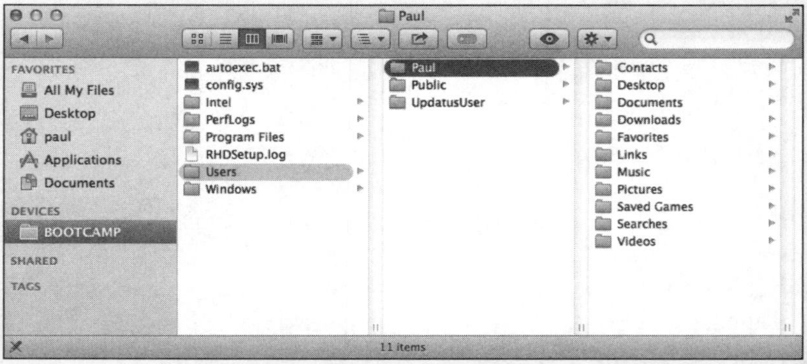

OS X understands the Windows file system, so you can work with your Windows files from within OS X. You can see your Windows files by selecting the BOOTCAMP device in Finder and then navigating the Windows folders just as though they were OS X folders. Note, however, that because the Boot Camp partition uses the NTFS file system, you can only view the Windows files; you cannot make any changes to the existing files or add new files.

Work with OS X Files in Windows

Unfortunately, Windows cannot work with the OS X file system, so it is not possible to see the Mac Pro hard drive in Windows. However, there are a couple of workarounds you can use. For example, you can connect an external hard drive and then use Windows to format the drive using the FAT32 file system. You can then move files from your Mac Pro's hard drive to the external hard drive and access them from Windows. Alternatively, store the files in a shared network folder accessible from both OS X and Windows.

Using a Keyboard

One of the problems you face when you boot into Windows using your Mac Pro is how you press Windows-specific keys using your Mac Pro keyboard. If you happen to have a USB PC keyboard, connect it to a USB port on your Mac Pro — this solves the problem because the PC keyboard works properly in Boot Camp. Alternatively, you can connect a wireless PC keyboard to Windows.

Keyboard Alternatives

If you have only your Mac Pro keyboard, you can still use it in Windows because Boot Camp installs a keyboard driver that translates certain Mac keyboard combinations into equivalent Windows keys. The following table lists the key combinations you can use.

Mac Keyboard Techniques to Use in Windows

To get this Windows key	Press this on the Mac Pro keyboard
Windows	⌘
Alt	Option
Right Alt	Right Option
Ctrl	Control
Ctrl+Alt+Delete	Control+Option+Fwd Delete
Enter	Return
Backspace	Delete
Delete	Fwd Delete
Insert	Fn+Enter
Num Lock	Clear
Print scrn	F14
Print Active Window	Option+F14
Scroll Lock	F15
Pause/Break	F16

Index

D

E

F

I

K

L

M

N

O

P

Q

R

S

Y

Z

Office

InDesign®

Facebook®

THE WAY YOU WANT TO LEARN.

HTML

Photoshop

DigitalClassroom.com

Flexible, fast, and fun, DigitalClassroom.com lets you choose when, where, and how to learn new skills. This subscription-based online learning environment is accessible anytime from your desktop, laptop, tablet, or smartphone. It's easy, efficient learning — on ***your*** schedule.

- Learn web design and development, Office applications, and new technologies from more than 2,500 video tutorials, e-books, and lesson files
- Master software from Adobe, Apple, and Microsoft
- Interact with other students in forums and groups led by industry pros

Learn more! Sample DigitalClassroom.com for free, now!

We're social. Connect with us!

facebook.com/digitalclassroom
@digitalclassrm

DIGITAL CLASSROOM